PROTEST, REFORM, AND REVOLT

A Reader in Social Movements

EDITED BY

JOSEPH R. GUSFIELD

University of California, San Diego

JOHN WILEY & SONS, INC.

NEW YORK · LONDON · SYDNEY · TORONTO

Copyright © 1970, by John Wiley & Sons, Inc.

All rights reserved. No part of this book may be reproduced
by any means, nor transmitted, nor translated into a machine
language without the written permission of the publisher.

10 9 8 7 6 5 4 3 2 1

Library of Congress Catalogue Card Number: 70-94913

SBN 471 33685 8

Printed in the United States of America

To Julie, Dan, and Ilene—three who change the world

Preface

The study of social change through collective action has been one of the great *terra incognita* of sociology. Introductory texts usually have devoted one or two chapters to "social change" and consequently have given the illusion that society was largely a static and unchanging system of relationships, norms, and values. Certainly social scientists have recognized this as illusory, but we have been far less able to develop analytical tools with which to study change. As a result, a great deal of the analysis of social change has consisted in the study of large-scale theories such as those of Marx, Veblen, or Sorokin. A great deal of the writing and research in the area of social change has dealt with latent and undirected developments, especially those emerging under the impact of technology. The salient work of William Fielding Ogborn is an excellent illustration of significant and influential development. In recent years the emphasis on nation-building, modernization, and economic growth has again brought into focus the concern for basic shifts in forms of societies and for studying the implications of technology and industrialization.

This general approach to social change (although highly important and useful) nevertheless has led us to neglect the extent to which human purpose, deliberate design, and organization have played a crucial role in the direction and redirection of societies. During the 1950's, when I began teaching, writing, and researching in reform movements, this area was still a marginal field for sociologists. Not many students were working on the analysis of social movements and not many universities had courses concerned with this area in their sociology departments. Historical writings were largely descriptive, and the sociologist's concern was represented by a field loosely called "collective behavior and social movements." This was the case, despite the enormous significance and importance that early writers, like Marx and De Tocqueville, had given to the study and analysis of revolution and revolt.

In more recent years the study of collective action and its implications for social change has again moved into the foreground of social sciences. The black revolution in the United States, widespread student unrest in many countries, and the development of independence movements in Asia and Africa have again focused enormous attention on reform, rebellion, revolt, and protest as important forms of social and political behavior. The importance of social and political conflict, as processes through which society is shaped, has become a major area in social research. By viewing social movements and collective action in the context of social change and conflict, we are redressing a balance which, in the past, has minimized the importance that human volition gives to the direction of change in societies. To the long-run analysis of trends and latent elements in change, the new emphasis adds a concern for crisis and the extent to which change comes about suddenly as well as continuously.

Social movements, because they exist in a political and ideological context, present the sociologist with difficult questions of the relationship between knowledge and action. These are less apparent when one studies social change as a continuous process manifested in long-run trends. Because what we do in our analytical capacities has immediate consequence for activities exhorting man to immediate action, the sociologist functioning in the area of social movements and collective action meets the issues of objectivity and detachment in a more puzzling and strident fashion. In this period of history, when students, professors, and publics are so deeply preoccupied with issues of revolt, reform, and dissent, I still hang firmly to a belief in the value of intellectual detachment and the virtues of disinterested analysis. When men are deeply in conflict with each other, it is difficult for the intellectual judgments of the scholar not to help this or that cause or to hinder others. It is more difficult than at other periods for the scholar to hold his own personal and political commitments in check and to apply the necessary doubts that are so central to scholarship and reason. Our aim in the volume is to indicate to students some of the tools in perspectives which he can utilize in understanding human activity and conflict. The relation between knowledge in the social sciences and political action is a more vital issue today than in the past decades, and each teacher and student must decide whether the position taken here is one that has merit.

This collection of materials reflects several intellectual and historical influences. My interest in the study of social movements goes back to graduate-school days at the University of Chicago in the early 1950's and to lectures and discussions with Herbert Blumer. His emphasis on processes of development and the rise of a new social order out of collective behavior has remained a major source for my understanding of collective action. This has been tempered by more structural orientations, which are traditional in sociology and reflect, in one way or another, the impact of such writers as De Tocqueville, Marx, and Weber. In recent years the study of social movements has gained much from the work of a number of social scientists that cut across historical periods, cultures, and academic disciplines. Here the work on millennial movements and European protest in the 18th and 19th centuries has been especially pertinent, and the writings of Norman Cohn, Eric Hobsbawm, Reinhard Bendix, and George Rudé have been most influential on my thinking. Some of these writers are represented in this volume. The writings of people involved deeply in political action have been another major source that has been a great influence on me and others in our thinking about the analysis of sources of discontents and the expressive elements in collective action. Here the work of Frantz Fanon, harkening back to Georges Sorel, is especially important. The renaissance of Marxian thought is again indicative of abiding issues that return again and again in the history of ideas.

Intellectual debts are always difficult to pay, since scholars seldom keep accurate ledgers. I owe a special debt, however, to David Riesman with whom I have worked over the past decade in studies of higher education. His intellectual curiosity and ability to observe the complexity with which the particular and the general cohere has been infectious. His influence on social scientists goes beyond the very great value of his own scholarly contributions.

Many people aided in the production of this particular volume. I especially thank Jonathan Eisen for considerable help in the development of the bibliography. Linda Hawley, Anice Duncan, and Julie Metzger were immensely valuable in the tasks of photocopying and typing. Without the help of Irma Gusfield this volume would probably still be in preparation. Finally, I am deeply grateful to Charles Tilly and Morris Janowitz whose very cogent criticisms led to revisions that I hope have greatly improved the final product.

La Jolla, California, 1970

Joseph Gusfield

Contents

PROTEST, REFORM, AND REVOLT

INTRODUCTION: A DEFINITION OF THE SUBJECT

Change and conflict are as much facts of human society as are stability and order. This collection of readings is based on recognition of these facts. Our title suggests people in motion, rejecting what has been accepted, dissenting from what is dominant, and acting to bring about new patterns of social life against the resistance of institutional rules, fixed beliefs, or social controls.

Efforts to bring about social change may be pervasive and may encompass many aspects of a society, as did the revolutions of France in 1789, Russia in 1917, and China in 1949. Others may involve less pervasive aspects of some institution, far less profound in their intensity or sweep. Such is the movement to expand the teaching of the new mathematics in American schools or to reform the selection and promotion of Civil Service personnel. Our topic includes a great many diverse actions and organizations—the reforms of the Civil Rights movements, antitrust enforcement, the nationalist movements of colonial countries, ghetto riots, and the creation of utopian settlements, to list some from among many. What these have in common is their character as collective actions to bring about change.

Historians, political scientists, and sociologists have published studies of the following phenomena: Liberalism, the American Revolution, the Chinese Revolution, the Methodist movement, Temperance, the Civil Rights movement, Populism, the Sepoy rebellion, the Taiping rebellion, the Labor movement, "cargo cults," McCarthyism, Pan-Africanism, the Peace Movement, Technocracy, Messianism, Zionism, the Free Love

1

movement, the New Right, the New Left, the Natural Childbirth movement, Surrealism, Feminism, Freudianism, Progressivism, Neorealism, and Antidisestablishmentarianism. All of these meet our criterion for social movements in being *socially shared activities and beliefs directed toward the demand for change in some aspect of the social order.* In explaining this definition we shall clarify the subject of our study.

While the concept of "social movement" is primary in our usage, we have coupled it with "collective action" in the title and will use the two terms throughout this reader. We do this for two reasons. (a) The term "social movements" has a certain looseness akin to that of "social trends," while "collective action" emphasizes a group component and a structured organized character. (b) While we shall distinguish social movements from the field of collective behavior—which includes such phenomena as crowds, mobs, riots, panic, and fashion—there is nevertheless a close relationship between episodes of collective behavior and the development of social movements. By using the term "collective action" we emphasize that our concern with collective behavior is its implications for social movements and social change. Collective action denotes this fact of group activity channeled into actions relevant for change.

THE PARTS OF THE DEFINITION

1. *Socially Shared*

Movements are group phenomena, and the beliefs and actions are carried by group members. Our interest is in group actions and not in individual, eccentric behavior. Social movements are products of the interaction of people mutually influencing each other. The current "student movement" in the United States is not the chance similarity of a number of individual actions as is the massing of automobiles on a city expressway at rush hour. Instead it is a movement formed by students whose actions and words are responded to by other students. It exists in the sharing of ideas and in cooperative actions on a campus or among students at different campuses. It is the action of a group of students.

2. *Activities and Beliefs*

The idea of movement suggests efforts toward achieving change. Effort consists in activities—demonstrations, meetings, literature, campaigns. A movement consists of more than the passive sense of discontent, however shared that may be. It also involves beliefs—perceptions of what is wrong with the society, the culture, or the institution, and what can and should be done about it. What the participants in a movement share are the activities and beliefs that distinguish it.

3. *Demands*

Collective action involves advocacy for action, be it a new legislative act, the adoption of a new technique in teaching, or the personal use of marijuana. Movements are more than expressive; they seek to change the society and thus put pressures on nonbelievers and opponents. Because of this, movements are focal points of conflict in society and usually generate public issues.

4. *Change*

Collective action implies discontent with an existent situation and some desire to create a new one. The idea of a demand for change indicates the element of discontent with the existent situation—a policy, a set of rules, values, or authorities. It is the expression of dissatisfaction with the status quo that makes protest activity relevant to the study of social movements and collective action as modes of producing change.

5. *Social Order*

The sociologist is concerned with the system of rules, relationships, and moral codes by which men act in concert. The demands for change which interest us in this volume as those related to changes in the system or the social order, rather than isolated events or aims not generalized beyond the immediate. The storming of the Bastille can be studied as an isolated instance of mob action. Its significance for social change lies in its relationship to the French Revolution, in what it helped bring about.

The current waves of ghetto riots and of student revolt are significant as parts of movements for change in racial relations, in politics, and in universities. In emphasizing the study of social action as a part of the analysis of social change we put great weight on explicit attempts to bring about change. Discontent with accepted policies and practices is accompanied by new programs and policies and the demand for their adoption. In social action men challenge authorities, institutions, and values which others cherish. These are not sporadic acts occurring only once; they take on momentum and growth. They call out responses in those who oppose them and defend the existent order. For this reason

the study of social movements and collective action is a central part
of the study of social conflict and change.

THE LIMITS OF DEFINITION

In the social sciences definitions are not fences, carefully separating
one field from another. Instead they are road signs pointing a direction
to be taken. Our definitions cannot always include all the phenomena
of our interest. Much is included in the definition of social movements
given above, but some things elude our efforts to define them within
fixed categories. For example, mob activity, demonstrations, and riots
may seem to be outside the scope of our definition. As they are sporadic
acts not necessarily linked to demands for change in the social order,
we need not develop categories for the analysis of these phenomena.
Yet we would be blind to the real world if we failed to recognize the
great significance of many such acts in generating social movements
or their role in relation to more articulate demands for change. We
realize that some mob acts—a riot over a soccer match decision, for
example—have little relation to social change or to the development
of organized social action, except as symptoms of a possibly latent discontent. Others, such as a riot precipitated by charges of police brutality
toward Negroes, may be deeply connected with the Civil Rights movement, both in its generation and in its consequences. The character
of action as a protest against a general pattern of supposed injustice
is different from the character of action protesting against a specific
decision. In the former there is an overlap between forms of collective
action. Though the protest action seems inexplicit and not an articulate
demand for change, it must nevertheless fall within the scope of our
study.

FINDING THE BOUNDARIES

The nature of the field can be clarified still further by a discussion
of subject areas with which it has much in common but from which
it is nonetheless distinguished. One of the most difficult lines to draw
is that between social movements and *social trends*. If we study the
drive for Social Security legislation in the United States, for example,
we quickly recognize that it was related to a wider change in social
attitudes and values that replaced individualistic conceptions of governmental and public responsibility with a more collectivist orientation.
This shift is sometimes summed up in the phrase "the rise of the welfare

state." At this point the study of individual and narrowly specific movements becomes entangled with the analysis of more pervasive shifts in opinions, attitudes, and values.

A way of analyzing this has been suggested by Herbert Blumer.[1] He distinguished between specific movements and general movements, in which specific ones may be included. Thus the drive for equal voting rights for women was a movement with a specific goal. At the same time suffrage was one of many diffuse changes in conceptions of women's rights and duties occurring in the United States during the late nineteenth and early twentieth centuries and which are included in the general movement among women which historians have labeled the Feminist movement. In this movement the general nature of woman's status was being refashioned in a number of life areas.

General movements, however related to specific ones, possess a diffuse quality that makes them difficult to study as group phenomena in the same way as articulated demands of specific and organized groups. They have much in common with other social trends which occur in undirected and inarticulate fashion. The trend toward Italian foods in the American diet, such as spaghetti, pizza, and lasagna, has not been the result of a program demanding a change in American diets. While the trend toward earlier marriage in the United States may have some relations to the Feminist movement, it has not been the consequence of articulate demands, nor has it met organized opposition. The growing autonomy of adolescent groups is another example of a trend clearly developing in many contemporary societies and has even been the object of organized concern. It has not been focused on as a social issue, a matter of controversy between advocates and opponents. There have been trends, but not movements, leading to the habit of eating pizza, of earlier marriage, and of adolescent autonomy in the United States.

A pristine concern for logical categories might rule general movements as outside the concern of our analysis. Yet again, realistic and pragmatic attention to social change and conflict cannot dispense with them entirely. Social trends are distinguished from social movements, yet at points they do overlap with the phenomena of our concern.

Neither are social movements coordinate with *public opinion*, although there are many points at which the two converge. The public is an aggregate of people distinguished by its common focus on an issue. Capital punishment, for example, is a public issue around which controversy exists. There is debate and discussion, and the attention of

[1] Herbert Blumer, "Collective Behavior." *In* Robert Park, ed., *An Outline of the Principle of Sociology*. New York: Barnes and Noble, Inc., 1939, pp. 256–259.

people is placed on the merits and demerits of capital punishment as a policy.

Certainly social movements contribute to the generation and form of public opinion. There are groups concerned with the modification or elimination of capital punishment. The planned execution of Caryl Chessman in the early 1960s drew large demonstrations and led to the formation of organizations dedicated to abolition of the death penalty in California. These groups engaged in collective action which helped restore the issue to public attention. In this fashion collective action is frequently involved in public opinion.

Collective action and public opinion are nevertheless distinguishable. "Publics," in the usage of public opinion analysts, are mass phenomena, the attitudes of individuals toward issues. They may display social organization, as in voting behavior, but by no means do publics necessarily or often involve the action of groups directed toward change. While some social movements may seek to gain the support of public opinion, to persuade others of their cause, not all movements do so. The two fields come together at the point at which movements seek to persuade publics or when movements are themselves the center of an issue, as is the Civil Rights movement today.

Similarly there is often a tendency to confuse the study of collective action and social movements with the study of *voluntary associations.* This is deceptive, since many movements, and many aspects of movements, do not display the degree of organization, definiteness, and permanent establishment enjoyed by such associations as churches, labor unions, political parties, and fraternal organizations. The fact that so many movements function as associational groups or grow into highly organized bodies has often meant that many case studies of collective action have also been studies of voluntary associations. To study the Christian Science movement it is necessary to study a church, for example. The famous last line of the legendary labor agitator Joe Hill attests to the search for organization as an almost inevitable stage in the development of collective action. As he died Hill is reputed to have said, "Don't mourn for me—organize!"

Yet many movements are not organizations, which people can join, which hold meetings, and adopt definite programs. McCarthyism (named for the activities and beliefs of the late Senator Joseph McCarthy and his supporters), for example, illustrates a fluid set of beliefs and activities without an organization. Its "members" are defined by what they did and what they believed. Many movements also contain a number of associations, often in conflict with each other. The Temperance movement in the United States has gained expression and leadership from a number of organizations, among them the Woman's Christian Temperance Union, the Anti-Saloon League, and the Prohibition Party. Often problems arise among movements when they become voluntary associations, but these are by no means typical of all movements nor do they exhaust the areas of analysis of them. Neither is a bowling team or an Elks Club (both voluntary associations) analyzable as a group oriented toward achieving change.

Lastly, and most importantly, it is necessary to distinguish the study of social movements and collective action from the study of *elementary collective behavior*. Sociologists have often included the study of social movements in this field and assumed a social psychological orientation common to that used in studying crowds, mobs, mass, public, and other phenomena representing sporadic and unstructured group behavior. (The 1967 *Directory of the American Sociological Association* lists this entire field under Social Psychology and titles it the subfield of "Collective Behavior and [italics ours—J.G.] Social Movements.") Yet much of the subject matter of collective behavior lies well outside our concerns with social change. A crowd at a baseball game may riot, as sports audiences have been known to do when enraged at a decision. The outbreak of fire may create panic in a public building. An audience at a theater is analyzable as a sporadic and highly suggestible group. Such behavior, however, has little significance for the system of rules and relationships we call social orders. None of these contributes to an understanding of conflicts and changes in society. The recent wave of racial riots in the United States, however, must be analyzed as part of the Civil Rights movement. In their generation and in their consequences, they are embedded in the protests and struggles of that attempt to change the pattern of Negro-white relationships in the United States. The analysis of crowds, fashions, fads, and other noninstitutionalized and even antisocial collective behavior, per se, lacks that relevance for the analysis of social conflict, conflict resolution, and change which is essential and so much in evidence in actual studies of social movements.

Nevertheless, there has been good reason for sociologists to have stressed the collective behavior aspects of social movements. It cannot be ignored, no more than can the overlap of the study of social movements with the other areas discussed above. First, a great many demands for change have emerged out of the stimulation and disruption of episodes of crowdlike action periods of protest, riot, and mutual suggestibility. Such acts, often involving attacks on authority, are both expressive of alienation from dominant values and themselves an attack on constituted authority. Second, the analysis of mutual influence, the impact of dramatic events, and the vivid conditions under which old norms and values become illegitimate is a major framework for studying the attachment to new symbols and beliefs. While we do believe that the sociological analysis of social movements has been hampered by too close an association with the study of collective behavior, the insistence on reshaping social symbols as a basic function of collective behavior has been of great value in correcting an exaggerated form of institutional determinism.

What constitutes the special character of the study of social movements is therefore its relation to the analysis of change and social conflict. Collective actions involve more or less explicit rejection of dominant practices or beliefs, and they attempt to bring about change against the resistance of prevalent belief and authority. Social movements and collective action thus possess both *structure*—some organization of people—and *sentiments*—beliefs about what ought to be and what will come to pass. While any exclusive definition will break down when applied too rigorously in this field, this emphasis on change and conflict enables us to take a viewpoint which helps organize our analysis.

Throughout this volume we emphasize that this definition of our subject matter carries with it a definite historical bias. It expresses the perspective of societies in which conflict and dissent have been partially organized and legitimate. Our focus on explicit demands for change and on the development of organization and association is most clearly applicable to movements that grow in size and significance, that attempt to achieve goals through peaceful political or moral persuasion, and that espouse their beliefs in doctrine and program. Such movements, whether they aim at partial reform or involve large-scale programs of revolutionary dimensions, participate in the process through which change and conflict are institutionalized. The movement for minimum-wage legislation in the United States was conducted in conflict with those who opposed such legislation, but its methods were legal and socially acceptable.

Sporadic protests, revolutionary violence, insurrections, conspiracies, and riots are a few examples of behavior which lie outside legitimate modes of conflict in many advanced, industrial societies. The use of reform as the model of change is therefore not a universal fact but is a method more likely to be found in societies whose institutions admit reform and dissent. Protest and other less organized forms of dissent may be more typical in other historical periods and social systems. The occurrence of such relatively peaceful forms of collective behavior on a wide scale in societies in which reform is a possible alternative poses a different analytical problem from the situation in societies where orderly mechanisms of controlling and expressing conflict are absent.

I.

DIFFERENTIAL
RESPONSES TO
SOCIAL CHANGE

In this initial section of the reader we describe social movements and collective action as responses to social change. To see them in this light emphasizes the disruptive and disturbing quality which new ideas, technologies, procedures, group migration, and intrusions can have for people. They may render old habits unrewarding, may introduce new interests and conflicts, may provide new opportunities for old aspirations or make impossible dreams now potential realities. "Each age," wrote the poet Arthur Symons, "is a dream that is dying or one that is coming to birth."

This sociological perspective views change as a seedbed for discontent, although for some it may also be a source of gratifications and contentment. In beginning to understand and analyze the appearance of discontent, the sociologist examines the context of changes which have occurred to those who now express dissatisfaction and disaffection with institutions or values which in the past have claimed either their loyalty or at least their passive assent. In the first reading the American historian David Donald analyzes the roots of the Abolitionist movement in the 1840s. To explain the emergence of militant antislavery agitation in New England he turns to the experience of a certain group of New Englanders. Not experience with slavery but their own loss of power and status generated the discontents of upper-class New Englanders, whose

Federalist parents had occupied the places of power and respect a generation before. Antislavery was their reaction to the new men who had risen to power in the period after Jefferson and Jackson. Such men seemed to the Abolitionists to lack the appropriate moral qualities for legitimate leadership, and their acceptance of slavery only made it evident. They found their world morally unclean and, in seeking to purify it, they sought their own superiority.

Bruce McCully adds to understanding of change by demonstrating how the diffusion of ideas can operate to change perceptions and judgments. In many countries that have recently achieved independence, the idea of national self-rule has been, in great part, a product of education conducted and supported by the colonial powers themselves. The long development and great power of the Indian independence movement is the model for this process. English education in India created a class of civil servants and professionals and provided a language and a forum for their union. Within this westernized class the nationalist idea of independence was learned, and it provided the emotional and ideological spark to light the fires of hostility to colonial status.

In Donald's analysis of Abolitionism two aspects are significant. First, collective action may be perceived as an attempt to solve problems which its adherents are facing. Whether they seek means of defense to maintain old habits against the blows of unfortunate changes or align themselves as proponents of new ideas and norms against the past, the partisans of social movements are grappling with problems that have emerged within their lives. The discontents which they express are one source by which the sociologist tries to understand what has prompted them to view their society, or some facet of it, as unjust, immoral, or illegitimate.

The second aspect of Donald's essay is that change and its resultant discontents and opportunities operates differentially. Not everyone undergoes the same experience, nor does social change have the same impact on everyone in a society. This fact of differential responses and effects is brought out in the next two readings. In his paper on Fascism in several countries, Seymour Martin Lipset exemplifies what is perhaps the major analytical method of the sociologist—the location of behavior in specific parts of the social structure. The strains of change and the discontents expressed in a movement are not randomly distributed. They do not, like "the gentle rain from Heaven," fall on all classes, religions, ethnic groups, ages, and occupations alike. Social movements draw their adherents from particular segments of the society, people whose experiences make them more receptive to a particular ideology than others, whose conditions of life make communication and organization more possible, or who experience events in sharper and more intense form. Fascism in Germany, France, Italy, and the United States appealed to the same groups of small agricultural landowners and lower-middle-class urban white-collar workers and shopkeepers. It had an ideology which appealed to their experiences with the upsetting and dispossessing character of industrial capitalism for just those classes.

The insight of differential responses has much in common with the folk adage, "It all depends on whose ox is being gored." What may be greeted with warmth and acceptance by one group is responded to with hostility and repulsion by those whose life conditions differ. The uneven quality of change is a source of conflict and thus discontent and collective action. Charles Tilly's study of counterrevolution, excerpted here, emphasizes the fact that the changes which generated the French Revolution elsewhere in France did not operate in the same intense fashion in the rural part of Southern France, the Vendée. The changes introduced by the French Revolution were responses, in part, to the urbanization which was occurring in France. Its occurrence, however, was less marked in the Vendée, and the new institutions and the new values were less acceptable and more a source of conflict there than elsewhere in Revolutionary France. They culminated in the outbreak of a revolt against the revolution in the Vendée in 1793.

Focus on differential response and on the disruptive nature of social change raises a problem which has claimed the study and attention of many sociologists: Is collective action more likely when men are at a low level of living and deprivation, or when they are gaining new levels of wealth, status, or other rewards? Both the readings by Donald and Lipset describe instances of social groups losing power, status, and wealth, but the opposite can also be observed. For example, the current militant drive for equality among American Negroes comes when migration and political power have already achieved a considerable long-run rise in absolute income and education. Similarly, economic growth may be accompanied by political instability, and the poor are often passive, uncomplaining, and slow to organize.

Alexis de Tocqueville surveys this issue in his study of the French Revolution. His viewpoint contrasts sharply with that of Karl Marx. Marx emphasized the shift toward increasing poverty as a basic source of potential worker revolt, while Tocqueville (in part of a selection in the following section) found the French peasant wealthier on the eve of the French Revolution than in earlier periods of his history. This is the phenomenon of *relative deprivations*. What is significant is not the absolute level of poverty or prosperity, but what people have come to feel is their just due as compared with their present or threatened future existence. As the American Negro has increased his education and his income, he has come to perceive a position of greater equality as rightfully his, as possible to attain, and thus his actual situation seems even more depriving than formerly. Furthermore, as his expectations have risen, so too have his skills for organizing—skills which increased urbanization, income, and education have made possible. Thus "progress" is not a guarantee of stability.

A.

Sources of Discontent

1.

TOWARD A RECONSIDERATION OF ABOLITIONISTS (1956)

DAVID DONALD

I

Abraham Lincoln was not a abolitionist. He believed that slavery was a moral wrong, but he was not sure how to right it. When elected President, he was pledged to contain, not to extirpate, the South's peculiar institution. Only after offers of compensation to slaveholders had failed and after military necessities had become desperate did he issue his Emancipation Proclamation. Even then his action affected only a portion of the Negroes, and the President himself seemed at times unsure of the constitutionality of his proclamation.

It is easy to see, then, why earnest antislavery men were suspicious of Lincoln. Unburdened with the responsibilities of power, unaware of the larger implications of actions, they criticized the President's slowness, doubted his good faith, and hoped for his replacement by a more vigorous emancipationist. Such murmurings and discontents are normal

SOURCE. David Donald, *Lincoln Reconsidered, Essays on the Civil War Era.* New York: Alfred A. Knopf, 1956, pp. 19–36. Copyright 1956 by Alfred A. Knopf. Reprinted by permission of Alfred A. Knopf, Inc., and the author.

in American political life; in every village over the land there is always at least one man who can tell the President how the government ought to be run.

But a small group of extreme antislavery men, doctrinaire advocates of immediate and uncompensated abolition, assailed the wartime President with a virulence beyond normal expectation. It was one thing to worry about the fixity of Lincoln's principles, but quite another to denounce him, as did Wendell Phillips, as "the slave-hound of Illinois." Many Republicans might reasonably have wanted another candidate in 1864, but there was something almost paranoid in the declaration by a group of Iowa abolitionists that "Lincoln, . . . a Kentuckian by birth, and his brothers-in-law being in the rebel army, is evidently, by his sympathies with the owners of slaves, checked in crushing the rebellion by severe measures against slaveholders." A man might properly be troubled by Lincoln's reconstruction plans, but surely it was excessive for a Parker Pillsbury to pledge that, "by the grace of God and the Saxon Tongue," he would expose the "hypocrisy and cruelty" of Lincoln and of "whatever other President dares tread in his bloody footsteps."

The striking thing here is the disproportion between cause and effect—between Lincoln's actions, which were, after all, against slavery, and the abuse with which abolitionists greeted them. When a patient reacts with excessive vehemence to a mild stimulus, a doctor at once becomes suspicious of some deep-seated malaise. Similarly, the historian should be alert to see in extraordinary and unprovoked violence of expression the symptom of some profound social or psychological dislocation. In this instance, he must ask what produced in these abolitionists their attitude of frozen hostility toward the President.

These abolitionist leaders who so excessively berated Lincoln belonged to a distinct phase of American antislavery agitation. Their demand for an unconditional and immediate end of slavery, which first became articulate around 1830, was different from earlier antislavery sentiment, which had focused on gradual emancipation with colonization of the freed Negroes. And the abolitionist movement, with its Garrisonian deprecation of political action, was also distinct from political antislavery, which became dominant in the 1840's. The abolitionist, then, was a special type of antislavery agitator, and his crusade was part of that remarkable American social phenomenon which erupted in the 1830's, "freedom's ferment," the effervescence of kindred humanitarian reform movements—prohibition; prison reform; education for the blind, deaf, dumb; world peace; penny postage; women's rights; and a score of lesser and more eccentric drives.

Historians have been so absorbed in chronicling what these movements did, in allocating praise or blame among squabbling factions in each, and in making moral judgments on the desirability of various reforms that they had paid surprisingly little attention to the movement as a whole. Few serious attempts have been made to explain why humanitarian reform appeared in American when it did, and more specifically why immediate abolitionism, so different in tone, method, and membership from its predecessors and its successor, emerged in the 1830's.

The participants in such movements naturally give no adequate explanation for such a causal problem. According to their voluminous memoirs and autobiographies, they were simply convinced by religion, by reading, by reflection that slavery was evil, and they pledged their lives and their sacred honor to destroy it. Seeing slavery in a Southern state, reading an editorial by William Lloyd Garrison, hearing a sermon by Theodore Dwight Weld—such events precipitated a decision made on the highest of moral and ethical planes. No one who has studied the abolitionist literature can doubt the absolute sincerity of these accounts. Abolitionism was a dangerous creed of devotion, and no fair-minded person can believe that men joined the movement for personal gain or for conscious self-glorification. In all truth, the decision to become an antislavery crusader was a decision of conscience.

But when all this is admitted, there are still fundamental problems. Social evils are always present; vice is always in the saddle while virtue trudges on afoot. Not merely the existence of evil but the recognition of it is the prerequisite for reform. Were there more men of integrity, were there more women of sensitive conscience in the 1830's than in any previous decade? A generation of giants these reformers were indeed, but why was there such a concentration of genius in those ten years from 1830 to 1840? If the individual's decision to join the abolitionist movement was a matter of personality or religion or philosophy, is it not necessary to inquire why so many similar personalities or religions or philosophies appeared in America simultaneously? In short, we need to know why so many Americans in the 1830's were predisposed toward a certain kind of reform movement.

Many students have felt, somewhat vaguely, this need for a social interpretation of reform. Little precise analysis has been attempted, but the general histories of antislavery attribute the abolitionist movement to the Christian tradition, to the spirit of the Declaration of Independence, to the ferment of Jacksonian democracy, or to the growth of romanticism. That some or all of these factors may have relation to abolitionism can be granted, but this helps little. Why did the "spirit of Puritanism," to which one writer attributes the movement, become manifest as militant abolitionism in the 1830's although it had no such effect on the previous generation? Why did the Declaration of Independence find fulfillment in abolition during the sixth decade after its promulgation, and not in the fourth or the third?

In their elaborate studies of the antislavery movement,[1] Gilbert H. Barnes and Dwight L. Dumond have pointed up some of the more immediate reasons for the rise of American abolitionism. Many of the most important antislavery leaders fell under the influence of Charles Grandison Finney, whose revivalism set rural New York and the Western Reserve ablaze with religious fervor and evoked "Wonderful outpourings of the Holy Spirit" throughout the North. Not merely did Finney's invocation of the fear of hell and the promise of heaven rouse sluggish souls to renewed religious zeal, but his emphasis upon good works and pious endeavor as steps toward salvation freed men's minds from the bonds of arid theological controversies. One of Finney's most famous converts was Theodore Dwight Weld, the greatest of the Western abolitionists, "eloquent as an angel and powerful as thunder," who recruited a band of seventy antislavery apostles, trained them in Finney's revivalistic techniques, and sent them fourth to consolidate the emancipation movement in the North. Their greatest successes were reaped in precisely those communities where Finney's preaching had prepared the soil.

Barnes and Dumond also recognized the importance of British influence upon the American antislavery movement. The connection is clear and easily traced: British antislavery leaders fought for immediate emancipation in the West Indies; reading the tracts of Wilberforce and Clarkson converted William Lloyd Garrison to immediate abolitionism at about the same time that Theodore Weld was won over to the cause by his English friend Charles Stuart; and Weld in turn gained for the movement the support of the Tappan brothers, the wealthy New York merchants and philanthropists who contributed so much in money and time to the antislavery crusade. Thus, abolition had in British precedent a model, in Garrison and Weld leaders, and in the Tappans financial backers.

Historians are deeply indebted to Professors Barnes and Dumond, for the importance of their studies on the antislavery movement is very great. But perhaps they have raised as many questions as they have answered. Both religious revivalism and British antislavery theories had a selective influence in America. Many men heard Finney and Weld,

---

[1] Gilbert H. Barnes, *The Antislavery Impulse, 1830–1844* (1933); Barnes and Dwight L. Dumond, eds., *Lettters of Theodore Dwight Weld, Angelina Grimké Weld and Sarah Grimké, 1822–1844* (2 vols., 1934); Dumond, ed., *Letters of James Gillespie Birney, 1831–1857* (2 vols., 1939); Dumond, *Antislavery Origins of the Civil War in the United States* (1939).

but only certain communities were converted. Hundreds of Americans read Wilberforce, Clarkson, and the other British abolitionists, but only the Garrisons and the Welds were convinced. The question remains: Whether they received the idea through the revivalism of Finney or through the publications of British antislavery spokesmen, why were some Americans in the 1830's for the first time moved to advocate immediate abolition? Why was this particular seed bed ready at this precise time?

II

I believe that the best way to answer this difficult question is to analyze the leadership of the abolitionist movement. There is, unfortunately, no complete list of American abolitionists, and I have had to use a good deal of subjective judgment in drawing up a roster of leading reformers. From the classified indexes of the *Dictionary of American Biography* and the old Appleton's *Cyclopaedia of American Biography* and from important primary and secondary works on the reform generation, I made a list of about two hundred and fifty persons who seemed to be identified with the antislavery cause. This obviously is not a definitive enumeration of all the important abolitionists; had someone else compiled it, other names doubtless would have been included. Nevertheless, even if one or two major spokesmen have accidentally been omitted, this is a good deal more than a representative sampling of antislavery leadership.

After preliminary work I eliminated nearly one hundred of these names. Some proved not to be genuine abolitionists but advocates of colonizing the freed Negroes in Africa; others had only incidental interest or sympathy for emancipation. I ruthlessly excluded those who joined the abolitionists after 1840, because the political antislavery movement clearly poses a different set of causal problems. After this weeding out, I had reluctantly to drop other names because I was unable to secure more than random bits of information about them. Some of Weld's band of seventy agitators, for instance, were so obscure that even Barnes and Dumond were unable to identify them. There remained the names of one hundred and six abolitionists, the hard core of active antislavery leadership in the 1830's.

Most of these abolitionists were born between 1790 and 1810, and when the first number of the *Liberator* was published in 1831, their median age was twenty-nine. Abolitionism was thus a revolt of the young.

My analysis confirms the traditional identification of radical antislavery with New England. Although I made every effort to include Southern and Western leaders, eighty-five percent of these abolitionists came from northeastern states, sixty per cent from New England, thirty per cent from Massachussets alone. Many of the others were descended from New England families. Only four of the leaders were born abroad or were second-generation immigrants.

The ancestors of these abolitionists are in some ways as interesting as the antislavery leaders themselves. In the biographies of their more famous descendants certain standard phrases recur: "of the best New England stock," "of Pilgrim descent," "of a serious, pious household." The parents of the leaders generally belonged to a clearly defined stratum of society. Many were preachers, doctors, or teachers; some were farmers and a few were merchants; but only three were manufacturers (and two of these on a very small scale), none was a banker, and only one was an ordinary day laborer. Virtually all the parents were stanch Federalists.

These families were neither rich nor poor, and it is worth remembering that among neither extreme did abolitionism flourish. The abolitionist could best appeal to "the substantial men" of the community, thought Weld, and not to "the *aristocracy* and fashionable worldliness" that remained aloof from reform. In *The Burned-Over District,* an important analysis of reform drives in western New York, Whitney R. Cross has confirmed Weld's social analysis. In New York, antislavery was strongest in those counties which had once been economically dominant but which by the 1830's, though still prosperous, had relatively fallen behind their more advantageously situated neighbors. As young men the fathers of abolitionists had been leaders of their communities and states; in their old age they were elbowed aside by the merchant prince, the manufacturing tycoon, the corporation lawyer. The bustling democracy of the 1830's passed them by; as the Reverend Ludovicus Weld lamented to his famous son Theodore: "I have . . . felt like a stranger in a strange land."

If the abolitionists were descendants of old and distinguished New England families, it is scarcely surprising to find among them an enthusiasm for higher education. The women in the movement could not, of course, have much formal education, nor could the three Negroes here included, but of the eighty-nine white male leaders, at least fifty-three attended college, university, or theological seminary. In the East, Harvard and Yale were the favored schools; in the West, Oberlin; but in any case the training was usually of the traditional liberal-arts variety.

For an age of chivalry and repression there was an extraordinary proportion of women in the abolitionist movement. Fourteen of these leaders were women who defied the convention that the female's place was at the fireside, not in the forum, and appeared publicly as antislavery apostles. The Grimké sisters of South Carolina were the most famous of these, but most of the antislavery heroines came from New England.

It is difficult to tabulate the religious affiliations of antislavery leaders. Most were troubled by spiritual discontent, and they wandered from one set to another seeking salvation. It is quite clear, however, that there was a heavy Congregational-Presbyterian and Quaker preponderance. There were many Methodists, some Baptists, but very few Unitarians, Episcopalians, or Catholics. Recent admirable dissertations on the antislavery movement in each of the Western states, prepared at the University of Michigan under Professor Dumond's supervision, confirm the conclusion that, except in Pennsylvania, it is correct to consider humanitarian reform and Congregational-Presbyterianism as causally interrelated.

Only one of these abolitionist leaders seems to have had much connection with the rising industrialism of the 1830's, and only thirteen of the entire group were born in any of the principal cities of the United States. Abolition was distinctly a rural movement, and throughout the crusade many of the antislavery leaders seemed to feel an instinctive antipathy toward the city. Weld urged his following: "Let the great cities *alone;* they must be burned down by *back fires.* The springs to touch in order to move them *lie in the country.*"

In general the abolitionists had little sympathy or understanding for the problems of an urban society. Reformers though they were, they were men of conservative economic views. Living in an age of growing industrialization, of tenement congestion, of sweatshop oppression, not one of them can properly be identified with the labor movement of the 1830's. Most would agree with Garrison, who denounced labor leaders for trying "to inflame the minds of our working classes against the more opulent, and to persuade men that they are contemned and oppressed by a wealthy aristocracy." After all, Wendell Phillips assured the laborers, the American factory operative could be "neither wronged nor oppressed" so long as he had the ballot. William Ellery Channing, gentle high priest of the Boston area, told dissatisfied miners that moral self-improvement was a more potent weapon than strikes, and he urged that they take advantage of the leisure afforded by unemployment for mental and spiritual self-cultivation. A Massachusetts attempt to limit the hours of factory operatives to ten a day was denounced by Samuel Gridley Howe, veteran of a score of humanitarian wars, as "emasculating the people" because it took from them their free right to choose their conditions of employment.

The suffering of laborers during periodic depressions aroused little sympathy among abolitionists. As Emerson remarked tartly, "Do not tell me . . . of my obligation to put all poor men in good situations. Are they *my* poor? I tell thee, thou foolish philanthropist, that I grudge the dollar, the dime, the cent I give to such men. . . ."

Actually it is clear that abolitionists were not so much hostile to labor as indifferent to it. The factory worker represented an alien and unfamiliar system toward which the antislavery leaders felt no kinship or responsibility. Sons of the old New England of Federalism, farming, and foreign commerce, the reformers did not fit into a society that was beginning to be dominated by a bourgeoisie based on manufacturing and trade. Thoreau's bitter comment, "We do not ride on the railroads; they ride on us," was more than the acid aside of a man whose privacy at Walden had been invaded; it was the reaction of a class whose leadership had been discarded. The bitterest attacks in the journals of Ralph Waldo Emerson, the most pointed denunciations in the sermons of Theodore Parker, the harshest philippics in the orations of Charles Sumner were directed against the "Lords of the Loom," not so much for exploiting their labor as for changing the character and undermining the morality of old New England.

As Lewis Tappan pointed out in a pamphlet suggestively titled *Is It Right to Be Rich?*, reformers did not object to ordinary acquisition of money. It was instead that "eagerness to amass property" which made a man "selfish, unsocial, mean, tyrannical, and but a nominal Christian" that seemed so wrong. It is worth noting that Tappan, in his numerous examples of the vice of excessive accumulation, found this evil stemming from manufacturing and banking, and never from farming or foreign trade—in which last occupation Tappan himself flourished.

Tappan, like Emerson, was trying to uphold the old standards and to protest against the easy morality of the new age. "This invasion of Nature by Trade with its Money, its Credit, its Steam, its Railroads," complained Emerson, "threatens to upset the balance of man, and establish a new universal monarchy more tyrannical than Babylon or Rome." Calmly Emerson welcomed the panic of 1837 as a wholesome lesson to the new monarchs of manufacturing: "I see good in such emphatic and universal calamity. . . ."

Jacksonian democracy, whether considered a labor movement or a triumph of laissez-faire capitalism, obviously had little appeal for the abolitionist conservative. As far as can be determined, only one of these abolitionist leaders was a Jacksonian; nearly all were strong Whigs. William Lloyd Garrison made his first public appearance in Boston to endorse the arch-Whig Harrison Gray Otis; James G. Birney campaigned throughout Alabama to defeat Jackson; Henry B. Stanton wrote editorials for anti-Jackson newspapers. Not merely the leaders but their followers as well seem to have been hostile to Jacksonian democracy, for it is estimated that fifty-nine out of sixty Massachusetts abolitionists belonged to the Whig party.

Jacksonian Democrats recognized the opposition of the abolitionists and accused the leaders of using slavery to distract public attention from more immediate economic problems at home. "The abolitionists of the North have mistaken the color of the American slaves," Theophilus Fisk wrote tartly; "all the real Slaves in the United States have pale faces. . . . I will venture to affirm that there are more slaves in Lowell and Nashua alone than can be found South of the Potomac."

III

Hert, then, is a composite portrait of abolitionist leadership. Descended from old and socially dominant Northeastern families, reared in a faith of aggressive piety and moral endeavor, educated for conservative leadership, these young men and women who reached maturity in the 1830's faced a strange and hostile world. Social and economic leadership was being transferred from the country to the city, from the farmer to the manufacturer, from the preacher to the corporation attorney. Too distinguished a family, too gentle an education, too nice a morality were handicaps in a bustling world of business. Expecting to lead, these young people found no followers. They were an elite without function, a displaced class in American society.

Some—like Daniel Webster—made their terms with the new order and lent their talents and their family names to the greater glorification of the god of trade. But many of the young men were unable to overcome their traditional disdain for the new money-grubbing class that was beginning to rule. In these plebeian days they could not be successful in politics; family tradition and education prohibited idleness; and agitation allowed the only chance for personal and social self-fulfillment.

If the young men were aliens in the new industrial society, the young women felt equally lost. Their mothers had married preachers, doctors, teachers, and had become dominant moral forces in their communities. But in rural New England of the 1830's the westward exodus had thinned the ranks of eligible suitors, and because girls of distinguished family heistated to work in the cotton mills, more and more turned to school-teaching and nursing and other socially useful but unrewarding spinster tasks. The women, like the men, were ripe for reform.

They did not support radical economic reforms because fundamentally these young men and women had no serious quarrel with the capitalistic system of private ownership and control of property. What they did question, and what they did rue, was the transfer of leadership to the wrong groups in society, and their appeal for reform was a strident call for their own class to re-exert its former social dominance. Some fought for prison reform; some for women's rights; some for world peace; but ultimately most came to make that natural identification between moneyed aristocracy, textile-manufacturing, and Southern slave-grown cotton. An attack on slavery was their best, if quite unconscious, attack upon the new industrial system. As Richard Henry Dana, Jr., avowed: "I am a Free Soiler, because I am . . . of the stock of the old Northern gentry, and have a particular dislike to any subserviency on the part of our people to the slave-holding oligarchy"—and, he might have added, to their Northern manufacturing allies.

With all its dangers and all its sacrifices, membership in a movement like abolitionism offered these young people a chance for a reassertion of their traditional values, an opportunity for association with others of their kind, and a possibility of achieving that self-fulfillment which should traditionally have been theirs as social leaders. Reform gave meaning to the lives of this displaced social elite. "My life, what has it been?" queried one young seeker; "the painting of a soul after eternity—the feeling that there was nothing here to fill the aching void, to provide enjoyment and occupation such as my spirit panted for. The world, what has it been? a howling wilderness. I seem to be just now awakened . . . to a true perception of the end of my being, my duties, my responsibilities, the rich and perpetual pleasures which God has provided for us in the fullfillment of duty to Him and to our fellow creatures. Thanks to the A[nti]. S[lavery]. cause, it first gave an impetus to my palsied intellect. . . ."

Viewed against the backgrounds and common ideas of its leaders, abolitionism appears to have been a double crusade. Seeking freedom for the Negro in the South, these reformers were also attempting a restoration of the traditional values of their class at home. Leadership of humanitarian reform may have been influenced by revivalism or by British precedent, but its true origin lay in the drastic dislocation of Northern society. Basically, abolitionism should be considered the anguished protest of an aggrieved class against a world they never made.

Such an interpretation helps explain the abolitionists' excessive suspicion of Abraham Lincoln. Not merely did the President, with his plebeian origins, his lack of Calvinistic zeal, his success in corporate law practice, and his skill in practical politics, personify the very forces

that they thought most threatening in Northern society, but by his effective actions against slavery he left the abolitionists without a cause.
The freeing of the slaves ended the great crusade that had brought
purpose and joy to the abolitionists. For them Abraham Lincoln was
not the Great Emancipator; he was the killer of the dream.

2.

ENGLISH EDUCATION AND INDIAN NATIONALISM (1940)

BRUCE MCCULLY

The foregoing survey of English education and the genesis of Indian
nationalism suggests certain unavoidable conclusions. It seems reasonably clear, in the first place, that the nationalism of the 'seventies and
'eighties was permeated with the strains of a foreign culture. National
feeling did not germinate of its own accord in the soil of India; rather
it was an exotic growth implanted by foreign hands and influences.
Without the existence of the British regime and the element of foreign
domination implicit in that system, the beginnings of Indian nationalism
would be difficult to envisage. In the course of time it is possible, had
the Mogul empire of the seventeenth century remained intact, that national feeling might have arisen as a result of ordinary commercial and
other contacts with Europe. The later history of China, Persia, Egypt,
Turkey and other non-European countries seems to countenance such
a supposition. But in this instance it is idle to speculate upon what
might have happened. The fact was that the British, by a combination
of good luck and good management, did gain control of the peninsula
during the eighteenth and nineteenth century. In India as elsewhere
foreign rule produced an atmosphere favorable to the growth of national
sentiment, and foreign education in time created a native intelligentsia
in whose rank such ideas found a ready welcome.

SOURCE. Bruce McCully, *English Education and Indian Nationalism*. New
York: Columbia University Press 1940, pp. 388–396. Copyright 1940 by Columbia
University Press, and 1966 by Bruce T. McCully. Reprinted by permission of the
author.

CHARACTERISTICS OF EARLY NATIONALIST THOUGHT IN INDIA

If the hand of the foreigner prepared the country for the reception of nationalist dogma, it also moulded the content of early nationalist thought. Much of the latter—as the writings of Banerjea and other exponents show—was European in origin, having been appropriated almost wholesale from the teachings of continental doctrinaires like Mazzini. The Liberal nationalists of India—the Banerjeas, the Naorojis, the Mehtas, the Ghoses, and others—invented little or nothing in the way of ideology. Their contribution to Indian nationalist thought consisted for the most part in expounding a modified version of doctrines which they had picked up as students in the Indian universities or acquired later while studying in England or abroad. Even the tactics of the European nationalists were imitated. Banerjea, it is true, prudently abandoned Mazzini's concept of mass insurrection as "impractical"; yet he attempted to emulate the methods of the Italian by organizing among the native students of Bengal and Upper India a kind of Young India modelled after Mazzini's Young Italy and Young Germany. The pattern of English party politics and to some extent the tactics of the Irish nationalists during the 'seventies furnished men of his stamp with fruitful examples of "constitutional" agitation. The study of English history and political theory indoctrinated the native intelligentsia with ideals and aspirations incompatible with the existing political order in India. Such notions previously had no currency at all in that land of shrines and temple.

The content of early Indian political and economic nationalist thought was therefore derivatory to considerable degree. Foreign learning and influences also contributed to the genesis of non-political nationalist doctrines. Hindu cultural nationalism was an outgrowth of the cultural conflict precipitated by the spread of English education among a people whose institutions, customs and traditions differed profoundly from those of Western Europe. From the days of Sir William Jones to those of Max Müller European scholars had been occupied in unveiling the learning and literature of ancient India. English and continental philologists traced the origins of Sanskrit back to a mysterious Indo-European tongue which they claimed had been the parent of most of the languages spoken in modern Europe. They showed how Europeans and Hindus were really distant kin-folk, since both peoples were presumably descended from the same tribes that once grazed their flocks on the grasslands near the Caspian Sea. Their researches revealed the greatness of the Aryan civilization that had flourished in the dim past ages in Upper India.

All this was seized upon by certain Hindus who, though themselves members of the educated class, distrusted the frank materialism of the civilization which the British were spreading throughout the land. Like the Slavophils of Russia, these Hindus turned their backs upon the enlightenment of Europe to romanticize about the superiority of their own Aryan ancestors. Their writings over-flowed with a mystical reverence for their racial past which was represented as a golden age of heroes, seers, and virtuous, upright tribes folk. Ceaselessly they prophesied the regeneration of India, but they made it abundantly clear that this could come about only through the revival of ancient Hindu values and ideals, and not by the adoption of those of nineteenth century Europe. And in sublime disregard for the Mohammedan and other native communities they talked confidently of the unity of India in terms of the Hindu race and Hindu civilization.

Thus two distinct strands appear in the fabric of early Indian nationalist theories. One school of thought, deeply imbued with English political and economic doctrines, drew its chief inspiration from contemporary European nationalism. The other school, alarmed by the steady penetration of foreign civilization throughout the peninsula, advocated a revival of ancient Hindu culture in order to check the threatened Europeanization of their country. Oddly enough both of these contradictory doctrines in some instances were expounded by the same persons. This paradox reflected that inner conflict which practically every educated native experienced at some time or other in the course of his life. Many members of the educated class never succeeded in resolving the conflict. To the end of their days some of them, like Keshub Chundra Sen and his cousin Norendranath Sen, the editor of the *Indian Mirror,* vacillated between these two poles of nationalist thought. Later dissensions in the Congress Party are traceable to the differences represented by the two opposing theories. Even native interpretations of the origins of Indian nationalism have mirrored this dualism, as a recent bibliographical study shows.

THE ROLE OF THE EDUCATED CLASS
IN THE NATIONALIST MOVEMENT

Why did such nationalist doctrines secure a following among a people like the Hindus with no vital political traditions and no genuine feeling for their own history? The answer would seem to lie in the group interests of the educated class which had emerged by the 'seventies and 'eighties. Detached from the soil or from the hereditary crafts of their

forefathers, many partially educated natives eked out a miserable existence as quill-drivers in the business houses and Government officies
of the larger urban centers in India. Lacking social position or property,
unable to rise above the status of petty clerks, they formed a kind
of rootless educated proletariat whose dissatisfaction with their lot was
only too well founded. Their intellectual superiors, the educated élite
who held degrees from one or another of the Indian universities, generally had little difficulty in keeping the wolf from the door. Nevertheless
they too nursed a grievance against the haughty foreigners who monopolized the highly-paid posts in the Government services. Common education drew the lower and upper strata of the educated class together
Mutual dislike of the Anglo-Indian bureaucracy cemented the alliance. It
was not hard to appeal to such natives with the slogan "India for the Indians"—the Civil Service agitation of 1877–1880 in Bengal showed that,
though it left the authorities unmoved. The interplay of idea and interest
became increasingly evident as political agitation began to bear fruit
in the form of more and more native recruits. The objects of the Indian
Association, the program of the Madras Mahajana Sabha, of the Bombay
Presidency Association, the agendas of sundry regional conferences cul-
minating in the first Indian National Congress at Poona, all bespoke
the political interests of educated India.

Here in the needs and urges of the latter is to be found the strength
and weakness of the nascent nationalist movement of the 1880's. The
native intelligentsia was bound together by ties of culture which set
its members apart from their less fortunate fellow-countrymen; it was
ambitious, capable and highly articulate; its leader knew what they
wanted and did not hesitate to make their voices heard. In the native
English and vernacular Press they possessed an instrument of propaganda by means of which public opinion in India could be moulded
in accordance with the views and interests of the educated community
at large. Indeed, the Press repeatedly claimed as its function the
right to speak in behalf of the governed and, in general, to interpret
the views of the country as a whole on the burning questions of the
day. Common interests no less than a common stock of ideas helped
to promote mutual aspirations among most educated Indians at that
time. Participation in an organized movement like the Indian National
Congress was therefore the logical step for the intelligentsia to take
if such ambitions were to be realized. Once the Congress was founded,
native political aspirations awoke outside the ranks of the educated
class. As the Congress movement with its all-India outlook gathered
headway, other elements—Mohammedan and Hindu princes, petty
traders, artisans and peasants—jumped on the band-wagon. "Each year,"

wrote Sir William Hunter of the Congress in 1888, "its electoral organization becomes better developed, its sense of responsibility and its consciousness of power increase, the Mohammedans take a more important share in its proceedings and it justifies more fully its claim to be considered a National Indian Congress." But for a long time the leadership of the Congress party remained in the hands of the Hindu intelligentsia and its allies.

This circumstance, taken in conjunction with other factors, operated to prevent Indian nationalism from partaking of the character of a mass movement. The citadel of the educated and professional classes was situated in urban India. In the 'eighties that part of the peninsula which was under British jurisdiction contained but 44 towns with upwards of 50,000 inhabitants each—altogether less than one-thirtieth of the total population. Hence the Congress party despite its claim to represent all India, could at most speak for only a small fraction of the people. From its infancy the nationalist movement bore the marks of its bourgeois origin. The very thing that made for homogeneity among educated natives—a common language—effectively inhibited the spread of nationalist sentiment among the vernacular-speaking masses. Like English education, Indian nationalism was an urban phenomenon, without meaning to the peasantry in a peasant country. When one considers that as late as 1930 not more than 2% of the Indian population could talk English, the essential weakness of the national movement is apparent. Wherever it became a mass movement, the foreign language played no part in its success.

It is an article of faith with modern Indian nationalists that their movement has the support of Mohammedan no less than of Hindu India. The contention has been vigorously challenged by critics of the Congress party. Whatever the truth may be today, in its infancy Indian nationalism was virtually synonymous with Hindu nationalism. Political organizations with avowedly nationalistic aims, such as the Indian Association, could boast few Moslem members. Regional political conferences in Calcutta, Bombay and Madras failed to attract any support from Mohammedan organizations until 1885. Only one Moslem "delegate" appeared at Poona to attend the inaugural meeting of the Indian National Congress which was overwhelmingly Hindu and Parsee in composition. Neither the organization nor the doctrines of Indian nationalism at that time seem to have appealed to Mohammedan tastes, despite the propaganda for "national unity" broadcast by the native Press.

This situation was due partly to the growing rivalry of Hindu and Mohammedan, and partly to the political apathy of all but educated Moslems. The latter could hardly show much enthusiasm for theories

of Hindu cultural nationalism which glorified the "Aryan" elements in
India's civilization and sought to invoke a highly un-Mohammedan set
of traditional values and ideals. Liberal nationalism won some recruits
among the Mohammedan community, but not many at that time since
few Moslems had sufficient education to share the aims and aspirations
that drew the Hindu intelligentsia into the nationalist movement. Mohammedan leaders were not indifferent to the nationalists' clamor that
the Indian Government ought to be liberalized, but they were more
concerned with the broad problem of overcoming the backwardness
of their co-religionists and of restoring them to the position which they
once enjoyed among the various Indian communities. Toward that end
they sought to promote equality of opportunity in education, in the
professions, in the Civil Service, in local and provincial government
bodies, and so on. Their agitation followed communal rather than nationalistic lines: witness the aims of the National Mohammedan Association which Syed Amir Ali organized in Bengal during the late 'seventies.
Educated Mohammedans were Mohammedans first and foremost and
Indian nationalists only secondarily; if forced to choose between an
all-embracing nationalism and the interests of the community to which
they belonged, they invariably chose the latter. This explains why so
sincere a champion of Hindu-Moslem unity as Sir Syed Ahmad Khan
broke with the Congress party soon after its establishment.

Thus English education failed to bridge the gap permanently between
the two great communities. Indeed, by qualifying disproportionate numbers of Hindus for Government service and professional employment,
it probably accentuated inter-communal rivalry. Such an atmosphere
was ill-calculated to turn Mohammedans into ardent Indian nationalists.
For Hindus and other communities on an equal footing with Hindus,
however, higher education provided an element of unity, a synthetic
force which transcended linguistic and regional differences and drew
its beneficiaries together into a fairly homogeneous grouping on the
basis of a common culture. Among educated natives, as the evidence
abundantly shows, the notion of an Indian nationality comprehending
the entirety of the peninsula crystalized and at length assumed tangible
expression in the Congress movement. It is difficult to see what other
agency could have performed this original creative function save foreign
schooling. Certainly not religion, not indigenous learning, not the traditional forms of social organization, nor all three together could have
done so. A common language or anything approaching it did not exist.
Yet some common factor was necessary in order to bring together in
a single cause natives of different provinces and localities, speaking
different tongues, and lacking any strong tradition of group action for

political ends. English education fulfilled such an integrating function and for that reason alone, as many native writers have since acknowledged, it played a major role in the genesis of the nationalist movement.

Schooled in a foreign culture, speaking a foreign tongue when occasion demanded, indoctrinated with foreign political, social and economic concepts, the native intelligentsia developed individual and collective aspirations very different from those once expected. Instead of being the staunch ally of the Anglo-Indian administration as Grant and Trevelyan had prophesied, educated natives became vigorous competitors of the bureaucracy. Instead of serving as a buttress of British imperialism, they had turned into its bitterest critics. Instead of dwelling with loving appreciation upon the benevolence of their rulers, they found constant fault with those in authority against whom they raised the cry of "India for the Indians." Finding their aspirations blocked by the opposition of bureaucrats and resident non-official Europeans, they denounced the racial prejudices of their foes and turned to the task of building their own political organizations. Such, in brief, were the origins of Indian nationalism.

B.

The Social Base of Movements

3.

FASCISM—LEFT, RIGHT, AND CENTER (1959)

Seymour Martin Lipset

The return of De Gaulle to power in France in 1958 following a military *coup d'état* was accompanied by dire predictions of the revival of fascism as a major ideological movement, and raised anew the issue of the character of different kinds of extremist movements. Much of the discussion between Marxist and non-Marxist scholars before 1945 was devoted to an analysis of fascism in power and focused on whether the Nazis or other fascist parties were actually strengthening the economic institutions of capitalism or creating a new post-capitalist social order similar to Soviet bureaucratic totalitarianism.

While an analysis of the actual behavior of parties in office is crucial to an understanding of their functional significance, the social base and ideology of any movement must also be analyzed if it is to be truly understood. A study of the social bases of different modern mass movements suggests that each major social stratum has both democratic and extremist political expressions. The extremist movements of the left, right, and center (Communism and Peronism, traditional authoritarianism, and fascism) are based primarily on the working, upper, and middle classes, respectively. The term "fascism" has been applied at one time or another to all of these varieties of extremism, but an analytical examination of the social base and ideology of each reveals their different characters.

The political and sociological analysis of modern society in terms of left, center, and right goes back to the days of the first French Republic when the delegates were seated, according to their political coloration, in a continuous semicircle from the most radical and egalitarian on the left to the most moderate and aristocratic on the right. The identification of the left with advocacy of social reform and egalitarianism; the right, with aristocracy and conservatism, deepened as politics became defined as the clash between classes. Nineteenth-century conservatives and Marxists alike joined in the assumption that the socio-economic cleavage is the most basic in modern society. Since democracy has become institutionalized and the conservatives' fears that universal suffrage would mean the end of private property have declined, many people have begun to argue that the analysis of politics in terms of left and right and class conflict oversimplifies and distorts reality. However, the tradition of political discourse, as well as political reality, has forced most scholars to retain these basic concepts, although other dimensions, like religious differences or regional conflicts, account for political behavior which does not follow class lines.[1]

Before 1917 extremist political movements were usually thought of as a rightist phenomenon. Those who would eliminate democracy generally sought to restore monarchy or the rule of the aristocrats. After 1917 politicians and scholars alike began to refer to both left and right extremism, i.e., Communism and fascism. In this view, extremists at either end of the political continuum develop into advocates of dictatorship, while the moderates of the center remain the defenders of democracy. This chapter will attempt to show that this is an error—that extremist ideologies and groups can be classified and analyzed in the same terms as democratic groups, i.e., right, left, and *center*. The three positions resemble their democratic parallels in both the compositions of their social bases and the contents of their appeals. While comparisons of all three positions on the democratic and extremist continuum are of intrinsic interest, this chapter concentrates on the politics of the center, the most neglected type of political extremism, and that form of "left" extremism sometimes called "fascism"—Peronism—as manifested in Argentina and Brazil.

---

[1] In spite of the complexities of French politics, the foremost students of elections in that country find that they must classify parties and alternatives along the left-right dimension. See F. Goguel, *Géographie des élections françaises de 1870 à 1951, Cahiers de la fondation nationale des sciences politiques*, No. 27 (Paris: Librairie Armand Colin, 1951).

The center position among the democratic tendencies is usually called liberalism. In Europe where it is represented by various parties like the French Radicals, the Dutch and Belgian Liberals, and others, the liberal position means: in economics—a commitment to *laissez-faire* ideology, a belief in the vitality of small business, and opposition to strong trade-unions; in politics—a demand for minimal government intervention and regulation; in social ideology—support of equal opportunity for achievement, opposition to aristocracy, and opposition to enforced equality of income; in culture—anticlericalism and antitraditionalism.

If we look at the supporters of the three major positions in most democratic countries, we find a fairly logical relationship between ideology and social base. The Socialist left derives its strength from manual workers and the poorer rural strata; the conservative right is backed by the rather well-to-do elements—owners of large industry and farms, the managerial and free professional strata—and those segments of the less privileged groups who have remained involved in traditionalist institutions, particularly the Church. The democratic center is backed by the middle classes, especially small businessmen, white-collar workers, and the anticlerical sections of the professional classes.

The different extremist groups have ideologies which correspond to those of their democratic counterparts. The classic fascist movements have represented the extremism of the center. Fascist ideology, though antiliberal in its glorification of the state, has been similar to liberalism in its opposition to big business, trade-unions, and the socialist state. It has also resembled liberalism in its distaste for religion and other forms of traditionalism. And, as we shall see later, the social characteristics of Nazi voters in pre-Hitler Germany and Austria resembled those of the liberals much more than they did those of the conservatives.

The largest group of left extremists are the Communists, whose appeal has already been discussed in some detail and who will not concern us much in this chapter. The Communists are clearly revolutionary, opposed to the dominant strata, and based on the lower classes. There is, however, another form of left extremism which, like right extremism, is often classified under the heading of fascism. This form, Peronism, largely found in poorer underdeveloped countries, appeals to the lower strata against the middle and upper classes. It differs from Communism in being nationalistic, and has usually been the creation of nationalist army officers seeking to create a more vital society by destroying the corrupt privileged strata which they believe have kept the masses in poverty, the economy underdeveloped, and the army demoralized and underpaid.

Conservative or rightist extremist movements have arisen at different periods in modern history, ranging from the Horthyites in Hungary, the Christian Social party of Dollfuss in Austria, the Stahlhelm and other nationalists in pre-Hitler Germany, and Salazar in Portugal, to the pre-1958 Gaullist movements and the monarchists in contemporary France and Italy. The right extremists are conservative, not revolutionary. They seek to change political institutions in order to preserve or restore cultural and economic ones, while extremists of the center and left seek to use political means for cultural and social revolution. The ideal of the right extremist is not a totalitarian ruler, but a monarch, or a traditionalist who acts like one. Many such movements—in Spain, Austria, Hungary, Germany, and Italy—have been explicitly monarchist, and De Gaulle returned monarchical rights and privileges to the French presidency. Not surprisingly, the supporters of these movements differ from those of the centrists; they tend to be wealthier, and—more important in terms of mass support—more religious.

The thesis that fascism is basically a middle-class movement representing a protest against both capitalism *and* socialism, big business *and* big unions, is far from original. Many analysts have suggested it ever since fascism and Nazism first appeared on the scene. Nearly twenty-five years ago, the economist David Saposs stated it well:

√ Fascism . . . [is] the extreme expression of middle-classism or populism. . . . The basic ideology of the middle class is populism. . . . Their ideal was an independent small property-owning class consisting of merchants, mechanics, and farmers. This element . . . now designated as middle class, sponsored a system of private property, profit, and competition on an entirely different basis from that conceived by capitalism. . . . From its very inception it opposed "big business" or what has now become known as capitalism.

Since the war the death knell of liberalism and individualism has been vociferously, albeit justly, sounded. But since liberalism and individualism are of middle-class origin, it has been taken for granted that this class has also been eliminated as an effective social force. As a matter of fact, populism is now as formidable a force as it has ever been. And the middle class is more vigorously assertive than ever. . . .[2]

[2] David J. Saposs, "The Role of the Middle Class in Social Development: Fascism, Populism, Communism, Socialism," in *Economic Essays in Honor of Wesley Clair Mitchell* (New York: Columbia University Press, 1935), pp. 395, 397, 400. An even earlier analysis by André Siegfried based on a detailed ecological study of voting patterns in part of France from 1871 to 1912, suggested that the petty bourgeoisie who had been considered the classic source of French democratic ideology were becoming the principal recruiting grounds for extremist movements. Siegfried pointed out that though they are "by nature egalitarian democratic, and envious . . . they are fearful above all of new economic conditions which threatened to eliminate them, crushed between the aggressive capitalism of the great companies and the increasing rise of the working people. They place great hopes in the Republic, and they do not cease being republican or egalitarian. But they are in that state of

And although some have attributed the lower middle-class support for Nazism to the specific economic difficulties of the 1930s, the political scientist, Harold Lasswell, writing in the depths of the Depression, suggested that middle-class extremism flowed from trends inherent in capitalist industrial society which would continue to affect the middle class even if its economic position improved.

> Insofar as Hitlerism is a desperation reaction of the lower middle classes, it continues a movement which began during the closing years of the nineteenth century. Materially speaking, it is not necessary to assume that the small shopkeepers, teachers, preachers, lawyers, doctors, farmers and craftsmen were worse off at the end than they had been in the middle of the century. Psychologically speaking, however, the lower middle class was increasingly overshadowed by the workers and the upper bourgeoisie, whose unions, cartels and parties took the center of the stage. The psychological impoverishment of the lower middle class precipitated emotional insecurities within the personalities of its members, thus fertilizing the ground for the various movements of mass protest through which the middle classes might revenge themselves.[3]

As the relative position of the middle class declined and its resentments against on-going social and economic trends continued, its "liberal" ideology—the support of individual rights against large-scale power— changed from that of a revolutionary class to that of a reactionary class. Once liberal doctrines had supported the *bourgeoisie* in their fight against the remnants of the feudal and monarchical order, and against the limitations demanded by mercantilist rulers and the Church. A liberal ideology opposed to Throne and Altar and favoring a limited state emerged. This ideology was not only revolutionary in political terms; it fulfilled some of the functional requirements for efficient industrialization. As Max Weber pointed out, the development of the capitalist system (which in his analysis coincides with industrialization) necessitated the abolition of artificial internal boundaries, the creation of an open international market, the establishment of law and order, and relative international peace.[4]

---

discontent, from which the Boulangisms marshal their forces, in which reactionary demagogues see the best ground in which to agitate, and in which is born passionate resistance to certain democratic reforms." André Siegfried, *Tableau politique de la France de l'ouest sous la troisième république* (Paris: Librairie Armand Colin, 1913). p. 413.

[3] Harold Lasswell, "The Psychology of Hitlerism," *The Political Quarterly*, 4 (1933), p. 374.

[4] See also Karl Polanyi, *The Great Transformation* (New York: Farrar and Rinehart, 1944).

But the aspirations and ideology which underlay eighteenth- and nine-teenth-century liberalism and populism have a different meaning and serve a different function in the advanced industrial societies of the twentieth century. Resisting large-scale organizations and the growth of state authority challenges some of the fundamental characteristics of our present society, since large industry and a strong and legitimate labor movement are necessary for a stable, modernized social structure, and government regulation and heavy taxes seem an inevitable concomi-tant. To be against business bureaucracies, trade-unions, and state regu-lation is both unrealistic and to some degree irrational. As Talcott Par-sons has put it, the "new negative orientation to certain primary aspects of the maturing modern social order has above all centered in the symbol of 'capitalism'. . . . The reaction against the 'ideology' of the rationaliza-tion of society is the principal aspect at least of the ideology of fascism."[5]

While continuing conflict between management and labor is an in-tegral part of large-scale industrialism, the small businessman's desire to retain an important place for himself and his social values is "reaction-ary"—not in the Marxist sense of slowing down the wheels of revolution, but from the perspective of the inherent trends of a modern industrial society. Sometimes the efforts of the small business stratum to resist or reverse the process take the form of democratic liberal movements, like the British Liberal party, the French Radicals, or the American Taft Republicans. Such movements have failed to stop the trends which their adherents oppose, and as another sociologist, Martin Trow, recently noted: "The tendencies which small businessmen fear—of concentration and centralization—proceed without interruption in depression, war and prosperity, and irrespective of what party is in power; thus they are *always* disaffected. . . ."[6] It is not surprising, therefore, that under cer-tain conditions small businessmen turn to extremist political movements, either fascism or antiparliamentary populism, which in one way or an-other express contempt for parliamentary democracy. These movements answer some of the same needs as the more conventional liberal parties; they are an outlet for the stratification strains of the middle class in

[5] Talcott Parsons, "Some Sociological Aspects of the Fascist Movement," in his *Essays in Sociological Theory* (Glencoe: The Free Press, 1954), pp. 133–134. Marx himself pointed out that "the small manufacturer, the small merchant, the artisan, the peasant, all fight against the [big] bourgeois, in order to protect their position as a middle class from being destroyed. They are, however, not revolutionary, but conservative. Even more, they are reactionary, they look for a way to reverse the path of history," quoted in S. S. Nilson, "Wahlsoziologische Probleme des National-sozialismus," *Zeitschrift für die Gesamte Staatswissenchaft*, 110 (1954), p. 295.

[6] Martin A. Trow, "Small Businessmen, Political Tolerance, and Support for McCarthy," *American Journal of Sociology*, 64 (1958), pp. 279–280.

a mature industrial order. But while liberalism attempts to cope with the problems by legitimate social changes and "reforms" ("reforms" which would, to be sure, reverse the modernization process), fascism and populism propose to solve the problems by taking over the state and running it in a way which will restore the old middle classes' economic security and high standing in society, and at the same time reduce the power and status of big capital and big labor.

The appeal of extremist movements may also be a response by different strata of the population to the social effects of industrialization at different stages of its development. These variations are set in sharp relief by a comparison of the organized threats to the democratic process in societies at various stages of industrialization. As I have already shown, working-class extremism, whether Communist, anarchist, revolutionary socialist, or Peronist, is most commonly found in societies undergoing rapid industrialization, or in those where the process of industrialization did not result in a predominantly industrial society, like the Latin countries of southern Europe. Middle-class extremism occurs in countries characterized by both large-scale capitalism and a powerful labor movement. Right-wing extremism is most common in less developed economies, in which the traditional conservative forces linked to Throne and Altar remain strong. Since some countries, like France, Italy, or Weimar Germany, have possesed strata in all three sets of circumstances, all three types of extremist politics sometimes exist in the same country. Only the well-to-do, highly industrialized and urbanized nations seem immune to the virus, but even in the United States and Canada there is evidence that the self-employed are somewhat disaffected.

The different political reactions of similar strata at different points in the industrialization process are clearly delineated by a comparison of the politics of certain Latin-American countries with those of Western Europe. The more well-to-do Latin-American countries today resemble Europe in the nineteenth century; they are experiencing industrial growth while their working classes are still relatively unorganized into trade-unions and political parties, and reservoirs of traditional conservatism still exist in their rural populations. The growing middle class in these countries, like its nineteenth-century European counterpart, supports a democratic society by attempting to reduce the influence of the anticapitalist traditionalists and the arbitrary power of the military.[7]

[7] For an analysis of the political role of the rapidly growing Latin-American middle classes see John J. Johnson, *Political Change in Latin America—the Emergence of the Middle Sectors* (Stanford: Stanford Univesity Press, 1958). The different political propensities of a social group at successive stages of industrialization are indicated by James Bryce's comment in 1912 that "the absence of that class

To the extent that there is a social base at this stage of economic development for extremist politics, it lies not in the middle classes but in the
growing, still unorganized working classes who are suffering from the
tensions inherent in rapid industrialization. These workers have provided
the primary base of support for the only large-scale "fascist" movements
in Latin America—those of Peron in the Argentine and Vargas in Brazil.
These movements, like the Communist ones with which they have sometimes been allied, appeal to the "displaced masses" of newly industrializing countries.

The real question to answer is: which strata are most "displaced"
in each country? In some, it is the new working class, or the working
class which was never integrated in the total society, economically or
politically; in others, it is the small businessmen and other relatively
independent entrepreneurs (small farm owners, provincial lawyers) who
feel oppressed by the growing power and status of unionized workers
and by large-scale corporative and governmental bureaucracies. In still
others, it is the conservative and traditionalist elements who seek to
preserve the old society from the values of socialism and liberalism.
Fascist ideology in Italy, for example, arose out of an opportunistic
movement which sought at various times to appeal to all three groups,
and remained sufficiently amorphous to permit appeals to widely different strata, depending on national variation as to who were most "displaced."[8] Since fascist politicians have been extremely opportunistic in
their efforts to secure support, such movements have often encompassed
groups with conflicting interests and values, even when they primarily
expressed the needs of one stratum. Hitler, a centrist extremist, won
backing from conservatives who hoped to use the Nazis against the
Marxist left. And conservative extremists like Franco have often been
able to retain centrists among their followers without giving them control
of the movement.

---

of small landowners which is the soundest and most stable element in the United
States and in Switzerland and is equally stable, if less politically trained, in France
and parts of Germany, is a grave misfortune for South and Central America." This
may have been true in an early period, before the impact of large-scale organization
of the farms meant economic competition for small farmers and added them to the
rank of the potential supporters of fascism, as the data on Germany and other
countries discussed here show. See James Bryce, *South America: Observations and
Impressions* (New York: Macmillan, 1912), p. 533.

[8] A comparison of the European middle class and the Argentine working class,
which argues that each is most "displaced" in its respective environment, is contained
in Gino Germani, *Intergracion politica de las masas y la totalitarismo* (Buenos Aires:
Colegio Libre de Estudios Superiores, 1956). See also his *Estructura social de la
Argentina* (Buenos Aires: Raigal, 1955).

In the . . . chapter on working-class authoritarianism I tried to specify some of the other conditions which dispose different groups and individuals to accept more readily an extremist and demonological view of the world.[9] The thesis presented there suggested that a low level of sophistication and a high degree of insecurity predispose an individual toward an extremist view of politics. Lack of sophistication is largely a product of little education and isolation from varied experiences. On these grounds, the most authoritarian segments of the middle strata should be found among the small entrepreneurs who live in small communities or on farms. These people receive relatively little formal education as compared with those in other middle-class positions; and living in rural areas or small towns usually means isolation from heterogeneous values and groups. By the same token, one would expect more middle-class extremism among the self-employed, whether rural or urban, than among white-collar workers, executives, and professionals.

The following sections bring together available data for different countries which indicate the sharp difference between the social roots of classic fascism and populism and those of right-wing movements.

GERMANY ✓

The classic example of a revolutionary fascist party is, of course, the National Socialist Workers' party led by Adolf Hitler. For Marxian analysts, this party represented the last stage of capitalism, winning power in order to maintain capitalism's tottering institutions. Since the Nazis came to power before the days of public opinion polls, we have to rely on records of the total votes to locate their social base. If classic fascism appeals largely to the same elements as those which back liberalism, then the previous supporters of liberalism should have provided the backing for the Nazis. A look at the gross election statistics for the German Reich between 1928 and 1933 would seem to verify this (Table 1).

Although a table like this conceals changes by individuals which go against the general statistical trend, some reasonable inferences may be made. As the Nazis grew, the liberal bourgeois center parties, based on the less traditionalist elements of German society—primarily small business and white-collar workers—completely collapsed. Between 1928 and 1932 these parties lost almost 80 per cent of their vote, and their proportion of the total vote dropped from a quarter to less than 3 per

[9] See pp. 108–14 of Chap. 4. (Ed. note: original volume)

TABLE 1   PERCENTAGES OF TOTAL VOTE RECEIVED BY VARIOUS GERMAN
PARTIES, 1928–1933, AND THE PERCENTAGE OF THE 1928 VOTE
RETAINED IN THE LAST FREE ELECTION 1932[a]

Party	Percentage of Total Vote					Ratio of 1928 to Second 1932 Election Expressed as Percentage
Conservative Party	1928	1930	1932	1932	1933	
DNVP	14.2	7.0	5.9	8.5	8.0	60
Middle-class Parties						
DVP (right liberals)	8.7	4.85	1.2	1.8	1.1	21
DDP (left liberals)	4.8	3.45	1.0	.95	.8	20
Wirtschaftspartei						
(small business)	4.5	3.9	0.4	0.3	1	7
Others	9.5	10.1	2.6	2.8	.6	29
Total proportion of middle-class vote maintained:						21
Center (Catholic)	15.4	17.6	16.7	16.2	15.0	105
Workers' Parties						
SPD (Socialist)	29.8	24.5	21.6	20.4	18.3	69
KPD (Communist)	10.6	13.1	14.3	16.85	12.3	159
Total proportion of working-class vote maintained:						92
Fascist Party						
NSDAP	2.6	18.3	37.3	33.1	43.9	1277
Total proportion of increase in Fascist party vote:						1277

[a] The basic data are presented in Samuel Pratt, *The Social Basis of Nazism and Communism in Urban Germany* (M.A. thesis, Dept. of Sociology, Michigan State University, 1948), pp. 29, 30. The same data are presented and analyzed in Karl D. Bracher, *Die Auflösung der Weimarer Republik* (Stuttgart and Düsseldorf: Ring Verlag, 1954), pp. 86–106. The 1933 election was held after Hitler had been chancellor for more than a month.

[b] The *Wirtschaftspartei* did not run any candidates in the 1933 elections.

cent. The only center party which maintained its proportionate support was the Catholic Center party whose support was reinforced by religious allegiance. The Marxist parties, the socialists and the Communists, lost about a tenth of their percentage support, although their total vote dropped only slightly. The proportionate support of the conservatives dropped about 40 per cent, much less than that of the more liberal middle-class parties.

An inspection of the shifts among the non-Marxist and non-Catholic parties suggests that the Nazis gained most heavily among the liberal middle-class parties, the former bulwarks of the Weimar Republic. Among these parties, the one which lost most heavily was the *Wirtschaftspartei,* which represented primarily small businessman and artisans.[10] The right-wing nationalist opponent of Weimar, the German National People's party (DNVP), was the only one of the non-Marxist and non-Catholic parties to retain over half of its 1928 proportion to the total vote.

The largest drop-off in the conservative vote lay mainly in the election districts on the eastern border of Germany. The proportion of the vote obtained by the German National People's party declined by 50 per cent or more between 1928 and 1932 in ten of the thirty-five election districts in Germany. Seven of these ten were border areas, including every region which fronted on the Polish corridor, and Schleswig-Holstein, fronting on the northern border. Since the party was both the most conservative and the most nationalist pre-Nazi opponent of the Versailles Treaty, these data suggest that the Nazis most severely weakened the conservatives in those areas where nationalism was their greatest source of strength, while the conservatives retained most of their voters in regions which had not suffered as directly from the annexations imposed by Versailles and in which, it may be argued, the party's basic appeal was more conservative than nationalist. The German-American sociologist Rudolf Heberle has demonstrated in a detailed study of voting patterns in Schleswig-Holstein that the conservatives lost the backing of the small property owners, both urban and rural, whose counterparts in nonborder areas were most commonly liberals, while they retained the backing of the upper-strata conservatives.[11]

Some further indirect evidence that the Nazis did not appeal to the same sources as the traditional German right may be found in the data on the voting of men and women. In the 1920s and 1930s the more conservative or religious a party, the higher, in general, its feminine support. The German National People's party had more female backing than any party except the Catholic Center party. The Nazis, together

[10] Karl D. Bracher, *Die Auflösung der Weimarer Republic* (Stuttgart und Düsseldorf: Ring Verlag, 1954), p. 94. The parliamentary delegation of this party was almost exclusively composed of businessmen who were active in the interest group associations of small business. See Sigmund Neumann, "Germany: Changing Patterns and Lasting Problems" in S. Neumann, ed., *Modern Political Parties* (Chicago: University of Chicago Press, 1956), p. 364.

[11] Rudolf Heberle, *From Democracy to Nazism* (Baton Rouge: Louisiana State University Press, 1945).

with the more liberal middle-class parties and Marxist parties, received disproportionate support from men.[12]

More direct evidence for the thesis is given in Heberle's study of Schleswig-Holstein, the state in which the Nazis were strongest. In 1932 *the Conservatives were weakest where the Nazis were strongest and the Nazis were relatively weak where the Conservatives were strong.* The correlation in 18 predominantly rural election districts between percentages of votes obtained by the NSDAP [Nazis] and by the DNVP [Conservatives] is negative (minus .89). . . . It appears that the Nazis had in 1932 really succeeded the former liberal parties, like the *Landespartei* and Democratic party, as the preferred party among the small farmers . . . while the landlords and big farmers were more reluctant to cast their vote for Hitler."[13]

A more recent analysis by a German political scientist, Günther Franz, identifying voting trends in another state in which the Nazis were very strong—Lower Saxony—reported similar patterns. Franz concluded:

> The majority of the National Socialist voters came from the bourgeois center parties. The DNVP [conservatives] had also lost votes, but in 1932, they held the votes which they received in 1930, and increased their total vote in the next two elections. They were (except for the Catholic Center) the only bourgeois party, which had not simply collapsed before the NSDAP. . . .[14]

This situation in Schleswig-Holstein and Lower Saxony also existed in Germany as a whole. Among the thirty-five electoral districts, the rank-order correlation of the proportionate Nazi gain with the liberal parties' loss was greater (.48) than with the conservatives' loss (.25).[15]

Besides the liberal parties, there was one other group of German

[12] The most comprehensive set of German election data presenting party vote in different elections by sex may be found in Maurice Duverger, *La Participation des femmes à la vie politique* (Paris: UNESCO, 1955), pp. 56–63; and Gabriele Bremme, *die politische Rolle der Frau in Deutschland* (Göttingen: Vandenhoeck and Ruprecht, 1956), pp. 74–77, 111, 343–52; see also Heinrich Striefler, *Deutsche Wahlen in Bildern und Zahlen* (Düsseldorf: Wilhelm Hagemann, 1946), pp. 20–22; Günther Franz, *Die politischen Wahlen in Niedersachsen 1867 bis 1949* (Bremen-Horn: Walter Dorn Verlag, 1957), pp. 28–32; Karl D. Bracher, *op. cit.*, p. 476; Herbert Tingsten, *Political Behavior: Studies in Election Statistics*, London: P. S. King & Son, 1937), pp. 37–65.

[13] Rudolf Heberle, *op. cit.*, pp. 113, 114, 119 (emphasis supplied).

[14] Günther Franz, *op. cit.*, p. 62.

[15] The six eastern border districts in which Nazi gain and conservative loss were both high account for the small positive correlation between the two. Without these six districts, the correlation is actually negative.

parties, based on the *Mittel-stand*, whose supporters seem to have gone over almost en masse to the Nazis—the so-called "federalist" or regional autonomy parties.[16] These parties objected either to the unification of Germany or to the specific annexation of various provinces like Hesse, Lower Saxony, and Schleswig-Holstein to Prussia. In large measure they gave voice to the objections felt by the rural and urban middle classes of provincial areas to the increasing bureaucratization of modern industrial society and sought to turn the clock back by decentralizing government authority. At first glance, the decentralist aspirations of the regional autonomy parties and the glorification of the state inherent in fascism or Nazism seem to reflect totally dissimilar needs and sentiments. But in fact both the "state's rights" ideology of the regionalists and the Nazis' ideological antagonism to the "big" forces of industrial society appealed to those who felt uprooted or challenged. In their economic ideology, the regional parties expressed sentiments similar to those voiced by the Nazis before the latter were strong. Thus the *Schleswig-Holsteinische Landespartei*, which demanded "regional and cultural autonomy for Schleswig-Holstein within Germany," wrote in an early program:

> The craftsman [artisan] has to be protected on the one hand against capitalism, which crushes him by means of its factories, and on the other hand against socialism, which aims at making him a proletarian wage-laborer. At the same time the merchant has to be protected against

---

[16] In Schleswig-Holstein, the regionalist *Landespartei* was strong in 1919 and 1921 in the same districts in which the liberal Democratic party secured its greatest vote. These were the same areas which went most heavily Nazi in the 1930s. See R. Heberle, *op. cit.*, pp. 98–100; in Lower Saxony, an examination of the vote suggests that the supporters of the *Welfen*, the Hanoverian regionalists, who were a major party in the state until 1932, went over to the Nazis. Those "middle-class and rural voting districts . . . in which the Welfen secured their largest vote, became the earliest and strongest centers of Nazism." See G. Franz. *op. cit.*, pp. 53–54, also p. 62. In Bavaria, a somewhat comparable party, the *Bayerischer Bauern und Mittelstandsbund*, dropped from 11.1 per cent in 1928 to 3.3 per cent in 1932. And a study of Bavarian voting patterns suggests that it, like the other regionalist parties, lost its voters predominantly to the Nazis. See Meinrad Hagman, *Der Weg ins Verhängnis, Reichstagswahlergebnisse 1919 bis 1933 besonders aus Bayern* (München; Michael Beckstein Verlag, 1946), pp. 27–28. A sympathetic analysis of the way in which an agrarian regionalist movement paved the way for Nazi electoral victory in Hesse is Eugen Schmahl, *Entwicklung der völkischen Bewegung* (Giessen: Emil Roth Verlag, 1933). This book contains an appendix which analyzes electoral shifts from 1930 to 1932 by a Nazi, Wilhelm Seipel, "Entwicklung der nationalsozialistischen Bauern-bewegung in Hessen," pp. 135–67. In the elections for the provincial assembly in 1931, the Hessen Landbund's representation dropped from 14 per cent to 3 per cent, and the organization shortly thereafter withdrew as a political party, and made an agreement with the Nazis. *Ibid.*, pp. 163–65.

capitalism in the form of the great department stores, and the whole retail trade against the danger of socialism.[17]

The link between regionalism as an ideology protesting bigness and centralization, and the direct expression of the economic self-interest of the small businessmen may be seen in the joining of the two largest of the regional parties, the Lower Saxon *Deutsch-Hanoverischen Partei* and the Bavarian *Bauern und Mittelstandsbund,* into one parliamentary faction with the *Wirtschaftspartei,* the party which explicitly defined itself as representing the small entrepreneurs. In the 1924 elections the Bavarian regionalists and the small businessmen's party actually presented a joint electoral ticket.[18] As Heberle points out about these parties: "The criticism of Prussian policy . . . the demand for native civil servants, the refusal to accept Berlin as the general center of culture, were all outlets for a disposition which had been formed a long time before the war. . . . At bottom and criticism against Prussia was merely an expression of a general antipathy against the social system of industrial capitalism. . . ."[19]

The appeal of the Nazis to those elements in German society which resented the power and culture of the large cities is also reflected in the Nazis 'success in small communities. A detailed ecological analysis of voting in German cities with 25,000 or more population, in 1932, indicates that *the larger the city, the smaller the Nazi vote.* The Nazis secured less of their total vote in cities over 25,000 in size than did any of the other five major parties, including the Catholic Center and the conservative DNVP.[20] And Berlin, the great metropolis, was the only predominantly Protestant election district in which the Nazis received under 25 per cent of the vote in July 1932.[21] These facts sharply challenge the various interpretations of Nazism as the product of the

[17] Cited in R. Herberle, *op. cit.,* p. 47. The *Hessische Volksbund* expressed similar sentiments in Hesse. *Ibid.,* p .52.
[18] F. A. Hermens, *Demokratie und Wahlrecht* (Paderborn: Verlag Ferdinand Schöningh, 1933), pp. 125–26; and Günther Franz, *op. cit.,* p. 53.
[19] R. Heberle, *op. cit.,* p. 49.
[20] Samuel A. Pratt, *op. cit.,* pp. 63, 261–66; Herberle also reports that within Schleswig-Holstein, "An analysis of election returns by communities showed a rather strong inverse correlation between the size of the community and the percentage of votes obtained by the NSDAP." R. Herberle, *op. cit.,* p. 89; Bracher, differentiating the 35 large election districts into those which were high or low in voting Nazis, found that the high Nazi districts were more rural than the low ones. This parallels Pratt's findings. See Karl A. Bracher, *op. cit.,* pp. 647–48.
[21] All the studies agree that religion affected support of the Nazis *more* than any other factor. The Nazis were weak in Catholic regions and cities, and secured majorities in many Protestant small communities.

growth of anomie and the general rootlessness of modern urban industrial society.

Examination of the shifts in patterns of German voting between 1928 and 1932 among the non-Marxist and non-Catholic parties indicates, as we have seen, that the Nazis gained disproportionately from the ranks of the center and liberal parties rather than from the conservatives, thus validating one aspect of the thesis that classic fascism appeals to the same strata as liberalism. The second part of the argument, that fascism appeals predominantly to the self-employed among the middle strata, has been supported by three separate ecological studies of German voting between 1928 and 1932. Two American sociologists, Charles Loomis and J. Allen Beegle, correlated the percentage of the Nazi vote in 1932 in communities under 10,000 in population in three states with the percentage of the labor force in specific socioeconomic classes and found that "areas in which the middle classes prevailed [as indicated by the proportion of proprietors in the population and the ratio of proprietors to laborers and salaried employees] gave increasingly larger votes to the Nazis as the economic and social crises settled on Germany."

This high correlation between Nazi vote and proprietorship holds for farm owners as well as owners of small business and industry in Schleswig-Holstein and Hanover, but not in Bavaria, a strongly Catholic area where the Nazis were relatively weak.[22] Heberle's study of Schleswig-Holstein, which analyzed all of the elections under Weimar, concluded that "the classes particularly susceptible to Nazism were neither the rural nobility and the big farmers nor the rural proletariat, but rather the small farm proprietors, very much the ura equivalent of the lower middle class or petty bourgeoisie (*Kleinbuergertum*) which formed the backbone of the NSDAP in the cities."[23]

The sociologist Samuel Pratt's excellent study of urban voting prior to the Nazi victory related the Nazi vote in July 1932 to the proportion of the population in the "upper middle class," defined as "proprietors of small and large establishments and executives," and the proportion

[22] Charles P. Loomis and J. Allen Beegle, "The Spread of German Nazism in Rural Areas," *American Sociological Review*, 11 (1946), pp. 729, 730. Catholic affiliation constantly overrides class or other allegiances as a major determinant of party support in practically all election data for Germany, in both the Weimar and Bonn republics. The Nazis' largest support in Bavaria and other Catholic areas came from Protestant enclaves, a fact which makes ecological analysis that does not hold religious affiliation constant relatively useless in such regions.

[23] R. Heberle, *op. cit.*, p. 112; Franz also reports that in Lower Saxony, " It was the bourgeois middle-class in the cities, and the farm-owners on the land who supported the NSDAP." Günther Franz, *op. cit.*, p. 62.

TABLE 2   THE RATIO OF THE PERCENTAGE OF MEN IN THE NAZI
PARTY TO THE PERCENTAGE IN THE GENERAL POPULATION
FROM VARIOUS OCCUPATIONS, 1933[a]

Occupational Category	1933
Manual workers	68%
White-collar workers	169
Independents[b]	187
Officials (civil servants)	146
Peasants	60
Domestic servants, and nonagricultural family helpers	178

[a] Computed from a table in Hans Gerth, "The Nazi Party: Its Leadership and Composition," in Robert K. Merton, *et al.*, eds., *Reader in Bureaucracy* (Glencoe: The Free Press, 1952), p. 106.

[b] Includes self-employed businessmen, artisans, and free professionals.

in the "lower middle class," composed of "civil servants and white-collar employees." The Nazi vote correlated highly with the proportion in both middle-class groups in different-size cities and in different areas of the country, but the correlations with the "lower middle class" were not as consistently high and positive as those with the "upper middle." As Pratt put it: "Of the two elements of the middle class, the upper seemed to be the more thoroughly pro-Nazi."[24] The so-called upper class, however, was predominantly composed of small businessmen, so that the correlation reported is largely that of self-employed economic status with Nazi voting.[25] This interpretation is enhanced by Pratt's finding that the Nazi vote also correlated ($+.6$) with the proportion of business establishments with only one employee—in other words, self-employment. "This would be expected, for plants of one employee are another measure of the proprietorship class which was used in measuring the upper middle class."[26]

The occupational distribution of the membership of the Nazi party in 1933 indicates that it was largely drawn from the various urban middle-class strata, with the self-employed again being the most overrepresented (Table 2). The second most overrepresented category—domestic servants and nonagricultural family helpers—also bears witness to the

[24] See Samuel A. Pratt, *op. cit.*, p. 148.

[25] Examination of the German census for 1933 reveals that over 90 per cent of the "upper middle-class" category used by Pratt is filled by "proprietors," with only a small proportion coming from employed groups.

[26] Samuel A. Pratt, *op. cit.*, p. 171.

party's appeal to small business, since this category is primarily composed of helpers in family-owned small businesses.

The relation of German big business to the Nazis has been a matter of considerable controversy, particularly since various Marxists have attempted to demonstrate that the movement was from the outset "fostered, nourished, maintained and subsidized by the big *bourgeoisie,* by the big landlords, financiers, and industrialists."[27] The most recent studies suggest that the opposite is true. With the exception of a few isolated individuals, German big business gave Nazism little financial support or other encouragement *until* it had risen to the status of a major party. The Nazis did begin to pick up financial backing in 1932, but in large part this backing was a result of many businesses' policy of giving money to all major parties except the Communists in order to be in their good graces. Some German industrialists probably hoped to tame the Nazis by giving them funds. On the whole, however, this group remained loyal to the conservative parties, and many gave no money to the Nazis until after the party won power.[28]

The ideal-typical Nazi voter in 1932 was a middle-class self-employed Protestant who lived either on a farm or in a small community, and who had previously voted for a centrist or regionalist political party strongly opposed to the power and influence of big business and big labor. This does not mean that most Nazi voters did not have other characteristics. Like all parties looking for an electoral majority, the Nazis tried to appeal to some degree to every large group of voters.[29]

---

[27] R. Palme Dutt, *Fascism and Social Revolution* (New York: International Publishers, 1934), p. 80.

[28] See F. Thyssen, *I Paid Hitler* (New York: Farrar and Rinehart, 1941), p. 102; Walter Gorlitz and Herbert Quint, *Hitler, Eine Biographie* (Stuttgart: Steingrubben Verlag, 1952), pp. 284, 286; Edward Norman Peterson, *Hjalmar Schacht for and against Hitler* (Boston: The Christopher Publishing House, 1954), pp. 112–17; for general discussion and documentation see also August Heinrichsbauer, *Schwerindustrie und Politik* (Essen: Verlag Glückauf, 1948); Arild Halland, *Nazismen i Tyskland* (Bergen: John Griegs Forlag, 1955); and Louis P. Lochner, *Tycoons and Tyrants, German Industry from Hitler to Adenauer* (Chicago: Henry Regnery Co., 1954).

[29] An analysis of the sources of the vote for the Social Democratic party in 1930 estimated that 40 per cent of the SPD voters were not manual workers, that the party was backed in that year by 25 per cent of the white-collar workers, 33 per cent of the lower civil servants, and 25 per cent of the self-employed in artisan shops and retail business. But the core of the SPD support was employed, skilled manual workers, while the core of the Nazi strength was small owners, both urban and rural. See Hans Neisser, "Sozialstatistischen Analyse des Wahlergebnisses," *Die Arbeit,* 10 (1930), pp. 657–58.

They clearly had a great deal of success with other middle-class groups, particularly the unemployed.[30] And at the low point of the Great Depression, which affected Germany more than any other industrial nation, discontent with the "system" was widespread throughout the society. However, as a movement, Nazism was most attractive to those with the characteristics summarized above.

4.

THE ANALYSIS OF A
COUNTER-REVOLUTION (1963)

CHARLES TILLY

Just as a theory of heredity which could not account for the occasional appearance of dramatically new genetic traits would be considered incomplete, a theory of revolution, or an analysis of a specific revolution, which provides no understanding of the presence of counter-revolutionary forces in the midst of a society in revolt must leave us unsatisfied. If a theory purports to tell us when and why a society is ready for rebellion, it also ought to tell us which sectors of the society will resist the rebellion, and why. Exceptions prove the rule. Counter-revolutions test our explanations of revolutions.

If this is true, it is of no small interest to examine the ways that historians have handled the problem of counter-revolution. There is no "theory of counter-revolution" as such, but most analyses of counter-revolutions have relied implicitly on general conceptions of the nature of revolution. Almost always, furthermore, the historian's attitude toward the revolution in question has shaped his understanding of the counter-revolution which arose in its shadow.

One might think that everyone would agree with Meusel's description of counter-revolution as "an attempt to reverse the transformations effected in a revolution; its success signalizes the triumph of the upper class, which has been endangered and temporarily displaced by the

SOURCE: Charles Tilly, "The Analysis of a Counter-Revolution." *History and Theory*, **III** (1963–64), pp. 30–37; 45–58.

[30] Pratt reports a high positive correlation between white-collar unemployment and the Nazi vote in the cities. See S. Pratt, *op. cit.*, Chap. 8.

revolution." Yet this description rests on a particular (if popular) theory of revolution, one which leads to the conclusion that "When a great revolution finally breaks, it encounters virtually no internal opposition; it appears to unite the people rather than to separate them into hostile camps." It no longer seems indubitable that this is the case, even for the most frequently cited model, the great French Revolution. There is accordingly room for doubt about the corollary propositions on the nature of counter-revolution.

One reasonable way to deal with this doubt would be to assemble information about a number of counter-revolutions, in order to discern any uniformities in their personnel, circumstances or organization. That would be an absorbing venture, but it is not the task of this paper. For there is another problem, more obscure but equally interesting, whose outline is flickering in the background. How have historians conceived the problem of explaining counter-revolution, and how have their conceptions of the problem influenced the results they have obtained? If we were lucky enough to stumble onto valid answers to these questions, we would greatly increase our ability to evaluate the available explanations, both general and particular, of revolution and counter-revolution. I wish to present some possible answers to these questions. They are derived very largely from reflection on one major instance of resistance to the French Revolution, and therefore cry out for comparison and correction.

I

The instance is the counter-revolution of the Vendée. Despite the eagerness with which they have disagreed over the origins of the Vendée, historians have commonly agreed on what was to be explained. They have displayed a bent that is at once psychological and judicial, seeking to accumulate evidence on the mentalities and motives of a very limited number of "actors" (consisting of either outstanding personalities or groups seen as moving in unison), and striving by means of judgments of motives to assign responsibility for the events. The motives supplied have often been in the form of articulated beliefs about the nature of the world—ideologies. Perhaps the most important point is that these conceptions of the nature of the problem have strongly influenced the kinds of explanations that have been seriously considered, the forms of historical craftsmanship that have been employed, and the conclusions at which students of the counter-revolution have arrived. There are other ways of defining the problem, and they lead to other sorts of explanations, other methods of dealing with the available documents, even to somewhat different conclusions. I shall attempt to substantiate this claim by displaying the results of defining the problem as many sociologists would be inclined to see it.

The case for discussion, the counter-revolution of the Vendée, is important in itself. The first, and probably the most potent, concentration of provincial opposition to the Revolution, the revolt in the West which began in 1793 threatened the work of the new regime, hindered the prosecution of the war, provided the occasion for enactment of some of the terrible legal instruments of the Terror, and intermittently distracted the central government from other tasks until 1799. In the course of the year 1793, there were at one time or another 50,000 to 100,000 rebels under arms in the section of western France south of the Loire. The inhabitants of the area most intensely involved in the counter-revolution—below the Loire—comprised some 2% of the entire population of France. By its sheer bulk, the Vendée rebellion commands attention.

How shall we explain the existence of this massive counter-revolution? The commonsense answer is: find out exactly who rebelled, and then look for evidence of their motives when the rebellion began. This is, in large part, what historians of the Vendée have sought to do.[1] Their agreement on the task at hand does not mean they have reached a happy consensus on the identities of those most responsible, or on their motives. Writers on the Vendée have generally been just-as-partisan as their zealous protestations of impartiality would lead a cynic to suspect. Yet until the very recent and very important work of Paul Bois, they had uniformly sought to place the *responsibility* for the Vendée on one group or another.[2] This was true whether they thought this

---

[1] The main works to which the following discussion applies are: H. Baguénier-Désormeaux, *Les origines et les responsabilités de l'insurrection vendéenne* (Fontenay-le-Comte, 1916); Alphonse de Beauchamp, *Histoire de la Guerre de la Vendée* (Paris, 1820), 4 vols.; P. V. J. Berthre de Bourniseaux, *Histoire des guerres de la Vendée et des Chouans* (Paris, 1819), 3 vols.; Ch.-L. Chassin, *La préparation de la guerre de Vendée* (Paris, 1892), 3 vols.; Joseph Clémenceau (F. Uzureau, ed.), *Histoire de la guerre de la Vendée (1793–1815)* (Paris, 1909); J. Crétineau-Joly, *Histoire de la Vendée Militaire* (Paris, 1851), 4 vols.; Félix Déniau, *Histoire de la Guerre de la Vendée* (Angers, 1878), 6 vols.; Léon Dubreuil, *Histoire des insurrections de l'Ouest* (Paris, 1929), 2 vols.; Émile Gabory, *La Révolution et la Vendée* (Paris, 1925), 3 vols; Pierre de la Gorce *Histoire religiouse de la Révolution française* (Paris, 1911), vol. II; Théodore Muret, *Histoire des guerres de l'Ouest* (Paris 1848), 3 vols.; Henri de Malleray, *Les Cinq Vendées* (Angers and Paris, 1924); Célestin Port, *La Vendée angevine* (Paris, 1888), 2 vols.; J. J. M. Savary, *Guerres des Vendéens et des Chouans contre la République française* (Paris, 1824–27), 6 vols.

[2] Paul Bois, *Paysans de l'Ouest* (Le Mans, 1960); Bois, *Cahier de doléances du tiers état de la Sénéchaussée de Château-du-Loir pour les États généraux de 1789* (Gap, 1960); Bois, "Réflexions sur les survivances de la Révolution dans l'Ouest," *Annales historiques de la Révolution française*, XXXIII (Avril-Juin, 1961), 177–186.

responsibility a badge of honor or a mark of shame. To assign the responsibility, they undertook the almost-judicial reconstruction of the motives and conscious actions of the relevant groups: the peasants, the nobles, the clergy. It is no great surprise to learn that Célestin Port, in his introduction to his partisan, lively and valuable *Vendée angevine,* presented what he regarded as the most important conclusion of the book in these terms:

> For my part, I pursued this study for a long time with the considered prejudice that the whole war had been fomented by the clergy. I have left it with a contrary conviction.[3]

The conviction was that the nobility, by means of a far-flung plot, had done the job themselves. In his change of views, Port had not left behind the assumption that explanation meant finding a responsible group, and proving that responsibility by reconstructing its motives and intentional activities.

Even those willing to present as forthright an explanation as Célestin Port's have to contend with the fact that a large number of men who were neither nobles nor priests took up arms in the rebellion. As a result, almost all analysts of the Vendée have tried to reconstruct the mentality of the mass of the rebels, considering them to be a representative selection of the region's peasantry. And this raises a new problem. It is not easy to argue that narrow self-interest—often taken for granted in the case of nobles or priests—drove the bulk of the population into counter-revolution. Mathiez, to be sure, made a gesture in that direction, but in the end his analysis came to: a) deep peasant malaise, plus b) agitation by priests and nobles. It is possible, however, to insert an ideology into the same logical structure. One can explain a group's behavior on the basis of its distinctive beliefs and attitudes, even if one finds those beliefs and attitudes tainted.

In this context, the problem of ideology is not the usual (if horrendously complex) one of analyzing the origins and functions of a set of beliefs about the social world. Rather, the (no less vexing) question is the extent to which it is possible to explain major actions of large collections of men by reference to such beliefs. Certainly historians of both the Revolution and the counter-revolution have undertaken such explanations; witness Crane Brinton's insistence on the analogy between the revolutionary view of the world and eschatological religion, as well as Gabory's portrayal of the counter-revolutionary peasants as defenders of their own view of organized religion. The most fully ideological ex-

---

[3] Port *op. cit.,* I, xii–xiii.

planations of the Vendée have been the work of writers, like Gabory, sympathetic to the counter-revolution. In response to such explanations, historians closer to the Republican mainstream have often been moved to distinguish, with disconcerting confidence, between "true religion," on the one hand, and superstition, mindless fanaticism or blind ritualism, on the other. In his illuminating review of counter-revolutionary doctrine and action in France, for example, Jacques Godechot remarks that ". . . generally speaking, the peasant of the West was quite attached to religious practice, if not to religion itself . . ."—an echo to Savary's contention, a century and a half earlier, that to the Vendean peasant, religion meant lighting "a candle for St. Michael, and one for his serpent."

Why these inquiries into faith and reason? Pro-revolutionary historians appear to be uncomfortable with *any* assertion that the Vendeans acted in accordance with a well-articulated set of beliefs. Perhaps that is because such a conclusion raises some doubt about the universal acceptability of the Revolution's point of view to the French masses. At any rate, rejection of the premise that an ideology existed has barred pro-revolutionary historians from seriously considering the character of the Vendean *Weltanschauung*. Those who have not rejected the premise (who are, of course, mainly counter-revolutionary in their leanings) have considered the Vendean view of the world to be so evident that they, too, have neglected to analyze it in any detail. The bizarre outcome is that no one has presented a careful and cogent argument that the rebels acted in accordance with a distinctive ideology. If it is true, as Peter Paret contends, that "in the Vendée the young Republic for the first time encountered an opponent possessing a somewhat comparable ideological élan," this is a remarkable oversight.

Ideology, in short, has appeared in accounts of the Vendée as an alternative to a) interest, b) other attitudes and feelings excited by the Revolution. It has been an explanatory device, rather than an object of study. And its use confirms the general tendency to see the crucial problem in explanation as the identification of the states of mind of the principal participants at the moments of decisive action. The historiography of the Vendée offers a fairly pure example of the common propensity to conceive of historical process and historical explanation psychologically. This propensity is certainly far from disreputable. It is, indeed, the foundation of such well-built philosophies of history as Collingwood's: "Reflective acts may be roughly described as the acts which we do on purpose, and these are the only acts which can become the subject-matter of history." But it is a foundation on which one cannot build any sort of structure one pleases.

This simple observation returns us to the main point. The "psychological" conception of the problem of explanation implies a distinctive form of argument. It implies the selection of units of analysis which can reasonably be thought of as acting consciously and collectively, the identification of a limited number of principal actors, the attribution of suitable motives, and the assignment of a personal sort of responsibility for critical events. These features of the argument, in turn, encourage the investigator to select, use and present those data which can be taken most directly as evidence of the intentions of participants in the critical events. Finally, they increase the probability that the major issues over which historians will disagree will be questions of motivation and responsibility. There is an internal logic to the Vendée's historiography.

The first element of this logic is the selection of the units whose action is to be explained. From the beginning, there have been three groups almost no writer on the Vendée has neglected: the nobles, the priests and the peasants. As early as the year of the rebellion itself, Momoro was declaring:

> Criminal priests, taking advantage of the credulity of the inhabitants of the country, succeeded in making them rebel against the authority of the nation in the name of religion. But those priests, the horror of all humanity, remained hidden behind a screen, as did the former nobles who crowded into the region from the four corners of France; they waited for the favorable moment to appear and put themselves at the head of the rebellious peasants.

The language has moderated since that time, but the principle has not changed very much: identify a small number of groups whose members can be thought of as acting collectively, with common intentions. Generally, these are groups which were already acting collectively before the Revolution rather than, for example, latent interest groups suddenly sensing their common destinies, or organizations formed and recruited from diverse origins during the Revolution itself. In the account offered by the soundest of the "Catholic" historians, Gabory, the cast of characters consists of the clergy, the nobles, the peasants and the bourgeoisie:

> In the Vendée, resistance to the Revolution was in a way the struggle of the nobles and the peasants against the bourgeois . . .
> Much more so than the nobles, the clergy contributed *indirectly* to the uprising.

But as Gabory's account proceeds, the bourgeois role shrinks to that of an unhappy target, rather than an active participant.

In the years since the Revolution, the number of actors that historians have felt compelled to distinguish in order to account for its general course has greatly increased. With Michelet, there is only one: The People. By the time we reach Taine, we must at least distinguish the plotting bourgeois from the furious masses. The heirs of Jean Jaurès have worked persistently at increasing the cast by dividing up the role once assigned to a single player, the Third Estate. Georges Lefebvre separates the Aristocratic Revolution, the Bourgeois Revolution, the Popular Revolution and the Peasant Revolution from each other. And now a new generation of historians is at work subdividing the role of the urban populus.[4] The parallel evolution in the historiography of the Vendée has been much more irregular and sluggish. (Maybe if more historians in sympathy with the Left could interest themselves in such a reactionary movement, the process of subdivision would advance more rapidly.) In the last significant general history of the counter-revolution, now more than thirty years old, Dubreuil offered distinctions between the upper and lower clergy, among several types of bourgeois, and even among a few different kinds of peasants. But these distinctions faded in the course of the analysis, leaving Dubreuil with the traditional nobles, peasants, priests and bourgeois.

One of the postulates of this type of analysis is that the groups distinguished are homogeneous in motivation. The model group assumed by the author resembles a single-minded individual more than it does, say, a modern political party composed of people from a variety of social positions or a factory within which conflict and contention flourish. As a result, the existence of a few individuals who do not fit the pattern (such as nobles who buy church properties) often embarrasses the author a good deal. For the advantage of working with a small number of actors is that it is possible to define their motives boldly and simply, and then to watch them blend or clash.

The motives assigned are critical, because so many writers treat them as the fundamental causes of the counter-revolution. Therefore, to make explanation of the Vendée convincing, one should offer some evidence that one has attributed the correct motives to the actors. The motivations of the nobles have almost always been taken to be self-evident, and this has often been the case for the clergy. The motives of the

---

[4] Jules Michelet, *Histoire de la Révolution française* (Paris, 1847–53), 7 vols.; Hippolyte Taine, *La Révolution* (Paris, 1878–84), 3 vols.; Jean Jaurès, *Histoire socialiste de la Révolution française* (Paris, 1901–1904), 4 vols.; Albert Mathiez, *La Révolution française* (Paris, 1924–27), 3 vols.; Georges Lefebvre, *The Coming of the French Revolution* (Princeton, 1947); Lefebvre, *La Révolution française* (Paris, 1951); Albert Soboul, *Les Sans-culottes parisiens en l'an II* (La Roche-sur-Yon, 1958); George Rudé, *The Crowd in the French Revolution* (Oxford, 1959); Kare Tønnesson, *La Défaite des sans-culottes* (Oslo and Paris, 1959).

bourgeois have received little attention, and that mainly in the form of attributing personal ambition, frustration or enlightened patriotism to them on general grounds, without specific evidence. It is the motives of the peasants—or rather of everyone but the nobles, clergy and bourgeois—that have attracted the greatest interest.

A weak, if common, form of argument for a particular motive is the simple assertion that it is consistent with all the actions of the group in question. A closely related tactic is first to provide a description of the "character" of the inhabitant of the counter-revolutionary area, and then to use that character as an explanation of his actions in 1793; that is the procedure of the Abbé Déniau:

> Confined in their Bocage as a result of the difficulties of communication with the adjoining territories, the Vendeans lived a familial existence; people from the same neighborhood ordinarily met only on Sunday and the days of markets or fairs. . . . These sedentary habits had naturally preserved them from the pernicious influences of the so-called civilization of the time; so they were profoundly religious, full of lively and simple faith, always faithful to their Christian duties: celebration of all the holy days, prayers morning and evening, participation in the sacraments, fasts and abstinence, recitation, at vespers, at Rosary, everything was accomplished punctually and with the most edifying piety.

After a good deal more description in this vein, the author goes on to portray the Vendean as the spontaneous defender of wronged religion.

When there is specific evidence offered for motivations, as one might expect, it is ordinarily in the form of informed observation on the mood and intentions of the rebels, or actual declarations of the counter-revolutionary leaders. The 1791 report of the emissaries of the National Assembly, Gallois and Gensonné, who reported that it was mainly the recent religious changes that were agitating the West, has been cited innumerable times as evidence that the basic motivations of the counter-revolution were religious. The response of the Vendean generals to British inquiries about their intentions has had a similar popularity.

It is precisely at this point that the lines between causes, motives and ideologies have become hopelessly smudged. One of the key passages in Muret's explanation of the counter-revolution runs:

> When the news of the king's death resounded like a thunderbolt through the Bocage, it aroused a sentiment of horror and deep shock. . . . Everything that had happened in the last three years must have accustomed men's minds to crimes, and yet this one was beyond imagining. People could hardly believe that the scoundrels had dared to stain their hands with the blood of the Lord's annointed, and they wondered what plague would strike the earth after such a transgression. No more

than an occasion was needed to touch off the emotions that were boiling in everyone's heart.

With the greatest of ease, Muret swings among the levels of ideology (royalism), motives (righteous indignation) and causes (this state of mind plus the "occasion" offered by the imposition of conscription). These gymnastics are quite impressive, since they allow the author to judge the counter-revolution, assign the responsibility for its occurrence, judge the intentions of the principal participants, and explain it, all at the same time. . . .

III

It is no news that historians have disagreed about the Vendée, or that their positions have been related to their general attitudes toward the Revolution. The point I want to urge is that the deeply divisive issues are judgments of the motives of the principal participants—rather than such still-open questions as the distribution of power before 1789 or the extent of the actual participation of various elements of the population in the counter-revolution—and that the accentuation of these issues is the result of a structure of explanation in terms of intention and responsibility.

This way of seeing the problem of explanation has some serious drawbacks. For one thing, it seems to discourage the analyst from making careful distinctions among the groups whose behavior he is explaining. The egregious example is the "peasantry." When looked at close up, the non-noble, non-clerical mass of the rebels turns out to be quite heterogeneous, and far from strictly peasant in composition. The prominence of such chiefs as Stofflet (a game warden), Cathelineau (a carter), Cady (a physician), and Souchu (a minor official), gives fair warning of that fact. A large proportion of the rebels were rural artisans (around 40 percent, according to the best estimates I have been able to prepare for Southern Anjou). And the peasants themselves ranged from landless laborers to substantial leaseholders. It is not evident *a priori* that one can attribute a uniform set of motives to such a group, even if they did all join the rebellion. Yet the method of analysis itself resists the conception of the rebels as a collection of men with diverse, even inconsistent, intentions, varying over time, linked by power, personal influence or common enemies—as reasonable as such a description might seem for contemporary rebellions, armies or political factions. Even Dubreuil, who begins with a description full of nuances, ends by abandoning all but the most elementary distinctions.

Another difficulty is that a whole range of problems tends to evaporate in the course of the analysis, even when the writer intuits their importance. They are the problems that cannot be readily subsumed under the states of mind of the principal actors during the times of critical actions: the effects of kinship ties, the residues of previous conflicts, the existence of party alignments, the presence of group pressures, and so on. The tension between urban and rural is such a problem in the Vendée. Both Dubreuil and Gabory sensed its importance, Gabory labeling the counter-revolution a "struggle of the countryside against the cities." But except as the analysis of bourgeois and "peasant" behavior absorbed it, nothing more came of the insight. The consequence is that the historians of the counter-revolution (even those who, like Célestin Port, had plenty of evidence before them) have neglected the significance of local rural-urban conflicts in the process that led to rebellion.

The problem of ideology also disappears, all too quickly. Of course, many writers have felt the importance of a distinctive view of the world in the Vendée; military historians seem to have been particularly sensitive to it, perhaps because they had to explain how "insurgents beginning without cannon, without cavalry, without material, without munitions, armed in part with scythes, with sickles and with ploughshares, operating in a small theater that one can cross in four marches, [accumulated] triumph after triumph, not in simple skirmishes . . . but in pitched battles." General Turreau, who was in a position to know the ferocity of the Vendeans, hinted that their particular way of looking at the world was important:

> A way of fighting that no one had known before . . . an inviolable attachment to their party; unlimited confidence in their chiefs; such fidelity to their promises that it could take the place of discipline; indomitable courage . . . this is what made the Vendeans fearsome enemies and has placed them in history among the first rank of warrior peoples.

Despite all this, no historian of the Vendée has distinguished sharply enough among motives, causes and ideology to investigate how and when the distinctive outlook of the rebels was formed, how widely it was accepted, and in what way (if any) it constrained the course of the counter-revolution.

Explanation via intention and responsibility contains an even more serious defect, its discouragement of comparative analysis. So long as one holds an individualistic, psychological view of the actors, he will find it hard to see the relevance of systematic comparison with other actors: what seems to matter is the sympathetic understanding of those who did something, not of those who did not. Many writers have noted that the people of the larger cities, the Loire Valley and the plains surrounding the Vendée generally supported the Revolution. Then they have passed on to what they regarded as the business at hand, the description of the men who resisted the Revolution. They have not given serious attention to the most searching question of all: why the Vendée, and not somewhere else? In the rush away from this question, historians of the counter-revolution have also left behind the tasks of delineating accurately the territory whose inhabitants took active part in the fighting, as well as determining exactly what sorts of people participated most vigorously. Without these tasks accomplished, it is hard to see how a valid explanation could even begin. And until statements of the order of "The peasants were religious" are translated at least into others like "The peasants were *more* religious than those elsewhere, and religious peasants are more likely to resist revolution," it is even harder to see how any explanation could be verified.

The viewpoint that has prevailed in the analysis of the Vendée involves an extremely rationalistic model of human behavior—at least that part of human behavior which is worthy of historical analysis—and sets the historian the immensely difficult task of reconstructing states of mind. It drastically limits the part that systematic theory can play in historical explanation, since the relevant theories must be of a very special sort: theories of motives and states of mind. Instead, it encourages the analyst to introduce, implicitly, general propositions of an exceedingly simple order (e.g. "Men act in accordance with their material interests"). Furthermore, it draws the historian's attention away from alternative ways of defining his problem which may be equally profitable, and less likely to draw him into bootless debate. Perhaps it is significant that just as it was de Tocqueville, who never wrote a history of the Revolution itself, but brilliantly anticipated later forms of analysis of the Revolution, it was André Siegfried, who never wrote a history of the Vendée, who provided the most exciting ideas for further research on the counter-revolution. For it is Siegfried's intuitive, journalistic, often inaccurate observations on the relationship between social organization and political action in the West that offer the beginnings of a comparative sociological analysis of the counter-revolution.

A critical examination of what Siegfried had to say, in the course of which a great many of the important details turned out to be entirely wrong, started Paul Bois on his monumental comparative study of political life in the Sarthe. The re-examination of Siegfried eventually led him to reject some of the most cherished assumptions writers have made about rural life in the West: the predominance of noble landlords, the frequency of noble residence in the countryside, peasant resistance to the sale of church properties, and so on. Not all of Bois' conclusions are definitely established, but they are certainly powerful enough to expose the feeble foundation on which a great deal of previous writing has been based.

Bois' study of the Sarthe shows unremitting labor. However, it is not its thoroughness which is its most distinctive feature. The author did not just offer a "new interpretation." He asked new questions. The questions he asked did not focus on intention and responsibility, but on the characteristics that distinguished the areas of counter-revolutionary activity (in this case, the guerrilla of Chouannerie rather than the full-scale war of the Vendée) from those that remained calm after 1793. In doing so, he painstakingly tested each of the major variables Siegfried and other commentators had alleged to be related to the presence or absence of rightist politics and counter-revolutionary spirit. One by one, the idols fell: there was no correlation between large property and rightist voting; no fatal relationship between dispersed settlement (that producer of "independent character" and preserver of "religious spirit") and counter-revolution; nothing to the supposed influence of sharecropping in maintaining patriarchal relations between nobles and their tenants. There is room for doubt whether the data justify all the conclusions—for instance, the allegedly greater rivalry between bourgeois and peasants for the acquisition of land in the areas that were vigorously counter-revolutionary. It is far from certain that the conclusions can be transferred wholesale to the Vendée. And the final element of the analysis, an ill-defined *prise de conscience* on the part of the substantial peasantry of one section of the department, is a reversion to unverified explanations in terms of states of mind. Still, a new logic is there, and it works magnificently in clearing away the debris of earlier discussions of counter-revolution in the West.

The new logic is not, of course, entirely of Bois' invention. With all his inaccuracies, Siegfried saw clearly enough the principle that regional variations in political orientation in the West should be related to variations in social organization. Jacques Godechot has recently stressed the necessity of analyzing the "economic and social structure of the insurgent areas," an observation anticipated by Marc Bloch, thirty years before. Over the last few years, a number of careful scholars have been working to accumulate the essential information on local social organization and regional variation in the West. The great tradition represented by the *Annales* is finally making its weight felt.

The basic logic is one that is almost second nature to sociologists. When explaining the existence of a phenomenon, a sociologist is likely to begin by asking of exactly what kind of social unit (traditional bureaucracies? marginal individuals? high-ranking cliques?) it is characteristic. He is likely to proceed immediately to an analysis of the distinguishing characteristics of such social units (elaborate hierarchy? dual allegiances? powerful controls over membership?) and thus to a systematic comparison of units which display the phenomenon with otherwise comparable units which do not. He tends to search for reliable evidence (often, but by no means necessarily, in the form of quantitative measures) that the differences actually exist. Then he seeks to explain the phenomenon in question in terms of the distinguishing characteristics of the unit in which it appears. This leads him to an analysis of the way the elements of that unit fit together, or the subsumption of the case at hand under some broader generalization, or (more likely) both.

There is nothing occult, or even uncommon, about such a logical procedure. The important elements to retain are: the careful identification of the units of analysis, the concern for the identification of reliable differences, the use of generalizations already established, the stress on systematic comparison. These have obvious implications for the study of a counter-revolution. The most powerful new questions they lead to are these: 1) What were the real differences between the areas in which the counter-revolution sprang up in 1793 and those which remained calm, a) under the Old Regime, b) during the early Revolution? 2) What was distinctive about both the organization and the composition of the *groups* which actively supported the Revolution, and those which actively resisted it, over the period 1789–93? 3) What significant changes in the social situation occurred during the same period? 4) Is there any general knowledge available that helps to assemble coherently the answers to these three questions and the fact of counter-revolution?

These questions are by no means already definitely answered, but the very fact that they are now being asked is leading to rapid increases in our understanding of the Vendée. Like Bois immense study of Chouannerie in the Sarthe, my own more modest work on the counter-revolution in Southern Anjou illustrates the utility of asking new questions. Within the section of Anjou south of the Loire, some 700 square kilometers in area, appeared the most concerted counter-revolutionary outburst of 1793, as well as sharp divisions between the areas and the groups supporting and opposing the counter-revolution. A valid explanation should account for these divisions. It should also relate them to the process which culminated in counter-revolution.

Even asking the prior question—"Precisely what *are* the divisions to be explained?"—is quite useful. Although characterizations of the rebels are legion, the only studies remotely approaching the careful description of the supporters of revolution and counter-revolution in the West are Donald Greer's valuable compilations, by department and social category, of individuals officially designated as émigrés, and of people executed during the Terror. Those studies yield the following statistical description of these two categories of presumed opponents of the Revolution for all of western France:

Category	Percent of All Émigrés	Percent of Those Executed
Clergy	35	2
Nobility	23	2
Upper middle class	5	3
Lower middle class	2	3
Working class	10	41
Peasants	20	48
No status given	5	1
Total	100	100

Even when taken for individual departments, these figures provide only the most unreliable of guides to the divisions to be explained, since they necessarily mix counter-revolutionary and revolutionary sections of departments; since they comprehend only opponents, not supporters, of the regime; since the categories themselves do not correspond closely to the major social divisions in the West; since they do not indicate which categories had more than their shares of execution and emigration; and since neither emigration nor execution is tantamount to participation in the rebellion. We need other social categories, finer geographic divisions, further measures of opposition and support.

There are, as it happens, quite a few materials in the archives which will with careful handling turn themselves into measures of this sort. Eighteenth-century records of births, deaths and marriages, voting lists for 1790 and 1791, and population enumerations from the early Revolution all make possible some estimates of the distribution of occupations and its variation from one section to another, in Southern Anjou. Rosters of the National Guard, records of enlistments in the army, local election returns, and some curious *listes des bons patriotes* provide some information as to the identities of the supporters of the Revolution. The lengthy interrogations of refugees and prisoners during the counter-revolution, the registers made up from them, and the captured rosters of counter-revolutionary army units offer information on the character of the rebels. Some of the more easily handled items of this sort are in the following table, summarizing tentative findings for all of Southern Anjou:

PERCENT DISTRIBUTION BY MAJOR SOCIAL CATEGORY

Category	Estimated Occupational Distribution of Adult Males Rural Communes	Army Volunteers 2792	Bearing Arms with Rebels (Revolutionary Sources)	Bearing Arms with Rebels (Counter-Rev. Sources)	Aiding Rebels (All Sources)
Noble	0.29	0.0	0.61	0.0	1.95
Priest	1.28	0.0	0.0	0.0	8.87
Bourgeois	8.03	28.96	14.72	1.62	21.00
Hired hand	14.28		6.75	9.43	3.68
		4.52			
Other peasant	44.77		20.86	53.91	37.88
Weaver	10.62		31.29	14.56	8.44
		66.51			
Other artisan	20.73		25.77	20.48	18.18
Number identified	—	221	1121	841	801

The statistics do not speak for themselves, but they do seem to make muffled noises. They suggest, for example, the nearly total absence of peasants, nobles and priests from the patriotic camp. They raise serious reservations about the depiction of the Vendée as a "peasant" rebellion. They tend to confirm Greer's general conclusions about the victims of the Terror in the West. And the discrepancies between the revolutionary and counter-revolutionary sources of information about the rebels (undoubtedly affected by the fact that the counter-revolutionary sources are communal rosters, while the revolutionary ones are mainly the minutes of interrogations and depositions) bring into play some absorbing new problems. Not the least of the fruits of this sort of investigation are the inquiries it stimulates concerning the actual social relations among the diverse groups actively opposing the Revolution. It leads naturally to an analysis of the structures and relations of the revolutionary and counter-revolutionary parties of Southern Anjou.

In order to understand the party divisions, however, one must understand the regional divisions. A number of writers have, with apparent nonchalance, joined maps displaying the boundaries of the insurrection to their accounts of its course. The basis of such historical cartography is almost always a mystery. But there are some ways to reduce the mystery. For most of the period of the Revolution that concerns us here, the province of Anjou (alias the department of Maine-et-Loire) was divided into districts averaging some 60,000 persons, which were subdivided into cantons, themselves generally composed of three or four communes and four or five thousand people. The districts, cantons, and communes provide a convenient standard set of units for a wide variety of comparisons.

Given these units for comparison, the first task is the uneasy one of designating them as "revolutionary" and "counter-revolutionary." Paul Bois identified the significant divisions in the Sarthe by classifying official reports on the political tempers of the various cantons of the department. In the Vendée, one may also map the reported incidence of armed opposition to the Revolution in the first weeks of 1793's great outbreak. The same can be done with the counter-revolutionary incidents of 1790 and 1791. Likewise, it is possible to map the residences of the rebels identified in the documents already discussed, and to use the numerous claims for reward presented during the Restoration by Vendean veterans for the same purpose. These various tests agree with each other fairly well, and therefore identify the groups of communes, cantons and districts whose characteristics must be compared.

For purposes of illustration, one of the more easily quantifiable of these criteria appears in the following table with some measures of other forms of significant response to the Revolution. The units, in this case, are the most uniformly counter-revolutionary district of Southern Anjou (Cholet) and the most undividedly revolutionary district (Saumur):

	Counter-Revolutionary	Revolutionary
Number of reported rebels per 1,000 population	9.83	0.04
Émigrés reported per 1,000 population	4.1	7.1
Percent of priests taking Civil Constitution oath	5.3	64.7
Army enlistments per 1,000 population, 1791–92	2.3	7.0

The table has the virtue of being disconcerting. Considering that emigration is so widely taken as a sign of opposition to the Revolution, that the counter-revolutionary sections of Anjou have so often been portrayed as teeming with resident nobles in *bonne entente* with their peasants, and that the persecution of the clergy is supposed to have driven so many of them out of the country, one might have expected a much higher rate of emigration for those sections. Not so. This bit of serendipity leads to a re-examination of the question of noble residence, and to the (tentative) conclusion that the gentlemen were actually more numerous in the revolutionary sections of Southern Anjou, as well as to the hunch, plausible but untested, that emigration was most frequent where a determined counter-revolutionary minority met a determined revolutionary majority. One of the advantages of using systematic comparison and well-defined measures is that the results so often prove one's easy assumptions wrong.

Despite a few such contretemps, however, the general result of a variety of comparisons is to reinforce the conclusions a) that there was a relatively well-defined boundary between revolutionary and counter-revolutionary sections of Southern Anjou; b) that the two areas differed significantly in political behavior for several years before the counter-revolution; c) that it therefore makes sense to investigate further the contrasts in social organization between the two areas defined in this way.

At this point, a sociological view of the problem is especially useful. Many commentators, especially those mainly concerned with writing descriptions, rather than histories, of the region, have detailed their intuitions of a drastic difference:

> Between the Mauges and the neighboring Saumurois on the east, the difference is great. Distant, wide horizons succeed the plateau cut with valleys and ravines; wastes and orchards disappear, replaced by rich fields of hemp and vineyards. After a dark, rather hard Anjou comes a bright, light, sunny, blooming, flowering Anjou, a country of small property, a country of substantial people, individualistic, conscious of their liberty, egalitarian, a place where the Vendean insurrection was never able to take serious root.

The intuition of a contrast appears in a slightly different form in the frequent assertion of the intense isolation of the Vendée. But no one could seriously hold that the West as a whole, the setting of such cities as Nantes, Angers, La Rochelle, Niort, Laval, Saint-Malo or Le Mans, was completely rural or completely isolated. Nor was the counter-revolution simply the response of the most "backward" sections to the Revolution. One element of the contrast, to be sure, was the difference between localized, subsistence agriculture (in the Vendée) and market-oriented, rationalized agriculture (in the surrounding area). But another, often neglected, element is the eighteenth-century development of nuclei of trade and manufacturing in the midst of the traditional farming areas. One more statistical fragment, again comparing the extreme districts of Southern Anjou, shows the results:

ESTIMATED OCCUPATIONAL DISTRIBUTION OF ADULT
MALES; RURAL COMMUNES (PER CENT)

Category	Revolutionary	Counter-Revolutionary
Noble	0.47	0.16
Priest	1.42	1.10
Bourgeois	1.69	8.43
Hired hand	29.19	11.26
Other peasant	51.11	41.13
Weaver	2.35	21.27
Other artisan	13.77	16.64

The important fact to notice is the higher proportion of artisans and bourgeois (largely merchants and petty manufacturers) in the counter-revolutionary section, surrounded by peasants little involved in the money economy (as the low proportion of hired hands suggests). To put the matter all too baldly, such a social situation is much more favorable to violent local conflict between "old" and "new," "backward" and "progressive" than is a uniformly advanced, or a uniformly backward, social setting. In fact, it is not far off the mark to say that throughout the West, the peaks of counter-revolutionary activity were not in the backward sections so much as at the junctions of rural and urban ways of life.

Even if this simple formula explained the variation from revolutionary to counter-revolutionary sections of the West, it would still be necessary to analyze the changes in the social situation from 1789 to 1793. This returns us to one of the traditional issues, but from a new direction. Rather than asking whether the *cahiers* of the Vendée asked for any reform (when, after all, each commune was asked explicitly to state its grievances), we may ask whether there was any significant difference in the *cahiers* of the two sections of Southern Anjou that were later to disagree so acridly over the Revolution. The answer: yes. On almost every significant issue on which there was a difference, the counter-revolutionary section made fewer demands for reform. In this case, a statistical criterion does barbaric injustice to the pithy content of the cahiers, but is still convenient. 63% of the revolutionary communes opposed the *droit de chasse,* while 13% of the counter-revolutionary communes opposed it. On the question of reform or suppression of the manorial courts it was 31% against 22%. When it came to opposing the fiscal rights of the seigneurs, it was 52% versus 15%. 14% of the *cahiers* of communes from the revolutionary area proposed the sale of church lands, and 26% complained about the tithe collected by outsiders, while the figures for the counter-revolutionary territory were 2% and 11%. In short, in regard to issues that mattered a great deal in the years to follow, there were already notable differences in the positions taken in 1789 by the spokesmen of communities of the two sections of Southern Anjou.

Nevertheless, clearly defined revolutionary and counter-revolutionary *parties* did not form in the area until later. To summarize very briefly, a nucleus of revolutionary leaders, drawn especially from the mercantile bourgeoisie, emerged fairly early in the section that joined the counter-revolution, and steadily increased its share of the available public offices, and its control of the political apparatus. The organized opposition to the revolutionaries crystallized much more slowly, locally and erratically. That opposition was a good deal more heterogeneous than the revolutionary nucleus. A series of public issues drove more and more of the population into commitment to one party or the other, and increasingly drastic conflict both reinforced that commitment and drove the parties further apart. This happened somewhat independently within most localities of the Vendée. In fact, a process like that which Gregory Bateson calls schismogenesis—the increasing polarization of the norms of two groups as a result of their interaction—occurred. The level of conflict mounted erratically to the apex, counter-revolution.

IV

My purpose in laying out these segments of an analysis of the Vendée here is not to present a convincing and comprehensive explanation of the counter-revolution, but to demonstrate that a sociological conception of what is to be explained, and how it is to be explained, leads to different ways of dividing up the problem, different types of data, different methods of handling the data, different crucial issues, and new conclusions. It clarifies a number of the traditional debates that historians who begin by concentrating on the personal motives of the rebels get into, and deflates the importance of some of those debates. For example, the dilemma of "plot" vs. "spontaneity" in the explanation of the rebellion appears unreal when one considers the numerous, bitter combats between the parties in the years before 1793. As a result, even those who ask the traditional questions have something to gain from the sociological approach.

Some caveats are in order. A sociological approach does not banish motives. Sociologists (and the numerous historians who share the general method I have called "sociological," many of whom would reject both the appellation, and the implication of a prior claim by sociology) discuss motives, norms, values, and interests with considerable confidence. But they see motives as differentiated, complex and variable, as strongly limited and influenced by social structure, and they do not give the detection of motives nearly the prominence in their methods of explanation that traditional political historians do.

Furthermore, a sociological approach by no means sweeps away the problem of ideology. Instead, it reduces the indiscriminate use of articulated beliefs as explanations of collective social actions, and calls attention to the necessity of analyzing the development of an ideology, its function for the group which adheres to it, and, more generally, the conditions under which a group of men will fight in the name of a set of beliefs. In the case at hand, it seems that the beliefs about the virtues of the old regime and the intentions of the rebellion which have so often been retroactively imputed to the rebels actually emerged from the stress of battle, that once defined they did influence the movement, that they were later elaborated by elite apologists of the old regime and powerfully affected the region's political life in the nineteenth century. It does not seem that one can explain the counter-revolution by alleging the personal attachment of the peasants to Throne and Altar.

Of course, to the extent that one wishes to assign moral responsibility for historical events, or to encourage modern readers to empathize with historical figures, a sociological conception of explanation is unsatisfying. Either of these is a legitimate end for an historian to pursue. They are, however, ends which are declining in importance—or at least, whose pursuit is becoming more and more subtly blended with other aims—in the historiography of the French Revolution. The important new work of historians like Cobb, Rudé and Soboul stresses a range of questions whose significance stands out boldly in the light of the previous discussion: Exactly who were the participants in crucial actions of the Revolution? How did they differ from other people? How were they organized? What were their relations to other significant groupings? And only then comes the old question: what were their motives? The result is that great masses of new sorts of documents (long available but rarely explored before), new methods of handling the documents, and even new ways of presenting analyses of the Revolution are coming into use. The increasing prominence of expert demographers like Marcel Reinhard among the historians of the Revolution is itself a sign of the change.

What seems likely to result from this trend in the historiography of the Revolution and the parallel, if weaker, trend in the historiography of the counter-revolution is a much greater integration of our knowledge of the two of them. Both can be subsumed under an unsubtle question with subtle ramifications: in France as a whole, what social conditions led to acceptance or rejection of the Revolution and the party in power? This question, in turn, opens the way to a comparative sociology of political upheaval and change. No doubt it would be an act of sociological chauvinism to declare that this should be the aspiration of all studies of the Revolution. Yet I cannot escape the conviction that it is a worthy aim, and a feasible one.

No so long ago, Alfred Cobban remarked that, with increasing awareness of the multilithic character of the Revolution they once treated as a monolith, historians are enormously complicating their explanations, and that the "result may be something which it is difficult to list as a series of causes in a text-book, and in this sense the search for causes of the French Revolution may well be at an end." This is surely true. What seems to be happening, however, is not so much the withering of all causal inquiry as the following of a new understanding of the way to explain the events of the great revolution and, indeed, of all revolutions and counter-revolutions.

C.
Relative Deprivation

5.
THE OLD REGIME AND THE FRENCH REVOLUTION (1858)

Alexis de Tocqueville

What did the French Revolution accomplish?

The object of the foregoing pages was solely to throw light on the subject in a general way and make it easier to understand my answers to the questions raised in a previous chapter. What was the true aim of the Revolution? What was its specific character? Why did it take place and what exactly did it achieve?

The aim of the Revolution was not, as once was thought, to destroy the authority of the Church and religious faith in general. Appearances notwithstanding, it was essentially a movement for political and social reform and, as such, did not aim at creating a state of permanent disorder in the conduct of public affairs or (as one of its opponents bitterly remarked) at "methodizing anarchy." On the contrary, it sought to increase the power and jurisdiction of the central authority. Nor was it intended, as some have thought, to change the whole nature of our

SOURCE. Alexis de Tocqueville. *The Old Regime and the French Revolution.* Trans. by Stuart Gilbert, Garden City, New York: Doubleday and Co., Inc., 1955, pp. 19–32, 203–211. Doubleday Co., 1955. Reprinted by permission of Doubleday and Co., Inc.

traditional civilization, to arrest its progress, or even to make any vital
change in the principles basic to the structure of society in the Western
World. If we disregard various incidental developments which briefly
modified its aspect at different periods and in different lands, and study
it as it was essentially, we find that the chief permanent achievement
of the French Revolution was the suppression of those political institutions, commonly described as feudal, which for many centuries had
held unquestioned sway in most European countries. The Revolution
set out to replace them with a new social and political order, at once
simple and more uniform, based on the concept of the equality of all
men.

This in itself was enough to constitute a thorough-paced revolution
since, apart from the fact that the old feudal institutions still entered
into the very texture of the religious and political institutions of almost
the whole of Europe, they had also given rise to a host of ideas, sentiments, manners, and customs which, so to speak, adhered to them. Thus
nothing short of a major operation was needed to excise from the body
politic these accretions and to destroy them utterly. The effect was to
make the Revolution appear even more drastic than it actually was;
since what it was destroying affected the entire social system.

Radical though it may have been, the Revolution made far fewer
changes than is generally supposed, as I shall point out later. What
in point of fact it destroyed, or is in process of destroying—for the
Revolution is still operative—may be summed up as everything in the
old order that stemmed from aristocratic and feudal institutions, was
in any way connected with them, or even bore, however faintly, their
imprint. The only elements of the old régime that it retained were
those which had always been foreign to its institutions and could exist
independently of them. Chance played no part whatever in the outbreak
of the Revolution; though it took the world by surprise, it was the
inevitable outcome of a long period of gestation, the abrupt and violent
conclusion of a process in which six generations had played an intermittent part. Even if it had not taken place, the old social structure
would nonetheless have been shattered everywhere sooner or later. The
only difference would have been that instead of collapsing with such
brutal suddenness it would have crumbled bit by bit. At one fell swoop,
without warning, without transition, and without compunction, the Revolution effected what in any case was bound to happen, if by slow
degrees.

Such then was the achievement of the Revolution, and it may appear
surprising that even the most clear-sighted contemporaries should have
missed the point of an event whose purport seems so clear to us today.

Even Burke failed to understand it. "You wish to correct the abuses of your government," he said to the French, "but why invent novelties? Why not return to your old traditions? Why not confine yourselves to a resumption of your ancient liberties? Or, if it was not possible to recover the obliterated features of your original constitution, why not look towards England? There you would have found the ancient common law of Europe." Burke did not see that what was taking place before his eyes was a revolution whose aim was precisely to abolish that "ancient common law of Europe," and that there could be no question of putting the clock back.

But why did the storm that was gathering over the whole of Europe break in France and not elsewhere, and why did it acquire certain characteristics in France which were either absent in similar movements in other countries, or if present, assumed quite different forms? Obviously this question raises points of much importance; these will be dealt with at some length in the second part of this work.

Why Feudalism Had Come to Be More Detested in France than in Any Other Country

At first sight it may appear surprising that the Revolution, whose primary aim, as we have seen, was to destroy every vestige of the institutions of the Middle Ages, should not have broken out in countries where those institutions had the greatest hold and bore most heavily on the people instead of those in which their yoke was relatively light.

At the close of the eighteenth century serfdom had not yet been completely abolished anywhere in Germany; indeed, in most parts of that country the peasants were still literally bound to the land, as they had been in the Middle Ages. The armies of Frederick II and Maria Theresa were composed almost entirely of men who were serfs on the medieval pattern.

In most German states in 1788 the peasant was not allowed to quit his lord's estate; if he did so, he was liable to be tracked down wherever he was and brought back in custody. He was subject to the jurisdiction of his lord, who kept a close eye on his private life and could punish him for intemperance or idleness. He could neither better his social position, change his occupation, nor even marry without his master's consent, and a great number of his working hours had to be spent in his master's service. The system of compulsory labor, known in France as the *corvée*, was in full force in Germany, and in some districts entailed no less than three days' work a week. The peasant was expected to keep the buildings on his lord's estate in good repair and to carry the produce of the estate to market; he drove his lord's carriage and carried his messages. Also he had to spend some years of his youth in his lord's household as a member of the domestic staff. However, it was possible for the serf to become a landowner, though his tenure was always hedged round with restrictions. He had to cultivate his land in a pre-scribed manner, under his lord's supervision, and could neither alienate nor mortgage it without permission. In some cases he was compelled to sell its produce, in others forbidden to sell it; in any case he was bound to keep the land under cultivation. Moreover, his children did not inherit his entire estate, some part of it being usually withheld by his lord.

It must not be thought that I am describing ancient or obsolete laws; these provisions can be found even in the code drawn up by Frederick the Great and put in force by his successor at the very time when the French Revolution was getting under way.

In France such conditions had long since passed away; the peasants could move about, buy and sell, work, and enter into contracts as they liked. Only in one or two eastern provinces, recent annexations, some last vestiges of serfdom lingered on; everywhere else it had wholly dis-appeared. Indeed, the abolition of serfdom had taken place in times so remote that its very date had been forgotten. However, as a result of recent research work it is now known that as early as the thirteenth century serfdom had ceased to exist in Normandy.

Meanwhile another revolution, of a different order, had done much to improve the status of the French peasant; he had not merely ceased to be a serf, he had also become a landowner. Though this change had far-reaching consequences, it is apt to be overlooked, and I propose to devote some pages to this all-important subject.

Until quite recently it was taken for granted that the splitting up of the landed estates in France was the work of the Revolution, and the Revolution alone; actually there is much evidence in support of the contrary view. Twenty years or more before the Revolution we find complaints being made that land was being subdivided to an unconscion-able extent. "The practice of partitioning inheritances," said Turgot, writ-ing at about this time, "has gone so far that a piece of land which just sufficed for a single family is now parceled out between five or six sons. The result is that the heirs and their families soon find that they cannot depend on the land for their livelihood and have to look elsewhere." And some years later Necker declared that there was "an inordinate number" of small country estates in France.

In a confidential report made to an Intendant shortly before the Revo-lution I find the following observations: "Inheritances are being subdivided nowadays to an alarming extent. Everybody insists on having his share of the land, with the result that estates are broken up into innumerable fragments, and this process of fragmentation is going on all the time." One might well imagine these words to have been written by one of our contemporaries.

I have been at great pains to make, as it were, a cadastral survey (i.e., of the distribution of land) of the old régime and have to some extent, I think, succeeded. Under the provisions of the law of 1790, which imposed a tax on land, each parish was required to draw up a return of all the privately owned land within its boundaries. Most of these documents are lost, but I have discovered some in certain vil- 'lages and on comparing them with their modern equivalents have found that in these villages the number of landowners was as high as half, often two thirds, of the present number. These figures are impressive, and all the more so when we remember that the population of France has risen by over twenty-five per cent since that time.

Then, as in our own day, the peasant's desire for owning land was nothing short of an obsession and already all the passions to which possession of the soil gives rise in present-day France were active. "Land is always sold above its true value," a shrewd contemporary observer remarked, "and this is due to the Frenchman's inveterate craving to become a landowner. All the savings of the poorer classes, which in other countries are invested in private companies or the public funds, are used for buying land."

When Arthur Young visited France for the first time, among a multitude of new experiences, none impressed him more than the extent to which ownership of the soil was vested in innumerable peasant proprietors; half the cultivable land was owned by them. "I had no idea," he often says, "that such a state of affairs existed anywhere"—and in fact none such existed outside France.

There had once been many peasant proprietors in England, but by now their number had greatly dwindled. Everywhere in Germany and in all periods a limited number of free peasants had enjoyed full ownership of the land they worked. The special, often highly peculiar laws regulating the cultivator's ownership of land are set forth in the oldest German *Books of Customs,* but this type of ownership was always exceptional, there never were many of these small landed proprietors.

It was chiefly along the Rhine that at the close of the eighteenth century German farmers owned the land they worked and enjoyed almost as much freedom as the French small proprietor; and it was there, too, that the revolutionary zeal of the French found its earliest adepts and took most permanent effect. On the other hand, the parts of Germany which held out longest against the current of new ideas were those where the peasants did not as yet enjoy such privileges—and this is, to my mind, a highly suggestive fact.

Thus the prevalent idea that the breakup of the big estates in France began with the Revolution is erroneous; it had started long before. True, the revolutionary governments sold the estates owned by the clergy and many of those owned by the nobility; however, if we study the records of these sales (a rather tedious task, but one which I have on occasion found rewarding) we discover that most of the parcels of land were bought by people who already had land of their own. Thus, though estates changed hands, the number of landowners was increased much less than might have been expected. For, to employ the seemingly extravagant, but in this case correct, expression used by Necker, there were already "myriads" of such persons.

What the Revolution did was not to parcel out the soil of France, but to "liberate" it—for a while. Actually these small proprietors had much difficulty in making a living out of the land since it was subject to many imposts from which there was no escaping.

That these charges were heavy is undeniable, but, oddly enough, what made them seem so unbearable was something that, on the face of it, should have had the opposite effect: the fact that, as in no other part of Europe, our agriculturists had been emancipated from the control of their lords—a revolution no less momentous than that which had made them peasant proprietors.

Although the old régime is still so near to us in time—every day we meet persons born under its auspices—it already seems buried in the night of ages. So vast was the revolution that has intervened that its shadow falls on all that it did not destroy, and it is as if centuries lay between the times we live in and the revolutionary epoch. This explains why so few people know the answer to the quite simple question: How was rural France administered previous to 1789? And indeed it is impossible to give a full and accurate answer without having studied not the literature but the administrative records of the period.

I have often heard it said that though they had long ceased to play a part in the government of the country as a whole, the nobility kept in their hands, right up to the end, the administration of the rural districts; that, in fact, the landed proprietor "ruled" his peasants. This idea, too, seems based on a misconception of the true state of affairs.

In the eighteenth century all that touched the parish, the rural equivalent of the township, was under the control of a board of officials who were no longer agents of the seigneur or chosen by him. Some were nominated by the Intendant of the province, others elected by the local peasantry. Amongst the many functions of these officials were those of assessing the tax to be paid by each member of the community, of keeping churches in repair, of building schools, of summoning and presiding over the parish assemblies. They supervised the municipal funds, decided how these were to be expended, and in litigation to which the parish was a party acted as its representatives. Far from controlling the administration of parish affairs the lord had no say at all in them. All members of the parish councils were ex officio public servants or under the control of the central power (as will be explained in the following chapter). As for the lord, he rarely figured as the King's representative in the parish or as an intermediary between him and its inhabitants. He was no longer expected to see to the maintenance of law and order, to call out the militia, to levy taxes, to publish royal edicts, or to distribute the King's bounty in times of shortage. All these rights and duties had passed into the hands of others and the lord was in reality merely one of the inhabitants of the parish, differentiated from the others by certain exemptions and privileges. His social rank was higher, but he had no more power than they. In letters to their subdelegates the Intendants were careful to point out that the lord was only "the first resident."

When we turn from the parish to the larger territorial unit, the canton, we find the same arrangement; the nobles play no part, collectively or individually, in the administration of public affairs. This was peculiar to France; in all other countries what was the chief characteristic of ancient feudalism persisted to some extent and possession of the land carried with it the right to govern the people living on it.

England was administered as well as governed by the great landed proprietors. Even in those parts of Germany, for example Prussia and Austria, where the ruling Princes had been most successful in shaking off the control of the nobility in the conduct of affairs of State, they had allowed the nobles to retain to some extent the administration of the rural areas. Though in some places they kept a firm hand on the local lord, they had not, as yet, supplanted him.

The French nobility, however, had long ceased to play any part in public administration, with one exception: the administration of justice. The leading nobles retained the right of delegating to judges appointed by them the trial of certain kinds of suits and still issued police regulations, from time to time, that held good within the limits of their domains. But the central authority had gradually curtailed and subordinated to itself the judicial powers of the landed proprietor; to such an extent that the lords who still exercised them regarded them as little more than a source of revenue.

The same thing had happened to all the special powers of the nobility; on the political side these powers were now defunct and only the pecuniary advantages attaching to them remained (and in some cases had been much increased). At this point something must be said about those lucrative privileges which our forefathers usually had in mind when they spoke of "feudal rights," since it was these that most affected the life of the general public.

It is hard to say today which of these rights were still in force in 1789 and in what they consisted. There had been a vast number of them and by them many had died out or been modified almost out of recognition; indeed, the exact meaning of the terms in which they are described (about which even contemporaries were not very clear) is extremely hard to ascertain today. Nevertheless, my study of works by eighteenth-century experts on feudal law and my researches into local usages have made it clear to me that the rights still functioning in 1789 fell into a relatively small number of categories; others survived, no doubt, but they were operative only in exceptional cases.

Of the old seigneurial *corvée,* of statutory labor obligation, traces remained everywhere, but half obliterated. Most of the toll charges on the roads had been reduced or done away with, though there were few provinces in which some had not survived. Everywhere the resident seigneur levied dues on fairs and markets, and everywhere enjoyed exclusive rights of hunting. Usually he alone possessed dovecotes and pigeons, and it was the general rule that farmers must bring their wheat to their lord's mill and their grapes to his wine press. A universal and very onerous right was that named *lods et ventes;* that is to say an impost levied by the lord on transfers of land within his domain. And throughout the whole of France the land was subject to quitrents, ground rents, dues in money or in kind payable by the peasant proprietor to his lord and irredeemable by the former. Varied as they were, all these obligations had one common feature: they were associated with the soil or its produce, and all alike bore heavily on the cultivator.

The lords spiritual enjoyed similar privileges. For though the Church derived its authority from a different source and had aims and functions quite different from those of the temporal power, it had gradually become tied up with the feudal system and, though never fully integrated into it, was so deeply involved as to seem part and parcel of it.

Bishops, canons, and abbots owned fiefs or quitrents in virtue of their ecclesiastical status, and usually monasteries had seigneurial rights over the villages on whose land they stood. The monastery had serfs in the only part of France where serfdom had survived, employed forced labor, levied dues on fairs and markets had the monopoly of the communal wine press, bakehouse, mill, and the stud bull. Moreover, the clergy enjoyed in France—as indeed in all Christian Europe—the right of levying tithes.

The point, however, on which I would lay stress is that exactly the same feudal rights were in force in every European land and that in most other countries of the continent they pressed far more heavily on the population than in France. Take, for example, the lord's right to forced labor, the *corvée*. It was rarely exercised and little oppressive in France, whereas in Germany it was stringent and everywhere enforced.

Moreover, when we turn to the feudal rights which so much outraged our fathers and which they regarded as opposed not merely to all ideas of justice but to the spirit of civilization itself (I am thinking of the tithe, irredeemable ground rents, perpetual charges, *lods et ventes,* and so forth, all that in the somewhat grandiloquent language of the eighteenth century was styled "the servitude of the land"), we find that all these practices obtained to some extent in England and, indeed, are still found there today. Yet they do not prevent English husbandry from being the best organized and most productive in the modern world; and, what is perhaps still more remarkable, the English nation seems hardly aware of their existence.

Why then did these selfsame feudal rights arouse such bitter hatred in the heart of the French people that it has persisted even after its object has long since ceased to exist? One of the reasons is that the French peasant had become a landowner, and another that he had been completely emancipated from the control of his lord. (No doubt there were other reasons, but these, I think, were the chief ones.)

If the peasant had not owned his land he would hardly have noticed many of the charges which the feudal system imposed on all real estate. What could the tithe matter to a man who had no land of his own? He could simply deduct it from the rent. And even restrictions hampering agriculture mean nothing to an agriculturist who is simply cultivating land for the benefit of someone else.

Moreover, if the French peasant had still been under his lord's control, the feudal rights would have seemed much less obnoxious, because he would have regarded them as basic to the constitution of his country.

When the nobles had real power as well as privileges, when they governed and administered, their rights could be at once greater and less open to attack. In fact, the nobility was regarded in the age of feudalism much as the government is regarded by everyone today; its exactions were tolerated in view of the protection and security it provided. True, the nobles enjoyed invidious privileges and rights that weighed heavily on the commoner, but in return for this they kept order, administered justice, saw to the execution of the laws, came to the rescue of the oppressed, and watched over the interest of all. The more these functions passed out of the hands of the nobility, the more uncalled for did their privileges appear—until at last their mere existence seemed a meaningless anachronism.

I would ask you to picture to yourself the French peasant as he was in the eighteenth century—or, rather, the peasant you know today, for he has not changed at all. His status is different, but not his personality. See how he appears in the records from which I have been quoting: a man so passionately devoted to the soil that he spends all his earnings on buying land, no matter what it costs. To acquire it he must begin by paying certain dues, not to the government but to other landowners of the neighborhood, who are as far removed as he from the central administration and almost as powerless as he. When at long last he has gained possession of this land which means so much to him, it is hardly an exaggeration to say that he sinks his heart in it along with the grain he sows. The possession of this little plot of earth, a tiny part, his very own, of the wide world, fills him with pride and a sense of independence. But now the neighbors aforesaid put in an appearance, drag him away from his cherished fields, and bid him work elsewhere without payment. When he tries to protect his seedlings from the animals they hunt, they tell him to take down his fences, and they lie in wait for him at river crossings to exact a toll. At the market there they are again, to make him pay for the right of selling the produce of his land, and when on his return home he wants to use the wheat he has put aside for his daily needs, he has to take it to their mill to have it ground, and then to have his bread baked in the lord's oven. Thus part of the income from his small domain goes to supporting these men in the form of charges which are imprescriptible and irredeemable. Whatever he sets out to do, he finds these tiresome neighbors barring his path, interfering in his simple pleasures and his work, and consuming the produce of his toil. And when he has done with them, other fine gentlemen dressed in black step in and take the greater part of his harvest. When we remember the special temperament of the French peasant proprietor in the eighteenth century, his ruling interests and passions, and the treatment accorded him, we can well understand the rankling grievances that burst into a flame in the French Revolution.

For even after it had ceased to be a political institution, the feudal system remained basic to the economic organization of France. In this restricted form it was far more hated than in the heyday of feudalism, and we are fully justified in saying that the very destruction of some of the institutions of the Middle Ages made those which survived seem all the more detestable.

How, Given the Facts Set Forth in the Preceding Chapters, the Revolution Was a Foregone Conclusion

My object in this final chapter is to bring together some of those aspects of the old régime which were depicted piecemeal in the foregoing pages and to show how the Revolution was their natural, indeed inevitable, outcome.

When we remember that it was in France that the feudal system, while retaining the characteristics which made it so irksome to, and so much resented by, the masses, had most completely discarded all that could benefit or protect them, we may feel less surprise at the fact that France was the place of origin of the revolt destined so violently to sweep away the last vestiges of that ancient European institution.

Similarly, if we observe how the nobility after having lost their political rights and ceased, to a greater extent than in any other land of feudal Europe, to act as leaders of the people had nevertheless not only retained but greatly increased their fiscal immunities and the advantages accruing to them individually; and if we also note how, while ceasing to be the ruling class, they had remained a privileged, closed group, less and less (as I have pointed out) an aristocracy and more and more a caste—if we bear these facts in mind, it is easy to see why the privileges enjoyed by this small section of the community seemed so unwarranted and so odious to the French people and why they developed that intense jealousy of the "upper class" which rankles still today.

Finally, when we remember that the nobility had deliberately cut itself off both from the middle class and from the peasantry (whose former affection it had alienated) and had thus become like a foreign body in the State: ostensibly the high command of a great army, but actually a corps of officers without troops to follow them—when we keep this in mind, we can easily understand why the French nobility, after having so far weathered every storm, was stricken down in a single night.

I have shown how the monarchical government, after abolishing provincial independence and replacing local authorities by its nominees in three quarters of the country, had brought under its direct management all public business, even the most trivial. I have also shown how, owing to the centralization of power, Paris, which had until now been merely the capital city, had come to dominate France—or, rather, to embody in itself the whole kingdom. These two circumstances, peculiar to France, suffice to explain why it was that an uprising of the people could overwhelm so abruptly and decisively a monarchy that for so many centuries had successfully withstood so many onslaughts and, on the very eve of its downfall, seemed inexpugnable even to the men who were about to destroy it.

In no other country of Europe had all political thought been so thoroughly and for so long stifled as in France; in no other country had the private citizen become so completely out of touch with public affairs and so unused to studying the course of events, so much so that not only had the average Frenchman no experience of "popular movements" but he hardly understood what "the people" meant. Bearing this in mind, we may find it easier to understand why the nation as a whole could launch out into a sanguinary revolution, with those very men who stood to lose most by it taking the lead and clearing the ground for it.

Since no free institutions and, as a result, no experienced and organized political parties existed any longer in France, and since in the absence of any political groups of this sort the guidance of public opinion, when its first stirrings made themselves felt, came entirely into the hands of the philosophers, that is to say the intellectuals, it was only to be expected that the directives of the Revolution should take the form of abstract principles, highly generalized theories, and that political realities would be largely overlooked. Thus, instead of attacking only such laws as seemed objectionable, the idea developed that *all* laws indiscriminately must be abolished and a wholly new system of government, sponsored by these writers, should replace the ancient French constitution.

Moreover, since the Church was so closely bound up with the ancient institutions now to be swept away, it was inevitable that the Revolution, in overthrowing the civil power, should assail the established religion. As a result, the leaders of the movement, shaking off the controls that religion, law, and custom once had exercised, gave free rein to their imagination and indulged in acts of an outrageousness that took the whole world by surprise. Nevertheless, anyone who had closely studied the condition of the country at the time might well have guessed that there was no enormity, no form of violence from which these men would shrink.

In one of his eloquent pamphlets Burke made no secret of his consternation. What particularly surprised him was there was no one anywhere who could stand surety for the smallest group of his fellow citizens or even for a single man, the consequence being that anyone could be arrested in his home without protest or redress, whether the offense alleged against him were royalism, "moderatism," or any other political deviation.

Burke failed to realize how things were in the kingdom which the monarchy (whose downfall he deplored) had bequeathed to its new masters. Under the old order the government had long since deprived Frenchmen of the possibility, and even the desire, of coming to each other's aid. When the Revolution started, it would have been impossible to find, in most parts of France, even ten men used to acting in concert and defending their interests without appealing to the central power for aid. Thus once that central power had passed from the hands of the royal administration into those of irresponsible sovereign assemblies and a benevolent government had given place to a ruthless one, the latter found nothing to impede it or hold up its activities even momentarily. The same conditions which had precipitated the fall of the monarchy made for the absolutism of its successor.

Never had religious tolerance, the lenient use of power and kindness toward one's neighbor been preached so earnestly and, to all appearances, so generally practiced as in the eighteenth century. Even the rules of war, last resort of the will to violence, had been humanized. Yet it was in this humanitarian climate that the most inhuman of revolutions took its rise. Nor must it be thought that these amiable sentiments were merely feigned; once the Revolution had run its headlong course, these same feelings came to the fore again and promptly made their presence felt not only in legislation but in all the doings of the new government.

This contrast between theory and practice, between good intentions and acts of savage violence, which was a salient feature of the French Revolution, becomes less startling when we remember that the Revolution, though sponsored by the most civilized classes of the nation, was carried out by its least educated and most unruly elements. For, since the members of the cultured elite had formed a habit of keeping to themselves, were unused to acting together, and had no hold on the masses, the latter became masters of the situation almost from the start. Even where the people did not govern *de facto* and directly, they set the tone of the administration. And in view of the conditions in which these men had been living under the old régime, it was almost a foregone conclusion how they now would act.

Actually it was to these very conditions that our peasantry owed some of their outstanding qualities. Long enfranchised and owning some of the land he worked, the French peasant was largely independent and had developed a healthy pride and much common sense. Inured to hardships, he was indifferent to the amenities of life, intrepid in the face of danger, and faced misfortune stoically. It was from this simple, virile race of men that those great armies were raised which were to dominate for many years the European scene. But their very virtues made them dangerous masters. During the many centuries in which these men had borne the brunt of nation-wide misgovernment and lived as a class apart, they had nursed in secret their grievances, jealousies, and rancors and, having learned toughness in a hard school, had become capable of enduring or inflicting the very worst.

It was in this mood that gripping the reins of power, the French people undertook the task of seeing the Revolution through. Books had supplied them with the necessary theories, and they now put these into practice, adjusting the writers' ideas to their lust for revenge.

Readers of this book who have followed carefully my description of eighteenth-century France will have noticed the steady growth amongst the people of two ruling passions, not always simultaneous or having the same objectives. One of these, the more deeply rooted and long-standing, was an intense, indomitable hatred of inequality. This inequality forced itself on their attention, they saw signs of it at every turn; thus it is easy to understand why the French had for so many centuries felt a desire, inveterate and uncontrollable, utterly to destroy all such institutions as had survived from the Middle Ages and, having cleared the ground, to build up a new society in which men were as much alike and their status as equal as was possible, allowing for the innate differences between individuals. The other ruling passion, more recent and less deeply rooted, was a desire to live not only on an equal footing but also as free men.

Toward the close of the old régime these two passions were equally sincerely felt and seemed equally operative. When the Revolution started, they came in contact, joined forces, coalesced, and reinforced each other, fanning the revolutionary ardor of the nation to a blaze. This was in '89, that rapturous year of bright enthusiasm, heroic courage, lofty ideals—untempered, we must grant, by the reality of experience: a historic date of glorious memory to which the thoughts of men will turn with admiration and respect long after those who witnessed its achievement, and we ourselves, have passed away. At the time the French had such proud confidence in the cause they were defending, and in themselves, that they believed they could reconcile freedom with equality and interspersed democratic institutions everywhere with free institutions. Not only did they shatter that ancient system under which men were divided into classes, corporations, and castes, and their rights were even more unequal than their social situations, but by the same token they did away with all the more recent legislation, instituted by the monarchy, whose effect was to put every Frenchman under official surveillance, with the government as his mentor, overseer, and, on occasion, his oppressor. Thus centralization shared the fate of absolute government.

But when the virile generation which had launched the Revolution had perished or (as usually befalls a generation engaging in such ventures) its first fine energy had dwindled; and when, as was but to be expected after a spell of anarchy and "popular" dictatorship, the ideal of freedom had lost much of its appeal and the nation, at a loss where to turn, began to cast round for a master—under these conditions the stage was set for a return to one-man government. Indeed, never had conditions been more favorable for its establishment and consolidation, and the man of genius destined at once to carry on and to abolish the Revolution was quick to turn them to account.

Actually there had existed under the old régime a host of institutions which had quite a "modern" air and, not being incompatible with equality, could easily be embodied in the new social order—and all these institutions offered remarkable facilities to despotism. They were hunted for among the wreckage of the old order and duly salvaged. These institutions had formerly given rise to customs, usages, ideas, and prejudices tending to keep men apart, and thus make them easier to rule. They were revived and skillfully exploited; centralization was built up anew, and in the process all that had once kept it within bounds was carefully eliminated. Thus there arose, within a nation that had but recently laid low its monarchy, a central authority with powers wider, stricter, and more absolute than those which any French King had ever wielded. Rash though this venture may have been, it was carried through with entire success for the good reason that people took into account only what was under their eyes and forgot what they had seen before. Napoleon fell but the more solid parts of his achievement lasted on; his government died, but his administration survived, and every time that an attempt is made to do away with absolutism the most that could be done has been to graft the head of Liberty onto a servile body.

On several occasions during the period extending from the outbreak of the Revolution up to our time we find the desire for freedom reviving, succumbing, then returning, only to die out once more and presently blaze up again. This presumably will be the lot for many years to come of a passion so undisciplined and untutored by experience; so easily discouraged, cowed and vanquished, so superficial and short-lived. Yet during this same period the passion for equality, first to entrench itself in the hearts of Frenchmen, has never given ground; for it links up with feelings basic to our very nature. For while the urge to freedom is forever assuming new forms, losing or gaining strength according to the march of events, our love of equality is constant and pursues the object of its desire with a zeal that is obstinate and often blind, ready to make every concession to those who give it satisfaction. Hence the fact that the French nation is prepared to tolerate in a government that favors and flatters its desire for equality practices and principles that are, in fact, the tools of despotism.

To those who study it as an isolated phenomenon the French Revolution can but seem a dark and sinister enigma; only when we view it in the light of the events preceding it can we grasp its true significance. And, similarly, without a clear idea of the old régime, its laws, its vices, its prejudices, its shortcomings, and its greatness, it is impossible to comprehend the history of the sixty years following its fall. Yet even this is not enough; we need also to understand and bear in mind the peculiarities of the French temperament.

When I observe France from this angle I find the nation itself far more remarkable than any of the events in its long history. It hardly seems possible that there can ever have existed any other people so full of contrasts and so extreme in all their doings, so much guided by their emotions and so little by fixed principles, always behaving better, or worse, than one expected of them. At one time they rank above, at another below, the norm of humanity; their basic characteristics are so constant that we can recognize the France we know in portraits made of it two or three thousand years ago, and yet so changeful are its moods, so variable its tastes that the nation itself is often quite as much startled as any foreigner at the things it did only a few years before. Ordinarily the French are the most routine-bound of men, but once they are forced out of the rut and leave their homes, they travel to the ends of the earth and engage in the most reckless ventures. Undisciplined by temperament, the Frenchman is always readier to put up with the arbitrary rule, however harsh, of an autocrat than with a free, well-ordered government by his fellow citizens, however worthy of respect they be. At one moment he is up in arms against authority and the next we find him serving the powers-that-be with a zeal such as the most servile races never display. So long as no one thinks of resisting, you can lead him on a thread, but once a revolutionary movement is afoot, nothing can restrain him from taking part in it. That is why our rulers are so often taken by surprise; they fear the nation either too much or not enough, for though it is never so free that the possibility of enslaving it is ruled out, its spirit can never be broken so completely as to prevent its shaking off the yoke of an oppressive government. The Frenchman can turn his hand to anything, but he excels in war alone and he prefers fighting against odds, preferring dazzling feats of arms and spectacular successes to achievements of the more solid kind. He is more prone to heroism than to humdrum virtue, apter for genius than for good sense, more inclined to think up grandiose schemes than to carry through great enterprises. Thus the French are at once the most brilliant and the most dangerous of all European nations, and the best qualified to become, in the eyes of other peoples, an object of admiration, of hatred, of compassion, or alarm—never of indifference.

France alone could have given birth to revolution so sudden, so frantic, and so thoroughgoing, yet so full of unexpected changes of direction, of anomalies and inconsistencies. But for the antecedent circumstances described in this book, the French would never have embarked on it; yet we must recognize that though their effect was cumulative and overwhelming, they would not have sufficed to lead to such a drastic revolution elsewhere than in France.

Thus I have brought my readers to the threshold of this memorable revolution; for the present I shall halt at this point, though I may perhaps go further in a subsequent work and study not its causes but the French Revolution itself and endeavor to appraise the new social order which issued from it.

II.

REJECTIONS OF THE SOCIAL ORDER AND THEIR DIRECTION

In a seminal essay on world religions, Max Weber described the diverse orientations which religions have displayed in their conflict with prosaic and worldly values of material success and sensual pleasure. The asceticism of the Buddhist, who rejects the workaday world and retreats to a monastery to contemplate, is very different from the asceticism of the Puritan, who sought to reach salvation through hard work and amassing wealth while rejecting pleasure or cash. In a similar fashion, the ways in which men have responded to change, conflict, and deprivation are myriad. Political agitation is only one among several major orientations. Religious rejection of the world, spontaneous protest, utopian cults, and revolutions all represent different routes to change, different "solutions" to the problems entailed by response to a society perceived as flawed and unworthy of allegiance. Uniting to achieve institutional or cultural change is also only one possibility among many. Presumably men endure many frustrations and injustices with resignation and apathy while they combat others through social movements and collective action. In this section we consider several common alternative forms of collective response as different modes of rejecting the established social order.

The four types of movements illustrated in the materials of this chapter (withdrawal, protest, reform, and revolution) differ from each other largely in the direction and scope of change with which each is associated. *Withdrawal movements* are only indirectly preoccupied with producing change in institutions or in cultural values. The religious sects withdraw in two ways: they do not seek to reform or change other institutions or established churches from which they may have sprung, nor do they find solutions to common problems by political action or social change; instead they preach a search for internal and spiritual changes in the person. In a similar fashion, David Plath describes certain utopian communities in contemporary Japan as reactions to the threat of modernization to communal values. By constructing their own communities and physically separating from the larger society, these communitarians hope to maintain their values in a society moving in an opposite direction. Both movements have this characteristic of withdrawal in common with cults and subcommunities such as bohemian neighborhoods, nature cults, and the holy wanderers of India. The current Hippie movement and its subcommunities in the United States and other industrial societies is illustrative of a withdrawal movement with a specific ideology of separation: "Tune in, turn on, drop out," the motto of the LSD user and his advice of cultural rejection.

Protest movements are episodic rather than permanent forms of collective action. They take on significance as agents of change, as precursors of movements, in connection with a series of episodic actions, as they may bring about specific changes or as they become interpreted in broader and more general transformations of the social order. Taken by themselves they are diffuse and vague, often seeming to express hostility rather than to advocate any form of change.

Riots, insurrections, spontaneous demonstrations, and strikes often seem unrelated to programs or goals. In his analysis of crowd behavior in France and England during the eighteenth and nineteenth centuries, George Rudé shows that this was often not true. Such protests, though spontaneous, unplanned, and episodic, operated as reactions to specific acts of authority and frequently led to changes which alleviated the stresses and strains to which they responded. This kind of protest can be seen as analogous to the more organized and continuous social movement in its function in "advocating" change. We shall examine this again in Part III, when we contrast protest and reform as products of different historical periods and political contexts.

Much of our definition of social movements, presented in the introduction, is most clearly applicable to *reform movements,* such as the Abolitionist movement, discussed in Section B, the Civil Rights movement, the Labor movement, or the current movement for firearms control or abolition of capital punishment in the United States. What characterizes reform is its gradualist and legitimate status. Operation within the institutional structure for conflict regulation, the "rules of the game," is a major form of reformist action. What is sought are usually changes in specific institutions—the eradication of slavery or the registration of firearms—rather than general shifts in major social values or in the forms of authority. In these respects reform contrasts both with the episodic and sometimes illegal nature of protest and with the general and also immediate demand of revolutionary action. In the next section we shall consider the specific historical and structural context of reform. Here the American historian Arthur M. Schlessinger, Sr., discusses the historical climate which has made the United States so often a land of many reformists movements. While he is more concerned with the sources of dissent, he also considers the gradualism of reform and the absence of more violent and revolutionary forms of social action as part of the American social climate.

The reading from Alexis de Tocqueville's *The Old Régime and the French Revolution* (Part I) is an analysis of the classic case of revolution in Western history. The term *revolution* has been very difficult for scholars to define, and a large literature has developed on the subject. We stress two aspects of revolutionary movements: their totality of aim and their attack on the legitimacy of established authorities. Both were part of Tocqueville's description. The French Revolution swept across all elements and institutions in French life, transforming values and procedures. It attacked the power and legitimate authority of nobility and king and created new "rules of the game." It did so with suddenness and immediacy and not with gradual or piecemeal change.

The French Revolution has remained a model of the total transformation of a society through sudden and deliberate change. In our excerpt from his book, *The Opium of the Intellectuals,* the French sociologist and political analyst Raymond Aron examines this model and the idea of revolution as a solution to social issues, contrasting it with the reformist view of gradual change.

The typology of movements we have presented has utility in the analysis of diverse forms of movements and, as we shall see in the following section, in understanding the typicality and appearance of particular types of movements in specific contexts. In the analysis of specific movements, however, the different directions by which the social order can be rejected often emerge as alternative choices. Withdrawal, protest, reform, insurrection, and even revolution may all coexist among partisans of a movement, as separate organizations, events, or "wings." Each may affect the other. The current movement toward racial equality in the United States has had, and still has, such a diversity of advocates and programs. In his analysis of the history and contemporary phase of the movement, Michael Lewis is sensitive to ways in which current discussion is paralleled by the past. Thus the separatists among black Americans today have their analogues in the earlier Garvey movement. The interconnection of types within a movement is clearly seen in the relation between ghetto riots and consequent resistance to or acceptance of reformist aims by white society.

Our description of types of collective action includes five dimensions of action which pose alternative choices as forms of response to discontent. *Communal separation–societal change* represents one dimension of answer to the question: Shall we try to change the society to meet our needs and values or shall we withdraw and live our lives apart from the society? Obviously the utopian communities and sectarian movements have chosen the former direction.

Another dimension is given by the distinction between protest and reform or revolutionary movements. This is the continuum of *episodic-established*. The intermittent quality of riots, mob behavior, and spontaneous demonstrations contrasts with the organized form which most movements assume in developing semipermanent associational structures such as the Woman's Christian Temperance Union, the Students for a Democratic Society, and the Nudists Association of America.

Another question posed for the adherent of a movement is: How much of the society should be changed? The episodic movement is also a highly specific one, reacting to particular events and pressing for specific remedies. A fall in the price of bread, an alleged act of police brutality, or the decision of college authorities is a highly specific event. The responses of protest action are either diffuse and expressive, as in generalized looting, or they seek to redress a specific grievance. New rules and institutions are not the primary focus. Thus the scope of change is a major dimension in the analysis of the aims of social movements. Protests seem the narrowest type of collective action along the continuum of *narrow change–broad change*. Other types can't be clearly distinguished along this dimension, since utopian communities and religious sects may often entail very broad aspects of the adherent's life. Some reforms, such as the New Deal, may be more far-reaching than revolutionary *coups d'état*. However, in most cases, the revolution aims at the broadest of change while reformist movements are somewhere between them and protest.

Still another dimension is inherent in our description of reformist movements as gradualist. Some movements, especially protest action, seek immediate and sudden remedies. Revolutions are characterized in this fashion also, although the electoral orientation of the Communist

Party in France and Italy during the past two decades shows that this is not necessarily the case. The dimension of *gradual realization–immediate realization* is one to which we give more attention in later sections, when we assess the role of myth in social movements. Here the question asked by the partisan is: Can we, or must we, reach our aims now, or can we afford patience and evolution?

Lastly, we distinguish movements and collective actions along a continuum of legal-illegal. Here we recognize the peculiar role of reform movements as legitimate and accepted procedures for attacking the legitimacy of institutions and values making up the established social order. While many forms of protest and even revolutionary movements may act through legal means, these are more likely to function outside societally sanctioned procedures. As a consequence they are often marked by more violence than is true of reform. Along this dimension the adherent faces the question: Can we achieve our goals within the legally sanctioned system of conflict resolution, or must we operate outside the boundaries of law?

A.
Movements of Withdrawal

1.
MODERNIZATION AND ITS DISCONTENTS: JAPAN'S LITTLE UTOPIAS (1968)

David W. Plath

> The superior individual . . . undoubtedly plays a major role in the shaping of a nation. But so do the individuals at the other extreme: the poor, the outcasts, the misfits, and those in the grip of some overpowering passion. . . . They crave to merge their drab, wasted lives into something grand and complete.
>
> Eric Hoffer, *The Ordeal of Change*

Utopian groups have sung a counterpoint of discontent with modernization in the West since the eighteenth century. Their performances are widely known, and often have attracted popular curiosity as well as scholarly scrutiny. Utopian groups also exist in modern Japan, although few non-Japanese are aware of them. The origins of these little Japanese utopias, the themes of discontent they articulate, and their effects on the greater society, all raise intriguing questions about the nature of utopianism and the success of Japan's modernization.

SOURCE. Original publication.

IS UTOPIA WESTERN?

Western writers like to claim parochial patents for utopia and utopianism. To cite but one example, Ernest Tuveson asserts that "The phenomenon of utopianism—the attempt to realize an ideal state of affairs in this world and in this life—is unique to modern European countries. That fact alone would indicate that some idea was present in the European tradition and in no other high civilization" (1963: 467). We could, of course, define utopian phenomena strictly in terms of their Western forms. But doing so would limit us to making comparative studies of form only. It would bar the way to comparisons among the wide array of collective images and collective efforts that serve similar functions, or occur under similar conditions, in many other cultures—or for that matter in other corners of our own tradition.

Thomas More's famous utopography and its many successors do seem to combine a particular set of formal elements. These Western utopias present (1) a depiction of an ideal way of life, (2) that is nowhere close at hand, (3) but is enjoyed by real and ordinary humans, (4) and is reported first-hand by travelers or native informants. This combination may have originated with More but its elements occur elsewhere, before and since, alone or in other combinations. The human animal everywhere seems addicted to visions of ideal nowheres, although I grant that many of these otherworlds can be reached only in dreams or by death-and-transfiguration, and that many are populated only by parahuman angels or ancestral shades or chartreuse spaceniks. Nevertheless, men use these otherworlds as models for measuring their own everyday scene and as communicable symbols of dis-ease with it. They make similar use of nonfictional accounts of other cultures distant in time or space.

Indeed visions of utopia often seem to be stirred by culture shock and new exposure to human otherness, although the problem has not been carefully studied. More wrote his *Utopia* at a time when the voyages of discovery were dramatically expanding European cultural horizons. Conversely, upon being confronted by Europeans people around the world have invented all manner of new views of alternative futures—ranging from humble Melanesian hopes for a great cargo ship to the more stately Chinese mansions of an elaborate construct such as K'ang Yu-wei's *Ta-t'ung Shu*. In Japan, for example, an awareness of the West as glimpsed dimly through the lens of "Dutch Studies" creeps into idealist writings of the seventeenth century and may have helped stimulate them (Norman, 1949; Craig, 1965). And a much more dramatic reaction follows the renewed and intensified Japanese-Western contacts of the mid-nineteenth century. Judging from the number of original books as well as translations that appeared, Japanese in the 1880s and 1890s were as fond of reading and writing about utopia as were Westerners of the same era (Sansom, 1949: 398–399, 415–420; Okazaki, 1955: 131–142; Yanagita, 1964).

In its broadest sense utopia can be regarded as an element of any human action. Mex Weber epitomizes this in his remark that every ideal-type is a utopia: it envisions a society that operates, in some way or other, more perfectly than the society we experience in the daily frustrations of the human barnyard. Much of current "voluntarist" social and cultural theory builds along these lines, on the assumption that we can best account for human behavior by starting with the ideals and values that people strive to realize. This kind of striving certainly is not peculiarly European, and in this sense neither is utopia, although it may be peculiarly human.

VARIETIES OF UTOPIANS

We seldom use "utopian," though, simply as a synonym for "idealist." We tend to see the utopian as one who envisions drastic, even total, change; who rejects mere tinkering with culture patterns or resorting to planning committees; who believes that an ideal society is impossible within the range of potentials inherent in present institutions and personality types. As Fred Polak puts it:

> The utopian rejects (explicitly) the existing order as unnatural, unreasonable and immoral, as inconsistent with the unfolding ideals of human dignity and perfection. The utopian does not answer any *last* question, but rather poses a *first* question, that of the problematical worth of the present social structure; its solution leads man outside the existing framework of society into another, imaginatively constructed setting. . . . Politics is the art of the immediately possible, the concrete compromise and short-run muddling through. Utopianism is the art of the impossible as a long-run possibility, of visionary planning for a non-political society based on human altruism and solidarity (1961: vol. I, 426).

If he is more than just a beautiful dreamer the utopian may be able to inspire collective action; found a revitalization movement (Wallace, 1956; 1961: 143–156). He may hope to alter many features of society, eventually of the whole world, but as a practical matter he is likely to concentrate upon one or another "operating unit" as his main locus for trying to effect change. He might favor a class of persons, as does the Marxist or Maoist utopian in his vision of uniting workers or peasants of the world. He might favor an institutional complex, as does the Adam Smith utopian in his vision of the transmuting power of the unseen hand of the marketplace. He might favor the people of a region, as did utopian proponents of a Greater East Asian Co-Prosperity Sphere. He might favor a particular nation-state, as do utopian nation-builders on several continents today. He might favor a pilot-plant little community, as did Fourier and Robert Owen. Or he might, lastly, bypass organizations and favor the transforming of personal relationships, as does Japan's Nishida Tenkō with his stress upon selfless service. (For other ways of classifying utopian action see Egbert and Persons, 1952.)

Logically all of these could be examined as types of utopian action; historically the term usually has been reserved for the small-scale "experimental" or "communitarian" variety. (And usually applied in denigration, thanks to Marx and Engels with their disdain for small-scale socialism, which looked unscientific in their eyes because it blurred the distinction between owners and workers.) All of these types exist in modern Japan; our topic here is the small-scale variety.

This latter kind of utopian might be called, in Arthur Bestor's phrase, an "apostle of small-scale social experiment" (1953: 505). With qualifications, though. Some groups openly favor little collective settlements as an ideal—for example the *kibbutzim* in Israel, the Yamagists in Japan. But the majority appear to be small by default, a combination of sluggish recruiting, an indifferent social milieu, and a determination to begin building the better world right here and now even with a mere handful of workers. The logic of demonstration also is a factor for some. They may not forswear all political action but they bend their initial efforts along parapolitical lines. Instead of trying to win the power of the state, they pin their hopes on the winning power of their little sample. This need not mean that they have small ambitions: many groups believe that their efforts deserve global emulation, and some of them strive to bring it about. The Yamagists put it in a slogan. They have undertaken, they say, the "Z revolution"; it will prove to be the last one in the world as in the alphabet.

In any case, the utopian's first loyalty is to the primordial group of fellow-strivers who are developing a new style of life that they believe will prove superior to any yet known. For this they often are accused of escapism and snobbery. I find them no more sinful on this account than any group of enthusiasts, perhaps less. They seldom claim that their community is an end unto itself, for members only—in contrast to some exclusivistic religious sects of the "God's little band" type. Instead they see their work as paving the way to a more ideal life for others as well. Thus they do not claim that their community stands as a completed model so much as a locus for further improvements. They are "experimental" in a rough and ready way, although not rigidly like the scientific methodists of Skinner's *Walden Two*. (The Yamagists like to toy with this style of rhetoric, referring to themselves as human guinea pigs, to their settlements as testing stations.) Nishida speaks of his Ittōen as a gateway, Owen referred to New Harmony as a halfway house.

Furthermore, few of these groups begin by drawing detailed plans for the new life. Bestor overstates the case when he speaks of them as "patent-office models of the good society." None of the Japanese leaders did much programming, nor did many Western utopians other than Fourier and Cabet. Most of them set out with nothing more than a small fund of general principles—all things in common, or selfless service, or natural living—plus a great fund of discontent with the status quo, and a reservoir of determination to change it drastically. Hence it is a mistake to see little utopias merely as pursuits of perfection; as revitalization movements they are products of, and responses to, the social soil wherein they grow.

UTOPIAN ORIGINS

The little utopias first appear, generally speaking, in the springtime of modernization. They are part of the blossoming of discontent that is a product of the very process of development itself. They are, in a sense, elements in a greater struggle to reform and revitalize routines of living that are being disrupted by the corrosive institutions of mass society. This is clear for the United States, and it seems to hold true for Japan in a similar way—approximately a century later—although there the evidence is less ample. Whether or not it would hold for other cases of modernization, or in what ways, is a good question for future inquiry.

Temporally, utopian movements first emerge in the United States during the early decades of the nineteenth century, in Japan during the early decades of the twentieth. As time goes on, many of them do not, but new ones continue to be formed at a variable rate. Spatially, they most often seem to emerge in what we might call—generalizing Whitney Cross' term (1950)—the burned-over districts. These are areas flaming with reformism, religious and political as well as utopian, much of the heat being generated by the rasp of new institutions against the flinty primordial ground of preindustrial living arrangements. As the mass society expands, the utopians tend to move on with it.

Seymour Bassett points out that secular utopian groups began to be organized in the United States

> . . . when the strains caused by American expansion were most acute. The shocks of this period were delivered by a new industrial system which was recognized but little understood and which operated in an unevenly but swiftly broadening market area. . . . Secular utopianism and the equally ineffectual contemporary trade unionism and native agrarianism were the three movements in the North which first organized the opposition to American commercial and industrial capitalism (1952: 156).

To this we might add in the somewhat more effectual activities of Jacksonian democracy and religious revivalism.

A century later across the Pacific, the Japan of late-Meiji early-Taisho years was similarly being shaped by nation-building political integration and an aggressive industrial-economic "drive to maturity." There too we find a similar cluster of democratic reformers, agrarianists, unionists, new-religionists, and utopians. The first of the utopians, so far as I know, was Nishida, who founded his Ittōen ("Garden of The Light") in 1906. Mushakōji Saneatsu followed a decade later in 1917 with Atarashiki Mura ("New Village"). Neither group has attracted a vast following, but both remain active, a longevity record matched by very few of the American groups and surpassing, in the case of Ittōen, that of the *kibbutzim.*

The American communities first appeared in burned-over districts of the North Atlantic and North Central states; later they spread west and south with the expanding commercial system. Japanese utopianism first appeared in the burned-over region between Nagoya and Osaka, the region where modern industry first took root and where there had been a highly commercialized economy even before industrialization began. Later, utopian offshoots went overseas with the growing Empire; and in the years since the Pacific war they have appeared in almost all parts of the nation.

In one of his studies of the American groups Bestor points out that although they often are said to be a Turnerian "frontier" phenomenon, in fact most of them located behind the frontier. (Cross argues in a similar vein for religious revivalism.) For example, Bestor shows that of 36 known Owenite and Fourierist groups, ten happened to migrate but only three of them went to the frontier. The greatest number, 26, stayed at home. "Clearly enough," he concludes, "communitarianism as a secular doctrine of social reform made its impact in already settled areas and it inspired its inhabitants to act in their own neighborhoods far more frequently than it led them to seek the Frontier" (1953: 511).

Japanese cases are far too few in number, and as yet too poorly studied, to be statistically satisfying. But I would argue, in the spirit of the tantalizing hypothesis, that they suggest a similar distribution. Nishida, for instance, was first distressed by his own tribulations as leader of a group of new settlers on the Hokkaido frontier. But he returned home to Nagahama in Shiga prefecture, and started Ittōen there and in the nearby city of Kyoto. Mushakōji happened to pick an isolated site in southern Kyushu for the first Atarashiki Mura precisely because he wanted to be well away from urban-industrial distractions. (Later, though, when a power-dam reservoir inundated much of its best land the community moved to the outskirts of Tokyo.) However, Mushakōji also grew up in Shiga and his first proposals for a new village were published in an Osaka daily newspaper.

The most flourishing of the postwar groups, the Yamagishi Association, also grew from the same region. It was founded in Kyoto in 1953, and its largest community (and national headquarters) is in nearby Mie prefecture. However, the Yamagists also have a smaller community in Hokkaido, a mission station near Tokyo in Nikko, and more than a score of affiliated collectivist "testing stations" (jikkenchi) spread across the nation. I know of a handful of other recent efforts in Hokkaido and in central and northeastern Honshu. And although the Japan Kibbutz Association has not yet broken ground for a community, it intends to organize one soon along kibbutz lines. It probably will be located in Hokkaido or northeastern Honshu, and will be staffed by the young people that the Association has been sending to Israel for on-the-job training.

In short, the utopian sometimes is drawn to the frontiers, to colonies, or to the backwoods. Such places have obvious advantages: cheaper land and less likelihood of interference from the political and economic centers of control, hence a better chance for a radically different style of life to take shape. Sometimes, too, the utopian has agrarian longings, although I have been surprised by how seldom he fits the popular stereotype of him as a Luddite, neo-peasant, or nature-boy escapist. This stereotype applies best to some of the "sectarian socialist" sects such as the Shakers, Rappites, or Amana Inspirationists. Such groups antedate modernization; often reject some of its features; and are less concerned with improving upon them than with avoiding them lest they distract from one's proper concern with the afterlife. The secular utopian, on the other hand, is more likely to be where the action is—in the existential hellfires of modernity itself.

POSING FIRST QUESTIONS

Little utopias grow like burls on the cambium edge of the modern social system; they are partly reactions against it. They articulate doubts about some of its blessings and they offer signposts along the road to reconstruction. They join the wider search that Adam Ulam describes as a "search for a haven of peace and contentment where science and technology could reign and bestow their benefactions, but from which their fellow travellers, business and competition, would be sternly excluded" (1965: 382).

Dismay with the modern present need not imply arcadian longings for the pastoral past: as future-seekers the utopians are as likely to reject the weaving of homespun as well as the wearing of neckties. They regard the principles they have discovered, or are discovering, as timeless and presumably universal, not just improvements on modernity but inherent in the nature of things or the nature of culture. "We don't feel that Atarashiki Mura developed just as a reaction to capitalism," said Watanabe Kanji, current leader of the Saitama community, in a public lecture I heard in 1965. "It is a reaction to the facts of human existence; man wants to live in truth." Or consider the very title of Nishida's *Ichi Jijitsu*, a short statement which sets forth the kernel of the Ittōen outlook and which members recite in unison every morning. It can be translated variously as "the One Reality," or "The One Great Truth," or even "The One Fact of Life." These truths are held to be self-evident; by them one can gauge how badly both the human past and present alike are distortions of the ultimate human potential.

The Japanese groups differ widely over the particular faults they find and hopes they raise. A detailed exposition of the "critiques" they enunciate or embody will demand more intensive investigation, but in a preliminary and heuristic spirit let me mention a few prominent themes.

The most obvious and central concern for Japanese utopians as for Western ones is to eliminate exploitation and replace it with mutual aid. Western ones approach the problem with arguments drawn from socialism and Christian siblingship; Japanese ones blend socialist elements with Buddhist-Bushidō attention to selflessness. Whatever the reasoning, a profit-motivated economy is held to foster mutual theft and mutual competitiveness. To avoid it, dispense with market exchange and develop personalities and institutions that nourish mutualism. Widespread communal control of goods and services—all things common— thus becomes a first principle for almost all little utopias (Atarashiki

Mura is an exception) although none of them applies it literally down to the last toothpick.

As small collectivities take over the functions of the market in allocating economic factors, the joys of mutualism are to supplant the egotistic allures of the profit motive. Western utopianists tend to be more interested in the former part of the issue, Japanese in the latter. Western ones lavish their wit upon the devising of labor-credit systems (witness Fourier and the Associationists, or *Walden Two*), Japanese ones upon the devising of methods for "clarifying the self" until it sees the truth of mutual dependency.

The Yamagists do this by a group inquiry method created by founder Yamagishi Miyozō (cf. Plath, 1967). It is unique in some features but draws upon Zen-method traditions. It also has points in common with group psychotherapy, Maoist "struggle" meetings, or the mutual-criticism sessions practiced in the Oneida community a century ago in New York state.

Ittōen members strive to eradicate selfishness by submitting to moral tutelage, originally that of Nishida himself, now that of his representatives. They test themselves frequently by venturing out penniless and cheerfully offering to perform humble and unpleasant tasks—such as scrubbing toilets—for strangers, without expecting any direct reward. They also try to live frugally. Meals in the communal dining room, for example, consist of plain fare which one eats quickly and silently while sitting upon a bare wood floor. Living space in the community ideally should not exceed 1½ mats per person, or about 27 square feet. This is partly for discipline, partly so as not to survive at the expense of others. However, it does not imply an argument for counterproductivity. As the *Ichi Jijitsu* says of the true man, "Though he has no desire for possessions he delights in the production of plenty." (For a full translation see Thomsen, 1963: 227–228.) Nishida often uses the image of mother-and-nursling: when in need, ask and it will be given; when able, offer to help those in need. This is neither egoism nor altruism; a society based upon it will have no exploitation.

At Atarashiki Mura self-clarification methods are left to personal preference but there also is a strong stress upon mutual nonsacrifice. A man should neither sacrifice another's joy of living for his own sake nor his for another's sake—Mushakōji explained to me one day—because the first results in exploitation, the second in martyrdom; both are in error.

This must not be confused with communism, say the Japanese utopians, stung by years of being misunderstood and spied upon. Communism is only a mechanical and dictatorial equalizing of shares, they say, which in its own way clouds the self as badly as does the reciprocal robbery of capitalism. Clarified selves need no coercion; their actions are wholly voluntary and yet at the same time are full of a sense of involvement with others. Only in such a society will true self-realization become possible for the first time.

Likewise this kind of society will provide the first true integration. It will not be just a linking-up of monad selves; it will be, in the Yamagist phrase, an *ittai seikatsu*, a "unitary way of life," a "way of living-as-one-body." Another image favored by all groups is that of family harmony: all society, all mankind, will come to feel—as members of the little utopia already do—the homey warmth of a greater familyhood. (Sibling rivalry and intergeneration hostility are, of course, not mentioned.) Only Ittōen takes this rather literally; it has persuaded the census office to commit the statistical horror of tabulating it as a single household of some 300 persons.

More free and perfect personal expression, yes. But even utopian Japanese see this as taking place within a firm interpersonal framework—a point that will surprise no one acquainted with Japanese ethical tradition. They avoid the idioms of individualism and art-for-art's-sake familiar in the West. The founder of Fujisawa Nōjo did advocate a need for greater individualism among the Japanese, but within two years his experiment was defunct (quite possibly, of course, for other reasons as well).

Atarashiki Mura probably comes closest to the Western outlook in its attention to artistry, as befits a movement grown in the shadows of one of Japan's most popular artist-authors of the twentieth century. Every member of the village is expected to share the work but also to share his works. He is encouraged to develop his talents in music, writing, the visual arts—and learn to do so without sacrifice to his fellowmen. One member explained it to me this way:

> Artists like to talk about self-expression, but by that they usually mean rampant individualism. I admire Beethoven and Rembrandt because they were truly alive as artists but I wonder if they ever truly lived as human beings. All past civilizations have been built on the sacrifices of slaves; it inevitably ends in warfare. How can any man truly feel alive, how can he be happy to have been born human, so long as a single slave remains? This village is tiny yet but it shows that there is a way out.

What of the machine? For these utopianists the human productive potential is what is at stake, not the productive potential of the machine. The latter is not avoided or scorned; on the contrary, it is advocated. These groups seem every bit as eager as other Japanese are to benefit from the latest scientific and technological blessings. They tend to take such blessings for granted, perhaps because they are children of the twentieth century. Few of them extol the machine and mass fabrication with the optimism of an Owen or a Cabet, but none of them seems to fear it with the pessimism of a Ruskin or a William Morris. All take advantage of late-model gadgetry. Atarashiki Mura, for instance, currently is raising 20,000 hens by American style mass methods, using all-but-automated henneries. However, only Shinkyō and the Kibbutz Association incorporate technological motifs in their public imagery, and even for them what counts is that machines, like the Sabbath, be used to make life more comfortable.

UTOPIANS IN ACTION

The utopian may envision a way of life that is peaceful and noncompetitive; to enact it he must do battle in the competitive markets of ideas and power. He faces double difficulties. On the one hand he must build a pilot plant that both tests and demonstrates his ideals; on the other hand he must do so with imperfect people in an imperfect social setting that may at best be permissive, at worst repressive. A setting that can stimulate utopian visions need not be a setting that sustains their enactment. To continue in motion the utopian and his fellows must somehow cling to their vision and organize themselves to advance it, but they must also develop tactics for adapting to demands made by the local power structure (Plath, 1966). The fact that some groups are able to endure may be testimony to their adaptivism as much as to their idealism.

Like social movements generally, Japan's little utopias often include both a core of dedicated activists and a peripheral network of sympathizers. The activists usually live in the community itself but may be posted out on recruiting duty for extended periods, as at the Yamagist mission in Nikko. The activist group can be examined as a community in the usual sense, a co-resident organization with a more or less coherent and interdependent system of roles and rules embracing most of the usual domains of life. Detailed analysis of this, as of the utopian visions I touched upon earlier, will depend upon deeper field study. But on the basis of short-term observation in a half-dozen of these Japanese communities I venture these preliminary points.

The most populous communities have about 300 members each— Ittōen and the Yamagist center in Mie. All the rest have fewer than 100 members each. Much of everyday life in the community thus can easily take place in a personalized or "particularized" mode; so-called "secondary" or impersonal media (e.g. money, the written word) can be avoided with little strain. This is a major principle for utopian groups elsewhere: the *kibbutzin*, for example, set an upper limit of about 1000 members per community. Some of the Japanese groups speak of setting similar limits, but as yet their virtue has not been tried.

In any event, much of the daily round and much of the decision making are carried on informally, as in little communities all over the world. Ittōen has elaborated a more formal complex of daily services, and official dress and greetings. But the latter seem to be mainly used in collective presentations of self to outsiders, and often are ignored when members interact only with members. In some of the communities one sees orders posted: "Let's Not Pick The Flowers," "Authorized Personnel Only," "Silence." Apart from that, written communiques and monetary transactions are uncommon. Not so with outsiders, of course. The communities must use coin of the realm for taxes and due-bills: members usually have petty cash allowances for personal purchases. And four groups issue books and periodicals for the benefit of their supporters and more generally for public information and education.

Role relationships in the communities tend heavily to be aligned in hierarchal modes. It is tempting to explain this as a result of the vertical stress that is so much a feature of Japanese tradition. But the reasons may be more complex, since strong leader-follower ties of an asymmetric sort are so common in activist movements in other cultures too. In any case, this de facto asymmetry runs counter to the egalitarian and symmetric visions propounded by some of the Japanese groups, or for that matter the general democratic tenor of Japanese ideals over the past 20 years. Some deliberative assemblies do exist in all of the little utopias. They appear to be most active among the Yamagists, who after all lost their charismatic founder a half-dozen years ago. (Which in turn led to the departure of 80 members to a new community in Ōtsū, in the footsteps of his widow.) They appear to be least active at Ittōen, whose "council of elders" only recently has been encouraging them, now that the 96-year-old Nishida no longer can rule directly because of age, and no magnetic successor is in sight.

Many Japanese social critics in the postwar years have carped about the persistence of familism in a democratic society. The utopians seem to have been somewhat more effective in combating it than the rest of their countrymen, although none of the groups has seriously attacked monogamy, and their sporadic efforts to separate parents and children seem feeble by *kibbutz* standards. Their greatest achievement probably has been the elimination of inheritance, by merging family property into the collectivity. But many recognize that the struggle may not yet be over, since the communities for the most part still are in their first generation.

The fans and fellow-travelers are scattered outside the community, in ordinary walks of life. They are valuable to the movement as direct sources of material and moral support, and as indirect bearers of its light to a darkened world. Ittōen, with its fondness for luminary images, terms them Friends of the Light. Atarashiki Mura calls them Second Class Members (only First Class Members live in the community). Even Mushakōji himself is a Second Class Member: he left the community about a decade after he had founded it, although for the four succeeding decades he has continued to advocate it in his writings and aid it with his royalties. On this side of the Pacific, Robert Owen similarly poured much of his fortune and his energies into supporting New Harmony, even though he himself didn't seem eager to spend much time there. Horace Greeley and Arthur Brisbane were major propagandists for the Associationist movement.

Directly and indirectly the little Japanese utopias shed their light far beyond the dozen communities themselves and their aggregate of some 2000 members. It spreads most directly through the supporters, then through other people that they persuade to visit the community, sample its literature, audit its public lectures, or even take part in its training sessions. Ittōen and the Yamagists offer such sessions frequently and have reached several thousand people in this way over the past decade. (For a description of a Yamagist session, see my 1967 essay.) People who attend are urged that even if they do not see fit to join the movement itself they should strive to practice its ideals in their own daily lives. Some large business firms—such as Chichibu Cement and Noritake China—regularly send teams of employees to the Ittōen sessions, and are said to temper their commercial activities with Nishida's principles of selflessness. (The cynic may prefer to interpret this as simple cow sociology.) And thus in one sense some of the utopian endeavors shade off into moral rearmament campaigns.

Quite apart from the sessions, visitors are a common sight, singly or by the tourist busload, in many of the communities. Some people stay long enough to reap considerable influence. For example, author Kurata Hyakuzō, utopianist Yamogishi, and the founders of several religious sects all are said to have been shaped by their experiences at Ittōen. Ittōen and the Yamagists also have drawn a number of overseas visitors, some of whom have tarried for several months. (One Yamagist greeted me as a hoped-for first missionary to the Americans.)

Through the media of mass communications the utopian message is broadcast even more widely. Hundreds of thousands of Japanese have read Nishida's essays on altruism, millions have read Mushakōji on natural living. (Unfortunately, as yet little of this has been translated into English, other than fragments of Nishida's work in Ittōen pamphlets. Some of Mushakōji's novels and dramas have been translated, but none of his utopian essays.) And as for the more rapid media, in several communities the arrival of reporters and cameramen is so routine an event that it scarcely draws notice.

LESSONS FROM FAILURE

Are they, then, just beautiful failures? Twentieth-century utopian motions have been made, and sometimes seconded, but never yet carried by the majority of Japanese. The utopian activists have not yet "routinized their charisma" and remade Japan, much less the world. In fact, all of their efforts together have not won as many adherents or even as many headlines as any of the dozen or so most powerful of the new Japanese religions. Nor have they politicized and sought electoral power, a frequent outcome of social movements (cf. the *kibbutzim*), although Nishida did serve one term in the Diet shortly after the Pacific War.

The little utopias *have* achieved a degree of institutionalization, as tolerated if not always favored "internal strangers," watched by the state more with indifference than with hostility, scanned by the public less from conviction than from curiosity. They have continued to grow in numbers and influence, albeit slowly, and they have never been forcibly disbanded. Considering the backlog of discontent with modernization in Japan as in other "developed" nations, the utopian motion may be far from having spent its momentum. Japanese intellectuals and the less erudite as well are not above scanning it for suggestions as to how to knit the raveled sleeve of anomie (see the special issue "Let's Search for Utopia" of the journal *Shisō no Kagaku*, vol. 6, no. 9, 1962).

Retrospectively the little utopias are useful to the student of modern Japan in the way that any dramatic episode is useful: by oversimplifying issues it makes them stand open to scrutiny. The utopias are a strategy sample, not a statistician's random one. A minor backwash to modernization by themselves, they help us gauge how that major surge of integrative energy that we call "development" churns up the primordial ground of an established social order.

For example, small as the evidence is, utopian activism seems to reflect—or be a part of—changing phases in Japan's socioeconomic growth.

If we use the Ohkawa-Rosovsky formulations, Japanese development as measured by economic indices took major new turns about 1906 and again about 1953 (Ohkawa, 1966; Ohkawa and Rosovsky, 1965). Each of these new turns saw the crystallizing of new institutions. Each saw, likewise, a spate of utopian activism. I have already mentioned the emergence of Ittōen and Atarashiki Mura in the years after 1906. All the other present-day little utopias have sprouted since 1953: the Yamagishi Association that very year, the rest in the 1960s.

The utopian evidence itself is so slight that it may be dismissed as fortuitous. But if we add in the evidence of other movements of discontent with modernization, the case would grow much stronger. I am thinking here of the rise of new kinds of protest and reform efforts in the years following the Russo-Japanese War (labor and tenancy disputes, socialism, proletarian publications, new religions), and again since the early 1950s (Zengakuren, Sōka Gakkai, or even hippyism). Further evidence might better support some different periodization; I am not insisting on the 1906/1953 turning-points per se. What I am saying is that with a bit of inventiveness we may be able to measure the course of Japan's modernization by productivity indices of protest as well as of pig iron. The two might not directly correlate; either way we would be challenged to probe deeper into the human costs of material abundance. And a total lack of correlation would seriously call into question our usual statements about the interrelatedness of human affairs. Eisenstadt approaches the issue from a different perspective, but his concept of a modernizing society's changing capacity for the absorption of discontent is another way of attacking the problem (Eisenstadt, 1966).

The utopian evidence may also teach us the need for a more balanced evaluation of Japan's success in modernizing. Japan's achievements have been admirable enough in terms of central political and economic institutions, certainly when contrasted with much of Afro-Asia. The perduring Japanese difficulty has not been to create primordial loyalty to the central institutions but to restrain it. Damping it, and at the same time bolstering the peripheries, was the nub of Occupation policy in reconstructing the nation after 1945; it has been a continuing worry to Japanese reformers ever since.

Lately a number of analysts have been suggesting that Japan's central-level success was built on an "enlightened conservatism" that trusted the lower levels to resolve their own primordial conflicts. It was confident that traditional ties within villages and paternalistic workshop groups would furnish a solid base of social-psychological continuity (cf. Bellah, 1962: 32–33; Bennett and Ishino, 1963: chap. 10), or a buffer against the onslaughts of political and economic rationalization (Maruyama, 1964: 55). "On the foundations provided by the strong persistence of traditional institutions in the agricultural villages," writes Ōtsuka Hisao, "the towering edifice of modern industrial enterprise was laid" (1966: 55).

This may be valid for the early Meiji decades; it seems doubtful for the twentieth century. The very effectiveness of the central "integrative revolution" (a term coined by Geertz, 1963) itself undermined the traditional patterns, as Silberman has shown for some institutions (1967). Concern for new forms of lower-level solidarity has been a continuing feature of the Japanese scene since the turn of the century. The little utopias themselves are one small indication of it; it is manifested in many other movements such as trade-unionism, the new religions, or Kagawa's "brotherhood economics," to cite only three. Perhaps we could write "recipes for modernization" based on Meiji Japan and offer them to third-world nation-builders. When we study twentieth-century Japan, however, we need to examine not only the bases for Japanese success but also the responses to her failures.

UTOPIA IS NOWHERE

I mean nothing invidious by that last remark. If utopia yet is nowhere in Japan, the same can be said for all other "successful modernizers." The little utopian often is accused of being politically naive because of his indifference to the problems of central institutions; he might well reverse the charges. If he is guilty of wishful thinking about superstates and economic empires, leaders of the latter can be equally guilty of wishful thinking about problems at lower levels. Americans like to rest smug about their "democratic tradition" that is supposed to resolve these messy questions of community by providing citizens with a feeling that the future rests in their hand as it pulls the lever on the voting machine. We now are being repaid with interest for our domestic blindness.

In *Civilization and Its Discontents* Freud mentions the "advantage, not to be undervalued, in the existence of smaller communities, through which the aggressive instinct can find an outlet in enmity towards those outside the group" (1958: 64). This narcissism of petty differences, he argues, is a relatively innocent way to simultaneously satisfy aggressive tendencies and strengthen group mutuality. On this count the little utopain, political failure that he is, may have a lesson to teach the sophisticated and successful nation-builders.

REFERENCES

BASSETT, T. D. Seymour. 1952. The secular utopian socialists. *In* Egbert and Persons (1952), vol. I: 153–211.

BELLAH, Robert N. 1962. Values and social change in modern Japan. *Asian Cultural Studies* 3: 13–56.

BENNETT, John W., and ISHINO, Iwao. 1963. *Paternalism in the Japanese Economy, Anthropological Studies of Oyabun-Kobun Patterns.* Minneapolis: University of Minnesota Press.

BESTOR, Arthur. 1953. Patent-office models of the good society: some relationships between social reform and westward expansion. *American Historical Review* 58: 515–526.

BOGUSLAW, Robert. 1965. *The New Utopians, a Study of Systems Design and Social Change.* Englewood Cliffs, N.J.: Prentice-Hall, Inc.

CRAIG, Albert. 1965. Science and Confucianism in Tokugawa Japan. *In* Marius B. Jansen, *Changing Japanese Attitudes toward Modernization,* pp. 133–60. Princeton, N.J.: Princeton University Press.

CROSS, Whitney R. 1950. *The Burned-Over District; the Social and Intellectual History of Enthusiastic Religion in Western New York, 1800–1850.* Ithaca, N.Y.: Cornell University Press.

EGBERT, Donald D., and PERSONS, Stow (eds.). 1952. *Socialism and American Life.* Two vols. Princeton, N.J.: Princeton University Press.

EISENSTADT, S. N. 1966. *Modernization: Protest and Change.* Englewood Cliffs, N.J.: Prentice Hall, Inc.

FREUD, Sigmund. 1958. [1930]. *Civilization and Its Discontents.* Garden City, N.Y.: Doubleday and Co. (Anchor edition).

GEERTZ, Clifford. 1963. The integrative revolution, primordial sentiments and civil politics in the new states. *In* Clifford Geertz (ed.), *Old Societies and New States,* pp. 105–157. New York and London: The Free Press.

HOFFER, Eric. 1964. *The Ordeal of Change.* New York: Harper and Row (Colophon edition).

MARUYAMA, Masao. 1964. Japanese thought. *Journal of Social and Political Ideas in Japan* 2: no. 1 (April), 41–48.

NITOBE, Inazo. 1909. The influence of the West upon Japan. *In* Count Shigenuma Okuma (compiler), *Fifty Years of New Japan,* vol. II: 458–476. London: Smith, Elder and Co.

NORMAN, E. H. 1949. Andō Shōeki and the anatomy of Japanese feudalism. *Transactions of the Asiatic Society of Japan.* 3rd series, vol. II.

OHKAWA, Kazushi. 1966. Agriculture and turning-points in economic growth. *In* Seiichi Tōbata (ed.), *The Modernization of Japan,* vol. I, pp. 137–154. Tokyo: Institute of Asian Economic Affairs.

OHKAWA, Kazushi, and ROSOVSKY, Henry. 1965. A century of Japanese economic growth. *In* William W. Lockwood (ed.), *The State and Economic Enterprise in Japan,* pp. 47–92. Princeton, N.J.: Princeton University Press.

OKAZAKI, Yoshie. 1955. Japanese literature in the Meiji era. (Translated and adapted by V. H. Viglielmo.) Tokyo: Ōbunsha.

OTSUKA, Hisao. 1966. Modernization reconsidered—with special reference to industrialization. *In* Seiichi Tōbata (ed.), *The Modernization of Japan*, vol. I, pp. 49–66. Tokyo: Institute of Asian Economic Affairs.

PASSIN, Herbert. 1965. *Society and Education in Japan*. New York: Teachers College and East Asian Institute, Columbia University.

PLATH, David W. 1966. The fate of utopia: adaptive tactics in four Japanese groups. *American Anthropologist* 68: no. 5 (October), 1152–1162.

———. 1967. Utopian rhetoric: conversion and conversation in a Japanese cult. In June Helm (ed.), *Essays on the Verbal and Visual Arts: Proceedings of the 1966 Annual Spring Meeting of the American Ethnological Society*, pp. 96–108. Seattle: University of Washington Press.

POLAK, Fred. 1960. *The Image of the Future*. New York: Oceana Press.

REED, John Paul. 1937. Kokutai: a study of certain sacred and secular aspects of Japanese nationalism. Doctoral dissertation (Sociology), University of Chicago.

SANSOM, George B. 1949. *The Western World and Japan*. New York: Alfred Knopf.

SILBERMAN, Bernard B. 1967. Structural and functional differentiation in the political modernization of Japan. *In* Robert Ward (ed.), *The Political Development of Modern Japan*. Princeton, N.J.: Princeton University Press.

THOMSEN, Harry. 1963. *The New Religions of Japan*. Tokyo and Rutland, Vt.: Charles E. Tuttle.

TUVESON, Ernest. 1963. The power of believing. *Comparative Studies in Society and History* 5: no. 4 (July), 466–477.

ULAM, Adam. 1965. Socialism and utopia. *Daedalus* 94: no. 2 (Spring), 382–400.

UYEHARA, Cecil B. 1959. *Leftwing Social Movements in Japan, an Annotated Bibliography*. Tokyo and Rutland, Vt.: Charles E. Tuttle.

WALLACE, Anthony F. C. 1956. Revitalization movements. *American Anthropologist* 58: 264–281.

———. 1961. *Culture and Personality*. New York: Random House.

YANAGITA, Izumi. 1964. Meiji Nihon no yūtopia shisō [Utopian ideas in Meiji Japan]. *Sekai* (January), 240–248.

B.
Episodic Protest

2.
THE PRE-INDUSTRIAL CROWD (1964)
George Rudé

As long as the crowd in history was considered unworthy of serious attention, it was natural that the study of its motives should have been somewhat superficial. Explanations of why the crowd rioted or rebelled have naturally tended to vary with the social attitudes or *values* of the writer. To those to whom the crowd's actions were wholly reprehensible, the crowd would appear to be prompted by the basest motives, by the lure of loot, gold, rape, or the prospect of satisfying other lurking criminal instincts. To those to whom the crowd seemed, on balance, to be an object worthy of sympathy or compassion rather than of reprobation (though this would vary with the occasion), noble ideals, particularly those of sound middle-class and liberal inspiration, would play an important part. To others again, those whom Marx in his day termed the proponents of a "vulgar" materialism, short-term economic factors seemed the most valid explanation of all types of popular unrest, and every disturbance became almost by definition a hunger riot, or *émeute de la faim*.

SOURCE. George Rudé, *The Crowd In History*. New York: John Wiley & Sons, Inc., 1964, pp. 214–223 231–234. Copyright 1964 by John Wiley & Sons, Inc. Reprinted by permission of John Wiley & Sons, Inc., and the author.

None of these explanations are wholly without merit, yet all are either superficial or misleading. Why this is so will, I hope, appear in the course of the present chapter. But a preliminary word needs to be said about the first of these interpretations, which, being the most pervasive of the three, calls for a separate comment. Its underlying assumption appears to be that the masses have no worthwhile aspirations of their own and, being naturally venal, can be prodded into activity only by the promise of a reward by outside agents or "conspirators." "In most popular movements," writes Mortimer-Ternaux, a historian of the French Revolutionary Terror, "money plays a greater role than feeling or conviction (*la passion*)"; and Taine and his school offer similar explanations of why the Bastille fell or the French monarchy was overthrown. But such a view, with its evident social bias, was by no means the invention of these writers: on the contrary, it receives ample confirmation from the opinions of contemporary observers. For as long as no serious attempt was made to probe the deeper aspirations of the poor, their periodic outbursts in riot or rebellion were liable to be attributed to the machinations of a political opponent or a "hidden hand."

Such an attitude was shared by all in authority, whether aristocratic or middle class, conservative, liberal, or revolutionary, though the sort of outbreak that might, exceptionally, be condoned would naturally vary from one class or party to the other. Where Sir Robert Walpole, the King's Chief Minister, attributed the riots of 1736 in England to a Jacobite conspiracy and some of his agents spoke darkly of "high church" or "popish priests," Lord Granville, an opposition peer, was willing to ascribe such "tumults" to "oppression." Again, where George III's ministers and their agents hinted that the Gordon Riots might have been instigated by French or American gold, some opposition leaders were inclined to blame the government itself for deliberately fostering riot as a pretext for calling in the army and imposing martial law. Indeed it was common in eighteenth-century England for one party to accuse the other of "raising a Mob." In France, Voltaire, being a critic of aristocracy and a friend of Turgot, convinced himself that the grain-rioters of 1775 were in the pay of Turgot's enemies at Court. During the French Revolution, both revolutionary leaders and their royalist or aristocratic opponents were remarkably liberal with such charges when it suited them: Montjoie, a royalist journalist, claimed to have first-hand proof (which proved to have little foundation) that the Réveillon rioters of 1789 had been bribed with *louis d'or;* and Girondins and Jacobins alike were disposed to believe that food rioters like those that invaded Paris grocery shops in February 1793 had been paid by agents of Pitt or the "aristocrats." Thirty or forty years later, such simple explanations had lost much of their force: we have but to read English parliamentary debates on the Luddites and Chartists to appreciate the difference; but, throughout the eighteenth century, the police—the French perhaps more stubbornly than the English—clung to their conviction that the twin agents of riot and rebellion were bribery and "conspiracy."

To illustrate the point, we quote the remarkable cross examination by the Beauvais police of a woolen worker arrested in the market town of Mouy at the time of the corn riots of 1775:

Q. How was it known that there were riots elsewhere?
A. Everybody said so in the market at Mouy.
Q. Did any "strangers" come by who urged the people to riot?
A. He saw none.
Q. What did these "strangers" look like?
A. Repeats that he saw none.
Q. What did they talk about?
A. Repeats that he saw no "strangers."
Q. Did they claim to be bearers of the King's orders and did they produce papers purporting to prove it?
A. Repeats that he saw no "strangers."
Q. Did you give, lend, or promise money?
A. He saw no one offering money.
Q. Did any of them produce mouldy bread . . . to stir up the people?
A. He saw no mouldy bread.
Q. Does he know where and by whom this mouldy bread was baked?
A. Repeats that he saw no mouldy bread.
Q. How was it that the inhabitants of each village assembled on the same day and at the same hour?
A. This was always so on market days.
Q. Had he seen bills posted up or distributed?
A. No.
Q. Were they printed or written by hand?
A. Repeats that he saw none.
Q. Does he know where they were printed?
A. Repeats that he saw none.
Q. Does he recognize the writing on those written by hand?
A. Repeats that he saw none.
Q. Where had they been drinking, with whom, and who paid for the drinks?
A. Repeats that he saw no one.

It is remarkable that such searching and persistent questioning should, in this and other cases, have yielded almost entirely negative results. Occasionally a prisoner or a witness, unlike the prisoner in the present instance, admits to having heard rumors about money having been distributed to provoke disorder; but never once does he appear to have been present at the transaction or to have been personally involved. This is not to argue that such rumors were all equally without foundation, though it strongly suggests that cases of bribery in popular movements were not so frequent as the authorities supposed they were. Nor does it exclude the fact of bribery in other cases, as when gangs of strong-arm men were recruited by a man of "quality" to beat up or intimidate a political opponent. Such was the case at the Middlesex election of December 1768, when the Court candidate, Sir William Beauchamp Proctor, hired a band of Irish chairmen—at the rate of 2 guineas a day, it was claimed by their leader—to drive his radical opponent's supporters off the hustings. This was the well-known device of "raising a Mob"; but it has nothing to do with the sort of popular movement we are here discussing.

In any case, such explanations, even where they contain a more solid substance of truth, are grossly oversimplified. The crowd may riot because it is hungry or fears to be so, because it has some deep social grievance, because it seeks an immediate reform or the millenium, or because it wants to destroy an enemy or acclaim a "hero"; but it is seldom for any single one of these reasons alone. Of course, it would be ludicrous to reject the simple and obvious answers merely because they are so. Economic motives, for example, may be presumed to be dominant in strikes and food riots, as political issues play a part of varying importance in both radical reform movements and movements directed against radical reform, such as the Priestley riots in Birmingham in 1791. When Cornish tin miners or West Country weavers burn down their employer's house or mill or destroy his machinery in the course of an industrial dispute, we need no particular powers of divination to conclude that, whatever the form of disturbance, it is higher wages that they are after. Similarly, when food rioters threaten bakers, invade markets, and rip open sacks of flour or grain, we may assume that the real purpose is not so much to intimidate or destroy as to bring down the price of food. Again, when Parisians assault and capture the Bastille and Londoners "pull down" Catholic houses and chapels, we must suppose that they intended to do precisely this. In looking for motives we must, therefore, not be so subtle or devious as to ignore the overt or primary intention.

The latter, however, only gives us a clue to the general nature of a disturbance; and here we are not so much concerned with this as with what prompted people, often of different social groups, occupations, and beliefs to take part in the event. Even if the immediate or overt motives leap to the eye, we still have to explore those that lie beneath the surface; and if persons of differing classes or creeds are involved, some may be impelled by one motive and some by another. Motives will, therefore, vary not only between one action and the next but between different groups participating in the same disturbance. Even so, we shall become hopelessly confused if we do not attempt to make some distinction between what we may term dominant and underlying motives or beliefs. Here, for the sake of clarity, it is proposed to divide the former into "economic" and "political" and to consider what part they played, both separately and in association, in the activities of the pre-industrial crowd.

Let us begin with those disturbances in which economic issues were clearly paramount. Such were food riots (at this time, the most frequent of all), strikes, peasant attacks on châteaux, the destruction of gates and fences, the burning of hayricks and the wrecking of industrial and agricultural machinery. These account, as we have seen, for the vast majority of disturbances in which the pre-industrial crowd in France and England was actively engaged. And in these we must assume (unless we have evidence to the contrary) that the common people of town and countryside were impelled by the urge to maintain or improve living standards, to raise or prevent reductions in wages, to resist encroachments on their holdings in land or their rights of common pasture, to protect their means of livelihood against the threat of new mechanical devices, and, above all, to ensure a constant supply of cheap and plentiful food. Yet bad, even abysmal, economic conditions were not an automatic "trigger" to disturbance. In England, strikes and trade-union activity tended to occur not at moments of deepest trade depression and unemployment, but rather on the upswing of a boom: as in 1792, 1818, 1824, and 1844–6 (the year 1768 appears to have been an exception). During the French Revolution, we noted, the most protracted industrial disputes were those of 1791 and 1794, which were years of comparative prosperity; and that when runaway inflation and unemployment set in, as in the winter of 1794–5, strikes came to an end and food riots took over. Food riots, unlike strikes, were the direct product of bad harvests and trade depression, rising prices and shortage of stocks; but they did not necessarily occur at the peak of a cycle of rising prices: we saw rather that they tended, as in the largest disturbances of their kind before 1789—those of 1766 in England and 1775 in France—to arise as the result of a sudden sharp upward movement leading to shortage and panic buying. Again, strikes, food riots, and peasant movements, even when the prevailing issues were purely economic, might take place against a political background that gave them a greater intensity or a new direction. In London in 1768, already existing industrial disputes were touched by the Wilkite political movement: we find striking weavers and coal heavers acclaiming John Wilkes; and, in France in 1789, it seems unlikely that the peasants would have chosen that particular moment to settle accounts with their landlords if the general political conditions had not been what they were.

Conversely, economic motives often impinged on movements that were, in their essence, political. City riots, upon which political issues usually obtruded, frequently took place against a background of rising prices or food shortage: we saw examples from Paris in 1720, 1752, and 1788, and from London in 1736, 1768, and 1794; though, here, the Gordon Riots and the later Wilkite disturbances appear to have been exceptions. Similarly, the French revolutions of 1830 and 1848 broke out during periods of food shortage and trade depression; and we have noted the particular part played by the unemployed in Paris in June 1848. The same intrusion of economic issues is evident in English disturbances of the early nineteenth century; Professor Rostow has vividly illustrated the point in his "social tension chart" for the years 1790 to 1850.

On such occasions, the shortage and high price of bread and food appear to have acted as a stimulus to popular participation in movements that were obstensibly concerned with other objects and issues. During the first French Revolution concern for the price of bread runs like a constant thread through every phase of the struggle of parties and through nearly every one of the great popular *journées,* and accounts, perhaps more than any other factor, for the unity and militancy of the Parisian sans-culottes. The revolutionary crisis of 1789 broke out against a backcloth of steeply rising bread prices: we saw how the peasant movement began with raids on markets, millers, and granaries before turning into a war against the landlords; and the Réveillon rioters, who destroyed the houses of two unpopular manufacturers, also raided food shops and demanded a reduction in the price of bread. In October, the women of the markets who marched to Versailles to fetch the royal family to Paris chanted as they marched (or, at least, so tradition has it), "let us fetch the baker, the baker's wife and the little baker's boy"; and Barnave, in describing the day's proceedings to his *Dauphinois* constituents, wrote that while "the bourgeoisie" were mainly preoccupied with the political issues, "the people" were equally concerned with the shortage of food. The outbreak of war brought further problems: not only bread, but meat, wine, coffee, and sugar began to disappear from the shops, and in Paris food riots preceded or accompanied each one of the political *journées* of 1792 and 1793. In September 1793, as we saw, it was as the direct result of the popular agitation in the markets, streets, and Sections that the National Convention adopted the law of the General Maximum that placed a ceiling on the prices of most necessities. And, after the Jacobins had fallen and the *maximum* had been abandoned, the insurgents of May 1795 wore on their caps and on their blouses the twin slogans, "The Constitution of 1793" and "Bread."

We are certainly not arguing that short-term economic factors eclipsed all others and that all popular movements of this period, even such politically oriented movements as those of the French Revolution, were really food riots in disguise. We saw in an earlier chapter that even before 1789 the political ideas of the *parlements* in Paris and of the Common Council of the City of London played a part in popular disturbance. Mr. Edward Thompson claims that the London crowd of the 1760's and 1770's "had scarcely begun to develop its own organization or leaders" and, that, having little theory distinct from that of its middle-class "managers," was as yet as unreliable instrument of radical policies. This is true enough, and the proof lies in the fact that the same crowd that had shouted for "Wilkes and Liberty" in 1768 was, a dozen years later, directing its energies into channels that were hardly propitious for the radical cause—destroying Catholic houses and chapels. Nevertheless, the political lessons learned were not entirely forgotten, and they revived and were enriched under the impact of the French Revolution. For, both in England and France, the Revolution of 1789, by posing sharply in their multiform aspects the new concepts of the "rights of man" and the "sovereignty of the people," added a new dimension to popular disturbance and gave a new content to the struggle of parties and classes.

Some historians have doubted the depth of the penetration of these political ideas among the common people. Professor Cobban, for example, has questioned the importance of the circulation of a few political slogans, for (he writes) "one knows how easily a crowd can be taught to chant these and how little serious political content they can have." This would be true enough if it were only a matter of mouthing borrowed slogans, though even these were of some importance in mustering popular support for a radical cause: it is surely significant, for example, that even before the Estates General assembled at Versailles on May 5, 1789, Parisian crowds had taken up the rallying cry of *Vive le Tiers Etat!* and (like Arthur Young's peasants of a few months later) given it a special meaning of their own. And such ideas and slogans were certainly not kept on ice, as it were, for the great political occasions: on the contrary, there is ample evidence that they permeated ever more deeply and widely as the Revolution progressed. Already in August 1789, we find a journeyman gunsmith arrested at Versailles for speaking slightingly of General Lafayette supporting his claim to a fair hearing with an appeal to the "rights of man"; and Malouet, a hostile observer, relates how at this time chairmen at the gates of the National Assembly were eagerly discussing the rights and wrongs of the case for a royal right of "veto." A year later, the democrats of the Cordeliers Club were forming popular clubs and societies through which they began to give systematic instruction to small craftsmen and wage earners in the more advanced revolutionary doctrines; and, in police records, we read of journeymen and domestic servants subscribing to the radical press and even taking out subscriptions to the more exclusive Jacobin Club. Under this impetus, the sans-culottes not only formed political organizations of their own but later, when they dominated the Paris Sections and Commune, began to advance policies and solutions that proved highly embarrassing to their Jacobin allies. And not only that; for, having assimilated their ideas, they gave them a new content that corresponded more with their own interests than with those of their middle-class teachers.

The sans-culotte movement ended, as we have seen, in the final outbreak and disaster of May 1795, and when it reappeared in the 1830's it had acquired a new social content and the new battle cries and slogans. As we noted in Chapter 11 it was the advent of the industrial revolution and the growth of a working-class movement in the intervening years that were largely responsible for the transformation. Babeuf had already, during the first of the political revolutions, given a new socialist twist to the ideas of 1789, but he had come too late to find an effective audience among the sans-culottes. It was only after 1830 that his ideas and ideas similar to his evoked a deep response among the clubs and workers' organizations that sprang up in Paris and played so large a part in the events of 1848. What was new now was not only the content of the ideas themselves but the class of men who voiced them. Among those arrested after the June "days" of that year was Antoine Bisgambilia, an obscure and illiterate mechanic (*mécanicien*), who, in a note dictated to the police from La Roquette prison, expressed his political convictions as follows:

> Everybody knows that I don't compromise with my conscience and that, as long as I have breath left in my body, I shall use it for the triumph of the Democratic and Social Republic.

Admittedly, this declaration appears in an isolated document and we should hardly expect to find many others of the kind; but the nature of the June revolt and the large number of those arrested and convicted suggest that such views were shared by many others. What is certain is that, by now, wage earners—railwaymen, building workers, and journeymen of the traditional crafts—were playing a far larger part in political movements than they had in the first revolution, and were even (like the shopkeepers and craftsmen of 1793) voicing political demands of their own.

A similar evolution had taken place in England; and in some respects it had proceeded more rapidly than in France. As England went through no revolution of her own, the new revolutionary ideas of the rights of man and popular sovereignty were largely borrowed from across the Channel. Through the works of Thomas Paine and others, these began, from early in 1792, to circulate among democrats, dissenters, and the master craftsmen, and journeymen of the big cities and industrial towns. This was also the year that Thomas Hardy's London Corresponding Society began to meet at The Bell in Exeter Street, with its membership of small urban tradesmen and artisans: similar in its social composition to those who met in the clubs and committees of revolutionary Paris. Yet, in some of the English societies like that of Sheffield, there appears to have been a larger percentage of "the inferior sort of Manufacturers and Workmen" than in similar bodies in France. To that extent, it may perhaps be claimed that in England the new revolutionary ideas met with a proportionately greater response among wage earners than in France herself. The English societies were, however, short lived, succumbed to early repression, and had little opportunity of making recruits among the newly emerging factory population.

Jacobin ideas survived, however, gradually found a wider audience and, "driven into weaving villages, the shops of the Nottingham framework knitters and the Yorkshire croppers, the Lancashire cotton-mills, were propagated in every phase of rising prices and of hardship." They emerged on the surface again in the freer political atmosphere of the Westminster election of 1807, when the radicals Burdett and Cochrane were borne to victory by the popular vote; and they inspired the Lancashire weavers who were cut down by the Manchester yeomanry at the great parliamentary reform meeting in St. Peter's Fields in August 1819. After this, the Jacobin-radical tradition, enriched by memories of "Peterloo," took on a new form with the advent of the socialist ideas propounded by Robert Owen and others. It was such a mixture of ideas that moulded the political thought of men like George Loveless, the trade unionist and Tolpuddle Martyr of 1834, who, some years before Marx, wrote that "nothing will be done to relieve the distress of the working classes, unless they take it into their own hands." And, on a far wider canvas, they were carried forward into the nationwide agitation for the People's Charter, which, as we have seen, both drew its inspiration from the past and looked forward to the future. . . .

Millenarial and religious ideas also clearly played a part in popular disturbance. The millenium might assume a secular or a religious form, though (unlike the Wesleyan ideal) it was generally to be realized on earth rather than in heaven. Millenarial fantasies no doubt underlie many of the actions of the poor in the course of the French Revolution; but in none are they so clearly evident as in the sudden upsurge of hope aroused among them by the news that the Estates General should meet in the summer of 1789. The news fostered what French historians since Taine have called *la grande espérance:* the hope that, at last, past promises would be fulfilled and the burdens, particularly the hated *taille,* lifted off the peasants' backs, and that a new golden era would begin. The state of exaltation thus engendered equally produced its corollary, the conviction, once these hopes appeared to be endangered, that their realization was being frustrated by a *complot aristocratique.* This dual phenomenon, it has been argued, does a great deal to explain the almost mystical fervor with which the *menu peuple* pursued their "aristocratic" enemies during the Revolution. Or, as in England, millenarial fantasies might be clothed in the poetic imagery of Blake's "Jerusalem" or the apocalyptic extravagances of a Richard Brothers, whose *Revealed Knowledge of the Prophesies and Times* was published in London in early 1794. This was a time when Jacobin ideas were still making headway among the "lower orders"; and it has been suggested that men like Brothers, who interlaced their talk of "the whore of Babylon" and the "Antichrist" with denunciations of the high and mighty, may have nourished similar political aspirations to those nourished by Tom Paine's *The Rights of Man.* But millenarial ideas, while they might, under certain circumstances, stimulate rather than weaken an already existing political movement, might equally act as an antidote to popular militancy or as a consolation for a political defeat. This may have been the case in France after Waterloo and, in England in 1838, in the strange affair of "the battle in Bossenden Wood."

In the latter case, a number of Kentish laborers believed implicitly that their leader, the spurious Sir William Courtenay, was the Messiah. But this is only one guise in which the religious motive may appear in riots. At other times, though overtly proclaimed, it might not be so profound as it was made to appear; or conversely it might lie submerged beneath the surface of events. Of the first kind "No Popery" riots, "High Church" attacks on Methodist or Presbyterian meeting halls and chapels, and urban "Church and King" explosions are obvious examples. Quite apart from their social undercurrents, such movements were never quite what they seemed. We have seen that the ill-assorted slogans "destruction to Presbyterians" and "No Popery" appeared side by side in the Birmingham riots; and one of those sentenced to death for his part in the Gordon Riots said, when questioned: "Damn my eyes, I have no religion; but I have to keep it up for the good of the cause." It is not so much that in such movements the religious element is non-existent or a mere cloak for other issues (though this was firmly believed by some contemporaries) as that in them religious, social, and political motives are bewilderingly interwoven. Perhaps, in view of their proclaimed purpose to maintain an established Church as part of an established order, we should treat them less as religious movements than as anti-radical political demonstrations.

The case is somewhat different where a dissenting religious tradition serves as an undercurrent rather than as a proclaimed object of disturbance. In London and England's West Country, in particular, religious dissent and popular radicalism had had a long association; and Methodism, even when it professed to stave off riot and lay up its treasures solely in heaven, brought with it a new fervor and moral purpose that, sooner or later, were bound to leave their mark on popular social movements. Such was certainly the case in England and Wales in the disturbances of 1830 and the 1840's: in the "Swing" and Rebecca riots and in the Welsh Chartist movement Protestant nonconformity, both Wesleyan and other, played a part.

Nor must we assume that such secular, rationalist ideas as the "rights of man" and other products of the Enlightenment would, when they gripped the common people, necessarily serve as an antidote to religion. This was no doubt the intention of many rationalist thinkers and middle-class and aristocratic reformers or revolutionaries in England and France in the eighteenth century; and there were moments during the French Revolution when they appeared to have been successful. Certainly, the monopoly and authority of the established Catholic Church were successively undermined and broken—and these were never fully recovered; and Parisian crowds demonstrated to shouts of *A bas la calotte!* ("Down with the priests!") and played a part at the height of the "de-christianization" movement in the autumn of 1793, in closing down every church in the city. Yet the popular anti-religious (as distinct from the anti-clerical) movement was comparatively short lived; as late as June 1793, Parisians in the revolutionary Faubourg St. Antoine demonstrated for the right to preserve the traditional Corpus Christi procession; and Robespierre himself sought to win further popular support for the Revolutionary Government by launching a brand-new religious cult, the Cult of the Supreme Being. This was only the most highly publicized of numerous attempts to affect a fusion between religion and the current political ideas. In many districts, the people took the initiative themselves and the Revolution saw a remarkable upsurge of new religious cults; and solemn ceremonies, accompanied by all the *mystique* of the old religious practices, were dedicated to new local "saints" or to the great popular martyrs of the Revolution, Marat, Chalier, and Lepeletier. Yet once the Revolution was over, such cults appear to have left few traditions; and neither they nor the re-established Catholic Church, nor the religious minority groups, appear to have played any significant part in the revolutions of 1830 and 1848.

The analysis might be carried even further; but to spare the bewildered reader's feelings I propose to stop it here. What we have seen is a rich variety of motives and beliefs, through which economic issues and appeals to customary rights exist side by side with new conceptions of man's place in society and the search for the millenium. Such a medley of seemingly ill-assorted beliefs and aspirations is by no means a feature peculiar to the pre-industrial crowd: it appears as evidently, though with different emphases and variations, in the disturbances of today as it does in those of ancient or medieval times. But through the confusion a certain common pattern peculiar to the age emerges. We shall, however, hardly be aware of it unless we place the riots and rebellions in their historical context and compare those of the early and middle years of the eighteenth century with those of the French Revolution and those that followed later. Even when we do so, we shall not see a steady, gradual disappearance of appeals to custom and millenarial fantasies: these persist, though at times with abated vigor, throughout the period that we are concerned with. But there are significant turning points at which new conceptions enter and, while not eclipsing the old ideas entirely, transform them or reduce their relative importance. Such turning points are the revolution of 1789 in France and the growth of independent working-class movements in the 1830's.

Recently, Professor Reinhard Bendix has stressed the contrast between types of popular protest arising in the "pre-democratic" and those arising in the "democratic" period of West European history. The point is an important one, for once the new and essentially forward-looking ideas of the "rights of man" and "popular sovereignty" had gripped the popular imagination, riots and disturbances tended to acquire a new dimension and to assume a stable social-ideological content that they had lacked before. But, equally, emerging industrial society in France and England created an industrial working class, working-class movements, and working-class political ideas. Thus further new ideas and further social forces, unknown in 1789, began to come to the fore: we have seen examples in the French revolution of 1848 and in the Chartist movement in England. These stepping stones are no less significant because many of the old and backward-looking ideas persisted and old forms continued to rub shoulders with the new. Moreover, traditional beliefs might, instead of becoming abandoned, be transformed and adapted to meet new needs: in this sense, there is no radical departure from the old yearning for "protection" in the socialist ideal of a more fully collectivist society.

Thus, gradually, the pattern of popular protest, and the ideas that underlay it, would suffer a sea-change. In 1848, this process was by no means completed; but the new "industrial" crowd, with its richer stock of forward-looking concepts, was already clearly visible on the horizon.

C.
Reform

3.

THE HISTORICAL CLIMATE
OF REFORM (1950)

Arthur M. Schlesinger, Sr.

"I wish to offer to your consideration some thoughts on the particular and general relations of man as a reformer." Ralph Waldo Emerson thus opened a famous address in 1841 on the first great upsurge of social reform in United States history. At the time American society along the seaboard was two centuries old. The people had subdued the savages, reshaped their physical environment, won political independence, established representative institutions, founded towns and cities, developed agriculture and trade, entered upon manufacturing. The country had attained a provisional maturity, and despite the more primitive conditions on the western frontier, thinking men were taking stock of the achievements and conducting what the speaker called a "general inquisition into abuses." And so, as Emerson went on to say, "In the history of the world the doctrine of Reform had never such scope as at the present hour." It seemed to him that every human institution was being questioned—"Christianity, the laws, commerce, schools, the

SOURCE. Arthur Schlesinger, Sr., *The American as Reformer*. Cambridge: Harvard University Press, 1950, pp. 3–27. Reprinted by permission of Harvard University Press.

farm, the laboratory"—and that not a "town, statute, rite, calling, man, or woman, but is threatened by the new spirit."

A hundred years afterward, Emerson's words sound as if they had been uttered of our own age, though whether the spirit of reform be deemed a threat or promise is a matter of personal opinion, and Emerson's other remarks attest that he himself regarded it as vital to social health. Between his time and ours of course much has happened. Cycles of reform and repose have come and gone until by a giant turn of the wheel the American people again find themselves in a period when in the history of the world the doctrine of reform had never such scope as at the present hour. In venturing to treat Emerson's theme a century later I need hardly say that I do so without Emerson's intuitive wisdom and philosophic acumen. Instead, I bring to it the poorer gifts of the historical scholar, those of the foot soldier rather than of the air pilot. I can only hope that the longer span of national experience since his day, plus the historian's special approach, will add something, however slight, to an understanding of the conditions and nature of the reform impulse in the United States.

The reform urge has obviously not been an American monopoly, nor has the nation ever been immune to struggles for human betterment elsewhere. In particular there has been a like-mindedness with England. The colonists were deeply indebted to the mother country for their notions of individual liberty and free institutions, as well as for that "salutary neglect"—Burke's phrase—which enabled them to develop these conceptions yet farther. Even after Independence this kinship continued, as it has to the present time. Ideologically America has never been isolated from Europe nor Europe from America, and the cross-fertilization of ideals and practices has yielded mutual benefit.

The United States, however, until very recent times has nearly always set the pace for the Old World in reform zeal. The outstanding exception has been in solutions for the social maladjustments arising from industrialization, where Britain as the older country faced these problems in acute form before America was hardly aware of them. The English, for example, led in factory legislation, the mitigation of child labor and the legalizing of trade-unions. Another but less conclusive instance in a different field was England's earlier abolition of Negro servitude. The two governments, obeying a common impulse, acted simultaneously in 1807 to outlaw the African slave trade; then Britain ended human bondage throughout the Empire in 1833, whereas the United States waited until 1865. This delay was not due to any lack of will on the part of the American humanitarians, however, but to the fact that the circumstances in the two lands were so very different. In England's case the institution existed some thousands of miles away. Moreover, Parliament had full power to deal with it, and the colonies affected were in a static or decaying economic condition. In America, on the other hand, slavery not only existed at home, but it was anchored in state and local law and was recognized by the Federal Constitution. It was also bound up, directly or indirectly, with the material welfare of a large part of the nation. Nonetheless Britain's action inspired the immediate formation of the American Anti-Slavery Society and so threw the American movement into higher gear.

In the case of most other social innovations, however, America has stood at the forefront. Thus (white) manhood suffrage was attained in the United States by the middle of the nineteeth century but not in England until the early twentieth. In like manner America outstripped the older country in regard to liberty of the press, the separation of church and state, the abolition of barbarous punishments, restraints on the liquor traffic, public education and prison reform, not to mention other achievements.

II

The basic reason for the generally faster pace of reform may be found in two conditions. In the first place, men were not burdened to the same extent by the weight of tradition. Less energy had to be used in tearing down the old and revered, more was left for building anew, and the large measure of self-government enjoyed even by the colonists simplified the process. As Emerson put it on one occasion,

> America was opened after the feudal mischief was spent, and so the people made a good start. . . . No inquisition here, no kings, no nobles, no dominant church. . . . We began with freedom, and are defended from shocks now for a century by the facility with which through popular assemblies every necessary measure of reform can instantly be carried.

The second factor was the kind of people who emigrated to America, not only the original settlers but also their successors, the far greater number of immigrants. Early or late, these transplanted Europeans were men who rebelled against conditions as they found them in their home-lands—against a class society, against religious, political and economic oppression—and, unlike their more docile neighbors, they carried their rebellion to the point of going to a distant continent where life was strange, dangers abounded and new careers must be sought. The departure of such folk slowed down the impetus to change at home, just as it tended to quicken it in the adopted country.

Given these two circumstances, the surprising thing is that the tempo of reform in America was not far more precipitate. As Anthony Trollope observed with particular reference to the Revolutionary era, "this new people, when they had it in their power to change all their laws, to throw themselves upon any Utopian theory that the folly of a wild philanthropy could devise, . . . did not do so." He attributed this caution to their inherited English practicality, but there was more to it than that. By starting life in a new state they acquired a new state of mind. Those who had fled from religious bigotry could now worship as they wished, those who had suffered political discrimination were generally free to vote and run for office, while all could make an easier living and attain a greater human dignity. To revise an old proverb, nothing sobers like success. The owner of property, however eager to improve society, has a personal investment in orderly change, and under conditions of self-government a legislative body is, as Emerson remarked in the essay just quoted, "a standing insurrection, and escapes the violence of accumulated grievance."

In other words, virtually every newcomer to America underwent a sea change. No matter how desperate his lot had been in Europe, he quickly displayed what impatient extremists despise as a middle-class attitude toward reform. Being even surer of the future than of the present, he could not love innovation for its own sake, or be willing to risk all existing good in a general overturn. Hence he threw his weight on the side of piecemeal progress.

This temper has continued to dominate the American mind. Despite the growing industrialization and maldistribution of wealth of the last seventy-five years, despite the one third of the nation "ill-housed, ill-clad, ill-nourished," à Gallup poll a few years ago indicated that about nine out of every ten people still regard themselves as belonging to the great middle class. This means, in contrast to most European countries, that there is no large self-conscious group which feels so inferior or so handicapped as not to be able to better itself by constitutional methods.

If this is an overstatement as regards the Negro, it is not so as regards the army of labor, whose leaders avoid the expression "working class" because it implies permanent attachment to a status. American wage earners are, and always have been, capitalists on the make, and there are some observers who would say they have already arrived, since a number of the national unions possess bigger financial resources than many a college or university. The aggregate assets of all national and local labor organizations, including the funds for defense, pensions, welfare and other purposes, have recently been estimated at between three and four billion dollars. The United Mine Workers, for example, whose president on a $50,000 salary looks, acts and lives like a "robber baron" of the nineteenth century, help manage a miners' welfare fund increasing by $140,000,000 a year, and are able to contribute $420,000 to a national political campaign and offer million-dollar loans to other unions as well as to pay a court fine of $1,400,000.

The national preference for evolution over revolution, whether the revolution be peaceable or violent, has given the United States midway in the twentieth century the reputation abroad of being the last bulwark of conservatism. The kaleidoscopic disruptions of the two world wars have driven Europe to extreme measures of recovery and social reconstruction. By Communists the American method of progress is contemptuously dubbed "bourgeois liberalism," while even the democratic Socialists of Western Europe find little good in our way of making haste slowly. Yet the mass of Americans remain unconvinced. In their own lifetime they have witnessed a Square Deal followed by a New Freedom followed by a New Deal and then a Fair Deal, each yielding social gains, and they know that the flame of reform burns as fiercely as ever and is as menacing to special privilege. Until events demonstrate the failure of this pragmatic approach, they may be counted upon not to try any different method.

Another historical factor working against headlong change has been freedom of speech and print. Practiced even in colonial times, it was enshrined in the basic law of the states and nation after the Revolution. Liberty of expression may not at first seem a moderating influence, since it is an open invitation to all malcontents to agitate their grievances. But that is just the point. For orderly progress it is better that crackpots rant in public than plot in private, and the very act, moreover, subjects their beliefs to comparison with the more constructive ideas of others. Only in this way can the critics be criticized, their proposals cut down to size, and an appropriate course be arrived at democratically.

Infringements on freedom of utterance almost invariably defeat their purpose either by attracting attention to the cause involved or by creating indignation over the denial of constitutional rights. For example, the murder of the abolitionist editor Elijah Lovejoy and the "gag resolution" of the House of Representatives against antislavery petitions brought to the antislavery standard countless persons who had been unmoved by the woes of the Negro. Our wisest conservatives have always understood this function of free speech. Alexander Hamilton, Daniel Webster, Charles E. Hughes and Wendell Willkie, to name no others, championed the liberty to express views which they themselves hated. Through this process of keeping the windows of discussion open, many a plausible reform has died of exposure, while others, more responsibly conceived, have won their way to public acceptance.

III

Whence has American reform derived its abiding vitality? Many rivulets have contributed to the stream, some with constant flow and others intermittently. None, however, has been more potent than religion. As Edmund Burke observed, "All Protestantism, even the most cold and passive, is a sort of dissent," but the men who settled the colonies represented "the dissidence of dissent and the Protestantism of the Protestant religion."

Did this fact, however, always denote a general open-mindedness toward human rights and hopes? The Puritans, it has often been pointed out, though demanding freedom of conscience for themselves in England, denied it to others upon going to Massachusetts. But that is not the whole story. The core of Puritanism, once the theological husks are peeled away, was intense moral zeal both for one's own salvation and for that of the community. This attitude, as in the instance noted, could engender intolerance, but by the same token it could also engender intolerance of intolerance; and the history of the Puritan spirit as a social force in America shows that the disposition to challenge vested injustice was the more significant aspect.

Roger Williams and Anne Hutchinson are outstanding early examples. The New England clergymen who preached defiance of England as the Revolution approached exhibited the same quality in the political field. A Tory called them "Mr. Otis's black Regiment" who "like their Predecessors of 1641 . . . have been unceasingly sounding the Yell of Rebellion in the Ears of an ignorant & deluded people." In like manner a later generation of the strain abetted most of the humanitarian crusades of Emerson's period, earning Bronson Alcott's affectionate encomium of being "the Lord's chore boys." With equal ardor laymen of Puritan stock were at the same time promoting the public-school movement in New England and the newly settled West, thus enriching significantly the concept of democracy.

A similar concern for the public welfare galvanized most of the other religious groups. They too strove to comfort the afflicted and afflict the comfortable. In answer to protests against such activities a church-gathering in Peterboro, New York, resolved,

> That the correctness of this opinion turns wholly on the character of the politics which are preached: for whilst it is clearly wrong to preach anti-Bible or unrighteous politics on the Sabbath or on any other day, nothing can be clearer than that no day is too holy to be used in preaching the politics which are inculcated in the Bible.

The Quakers in particular wielded an influence out of proportion to their numbers.

To be sure, the more breathless reformers sometimes rebuked the churches for faintheartedness, notably in the case of antislavery which created special difficulties by splitting the national bodies along sectional lines. It is also true that the foes of reform, no less than the friends, resorted to the Bible for vindication. Not only the defenders of slavery but the opponents of temperance, of women's rights and of the peace movement managed to dig up scriptural authority. This, however, was something like the homage which vice pays to virtue, for the advantage rested inevitably with those who interpreted God as love, not as greed or oppression. Even the censorious William Lloyd Garrison was impressed when the two great popular churches, the Methodist and the Baptist, anticipated the political disruption of the Union by separating into Northern and Southern branches in 1844–1845 over a question involving slavery.

If America has been less ostensibly religious in more recent times, the teachings of Jesus have nevertheless continued as vitally to fuel humanitarian enterprises. Churchgoers have been at the van of all such undertakings, and the clergy by espousing the "social gospel" have opened minds to new human needs and persistently pricked the popular conscience. In short, religion, in America at least, has not been the opiate of the masses.

Even in politics liberal movements have turned constantly to Holy Writ for inspiration. William Jennings Bryan in the greatest convention speech in American history denounced the business magnates who would press down upon the brow of labor a "crown of thorns" and "crucify mankind upon a cross of gold." Theodore Roosevelt, defying the reactionary leaders of the Republican party, declared he stood at Armageddon and battled for the Lord. Woodrow Wilson, a religionist in the Scottish Covenanter tradition, always kept his Bible by his bedside. And the latest surge of political reform, the New Deal took as its slogan "the more abundant life." President Truman merely voiced a common opinion when he declared in a recent address, our "belief in the dignity and the freedom of man" is "derived from the word of God, and its roots are deep in our spiritual foundations."

IV

This belief, however, had independent support in the doctrines derived from Europe's Age of Englightenment. These eighteenth-century avowals of human excellence and man's boundless capacity for progress found instant and permanent lodgment in America, where they confirmed common observation as well as the more enlightened religious teachings. Incorporated in the Preamble of the Declaration of Independence, they not only served their immediate purpose, but resounded back to the Old World, where they still reverberate. At home the Preamble was more a great editorial than a factual report, as none knew better than its slaveholding author Thomas Jefferson, but it proved an incomparable rallying cry for reformers then as it has ever since.

If all men are created equal, demanded the abolitionists in their day, why are black men held in bondage? If all are created equal, cried the feminists in their time, why are women denied their rights? If human beings are equally entitled to life, liberty and the pursuit of happiness, asked others in their turn, how justify the plight of the distressed farmers, underprivileged children, the hungry poor, the innocent victims of war? Not many years ago Roger Baldwin of the American Civil Liberties Union was arrested for attempting to read the Declaration of Independence in front of the City Hall during a labor outbreak in Paterson, New Jersey. However benighted the policeman's action may seem, he and his superiors should at least be given credit for recognizing the great manifesto as an irrefutable challenge to a repressive *status quo*.

That indeed has been its historic function. No one has stated the case more tellingly in our own generation than a citizen of foreign birth.

> If I ask an American [writes Mary Antin] what is the fundamental American law, and he does not answer me promptly, "That which is contained in the Declaration of Independence," I put him down for a poor citizen. . . . What the Mosaic Law is to the Jews, the Declaration is to the American people. It affords us a starting-point in history and defines our mission among nations. . . . Up to the moment of our declaration of independence, our struggle with our English rulers did not differ from other popular struggles against despotic governments. Again and again we respectfully petitioned for redress of specific grievances, as the governed, from time immemorial, have petitioned their governors. But one day we abandoned our suit for petty damages, and instituted a suit for the recovery of our entire human heritage of freedom; and by basing our claim on the fundamental principles of the brotherhood of man and the sovereignty of the masses, we assumed championship of the oppressed against their oppressors, wherever found. . . . The American confession of faith, therefore, is a recital of the doctrines of liberty and equality.

It is true that the sober findings of science and scholarship since 1776 have shaken the foundations of the natural-rights philosophy on which the Declaration was based, but the aspiration to realize the dream it held forth has nevertheless continued as strong as ever. As President Truman put it in his State of the Union message in January 1950, "At every point in our history, these ideals have served to correct our failures and shortcomings, to spur us on to greater efforts, and to keep clearly before us the primary purpose of our existence as a nation. . . . These principles give meaning to all that we do."

V

Thus two basic sets of ideas or ideals, the one stemming from the Christian religion and the other from the Declaration of Independence, have sustained and refreshed the reform impulse. But great national crises, though less constant in effect, have also played a role. One may sympathize with Benjamin Franklin's view that there never was a good war or a bad peace and still recognize that the Revolutionary War—thanks partly to the lapse of British control—brought about such human gains in various states as a more democratic redistribution of land, the separation of church and state, the abrogation of primogeniture and entail and the first restraints on slavery and the slave trade. In like fashion the Civil War wrote into the Constitution the greatest of all American reforms, the total abolition of slavery. This showing, of course, can in no sense justify the spiritual and material costs of war. Probably most of these advances would have come sooner or later in any event, and the Civil War, moreover, actually set back such burgeoning reforms as temperance, women's rights and international peace. Besides, the moral letdown following an armed conflict often militates against social progress, as notably in the 1920's. Yet war, within such limits, has actually contributed to human betterment.

The peacetime crises known as depressions have exerted a more positive influence. In periods of general social dislocation, injustices long endured become intolerable, and men in their despair may even seek a passport to Utopia. The hard times following the Panic of 1837, for example, hurried many states into abolishing lotteries and imprisonment for debt, helped remove the restrictions on wives as to property rights, and generated forty or more short-lived collectivist communities. Similarly, the economic slump dating from 1873 speeded the movement for railroad regulation and for "cheap money," raised the Knights of Labor to national importance, and begot the Socialist Labor party as well as Henry George's panacea of the single tax. One need only recall the Great Depression of 1929, however, to realize to what extent a general economic collapse accelerates reform. It may appear unfortunate that so much of our social thinking has been done in abnormal times, but often the mind functions most clearly when action is imperative.

VI

Finally, it should be noted that the rhythm of reform has differed in different parts of the country; not all parts have advanced at the same speed or at the same time. In a nation nearly as large as Europe and almost as diversified as to local circumstances and interests, this is hardly surprising.

More than any other section, however, the South has resisted innovation. As slavery tightened its hold on the region and dimmed the ideals of the Revolutionary era, the people came to fear reform in general through fear of reform in particular—that one which would destroy the rock on which their society rested. Hence they derided as "glittering generalities" the "self-evident" truths proclaimed by their own Jefferson in 1776, defended slavery as the most Christian of institutions, and erected an intellectual dike against "subversive" Northern "isms." Since the Civil War this conservative tradition has been sustained by the persisting race problem, the drain of potential dissidents into other parts of the country and the lack of material means to carry through reforms dependent on public funds. Hence the South, despite some signs to the contrary, continues to lag behind the procession of states.

It is more difficult to assess the reform roles of the two geographic sections lying north of the Mason and Dixon Line. Indeed, it is hardly worth trying, since between East and West there was a constant shuttling and sharing of experience. Despite a common impression that the West has always acted first, one need only recall that antislavery scored its initial victories on the Atlantic Seaboard before there was an established West, and that Congress, without consulting the people concerned, extended the blessings of freedom to the settlements in the territory north of the Ohio.

A truer view suggests that each region led in the reforms dictated by its local conditions or needs. For example, the agricultural West, as the years went on, championed a progressively liberal public-land policy and currency reform and initiated government control of grain elevators and railroads. It also embarked first upon woman suffrage, perhaps because the undersupply of women in the newly settled parts of the country spurred the men to vie for their favor, whereas in the older East men preferred to treat women as their "superiors" rather than their equals. The East, on the other hand, focused on curing the evils created or intensified by its more complex industrial society: pov-

erty, illiteracy, woman and child labor, low wages and bad factory conditions. In matters of common concern, however, like (white) manhood
suffrage and "trust busting," the two sections acted almost
simultaneously.

VII

This freedom of the various states to deal with their own problems
in their own way has been a consequence of the American federal system. The Constitutional Convention of 1787 considered a consolidated
type of government, but wisely settled upon the plan of limited national
authority. Nothing could have proved a greater lubricant of social
change. Federalism, as James Bryce remarked in *The American Commonwealth*, has allowed the people "to try experiments in legislation and
administration which could not be safely made in a large centralized
country," and this has enabled the whole group of states to "profit by
the experience of a law or a method which has worked well or ill in
the State that has tried it."

Almost any successful reform would illustrate the point. Negro emancipation is not the best example because, though the Northeastern states
pioneered the innovation, similar action by the other Northern states
had in nearly every instance been assured by Congressional legislation
eliminating slavery while they were territories. In the case of manhood
suffrage, however, the principle had unrestricted play. The ballot, which
was limited at the time of the adoption of the Constitution to property
holders and taxpayers, was steadily liberalized state by state until at
the time of the Civil War any white male citizen could vote. In like
manner the states cut paths for each other in regard to public education,
the regulation of the liquor traffic, the curbing of corporations, labor
legislation and an endless number of other matters.

At certain points, however, federal action has supplemented state action, and this tendency increased as the country aged. The motive has
been either to universalize a social change already well tested locally,
or to protect progressive commonwealths against the harmful effects
of inferior standards in other states, or to help poorer states carry the
financial burden of reforms they could not otherwise afford. Sometimes
the federal intervention has even involved altering the Constitution.
Thus the three Civil War amendments conferred freedom and its attendant rights on the Negro in all the states, and the Nineteenth Amendment similarly extended the suffrage to women in all the states.

But experience with the prohibition amendment shows that action
from above may overreach itself. This episode is a puzzling one. Not
only was national prohibition preceded by a hundred years of local

experimentation, but at the time of its adoption two thirds of the people—and over 95 per cent of the land area—had banned the liquor traffic in one way or another, and the amendment was ratified by ten more states than were required, just two short of the entire forty-eight. Yet it was repealed with equal alacrity less than fourteen years later. Perhaps the reason was that it had to breast the abnormal conditions created by the moral slump following World War I, when the law-abiding easily became law-breaking and the government itself was half-hearted about enforcement—a period, moreover, that was climaxed by the onset of the Great Depression. Besides, the prohibition amendment diverged from all others in seeking to police private and personal habits.

In a different way the amendments to guarantee civil and political equality to the Negro did not work as expected. In this instance, however, they were not repealed, and by remaining in the Constitution they are serving in our own lay as a lever to secure the rights so long and wrongfully withheld.

VIII

For the most part, however, the general government has furthered reform by exercising powers already to be found in the Constitution. The first notable moves occurred when industrialization changed the face of the country and overran political subdivisions. The Interstate Commerce Act of 1887 and the Sherman Antitrust Law of 1890 came after efforts by individual states to solve these problems had failed. In the case of trusts, for example, the stubbornness of three states in chartering monopolies, which under the Constitution could do business also in all the other commonwealths, had confounded the attempts at local regulation. Stronger action by Congress along these lines followed in later years, together with a growing body of legislation to improve the economic position of wage earners, farmers and other groups. The constitutional basis for such measures was generally the interstate-commerce clause, which attained horizons of meaning undreamed of in simpler times. Thus Congress's prohibition of child labor in 1938, supplementing state measures, took the form of banning from interstate shipment goods manufactured by companies employing children under sixteen years of age, or, in hazardous occupations, under eighteen.

Congress has also used its revenue power to abet reform. The Constitution all along had authorized the lawmaking branch to lay taxes to provide for "the general welfare," but not till the twentieth century, and particularly after the income-tax amendment, did the government take multiple action along these lines. On the one hand, it has levied taxes on incomes, inheritances and corporate earnings so graduated as to bear most heavily upon the higher amounts and thus promote a redistribution of wealth. On the other hand, it has devoted national funds to assisting or bribing states to be more progressive. During the Great Depression it exceeded even these bounds and spent millions to provide the jobless with food and work.

The system of subsidies to states affords perhaps the most striking evidence of federal leadership in reform. Though the precedents go back to the early land grants for schools and colleges, the passage of years has gradually broadened the program, added the feature of national standards which the recipients must adopt, and in most instances has come to include reciprocal contributions from the states themselves. The New Deal greatly stepped up this reform strategy, offering grants-in-aid and low-interest loans to states and municipalities not only for the older purposes, but also such things as slum clearance, housing projects, old-age assistance and the public ownership of power plants. There can be no doubt as to who occupies the driver's seat because, if the national conditions are not agreed to, the funds are withheld.

Thus, as time has gone on, the balance in the federal system has shifted more and more toward the general government in the sphere of reform, as in so many others. Has this change gone so far as to deprive the states of their function as laboratories of social innovation? Interestingly enough, the present division of the Supreme Court between so-called conservative and liberal wings turns in considerable degree on this point. In principle both groups lean toward reform objectives, but the one wishes to preserve the traditional freedom of the states to make their own decisions, including the right to be wrong, while the other inclines to impose on them its own notions of expediency or wisdom.

The advantages of federal intervention and leadership have already been noted, and certainly the expansion of national power on which it rests springs naturally from modern conditions. The critics, however, stress the tendency of centralized direction and bureaucratic control to sap local initiative and variety to the nation's loss. That this point has not yet been reached is indicated by Nebraska's adoption of a unicameral legislature in the 1930's and Georgia's recent granting of the suffrage to eighteen-year-olds. Nevertheless the need somehow to combine the benefits of local creativeness and federal interposition, without the drawbacks of either, is one of the crucial challenges to the American public today. It is an aspect of our national evolution which demands the most thoughtful and continuous study.

D.
Revolution

4.
THE MYTH OF THE REVOLUTION (1955)
Raymond Avon

The idea of Progress is implicit in the myth of the Left, which feeds on the idea of a continuous movement. The myth of the Revolution has a significance which is at once complementary and opposed to this: it fosters the expectation of a break with the normal trend of human affairs. The second myth, like the first, it seems to me, is born of a rethinking of the past. The men who seem to us, looking back, to have been the precursors of the French Revolution because they disseminated a way of thought incompatible with that of the *Ancien Régime,* neither heralded nor desired the apocalyptic collapse of the old world. Almost all of them, though bold in theory, showed the same prudence as did Jean-Jacques Rousseau in the role of counsellor to the Throne or legislator. Most of them were inclined towards optimism: once tradition, prejudice and fanaticism were put aside, once men were enlightened, the natural order of things would assert itself. By 1791 or 1792, the Revolution was felt by most contemporary thinkers, including the *philosophes,* to have been a catastrophe. In retrospect, however, people came to

SOURCE. Raymond Avon, *The Opium of the Intellectuals,* translated by Terence Kilmart: v. New York: W. W. Norton and Co., 1962, pp. 35–50, 64–65. Reprinted by permission of Doubleday & Co.

lose the sense of catastrophe and to remember only the grandeur of the event.

Among those who followed the party of progress, some did their best to forget the terror, the despotism, the cycle of wars, all the blood-soaked vicissitudes of which the bright, heroic days of the storming of the Bastille or the Feast of the Federation had been the starting point. had merely been the accidental accompaniment of the Revolution. The The internecine struggles, the military glories and the military defeats, irresistible drive towards the liberation of mankind and the rational organisation of society, interrupted by royalist or religious reaction, would continue notwithstanding, peacefully perhaps, with a limited use of force if need be.

Others put the accent on the seizure of power, on subversion and the overthrow of the State; they had faith in violence as the only means of knocking the future into shape. The champions of the revolutionary myth mostly subscribe to the same system of values as the reformists; they envisage the same end—a peaceful, liberal society governed by reason. But for them mankind will never realise its vocation, will never control its own destiny, except by a promethean gesture, which becomes a valid end in itself as well as an essential means.

Are revolutions worthy of so much honour? The men who conceive them are not those who carry them out. Those who begin them rarely live to see their end, except in exile or in prison. Can they really be the symbol of a humanity which is the master of its own destiny if no man recognises his handiwork in the achievement which results from the savage free-for-all struggle?

REVOLUTION AND REVOLUTIONS

The word revolution, in the current language of sociology, means the sudden and violent supplanting of one régime by another. If we accept this definition, we must reject certain usages of the term which are ambiguous or misleading. In an expression such as "industrial revolution," the term simply suggests profound and rapid changes. To speak of a "working-class revolution" in England is to emphasise the importance, real or alleged, of the reforms carried out by the British Government between 1945 and 1950, although these changes, being neither violent nor unconstitutional cannot be placed in the same historical category as the events which took place in France between 1789 and 1797, or in Russia between 1917 and 1921. Labour's achievement, in essence, is certainly *not* revolutionary in the sense in which this epithet can be applied to that of the Jacobins or of the Bolsheviks.

Even if one discards fallacious usages, some ambiguity remains. Concepts never exactly fit the facts: the former are precise, the latter vague. One could think of innumerable cases where hesitation would be justified. The accession to power of National Socialism was legal and the subsequent violence was ordained by the State. Can one, in spite of its legal nature, call this transition a revolution because of the suddenness of the changes brought about in the personnel of the Government and the form of the country's institutions? At the other extreme, do the *pronunciamientos* of the South American republics deserve to be called revolutions when all they do is to replace one officer by another or at most a soldier by a civilian or vice versa, without effecting any real change either from one ruling class to another or from one form of government to another? Legal continuity has been broken, but there has been no real constitutional upheaval; the changeover, with or without bloodshed, from one leader to another, the comings and goings between palace and prison, are accompanied by no institutional changes.

It is not vitally important to give a dogmatic answer to these questions. Definitions are not true or false, but more or less useful or convenient. There is no such thing as an unalterable essence of revolution: the concept merely provides us with a means of grasping the significance of certain phenomena and of thinking clearly about them.

It seems too me to be reasonable to apply the term *coup d'état* either to a change of constitution illegally decreed by the holder of power (e.g. Napoleon III in 1851) or to the seizure of the State by a group of armed men which does not (whether it involves bloodshed or not) involve the introduction of a new ruling class or a different form of government. Revolution is more than a matter of "Box and Cox." On the other hand, the accession of Hitler is no less revolutionary because he was legally appointed Chancellor by President Hindenburg. The use of violence followed rather than preceded his accession, and, as a result of this, certain juridical characteristics of the revolutionary phenomenon were lacking. Sociologically, however, the essential traits are there: the exercise of power by a minority which ruthlessly suppresses its adversaries, creates a new State, and dreams of disfiguring the nation.

In themselves, these verbalistic arguments are of very minor significance, but discussions about the meaning of words often reveal the heart of the matter. I remember how in Berlin in 1933 the favourite argument among Frenchmen revolved around the question of whether or not what was happening was a revolution. They did not ask themselves whether or not the appearance or the masquerade of legality precluded reference to the precedents of Cromwell or of Lenin. Instead they denied with fury, as one of my colleagues did at the *Société Française de Philosophie* in 1938, that the noble term of revolution could be applied to such prosaic events as those which shook Germany in 1933. And yet, what more does one need to qualify as a revolutionary than to have brought about changes of personnel, ruling class, constitution and ideology?

To such a question, my compatriots in Berlin would have replied that the legality of the January 30 appointment and the absence of disorders in the streets represented a fundamental difference between the accession of the Third Reich and that of the Republic in 1792 or of Communism in 1917. But surely, in the last analysis, it matters little whether one sees them as two kinds of the same species or as two different species.

Others denied that National Socialism had brought about a revolution, because they regarded it as counter-revolutionary. It is permissible to speak of counter-revolution when the old regime has been restored, when the men of the past return to power, when the ideas or institutions which the revolutionaries of today bring with them are those which the revolutionaries of yesterday had abolished. There again, marginal cases are legion. A counter-revolution is never exclusively a restoration, and since every revolution repudiates to a certain extent the one which preceded it, it is bound to reveal certain counter-revolutionary characteristics. But neither Fascism nor National Socialism was entirely, or essentially, counter-revolutionary, though both borrowed a good deal of their terminology from the conservatives. The Nazis attacked not only the religious traditions of Christianity, but also the social traditions of the aristocracy and of bourgeois liberalism: the "Germanisation" of Christianity, the regimenting of the masses, the "leader principle" have a strictly revolutionary significance. National Socialism did not represent a return to the past; it broke with the past as radically as Communism.

The truth is, of course, that when people speak of revolution, when they ask themselves if such and such a sudden and violent upheaval is worthy to enter the temple in which 1789, the *Trois Glorieuses* and the "ten days which shook the world" occupy the places of honour, they base themselves, consciously or unconsciously, on two ideas: first, that revolutions, wherever they occur, whether they involve bloodshed or not, and whether they are successful or abortive, can be included in the sacred canon only in so far as they can be squared with the ideology of the Left, humane, liberal and egalitarian; and second, that they fulfil their object and justify themselves only if they result in a reversal of the existing system of ownership. In the perspective of history, these two ideas are prejudices pure and simple.

Every sudden and violent change of régime entails economic gains and losses which are equally unjust, and accelerates the circulation of wealth and property between the classes. But it does not necessarily introduce a new conception of property rights. According to Marxism, the abolition of private ownership of the means of production constitutes the essential characteristic of a revolution. But neither in the past nor at the present day has the downfall of thrones or republics, the overthrow of the State by active minorities, always coincided with a disruption of juridical norms.

It would be wrong to suggest that violence is inseparable from the values of the Left: in fact the opposite is nearer the truth. Revolutionary power is by definition a tyrannical power. It operates in defiance of the law, it expresses the will of a minority group, it is not, and cannot be, concerned with the interest of this or that section of the people. The duration of the tyrannical phase varies according to the circumstances, but it is never possible to dispense with it—or, more exactly, when it is avoided, there has been reform but no revolution. The seizure and excercise of power by violence presuppose conflicts which negotiation and compromise have failed to resolve—in other words the failure of democratic procedures. Revolution and democracy are contradictory notions.

It is therefore equally unreasonable either to condemn or to exalt revolutions in principle. Men and groups being what they are—obstinate in the defence of their interests, slaves of the present, rarely capable of sacrifices even when these would safeguard their future, inclined to oscillate between resistance and concessions rather than make a decisive stand—revolutions will probably remain inseparable from the ways of human societies. Too often, a ruling class betrays the community for which it is responsible, refuses to recognise the signs of new times. The Meiji reformers in Japan and the Kemalists in Turkey ousted a decaying ruling class in order to rebuild a political and social order. They could not have carried out their task and in such a short time had they not crushed all opposition and imposed by force a régime which the majority of the nation would probably have rejected. Rulers who violate tradition and legality in order to regenerate their countries are not always tyrants. Peter the Great and the Emperor of Japan were legitimate sovereigns when they undertook a task comparable with that of Kemal Ataturk and even, up to a point, that of the Bolsheviks.

Recourse to violence by a minority is often made inevitable, and sometimes desirable, by the inertia of the State, the decline of the élite, or anachronistic institutions. The man of reason, especially the man of the Left, must surely prefer therapeutic methods to the surgeon's knife, must prefer reform to revolution, as he must prefer peace to war and democracy to despotism. Revolutionary violence may seem to him sometimes to be the inevitable accompaniment or the essential condition of changes which he desires. He can never regard it as good in itself.

Experience, which sometimes excuses violence, also proves the disconnection between governmental instability and the transformation of the social order. France in the nineteenth century experienced more revolutions but a much slower economic evolution than Great Britain. A century ago, Prévost-Paradol deplored the fact that France so often indulged in the luxury of a revolution yet was incapable of achieving the reforms which most thinking people agreed were necessary. Today, the word revolution is extremely fashionable, and the country seems to have fallen back into the old rut.

The United States on the other hand has preserved its constitution intact for nearly two centuries; indeed it has gradually come to acquire an almost mystical prestige. And yet American society has never ceased to undergo continuous and rapid transformation. Economic expansion and the social melting-pot have been absorbed into a constitutional framework without weakening or modifying it. A federation of agrarian States has become the greatest industrial power in the world without any recourse to illegality.

It is no doubt true that colonial civilisations are subject to different laws from those of civilisations which have a long history behind them and are geographically confined. Constitutional instability remains none-the-less a sign of sickness rather than of health. Régimes which fall victim to popular uprisings or *coups d'état* have proved themselves guilty not of moral vices (they are often more humane than their conquerors) but of political errors. They have been incapable of giving way to an opposition, or of crushing the resistance of their own diehards, or of offering the prospect of reforms likely to appease the discontented or to satisfy the ambitious. Régimes such as those of Great Britain or the United States which have survived the onrush of historical change have given proof of the supreme virtue, which is a mixture of steadfastness and flexibility.

An "advanced" intellectual would surely admit that the constant recurrence of *coups d'état* in various South American States is a symptom of crisis and a caricature of the progressive spirit. Perhaps he would even acknowledge, though not without reluctance, that constitutional continuity since the eighteenth century has been, for Great Britain and the United States, a great good fortune. And he would readily concede that the seizure of power by Fascists or National Socialists proves that the same means—violence and single party government—are not good in themselves but can be used for abominable ends. But he would reaffirm his faith in one final Revolution, the only authentic one, which would aim not to replace one power by another but to overthrow or at least to humanise all power.

Unfortunately, experience has so far failed to provide an example of a revolution which lives up to Marxist prophecies or the hopes of the humanitarians. The first Russian Revolution, the February Revolution, brought about the collapse of a dynasty already undermined by the contradictions between traditional absolutism and the progress of ideas, by the incapacity of the Czar and by the consequences of a long-drawn-out war; the second, the November Revolution, consisted of the seizure of power by an armed minority taking advantage of the disorganisation of the State and the people's longing for peace. The industrial proletariat, small in number, played an important part in the second revolution; during the Civil War, the peasants' hostility to the counter-revolutionaries was probably decisive. In China, the industrial proletariat, even less numerous, did not provide the bulk of the Communist troops. It was in the countryside that the Party established itself, and it was there that it recruited its soldiers and prepared its victory: it was the intellectuals rather than the factory workers who provided the Party's cadres. The idea of a procession of the social classes, passing on the torch from one to the other, is no more than an illustration in a children's picture book.

The Marxist type of revolution has never come about because its very conception was mythical: neither the development of productive forces nor the coming of age of the working class paves the way for the overthrow of capitalism by the labouring masses, conscious of their mission. Proletarian revolutions, like all the revolutions of the past, merely entail the violent replacement of one élite by another. They present no special characteristic which would justify their being hailed as "the end of pre-history."

THE PRESTIGE OF REVOLUTION

The French Revolution belongs to the national heritage. Frenchmen have a weakness for the word revolution because they cherish the illusion of being associated with past glories. A writer like François Mauriac, when he talks about "the Christian and Socialist revolution" which failed after the Liberation, disregards the claims of accuracy and proof. The expression arouses emotions, evokes memories and visions; no one could possibly define it.

A reform once accomplished changes something. A revolution seems capable of changing everything, since no one knows precisely what it will change. To the intellectual who turns to politics for the sake of diversion, or for a cause to believe in or a theme for speculation, reform is boring and revolution exciting. The one is prosaic, the other poetic, one is the concern of mere functionaries, the other that of the people risen up against their exploiters. Revolution provides a welcome break with the everyday course of events and encourages the belief that all things are possible. The quasi-revolution of 1944 in France has bequeathed to those who lived through it (on the right side of the barricades) the nostalgic memory of a time of hope. They look back regretfully at the lost, lyrical illusion, they cannot bring themselves to criticise it; the "others"—the men at the top, or the Soviet Union, or the United States of America—are responsible for the deception.

In love with ideas and indifferent to institutions, uncompromising critic of private life and unamenable, in politics, to reason and moderation, the Frenchman is quintessentially the revolutionary in theory and the conservative in practice. But the myth of the revolution is not restricted to France or the French intellectuals alone. It seems to me to have benefited from the prestige of other ideas and fetishes more often borrowed than authentic.

In the first place, it has benefited from the prestige of aesthetic modernism. The artist who denounces the philistines, and the Marxist who denounces the bourgeoisie, could consider themselves united in battle against a single enemy; and indeed the artistic *avant-garde* and the political *avant-garde* have often dreamed of a joint mission for the liberation of mankind.

In fact, however, during the nineteenth century the two vanguards were more often in a state of divorce than of wedlock. None of the big literary movements as such were involved with the political Left. Victor Hugo in his old age became the self-appointed oracle of democracy: in earlier days he had sung the praises of the past and he was never a revolutionary in the modern sense of the word. Among the foremost writers of the time, some, like Balzac, were reactionaries, others, like Flaubert, fundamentally conservative. The *poète maudit* was anything but revolutionary. The Impressionists, in spite of their advanced aesthetic ideas and their struggle with academism, never dreamed of challenging the social order or of drawing doves for the organisers of the "night of the long knives." The Socialists, for their part, whether theorists or militants, did not always subscribe to the system of values held by the literary or artistic *avant-garde*. Léon Blum, for example, considered Porto-Riche as one of the greatest writers of his time. On the advanced literary magazine *La Revue Blanche*, Blum was one of the few contributors with left-wing tendencies. The inventor of scientific socialism had old-fashioned tastes when it came to artistic matters.

It was only after the First World War that the alliance between the two *avant-gardes* really came for a time into its own. In France, the symbol of this alliance was surrealism; in Germany, the denizens of the literary coffee houses and the experimental theatre joined forces with the extreme Left, even with the Bolsheviks, to attack artistic conformism, moral conventions and the tyranny of money. Religion was as much the enemy as was capitalism.

This alliance did not last long. Ten years after the Russian Revolution, modernist architects had been sacrificed on the altar of neo-classicism, and I can still hear the voice of Jean-Richard Bloch declaring, with the passionate faith of the convert, that if the return to columns and porticos represented an artistic regression it was certainly a dialectical advance. All the most outstanding members of the literary and artistic *avant-garde* in the Soviet Union had disappeared by 1939. Painting had reverted to the standards of the *Salon* of fifty years ago; composers had been made to toe the academic line. Thirty-five years ago, the Soviet Union was the pride of the aesthetic Left which vaunted the genius and daring of its film directors, poets and theatrical producers; today the fatherland of the Revolution has become the home of a reactionary artistic orthodoxy.

Abroad, there were poets like Aragon who moved from Surrealism to Communism and became the most diligent of party hacks, prepared impartially to vilify or to extol the French Army, and others like André Breton who remained loyal to the non-conformist ideals of their youth. By adopting the bourgeois values of academism, the Soviet Union clarified the issue and revealed the disparity between genuine idealism and the all-powerful Party. But what was there left to cling on to when the world seemed to be divided between two opposing "reactions"? The writer was reduced to solitude or sectarianism; the painter could pay lip service to the Party while ignoring its aesthetic doctrines.

The alliance of the two *avant-gardes* was born of a misunderstanding and exceptional circumstances. Out of a horror of conformism, artists join the party of revolt, but the ruling class which takes over the post-revolutionary society is hungry for stability, prestige and respect. There are obvious similarities between the bad taste of the Victorian bourgeoisie and that of the Soviet bourgeoisie of today, equally proud of

their material success. Whether capitalist or managerial, the first generation to go through the stage of primary industrialisation demands solid
furniture and imposing façades. The personality of Stalin also helps
to explain the extremes of obscurantism in the Russia of his day.

The connection between the revolutionary myth and the fetish of
moral non-conformism is based on the same misunderstanding. Literary
Bohemia felt itself to be linked to the extreme Left by a common hatred
of bourgeois hypocrisy. At the end of the last century and the beginning
of the present one, libertarian conceptions of morality—free love, legal
abortion, etc.—were current in advanced political circles. Couples used
to make it a point of honour not to present themselves before the civil
authorities for the marriage ceremony, and the term "partner" or "mate"
sounded better than "wife" or "husband," which stank of bourgeois
respectability.

All that has been changed. Marriage and the family virtues are now
exalted in the fatherland of the Revolution, and while divorce and abortion remain legal in certain circumstances, official propaganda is at pains
to discourage them and to revive in the individual citizen a sense of
the duty he has to subordinate his pleasures or his passions to the good
of society as a whole. The traditionalists could hardly have demanded
more.

Historians have often emphasised the puritanical tendencies of revolutionaries. Like the English Puritans and the Jacobins, the Bolsheviks
have always strongly disapproved of moral laxity. The debauchee is
suspect in their eyes, not because he violates the accepted code but
because he abandons himself to vice at the expense of the common
good, because he devotes too much time and energy to an unproductive
activity.

The restoration of the family is quite a different phenomenon; it symbolises the return to ordinary life after the ferment of the Revolution
and the obsessive preoccupation with politics. The family as an institution has a habit of outlasting the upheavals of states and societies. Shaken
to its foundations by the collapse of the old order, it re-establishes itself
as soon as the new order shows signs of lasting and the victorious élite
acquires confidence in itself and its future. Sometimes the break-up
leaves a heritage of liberation. In Europe, the authoritarian structure
of the family was to some extent historically linked to the authoritarian
structure of the State. The philosophy which advocates the right to
vote is also in favour of the right to be happy. Whatever the future
of Communism in China, the structure of the family will never be the
same as it was— the emancipation of women is likely to be a permanent
acquisition.

If the opposition to conventional morality served as a link between the political and the literary *avant-garde,* atheism would seem to be the link between the metaphysic of Revolt and the politics of the Revolution. There again, I think, the Revolution has been accorded an undeserved prestige: it is wrongly considered to be the inevitable offspring of humanism.

Marxist doctrine arose out of a criticism of religion which Marx had picked up from Feuerbach. Man "alienates" himself by projecting on to God the perfections to which he aspires. God, far from being the creator of mankind, is himself merely an idol of the human imagination. Men must seek to attain on this earth the perfection which their imaginations have conceived but which still eludes them. The criticism of religion leads to the criticism of society. But why should this criticism necessarily lead to the revolutionary imperative?

Revolution cannot be equated with the essence of action; it is merely a modality thereof. Every action is in effect a negation of the "given," but in this sense a reform is no less an action than is a revolution. The events of 1789 suggested to Hegel one of the themes of what has become the revolutionary myth: violence in the service of reason. But, unless one allows the class struggle a special intrinsic value, the effort to abolish anachronisms and build a society which conforms to the demands of reason does not require a sudden breach or a civil war. Revolution is neither a vocation nor a predestined end; it is a means.

In Marxism itself, one finds three divergent conceptions of revolution: first, a Blanquist conception, that of the seizure of power by a small group of armed men who, once they are masters of the State, proceed to transform its institutions; second, an evolutionary conception, according to which the society of the future must gradually mature within the present society until the final redeeming crisis arrives; and thirdly, the conception which has become that of the permanent revolution, according to which the proletarian party exerts a constant pressure on the bourgeois parties, taking advantage of the reforms grudgingly conceded by the latter to undermine the capitalist order and to prepare at once its own victory and the advent of socialism. Each of these three conceptions presupposes the necessity for violence, but the second, which is the least in harmony with the temperament of Marx himself and the most consistent with Marxist sociology, would postpone the final outbreak to an indefinite future.

At any given period a society, when considered realistically, reveals elements of different periods and styles which one might easily judge to be incompatible. Monarchy, parliament, trade unions, free health service, conscription, nationalised industries, Royal Navy—all these co-exist in present-day Britain. If historic régimes were as homogeneous as we make them out to be, revolutions would perhaps be inevitable in order to change from one to the other. From a watered-down capitalism to a pseudo-socialism, from aristocratic and bourgeois parliamentarianism to assemblies in which the unions and the mass parties are represented, the transition does not, in theory, involve bloodshed. It is circumstances which decide that.

An historical humanism—man in search of himself through successive régimes and empires—should not necessarily lead to the cult of revolution; only a dogmatic confusion between permanent aspirations and a certain technique of action can explain such an aberration. The choice of methods derives not from philosophic reflection but from experience and wisdom, unless it be granted that the class struggle has to pile up corpses in order to fulfil its role in history. Why should the victory of a single class result in the reconciliation of all mankind?

Marx progressed from atheism to revolution by way of a dialectic of history. Many intellectuals who will have nothing to do with the dialectic also arrive at the same conclusion, not because the Revolution promises to reconcile mankind or to solve the riddle of history, but because it destroys a hateful or mediocre world. The literary and the political *avant-garde* are brought into a kind of collusion by their common hatred of the established order or disorder. In other words, the Revolution benefits from the prestige of Revolt.

The word revolt, like the word nihilism, is today rather fashionable. It is used so frequently and loosely that people have come to forget precisely what it means. One wonders whether the majority of writers would not subscribe to the dictum of André Malraux: "The fundamental dignity of thought lies in the challenging of life and destiny, and any thought which really justifies the universe is worthless unless it is based on hope." In the twentieth century, it is certainly easier to condemn the world than to justify it.

As a metaphysic, the concept of revolt denies the existence of God, the foundations which religion or animism have traditionally given to moral values; it also emphasises the absurdity of the world and of human existence. As a historical analysis, it challenges society as such or the society of the present. The one often leads to the other, but neither is bound to lead to revolution or to the values which the revolutionary cause claims to represent. He who protests against the fate meted out to mankind by a meaningless universe sometimes finds himself in sympathy with the revolutionaries, because indignation or hatred outweigh all other considerations, because, in the last resort, violence alone can appease his despair. But, just as logically, he might aim to dispel the illusions created by those incorrigible optimists who are so busy fighting the social symptoms of the human plight that they remain oblivious of its real depths. Some rebels regard action for its own sake as a suitable aim for an aimless destiny, others regard it merely as a contemptible diversion, an attempt by Man to conceal from himself the true vanity of his condition. The party of the Revolution pours scorn on the descendants of Kierkegaard, Nietzsche or Kafka as the intellectual jeremiahs of a bourgeoisie which cannot console itself for the death of God because it is so conscious of its own death: the revolutionary, not the rebel, holds the key to transcendence and meaning—the historic future.

True, the rebels, the men of Revolt, also rebel against the established order. They regard most social rules and prohibitions as mere convention or hypocrisy. But many of them nevertheless subscribe to the values currently accepted in their social milieu, while others revolt against their own epoch but not against God or Fate. In the name of materialism and egoism, the Russian nihilists of the mid-nineteenth century in fact went along with the bourgeois socialist movement. Nietzsche and Bernanos, the one a believer and the other proclaiming the death of God, are authentic non-conformists. Both reject democracy, socialism, the adulation of the common man—the one in the name of an intuitive vision of the future, the other by invoking an idealised conception of the *Ancien Régime*. They are hostile or indifferent to the raising of living standards, the expansion of bourgeois materialism, the progress of technology. They are horrified by the vulgarity and baseness which seem to be part and parcel of electioneering and parliamentary practices—Bernanos hurled his invective at the pagan State, the garrulous Leviathan.

Since the defeat of the Fascist movements, most intellectuals of the Revolt and all those of the Revolution bear witness to an irreproachable conformism: they do not renounce the values of the societies they condemn. The French settler in Algeria, the Corsican functionary in Tunisia, may treat the natives with scant respect and scorn the idea of racial equality; but a right-wing intellectual in France would hardly dare to develop a philosophy of colonialism, any more than a Russian intellectual would develop a philosophy of slave labour. The supporters of Hitler, Mussolini and Franco aroused indignation because they refused to bow down to modern ideas: democracy, equality between men of every class and race, economic and social progress, humanitarianism and pacifism. The revolutionaries of the 1950's may sometimes frighten, but they never shock.

There is not a Christian today, however reactionary, who would dare to say or even to think that the standard of living of the masses is of no importance. The so-called left-wing Christian is not so much a man who shows courage and freedom of thought as a man who has consented to absorb the strongest dose of the ideas current in secular circles. In the last resort, the "progressive" Christian will consider a change of régime or an improvement in the material condition of the masses as indispensable for the propagation of Christian truth. The message of Simone Weil is not a left-wing message; it is a non-conformist message, reminding us of truths which we were no longer accustomed to hear.

It would be difficult to find, in present-day France, two truly incompatible philosophies such as those of the *Ancient Régime* and of Rationalism. The adversaries of today—apart from a few left-overs from Fascism—are brothers beneath the skin. Implicitly, Soviet Russian society may contain a system of values opposed to that of the West; explicitly, these two worlds mutually upbraid one another for violating their common values. The controversy about property rights and planning is concerned with means rather than ends.

Rebels or nihilists criticise the modern world, some for being what it wants to be, others for not being true to itself. The latter are today more numerous than the former. The most lively polemics break out not between these two but between intellectuals who are agreed on the essentials. To go for one another, they need not disagree about ultimate aims, they have merely to differ over the sacred word: Revolution. . . .

The concept of Revolution will not fall into disuse any more than the concept of the Left. It, too, expresses a nosatalgia, which will last as long as societies remain imperfect and men eager to reform them. Not that the wish for social progress must lead logically or inevitably to the will to revolution. A certain degree of optimism and impatience is also needed. There are some who are revolutionaries out of hatred of the world or a perverse love of disaster; more often, revolutionaries are guilty of excessive optimism. Every known régime is blameworthy if one relates it to an abstract ideal of equality or liberty. Only revolution, because it is an adventure, or a revolutionary régime, because it accepts the permanent use of violence, seems capable of attaining the goal of perfection. The myth of the Revolution serves as a refuge for utopian intellectuals; it becomes the mysterious, unpredictable intercessor between the real and the ideal.

Violence itself attracts and fascinates more than it repels. Socialism on the English model or the "classless Scandinavian society" have never enjoyed the same prestige among the continental, especially French, left-wingers as has the Russian Revolution—despite the civil war, the horrors of collectivisation, and the great purges. Or should one say because of? For it sometimes seems as if the price of the Revolution were placed on the credit rather than on the debit side of the balance sheet.

No one, as Herodotus says, is insane enough to prefer war to peace. The observation should also be applicable to civil wars. And yet, although the romance of war was buried in the mud of Flanders, the romance of civil war has managed to survive the dungeons of the Lubianka. There are times when one wonders whether the myth of the Revolution is not indistinguishable from the Fascist cult of violence. At the end of Sartre's play, *Le Diable et le Bon Dieu,* Goetz cries: "The reign of man has come at last. And a good beginning, too! Come on, Nasty, let's do some killing. . . . We've got this war to fight and I'll fight it."

Must the reign of men be the reign of war?

E.
Multiple Alternatives

5.
THE NEGRO PROTEST IN
URBAN AMERICA (1968)

MICHAEL LEWIS

INTRODUCTION

If one were to seek the prototypical victim, he would have to look no farther than the Negro American. For over 300 years, those sharing in this identity have absorbed countless blows to both their personal dignity and their institutional life. No area of the Negro's existence in American society—not his economic condition, his education, his political presence, nor his family—has been protected from abuse, both calculated and wanton. The object of the essay undertaken in these pages is the analysis of a major facet of the Negro's response to such victimization, the organization and expression of his protest in urban America.

However, before proceeding to the main body of the essay, some prefatory remarks are in order. What we shall call the *Protest* is not really a social movement in the orthodox sense of the concept. We would be hard put—for example—to use Blumer's conception of the natural stages or *career* of the social movement. It would be doing

SOURCE. Original publication.

149

great violence to the history of the *Protest* to trace, in a unitary manner, its progression from amorphous, poorly organized dissidence to a highly organized corporate entity with "a body of customs and traditions, established leadership [and] an enduring division of labor."[1] During its history the *Protest* as a whole has never been characterized by a leadership which could be called "established" in the sense that it could claim the universal loyalties (or at least the deference) of those who in one manner or another have identified themselves with it. On the contrary it would seem that as the *Protest* has intensified, as its importance has increased in the American city, it has likewise been characterized by conflict among its leaders and the proliferation of sectarian loyalties. As this has been the case it has also been true that for the most part the *Protest* cannot be described in terms of its emerging corporateness.

Behind the question of leadership and corporate development is the problem of ideological solidarity. In attempting to set forth the defining characteristics of a social movement Rudolph Heberle noted the *necessity* of such solidarity. He wrote:

> A *genuine* [emphasis mine] social movement . . . is always integrated
> by a *set* [emphasis mine] of constitutive ideas, or an ideology. . . .[2]

In surveying the emergence of the *Protest* it is clear that no single set of constitutive ideas or ultimate justifications for political action has been dominant. In large measure (although not in every case) the sectarianism which has been characteristic has been the function of differing ideological postures, of multiple and often conflicting ideological responses. For some, salvation has seemed to be attainable only by forsaking American society entirely; for others, political, economic, and social salvation has been viewed as divinely ordained; for others still, it has seemed to be a matter of far-reaching economic and social change in American society as a whole, of the transition from capitalism to socialism; and finally, it has seemed for some to be a matter of reform, a matter of simply making existing institutional arrangements function more equitably.

Thus if we conceive of a social movement in a unitary sense, if we conceive of its emergence in terms of the development of a corporate body committed to action in behalf of dictates emanating from a monistic ideological core, then the Negro's urban *Protest* would not fit such a conception.

[1] Herbert Blumer, "Social Movements." In *Principles of Sociology.* A. M. Lee, ed. (New York: Barnes and Noble, Inc., 1955), p. 199.
[2] Rudolph Heberle, *Social Movements: An Introduction to Political Sociology* (New York: Appleton-Century-Crofts, Inc., 1951), p. 11.

But if the *Protest* is not a social movement then how shall it be classified? In reality the *Protest* is a *class* of social movements. When we view the events and the organizational developments which constitute its history, it is clear that although there is enough concrete differentiation and conflict to sustain a conception of the *Protest* in terms of discrete units, there are also characteristics which seem to unify, in some measure, even the most disparate of these units. It is the presence of these characteristics which allows us to conceive of the discrete units of the *Protest* as belonging to the same *class* of sociohistorical phenomena.

To begin with, in spite of differing ideological responses, the discrete movements (i.e., the *Universal Negro Improvement Association*, the *Black Muslims*, the *March on Washington Movement*, etc.) have all emerged out of the same set of circumstances: the Negro's victimization—particularly in urban settings. They are all, therefore, expressions of the *same* discontent. Whatever the differences in their planned solutions, they have all tapped a single motivational core—the desire to be rid of the victimizing circumstances and concomitantly the desire for economic, political, and social equity. As a result of this, even those factions or discrete units which have seemed most in conflict have at times had elements of response in common. For example, even such an antagonist of black nationalism as A. Philip Randolph could commit the *March on Washington Movement* to a course intended to exclude the active participation of sympathetic whites.

On another level, the discrete units of the *Protest*—whatever the differences in their ideological commitments and between their leaders—have had a basic strategic proclivity in common: the tendency to act beyond the constraints of institutionalized political process.

Institutionalized (or party) politics in American society is characterized by the emphasis on achieving the "possible," on compromise and the art of "give and take." In all the movements comprising the *Protest*, compromise has counted for very little. Achieving the "possible" has been taken to mean settling for that which the white "power structure" of its own volition has been willing to give up. Because Negroes have been deprived of so much, in the eyes of the dissidents they have needed (and need today) so much more than the whites have been (and are) willing to give. In their view the "possible" has represented little more than token commitment to changes in the status quo—an open housing ordinance which permits the economically advantaged few to reside in previously all-white areas but which leaves the housing problems of the masses unsolved, a local Fair Employment Practices law which ostensibly opens up job opportunities but which is really ineffective because of outsized problems of enforcement, or the development of special programs for "culturally deprived" children which often seem to put the onus of failure on the children themselves rather than upon the school systems which have been insensitive to their own failures. Needing *"the impossible"*—that which white society has been unlikely to allow of its own volition—urban Negroes have attempted to obtain equity for themselves by organizing into groups whose basic strategies have rather consistently signified an absence of faith in the possibility of significant change as the result of "politics as usual." Whatever the preferred solutions championed by the discrete units, expressive symbolism and the "demonstration" (the "lie-in," the "shop-in," the boycott, etc.) rather than the vote and the party caucus have been their major levers of protest and hope for change.

There is finally another sense in which the discrete units of the *Protest* may be taken as constituting a class of social movements. Historically they have themselves constituted major segments of each other's significant environment. Some, like Marcus Garvey's *UNIA* (Universal Negro Improvement Association) or the *MOWM* (March on Washington Movement), because of their ideological or tactical innovations, have served as historical progenitors of other units of the *Protest.* The UNIA is the direct descendent of a number of lesser groups. And beyond this its ideological influence can be seen in such groups as the Black Muslims and the newly emerged Black Power advocates. The MOWM's predisposition to employ direct action presaged later tactical developments which have become characteristic of the *Protest* as a whole.

When there has been conflict among some of the movements each has had to organize not merely in terms of the goals to be achieved and the expected white opposition to their achievement, but also in terms of the ideological challenge created by its competitors. Because, as we noted earlier, each of the movements has tapped a common motivational core, it has been impossible to ignore competing ideological lures. Each unit of the *Protest* has had the problem of establishing the superiority of its program over others competing from the same loyalties. In this manner even disparate groups have influenced each other's ideological products.

There are thus at least three grounds for considering the units of the *Protest* as constituting a class of movements: (1) their common motivational base, (2) their consistant action beyond the limits of institutionalized politics, and (3) their environmental relevance for each other. It must be remembered, however, that in spite of such relatedness the units of the *Protest* have often been in conflict. And, moreover, that this conflict within the class has been and continues to be a serious problem, one that has impeded the *Protest* in the past and threatens its progress in the future.

Keeping these prefactory remarks in mind, let us now turn to an examination of the emergence of the *Protest* per se.[3]

THE DEVELOPMENT OF THE URBAN PROTEST

The Promised Land and the Dream Denied

In order to fathom the source of the urban *Protest,* one has to have an appreciation of the profound disenchantment which has emerged among urban Negroes as a product of their sensitivity to the disparity between promise and reality in the city. In the rural South up until recently there was no promise. Gross victimization and petty indignities were institutionalized into a way of life awful in its physical and spiritual toll—but nevertheless a way of life to which there was no realistic local alternative. The whites monopolized the rewards of full social participation while the Negroes suffered the burdens of institutionalized oppression. The "trouble"[4] of racial victimization dominated Southern culture and no one—black or white—could seriously entertain the promise of its demise. If there was no possibility of change in the South, there was, however, a promised land in the Northern cities. But these Zions—whether New York, Chicago, or any of the others—have turned out to be provinces of paradox and confusion. In these cities, the Negro has indeed been encouraged to pursue a dream of full participation—and has even been rebuked at times for the absence of ardor in its pursuit—but at the same time, he has been confronted with insurmountable obstacles to its realization.

The mass migrations to the cities began during the decade surrounding the First World War. A combination of agricultural depression in the South and war-induced labor shortages in the urban North pushed and pulled the Negroes from their traditional rural moorings. Labor recruiters from the North aided by the editorializing of Negro newspapers—such as the *Chicago Defender*—descended upon the impoverished black peas-

[3] The body of this paper must be taken more as an interim report than anything else. At this writing the *Protest* goes on, its conclusion, whether in success or in the despair of failure, is as yet out of sight.

[4] Lillian Smith uses this term to poignantly evoke the institutionalization of racism in the South. See the revised and enlarged edition of Lillian Smith, *Killers of the Dream* (Garden City: Anchor Books, 1961)..

ants with promises of jobs and a better life. And although the Southern whites tried—not uncommonly by means of terror and violence—to prevent an exodus, the Negroes began to leave in great numbers. . . .

The end of the war brought a period of economic retrenchment. In the industrial cities Negroes found themselves losing jobs to the returning whites. Organized labor for the most part turned its back on them. Quite often if a Negro worked at all he worked as a scab—a role he was forced to embrace in order to survive. The unions, themselves largely responsible for this state of affairs, nevertheless used it to justify their enmity toward and consequent exclusion of Negro workers.

Perhaps of even greater significance was the physical rejection which resulted in the Negro's imprisonment in the urban slum-ghetto. The slum-ghetto is not simply the result of enforced poverty although it has characteristically housed the poverty-stricken; it has been the physical manifestation of generalized antipathy toward the Negroes expressed by urban whites. In the Northern cities physical rejection in the absence of an institutionalized racial etiquette soon became the white man's "status-protection." Negroes who have challenged this rejection by moving into previously all-white areas have rarely met with success while they have frequently found themselves assaulted by hate-filled mobs. . . .

The pattern set during the twenties has remained remarkably stable; approximately 40 years after the "white retrenchment" the Negro's dream is still denied. In spite of liberalizing tendencies—FEPC legislation, the emergence of the racially universal CIO, and the "color-blind" civil service—urban Negroes still find themselves for the most part at the bottom of the economic ladder. In spite of court decisions which have destroyed the legal facade of restrictive housing practices,[5] most urban Negroes today find themselves living in ghettos—particularly slum-ghettos. Finally, the maintenance of the ghettos has meant the concomitant de facto segregation of Negro children in schools which are often poorly equipped and understaffed. Nevertheless, the swelling ranks of urban Negroes have been caught up in a "revolution of rising expectations." In the cities, for the first time, the Negro has come to view himself as a legitimate competitor for rewards which the whites have traditionally monopolized. It is crucial to remember that if nothing else and social context of the urban North has *integrated* aspiration and imagination. Seeing himself denied those opportunities and rewards which he

---

[5] For example, the Supreme Court of the United States ruled that restrictive covenants were unconstitutional in 1948.

recognizes as legitimately his, the urban Negro has reacted with increasing intensity. Thus the *Protest* was born and has continued to develop.

The Emerging Response

1. THE NATIONAL ADVOCATES. Nationally, the mainstream of the Negro protest has always appeared to have as its minimum goal the *desegregation* of opportunity and as its maximum goal the emergence of an *integrated* society in which race is essentially irrelevant as an identifying characteristic. The most widely known of the advocate organizations—the NAACP and the National Urban League—have from their beginnings championed such ends.

In the summer of 1905 twenty-nine Negro intellectuals led by W. E. B. Du Bois met on the Canadian side of Niagara Falls (they went to Canada after they were unable to secure adequate accommodations on the American side) to map an alternative to the accommodating leadership of Booker T. Washington. Washington, the most widely known and respected Negro American of his time, had publicly eschewed desegregation as an immediate goal for Negroes. Instead he had embraced a policy which emphasized the necessity of economic self-development for Negroes. To this end he became the primary architect of the Tuskeegee program of "industrial education."[6] Because of his personal charisma and because his views on desegregation posed no threat to the racial status quo, Washington attracted the support of white philanthropists. With such support he was able to build Tuskeegee Institute into an impressive training school.

Washington's personal achievements made him an international figure and in the circles of white power in the United States he was regarded as *the* spokesman for the Negroes. It was in this role that Washington generated opposition among many of the Negro intelligentsia. When, as spokesman, he pressed eloquently for extended aid to self-improvement programs in lieu of an attack on the racial dichotomy itself, he forsook those concerns which impinged most intensely on the intelligentsia. Highly trained themselves, they were little concerned with the need for developing essentially manual skills. Their need was for acceptance in the world beyond the plantation and the black ghettos. A man with the talent and education of W. E. B. Du Bois, for example, would not be a man inclined to accept separation from the cosmopolitan re-

[6] Industrial education was for the most part education in the crafts essential and ancillary to agriculture, i.e., wheelwrighting, blacksmithing, etc.

wards proffered freely to white men, these often with considerably less talent. The Negro intelligentsia was simply not prepared to accept the limitations of caste which Washington was willing to accept—for the time being at least—as an essentially unalterable reality.

Thus when 29 of these men met in the summer of 1905, they were concerned with providing the Negroes with a voice other than Washington's—a voice that would press for full equality of the Negro and full access to the opportunities and rewards of American society. Out of this meeting came an organization known as the Niagara Movement. Faced with the combined opposition of the Washington "establishment" and its powerful white allies, the movement itself accomplished little in substance. However, its basic philosophy did become the ideological beacon of the NAACP, which was formed in 1910 out of an alliance between the remnants of the Niagara group and sympathetic white liberals.[7]

Over the years the NAACP has become the most prominent advocate for the Negro. In Washington's stead it has produced such articulate spokesmen as W. E. B. Du Bois, Walter White, Thurgood Marshall, and Roy Wilkins. And since its inception it has won significant victories consistent with its antisegregation position, the best known being the Supreme Court school desegregation decision in 1954.

The Urban League came into existence in 1911 with the merger of three social welfare groups. Like the NAACP, the League has always been an interracial organization. The primary objective of the League has not been protest alone; it has instead operated as a social service organization with particular emphasis upon opening job opportunities for Negro labor. In reality the League has been a federation of autonomous local organizations—each self-supporting and each with its own board of directors. Thus its militancy in the pursuit of desegregated opportunity has varied from community to community.

While the NAACP and the Urban League have generally been recognized by whites (friend and foe alike) as the major advocates for the Negro interests, neither organization has ever had anything approaching a mass constituency among the Negroes themselves. In spite of their significant contributions to the Negro's welfare—the successful campaigns against illegal barriers to opportunity of the NAACP, and job training, employment securing, and social welfare efforts of the Urban League—neither organization has ever fired the loyalties of the rank and file. Court tests, behind-the-scenes negotiations, and educational

[7] For a treatment of this development, see Arnold Rose, *The Negroes' Morale* (Minneapolis: University of Minnesota Press, 1949), pp. 32–33.

efforts are not the kinds of activities which evoke passionate commitments from those who live their lives largely outside the middle-class context. For the Negro masses, these organizations have represented a somewhat vague benevolence bestowed from beyond the boundaries of their personal world.

2. MARCUS GARVEY AND THE UNIA. The first protest movement to attract a mass following was Marcus Garvey's urban-based *Universal Negro Improvement Association* (UNIA). It deserves special attention not only because of its mercurial success and equally mercurial failure as a movement, but also because elements of its ideological syntax have remained credible to a segment of the current protest leadership.

Marcus Garvey, a black West Indian, came to the United States with a background in labor leadership and social reform. A British subject, he had, moreover, spent two years in London, where (in contact with other West Indians and Africans) he learned of the universal plight of people of color and of their common if largely unknown heritage in the vast reaches of Africa.[8] During the decade following his arrival in 1916, Garvey catapulted himself and his organization into the forefront of the Negro-American scene. His adventures as well as his misadventures brought him notice in the world beyond the ghetto.

During the first half of the decade of the twenties Garvey claimed a membership for the UNIA of up to six million. While this figure has been disputed there can be little doubt that the UNIA had a largely urban-based membership approximating one million.[9] Also during this period Garvey captured the imagination of the black masses beyond the UNIA membership with such schemes as his plan for African colonization and the ill-fated but pride-bestowing operation of the Black Star Steamship Line.

The UNIA should be evaluated on two levels. First, what was the character of its ideological appeal—an appeal which rallied a mass of people and which has demonstrated the remarkable capability of outliving the movement itself? And second, what was the nature of the movement's organizational experience, of its rapid growth and decline?

It is quite clear, at the outset, that Marcus Garvey was the sole architect of the UNIA's ideology.[10] Garvey possessed an almost uncanny sensitivity to the unsatisfied psychic needs of the Negro masses. His ideolog-

[8] Edmund D. Cronon, *Black Moses: The Story of Marcus Garvey and the Universal Negro Improvement Association* (Madison: The University of Wisconsin Press, 1959), pp. 13–15.
[9] John Hope Franklin, *From Slavery to Freedom: A History of American Negroes* (New York: Alfred A. Knopf, 1941), p. 482.
[10] Cronon, *op. cit.*

ical creation was thus a symbolic amalgam which—even if it could
not be translated into a realizable program—was satisfying to many
simply in its emphatic statement. The major tenets of Garveyism may
be stated as follows:

(a) Glory in all things black; pride in the black man's racial identity
and an emphasis on racial purity.

(b) Rejection of the black man's powerlessness in white societies
(particularly the USA), while working for the attainment of
power in the black man's ancestral home, Africa.

(c) Preparation for the return to Africa by developing economic self-
reliance and power.[11]

In demanding respect for the black man's racial characteristics, Garvey
sought to turn the visible source of the Negro-American's stigmatized
identity into the source of his personal worthiness. . . .

Garvey himself, a short squat "full-blooded black man" had suffered
because of his physical appearance in his native Jamaica—where only
the light-hued mulattoes had any access to the white man's system of
opportunity and reward.[12] However, while others might despise themselves in this situation, Garvey made the situation a source of creative
effort. Knowing personally the stigmatization which so many had suffered, he brought to them a message of almost Messianic power. Over
and over again he regaled his listeners and readers with prideful stories
of the heroic achievements of black civilizations and black men. If in
the past black men had pride in themselves, if they had struggled to
maintain or regain their autonomy as a people, then black men in the
present could and should do the same. A black skin was nothing to
be ashamed of. It was the symbol of its possessor's link with a glorious
heritage and an even more glorious future.[13]

The glorious future which Garvey envisaged for the downtrodden
Negro had nothing in common with the standard conceptions of equal
economic and social treatment which were the hallmarks of the NAACP
Urban League approach. For Garvey such nostrums were unrealistic in
the American context. He maintained that "political, social, and industrial America [would] never become so converted as to be willing to
share up equitably between black and white."[14] Moreover, he viewed

[11] Cronon, *op. cit.*

[12] Arna Bontemps and Jack Conroy, *They Seek a City* (Garden City: Doubleday,
Doran and Co., Inc., 1945) p. 62.

[13] Throughout his career in the United States, Garvey emphasized racial purity.
He raged against American mulattoes and even went so far as to equate integration
of the races with biological amalgamation.

[14] Marcus Garvey, *Philosophy and Opinions*, Vol. II, p. 46, as quoted in Cronon,
op. cit., p. 188.

these conceptions as the panderings of those "so-called" Negro leaders who were often mulattoes without race pride. He would turn Negroes away from such false prophecy and toward their true destiny—the re-establishment of the black man's province over his ancestral home, Africa.

In order to achieve justice for themselves, black men had first to achieve power for themselves. They needed to create in Africa a strong Negro nation. Justice between black and white could not be achieved so long as black men came to white men as supplicants. When Negroes had re-established their domain over the African motherland then and only then could they free themselves from the oppression of the whites; then could they represent themselves as the equals of the white race. If all the Negroes of the world did not return to the homeland (and Garvey himself did not envisage that they would), those who remained in other lands would be strengthened in their confrontation with the whites because the presence of a powerful black nation would afford them prestige and, if necessary, protection.

Garvey had been greatly influenced by the philosophy of Booker T. Washington. Garvey concurred in Washington's view that the Negro's salvation rested on his ability to improve himself economically. But, where Washington saw such a development more or less as an end in itself within the context of American society, Garvey saw it as preparation for the return to Africa. Whereas economic self-improvement, in Washington's view, was an accommodative strategy in the face of what he perceived to be the realities of the Negro's position in American society, in Garvey's view it was a necessary first step toward the realization of the radical plan to withdraw from American life and to establish national power in Africa. To Garvey, the future was not something that America's Negroes would passively inherit; the glories of Africa would be theirs only if they were prepared to seize them. To this end he enjoined his followers, and others who were sympathetic, to start their own businesses, to work hard and not squander their earnings on short-lived gratification, to sacrifice financially for the UNIA, and above all to patronize those businesses owned and run by Negroes.

Garvey's ideological creation is something of a paradox. While its aggressive call for a massive Negro withdrawal from white America might easily be characterized as extremely radical, its content—its value emphases, its depiction of political, social, and economic reality—was in fact a mirror image of the conventional American world view. In enjoining Negroes to take pride in their race, to glory in the past achievements of black men, Garvey was merely turning the white American's racial chauvinism on its head. His view of justice and world order was based upon a conception of national power which most white Americans, then as now, would embrace. Economically, Garvey's thinking was characterized by a bourgeois solidity which would not be out of place in a Sinclair Lewis novel. Except for its emphasis on the return to Africa, the only "radicalism" in Garvey's thought can be found in his basic assumption that black men could and would manage their affairs in the same manner as did white men.

It is highly probable that the paradoxical interplay of radicalism and conventionality in Garvey's thought was the source of its wide appeal. Garvey's amalgam appealed to the disenchanted urban Negro while at the same time it did not require prospective adherents to forsake the aspects of American conventionality with which they were familiar. It did not require its "true believers" to embrace a world view which was beyond their experience. Garvey understood that in spite of apparent evidence to the contrary most black Americans aspired to the conventionality of white Americans. The success of his ideological construction can be found in the fact that it legitimated such aspiration while at the same time it catered to a counter desire to be rid of the possessors of that same conventionality.

If Garvey was eminently successful as an ideologue and propagandist his organizational efforts met with considerably less good fortune.

The chronology of the UNIA's rise and fall is truly amazing for its rapidity. During the 1919–1920 period the UNIA established chapters in most of the urban centers which had been attracting large numbers of Negro migrants from the South.[15] In 1919 Garvey and his lieutenants embarked upon an audacious commercial adventure, incorporating the Black Star Line as an all-Negro steamship line. This venture was to prove costly for the UNIA and for Garvey's reputation. But at the outset it seemed to be an undertaking which demonstrated Garvey's commitment to the Negro's economic self-improvement in the service of African redemption. The Garvey Negro business program also led (during the same year) to the establishment of the Negro Factories Corporation. The NFC developed a number of businesses, chief among them a chain of cooperative grocery stores, a restaurant, a laundry, a tailor and dressmaking shop, a millinery store, and a publishing house.[16]

In August of 1920, the UNIA held its first international convention at Liberty Hall in Harlem. Delegates from 25 countries attended. Among the tangible results of the convention were (1) the drafting of a "Declaration of the Rights of the Negro Peoples of the World," which after listing Negro grievances against their white subjugators went on to de-

[15] Cronon, *op. cit.*, p. 44.
[16] Cronon, *op. cit.*, p. 60.

mand self-determination and African redemption, and (2) the formaliza-
tion of UNIA as the organizational instrument of such redemption.
Garvey himself was designated the Provisional President of the African
Republic with a cabinet of "Potentates" to assist him in his work of
destiny.

At the close of the convention the UNIA had reached its organizational
zenith. The grand promises had been made and the dreams of the black
masses had been fired. By 1922, however, the Black Star Steamship
Line failed with unequivocal finality and Garvey and his business associates were indicted for using the mails to defraud, a charge stemming
from representations they had made in soliciting stock purchases. The
colonization program to transport America's black multitudes to the African motherland also failed dismally. Garvey's colonization scheme involved the settlement of areas in Liberia by Negro Americans. After
showing some interest in the UNIA scheme, the Liberian government
grew progressively inhospitable. In part, this was probably the result
of diplomatic pressures brought to bear by European colonial powers
such as England and France, which looked negatively upon Garvey's
blueprint for African independence; and in part, this was the result
of the fears which Garvey engendered among Liberia's own ruling elite.[17]
By the end of 1924 the possibility of Liberian colonization had disappeared and for all practical purposes Garvey's program for African redemption was dead. In 1925 Garvey was imprisoned on the mail fraud
charges stemming from the Black Star fiasco. Two years later his sen-
tence was commuted, but he was deported to his native Jamaica. In
1929, in a dispute over the location of the UNIA's headquarters, a large
segment of the organization in the United States rejected Garvey's stewardship and with this schism the UNIA was finished as a mass movement. Garvey lived through the thirties in relative obscurity. He tried
unsuccessfully to rekindle the loyalties of his former followers. He continued to write, to harangue, to implore as he had in the past, but
it was of little avail. And on July 10, 1940, Marcus Garvey, who ironically
had never set foot in Africa, was dead, his passing almost unnoticed
in the crises of worldwide conflagration.

Garvey's failure with the UNIA can be understood as the product
of a confluence of circumstances which was only in part his own responsibility. In a very real sense the movement may be seen as a victim
of historical circumstances. If, for example, the redemption of Africa
was at the core of the UNIA's ideological appeal, it was nevertheless

[17] It is easy to understand how a strong UNIA would prove a threat to the
political dominance of the already entrenched Liberians. Garvey was not a man to
subjugate his dreams to any national sovereignty—even a black sovereignty.

an historical impossibility in the international context of the twenties. The European colonial powers (England, France, Belgium, etc.) simply were not yet prepared to relinquish their domination of Africa. However, this in itself need not have been a seriously damaging factor if the UNIA had pursued its goal of redemption in a manner which, however militant, eschewed the quality of immediacy. If Garvey and his associates had been prepared to press their demands without committing the UNIA to immediate colonization, they probably would have been able to continue to rally mass support. If they had merely propagandized, if they had simply continued to challenge the legitimacy of the African status quo, they could have kept alive the mystique of a Negro-controlled Africa. The millenium does not have to occur in the lifetime of the "true believer"—it need only seem that it *will definitely* occur. When the UNIA—with as much public notice as it could master—went ahead with its colonization plan, the risk of failure was high indeed. And when failure came, as it was almost certain to do, the mystique of African redemption (in so far as it was associated with the Garvey movement) was dealt a mortal blow. The failure demonstrated that the millenium was no certainty, perhaps not even a real possibility. The confrontation had come too soon and the UNIA could no longer be looked upon as the invulnerable instrument of the Negro's political destiny.

Rash overcommitment contributed to Garvey's (and the UNIA's) difficulties in yet another area. When the UNIA under Garvey's leadership entered the shipping business, it did so without the necessary capital to purchase and maintain seaworthy ships, without a reservoir of manpower experienced in the ways of seafaring, and without a managerial force with the experience necessary for an undertaking of such scope. The result was disaster. Unscrupulous ship brokers took advantage of the managerial inexperience of the Black Star Line to foist upon it ships of dubious quality at prices far beyond their true value. Inexperienced and frequently unreliable manpower made the operation of the line even more difficult. Desperate attempts to keep the line alive led to fiscal mismanagement and ultimately to Garvey's conviction for stock fraud.

The incorporation of the Black Star Line was symbolic of the UNIA's commitment to economic independence and power for Negroes. It was calculated to show that Negroes could, in fact, compete with white economic interests on their own terms. A more prudent man than Marcus Garvey would have appreciated the difference between symbol and reality and would have delayed committing the line to an undertaking (the actual shipping operation) which, inspired gesture though it was, had no chance of real success as a business enterprise. As was the case with the UNIA's colonization scheme, too early a commitment to action led to inescapable failure. And this failure damaged the credibility of the condition which the gesture was supposed to symbolize—the ability of Negroes to compete economically with whites on a grand scale.

Finally, the UNIA's organizational difficulties were compounded by the very lack of race solidarity it sought to instill. The fact that the whites had grouped all Negroes into a single pariah class did not mean that the Negroes thought of themselves as a single undifferentiated group. On the contrary, there existed during the twenties, as there do today, very distinct cleavages within the Negro group. The major cleavage existed between the mass of undereducated, economically exploited Negroes and those Negroes who had been fortunate enough to escape the brunt of racial victimization—the middle class and the intelligentsia. Members of the Negro middle class often saw in the Negro masses the stereotype of the Negro held by the whites. In their need to disassociate themselves from that stereotype they often rejected (consciously or unconsciously) any identification with the lower-class group.[18] Lower-class Negroes, on the other hand, resentful of the relative security of members of the privileged group, tended to work a counterrejection of them. Thus it is easy to understand how an organization like the UNIA, which had great popularity among the exploited masses, was unable to fire the enthusiasm of the Negro middle class and intelligentsia. The UNIA did not merely fail to attract wide support among the middle class and those whom W. E. B. Du Bois called the "talented tenth" (a failure which no doubt deprived the movement of the counsel of those who might have been able to prevent the telling strategic errors described above), but also, because of Garvey's virulent denunciations of those who refused to support his cause, the intelligentsia in particular were polarized into an active and articulate opposition. Ironically and perhaps tragically, it was the active opposition of men like Du Bois, Chandler Owen, A. Philip Randolph, George Schuyler—more than white opposition to the UNIA—which damaged the movement extensively.[19] The UNIA failed as a mass movement in part because it came into existence at a time when the possibility of realizing its goals was nil, in part because of the strategic errors committed by its leadership, and

[18] Rose, *op. cit.*, pp. 57–67.
[19] This is not to suggest that Garvey met with no opposition from the white power structure. That the UNIA was considered dangerous by whites can be seen in its citation as radical and revolutionary by a New York state investigating committee, *The Lusk Committee*, in 1920.

in part because of the inherent cleavages which destroyed the solidarity of the Negroes and prevented their unification in behalf of "one aim" and "one destiny."

3. Early Failures: Garvey's Competitors and Immediate Successors. If the UNIA was the most audacious of the early urban protest movements it did have competitors. During the twenties two of Garvey's most articulate critics, Chandler Owen and A. Philip Randolph, attempted to create a political alliance between urban Negroes and white labor interests.[20] In their publications, *Challenge* and *The Crusader,* they preached labor solidarity across racial lines. Their efforts, however, had little effect upon the majority of the urban Negroes. In the first place the economic facts of life militated against such an alliance. Labor unions had been excluding Negroes and the Negroes in turn had—as a matter of survival—been accepting jobs at income levels below those sought by labor interests.[21] Secondly, the Owen-Randolph position was a derivative of their own commitment to socialism. Since the tenets of the socialist world view—public ownership, redistribution of wealth, the brotherhood of workers—were beyond the urban Negro's immediate realm of experience, it is not surprising that an appeal for interracial solidarity based upon class interests made little headway.

During the twenties and the thirties the Communists also made an attempt—with little success—to attract the support of urban Negroes. A major tenet of their program was a proposal to establish a separate black republic in the deep South. Somehow, while it was possible for millions of Negroes to believe in Garvey's spirited demand for black domain over Africa, the call for Negro separatism in the United States failed to capture their imaginations. Perhaps the impossibility of such a scheme seemed undeniable to those who had so recently suffered under the white man's dominance in the very area which the Communists would cede to them. Then, of course, the tenets of Communism, like Socialism, demanded prospective adherents to eschew the conventional American world view. This few urban Negroes were prepared to do. While the Communists made some headway among the Negroes, particularly during the thirties, they were never able to excite mass support.[22]

After the "Garvey years"—during a period of national depression—the Urban Negro Protest became increasingly sectarian. A number of urban-

[20] Gunnar Myrdal, *An American Dilemma* (New York: Harper and Brothers, 1944), pp. 749–750.

[21] Rose, *op. cit.,* p. 45.

[22] For a discussion of Communist efforts during the thirties, see Roi Ottley, *New World A'Coming* (Boston: Houghton Mifflin Company, 1943).

based protest organizations emerged in the name of black nationalism. None, however, really captured the allegiance of the urban masses. Among these the following were prominent examples. In 1932 the Chicago-based *Peace Movement of Ethiopia* began a campaign in behalf of Negro repatriation to Africa. The Peace Movement went so far as to actively support white racists in their attempts to commit the Federal government to a course of African repatriation. Later in the decade another group, the *Ethiopian World Federation*, sought to enlist the aid of American Negroes in the Italo-Ethiopian War. More than this, however, it gave focus to some of the nationalistic feelings awakened more than a decade earlier by Marcus Garvey. Among the other sects of similar ideological inclinations were the *National Union for People of African Descent*, a Garvey derivative which emphasized black chauvinism and extraterritorial independence for Negroes within the United States, and the *National Movement for the Establishment of the 49th State*, which had as its goal the establishment of an independent Negro commonwealth within the boundaries of the United States.[23]

4. PROTEST ON A RELIGIOUS BASIS: THE MOORS AND THE BLACK MUSLIMS. Although it could not have seemed extremely significant at the time, a religio-political sect emerged in Detroit during the early thirties, the *Lost Found Nation of Islam*, or otherwise the Black Muslims. Eventually, the Muslims were destined to succeed Garvey's UNIA as the most widely known and most controversial of the urban-based Negro militants. . . .

The Muslims were not the first religio-political movement inspired by aspects of Islamic teaching to have taken hold among urban Negroes. The movement was preceded by the *Moorish Science Temples* led by the self-styled Prophet of Allah, Noble Drew Ali. Drew Ali established his first temple in Newark, New Jersey, during the second decade of this century, and by the late twenties the movement had spread through such urban centers as New York, Philadelphia, Pittsburg, Detroit, and Chicago.[24] The Moors, as it turned out, were more of a religious sect than a political movement. While he supported Marcus Garvey, Drew Ali's major concern was to re-establish the Negroes' true identity as the children of Allah. Whereas Garvey taught that the salvation of the black man would come with the earned redemption of Africa, Drew

---

[23] For a discussion of these movements, see Myrdal, *op. cit.*, p. 814. Also see E. V. Essien-Udom, *Black Nationalism: A Search for an Identity in America* (Chicago: University of Chicago Press, 1962), pp. 49–50.

[24] For descriptions of the Moorish Science Movement see Boutemps and Conroy, *op. cit.*, pp. 174–177. Also see C. Eric Lincoln, *The Black Muslims in America* (Boston: The Beacon Press, 1961), pp. 51–55.

Ali saw the black man's salvation as the ordained result of an apocalypse which would destroy the white man. Like Garvey, he sensed the Negroes' need for redefinition of self; unlike Garvey, his response stopped short of organized, politically motivated protest. After Drew Ali's somewhat mysterious death in 1929, the cult, which had been torn for some time by internal strife, split into a number of different groups, none potent enough to exert a major influence upon the black proletariat of America's cities.

It is difficult to say precisely what influence the Moors had upon the tenets of the Muslim confession. There are some similarities between the beliefs of both groups. Since the Muslims began in Detroit and Chicago, the two cities in which the Moors had their greatest popularity, it is probably true that at the very least their presence prepared the way for the more militant and better organized Muslims.

As a religio-political protest movement the *Lost Found Nation of Islam* emerged largely through the ideological and organizational efforts of three extraordinary men: W. D. Fard, the founder of the sect; Elijah Muhammed, the maker of the movement; and Malcolm X, the movement's most effective intellect and evangelical.

Fard, whose background prior to his emergence as a prophet of Islam is still a mystery,[25] first appeared in Detroit in 1930.[26] . . . Presenting himself as a purveyor of silks and trinkets, he soon began to proselytize among his customers for a radical conversion. The one true God, said Fard, was Allah, and consequently the one true religion was not Christianity, as the white man would have the Negroes believe, but the religion of their ancestors, Islam. The black man was the original man; the white man—whatever his apparent advantages in wealth and power—was nothing more than a hybrid usurper, a devil whose religion was false and who would ultimately be brought to his knees in retribution for his sins and excesses. According to Fard, there was no end to the evil the white man had perpetrated upon the black man. Aside from the obvious history of enslavement and exploitation, he had deprived the black man of his true heritage, kept him ignorant, abused his women, forced him to eat unclean and unhealthy foods, and had even coerced him into adopting false slave names instead of the Islamic names which were his birthright. The black man's salvation, he taught, would come

[25] According to Lincoln a number of legends about Fard's origins have emerged Among them are the following: that he was a Palestinian Arab with a history of international racial agitation; that he was educated in England for a career in the diplomatic service of the kingdom of Hejaz; that he was the son of wealthy Arabic parents (see Lincoln, *ibid.*, p. 12).

[26] Lincoln, *ibid.*, p. 10.

when he turned his back on the white man, when he withdrew his allegiance from those false institutions which the white man had designed for his torment and returned to the peace which was naturally his in the "Nation of Islam."

Within a short time Fard had a following counted in the thousands. Each of these believers ostensibly forswore the white man's society and all of its accouterments, opting instead for total commitment to the goals and values of Islam as interpreted and taught by the prophet. In its early stages, then, the movement took on a parochial cast, for its leadership consciously attempted to reorganize the lives of the faithful in terms of what they deemed to be the sacred teachings of Islam.

Gradually, as the sect gained momentum, Fard retreated into the background and finally, in June 1934, he disappeared as mysteriously as he had appeared. After a short period during which the movement seemed to languish, one of Fard's lieutenants, Elijah Muhammad, emerged as his heir. After moving his headquarters to Chicago, Muhammad attached himself to the lingering charisma of Fard and set out to extend the movement throughout the slum-ghettos of urban America. As the "Messenger of Allah," Muhammad has, in fact, accomplished a great deal. What was an exotic but little-known sect in the mid-thirties is now a movement which Negro leaders feel they must regard seriously whether in support or in opposition—and which whites fear. Whatever may be said of their ultimate impact upon the course of the urban protest, it cannot be denied that Muhammad's organizational efforts have transformed the Muslims into a highly disciplined national community whose existence symbolizes the ultimate in the Negro's resistance to continued victimization. This Muhammad has been able to effect by his ability to propagandize among lower-class Negroes with a resonance matched only by the efforts of the departed Marcus Garvey; by his ability to sustain the loyalties of talented functionaries in a hierarchy whose discipline is matched by few organizations in contemporary America; and, finally, by his ability to demonstrate concrete achievements, particularly in the economic sphere, while avoiding commitments which might, by overextending the movement, expose its weaknesses. The late Malcolm X summed up Muhammad's impact when he wrote: "To us [the Muslims], the Nation of Islam was Mr. Muhammad."[27]

To most non-Muslims, black or white, it was Malcolm himself who seemed to embody the promise and the threat of the *Nation of Islam* as a political movement. It was Malcolm who, in the late fifties and

[27] Malcolm X, *The Autobiography of Malcolm X* (New York: Grove Press, Inc., 1964), p. 288.

early sixties, emerged as the Muslims' most articulate spokesman. A former hustler and convict converted to the *Nation of Islam* while in prison, Malcolm X had an almost uncanny ability to attract attention among both Negroes and whites. His fiery condemnations of white society and black integrationists, his fierce honesty where others—even Muslims—might have been more diplomatic, and his natural mental agility all combined to make him the most widely recognized of the Muslim leaders. Malcolm X more than any other Muslim brought Muhammad's teaching to general notice and his personal impressiveness led many, who had scorned the *Nation of Islam* as just another lower-class Negro escapist sect, to an appreciation of the movement.

At the height of his recognition Malcolm was silenced by Elijah Muhammad for allegedly rebelling against his authority. For several months Malcolm submitted to the discipline of the movement, but a growing disenchantment with his colleagues in the Muslim hierarchy, and a concomitant fear that the stated cause for Muhammad's action was nothing more than a pretext for removing him permanently from the inner circle of the movement, led him to formally break his ties with the *Nation of Islam.* In 1964 Malcolm X became his "own man" and organized the *Muslim Mosque Incorporated.*[28] This was to be the final venture in a remarkable career, for while he was struggling to define the goals of his new movement, Malcolm was struck down by the bullets of three assassins.[29]

Several divergences from the Black Muslim position did seem to appear during the short period of Malcolm's apostasy. First, the new organization, while still legitimated in terms of Islamic teaching, would be more activist in its political orientation. Second, it would make fewer sacred demands in the private sphere of the lives of its adherents. Third, while racially militant (its membership excluded whites), the movement would be selective in its condemnation of whites and would seek alliances with the mainstream civil rights organizations when such alliances seemed profitable in the cause of eliminating racial victimization. The first two of these differences are particularly important because they unwittingly indicate an important paradox which is characteristic of

---

[28] For a depiction of the events leading to this action, see *Malcolm X, ibid.,* Chap. 16, "Out," pp. 288–317.

[29] This occurred at a public meeting in Harlem on February 21, 1965. Three men were later tried and convicted of his murder. They were identified as members of the *Nation of Islam.* Malcolm X expected to be assassinated after he left the Muslims but just prior to his death he expressed doubts about their involvement in a previous attempt on his life., *ibid.,* p. 431.

the *Nation of Islam:* the rigid parochialism which has been the source of its internal cohesion and discipline has also weakened its potential for mobilization of the embittered Negro masses. The use of the term parochialism here does not merely denote separation or secession from white society. It is used to denote special theological demands, the acceptance of which effectively has set the Muslims apart from other *Negroes* in this society. (In this sense the UNIA was separatist but not parochial, because membership in the movement did not depend upon the acceptance of a divinely sanctioned body of teaching calculated to remove the individual functionally and spiritually from the community of his previous experience.) In their intense parochialism the Muslims are an anachronism in modern society. While other creeds have become increasingly modest about the extent to which they expect the sacred to occupy an individual's life-space, while other creeds have grudgingly accepted a compartmentalized role in secular society, the Muslims have insisted upon extending the sacred into every facet of the life of the individual member. The Muslim leaders from the outset have aspired to more than revisions of creed in the religious life of the Negro. Like the nineteenth-century Mormons who were bent upon creating a Zion in preparation for the Second Coming, the Muslims have attempted to convert any willing Negro to a sacred community, to a nation within a nation. . . .

The individual who converts to the Muslim faith therefore must also become a member of the Muslim community. He must reorient himself so that the sacred precepts which constitute the moral and ethical basis for that community supersede all else in the patterning of his daily life. For example, whatever his previous tastes, he must forsake such food as pork and corn bread because they are ritually unclean. He may neither smoke nor drink. He must moderate his diet so that over-eating does not result in physical and mental torpor. He must make ablutions before each of his required five daily prayers. No Muslim may marry outside the community. No Muslim may be alone with a member of the opposite sex unless this person is his spouse. Men must accept their familial responsibilities as providers and leaders and women must be obedient and modest in their presentation of self. Only by faithful observance of these and other theologically sanctioned requirements does an individual identify himself as a member of the *Nation of Islam.*

Conversion to the Muslim faith is clearly not something undertaken lightly, it is a commitment of the total self to a series of stringent demands. In light of this, a serious question must be raised with regard to the Muslim potential for mass leadership. A movement aspiring to a mass following can not be successful if it places too many obstacles in the way of widespread allegiance to its basic ideological thrust. While it may be true that in making their demands the Muslims bestow a meaningful new sense of identity upon those willing to acquiesce to them, one is forced to wonder about the number of Negroes who are, in fact, willing to acquiesce. It is useful to compare the Muslims in this regard with Garvey's UNIA. Within a few years of its birth the UNIA was able to rally approximately one million adherents to an ideology which in its social-psychological parameters—i.e., its emphasis on race pride and eventual political salvation—was not dissimilar to the Muslim belief. After approximately 30 years of existence the best estimates of membership in the *Lost Found Nation of Islam* range from 10,000 to a quarter of a million.[30] Even granting some overestimation of the UNIA members hip, the disparity in the relative magnetism of the two movements is striking, particularly when one takes into account the length of time during which the Muslims have been actively proselytizing. It might be possible to attribute this disparity to differences in the social contexts of recruitment. This, however, does not seem fruitful, for despite some real gains by the Negro middle class over the 30-year period in question, the socioeconomic conditions of the Negro lower class (the prime audience for both the UNIA and the Muslims) have not significantly changed for the better. If anything, conditions in the urban slum-ghettos worsened during the depression of the thirties, a circumstance which on the face of it should have stimulated a manifold increase in Muslim membership. Ruling out social context, we can account for the disparity by reference to the fact that commitment to the UNIA was simply less taxing than commitment to the *Nation of Islam*. Garvey, for example, might have harangued his followers and prospective adherents on the necessity of personal thrift and economic effort for the success of African redemption but he never demanded such behavior on the basis of sacred precept. Garvey's thought and teaching were essentially secular[31] and as a consequence the UNIA was behaviorally permissive. The Muslims, on the other hand, have invoked the sacred to legitimate their movement. They have constituted a religious community which numbers among its beliefs the expectation of political dominance as the result of Allah's divine intervention in the

---

[30] Essien-Udom, *op. cit.*, pp. 5–6; Lincoln, *op. cit.*, p. 98. Lincoln estimates the membership base at 100,000.

[31] This in spite of his references to the Black Christ.

affairs of men. In this sense their politicality is second to their religiosity.[32] Thus although an individual Negro might embrace their indictment of white society and their political goals, this would not be enough—as it was with the UNIA—for acceptance into the movement. Acceptance into the *Nation of Islam* and continued recognition as a Muslim are contingent upon meeting the theologically based demands of the sacred community, inclusive of those which refer to the private sphere of the individual's life. Neglect of ritual observance, of dietary prohibitions, and of the prescribed rules for heterosexual decorum are in fact indications of sinfulness which are subject to the community's discipline; if continued, this behavior would certainly be grounds for expulsion. It seems, therefore, that for persons inclined to favor the political ends of the Muslims, the price of membership in the movement itself may be too high.

The Muslims' parochialism works against their potential for mass mobilization in still another way. In a society dominated by *secular* norms and pursuits, it would seem that a movement which promises worldly deliverance in return for total obedience to *sacred* injunctions has little chance of developing into a mass movement. A movement successful in converting a mass following to its cause cannot—in spite of its rejection of the established order of things—violate the basic parameters of the potential convert's experience. Unless it possesses the means of widespread coercion, no movement can effect a mass revolution in conscience which completely eschews the character of the prerevolutionary thoughtways and folkways.[33]

The mass movement is the child of the society it is intended to supersede. It thrives upon the rejection of the imperfect present for the realization of a perfect future. It is the salvation for those who have loved and lost because it provides them with an escape from disillusionment and nihilism by establishing, at least psychologically, the certainty of their ultimate victory. All of this implies that the goals of the movement and the existing state of affairs—no matter how antithetical they may seem—are derivatives of a common social grammar. Thus it would seem that in twentieth-century urban America no group legitimating itself as a sacred community can have very much success in recruiting a

---

[32] This view differs markedly with the position of C. Eric Lincoln, who sees the Muslims as primarily political (Lincoln, *op. cit.*, p. 27). The difference is crucial. Because Lincoln sees the movement as more political than religious, his estimate of its potential mass impact is in my view inordinately high.

[33] As noted earlier, it was precisely Garvey's understanding of this which made his ideology so attractive.

mass membership.[34] Such legitimation derives from a normative base which, in terms of the experience of the group's potential converts, has little salience. Sacred legitimation simply runs counter to the secular normative experience of most contemporary Americans, white or black.[35] . . .

The Muslims then are today a highly disciplined minority of a minority. For all this notoriety, however, they do not seem to be in a realistic position to spearhead the Negro protest. On the basis of the analysis presented here there is little reason to believe—unless one assumes divine intervention as they do—that their political goals are realizable in the foreseeable future.

5. THE MOWM: A TASTE OF "SUCCESS." The most impressive development of the forties occurred early in the decade at a time when the nation was in the throes of its preparation for war. *The March on Washington Movement,* while not in the strictest sense indigenous to urban areas, did derive a major portion of its support in such areas. The MOWM differed significantly from its urban-based predecessors in several respects. In the first place, it was a reformist movement with a single delimited goal—to open up opportunities for Negro labor in the burgeoning defense industries. Second, it was a broadly based movement drawing adherents from across class lines. And finally, it was so loosely organized that there is some question as to whether it was in fact a movement at all.

Although a number of prominent Negro leaders—among them Walter White of the NAACP and Lester Granger of the Urban League—supported the MOWM at one time or another, only one man, A. Philip Randolph, President of the Brotherhood of Sleeping Car Porters, dominated it. It was Randolph (the same Randolph who earlier had been a bitter antagonist of Marcus Garvey) who, in January of 1941, proposed that ten thousand Negroes march on Washington to wrest from a reluctant administration a guarantee of equal access to defense employment.

Today, when we have experienced a mammoth march of some 250,000 people to Washington in behalf of civil rights legislation, Randolph's original call seems modest indeed and certainly not a proposal likely

[34] The notion of mass membership is relative and hard to pin down. A large absolute membership in an organization may not constitute a numerical mass if it constitutes only an insignificant proportion of its potential membership.

[35] For all their apparent religiosity, urban Negroes nevertheless live in a society dominated by secular concerns. However, the fact of their religiosity perhaps serves to explain why some do find the Muslims appealing. See Joseph H. Fichter, "American Religion and the Negro," *Daedalus,* vol. XCIV (Fall 1965), pp. 1088–1106.

to generate a mass movement. Coming when it did, however, the proposal seemed anything but modest and the early reaction to it among the Negro leadership ranged from very cautious optimism to outright pessimism. Only Marcus Garvey approximately 20 years earlier had been able to effect a mass mobilization of black men. Although Negroes, particularly those in the cities, were bitter about their inability to get a real foothold in the defense industries, they had not had the experience of employing organized mass pressure in pursuit of redress. Furthermore, the government was reminding everyone that in this time of crisis it was necessary to put aside special pleas in a show of national unity. Finally, and not insignificantly, Randolph's proposal meant demonstrating against the administration of Franklin Delano Roosevelt, a man revered by most Negroes. By May, however, the reservations of the Negro leadership had given way to commitment to the march, which was to take place on July 1. March committees were formed in a number of cities, street meetings were held to whip up support, and the Negro press undertook a vigorous campaign in support of the proposed venture. This organized restiveness did not go unnoticed in Washington. A mass demonstration of black men seeking equal opportunity—particularly if such a demonstration took place in the nation's capital—would have undoubtedly been a major international embarrassment to a government so close to entering a war for the defense of democracy and human equality. Moreover, such a demonstration might very well have served to indicate to potential enemies that the nation was not unified and that consequently it was unprepared to wage a major struggle. Certainly such a demonstration would have transformed a minority disaffection into a polarizing national issue. Early in June the administration began to "bargain collectively" with Randolph and other MOWM leaders in an attempt to have the proposed march canceled. The leaders demanded that the President issue an Executive Order establishing a Fair Employment Practices Committee empowered to deal with the problems of equal opportunity in defense industries. On June 25th, the President issued such an order and the Washington demonstration scheduled for the following week was called off.

In most quarters the establishment of FEPC was considered a major victory. Those most closely associated with Randolph went so far as to proclaim it the "second Emancipation Proclamation." As it turned out, it was something less than that. The establishment of the FEPC did not eradicate the inequities which moved the Negro leadership to organize the march. In the year following its establishment the President's committee held hearings in several cities. A report issued by the Bureau of Employment Security in March 1942 indicated that many defense employment opportunities during this period remained closed to Negroes. The MOWM leadership maintained that the original march had never been canceled but rather had been postponed, and that given the absence of major gains the time had come to reactivate the movement on a mass basis. Randolph and those associated with him announced plans for a series of mass convocations to be held in cities such as New York, Chicago, and St. Louis. The movement, galvanized by Randolph's charisma, undertook the major organizational effort necessary to ensure a mass turnout for the planned events. Their efforts met with extraordinary success. On June 16, eighteen thousand people packed New York's Madison Square Garden for the MOWM rally, and ten days later twelve thousand more packed a similar rally in Chicago. In the glitter of these successes, it seemed that a militantly reformist Negro mass movement was about to become a major factor in American race relations. However, these rallies represented the high-water mark for the MOWM. The tide was soon to recede. Plans for a similar rally in Washington, D.C., never materialized. In September of 1942, Walter White (NAACP) and Lester Granger (Urban League) withdrew their support from the MOWM and the broadly based federation no longer existed. Randolph, going it alone, adopted two positions for the MOWM which drew increasing criticism. First, he held that the MOWM should be an all-Negro organization. While not eschewing interracial cooperation, he did maintain that it was important for Negroes to show what they could accomplish on their own. Second, he believed that a strategy of nonviolent civil disobedience might be employed by the movement with some effect. The first position aroused the displeasure of those who saw in it a residue of the kind of nationalism which Randolph himself had so vigorously condemned in his earlier opposition to Marcus Garvey. The second position seemed to many a dangerous gamble with little hope of success. By 1943 the MOWM had ceased to be much of a factor in the Negro Protest, urban or otherwise. While Randolph was able to sustain the MOWM throughout the remaining years of the war (the last national conference was held in 1946), it never developed into the permanent protest movement he had so optimistically envisaged.[36]

The MOWM experience, however, is instructive because during its short-lived course the movement demonstrated the feasibility of certain possibilities for the organization and expression of the urban Negro's protest. If nothing else, the MOWM demonstrated that it is possible

[36] The foregoing description has relied heavily on the account of the MOWM in Herbert Garfinkel, *When Negroes March* (Glencoe: The Free Press, 1959).

to mobilize a broadly based Negro constituency. While its following (it would be erroneous to talk of membership) was pre-eminently working class, it did strike a response among middle-class Negroes as well. While most of its following was made up of people who would in some measure endorse the goal of an interracial society, it also attracted those who might be designated as nationalists or racial separatists. In all probability, the MOWM's broad appeal can be attributed to the fact that its leadership focused upon a specific issue rather than upon such global concerns as the general state of the race itself or the possibility (or impossibility) of the Negro's ultimate salvation in American society. The issue, unfair exclusion from job opportunities in defense industries, served as a "common denominator," a condition which every Negro—irrespective of class identity or ideological predisposition—would be likely to condemn. In a very real sense the immediacy of the problem and its delimited scope left no room for factionalism, on any basis, to fully bloom. In this regard it should be remembered that it was only after apparent (if not real) victory that cleavages within the Negro community began to weaken the movement, i.e., the loss of support of the NAACP and the Urban League.

Beyond the question of broadly based mobilization, the MOWM experience also indicates how effective the strategy of mass mobilization might be. FEPC became a reality when and only when government authorities perceived the strong possibility that thousands of aroused black men would dramatize their demands for redress in such a way as to interfere seriously with the pursuit of national objectives. . . . In this case a demonstrable threat of mass action was enough, for a grave international crisis confronted the nation. In less severe circumstances the march leaders no doubt would have had to make good their threat before the government would have taken positive action. Nevertheless, the events which led to the establishment of the FEPC indicate that the representative of the majority polity *will* make accommodations to minority demands when disciplined protest in behalf of those demands threatens to interfere with (or actually does interfere with) the orderly realization of majority interests.

Finally it should be noted that the two positions for which Randolph and his closest followers were criticized—their desire to limit the movement to Negroes and their desire to use nonviolent direct action (civil disobedience)—presaged later developments in the national protest. Although he was accused of fostering black nationalism when he favored an all-Negro MOWM, Randolph maintained that he was really fostering the Negro's sense of his own ability to influence his own destiny. He maintained that, unlike the nationalists, he was not anti-white. He believed, however, that just as other minorities, like the Jews, had their own defense organizations, the Negroes too should have a movement they could feel was entirely their own. As we shall see, this position, more than the exotic anti-white nationalism of such as Marcus Garvey and the Muslim leaders, seems to be the direct antecedent of contemporary Black Power advocacy. The call to a nonviolent direct action was a new and radical departure—a bit too radical for many who previously supported the MOWM. Nevertheless, today, after the "sit-ins," the "lie-ins," and the freedom rides of the late fifties and sixties, assertive civil disobedience is commonly associated with both urban and national Negro protest.

6. QUIESCENCE AND RESURGENCE: THE LOCALIZATION OF THE PROTEST. Except for the MOWM no other movement of the forties and early fifties seemed to have the capacity for capturing the attention—let alone the loyalties—of the urban masses.

The early forties did see the emergence of the *Congress of Racial Equality (CORE)*—today one of the vanguard protest organizations—in the urban North. Until the late fifties, however, CORE was a minor protest group whose activities, while effective, were sporadic and little related to the basic problems of unending poverty and ghetto life which daily confronted the cities' black masses.[37] . . . Other than CORE and MOWM, indigenous urban protest during this period was restricted to the Muslims and smaller groups, many of which were the ideological stepchildren of Garvey's black nationalism.

Exhausted by their herculean war efforts, Americans, during the postwar period, seemed to turn from public issues to the private concerns of day-to-day living. Although the conditions of urban life had not changed markedly for the Negroes, they too—as Americans—seemed less than sanguine in the pursuit of redress for their public grievances.[38] The lacuna in the black man's protest was, however, only temporary. A chain of events beginning with the historic 1954 Supreme Court decision banning segregation in the public schools eventuated in the flowering of urban activism in the late fifties and sixties.

Aside from its manifest impact, this Supreme Court decision had the

---

[37] See Marvin Rich, "The Congress of Racial Equality and its Strategy," in the *Annals of the American Academy of Political and Social Science,* Vol. 357 (January 1965), pp. 113–118.

[38] This is not to say that there were no developments of magnitude in the postwar period. These developments, however, seemed to be the delayed outcomes of earlier petitions for redress; e.g., the Supreme Court in 1947 held the all-white primary to be unconstitutional. See John Hope Franklin "The Two Worlds of Race: A Historical View," *Daedalus,* Vol. 94, no. 4; (Fall, 1965), p. 914.

important ancillary effect of implying that a new balance was at hand in the power relationships between Negroes and whites. By holding that segregation in the schools meant the denial of equal education opportunities to Negroes and that such a denial could not be tolerated, the Court symbolically legitimized the protest against the denial of opportunity to Negroes in general. No previous event in the race's American experience—except perhaps the issuing of the Emancipation Proclamation—so well signified a permanent change in the Negro's status. No doubt this would have been the case with any striking Supreme Court ruling which favored the Negro's cause. The fact, however, that the ruling came in the area of education intensified its symbolic impact. By holding that Negroes must have unrestricted access to educational opportunity, the Court in fact demanded that Negroes must have unrestricted access to a major ladder of social mobility in contemporary America. Without a doubt, economic reward and status conferral in midcentury America have increasingly come to depend upon the level of technical competence which an individual has attained. And in large measure, the attainment of technical competence has come to depend upon the basic education and advanced training the individual has received. Thus the Court's decision, coming as it did in the area of education, indicated to many Negroes that a new era, replete with possibilities never before within effective reach, was at hand. . . .

The Negro's protest in the urban North during the late fifties and its continuing development during the sixties has for the most part been characterized by a significant departure from earlier urban-based efforts. This departure may be referred to as a change of scale and focus.

A major characteristic of the earlier urban protest efforts—and in particular those of the nationalists—was their unrelatedness to specific local grievances. They were urban-*based* rather than urban-*focused*. The UNIA, for example, did not involve itself in seeking redress in the cities for the grievances of the Negro. Garvey was a visionary who saw the black man's problems on a grand scale; consequently, he was little interested in solutions which were not equally grand. The sorrows of the Negro's urban condition—the poverty, poor educational and job opportunities, the despair born of being locked into a ghetto existence—Garvey knew and understood, but in his eyes they would only be obliterated by the black man's return to Africa. The result of such a view was the calculated neglect of direct action to force change in the immediate urban environment. The Muslims too have been nourished by the justifiable discontents of the urban Negro without committing themselves to a program for redress. Since their dogma foresees the apocalyptic fall of white society as the result of divine intervention, they have avoided direct remedial action on the local scene. Even the MOWM, with its direct action program, focused upon a national problem—denial of equal job opportunities in defense industries—to the neglect of issues of local genesis.

When viewed against their predecessors, the urban movements of the late fifties and sixties appear markedly reduced in scale. Their focus has generally been the community rather than the nation, the obliteration in the present of a specified evil or series of evils rather than the evocation of some future utopia. A few examples will make this abundantly clear.

New York City has been the scene of heightened protest activity since the late fifties. For the most part this protest has been organized and executed by independent groups (which, on occasion, have been aligned with local NAACP and CORE chapters) focusing upon three perennial problems of ghetto life—inadequate educational opportunities, a limited job ceiling, and the physical decrepitude of available housing.

During the period under consideration the protest against inadequate educational opportunities in New York has grown in intensity as the protesters have come to view the educational "establishment" as lacking in good faith. Many of the protest groups have adopted a nihilistic rhetoric and tactics best described as disruptive as they have come to view the Board of Education's plans and proposals as demagogic gestures designed to forestall an honest reckoning with the problem. What began as an effort to break the pattern of de facto segregation by getting the Board of Education to employ its administrative prerogatives has turned into a struggle for neighborhood control of the ghetto schools. Local parents' groups have gone so far as to demand the right to oversee the school curriculum and the right to select professional staff, including the principal.

In the early sixties a coalition of protest groups, involving among others local CORE chapters, began to use direct action tactics in an attempt to force the unions to accept Negro members and to open their apprenticeship programs to qualified Negro applicants. In the summer of 1963, the protesters began picketing construction sites, lying down in the paths of trucks in order to prevent them from unloading construction materials, and "sitting in" at the offices of the Mayor and Governor. . . .

For years the majority of New York's Negro population has been forced to live in the teeming slums of areas like Harlem and the Bedford-Stuyvesant–East New York section of Brooklyn A perusal of available housing statistics indicates in understatement what even casual observation in such areas reveals with shocking force—that the physical condition of the housing is abominable. In Harlem, for example, as of 1960, 49 per cent of the available housing was in need of major repair as compared with 15 per cent for New York City as a whole. Even these statistics do not convey just how desperate the situation really has been. The need for major repairs would be grave enough, but extensive overcrowding in such dwellings multiplies the seriousness of the situation. When an inadequate dwelling unit houses one family it is bad enough; when it houses two or even three families the wretchedness of the conditions is staggering.

Faced with intolerable conditions which seemed to be getting worse rather than better, the ghetto residents of Harlem and other similar areas decided to take matters into their own hands.[39] During the early sixties a number of tenants' associations were organized. For the most part, these groups adopted a direct action strategy. On the assumption that the slumlord will respond only to economic pressure, they have attempted to make ownership of slum buildings unprofitable by withholding rents until needed repairs have been undertaken.[40]

Similar examples of locally focused protest activity may be cited in cities other than New York during this same period. In Philadelphia, Negro ministers organized the *Selective Patronage Movement* (1960), which by using the consumer boycott as a direct action technique induced a number of local companies to start hiring more Negroes while upgrading those whom they already employed. In San Francisco, Negroes organized what might be labeled "shop-ins" against supermarkets which discriminated in their hiring practices (1964). Organized school boycotts and large-scale demonstrations have occurred in Boston and Chicago, where the local school systems have long been segregated on a de factor basis. In Cleveland, "lie-ins" have occurred at construction sites in protest against discriminatory hiring practices in the building trades. . . .

The cases cited here—and they by no means exhaust the list—have one major characteristic in common. They all represent attempts to change the course of events within the context of the local community. They may be taken as indicators of the scaling down and refocusing of the Negro's urban protest. Few of these efforts have met with immediate success but they nevertheless represent a certain amount of progress in the protest effort. Certainly the confrontation of conditions on a level amenable to change indicates a realism which the grand schemes,

[39] The mass media most likely increased the Negroes' sense of grievance by bringing to them a picture of how the "other half lives."

[40] It should be noted that as a result of the tenants' groups efforts, rent strikes have legal standing in New York State.

for all their symbolic attraction, lacked. This is not to say, however, that the strategy of immediate direct action as presently used in the urban context is without problems. Too often direct action efforts have been squandered meaninglessly, as in the case of the abortive CORE "stall-in"—an attempt to block the access roads to the New York World's Fair for little observable cause. Also, more often than not, direct action has been undertaken by cadres without the mass support necessary for the greatest impact. But the realization that local conditions may be remedied by confrontation politics and disciplined dissidence must be considered a step forward because—if nothing else—it means that urban Negroes are gaining a sense of control over their own destinies.

The problematic nature of mass support for the direct action efforts in the cities requires some analysis because such support—or the lack of it—is likely to be a crucial factor in the success or failure of the urban Negro's protest efforts. It should be noted that in all of the examples cited above, the activists have constituted a small minority of those who might potentially support such efforts. Moreover, a major characteristic of the direct action protest in the cities has been the problem of sustaining the activism of those who turn out to support any given demonstration. In part the inability to mobilize mass support and keep it mobilized is the paradoxical derivative of the scaling down and refocusing of the protest. This may be seen in the following ways. First, the scaling down of the protest deprives the leadership of those grand symbols which almost universally excite the imagination. None of the contemporary urban protests has been characterized by the élan which characterized Garvey's UNIA or even the MOWM. Whereas Garvey could thunder about the redemption of Africa and the emergence of a mighty black nation, whereas A. Philip Randolph could use a struggle against racial insanity in Europe as a dramatic backdrop upon which his demands for the Negro's economic equity were striking indeed, the leaders of the localized protests have generally found it difficult to express their goals in as compelling a manner. The very concreteness of their efforts—the focus on the apparently attainable—has left little room for the grand symbolic appeal; the limitation of intent and execution runs contrary to the evocation of the grand historical illusion.

Beyond the loss of symbolic power, there is yet another mobilization problem which seems associated with the community issue focus. Earlier, we noted that part of the MOWM's success in mobilizing adherents was due to its concern with an issue about which various segments of the Negro population could make common cause. The denial to Negroes of equal job opportunities in defense preparations at a time when the national economy was gearing up in just this sector was issue enough to unite middle class and working class, integrationists and nationalists. On the face of it, it would seem that there is a parallel between the MOWM experience and the localized urban protests. For like the MOWM the direct action efforts have also focused upon issues of immediate relevance. Thus it would seem that the localized protests should have similar success in effecting a broadly based mobilization. In point of fact, however, this has not been the case in most instances, because on the local level the issues seem most often to directly affect only certain segments of the Negro population. The MOWM's concern was a "bread and butter" issue which—given the direction of the national economy immediately prior to World War II (and during the war)—affected millions of Negroes. The protest was specific in that it was limited to the defense economy, but at the same time it was broad enough to cover various levels within the economy. The skilled and the unskilled, the blue-collar worker and the white-collar worker, could all perceive a gain for themselves in its successful outcome. Typically, the organized local protest has been *overspecified*. Allowing for a number of exceptions, which are striking just because they are exceptions (the school protests for one), the localized protest efforts have tended to focus *not* on an identifiable problem area itself, but on a highly specific *aspect* of the problem area. Thus direct action protest does not attack the full range of discriminatory hiring practices, but job discrimination at specific levels in specific industries, such as the building trades and the retail food stores; it does not lump all housing problems together into a single target, but focuses upon slum conditions in one instance and suburban discrimination in another.[41] The effect of such overspecification is to narrow the affected audience and consequently to limit the potential number of activities. It would, however, be erroneous to maintain that only those who stand to gain personally engage in localized protest activities. Nevertheless the overspecification described above does create a situation in which broadly based activism is less likely to be the case. In any given situation a large number of potential activists are unlikely to be mobilized simply because they feel relatively removed from the precise circumstances of the controversy. They may sympathize with the effort but out of a sense of common condition—in the way that most laboring people sympathize with the strikers in a dispute which does not involve them directly; they may give moral support, even financial support—but they themselves are not likely to become active participants. Those who do become active

[41] One notable exception to this is the recent SCLC activity in Chicago where Martin Luther King's "open city" protest has encompassed the range of housing problems.

are thus likely to come from two segments of the population, both of which, when taken together, are hardly likely to provide a source of mass mobilization—those who see a personal gain and those people, black or white, who make up the cadres of the "civil rights movement." In truth it is this latter group who, perceiving any specific confrontation as an aspect of the general struggle, most often provide the backbone for localized protest. It becomes apparent that the overspecification of the protest focus tends to operate against mass mobilization and in so doing often results in a weaker effort than is necessary for effecting the desired change.

Taken together, the absence of symbolic power and the overspecification of the localized urban protest have resulted in (1) little sustained dissidence—there are peaks and valleys in activism which is focused upon discrete issues; and (2) activism which for all its intensity has not been a mass phenomenon—there is no readily definable mass movement in any of the urban centers. The general absence of real success in the localized protest may be the result of these conditions. Without sustained mass protest the organized dissidence may be seen as falling short of the levels necessary to force the white power structure to accommodate the Negroes' demands.

7. BLACK POWER ADVOCACY. It is possible to see in the latest protest developments a response to the problems we have noted above. While it would probably be erroneous to attribute the emergence of "Black Power" advocacy to a conscious recognition of the difficulties blocking the success of localized urban protest, the adoption of such advocacy may indeed serve to remedy some of these difficulties. To many whites, the use of "Black Power" signifies racism in reverse. Many of those who sympathize with and even act in behalf of the Negro's cause see in this slogan a demand to abrogate the interracial coalition of which they have been a part. On the other hand, those who have actively or passively supported the social disenfranchisement of the Negro view the slogan as a threat of retaliation. There is no doubt some justification for these interpretations—if not the abrogation of the coalition then at least a major realignment; if not general retaliation certainly a threat of direct retaliation against those who perpetrate violence against Negroes. But it would seem that beyond the perceived organizational and personal threat,[42] "Black Power" advocacy is an attempt to restore symbolic power to the protest, an attempt to develop sustained mass action.

In this light it is interesting to note similarities as well as the significant differences between the emerging "Black Power" advocacy and the grand

---

[42] Such "perceptions" of personal threat may very well be the projections of guilt-ridden whites.

constructions of the major black nationalist ideologues, particularly Marcus Garvey. Like Garvey, the contemporary "Black Power" advocates eschew integration as irrelevant to the Negro's struggle for equity. Unlike Garvey, however, their denial of integration seems to be more a matter of perspective than a statement of ultimate principle. "Black Power" advocates, Stokely Carmichael of SNCC and Floyd McKissick of CORE, do not envisage the irrevocable separation of black from white. They do, however, insist upon the Negro's right to self-definition and self-determination. The hold that integration has been a white man's solution to the Negro's problems; that integration only means what the white man will have it mean; that white money pays for it, white legislators and white judges define its limits. Moreover this view holds that because Negroes cannot trust whites, they ought not commit themselves to a goal the realization of which is likely to depend upon the tenuous probability of the white man's good faith.

It would appear that in denying the relevance of integration, the "Black Power" advocates are operating psychologically rather than politically. A political denial of integration (which would certainly have important psychological concomitants) would necessitate the proposal of a realizable or utopian alternative. This was done by Garvey in his claim to Africa, by the Communists in their proposal for Negro control of the South, and by the Muslims in their demand for black domain over a segment of North America. The major "Black Power" advocates have not gone this far—at least not yet.[43] Politically, it is therefore difficult to distinguish between their notions of racial equity and those of the integrationists, like Martin Luther King, Jr. Like the integrationists, they apparently want access to the fullest range of opportunity in American society and there is nothing to suggest that they want anything other than a society in which race is socially, politically, and economically irrelevant.[44] Psychologically, however, their position *is* distinct. In rejecting integration as a white man's concept, they have attempted to dispel the "white is right" notion which is all too common among Negroes. It is not the goals of integration per se to which they object, but the fact that Negroes accept these goals as defined by whites. In doing this, they maintain, Negroes do not define their protest for

[43] The national conference on black power held in Newark, N.J., several days after the riots there in July 1967 produced a number of political demands of a separatist nature (including a call for a dialogue on the development of a black society in the United States). However, it does not appear that the resolutions adopted at the conference represent a universally accepted political standard.

[44] We should, however, be cognizant of the fact that some of this advocacy has been tied to a notion of radical reconstruction of American life. Stokely Carmichael seems to hold such a position.

themselves. The eschewal of integration is then an attempt to have Negroes determine their own protest objectives without regard for white reaction. It is an attempt to urge Negroes to shape their own destinies, to determine for themselves what it is they wish to accomplish.

Along with the demand for self-definition of protest objectives, the "Black Power" advocates have insisted that leadership should rest in the hands of the Negroes themselves. This is, of course, consistent with the demand for self-definition. It would be effectively impossible for a Negro-determined movement to be led by whites, a contradiction almost by definition. In this there is a superficial resemblance to the positions of Garvey and other nationalists, but it is just that! Whereas the nationalists would exclude whites from any active participation in their efforts, the "Black Power" advocates would only exclude them from leadership. They do not object to alliances with whites who wish to follow in the ranks.[45]

Marcus Garvey believed that the salvation of the Negro in a white-dominated society depended upon the existence of a powerful Black African nation-state. Such a state by its presence in the community of nations, he believed, would be able to exert enough pressure to ensure equitable treatment of black people no matter where they might reside. Such a state would establish the common peoplehood of all black men. Thus an offense against overseas black men would be regarded as an offense against a powerful African nation-state whose protective response would most certainly be forthcoming and could hardly be ignored. Garvey's basic assumption in such a view was that equity could not be achieved by appealing to the white man's sense of justice but only as the result of exerted leverage on the white man's interests. The powerful Black African state would be in a position to exert such leverage. "Black Power" advocates have adopted the basic Garvey assumption while modifying the proposed mode of its operationalization. They, too, despair of moral persuasion as a mechanism of basic change in American race relations and opt instead for a course intended to *wrest* an accommodation from the whites. While, however, the "Black Power" advocates have recognized in the emergence of the independent African states a possible source of leverage on the power structure of the United States, and while they consequently strive—in varying degrees—to forge a common sense of peoplehood with the Africans, the basic thrust of their strategy has not been geared to the possibility of African intervention in the Negro American's behalf. The relative powerlessness of these states,

[45] See the *New York Times*, August 11, 1967, "Political Alliances with Whites Urged by Negro Leaders." The call for such alliances was made by Floyd McKissick among others.

their internal instability, and the recognition that the sense of people-hood will not easily be attained do not encourage belief in the realism of such a possibility. Instead, leaders like Carmichael and McKissick have attempted to encourage the development of domestic sources of coercive leverage.

In the cities, "Black Power" seems to find its most ardent expression among the direct action groups who eschew institutionalized politics as a mechanism for change. . . . In Los Angeles, for example, there are groups (SLANT, US, Afro-American Citizen's Council, the Self-Determination Committee) which demonstrate quite well the playing out of "Black Power" themes. *SLANT* (Self-Leadership for All Nationalities Today), a small group of some 500 adherents, takes the position that without first building a consolidated black community, integration can only mean continued subservience to the whites. US, a more thoroughly nationalist group inspired by the memory of Malcolm X, goes even further. US demands the development of a separated local community within the boundaries of the city. Such a community would have its own language—Swahili, celebrate its own holidays—Malcolm's birthday, the Sacrifice of Malcolm Day, etc., and operate its own schools. The solidarity of the black community, the product of its isolation, would, in the view of the US leadership, create a power base which in turn would improve the black man's bargaining position in confrontations with the local white power structure.[46]

Similar groups have recently emerged in most major American cities where Negroes remain locked within the ghetto. However, while such groups have emerged, their impact does not as yet seem very great. This is probably true in part because—the summer riots notwithstanding—this is a period of mobilization, a period of building solidarity before the confrontation with the white power structure. But it is also probably true because on the local level no leaders have emerged who are sufficiently charismatic to attract mass followings. And in the absence of such leadership, the "Black Power" groups seem to dissipate much of their potential. . . . Thus the "Black Power" response as yet is not a dominant characteristic of the urban protest; the unified exercise of leverage on the urban white power structures still eludes the Negro.[47]

[46] See Andrew Kopkind, "Watts—Waiting for D-Day," *New Republic* (June 11, 1966), pp. 15–17.

[47] It is easy to be misled by the scale of the recent summer violence. While Black Power advocacy has been prominently associated—at least in the mass media—with these events, there is as yet no real evidence of its strength as a source of violent action which is intended as a rational tactic in the exercise of political leverage.

Finally, we must note that "Black Power" is ideological without really being an ideology. It is not, as we have seen, a fully adumbrated scheme of ultimate goals which sanction immediate action. Its advocacy is an attempt to provide the symbols necessary for sustaining mass mobilization, but these symbols have not yet been evoked with clarity. The term "Black Power" does itself seem to tap the welled-up aspirations of many Negroes for self-realization and even retribution against their white tormentors. Beyond this striking term, however, there are only those vague calls for black solidarity and pride in a common heritage —presumably African. The question remains as to whether a quasi-ideology will be enough to evoke a mobilization of Negroes in great enough numbers to make a dent in the walls of white recalcitrance. The question is a basic one because a quasi-ideology with its limited symbolism is likely to be all that will be forthcoming from the leading "Black Power" advocates, who are activists before they are ideologues. . . .

CONCLUSION: THE NEW VISIBILITY AND ITS PROBLEMS

The Negroes of our urban slums are no longer "invisible." Their increasingly intense protest activities, their articulate indictment of continuing racism, and even their violent expressions of frustration in the summer riots have forced us all to confront the unpleasant realities which are the products of the American racial dichotomy. The issue has been joined but whether or not the protest will ultimately result in racial equity is still a matter of some uncertainty.

We have already noted that the protest has developed outside the constraints of institutionalized politics. The practice of noninstitutional politics in American society is, however, severely limited by historical circumstance. It would seem, for example, that the only strategy available to Negroes with any possibility of success is the evocation and sustenance of *mass dissidence*.[48] Without mass support, an activist vanguard could theoretically achieve its ends by one of two alternative courses. If the committed few, as the result of historic good fortune, have intimate access to the inner circles of power, they may, by various covert activities, bring about the conditions they desire. Lacking such access, the ultimate success of the committed will depend upon their ability to seize power, most probably by acts of disciplined violence. For Negro activitists neither of these alternatives is possible. Certainly the vanguard

---

[48] At the Tenth Anniversary Convention of SCLC in August 1967, Martin Luther King seemed to recognize this in his call for mass disruptive action in the cities.

has but very limited access to the inner circles of power. In large part this is what the protest is about.[49] A seizure of power, on the other hand, is inconceivable except in a situation characterized by political anomie.[50] Despite recurrent crises there is nothing now present or in the foreseeable future which suggests an upheaval in American society of such cataclysmic proportions as to enable any group to violently seize power. . . . Thus, unless the protest leadership is willing to settle for the compromise solutions available through institutionalized channels, it would seem that they must ultimately undertake a campaign of mass dissidence.

Essentially mass dissidence refers to the large-scale projection of direct action. It implies the organization of a mass movement committed to large-scale tactical disruption of orderly social process. It would, in effect, unite two previously disparate characteristics of the Negro's urban protest: large-scale organization and participation (the UNIA, the MOWM, and perhaps the Black Muslims) and the techniques of militant civil disobedience (CORE, SNCC, SCLC, and the localized protest groups).[51] The strategic rationale for mass dissidence may be stated as follows. No social system can long endure the disruption of orderly social process even if the system's power structure[52] has the loyalty of the majority. The presistent dissidence of a numerically significant minority would throw the system into a state of crisis. If this occurred two alternatives would be open to the power structure. It must either "break the back" of the dissident minority by acts of repression, or accommodate the demands of the dissidents. On the assumption that repression of a large-scale Negro movement would be effectively impossible without a complete breakdown in the American legal system, the power structure would be forced to make an accommodation.

[49] Charles S. Silberman, *Crisis in Black and White* (New York: Vintage Books, 1964), p. 195.
[50] The Bolshevik seizure of power in Russia would have been impossible without the general breakdown of traditional political authority.
[51] The MOWM almost approximated such unification, but not quite. Martin Luther King, Jr., and his associates made a somewhat abortive attempt to unite these characteristics in their "open city" protest in Chicago, summer 1966. Although an agreement on open housing was signed with the Mayor and local civic leaders as a result of King's work, the movement lost its momentum, and its cadres—for the most part—withdrew from the Chicago scene (interview with Daniel Shienfeld, Institute for Juvenile Research, Chicago, June 1967).
[52] "Power structure" is an overused term. Although it is unclear whether in any empirical case a "power structure" exists as a monistic entity, we use the term as a shorthand for structure of political allocation which may in fact have several tracks and bases.

If mass dissidence is the only noninstitutional strategy which might eventuate in significant gains for the urban Negro, it is nevertheless a course faced with two significant difficulties, either one of which might foreclose the possibility of success. First, there is the problem of developing an ideological repertoire capable of evoking a broadly based activism. As we have seen, there has been only one urban-based Negro protest movement—the MOWM—which, for even a short time, had broad enough appeal to evoke consolidated mass action. . . .

Without the development of ideological solidarity, organized mass dissidence is unlikely to materialize. Without it the protest will continue to be the sporadic product of the alliance between civil rights cadres and those who are touched directly by given concrete issues.

Second, there is the problem of developing a stable leadership coalition. Historically the urban protest leadership has dissipated much of its energy in internecine warfare. In many instances—as was the case with the conflict between Garvey and men like Du Bois, Randolph, and Owen—such struggles have emerged out of meaningful disagreement over ideological postures. In other instances, however, such as the break of White and Granger with Randolph during the MOWM episode or the isolation of Malcolm X by the Muslim hierarchy, the conflicts seem to have been the derivatives of organizational or personal self-interest. If the tendency to factionalize is not overcome a coordinated program of mass dissidence will be impossible. Instead the protest will continue to be led on an idiosyncratic basis.

If the problems of ideology and leadership are overcome the chances for the successful exercise of mass dissidence will be multiplied. However, the ultimate success of the *Protest* will not thereby be assured. The tactical rationale for such a campaign assumes that the disruption of orderly social process will eventually elicit an accommodation from the majority power structure, that given the inherent protections of the American legal system, repression will be impossible. While this assumption may be borne out in the long run, the immediate response of the threatened white majority to mass dissidence on the part of the Negroes might be devastating to such a movement. There are, unfortunately, enough current examples of repressive white resistance to the Negro's direct action protest to give even the most optimistic observer pause. Even in the so-called liberal cities of the North this has increasingly been the case. . . . Heightened Negro protest apparently activates the dormant fears and prejudices of many whites to the point where they react with uncontrolled violence. If the discipline of the protesters should break down so that they respond to their tormentors in kind, a situation might easily arise in which the power structure might feel justified in opting for the repressive alternative.[53]

Any campaign of mass dissidence is likely to be faced with a threat of violent resistance, which, by virtue of its internal discipline, it must ignore. If it does not, formal repression may deal the movement a crippling, if not devastating, blow. That such discipline is possible is evident in the example of the Southern activists who have withstood intense pressure. Nevertheless, the probability of a breakdown in such discipline will be greater in a program of mass dissidence. Whereas the Southern activists have been selected cadres, the strategy of mass dissidence demands the widest range of participants. In the tinderbox situations which may be expected to arise if the strategy is initiated, one undisciplined response may destroy the movement's effectiveness.

Finally, even if mass dissidence should prove effective, even if a militant urban protest should ultimately wrest a meaningful accommodation from the majority power structure, unintended consequences would result. While the successful prosecution of mass dissidence would mean the lowering of formal barriers to full participation it would also probably result in a major increment in the already existing interracial estrangement. The strategy implies the creative use of conflict—and conflict can be expected to intensify the personal antipathy of members of one side for the other, particularly when the conflict generates violence. Thus, although greater equity of opportunity may be achieved, true integration—a state in which race is irrelevant—would yet be unrealized.

REFERENCES

BLUMER, Herbert. Social Movements. *In* A. M. Lee (ed.), *Principles of Sociology.* New York: Barnes and Noble, Inc., 1955.

BONTEMPS, Arna, and CONROY, Jack. *They Seek a City.* Garden City: Doubleday, Doran and Co., Inc. 1945.

CRONON, Edmund D. *Black Moses: The Story of Marcus Garvey and the Universal Negro Improvement Association.* Madison: The University of Wisconsin Press, 1955.

ESSIEN-UDOM, E. V. *Black Nationalism: A Search For an Identity in America.* Chicago: University of Chicago Press, 1962.

---

[53] The summer riots of 1967 indicate that repression is at least a real possibility when civil disorders erupts. In Plainfield, N.J., for example, National Guardsmen and police searched the homes of Negro residents in the riot area *without warrants* because of an alleged theft of guns.

Fichter, Joseph H. "American Religion and the Negro," *Daedalus,* Vol. 94 (Fall 1965).

Franklin, John Hope. *From Slavery to Freedom: A History of American Negroes.* New York: Alfred A. Knopf, 1947.

————. "The Two Worlds of Race: A Historical View," *Daedalus,* Vol. 94 (Fall 1965).

Garfinkel, Herbert. *When Negroes March.* Glencoe: The Free Press, 1959.

Heberle, Rudolph. *Social Movements: An Introduction to Political Sociology.* New York: Appleton-Century-Crofts, Inc., 1951.

Lincoln, C. Eric. *The Black Muslims in America.* Boston: The Beacon Press, 1961.

Malcolm X. *The Autobiography of Malcolm X.* New York: Grove Press, Inc., 1964.

Myrdal, Gunnar. *An American Dilemma.* New York: Harper and Brothers, 1944.

Ottley, Roi. *New World A'Coming.* Boston: Houghton Mifflin Company, 1943.

Rich, Marvin. "The Congress of Racial Equality and Its Strategy," *The Annals of the American Academy of Political and Social Science,* Vol. 357 (January 1965).

Rose, Arnold. *The Negroes' Morale.* Minneapolis: University of Minnesota Press, 1949.

Silberman, Charles S. *Crises in Black and White.* New York: Vintage Books, 1964.

Smith, Lillian. *Killers of the Dream.* Garden City: Anchor Books, 1961.

Thompson, Daniel C. "The Rise of the Negro Protest," *The Annals of the American Academy of Political and Social Science,* Vol. 357 (January 1965).

III.

THE STRUCTURAL
SOURCES OF PROTEST,
REFORM, AND REVOLT

In Part II we pointed out that our general characterization of social movements is most clearly applicable to reform movements. This formulation has reflected historical facts about American society, which has made the reform movement a major instrument through which change has occurred. In this chapter we examine the problematic nature of reform, indicating the special features of history and social structure which make it more frequent in certain societies and historical periods than in others, where protest, revolt, and revolution may be more likely forms of collective action.

Our point in this section of the volume is a conclusion derived from the general sociological insight that knowledge is itself produced under specific social conditions. Perspectives toward the study of social movements have given central place to reform because political institutions of American and European life have made such movements possible and typical.

Both reform and revolution of the kinds studied may, however, be products of modern Western society and not significant in other societies and earlier historical periods. They depend upon the emergence of modern, Western society and are not metaphysically fixed entities. This point of view has already found much support in George Rudé's account of eighteenth- and nineteenth-century crowd protest presented in Part II.

Rudé concluded that protest behavior was supplanted by organized working class movements when ideological conceptions of "rights of man" and industrialization produced a stable and politically involved working class to replace the heterogeneous and politically excluded "crowd."

The heart of this perspective is an analysis of how mechanisms within the social order deter or support the appearance of one or another form of collective action. In a society where even reformist sentiment is not permitted, open expression and association are prevented and shared dissent either fails to emerge as collective action demanding change or is forced into secret and illegal activity, militarized, and made revolutionary. Thus we can see that the replacement of protest by reform is one means by which dissent is given legitimacy and, by this process, both widened and pacified.

In the first reading in this section, Reinhard Bendix analyzes this process as one in which the lower classes in England and other parts of Europe were granted political representation as a means of regularizing and channeling protest into peaceful and less disruptive forms of social change. This politicization of protest involved *both* the widening of demands into more general criticisms of the society and the development of the social movement as a major form of organization to achieve group aims and realize interests. In this fashion the social institutions of political democracy functioned to regularize, accept, and legitimate conflict and dissent under prescribed forms. The applicability of this theory of reformist and revolutionary movements to all societies and to contemporary Western ones is the focus of the remaining readings in this section.

The gradualist and organized quality of reform has often been viewed as a major characteristic of American history, as A. M. Schlesinger indicated in Part II. The conditions of contemporary American society may be shifting the locus of initiative in reformist sentiment from self-interested groups within the society to the agencies of social control themselves. Daniel Patrick Moynihan reaches this conclusion in his paper, "The Professionalization of Reform." Moynihan observes that the new programs to eradicate poverty and extend equality and welfare have come as much, if not more, from the professional welfare intellectuals and executives in government and the universities as they have from the dispossessed and the poor. Is it possible that we are beginning to witness a new form of social movement, made possible by the centralization of welfare opportunities in governmental action? It would be a form congruent with the welfare state and the bureaucratic character of twentieth-century postindustrial societies.

No social observer writing in the 1960s could possibly maintain that sporadic and volatile protest has disappeared from modern societies. The student-led and -inspired riots and demonstrations in Europe (both East and West) and the ghetto riots and student "unrest" in the United States might even suggest that reformism as a major vehicle of change is undergoing severe transformation. The two readings on contemporary protest are more than descriptive or hortatory. Lee Rainwater's editorial article, written shortly after the Detroit riots, is an analysis of the conditions which have made for Negro protest through this channel. It suggests to us similarities between the preindustrial crowds described by Rudé and the present semiexcluded position of the Negro in America. Unlike those earlier events, however, modern conditions give the ghetto riot a greater political import and link it to a general movement for Negro equality.

In analyzing specific protest we need also to see those conditions which make for sporadic protest among certain parts of the society. There are particular reasons for Negro protest taking form through riot. Student unrest, although it takes particular forms in specific countries and periods, nevertheless derives from conditions of student life in many countries and historical eras. Philip Altbach thus addresses himself to the question of why students are generally a volatile and riotous group, less inclined to politicize protest than to move to insurrection, protest, and demonstration than is true of other segments of societies. Both Rainwater and Altbach give the reader some reasons for the fact that institutionalized methods for conflict regulation and resolution are not always utilized.

In recent years a number of social analysts, such as Hannah Arendt, Karl Mannheim, and William Kornhauser, have argued that structural features of modern life produce a weakening of the attachments between persons and the major institutions regulating conflict and the expression of aggressive impulse. The specific characteristics of "mass society" involve the diminution of emotional loyalties and group identifications. The result, in a society of large-scale organizations and democratic politics, may be a combination of disattachment and distrust toward authority with a mobilization of the "mass" around aggressive acts and symbols. The theory is formulated and discussed in the reading by Philip Selznick in a paper derived from his study of the Communist Party in Europe and in the United States.

Mass society theory is thus an analysis of the consequences of "breakdown" in the mechanisms which institutionalize conflict in modern societies. It is another way in which contemporary social scientists are examining the presuppositions of reformism and its applicability as an instrument of social reform in the modern world. Analysis of a non-Western but industrialized society shows us the importance of specifying the structure of conflict regulation in understanding the appearance of "mass politics" and protest action. Robert Scalapino's description and analysis of the Japanese political riots of 1960 form a vivid case study of "mass politics." The causes of that protest, however, are located in the nature of Japanese political parties, which function very differently from either the programmatic organizations of Europe or the coalitions and interest-representational ones of the United States. In both readings (Selznick and Scalapino) a significant aspect of the analysis recognizes the importance of the democratication of the citizen *and* the nature of social organizations as crucial variables in the development of forms of collective action.

In our final reading we consider the possibility that sporadic protest may operate as a more typical part of the process of change in underdeveloped countries than in present industrialized societies, where they appear as disruptive. David Bayley, in an analysis of riot and demonstration as part of Indian politics, suggests that such protest actions are now so much a predictable feature of Indian life that they are themselves becoming institutionalized and regulated. Perhaps this may be a step toward the development of reform movements as a more typical expression of dissent, as occurred in the West. Reform, with its assumption of wide communications, literacy, and organizational skills, may not be capable of utilization by many segments of the new nations. Democratic politics, under these conditions, is likely to share many traits with "mass politics" and popular participation through protest. It is necessary to recognize the distinct possibility that the historical era of reform may no longer exist. Conditions of a "mass society" may imply a very different setting for dissent and change—one that may impart a more violent and sporadic character to social movements.

A.

The Politicization of Protest

1.

THE LOWER CLASSES AND THE "DEMOCRATIC REVOLUTION" (1961)

Reinhard Bendix

This essay re-examines the problem of the political community with special reference to the position of the lower classes.[1] The vantage-point

SOURCE. Reinhard Bendix, "The Lower Classes and the 'Democratic Revolution,'" *Industrial Relations,* Berkeley: Institute of Industrial Relations, October 1961, pp. 91–116. Reprinted by permission of the Institute of Industrial Relations and the author.

[1] The two phrases used in the title demand a brief explanation. By "lower classes" I mean all those persons who have been excluded from political participation in most periods of history up to the development of universal suffrage. They often have few possessions, low income, little prestige, and few legal rights, although these things need not go together. The emphasis is on all those who are excluded from the privileges of a society, and a good many, *e.g.,* women and children, belong to this "class," even though they are not usually considered in these terms. The capacity of this "class" for collective action if any, is a subject for investigation, not a foregone conclusion. By "democratic revolution" I mean the "age of democratic revolution"—with due apologies to Professor R. R. Palmer whose superb book by this title is cited below—that is, the entire period since the French Revolution during which the "lower classes" have become equal citizens. The phrase is similar to Alexis de Tocqueville's term "age of equality" in that it refers to the destruction of previously existing legal, political, and social barriers. Naturally, I

is Western Europe, and the time-period extends from the eighteenth century towards the present. The purpose is to look backward in order to move forward in the comparative study of political and industrial development.

The period from the 1760's to the 1830's witnessed major transformations of Western society: the industrial revolution in England, the political revolutions in the United States and France, and the development of centralized government and national citizenship. The near coincidence of these transformations brought to the fore issues of the political community with which the democratic and industrial late-comers among the nations in Europe and elsewhere have had to grapple ever since. Among these issues the civic position of the lower classes was pre-eminent, in theory and practice, until well into the present century; in the industrialized societies of Western civilization it is pre-eminent no longer. Why? The following analysis attempts to answer this question, however tentatively. It seeks to advance the understanding of our own historical experience so as to improve our ability to cope intellectually with the spread of the "democratic revolution" around the world.

The lower classes were considered a threat to the established order of Europe, and hence a principal social problem, long before economic development had created conditions under which a working class proper could arise.[2] The reason for this preoccupation was the spread of egalitarian ideas at a time when society was still sharply divided into clearly distinguishable social ranks with their separate immunities and autonomous jurisdictions. Locke's idea that all men are born equally unformed, that sense-impressions and education imprint upon them such differences as we find among them, proved to be both the starting-point of the educational reforms of the French enlightenment and a new impetus to the idea of equal rights for all men. The conception of an equality of all men as citizens encouraged the formation of "new social classes" on the basis of common interests, challenged traditional privileges, and thus disrupted the established relations between rulers and ruled. And where "new men" were coming into positions of authority while the

---

am aware that this "democratic revolution" has often made use of "undemocratic" political methods. Since it is confusing to ignore common usage and dispense with accepted meanings of the term, we must distinguish democracy in the sense of [Equality from democracy in the sense of] a viable party system, protection constitutional liberties, and related institutions. By the phrase "democratic revolution" I refer to equality and by "pre-democratic period" I mean the period to the eighteenth century.

[2] Robert Michels has traced this preoccupation back to the seventeenth century in his *Die Verelendungstheorie* (Leipzig: Alfred Kröner, 1928).

lower classes were forced to accommodate themselves to a new position of subordination, the problem of redefining the relation between rulers and ruled, masters and servants, employers and employees, became by fits and starts a national political issue. . . .

POLITICAL COMMUNITY THEN AND NOW

The following discussion will emphasize the great transformation of Western European societies since the eighteenth century and in particular the changing civic position of the lower classes. For reasons discussed in an earlier paper, this transformation should be considered at the political level.[3] I begin, therefore, with as brief a characterization of the medieval and the modern political community in Western Europe as is necessary for background for the major topic of this paper: the changing position of the lower classes.

In medieval political life the exercise of public authority was in the hands of the king and his officials, of individuals who held land by virtue of their fealty relationship to the ruler, or of institutions like the Church which held land and exercised public functions by virtue of special grants of immunity. Landownership and/or a special grant of immunity were the preconditions of the exercise of public rights and active participation in political life. Government authority was indistinguishable from the political struggle, because the right to exercise authority *and* participate in the struggle over the distribution of rights and obligations was based on hereditary privilege, as in the case of noble families (though for a time a new act of homage and oath were required of the recognized heir), or on an institutional immunity, as in the case of the Church or later the municipal corporation. On this general basis the individual enjoyed rights and performed duties by virtue of his status, which could be defined by heredity (especially at the top and the bottom of the social hierarchy) or by membership in an organization possessing certain immunities or liberties. The status of a person typically encompassed *all* his rights and obligations, whether he stood in a personal service relationship or belonged to the Church,

---

[3] Much modern social science, along with Marxism, has denigrated politics and government as phenomena whose explanation must properly be sought in social and economic "forces." For a critique of this approach and a suggestion of an alternative, see my article "Social Stratification and the Political Community," *Archives Européenness de Sociologie*, I (1960), 181–210. The present essay is a sequel to that earlier publication; hence my restatement here is brief.

a municipality, or an association within a municipality. Except for a handful of the most powerful men (and the personal retainers of the king himself) status involved a mediated relation in the sense that the vast majority of persons did *not* stand in a direct legal or political relationship to the supreme authority of the king.

These conditions of medieval political life had a direct bearing upon the position of the lower classes. Because they did not own land, peasants and artisans were excluded from the exercise of public rights and in this sense were excluded from participation in political life. This is not to say that they were deprived of rights; rather, they enjoyed rights and performed duties by virtue of their fealty relationship to a lord or through their membership in an association or corporation possessing a more or less autonomous jurisdiction.

In this setting the rights and obligations of the lower classes provided one important arena for the struggles among politically active groups within society. A standardized example may illustrate the relations involved. Aristocratic landowners insisted upon complete authority over their own vassals as an essential ingredient of rights. In return they paid homage to the king and rendered him the services befitting their station. Rulers in the Middle Ages rarely granted this principle, although they often conceded it in practice. Wherever possible rulers would insist upon a share in the services and payments which members of the lower classes rendered their immediate overlords. The latter resisted this "encroachment" of the king with all the real and ideal weapons at their disposal. Hence a pattern of conflict was built into the traditional norms sanctioning the mediated relationship between the king, his noble vassals, and their lowly peasants. Frequently the burden of this conflict fell heavily upon the lower classes, although on occasion shifts in power relations also increased their rights. Though the rights and obligations of each lower-class person were defined by his status, the incidents of that status were subject, therefore, to modifications resulting from political struggles in which he had no right to participate.

In modern political life, as it has developed in the countries of Western civilization, the exercise of public authority is in the hands of citizens who are constitutionally elected officials of government and of appointed officials. They have authority to the extent that it has been delegated to them. Thus, citizenship, election, and appointment are the preconditions of the exercise of public rights, not inheritance and landownership. Moreover, governmental authority has become separated from the political struggle over the distribution of rights and obligations. The authority of government to exercise public functions is not itself an object of the political struggle because the attempts to shape policy in conformity with specific interests do not as a rule challenge that authority but only its exercise.

Furthermore, politics is no longer a struggle over national sovereignty. Despite some borderline phenomena, sovereignty today is vested in national governments which control foreign relations, currency, military recruitment, taxation, law enforcement, and other areas of public authority. Though policies are much debated, governmental control itself is beyond dispute. And consequently, the individual typically enjoys rights and performs duties by virtue of his status as a citizen, as defined by the national government. All citizens of a modern state hold certain rights and obligations in common and in this sense all citizens stand in a direct legal and political relationship to the supreme authority of state.

These general conditions of modern political life have a direct bearing upon the position of the lower classes. Today, *all* adults who meet certain minimum conditions are entitled to the exercise of basic rights of citizenship. These rights have become the foundation of political life, in which the distribution and redistribution of all rights and obligations *other than those of citizenship and the sovereignty of the national government* are overriding issues. In this setting it is still true that the rights and obligations of the lower classes provide an important arena of the political struggle, but now all politically active groups must take into account the public rights of the lower classes themselves. In the long run this has resulted in the modern welfare state, which underwrites a minimum standard of life for the weaker members of the political community, raises the recognized legal claims of the lower classes, and hence redefines the status of citizenship in their favor. This over-all change is a consequence of the direct legal and political relationship between all citizens and the supreme authority of government.

The contrast between the political community then and now provides the framework for the following discussion. I have suggested—albeit in very broad strokes—that medieval European societies excluded the lower classes from the exercise of public rights associated with land-ownership and, at a time when the authority for such exercise was indistinguishable from political action, from participation in political life. Where lower classes had their status defined by membership in associations and municipalities with immunity and authority to exercise public rights, they enjoyed indirect participation in political life. In both of these cases the lower-class *individual* stood in a mediated relation with the supreme authority of the realm and hence he could seek a redress of his grievances only by petitions submitted to his immediate ruler. As a response of the lower classes to this mediated position, collective protests typically took the form of direct action, whether this consisted in millenarian movements, social banditry, or populist legitimism. A brief survey of these types of protest will be useful, not for what it can tell us about politics in the Middle Ages, but because it provides us with a contrast-conception for the social unrest which followed the French Revolution and ushered in the novel structure of a national political community.

"PRE-DEMOCRATIC" TYPES OF UNREST

In his study of millenarian movements Professor Norman Cohn has shown that from the eleventh century onward popular unrest often involved acceptance of an image of a wholly evil world, as well as a recurrent enthusiastic faith in a new world of perfection in which evildoers would be destroyed utterly while a flock of true believers would come into a realm of perfect goodness and perfect happiness. Within Western civilization this type of response has tended to recur, because the Christian tradition encourages belief in a future fundamentally different from the present. Both despair of the present and hope for the future were couched entirely in religious terms. Thus, medieval millenarianism aimed at a wholly good world to come by virtue of its complete rejection of the existing religious community as defined by the Church.

In the modern world millenarian movements have recurred where Christian ideas have spread along with the political and industrial expansion of Western civilization. In many of these cases the indigenous social structure has been disrupted severely, while the affected population has remained apart from the religious and political community in which these disrupting influences originated. This experience appears to provoke a phantasy-destruction of the powers that be, a psychological withdrawal from all communication with these powers, and a wish-fulfilling belief in the sudden and terrestrial appearance of an age of plenty. Such religious responses have political implications, whether or not they "are" political; they constitute a religious paraphrase of a people's noncooperation with an "alien" and dominant government.

Such noncooperation verges on a second type of social unrest which Professor Hobsbawm has characterized as social banditry. In contrast to millenarian radicalism this is a fundamentally secular and conservative response to physically superior powers, which are conceived of as an alien interference with an established way of life that is as yet independent of governmental institutions. On this basis the social bandit finds illicit support among the peasants of his native village, who will condone his outlawry as long as he adheres to their own social code. Since the character of this local support will vary, however, social banditry may take on a more populist or a more conservative slant. The first is symbolized and idealized by Robin Hood, who resists the law and the government, who robs the rich to give to the poor, and who fuses personal courage and largesse with an implacable ruthlessness that is "justified" by the "evil" of the individuals and powers marked out for extermination. The second consists, in Sicily at least, in a "private government" (*Mafia*) organized with the support of landowners, who use it, albeit at a price, in opposition to the national government in order to support or extend their own dominion over the population.

Both the populist and the conservative variations of social banditry represent rejections of the prevailing political community, but their activities differ from simple crime *to the extent* that the collective support given the outlaws is not itself the product of coercion. As a form of protest against the political community social banditry has declined to the extent that relatively few areas and peoples within Western civilization have remained outside the institutional framework of citizenship.

There is a third type of social unrest, populist legitimism, which consists in violent protests against existing conditions for the purpose of setting to right an established order that has been willfully abused by those who exercise immediate authority. Like millenarianism and social banditry, this third type of protest has recurred throughout European history. But unlike the other types, populist legitimism accepts the established political order.

Though populist agitation easily becomes infused with millenarian elements, *e.g.*, in the peasant wars of sixteenth century Europe, the two types of unrest are distinct. The peasant rebellions of eighteenth century Russia are a case in point. These rebellions were justified on the ground that the Tsar's authority had been abused or that the Tsar who had authorized oppressive measures could not be the rightful ruler. The rebels used the claims made on behalf of the Tsar's authority as an argument against the use to which that authority had been put. By thus appealing to the official creed of the Tsarist order they justified violence on the ground that this order guaranteed the rights even of subordinate groups. Whether or not such claims have a foundation is less important than the belief that they do and that the rulers rather than the people have willfully violated the established order.

This specifically political idea, that customary rights have been abrogated unilaterally, often developed among subordinate groups which were moderately well-to-do, rather than among those living at the margin of subsistence. Men living above that margin have something to lose, are aware of their status and their degradation, and have the aspirations which can provide the basis for concerted action. Hence, they may be reluctant to follow a millenarian movement or practice outlawry simply because their subordinate social position involves a minimum of satisfactions. An appeal to ancient rights that have been violated by rulers may serve to minimize the psychological burdens of a revolt against a social order which is accepted as legitimate, but which particular abuses have made temporarily intolerable. In this sense subordinate groups may have a stake in a political community despite the fact that they are excluded from the exercise of public rights.

Of the three types of popular unrest which recurred in Europe prior to the "age of democratic revolution," the third, popular legitimism, may have been a transitional phenomenon. After the sixteenth century at any rate, the legitimist appeal to ancient rights assumed a new character. For, with the rise of absolute monarchies paternalism was transformed from a justification of domestic relations to an ideology of national government. The king became less an overlord of a feudal nobility and more the supreme ruler of the nation. Under these conditions a popular appeal to ancient rights suggested on occasion that the autocratic ruler who acted as the "father" of his people could rely on their loyalty in his struggle against the estates. The ideology and practices of "enlightened despotism" were in this sense a counterpart of "populist legitimism."

The incipient development of equalitarian ideas was given special momentum during the eighteenth century by economic changes as well as by major changes of intellectual life which are outside the limits of the present discussion. Instead, I wish to focus attention upon the relations between social ranks in this period of transition. To understand the emergence of the modern political community with its equality of citizenship we need a more intimate view of the crisis in human relations which results from the spread of equalitarian ideas in a society in which inequality is taken for granted. A proper understanding of such a crisis will make clear in what sense the "age of democratic revolution" has been going on since it began in eighteenth century Europe. To achieve this understanding was the fundamental concern of Tocqueville's lifework, which will be considered here in terms of his theory of "domestic government."

TRANSITION TO THE "AGE OF EQUALITY"

Tocqueville analyzed the revolutionary crisis of his time in terms of the relations between masters and servants. As a basis for comparison he referred to the "aristocratic nations" of the past, in which stable conditions of inequality had prevailed. In so doing he ignored the types of protest discussed in the preceding section and concentrated his attention upon a model or ideal type of fealty relationship between feudal lords and their personal servants. In such a relation masters and servants felt strongly identified with each other despite the immense social distance between them. The master's influence upon his servants was all-encompassing; from childhood on the servants were accustomed to "the notion of being commanded." In Tocqueville's view such complete domination and submission had important psychological consequences. Through intimate daily contact with the opinions and habits of their servants, the masters came to look upon them as "an inferior and secondary part" of themselves and "by a last stretch of selfishness" took an interest in their lot. And conversely, the servants complacently invested themselves with the wealth and rank of their masters. To make up for their obscurity and life-long obedience they tended to feed their minds with "borrowed greatness" and by means of this personal identification bridged the personal distance between themselves and their masters. Thus, masters and servants thought of each other as an inferior or superior extension of themselves.

In Tocqueville's view the facts and the ideals of this relation between aristocratic masters and their servants were destroyed by the spread of equalitarian ideas. As the social distance between masters and servants decreased, the points of personal disagreement between them sharply increased. In the "secret persuasion of his mind" the master continues to think of himself as superior, though he no longer dares to say so, and his authority over the servant is consequently timid. But the master's authority is also harsh, because he has abandoned the responsibilities of paternalism while retaining its privileges. The servant, on the other hand, rebels in his heart against a subordination to which he has subjected himself and from which he derives actual profit. "An imperfect phantom of equality" haunts his mind and he does not at once perceive "whether the equality to which he is entitled is to be found within or without the pale of domestic service." Obedience is no longer a divine obligation and is not yet perceived as a contractual obligation. The servant consents to serve because this is to his advantage; however, he blushes to obey because where all men are equal subordination is degrading.

Under these circumstances the servants

> . . . are not sure that they ought not themselves to be masters, and they are inclined to consider him who orders them as an unjust usurper of their own rights.
>
> Then it is that the dwelling of every citizen offers a spectacle some-

what analogous to the gloomy aspect of political society. A secret and internal warfare is going on there between powers ever rivals and suspicious of each other: the master is ill-natured and weak, the servant ill-natured and intractable; the one constantly attempts to evade by unfair restrictions his obligation to protect and to remunerate, the other his obligation to obey. The reins of domestic government dangle between them, to be snatched at by one or the other. The lines that divide authority from oppression, liberty from license, and right from might are to their eyes so jumbled together and confused that no one knows exactly what he is or what he may be or what he ought to be. Such a condition is not democracy, but revolution.

Tocqueville wrote this analysis of revolution in "domestic government" in the context of his contrast between revolutionary France and democratic America. The reactions of a hypothetical servant to the idea of equality symbolized by Tocqueville the unsettled conditions of French society in the nineteenth century. If France was to overcome her revolutionary fever and combine liberty with order, she would have to approximate the conditions of settled equality in the United States. There, servants regarded their masters as equals despite their manifest differences, but in lieu of loyalty they acknowledged the obligations of contract. In France, on the other hand, servants displayed neither loyalty nor a sense of contractual obligation. Economic need rather than an unalterably inferior status forced them to be subordinates. But when all men are equal, continued subordination appears to the servants as a blemish on their character (at least initially), while the availability of other opportunities makes them careless of pleasing and impatient of control. Thus the dominant concern of Tocqueville's servant is the consciousness of a position with claims and rights that are not acknowledged by the powers that be. The discrepancy between the servant's legal equality with his master and his subordinate economic position leads to a "confused and imperfect phantom of equality" that obliterates the difference between domestic and civic government. The protest against economic subordination can quickly assume a political character when the servants "consider him who orders them as an unjust usurper of their own rights." This reaction to the changing relations of masters and servants may be considered the basis for the appeal of socialist ideas of natural rights throughout Europe.

Tocqueville's paradigm also implies a second attitude to which a conservative theory of natural rights could appeal. In an earlier society servants either had derived some psychic and material satisfactions from their subordination to great men or such satisfactions seemed appealing in retrospect. Against this background of experience or nostalgia the establishment of formal equality necessarily appeared as a unilateral abrogation of claims and expectations to which the servants felt rightfully entitled. Hence, Tocqueville's paradigm implies the possibility that in an emerging equalitarian society the servants protest against their degradation by seeking to "re-establish" their position under the new conditions. Basically, this is a conservative response. It suggests a belief that the lower class makes a vital contribution to the society; and although this contribution is not a basis for claiming equality with the masters or justifying social reorganization, it is a basis for demanding that the position of the servant be respected as such.

It may be noted that Tocqueville attributed the crisis of "domestic government" to the spread of equalitarian ideas by men of letters. He maintained that in eighteenth century France this diffusion was facilitated by a gradual increase of economic prosperity rather than poverty. But while the diffusion of equalitarian ideas and their inherent revolutionary potential appeared inevitable to him, the actual development depended upon a nation's "moral and intellectual qualities given by nature and education." In contrast to Marx, Tocqueville did not attempt to predict the final outcome of the tendencies he discerned or to explain away ideas by a reference to some ultimate determinant like the organization of production. He sought to account for the frame of mind in which servants rejected the "rules of the game" on which the established society had been founded. To do this he formulated a theory of crisis in the relations of masters and servants: (1) in an earlier condition the socially inferior person possessed a recognized status, *i.e.*, Tocqueville's reference to the sense of "borrowed greatness" among the servants of aristocratic masters; (2) in the crisis of transition the masters retained their privileges but no longer performed their functions, while the servants retained their obligations but perceived new opportunities; (3) in consequence the servants considered that the traditional claims of their status had been abrogated unilaterally and/or that they were now entitled to an equality of rights with all other social ranks since in his capacity as a citizen every man was the equal of every other.

In Tocqueville's view this transformation of domestic government was part of a larger transformation of the political community and his attention was devoted to the ways in which a new reciprocity of rights and obligations could be achieved in the democratic nations. However, my present purpose is to take as my model Tocqueville's theory of crisis in domestic government, because it focuses directly on lower-class protest during the transition that initiated the "age of democratic revolution." To understand the changing position of the lower class in Western Europe it is necessary to recognize as critical the emergence of a national political community in which eventually all adult citizens would participate on formally equal terms.[4] During this crisis the lower classes frequently entered politics under circumstances in which universal adult participation in the political community became a national issue for the first time in history. One way of approaching this "entry into politics" is to contrast the types of lower-class protest characteristic of the predemocratic period of Western European history with the types of protest characteristic of this period of transition. It will be seen that the latter correspond to Tocqueville's characterization of "domestic government" in crisis: a new sense of right on the part of the lower classes, resistance to these claims for civic recognition, and—going somewhat beyond Tocqueville's model—groping efforts to define the position of the lower classes in the national political community. Just as Tocqueville focused attention on a transition in domestic relations, marked by a change in the terms of commands and obedience, so the following discussion will focus attention on a transition in group relations on the national level, marked by changing ideas concerning the rights and obligations of the lower classes.

LOWER-CLASS UNREST BECOMES POLITICAL: ENGLAND

We are accustomed to attribute political changes to economic changes and hence the changing position of the lower classes and the emergence

[4] Those analysts seem to me in error who counter Marx's theory that revolution is the end-product of industrial conflict in mature industrial societies with the observation that conflict is most intense at the beginning of industrialization. For an exposition of this view, see Clark Kerr, Frederick H. Harbison, John T. Dunlop and Charles A. Myers, "The Labour Problem in Economic Development," *International Labour Review*, LXXI (March, 1955), 232–234. Though it is true that industrial conflict has diminished, the argument tacitly accepts Marx's theory of history, according to which conflict is created by the clash of economic interests. The point is, as the following discussion seeks to show, that Marx's theory is wrong also; the frequent intensification of conflict at the "beginning" of industrialization is principally political and it is not industrialization as such but the widening of political participation which is the major issue. The same authors have modified their original thesis in Clark Kerr, and others, *Industrialism and Industrial Man* (Cambridge: Harvard University Press, 1960), and in the article of the same title in *International Labour Review*, LXXXII (September, 1960), 236–250, where they have shifted their emphasis from labor protest to a consideration of "industrializing elites" and the "web of rules" they establish. Yet the original theme regarding the changing position of the lower class is still a relevant issue, and the emphasis on elites and systems of rules cannot be handled intellectually without attention to the political community. However, the authors are by no means alone in the view that all advanced industrial societies are becoming more alike, nor are they singular in arriving at this conclusion by the simple device of ignoring the political process. For a trenchant criticism of this school of thought see Sheldon S. Wolin, *Politics and Vision* (Boston: Little, Brown, 1960), chaps. 9–10.

of national citizenship to the process of industrialization. This line of interpretation was developed at the end of the eighteenth century and appeared plausible in the sense that the revolutions in the United States and France accompanied the rise of bourgeoisie, while the industrial revolution in England led to the political mobilization of an emerging industrial work-force. However, these historical phenomena were made the basis of general principles by which all political events were construed as more or less direct by-products of social and economic processes. Yet today we know that elsewhere political revolutions have occurred in the absence (sometimes because of the absence) of an economically strong and politically articulate middle class, as for example in Japan and Russia. Again, the political mobilization of the lower classes has occurred, not as a result of industrialization, but rather as a prelude to it. Or indeed it has occurred as a means to achieve economic development, as for example in the United States, Italy, Russia, or many economically undeveloped countries today. Changes in the economic and political spheres are closely related, but their influence works in both directions. Hence we get little guidance if we tacitly accept as our model the case of Western Europe toward the end of the eighteenth century, where socio-economic changes did have a massive impact upon the political structure. It is true that democratic ideas and industrial institutions originated under these circumstances, but they have spread around the world ever since in the absence of similar circumstances. National citizenship and modern industrialism have been combined with a great variety of social structures; hence we should recognize democratization and industrialization as two processes, each distinct from the other however intimately they have been interrelated on occasion.

In England these two processes were closely linked. And since the English development has served for so long as a kind of tacit model for an understanding of political and economic modernization it may be well to show that even there it is possible to distinguish the political element in the midst of social and economic change. We saw that prior to the eighteenth century the lower classes might try to wring concessions from the powers that be by a "legitimist" posture mixed with violence; or that they might compensate for their exclusion from the exercise of public rights by millenarian phantasies and banditry. Different forms of lower-class protest became possible, however, after "enlightened despotism" and the philosophers of the Enlightenment had formulated the principle that all men possessed certain fundamental rights. The spread of this idea was certainly facilitated by industrialization, a fact which was recognized early:

> Of the working men, at least in the more advanced countries of Europe,
> it may be pronounced certain that the patriarchal or paternal system

of government is one to which they will not again be subject. That question was decided, when they were taught to read, and allowed access to newspapers and political tracts; when dissenting preachers were suffered to go among them, and appeal to their faculties and feelings in opposition to the creeds professed and countenanced by their superiors; when they were brought together in numbers, to work socially under the same roof; when railways enabled them to shift from place to place, and change their patrons and employers as easily as their coats; when they were encouraged to seek a share in the government, by means of the electoral franchise.

In this statement Mill described a relatively industrialized country and his references to dissenting preachers and the electoral franchise pointed to conditions which were more or less peculiar to England, certainly at this time. But he also noted several factors which have been rather generally associated with the recruitment of an industrial workforce: the literacy of workers, the spread of printed matter among them, physical concentration of work, increased geographic mobility, and the depersonalization of the employment relationship. Mill's descriptive account may be considered equivalent to Mannheim's statement that "modern industrial society"—by physically and intellectually mobilizing the people—"stirs into action those classes which formerly only played a passive part in political life."

Under the influence of ideas of equality this mobilization of lower-class protest came to be oriented, broadly speaking, towards realizing full participation in the existing political community or establishing a national political community in which such participation would be possible. This consideration may be applied initially to some of the popular disturbances in early nineteenth century England. For Marx these disturbances were similar to the sporadic rebellions in which for several centuries peasants and artisans had broken up machines as the most immediate instruments of their oppression. Later writers have shown that this violence was directed against bankers or money-lenders as much as against machines and that despite their obvious agitation the workers of early nineteenth century England showed a most surprising respect for property not directly connected with their distress. By distinguishing in practice between looting and a "justified" destruction of property the workers may be said to have engaged in "collective bargaining by riot" at a time when combinations were prohibited by law. Such evidence is compatible with the idea that the workers who engaged in violence desired at the same time to demonstrate their respectability. They were face to face with a manifest legal inequity; they were prevented from combining for peaceful collective bargaining, while combinations of employers were tolerated or even encouraged. Hence, "collective bargaining

by riot" easily accompanied the demand for civil rights which had been
denied despite acceptance of formal equality before the law.

Though very inarticulate at first, the appeal against legal inequities
came to involve a new dimension of social unrest. To get at the relative
novelty of this experience we have to rely on the circumstantial evidence
of the period. In the late eighteenth and throughout the nineteenth
century the civic position of the common people became a subject of
national debate in Europe. Elementary education and the franchise were
debated for decades in terms of whether an increase in literacy or of
voting rights among the people would work as an antidote to revolutionary propaganda or as a dangerous incentive to insubordination. It is
difficult to know what sentiments these debates aroused among the
people themselves. Faced with the inequity of their legal position and
this public debate over their civic reliability there was naturally much
vacillation. The insistence on ancient rights alternated with violent uprisings against the most apparent causes of oppression; protestations
of respectability, cries for bloody revolution, proposals for specific reforms, and utopian schemes of bewildering variety were all part of the
popular response. But such a diversity of manifestations can have a
common core in the transitional experience which Tocqueville characterized:

> . . . there is almost always a time when men's minds fluctuate between
> the aristocratic notion of subjection and the democratic notion of obedi-
> ence. Obedience then loses its moral importance in the eyes of him
> who obeys; he no longer considers it as a species of divine obligation,
> and he does not yet view it under its purely human aspect; it has to
> him no character of sanctity or justice, and he submits to it as to a
> degrading but profitable condition.

In England this ambivalence was resolved eventually at the political
level by the acceptance of the idea, however variously expressed, that
the people's rights as citizens had been denied unjustly because as working people they had rights by virtue of their contribution to the nation's
wealth.

There are several reasons for accepting the plausibility of this interpretation, even though it may be impossible to prove. One such reason
is that legal inequity and the public debate over the people's civic unreli-
ability were a kind of cumulative denial of their respectability which
occurred just when industrialization and the spread of equalitarian ideas
stirred "into action those classes which formerly only played a passive
part in political life" (Mannheim). On occasion this denial of respectability was even tantamount to a denial of the right to existence, as

in this passage from Thomas Malthus, which became a notorious object of socialist attacks:

> A man who is born into a world already possessed, if he cannot get subsistence from his parents on whom he has a just demand, and if the society do not want his labour, has no claim of right to the smallest portion of food, and, in fact, has no business to be where he is. At Nature's mighty feast there is no vacant cover for him. She tells him to be gone, and will quickly execute her own orders.

Extreme statements like this or like Burke's reference to the "swinish multitude" were made by intellectuals and may not have been widely known among the people at large. However, haughtiness and fear were widespread in middle-class circles, and it is reasonable to expect a growing sensitivity among the people, however inarticulate, in response to this public questioning of their respectability.

Contemporary observers frequently commented on a popular reaction. To be sure, these observers were often remote from working-class life, partisans in the debate concerning the "lower classes," and divided among themselves. Their biases were many, but partisanship can sensitize as well as distort understanding. In England such different observers as Thomas Carlyle, William Cobbett, Benjamin Disraeli, and Harriet Martineau commented on the feeling of injustice among the workers, on their loss of self-respect, on the personal abuse which the rulers of society heaped upon them, on the Chartist movement as the common people's expression of outrage at the denial of their civil rights, and on the workers' feeling of being an "outcast order" in their own country. Such a civic disaffection of the people was regarded with grave concern by prominent spokesmen in many European societies. In retrospect this concern appears justified in the sense that the position of the "masses" as citizens was indeed at issue.

The implicit or explicit denial of the peoples' civic respectability was countered rather naturally by an insistence on people's rights which should not and could not be abrogated. That insistence was founded in the first instance upon a sense of righteous indignation at the idea that labor which is "the Corner-stone upon which civilized society is built" is "offered less . . . than will support the family of a sober and orderly man in decency and comfort." This conception of a "right to subsistence" along with the ideas of "labor's right to the whole produce" and of each able bodied worker's "right to labor" (or "right to a job") were the three inherent or natural rights put in opposition to the contractually acquired rights that alone were recognized by the prevailing legal system. Although the theoretical elaborations of these concepts in the socialist literature do not reveal the thinking of the ordinary man, it is plausible to assume that such theories had an appeal because they asserted the workingman's claims as a citizen.

My thesis is that in England lower-class protests aimed at establishing for the working class full citizenship within the political community, a status which would command the respect which accrued to those who contributed to the wealth and welfare of their country and therefore had a right to be heard in its national councils. Except for occasional outbursts these demands never reached the revolutionary pitch in England that they did on the Continent, and this for several reasons. Throughout much of the nineteenth century England was the leader in industrialization and overseas expansion. Thus the "fourth estate" claimed its rightful place in the political community of the leading nation of the world. Within this favorable context the lower and upper classes continued to use the traditional language of religion in their national debate concerning the status of the "lower orders." If we relate these considerations to Tocqueville's concept of the "crisis of transition" we may infer that in England a new reciprocity of rights and obligations was established eventually at the national level because the idea of such a reciprocity was never entirely abandoned. Though many material factors favored this outcome in the case of England, the alteration of the national balance of right and duties was not accomplished easily even there.

An example from the field of industrial relations may serve to illustrate this retention of reciprocity in the English transition to a modern political community. At first glance, the legal prohibition of trade unions in the early nineteenth century gives no evidence of such reciprocity at all. Such combinations were said to curtail the employer's as well as the worker's formal legal rights, rights which were held sacrosanct regardless of the individual's actual ability to avail himself of them. However, the suppression of combinations was not universal despite this unequivocal legal prohibition. In their survey of early trade unionism, the Webbs concluded that the inefficient organization of the police, the absence of a public prosecutor, and the inaction of the employers were responsible for the widespread occurrence of illegal combinations.

More recently, a publication of documents on the early trade unions has revealed that the employers themselves were often responsible for the spread of trade unions because they would not resort to the legal remedies open to them, despite encouragement from government officials. Apparently, the employers wished the government to institute proceedings against illegal combinations. An opinion of the Attorney General, sent to the Home Secretary in 1804, is of special interest in this respect. The opinion sets forth details of the great evil of combinations among workmen throughout the country, combinations said to be clearly illegal and liable to prosecution. But if the government were to institute the prosecution in the case under consideration, the Attorney General states, applications for similar actions on the part of the government could be anticipated from every other trade, since "combinations exist in almost every trade in the kingdom."

> It will lead to an opinion that it is not the business of the masters of the trade who feel the injury to prosecute, but that it is the business of Government. . . . It must be admitted indeed that the offence has grown to such height and such an extent as to make it very discouraging for any individual to institute a prosecution—as the persons whom he would prosecute would be supported at their trial and during their imprisonment by the contributions of their confederates, and his own shop would probably be deserted by his workmen. But then it is clear that it is owing to the inertness and timidity of the masters that the conspiracy has reached this height, and it may well be feared that this inertness will be rather increased than diminished by the interference of Government. . . . When they once think the punishment of such offences to be the business of Government, they will think it also the business of Government to procure the evidence, and not theirs to give it, so that the future detection and prosecution of such offences would probably be rendered more difficult. Besides . . . the impartiality of Government would be awkwardly situated, if, after undertaking a prosecution at the instance of the masters against the conspiracy of the journeymen, they were to be applied to on the part of the journeymen to prosecute the same masters for a conspiracy against their men.

This opinion is instructive, even though its judiciousness cannot be considered representative.

Whatever their partiality toward the employers, the magistrates were responsible for maintaining law and order. And this task was complicated time and again by the reluctance of the employers to make use of the law which prohibited combinations, by their repeated attempts to induce the government to do it for them, by their tendency to connive in these combinations when it suited their purpose, and finally by their tendency to reject all responsibility for the consequences of their own actions in the belief that ultimately the government would maintain law and order and protect their interests. It is not surprising that the magistrates were often highly critical of the employers, holding that the latter acted with little discretion, that they could well afford to pay higher wages, and that the complaints of the workers were justified even though their combinations were illegal. Sometimes the magistrates even acted as informal mediators in disputes between employers and their workers in the interest of maintaining the peace. Thus, neither the partiality of the magistrates nor the principle of a hands-off policy nor the employers' evident opportunism wholly succeeded in eliminating the principle of reciprocity, even though in practice little was done to meet the workers' complaints except on terms calculated to injure their status as self-respecting members of the community.

In this period of transition Tocqueville saw a major revolutionary threat in the master's continued expectation of servility and rejection of responsibility for his servants together with the latters' claim of equal rights and growing intractability. At the societal level the English case approximates this model. Many early English entrepreneurs certainly rejected all responsibility for their employees and yet expected them to obey; they rejected all governmental interference with management, though they sought to charge government with responsibility for any untoward public consequences of their own acts. Government officials supported the entrepreneurs in many cases because all ruling groups were profoundly concerned with unrest and truculence, as they saw it, among the laboring classes.

But having said this, several reservations must be added which militate against the use of Tocqueville's model in the case of England. There were some manufacturers who acknowledged the traditional obligations of a ruling class. Among some magistrates the principle of noninterference by government was adhered to, as we have seen, by a detached and critical attitude, even in the first decades of the nineteenth century. Finally, the demand for equality of the developing working class was cast in a more or less conservative mold in the sense that on balance it added up to a quest for public acceptance of equal citizenship. In other words, English society proved itself capable of accommodating the lower class as an equal participant in the national political community, though even in England this development involved a prolonged struggle and the full implications of equality as we understand them today evolved only gradually.

B.
Structural Sources of Contemporary Protest

2.

OPEN LETTER ON WHITE JUSTICE AND THE RIOTS (1967)

Lee Rainwater

A great deal of the difficulty in understanding what causes riots and what might be done about them comes from a misunderstanding of exactly what their nature is. A riot seems almost always to begin with an incident in which the police make an effort at enforcing one or another law—whether the culprits involved be a tipsy driver, a traffic law violator, or the operators and patrons of a blind pig. In other words, riots grow out of efforts at social control where society's officials move in on behavior which the informal social controls of the community do not prove sufficient to contain.

As the police go about their business, a curious crowd gathers. The crowd watches what is going on and reflects on it, and some members come to deny the legitimacy of what the police are doing. Rather than responding with satisfaction to the smooth functioning of the social con-

SOURCE. Lee Rainwater. "Open Letter On White Justice & The Riots." *Trans-Action* (September 1967), pp. 22–23, 26–27, 30–32. Reprinted by permission of *Trans-Action* and the author.

trol forces, the crowd members respond with anger and resentment; they identify with the culprits rather than with the law. This identification often takes the form of a belief either that the culprits are innocent, or that they're being treated more roughly than is warranted or just.

The riot develops from this initial incident as the people in the crowd begin to express their anger in response to the situation—they throw rocks at the police, or make attempts to rescue the prisoners. Here they are only acting out the strong and unpleasant emotions stimulated by what they see and the meanings they assign to it. But as this process continues and people talk to each other about what has happened, the matter becomes more ideological—that is, the events are interpreted in an increasingly larger context. The incident becomes an example of a society in which whites do as they please, while Negroes are held accountable for every minor infraction, even those infractions involving behavior that is not really voluntary. For example, a man may get drunk because he is depressed and discouraged about his situation, or he may spend his time on the streets and get in trouble there because he has given up looking for a job. The fury of the rioters is probably exacerbated by their weariness at trying to manage their lives in such a way that they can avoid the attentive ministrations of the social control agents (and these include truant officers, welfare investigators, and personnel officers, as well as the police).

By now the guilt or innocence of the culprits, and the manner in which the police treat them, are no longer that central. Instead, the focus is on the crowd members' general feelings that they live in a world in which they are constantly held accountable to standards of justice which are not applied to others. They feel that the merchants with whom they deal cheat them, that employers are either indifferent or exploiting toward them, that the police are disrespectful and suspicious of them. Therefore, they feel that the police (as representatives of the society at large) are perpetrating the greater evil—an evil by comparison with which the minor peccadillos of the drunken driver, traffic violator, the blind-pig patron are, in human terms, irrelevant.

Further, as incidents like this multiply, and as sophistication about Negro victimization rises in the ghetto community, it becomes increasingly possible to generalize this process without a particular incident. Following the news of the Newark, Detroit, and East Harlem riots in July, a group of Negro teenagers went on a rampage after a rock and roll concert, smashing and looting several of New York's Fifth Avenue stores. They did not need the provocation of an actual encounter with the police to touch off this vivid rejection of legal authority. . . .

Riots are difficult to control precisely because of this voluntary division of labor among the participants. Because their many different sorts of activities require different sorts of responses, the riot becomes a highly complex event that can be brought under control only by a mass show of force (or perhaps by a show of no force at all). This, plus the fact that once the riot gets under way there is almost total denial of legitimacy to the police, means that the area must be *occupied* to be controlled—a process that calls ever further into question the legitimacy of the total society and its laws. The riots elicit from the official world exactly the kind of behavior that confirms the ghetto's estimate of white justice. The trigger-happy behavior of the National Guard and the police and the haphazard way in which arrests are or are not made deepens the conviction that being accorded justice depends more on luck than on the rule of law. The rising hysteria of the fatigued and frightened men in uniform seems to release all of their latent hostility to Negroes. In New Jersey, Los Angeles, and numerous smaller cities the civilian officials have hardly behaved better; it is to the credit of Detroit's Mayor Cavanaugh and his cabinet that no hint of such prejudice and bitterness has been apparent there.

Riots, then, provide different kinds of ghetto dwellers with different opportunities to pursue highly varied goals. The larger the riots get, the easier for individuals to become participants, and probably the more varied the goals they pursue.

In this context, it's quite clear from the data on the social characteristics of those arrested and convicted in Watts that the rioters are probably *not* exclusively "young hoodlums." For example, over half of those arrested in Watts were twenty-five years of age and over and as many as 40 per cent were over thirty. Further, about two-thirds of those arrested and convicted were employed. It is certainly true that those arrested were very familiar with the law; less than 30 per cent of them had no prior arrest. This, however, is not evidence that they are criminals, but only that they live in the ghetto. (Note, for example, that half of those arrested had never been convicted.) We would need more precise data to know what differences there might be between those who form some kind of active core of the rioters and those who take part more casually, by minor looting and the like. It might well be that the active core is more youthful and more solidly involved in delinquent activity than the others. But the most important fact here is that one could not make a riot of any size with the dominant proportion of the participants composed only of "young hoodlums."

There should be no mistake on this point. A very large proportion of the able-bodied members of any lower class Negro ghetto are potential participants in a riot. And, the riot has an ideological meaning for them;

it is not simply a diversion which allows for criminal activity. The man who steals a six-pack of beer or breaks a store window does it not out of "criminal" motivation (it would hardly be worth his while), but because he is expressing some important feelings about his world and trying to put these feelings "on the record." If in the process he can derive some material benefit, like a television set or a new G.E. range, that is all to the good because it makes his point even clearer. Everyone in America knows that money talks. The greater the damage in terms of the financial cost of the looting and burning, the more effectively the point has been made.

But just as a riot provides a wide range of opportunities, it also involves a wide range of costs—primarily those of being killed, arrested, or burned out. It is probably true that stable working class Negroes (who are often as much prisoners of the ghetto as lower class people) are much less interested in the opportunities of riots and more concerned about the costs. They often share the feeling that legal authority is neither just nor fair, but they also have material possessions and social positions to protect. They don't want their homes burned by rioters or strafed by the National Guard. And they are concerned that their children will become involved in the riot—that they will be treated as, and may come to think of themselves as, the "young hoodlums."

Because this more stable working class in the ghetto usually supplies its "community leaders," there is real danger that any investigating committee will be misled into believing that the riots represent the feelings of only a small minority. These "respectable" spokesmen for the area must not be allowed (no matter how honest their personal views might be) to mislead an investigating group in its analysis of the nature of riot participation.

There is always deep conflict and ambivalence in the ghetto over the issue of police protection versus police harassment. The ghetto is a dangerous place for its inhabitants, and they would like to have firm and competent police surveillance. On the other hand, that very surveillance carries with it the danger of unjust and unseemly behavior by the police. Police rationality dictates that anyone in the ghetto is more suspect of crime than anyone in a white middle class neighborhood. From the police point of view, then, ghetto residents should be more willing to cooperate by answering questions and accepting arrest. The conflict built into this kind of situation can perhaps be somewhat ameliorated by more integrated police forces, and by vigorous supervision of the police to see that they are not impolite or overly aggressive. But that is no real solution to the problem.

Further, riots may well become more frequent and larger as time goes on due to the diffusion of knowledge, almost technical in nature, about how a riot is carried on. It is not too fanciful to say that anyone who watches television and reads the newspapers learns from the coverage of Watts, Hough, Newark, Harlem, and Detroit how to participate in a riots. Therefore, *without any organization at all* in the sense of a command structure, people in all parts of the nation know what to do and what roles one might take should a riot opportunity present itself. Millions of Americans today could, on request, fashion Molotov cocktails, who a year or two ago would not have known the meaning of the term. Similarly, millions of Americans now know that many rioters are not arrested and that snipers are seldom caught. There is no way of preventing the diffusion of this knowledge; we can only try to prevent the need and willingness to use it.

Finally, the particular quality of the riots reflects the Negro cultural emphasis on expressivity over instrumentality—practical, goal-directed action. A WASP riot under similar conditions would probably be a much more hard-nosed and certainly much more bloody and violent event. The "carnival atmosphere" noted by observers at all major riots is probably a direct reflection of the expressive emphasis in all group activity among Negroes, whether it be church participation, the blues, a rock and roll concert, or street corner banter.

This is perhaps also part of the key to why the riots seem to be relatively unorganized, both locally and nationally. Discussion of an organized national conspiracy is probably a white projection. Whites find it very difficult to understand why Negroes aren't more efficient in their rebellion—why there is no national cadre, no command structure, no greater efficiency in doing damage. A good part of this may be because this is not the Negroes' preferred way of going about things. Rather, in the midst of an ineffable group solidarity, a kind of free enterprise prevails in which each individual works for himself, perhaps cooperating for short periods of time with others to accomplish some immediate goals, but in the main doing things his own way as an expression of his own feelings. The expressive focus may be very important in formulating an ideology, and thus ultimately have a strong effect on the frequency and nature of rioting. But, that effect is achieved not by *organization*, but rather through *communication* of a developing social doctrine.

Negro expressiveness may also account for the tremendous disjunction between the verbal communication of supposedly violent groups such as RAM and spokesmen for violence like H. Rap Brown, and the fact that organized paramilitary action seems to be virtually absent from the riots. They behave as if they were designed more for display to the white press and titillated or scandalized Negro audiences than for actual committed revolutionary action. I don't think this point about Negro expressive life style is particularly important in understanding or accounting for the riots except to the extent that it helps us understand and get behind the myths that some whites (particularly Senators Eastland and McClellan, the press, and law enforcement agencies) and some Negroes (like Carmichael in Havana) are putting forth. . . .

Much of the popular interpretation of riots has turned on an understanding of the really desperate situation of the worst off in the ghettos, of those who make up the "underclass," which may include anywhere between one-third and one-half of the ghetto population. Again, however, the figures on the Watts arrestees are instructive. Two-thirds of the men arrested and convicted were employed and perhaps as many as one-third of them were earning over $300 a month. Forty per cent (or over half of those who had ever been married) were living with their spouses. Thus, when a riot takes place, a significant portion even of those above the poverty line may well be drawn into participation. This should alert us to the fact that rioting is not exclusively a problem of poverty as currently defined.

One may talk about two major kinds of causative factors—one involving *class* (by which is meant simply economic deprivation and all of the cultural and social consequences that flow from it) and the other involving the inferior *caste* position of Negroes to whites. This latter factor is most directly expressed in ghetto hostility toward the police, but it is also involved in the attack the riots come to represent on the total white-dominated society. Even the Negro who is well off in class terms may feel a strong pull toward participation if he has had the experience of being interrogated and perhaps arrested in a ghetto area simply because his face is black. Where men have little to protect and where their experience of hostility and indifference from the white world is even more pervasive, as in the case of the lower class, the resistance to participation will be even less.

The fact that even a significant minority of the participants are members of seemingly stable families earning above poverty level incomes tells us something about what is involved in exclusion from ordinary American society in a city as prosperous as Detroit or Los Angeles. Whatever poverty as minimum subsistence may mean, it is quite clear that people with incomes as high as $5,000 a year are really not able to feel that they participate in the broad spectrum of average American affluence and satisfaction. A community in which the great majority of the families must exist on significantly less than the median family income for the nation is a community of failures. Inclusion in such a community, compounded as it is by belonging to a historically excluded group and the knowledge that there is a connection between racial exclusion and economic exclusion, is undesirable to those who live within its confines as well as to those outside.

Thus, the ghetto community has few informal social controls; people tend to minimize trouble by avoiding each other more than by building up informal social networks which ensure observance of common group standards. Everybody does pretty much what he wants as long as he can stay out of the clutches of the authorities. Thus, the individual has few effective sanctions available at the informal level. Even those who disapprove of rioting are powerless to do much about it by informally punishing those who participate. Any influence they might have is vitiated by the common perception of all that the authorities are just about as unjust as the law-breakers. Ghetto residents will, in desperation, call upon officialdom to punish those of their fellows who are directly making trouble for them, but they do it in much the same way that one might pay the neighborhood bully to discipline an enemy. The bully is called upon because of his power, not because of any legitimate authority.

The riots bring into high relief the ever present schism in the Negro community between those who feel they have nothing to lose, and those who want to protect what they have—while the former riot, the latter deluge the police and mayor's office with telephone calls demanding protection from the rioters, demanding that the riot be put down before their homes are burned, their community destroyed. The physical contrast in Detroit is particularly striking. Not three blocks from the 12th Street riot area are substantial homes on well-maintained tree-lined streets. Their residents, like other stable working and middle class Negro Detroiters, wanted the riots put down with all possible dispatch; the potential cost of getting even with Whitey was too great.

And then there are the Negro businessmen in the ghetto—the "soul brothers." Detroit's Grand River Boulevard, where the riot-damaged buildings string out for miles, has a great many soul brothers (and one soul mother) whose quickly inscribed signs protected them from damage while on either side the looting or burning seemed complete. But, one can't count the "soul brother" signs that are no longer there because the glass was broken; and an occasional sign is still observable when only one broken show window in a soul brother's store was required to accomplish the looting. The signs obviously provided some protection, but exactly how much they lower the risk is a moot point. If the protection is very high, it would suggest that the hostility of the more prosperous and respectable Negroes is not returned by the rioters; if protection is low the rioters might be saying, as those in Bedford-Stuyvesant are reported to have taunted Negro policemen, "Take off your black masks so we can see your white faces."

Summing up: (1) the root cause of the riots lies in a caste system deeply imbedded in our society that has created a situation in which (a) a very large proportion of Negroes are denied the opportunity to achieve an average American standard of living, and (b) even those Negroes who do, by dint of their own efforts, manage to come reasonably close to an average American standard are still subjected to special disabilities and insults because of their confinement to a ghetto community. (2) From the immediate point of view of the rioters, the most pervasive factor which prevents their achieving some sense of a decent life is that of living in poverty or near-poverty (as a rough rule from, say, having incomes less than one-half to two-thirds that of the median family income for the nation). This economic exclusion affects almost everything they do—their ability to purchase all those elements that make up the "standard package" that most American families deem their right. And the inability to earn more than this kind of poverty or near-poverty income affects the respect they are able to elicit from their own family members, members of their immediate community, and from the society at large.

It seems likely that the starting mechanisms for a riot are fairly dependent on the existence of pronounced poverty coupled with very high rates of unemployment. This, at least, would seem to be important to the extent that young men (say men under twenty-five) have a disproportionate influence on getting a riot going. This group is excluded not only from the availability of something like an average American life, but is excluded even within its own community. The older men do tend to be employed and to earn incomes reasonably close to the poverty line. It is the younger men in the ghetto who are most completely and dramatically excluded from any participation in the conventional rewards of the society.

If this diagnosis is correct—that the direct cause of participation in the riots (as opposed to the precipitating incidents) is economic marginality—it should put us on notice that no "community action" programs, whether they involve better police-community relations or rapprochement with the new black militant leaders, will prevent riots. Rather, the necessary condition for any permanent solution to the riot problem will be to provide a reasonable approximation of the "average American standard of living" for every family. This means managing the society so that poverty and near-poverty are eliminated. Only then can those who now participate in and support the riots find themselves in situations where rioting has become a meaningless, useless activity. This "income strategy" has two principal elements.

The more important of these is creating work. The demand for goods and services must be manipulated in such a way that private and public employers have more jobs which they are willing to offer to relatively unskilled and "undesirable" employees because they need these employees to satisfy the demands for their products. This is the aggregate demand solution to poverty argued by James Tobin, Hyman Minsky, and others. Such a solution has the advantage that it makes maximum use of what is already our main technique for distributing goods and services to families—that is, employment. A further advantage is that an aggregate demand, full employment situation tends to upgrade wages in low wage industries and thus alleviate the problem of near-poverty and poverty among employed workers.

An integral part of this strategy will probably have to be some direct planning by the government to make demand for unskilled workers roughly equal to that for more skilled workers. The most promising suggestions in this area involve the "new careers for the poor" proposals which create new kinds of jobs and avenues for advancement in public service activities. But it is very important that these programs not be developed as programs of "last resort employment," but rather as permanent programs which are productive for the entire society.

It might be well to design crash programs, as well as possible subsidized employment in private industry, for young workers. Such crash programs would be a dead end, however, unless they were part of an overall aggregate demand plus special-programs-for-unskilled-workers strategy.

It follows that the government agencies who should be responsible for solving the problems of the riots are not so much HEW, Labor, and OEO, as they are the Treasury Department, Council of Economic Advisors, and the Federal Reserve Board. OEO-type programs such as the Job Corps, which are designed only to train a small number of lower class individuals to compete more successfully within a system that offers them little or no opportunity as long as they remain unskilled, cannot hope to solve the massive income problems of the whole disadvantaged sector. Unless the power and skills of those agencies which set basic fiscal and economic policy are brought to bear (and backed, of course, by a committed President) it is very difficult to believe that we can solve the problem of rioting—or the more general problem of poverty, and the racial caste system it supports.

The second aspect of the income strategy will involve some form of guaranteed minimum income. We now know that the various particular plans that have been suggested—negative income tax, family allowance, upgraded welfare systems, and the like—all represent variations on a common system of income redistribution (see the work of Christopher Green recently published by The Brookings Institution). The important issue is not so much which of these plans is best as what the guaranteed minimum is to be and what the tax rate on the subsidy is to be. Given the amount of current research activity on income maintenance, the basic technical issues involved in a guaranteed income program will be resolved in the next two or three years. The real question is how we are to muster the political goodwill to put a program into effect.

A guaranteed minimum income program will be crucial for two reasons. First of all, there will always be families for whom the economy cannot provide a reasonable income on a regular and secure basis. Perhaps more important from a political point of view, a national commitment to a guaranteed minimum income will spur the government to maintain employment as fully as possible so that the maximum number of people will derive the maximum proportion of their incomes from their own earnings and not from the national dole. The political vulnerability of any group which over a long period of time derives a significant proportion of its income from government transfers will always be great. Therefore, income maintenance plans can only be a form of family insurance and national political insurance, not a major way of channeling income to families.

A solution to the Negro income problem is thus the sine qua non for a permanent solution to the problem of rioting. With this achieved, tremendous pressure will be generated to move out of the ghetto. I would guess that only a small minority of current ghetto residents would prefer to stay, given a choice. This pressure will itself facilitate the development of desegregated housing; but the government must also facilitate the dispersion of ghetto residents to a more integrated life away from the central city ghettos. That dispersion would to some extent be aided by fair housing laws, but perhaps more important would be the development of government-supported programs for the expansion of middle and lower middle income housing. This would maximize the range of choice available to anyone seeking a better place to live.

It is my belief that it will prove impossible to solve the many other problems of the ghetto until the income problem is solved. Further, I believe that these other problems—education, health, political participation, and the like—would be amenable to very different and much simpler solutions if the Negro families involved had decent incomes.

The ideological developments of the past ten years in connection with the situation of the Negro American pose a challenge to the government and to white society generally. Depending on how this challenge is met, we will move more slowly or more quickly toward the basic economic solutions offered above. I see the vague and often contradictory militant civil rights ideology which has developed over the past few years as a result of two factors. First, as the nation has become more prosperous, it has become increasingly obvious that it is not necessary to have a deprived and excluded group in our midst. The dynamics of affluence themselves call into question the old caste-like racial arrangements. As some Negroes participate in that prosperity, and as they look on the tremendous affluence of white society, there is a strong push in the direction of forcing the society to accord Negroes their share. This factor was perhaps the dominant influence in the early period of the new civil rights consciousness that started in the early '60's—suddenly it seemed ridiculous to most Americans that anyone should be excluded when we have so much.

Second, and more recently, has come a new wave of black populism. The common theme running through many of the ideas of the new black militants is that Negroes have a right to their own future and their own place in the sun, not just in economic terms but as full men in society. The emphasis on blackness is a reaction to the price that white society seems to want to exact for economic payoffs, a price that seems to involve a denial of oneself as Negro and to require a tame imitation of whatever the going definition of the proper white person is. Now there is a lot of nonsense these days about what Negro culture involves and what black autonomy might mean. But, at the core of the black populist movement is a denial of the right of whites to define who the Negro is and what he may become. This is not only healthy, but much more realistic than the earlier, simple-minded integrationist myth that dominated civil rights activity for so long.

There are now, and will probably continue to be for some time, conflicts between moving toward the economic goals of the civil rights movement and the black populist goals. The political challenge for white society is to thread its way through these conflicts without denying the validity of either factor, and to select those areas in which the government can further the Negro goals (to my mind, principally the economic area) and those areas in which the main effort at constructing a new social reality will have to be made primarily by Negroes themselves.

The danger here is that the reaction to the black populist goals on the part of the government and whites generally will be so hostile that Negro leaders who emphasize such aims will be progressively alienated and provoked into activities destructive to both sets of goals. In the main, however, the mutual alienation and viciousness that has tended to dominate the civil rights–white power structure dialogue for the past two years is more a result of the government's unwillingness to make major economic commitments than it is of any inherent tendencies in the black populist movement.

In short, the government cannot give Negroes a black culture or a black consciousness, but it can manage the society in such a way as to give them a "black affluence." If the government does not do what it can do, then we can only expect the courageous and the committed in the Negro community to become more aggressive and more destructive toward the larger society which has the necessary means, but refuses to use them.

3.

STUDENTS AND POLITICS (1967)

Philip G. Altbach

For more than a century, student movements have had an important place among the agents of social change. In some nations, students have succeeded in toppling governments or changing policies. In others, they have been instrumental in various kinds of cultural revivals. In the new nations of Asia, Africa, and Latin America, students are often instrumental in political, social, and cultural development. Students have provided inspired leadership to national liberation movements, political parties, and on a more mundane level, labor organizations and cultural groups. Not only have the leaders of the new states frequently come from student ranks, but the ideological base of many of the new societies has been influenced by the student movement.

While the organizational manifestation of student concern is the most dramatic indication of the power and importance of the student community, the day to day life of the student in these societies is also crucial to their development. The values which are obtained during the process

SOURCE. Philip G. Altbach, "Students and Politics," Chapter 3 of *Student Politics*, edited by Seymour Martin Lipset. New York: Basic Books, Inc., 1967. Copyright 1967 by Basic Books, Inc. Reprinted by permission of Basic Books, Inc., and the author.

of higher education and the quality of that education will inevitably have an impact on nations which have a very small reservoir of trained manpower.

While students in the industrially advanced nations of the West are important, their numbers are large and the society is sufficiently well developed so that the fate of an individual student or even fairly large group of students is not crucial. In most new nations, however, students often form an "incipient elite." In many of these societies, students assume political responsibility even before finishing their studies, thus bringing national politics onto the campuses in a very direct way. Governments are therefore conscious of the student population, trying to influence it or perhaps repress some of its leaders. It is hard to imagine that the head of a Western nation would engage in a protracted debate with student leaders in order to insure the loyalty of the student union. Yet, the President of the Ivory Coast recently engaged in just that kind of dialogue with student leaders, arguing with them, and finally threatening to suspend their government scholarships in order to insure the loyalty of the student organization. Because the government has financial and political power at its command, it can usually impose its will on the students. If all else fails, governments can, as has happened in Burma, close the universities for extended periods. The fact that governments in many of the new nations must either argue with or force the students to accept their policies is an indication of the potential power of the students.

The student population in many of the developing nations is numerically small, and is often very much cut off from the rest of its peer group by vastly differing experiences, "Western" ideas, and educational opportunities. This alienation from the peer group, as well as from the mainstream of the traditional society in many cases, often makes the student community self-reliant and at the same time unsure of its roots. In addition, students often have to develop their own traditions, since established patterns of "modern" educational political, and social behavior in many new states have not as yet evolved.

Although substantial attention has been given to the student organizations and higher education in the new nations, much of what has been said has been little more than uninspiring exhortation or political rhetoric. Obviously one must carefully analyze the student community, a vital segment of the population of the new states. Moving beyond the clichés of the politicians and the limited proposals of educators should enable us to apply historical and sociological principles to the consideration of the student population and its organizations.

CHARACTERISTICS OF STUDENTS AND STUDENT GROUPS

While the concept "student" has existed in the modern sense of the term since the Middle Ages, the individual student lost much of his importance in the West in an era of mass education. In medieval Europe, the student had something of an elite status with its accompanying freedom and prerogatives. Now, in the new nations, modern Western systems of higher education are being grafted onto traditional societies, recreating, in some aspects, older patterns of student life.

Studentship is a transitory state, usually lasting only three or four years, though perhaps extended by graduate study. While some student leaders have prolonged their affiliation with the student community, for the vast majority academic life is a short, although often highly intensive period. This makes the existence of on-going organizations and sustained leadership almost impossible. The problem is further aggravated by the fact that student participation in a movement is sporadic, for extra-curricular activity becomes difficult to pursue when the pressure of examinations grows intense, or when official disapproval is manifested. Moreover, because the student feels he is in a period of transition, he often does not develop deep ties to the student community. Academic life is seen as a brief way-station on the road to economic advancement by many, while for others it is a time of unparalleled freedom. The important difference in orientation between the generally career-minded and therefore apolitical science and professional students and the more intellectual orientation of many liberal arts students has had vital implications. A number of studies have pointed out that, in many nations, liberal arts students constitute the key element in political movements.[1]

The student days are one of the few times in the life of an individual when he is not burdened by financial or social responsibilities or subject to outside control. The concept of adolescence does not exist in many traditional societies; there is simply an abrupt transition from childhood to adult life. The young person anticipates with pleasure the freedom of his student career; however, he is often unprepared for this freedom. Relative freedom from parental and familial control, from financial responsibility (in some cases), and from outside work combine to make the academic environment a heady experience for many young people. Furthermore, many realize that the student years mark the end of youth and that adult responsibilities will necessarily follow graduation from the university.

Because of their freedom, students can often afford to take risks which others in the society, saddled with family and other responsibilities, cannot take. It is partly for this same reason that the student community is considered less corrupt than any other segment of the society. In the public image, student politics are supposedly unmarred by considerations of partisanship or personal material gain. In many nations, students have attempted to take upon themselves the leadership of the working classes, who are often unable to speak for themselves and have no tradition of organization. Students also have the reputation, perhaps justified, for having greater ideological "purity" than other elements in society, and it is true that they can often approach society without the biases of vested interests or social constraints and with a relatively high degree of intellectual honesty. They are relatively free agents in their thought and actions, often having the security of future employment because of their education and position in the elite class.

It is no coincidence that students have often been in the vanguard of revolutionary movements in various countries. The Russian student movement provided an important impetus to revolutionary activity, and students in Burma, India, Korea, and other nations have been a leading element in independence movements. Participation in revolutionary movements is often part of the generational conflicts which are so often evident among students. Advocacy of drastic social reforms is often seen as a means of fighting the authoritarian influence of the traditional family.[2] Because of their lack of outside responsibility, their openness to modernizing ideologies, and their desire to create a better society, students are often involved in social movements.

Because students deal with ideas and intellectualized concepts in their academic work, they are better able to understand abstract ideological systems than are persons who regularly work in concrete "non-intellectual" situations. As a result, students are often more receptive to ideologically oriented movements and causes. Having little or no experience in practical politics or the problems of economic development, they are often more naive about the key issues facing their societies, and are more likely to seek all-encompassing solutions to societal problems than are their elders. Because of this intellectual interest and urge to systematize, students seek an ideological system which will provide them with a *weltanschauung*, a guide to thought and action. Both left and right wing ideological movements have traditionally found strong student support, although in the developing nations the left far outweighs the right in popularity and influence.[3] This natural interest in intellectualized ideological systems has been an important factor in stimulating the growth of student movements and in providing them with some enduring impetus. In the non-student world, organizational initiative can help keep a movement alive. On the student level, ideological convictions among succeeding generations of students must suffice because of the rapidly changing nature of the student population.

In addition to the freedom which is naturally a part of student life, many societies, both traditional and advanced, have taken a permissive attitude toward student values and activity. Political acts which would be subjected to severe government repression if performed by labor unions or other groups, often go unheeded if done by students. The concept of "sowing wild oats," restricted to pranks in the United States, extends to politics in many nations, where it is assumed that students will take an active and often volatile role in politics. This tradition of intellectual, political and physical freedom which students enjoy in many societies acts as a reinforcing element to the student movement, permitting it to act with relative impunity. Understandably, the student community often has very little in common with other young people. For many college students in the developing nations college life is the first non-family experience. Physiologically and psychologically, the period of adolescence is one of adjustment and change, and this cannot but have repercussions on the educational, social, and political attitudes of the students. The need for independence and self-expression are great during this period, and the tendency toward rebellion against authority, particularly that represented by the father, is marked. Studies of youth in Japan and in India indicate that many of the same factors which have been documented in the West also operate in non-Western societies.[4]

In addition to the factors which lead the individual student in a political direction, there are various pressures on the student population which also drive in this direction. The existence of a large number of students at one location, with similar interests, and subject to similar stimuli from the environment, gives a powerful impetus to organizational activities of all kinds. It is difficult to imagine a more cohesive community from which to recruit members. The intellectual ferment which takes place as a natural result of the academic setting is also influential in moving students to action. While only a minority of any given group of students is likely to be interested in politics (or any other extra-curricular subject), the presence of substantial numbers of students in a single location tends to create a numerically significant group of dedicated and committed politicized students, even though the percentages involved may remain relatively small.

Communications within the student movement are usually quite good, especially when the majority of the students in a given area are congregated on one campus. Thus, when external conditions or ideological issues move students to action, it is easy to create a substantial movement in a relatively short time. Expensive and complex newspapers, radio programs, etc., are unnecessary; all that is needed is a mimeograph machine and a few strategically placed posters. It is difficult to overestimate the value of good communications in the development of student movements. Even in totalitarian societies, the students are one of the most difficult groups to control partly because of the ease with which they can communicate among themselves.

The sense of community which is often built up by the students because of their similarities in background and outlook and their common environment provides a basis for a student movement or organization. Without this sense of community the students would be unable to participate in political and cultural affairs to the extent that they have in the new nations. Indeed, there are indications that as the student population becomes larger and less homogeneous, it is more difficult to organize large scale student movements. In India, for example, as higher education became available to young people from middle and lower middle class backgrounds and the educational institutions expanded at a rapid rate, the student community lost its cohesive quality and it has been more difficult to organize the students.

Students have often been united by a common alienation from traditional patterns of society. Students are often one of the few representatives of "Western" culture and ideology in their societies. The structure and content of their educational institutions are largely imported, and many of their teachers are either foreigners or foreign-educated. There is much vacillation between tradition and modernity in the student community.[5] Intellectual trends often push the students further from traditional cultural and social patterns. As a result of these factors, the students feel alienated from and superior to their families and the society at large, but at the same time they feel guilty because of their rejection of the "true" values of their culture. While this alienation often disappears as the student takes his place in his society, it is an important factor during the student period.

This very sense of alienation serves to unite the student community. Alienation also has a politicizing effect, in that the values of the "modern" Western ideologies are often combined with elements of traditional culture to form the basis of new ideological movements. Elements of "African Socialism," 19th century Indian revivalism, and other ideological tendencies are part of this phenomenon. Regardless of the result of the sense of alienation, it is true that it is a powerful force on the students of the developing nations. Notions of deracination and cultural regeneration are recurrent themes in student discussions in many of the new states. Thus, regardless of the truth in the notions, they are important influences on students' thinking, and hence on their actions.[6]

The student population also provides an organizational base for student political and social action. Student unions and other organizations which have been set up by educational authorities or governments often provide a meeting place for students interested in ideological discussions or cultural activity. Often, more radical groups grow out of these "official" organizations. Even in totalitarian societies, the "official" youth movements often provide the basis for dissenting groups of various kinds. Much of the impetus for the political ferment in Poland in the late 'fifties came from the Polish student movement and its publications, which were officially sanctioned by the government.[7]

Despite the fact that students in the developing nations are usually privileged people and have a much higher standard of living than the average citizen, the student is often under severe pressure during his academic career. Sometimes economic, but more often academic or social, these pressures help to determine the scope and intensity of student social action. The most direct pressure on the student is from the educational institution itself. The need to pass the periodic examinations, to keep up with course work, and to achieve a high academic status are some of the main worries of any student. The educational institution often demands an outward show of loyalty from its students and occasionally asks for ideological and social conformity from them. In nations where university graduates are threatened by unemployment, and the quality of the instruction is perceived by the students as inadequate, there is likely to be a good deal of underlying discontent. There is often a substantial difference in student attitudes and involvement in politics from faculty to faculty within a university. In India, for example, academic standards and employment prospects are much better for science and technological students than for those in the liberal arts, and it is true that science students are not often involved in student "indiscipline." Where the academic program is challenging, the pressures of the university on the students (in the direction of academic excellence, for instance) are usually seen as justified. In faculties where a good deal of ambivalence about the future and a realization that standards of education are inadequate exists, there is likely to be discontent.

Academic standards and methods of university administration vary greatly in the developing nations. While some nations have worked hard to maintain educational standards and limit enrollments, other have engaged in rapid expansion of educational institutions with an accompanying lowering of standards. It is clear that educational policies imposed by governments have an important impact on the students, and that the nature of student organization is often determined by educational standards in various faculties, employment prospects, and other external factors.

Most traditional societies are family-oriented; the individual may be primarily a member of his family rather than a citizen of the state or nation. The family can and often does apply pressure on the student. Representing the traditional values in the society, the family may influence the student toward social conformity, adherence to traditional social and religious ideas, and retention of traditional values. In any case, the pressure from traditional elements within any society is often one of the major sources of stress in the life of the student.

While the government usually exercises a rather nebulous influence on the individual student, it can on occasion become a major force in his life. Government educational policies, particularly in the developing nations, have a profound impact on the educational system and, consequently, on the lives of individual students. Government pressure for political conformity, censorship and suppression affect the students. Since the latter are often impatient with the slowness and ineffectuality of government efforts in economic development, there is often opposition to the established regime. Government also represents the older generation, and in many cases, provides an obstacle to ambitious student leaders seeking quick advancement.

Politics exercise a strong attraction and a potent pressure among students. As a general rule, the political groups cannot apply the kind of direct pressure of which the educational authorities and the government are capable. In many of the developing nations, political issues have caused student uprisings and agitational campaigns. Students have sacrified their educational future in order to participate in political movements and such organizations on university campuses consume a great deal of time and energy. While it is difficult to include politics as another "pressure," it is often a major preoccupation of the student community.

Ideology attunes the student not only to the broader issues of his society, but makes him more willing to participate in campus-based movements. It is often true that an agitational campaign against an increase in university fees, ostensibly a campus-based issue, will be led by ideologically committed students. During the various struggles for independence and national liberation, students left the universities in substantial numbers to participate in labor and peasant movements as well as directly in the independence struggle. While not consisting of direct physical pressure on the student community, ideology and political movements provide the pressure and stimulus of ideas and all-encompassing answers to some of the important questions facing the developing nations.

The environment of the individual student usually provides pressure. Indeed, much of his behavior, and his ideological views as well, are shaped by his environment. Many students suffer from financial hardship during their educational careers and have to live in poor conditions. In many cases, college facilities are poor and do not provide even the basic necessities for higher education. Inadequate libraries, badly trained staff, and outmoded buildings mark many colleges in the developing nations. The impact of these conditions cannot but have an important influence on the student, his attitudes, and naturally his educational attainment. Students from the working and new middle classes, whose experience with Western values is shorter and whose families can ill afford the expense of a college education are usually affected by these factors most. The threat of unemployment hangs over the heads of many college students in the new nations, and this fear naturally has implications for the individuals involved.

STUDENT ORGANIZATIONS AND MOVEMENTS

Before discussing the "student movement" one must adequately define the term. It is not a fraternity, a social club, an academic society, or an extra-curricular cultural group, although under certain circumstances, it may encompass the activities and functions of such groups. We may define a student movement as an association of students inspired by aims set forth in a specific ideological doctrine, usually, although not exclusively, political in nature. A student movement may be generated by emotional feelings often associated with inter-generational conflicts, although it may also be motivated by positive goals; the members of a student movement, moreover, have the conviction that, as young intellectuals, they have a special historical mission to achieve that which the older generation has failed to achieve, or to correct imperfections in their environment.[8] A student movement is a combination of emotional response and intellectual conviction.

The student movement is almost invariably expressed in organizational terms, although not all student organizations are "movements." It is true that almost every student community has a nexus of organizations which involve individuals in various activities. These organizations exist regardless of the political composition of the student community or the form of government or educational authority which exists in the society.

There are, furthermore, numerous types of student organizations, many of which have overlapping memberships. Groups range from large officially sponsored organizations to clandestine informal study circles.

Almost every college or university abounds with various "official" student organizations, devoted to manifold causes. In many institutions, officially recognized student unions are an integral part of the university community and in some places, notably Latin America, students have a constitutional voice in academic affairs. Extra-curricular social, cultural, or service organizations also involve many students. These groups provide a potentially valuable adjunct to the education of the participants, and it is common for them to be financially aided by the university administration or by the governments concerned. These groups are often formed by the university authorities for specific purposes and are subjected to strict supervision. The popularity of such groups varies and it is a fact that many of the "official" student groups have minimal support or participation.

In many nations, an attempt has been made to create movements on the basis of the official student groups; however, such efforts have usually been unsuccessful. It is also true that educational administrators or government officials frequently try to use these groups to forestall or compete with student protest organizations which oppose the authorities. Almost without exception, the official student organizations become a natural and logical training and recruiting ground for political leadership. Occasionally, the official student groups develop into militant student movements, sometimes opposing their patrons. At different periods, the influence of these groups has varied from country to country; nevertheless, through sheer size and power, the official student organizations usually constitute an important part of the organized student community.

In addition to the official groups, most universities support a multitude of voluntary extra-curricular organizations. These are often recognized by the university authorities and may be required to have a faculty member as advisor, but they are usually student administered. Because they have no official patronage, they stand or fall on their own merits; the average life-span of many of them is very short. These organizations range from purely social gatherings to those devoted to politics, social service, discussion and debate, athletics, dramatics and culture. Many are organized by the members of a particular religious or linguistic community as social and cultural centers.

These organizations do not as a rule constitute movements, although they sometimes inspire more militant and massive organizational efforts. Students from a particular religious minority may, for example, in the course of discussions within an approved student group, formulate a broader religious or political creed which leads them to collaborate with or form a mass movement. Similarly, the political ideas which are discussed in such an organization can easily lead to more radical organizational activity.

Finally, there are often various kinds of unofficial and unapproved student organizations existing at a given university. Student movements are more often started by such groups than by the official organizations. Such unrecognized groups are often devoted to political issues or ideologies and are often militantly opposed to the power structure of their society. Some, however, may be of purely social nature, such as fraternities in the United States. The student "underground" may never reach an insurrectionary or an active stage; yet it undeniably plays an important part in influencing its membership even at the discussion-group stage.[9]

The membership of such unapproved student groups is in general much smaller than the approved organizations, although this is often compensated by a high level of commitment from the membership, and a great deal of loyalty to the peer group. These associations are sometimes, but not always, affiliated to or under the influence of outside organizations, such as political parties or larger student movements. Members of highly disciplined clandestine student groups may hold high offices in "respectable" groups, thereby enhancing their influence.

All of these types of student organizations can be important in specific situations, and it would be a mistake to overlook aspects of seemingly respectable groups in any evaluation of a student movement. There is often a good deal of interaction between these various elements of the organized student community, a fact of primary importance in investigating the web of personal contacts and ideologies within the student community. The overlap of membership in various types of organizations is often substantial, and there is often an accompanying overlap of ideas. Infiltration of official student groups by the student "underground" is not uncommon and often accounts for the radical nature of ostensibly respectable organizations. Thus, the ideology of the unofficial student organizations can permeate the entire student community without much difficulty regardless of the wishes of university officials.

A student movement need not have as its goal violent political change; it can, for example, press for a "cultural renaissance" within a society. It may also be concerned solely with educational or campus issues, without involving individuals or issues from the broader society. Thus, in searching for the roots of a student movement or agitational campaign, it may be fruitful to examine all organizations, not only the militantly politically motivated student groups, bearing in mind, however, that movements of a militant nature more often than not arise from ideologically committed groups.

Regardless of the type, function, or size, student groups are notoriously unstable. This is due mainly to the rapidly changing nature of the student population, but also to the changing interests of the students themselves. Even the large groups with lavish government support often lose much of their leadership and support in a short time due to changes in the interests of the students or the loss of key leaders. The clandestine organizations are still more vulnerable to changes in the winds of the student community or of the society at large. It is possible with intelligent student leadership and by careful planning and leadership training to insure a relatively long period of organizational continuity. In the last analysis, the transitory nature of the student groups is one of their dominant characteristics and a key element in the understanding of the student community. Even seemingly stable and militant student movements can lose their popular support in a short period; internal disputes and factional disagreements can destroy the core of leadership in a matter of days, and administrative restrictions can cause serious difficulties. Other factors, such as a university examination, a diverting event in the broader society, or the arrest of key student leaders can temporarily destroy a student organization or movement. Yet, it is entirely possible for a movement to recoup its losses in a very short time, thus suggesting that its ideology and program have survived a temporary organizational setback.

In recent years, there has been a growing realization of the importance of student activity in both educational and political development in many of the new nations.[10] Because of the fact that student political movements have had a dramatic influence in some of these nations, attention has been focused on them. It is possible to state, in capsule form, some of the general causes for student action which have been pointed out in recent studies, as well as those which have been observed in various student movements. Such an enumeration will help give an idea of the causes of student action.

It is almost a truism that the university is greatly dependent on its environment. The student community may be aroused or swayed by events in the outside world. Political leaders often take a direct and active interest in the students, occasionally guiding or exploiting student movements. It has been mentioned that the various national liberation movements received substantial support from the students. The struggle for independence influenced the university campus and transformed many universities into battle grounds for extended periods of time. Cultural trends in the society can also have an impact on the students, as can international events, economic crisis, or religious strife. The student is also influenced by his future prospects for employment and prestige in the society.

A tradition of independent political and social action among the students can help to determine the nature and direction of the student movement. Where the student community has few traditions to fall back on, its response to external events is unpredictable and inconsistent; where there is a tradition of apoliticism among the students, even severe social crisis often fails to move the students to action. Thus, the historical roots of the system of higher education and the student population itself both play an important part in the development of the student movement.

It is unlikely that movements stimulated by specific or isolated events will be able to sustain themselves over a long period of time. One would expect to encounter less ideological sophistication or broad political concern in them than in movements founded by politically conscious students with long range goals in mind.

These "spontaneous" movements may arise when the student movement feels directly threatened or challenged. The cause can be an imposed fee increase or an unusually difficult examination. In the past, administrative censorship, suppression or condescension have instigated demonstrations. Once students have taken action on some issue, it is difficult for them to quietly return to their routine academic life after having experienced the exhilaration of political agitation and contact with the centers of power in the society.

In the recent past much student unrest has been collectively described as "indiscipline," as the result of immaturity or the ever-present generational conflict. While it is true that much of the violence which takes place on the campus is a result of one or the other of the above factors, students often have legitimate grievances, and are capable of expressing their concern in a disciplined and at times effective manner. They are often in the vanguard of the political and social movements of their nations and their actions frequently reflect sensitivity to social reality rather than immaturity.

Students are driven by many motives, some of them contradictory. By using a variety of approaches, it may be possible to define these motives. Psychological examination and depth interviews will reveal facets of student behavior which an historical analysis of student activity could not, and sociologically oriented attitude surveys have much relevance. Yet, it would be a mistake to suggest that psychological and sociological methods are the only valid means for analyzing student movements, just as a sole dependence on historical analysis would be inadequate.

An examination of the student movement alone is insufficient to obtain a total picture of the student population. The social class background of the students will in part determine their attitudes toward education and occupation. Caste or tribal affiliations also influence student attitudes. The relationship between the student and society can also have an impact on the nature of the movement, since students will not tend toward political activism when there are few external causes for discontent. Where the society is marked by generational tension or by economic discontent, student political activism is more likely.

These are various types of student political activity which have been important in the new states. Each type is a response to a specific grievance or aimed at a particular goal. One important distinction is the difference between norm and value oriented student political action. Norm-oriented student movements generally aim at the correction of a specific grievance or at a particular goal, and do not often have broader ideological overtones. The norm-oriented movement is unlikely to maintain itself after its goal has been attained, although, as has been noted, such movements often provide an impetus for further activity.

ORIENTATIONS OF STUDENT GROUPS

While the norm-oriented movement is concerned with specific goals and is more likely a product of an emotional response to a specific limited issue, the value-oriented movement is concerned with broader ideological issues, and when it is involved in concrete actions, this activity is usually linked directly to a broader concern.[11] Most revolutionary political movements are value-oriented, and most of the on-going student political organizations, particularly "underground" groups, are value-oriented. A value orientation does not prevent students from participating in limited campaigns or agitations, although such participation is usually done for reasons transcending the specific objective. In the student community, a value-oriented movement has a more important influence in the long run, and is often a leading element in apparently norm-oriented actions. Both types of groups, the norm-oriented "cause-group" aimed at reducing fees or securing a change in college administration, and the value-oriented political organization committed to doctrines of Marxism, Hinduism, or other ideological concepts, exist side by side in the student community. Naturally, there is some overlap between these two types of groups and it is often difficult to make a clear distinction between them, since the leadership of a group which is seemingly norm-oriented may be ideologically sophisticated and able to turn the attention of the participants to broader issues.

What starts as a limited protest against some isolated issue may easily turn into a sustained movement, with concerns extending to the broader society. The leadership of the student movement is notably fluid, and it is very possible for a norm-oriented leadership to be supplanted by students interested in capitalizing on a particular movement for their broader political purposes. Thus, while the norm and value orientations offer some convenient models to work from, student movements often defy a tight definition of either category and care must be taken in applying these labels to various student movements and organizations.

In addition to the distinction between "norm" and "value" oriented movements, there is a related series of factors which can influence the direction of student organizations. A student movement may be concerned only with "campus" issues and have relatively little interest or impact on the external political situation. Such movements have been called "etudialist" because of their primary student orientation. They are often quite militant over issues of student welfare, fee increases, and administrative harrassment of students. They are occasionally interested in the broader issues of educational policy and reform, although generally student interests are confined to more limited areas. Contrasted to such movements are society-oriented student movements, which are concerned with societal issues-usually political, although occasionally social or cultural.[12]

There are similarities between the norm-value distinction and the "etudialist"-society orientation of the student movement. It is usually true that student organizations or movements interested in broader social issues are motivated by value orientations, although this is not always the case. Student groups affiliated to political parties usually have a value orientation and are often concerned with broader political issues. Yet, it is important to keep these two sets of criteria clear, since it is possible for student movements to manifest differing orientations over a period of time. The Zengakuren, Japan's militant student organization, is clearly a value-oriented student organization, adhering to extreme leftist ideological views.[13] Yet, this organization has alternatively taken part in "etudialist" and societal activities during its post-war history. Thus, while its orientation has been value directed, it has switched its tactics on a number of occasions to meet the needs of the students and/or of its political ideology. The Indian student movement shows similar examples of this relatively facile change of tactics. The Communist-sponsored student organization, the All-India Students' Federation, clearly a value-oriented movement, has alternatively taken part in broader political issues under the direction of the Communist Party and has participated in campus-oriented activity when such action has served its needs or has become of importance to the students. It is also possible for norm-oriented student groups to take part in societal activity. At various Indian universities, students have taken part in outside politics when such action has been deemed necessary to fulfill a student demand. Pressure on political leaders often can lead to amelioration of a campus problem.

These distinctions are often blurred, and are hardly ever clear in the minds of the students themselves. Yet, they are valuable tools for gaining an understanding of a specific student movement. The issue is further complicated by the fact that the orientation and direction of student organizations can and often do change rather radically in a short period of time. These changes usually occur in a relatively disciplined manner, and a knowledge of the general orientation of the movement can help to predict its direction, or can lead to a further understanding of its motives and goals.

Student political activity often contains an important non-student element, which sometimes provides direction and ideological sophistication to the movement. In most societies, the student community consists not only of students currently enrolled in institutions of higher education, but also of ex-students or part time students who wish to remain on the periphery of the student community. While a student *per se* may only remain at an institution for four years, non-student elements in the student community often remain for longer periods of time, providing something of an historical sense to the student movement. Political parties often assign young activists to the student work and seek to expand their influence in this way. Part of the "underground" of the student population, these elements cannot be overlooked as they are often of crucial importance to student movements.

FUNCTIONS OF STUDENT MOVEMENTS

The student movement, in addition to meeting certain emotional and intellectual needs of the students, also has a number of important functions within the framework of education and political development in the new nations. Student cultural and social organizations are often important sources of academic knowledge, since they sponsor well-attended lectures and other programs. These organizations provide the student community with one of the few opportunities for serious discussion and a chance to meet informally with professors and other academic persons. University authorities often try to include the "extra-curriculum" as an important part of the educational experience of the students, although quite often these groups are left to student initiative. In some cases, Western ideas are engendered through the activities of such groups. The various debating societies which are popular give valuable training in parliamentary methods, public speaking, and often in politics as well. The religiously based student groups often give the student a new insight into and perhaps identification with his religious tradition. Literary groups are sometimes as effective as formal courses in literature in providing the students with a background in this field.

One of the most important educational aspects of the student organizations is concerned with politics. Where they are permitted, most universities have active political discussion groups. Where there are constraints on student organization, such discussion groups often operate underground on a smaller scale. Such groups are usually the main source of political education for the students involved in them, and often have a vital and lasting effect on those involved. Student cultural organizations often provide training in drama, dancing, and other arts to students who go on to become well known in the cultural realm. Students who are active in the movement often have an advantage in such mundane affairs as business and commerce because of their training in human relations and organizational techniques. Indeed, it has been said that the alumni of the militant leftist Zengakuren in Japan often make very good businessmen after their revolutionary careers come to and end.[14]

The socializing role of the student movement has been implicit in much of the foregoing discussion. Student groups are often a primary element in the political socialization of whole student generations, thereby playing an important although indirect role in the shaping of the political life of the broader society. Even when students lose much of their youthful radicalism in later years, they retain something of the training they received in the movement. In India, for example, the organizational training provided by the Communist student movement has proved a valuable asset to the many former Communists who have achieved high business or government positions. Students occasionally make career choices on the basis of their experiences in the student movement, and many choose politics as a career because of their experiences in the student movement.[15]

Student organizations of all types often shape student attitudes. This is a particularly important consideration in societies in which the student community is surrounded by traditional value orientations. In such societies, the student movement is one of the few modernizing elements and can go a long way toward breaking down caste, religious and linguistic rivalries and building a sense of nationality. Thus, social views are shaped by the student movement as well as political outlooks. And again, while students leave the universities, they often retain something of the attitudes which they learned in the movement. In rigidly administered educational systems, the more informal structures of the student movement can be even more important.

The student movement has been a stimulus for nationalism in many of the new nations. Much of modern Indian nationalism was developed by individuals with Western educations, many of whom had studied in Europe. Many of the first generation of African nationalists were trained in the London-based West African Students' Union. Student groups in other areas have also been important training centers for nationalist leaders, and some nationalist ideology was developed within such organizations.

The student movement has occasionally achieved direct political results from its activity. Governments in Korea and Turkey were toppled by militant student movements although the military soon took over the reigns of government. Students in Japan forced the Kishi government to resign as a result of massive demonstrations. Students exercised an important influence on the Russian revolutionary movement and on the nationalist movements in India, Burma, and parts of Africa. Thus, the student movement can have a direct political function as well as a more diffuse educational impact. Students have never been able to successfully control a revolutionary movement, even in those instances when they have been primarily responsible for it.

The student movement is often a primary contact between the student population and the educational authorities, thus functioning as a means of communication between the two key elements in any system of higher education. Students have often taken a direct role in educational affairs by suggesting changes and reforms, which have occasionally been accepted. When the students feel strongly about an educational issue, they can force the hand of the authorities by demanding reforms and enforcing their wishes by agitational campaigns.

The student movement does not always play a radical role in the community, pressing for progressive reforms and backing left-wing politicians. It can also act as a reactionary force, supporting traditional elements in the society. Although it would seem that leftism is a more pervasive influence, strong conservative student organizations exist in many nations. As in politics, the cultural influence of the student movement can be conservative as well, and can help to build an identification of the students with traditional cultural patterns after an initial rebellion from them.

That student movements, political and non-political, have played an important and at times crucial role in the developing nations is clear. Generalizing about the nature of such movements is more difficult, since there are many differences between nations. One of the difficulties in analyzing student movements is their transitory nature—the student community as well as the interests of the students change rapidly. Organizations are often temporary, and leadership fluctuates. The emphasis of the movements shifts from campus to society and back again at rather regular intervals, and the movement itself can disappear for extended periods of time.

Interaction between the educational system, the broader political and economic situation, and the socio-psychological nature of the student community is complex, making any thorough understanding of the role of the students in politics and on the educational establishment difficult. Yet, it is of crucial importance that the student movement be thoroughly analyzed if an important aspect of economic and political development in the new nations is to be understood.

REFERENCES

[1] Metta SPENCER, "Professional, Scientific, and Intellectual Students in India," *Comparative Education Review*, June 10, 1966, p. 297.

[2] Seymour Martin LIPSET, "University Students and Politics in Underdeveloped Countries," *Comparative Education Review, ibid.*, p. 140.

[3] Glaucio A. D. SOARES, "The Active Few: Student Ideology and Participation in Developing Countries," *Comparative Education Review, ibid.*, p. 206.

[4] Lewis, FEUER, "A Talk with the Zengakuren," *New Leader*, XLIV (May 1, 1961), p. 17.

[5] Edward SHILS, "Indian Students: Rather Sadhus Than Philistines," *Encounter*, XVII (September, 1961), p. 15.

[6] Robert Jay LIFTON, "Youth and History: Individual Changes in Postwar Japan," *Daedalus*, 51 (Winter, 1962), p. 179.

[7] LIPSET, *op. cit.*, p. 136.

[8] Lewis FEUER, "Patterns in the History of Student Movements," (mimeographed, Berkeley: University of California, 1965), p. 4.

[9] Calvin TRILLIN, "Letter from Berkeley," in Michael Miller and Susan Gilmore (eds.), *Revolution at Berkeley* (New York: Dell Books, 1965), p. 261.

[10] Dwaine Marvick, "African University Students: A Presumptive Elite," in James S. Coleman (ed.), *Education and Political Development* (Princeton, N.J.: Princeton University Press, 1965), p. 491.

[11] Neil Smelser, *Theory of Collective Behavior,* New York: The Free Press, 1963, p. 275.

[12] James Petras, "General Remarks on Politics and Students" (unpublished paper, Berkeley: University of California, 1964), p. 2.

[13] Feuer, "Patterns of Student Movements," *op. cit.,* p. 17.

[14] Philip G. Altbach, "Japanese Students and Japanese Politics," *Comparative Education Review,* 7 (October, 1963), p. 184.

[15] Sagar Ahluwalia, "The Student Movement in India" (unpublished, Delhi, 1963), p. 20.

C.

Contemporary Societies and
"Mass Politics"

4.

THE PROFESSIONALIZATION
OF REFORM (1965)

Daniel Patrick Moynihan

When President Johnson delivered his famous civil rights speech at
Howard University in the summer of 1965, Daniel P. Moynihan had
helped prepare the speech, and the approach Johnson proposed closely
followed Moynihan's celebrated report on the Negro family. Both the
Moynihan report and Johnson's Howard University speech were special
examples of a general strategy of professionalized social reform.
Moynihan supplies us with a candid statement of this strategy in the
essay below. In it, he gives what is intended to be a heartening report
on the latest manifestation of the reform impulse in the United States.

Contemporary American social reform is the heir of a complex history.
There was in the nineteenth century a sturdy tradition of individualism—what Ralph Waldo Emerson called "an assertion of the sufficiency

SOURCE. Daniel Patrick Moynihan, "The Professionalization of Reform," *The
Public Interest,* I (Fall 1965), pp. 6–10. Copyright 1965 by National Affairs, Inc.
Reprinted by permission of National Affairs, Inc., and the author.

of the private man." But alongside the spirit of manly self-reliance, there was also a repressive and aristocratic aspect to American reform. Benevolent gentlemen, convinced that they enjoyed a mandate from on high to enlighten their less deserving fellow citizens, went about their philanthropic tasks in a spirit of "Moral Stewardship." In an infinitely more sophisticated way, the contemporary ideology of professionalized reform shares the elitism and tough-mindedness of nineteenth-century moral stewardship. But there is at least one important difference. In the twentieth century, benevolent purposes are often tied to the exercise of vast government power, whereas in the earlier period voluntary efforts were the major expression of reform. Harnessing state power to benevolence has become the goal of those in modern America who call themselves "liberal." With Moynihan, they are dedicated to the possibilities for expert social manipulation that an institutionalized welfare state supplies. Although he is no longer a member of the Johnson Administration, Moynihan provides an insiders' view of the establishment's conception of its own benevolence.

I

Our best hope for the future lies in the extension to social organization of the methods that we already employ in our most progressive fields of effort. In science and in industry . . . we do not wait for catastrophe to force new ways upon us. . . . We rely, and with success, upon quantitative analysis to point the way; and we advance because we are constantly improving and applying such analysis.

The passage above, as succinct a case for social planning as could be made, is not a product of either the thought or the institutions of the liberal left. It is, rather, a statement by the late mathematical economist Wesley C. Mitchell. And it has recently been approvingly reprinted at the beginning of a report on "The Concept of Poverty" published by—the Chamber of Commerce of the United States.

The report itself, the work of businessmen and scholars, is perhaps the most competent commentary on the government's antipoverty program yet to appear. It is replete with citations of articles in *Social Research* and *Land Economics,* and of data from *The Statistical Abstract of the United States;* the perspective ranges from friendly references to the works of Friedrich Engels, to more detached assessments of contemporary tracts. ("Michael Harrington, author of a widely read book on poverty, *The Other America,* has written, 'Any gain for America's minorities will immediately be translated into an advance for all the unskilled workers. One cannot raise the bottom of society without benefiting everyone above' This is almost precisely wrong.") But the report is less significant for what it says than for what it is: an example of the evolving technique and style of reform in the profoundly new society developing in the United States. Lacking a better term, it might be described as the professionalization of reform.

II

Writing for the British journal, *The New Society,* just prior to the assassination of President Kennedy, Nathan Glazer described the process:

> Without benefit of anything like the Beveridge report to spark and focus public discussion and concern, the United States is passing through a stage of enormous expansion in the size and scope of what we may loosely call the social services—the public programs designed to help people adapt to an increasingly complex and unmanageable society. While Congress has been painfully and hesitantly trying to deal with two great measures—tax reform and a civil rights bill—and its deliberations on both have been closely covered by the mass media, it has also been working with much less publicity on a number of bills which will contribute at least as much to changing the shape of American society.

The vast Mental Retardation Facilities and Community Mental Health Centers Construction Act had just become law. The no less enormous vocational education bill was moving steadily through the Congress. The Kennedy Administration had earlier obtained such measures as the Area Redevelopment Act, the Manpower Development and Training Act, and the Public Welfare Amendments of 1962. "Waiting in the wings" were a domestic peace corps and an ambitious youth conservation corps, while the community action programs developed by the President's Committee on Juvenile Delinquency and Youth Crime, established in 1961, were scheduled for new and expanded funding.

It is a special mind that can as much as keep the titles of those programs straight. But the most interesting thing about all this sudden expansion of social services was that it had behind it, as Glazer noted, "nothing like the powerful political pressure and long-sustained intellectual support that produced the great welfare measures of the New Deal—Social Security, Unemployment Insurance, Public Welfare, Public Housing." The "massive political support and intellectual leadership that produced the reforms of the thirties" simply did not exist; yet the reforms were moving forward.

Glazer accounted for this in terms of the emergence of a large body of professional persons and professional organizations that had taken on themselves the concern for the 20 to 30 per cent of the population that was outside the mainstream of American prosperity. Intellectuals knew little about the subject, and were not much interested. Organized labor, while both concerned and knowledgeable, had had but limited success in involving its membership in such efforts. As a result

> . . . the fate of the poor is in the hands of the administrators and the professional organizations of doctors, teachers, social workers, therapists, counselors and so forth. It is these, who, in a situation where the legislation and programs become ever more complex, spend the time to find out—or rather have brought home to them—through their work the effects of certain kinds of measures and programs, and who propose ever more complex programs which Congress deliberates upon in the absence of any major public interest. When Congress argues these programs, the chief pressures upon it are not the people, but the organized professional interests that work with that segment of the problem, and those who will benefit from or be hurt by the legislation.

The antipoverty program that was being developed even as Glazer wrote is far the best instance of the professionalization of reform yet to appear. In its genesis, its development, and now in its operation, it is a prototype of the social technique of action that will almost certainly become more common in the future. It is a technique that will not appeal to everyone, and in which many will perceive the not altogether imaginary danger of a too-powerful government. But it is also a technique that offers a profound promise of social sanity and stability in time to come.

There are two aspects of the poverty program which distinguish it from earlier movements of its kind: The initiative came largely from within. The case for action was based on essentially esoteric information about the past and probable future course of events.

The most distinctive break with the past is with regard to initiative. War on poverty was not declared at the behest of the poor. Just the opposite. The poor were not only invisible, as Michael Harrington described them, they were also for the most part silent. John F. Kennedy ventured into Appalachia searching for Protestant votes, not for poverty. There he encountered the incredible pauperization of the mountain people, most particularly the soft coal miners, an industrial work force whose numbers had been reduced by nearly two-thirds in the course of a decade—but with hardly a sound of protest. The miners were desperately poor, shockingly unemployed, but neither radical nor in any significant way restive. It may be noted that in 1964, in the face of the historic Democratic sweep, Harlan County, Kentucky, returned a freshman Republican Congressman.

True, the civil rights movement was well established and highly effective during this period, but it was primarily concerned with just that: the demand for the recognition of the civil rights of the Negro American. While the movement would clearly in time turn to the problem of poverty and of the economic position of the Negro, it had only begun to do so, as in the March on Washington in August 1963, and its economic demands were still general and essentially traditional, as for example, an increased minimum wage.

Apart from the always faithful labor movement, the only major lobbies working for any of the programs that came together to form the War on Poverty were the conservationists supporting the youth conservation camps and the National Committee on the Employment of Youth, an organization representing a variety of groups in the social welfare field. The essential fact is that the main pressure for a massive government assault on poverty developed within the Kennedy-Johnson Administration, among officials whose responsibilities were to think about just such matters. These men now exist, they are well paid, have competent staffs, and have access to the President. (Many of these officials, of course, were originally brought to Washington by the New Deal: they are by no means all *nuovi uomini*.) Most importantly, they have at their command an increasing fund of information about social conditions in the United States.

Almost all this information is public, but the art of interpreting it is, in a sense, private. Anyone is free to analyze income statistics, or employment data, or demographic trends to his heart's content. But very few persons in the beginning years of the present decade were able to perceive in those statistics the gradual settling of a poverty class in America. A number of officials in the Federal government (mostly academicians on leave) were. Leaving aside the question of whether or not they were right—a question which must always be open—it is clear that the judgment they reached was quite at variance, almost poles apart, from the general public understanding of the time.

Whereas the public, both high and low in the intellectual hierarchy, saw income distribution steadily compressing, saw the Negro American more and more winning his rightful place in society, saw prosperity spreading through the land, the men in the government saw something quite different: an income distribution gap that had not budged since the end of the war, and had in fact worsened sharply for Negroes, a rising measure of social disorganization among poor families and poor communities, a widening gap between the prospects of the poor and those of the middle class.

In President Johnson these officials found a chief executive who knew a good deal about poverty, and seemingly everything about politics. In a matter of weeks from the time he assumed office, the array of programs and bills Glazer had described as "waiting in the wings" were mustered into a coherent legislative program, reinforced by some entirely new ideas, and moved out under the banner of War on Poverty. It was an issue that united rather than divided, and the ranks of its supporters if anything swelled as it moved through the legislative process.

There is nothing, as such, startling about these developments. They have been foreseen, with either hope or fear, by many persons for many years. However, in recent times a number of events have occurred which very much hasten the process, and make it of greater moment. These have to do with the almost sudden emergence of the fact that the industrial nations of the world seem finally about to learn how to manage their economies, with the professionalization of the middle class, and with the exponential growth of knowledge.

III

The Economic Revolution

Recent years, with the steady advance of technology, have given birth to a good number of neo-apocalyptic views of the future of the American economy, most of them associated with the concept of automation. No one should doubt there is something called automation going on, and that it does change things. However, there is no evidence whatever that it is in fact transforming American society, or any other society. It is simply the newest phase in a process that has been under way for at least two centuries, and will presumedly go on and on, past any immediate concern of this age or the next.

At the same time, there is a good deal of evidence, if that is the term for what are little more than everyday impressions, that in the area of economic policy there has occurred a genuine discontinuity, a true break with the past: Men are learning how to make an industrial economy work.

What is involved is something more permanent than simply a run of good luck, or specially refined intuitions on the part of persons responsible for the economic affairs of one nation, or a group of nations. Rather it is the fact that for two decades now, since the end of World War II, the industrial democracies of the world have been able to operate their economies on a high and steadily expanding level of production and employment. Nothing like it has ever happened before in history. It is perhaps the central fact of world politics today. The briefest recollection of what happened to those economics in the two decades that followed World War I will suggest why.

Moreover, it is a development that has all the markings of a scientific event, of a profound advance in knowledge, as well as of an improvement in statecraft.

In the beginning was the theory. With but little data either to support or confound them, economic theories multiplied and conflicted. But gradually more and better data accumulated: progress begins on social problems when it becomes possible to measure them. As the data accumulated and technology made it possible to calculate more rapidly, the theories gradually became able to explain more, and these in turn led to the improvement in the data. John Maynard Keynes at King's College, Cambridge, and Wesley C. Mitchell at the National Bureau of Economic Research in New York, are supremely good symbols of the two processes that ended up in a deeply symbiotic relationship. And then one day it all more or less hangs together and the world is different, although of course not quite aware of the change. Governments promise full employment—and then produce it. (In 1964 unemployment, adjusted to conform more or less to United States' definitions, was 2.9 per cent in Italy, 2.5 per cent in France and Britain, and 0.4 per cent in Germany. Consider the contrast with post-World War I.) Governments undertake to expand their economy at a steady rate—and do so. (In 1961 the members of the Organization for Economic Cooperation and Development, which grew out of the Marshall Plan, undertook to increase their output by 50 per cent during the decade of the 1960s. The United States at all events is right on schedule.)

The ability to predict events, as against controlling them, has developed even more impressively—the Council of Economic Advisers' forecast of GNP for 1964 was off by only $400 million in a total of $623 billion; the unemployment forecast was on the nose.

There is a temptation, of course, to go too far in presuming what can be done with the economy. The international exchange system is primitive, and at the moment menacing. The stock market can be wildly irrational. There are, as Hyman Lewis points out, competing theories of investment which could bring us to unsettling dilemmas. We in the United States have not achieved full employment. We have accepted the use of federal taxing and spending powers as a means of social adjustment, but so far only in pleasant formulations. Our willingness to raise taxes, for example, is yet to be tested. In general, the political component of political economy remains very much uncertain. Thus the British, again to cite Lewis, have the best economists, but one of the less successful economies. But the fact remains that economics is approaching the status of an applied science.

In the long run this econometric revolution, assuming it works itself out, is bound to have profound effects on the domestic politics of all the nations involved. The central political issue of most industrial nations over the past century and a half has been how to make an economy work. Almost every conceivable nostrum, from the nationalization of the means of production, distribution, and exchange, to the free coinage of silver, has been proposed, and most have been tried. Usually without success. In the United States, for one administration after another, economic failure has led to political failure. But if henceforth the business cycle has a longer sweep, and fewer abrupt downturns, the rise and fall of political fortunes may follow the same pattern. Once in power, a party may be much more likely to remain so. Or in any event, the issues that elect or defeat governments could be significantly different from those of the past.

The more immediate impact of this econometric revolution in the United States is that the federal government will be endowed, more often than not, with a substantial, and within limits predictable, rise in revenues available for social purposes. Significantly, the War on Poverty began in the same year of the great tax cut. The President was not forced to choose between the measures; he was able to proceed with both. In that sense, the War on Poverty began not because it was necessary (which it was), but because it was possible.

The singular nature of the new situation in which the federal government finds itself is that the immediate *supply* of resources available for social purposes might actually outrun the immediate *demand* of established programs. Federal expenditures under existing programs rise at a fairly predictable rate. But, under conditions of economic growth, revenues rise faster. This has given birth to the phenomenon of the "fiscal drag"—the idea that unless the federal government disposes of this annual increment, either by cutting taxes or adding programs, the money taken out of circulation by taxes will slow down economic growth, and could, of course, at a certain point stop it altogether.

Thus, assuming the continued progress of the economy in something like the pattern of recent years, there is likely to be $4–5 billion in additional, unobligated revenue coming in each year. *But* this increment will only continue to come on condition that it is disposed of. Therefore one of the important tasks to which an Administration must address itself is that of devising new and responsible programs for expending public funds in the public interest.

This is precisely the type of decision making that is suited to the techniques of modern organizations, and which ends up in the hands of persons who make a profession of it. They are less and less political decisions, more and more administrative ones. They are decisions that can be reached by consensus rather than conflict.

The Professionalization of the Middle Class

"Everywhere in American life," Kenneth S. Lynn reports, "the professions are triumphant." The period since the G.I. Bill has witnessed an extraordinary expansion of higher education. In the United States, a quarter of the teenage population now goes on to some kind of college, and among specific class and ethnic groups the proportion is as high as three quarters. The trend is unmistakable and probably irresistible: in the course of the coming decades some form of higher education will become near to universal. But most importantly, for more and more persons the form of education will involve professional training. This is not the same thing as traditional higher education; it does not produce the same types of persons.

The difference has been most succinctly stated by Everett C. Hughes: "Professionals *profess*. They profess to know better than others the nature of certain matters, and to know better than their clients what ails them or their affairs." And he continues:

> Lawyers not only give advice to clients and plead their cases for them; they also develop a philosophy of law—of its nature and its functions, and of the proper way in which to administer justice. Physicians consider it their prerogative to define the nature of disease and of health, and to determine how medical services ought to be distributed and paid for. Social workers are not content to develop a technique of casework; they concern themselves with social legislation. Every profession considers itself the proper body to set the terms in which some aspect of society, life or nature is to be thought of, and to define the general lines, or even the details, of public policy concerning it.

As the number of professionals increase, so also do the number of professions, or neo-professions. More and more, middle-class persons are attracted by the independence of judgment, esoteric knowledge, and immunity to outside criticism that characterize professionals. As Everett Hughes puts it: "The YMCA secretary wants his occupation recognized not merely as that of offering young men from the country a pleasant road to Protestant righteousness in the city, but as a more universal one of dealing with groups of young people. All that is learned of adolescence, of behavior in small groups, of the nature and organization of community life is considered the intellectual base of his work."

There are now an extraordinary number of such persons in America. Those Americans classified as professional and technical workers have just passed the nine million mark—more than the number of "managers, officials, and proprietors," more than the craftsmen and foremen. And of this group, an enormous number is involved in various aspects of social welfare and reform. Through sheer numbers they would tend to have their way; but as professionals in a professionalizing society, they are increasingly *entitled* to have their way. That is how the system works.

One of the more powerful demonstrations of the influence of professional thinking on programs of social reform is the provision of the Economic Opportunity Act that community action programs be carried out with the "maximum feasible participation" of the poor themselves. This is one of the most important and pioneering aspects of the entire antipoverty program. But typically this measure was inserted in the legislation not because of any demand of the poor, but because the intellectual leaders of the social welfare profession had come to the conclusion that this was indispensable to effective social action. Typically also, the literature describes the process in terms of the use of the "indigenous nonprofessional"—persons identified by the fact that they are *not* professional. A somewhat ironical turn of events in this area is the role the community action programs are playing in re-creating the ethnic political-social organizations of the big city slums—the dismantling of which was for so long the object of political and social reformers in the United States!

The prospect of large-scale opposition to the new professions is, for the moment at least, limited because the professionalization of the middle class has led to a no less extraordinary opening up of careers to talent. The time when any considerable number of persons of great ability and ambition have found their way out of poverty blocked by their inability to obtain an education has all but passed. (There are still many, many persons whose natural abilities are stunted by poverty, but that is another matter.) A nationwide survey of 1960 high school graduates, Project Talent, found that about 97 per cent of those in the top 1 per cent in aptitude and 93 per cent of those in the top 5 per cent, entered college within a year. Among the next 5 per cent (the 90th to 94th percentile) 86 per cent did so. As a general propostion, ability is recognized and rewarded in America today as at no time in history. (Michael Young's forecast of the revolt of the lower quartile against the ultimate injustice of a society based on merit may not be discounted, but it is not on the other hand scheduled until 2031).

It is possible that this process, just because it is successful in drawing up talent from lower economic and social groups, will deprive those groups of much of their natural leadership, and make them all the more dependent on professionals. Kenneth Clark has noted that the degree of recruitment of civil rights leaders into "establishment" organizations verges on raiding—and has raised suspicions of hidden motives! On the other hand, there is rather a pronounced tendency for persons from such groups, when they do rise to the middle class, to settle into professions which involve work with the very groups they left behind. Thus, in a certain sense the poor are not so much losing their natural leaders as obtaining them through different routes.

The Exponential Growth of Knowledge

Among the complexities of life is the fact that the American business community, in a period when it was fiercely opposed to the idea of economic or social planning, nonetheless supported, even pressed for, the development of a national statistical system which has become the best in the world and which now makes certain types of planning and regulation—although quite different from the collective proposals of earlier eras—both feasible and in a measure inevitable. Much as mountains are climbed, so statistics are used if they are there. As an example, trade union wage settlements in recent years have been profoundly influenced by the wage-price guidelines set by the federal government. This could not possibly have occurred on an essentially voluntary basis were it not that the Bureau of Labor Statistics has developed the technique of measuring productivity—and has done so accompanied, step by step, by the business and labor advisory committees that work with the bureau. A measure of the near quantum change that has only recently occurred in the information available for social planning in the United States (the development work began long ago, but the pay-off has been rather recent) may be suggested by the fact that the nation went through the great depression of the 1930s without ever really knowing what the rate of unemployment was! This was then a measurement taken but once every ten years, by the census. Today, of course, employment and unemployment data are collected monthly, and debated in terms of the decimal points. Similarly, the census has been quietly transformed from a ten-times-a-century proceeding to a system of current accounts on a vast range of social data.

Most of the information that went into the development of the anti-poverty program was essentially economic, but the social data available to the President's task force was of singular importance in shaping the program, and in turn the program will greatly stimulate the collection of more such. The nation is clearly on the verge of developing a system of social statistics comparable to the now highly developed system of economic statistics.

The use of all such statistics is developing also. A vast "industry of discovery," to use William Haber's description of events in the physical sciences, is developing in the social sciences as well. Computer technology has greatly enhanced the possible uses of such data. Just as the effort to stimulate the American economy is now well advanced, the simulation of social processes, particularly in decision making, is also begun, and may be expected to produce important, if not indeed revolutionary insights. Such prospects tend to stir some alarm in thoughtful persons, but it may be noted the public has accepted with calm, even relish, the fact that the outcome of elections is now predicted with surpassing accuracy. If that most solemn of democratic rituals may be simulated without protest, there is not likely to be much outcry against the simulation of various strategies of housing integration, or techniques of conflict resolution, or patterns of child rearing.

Expenditure for social science research was somewhere between $500 and $600 million in 1964. This was only 10 per cent of the $6 billion spent in the same year on the life and physical sciences (including psychology), and much less a proportion of the $19 billion spent on research and development altogether. Nonetheless it represents a sixfold growth in a decade. There is, moreover, some indication that social scientists are not yet thinking in the money terms that are in fact available to them. Angus Campbell suggested recently that social scientists still think in budgets of thousands of dollars when they should be thinking of millions. "The prevailing format for social research is still the exploitation of opportunities which are close at hand, easily manageable, and inexpensive." But, he adds, "there are a good many social scientists who know very well how to study social change on a broad scale and are intensely interested in going about it." The Survey Research Center at the University of Michigan, which Campbell directs, has, for example, under way a year-long panel survey of the impact of the 1964 tax cut on the nation's taxpayers, a specific example of the use of social science techniques in the development of economic policy.

All in all, the prospect is for a still wider expansion of knowledge available to governments as to how people behave. This will be accompanied by further improvement of the now well-developed techniques of determining what they think. Public opinion polls are already a daily instrument of government decision-making (a fact which has clearly affected the role of the legislature). In combination, these two systems of information make it possible for a government to respond intelligently and in time to the changing needs and desires of the electorate. The day when mile-long petitions and mass rallies were required to persuade a government that a popular demand existed that things be done differently is clearly drawing to a close. Indeed, the very existence of such petitions and rallies may in time become a sign that what is being demanded is *not yet* a popular demand.

The Perils of Progress

The professionalization of reform will proceed, regardless of the perils it presents. Even in the face of economic catastrophe, which is certainly conceivable if not probable, the response will be vastly more systematic and informed than any of the past.

A certain price will be paid, and a considerable risk will be incurred. The price will be a decline in the moral exhilaration of public affairs at the domestic level. It has been well said that the civil rights movement of the present time has at last provided the youth of America with a moral equivalent of war. The more general effect of the civil rights movement has been a much heightened public concern for human dignity and welfare. This kind of passion could seep out of the life of the nation, and we would be the less for it.

The risk is a combination of enlightenment, resources, and skill which in the long run, to use Harold D. Lasswell's phrase, becomes a "monocracy of power."

But the potential rewards are not less great. The creation of a society that can put an end to the "animal miseries" and stupid controversies that afflict most peoples would be an extraordinary achievement of the human spirit. The argument may be made, for example, that had the processes described in this article not progressed as far as they had by 1961, the response of the federal government to the civil rights revolution would have been thoroughly inadequate: that instead of joining with and helping to direct the movement, the national government would have trailed behind with grudging, uncomprehending, and increasingly inadequate concessions that could have resulted in the problem of the Negro American becoming insoluble in terms of existing American society.

The prospect that the more primitive social issues of American politics are at last to be resolved need only mean that we may now turn to

issues more demanding of human ingenuity than that of how to put
an end to poverty in the richest nation in the world. Many such issues
might be in the area of foreign affairs, where the enormity of difficulty
and the proximity of disaster is sufficient to keep the citizens and political
parties of the nation fully occupied. And there is also the problem of
perfecting, to the highest degree possible, the *quality* of our lives and
of our civilization. We may not be accustomed to giving political priority
to such questions. But no one can say they will be boring or trivial!

5.

INSTITUTIONAL VULNERABILITY IN
MASS SOCIETY (1951)

PHILIP SELZNICK

The struggle for power in society poses the central question: How can
we preserve the integrity of social institutions when they become targets
in political combat? The current weakness of social and political theory
becomes manifest when we attempt to deal with this problem in scientific
terms.

In order to provide guides for research, the following analysis attempts
to bring to bear upon the problem of institutional vulnerability a reformulation of the idea of mass society.[1] It is suggested that a close inspection of our institutions from this standpoint will illuminate relevant
sources of weakness and of strength.

The approach taken here is clinical. We are necessarily interested
in social pathology, in appraising the capacity of institutions to meet,
within their own terms, the requirements of self-maintenance. "Self-maintenance," of course, refers to the preservation of central values and
purposes as well as to the bare continuity of organizational existence.

We shall approach a definition of mass society by considering (1)

SOURCE. Philip Selznick, "Institutional Vulnerability in Mass Society," *The
American Journal of Sociology*, LVI (January 1951) pp. 320–331. Reprinted by
permission of *The American Journal of Sociology* and the author.

[1] "Mass society" is used here as the best available substitute for a more abstract
term which would denote the qaulity of "massness"–possibly useful but infelicitous
expression.

the role of creative and culture-sustaining elites; (2) the quality of participation in mass society and mass organization; and (3) a catalogue of diagnostic symptoms of mass behavior. We proceed on the assumption that the achievement of adequate definitions reflects the close of this phase of inquiry rather than its beginning.

THE MASS AND CREATIVE ELITES

Critics of egalitarianism have sometimes put forward the view that the mass, incompetent and vulgar, is unable by definition to uphold the standards which sustain a culture or to participate effectively in political decision-making.[2] The mass is, moreover, a dire threat because what was once a passive multitude, a neuter element in the body politic, has now become dynamic. In this view the consequences of democratization are seen as the spread of incompetence into new areas and, indeed, the emergence of a type of man who may be found in all sectors of social life—the mass man.

The mass man, runs the anti-egalitarian complaint, exerts a heavy influence upon all areas of social life but is unqualified to do so. Whereas earlier the mass accepted its proper station, now it arrogates to itself the right to upset ideals of attainment and behavior established by traditional culture-bearing elites. The result is a cultural vacuum in which no group is able to give moral direction to society; there is an absence of standards to which appeal can be made; and resort to violence becomes characteristic of the age. In the words of a Nazi playwright: "When I hear the word 'culture,' I reach for my revolver." Bolshevik activism replaces "parliamentary mathematics." In the non-totalitarian countries, too, a leveling process in education, literature, and politics substitutes the standardless appetites of the mass market for the canons of refinement and sober restraint. The mass rejects tradition and, in doing so, avoids responsibility for the continuity of constitutional order and the arts. Hence the very souls of nations are placed in tragic jeopardy.

This critique is not limited to anti-egalitarian ideologists. Even among those who favor the general process of democratization, and who lack any feelings of contempt for the non-elite, there is some acceptance

[2] See José Ortega y Gasset, *The Revolt of the Masses* (New York: Norton, 1932), p. 120: "By mass . . . is not to be specially understood the workers; it does not indicate a social class, but a kind of man to be found today in all social classes, who consequently represents our age, in which he is the predominant, ruling power."

of the notion that the mass is inherently unqualified. Thus Mannheim, in tracing the "fundamental democratization" of society, saw negative consequences of the widespread intervention of intellectually backward elements into new areas of social life:

> The crisis in culture in liberal-democratic society is due, in the first place, to the fact that the social processes, which previously favored the development of the creative elites, now have the opposite effect, i.e. have become obstacles to the forming of elites because wider sections of the population under unfavorable social conditions take an active part in cultural activities.

Specifically, according to Mannheim, this democratization brings such undesirable results as (1) an increase in the number of elites to the point where "no group can succeed in deeply influencing the whole of society" and (2) a breakdown of the exclusiveness of elites—that insulation from day-to-day pressures which permits new ideas and skills to mature.

The import of Mannheim's critique is that creative elites are objectively necessary for the maintenance and development of culture. The mass is implicitly defined in contrast to these elites; hence it is conceived of as essentially unqualified. This is not to say that such elites are necessarily identical with traditional aristocracies. And, regardless of what one may think of a specific elite, it is, in this view, sociologically demonstrable that the creation and protection of elites are essential to a healthy society. A mass society is one which does not permit elites to carry out their cultural functions; hence it results in the sovereignty of the unqualified. Of course, "sovereignty" here does not refer to government but to the locus of decisive cultural influence. The rule of the masses is not inconsistent with elite control of the state, for that rule is expressed in the fact that the governing elite is itself formed in the image of the mass.

If we examine this conception of the mass as unfit, we see that judgments as to the inherent competence of various strata of society are in fact irrelevant. What is really identified is a social system in which the indispensable functions of creative elites cannot be performed. It is not the quality of the individuals which is in point but their roles; it is not so much that the mass is unfit in any literal sense as that the nature of the system prevents the emergence of an effective social leadership. In a sense, a mass society is one in which no one is qualified. This is so because the relationships involve a radical cultural leveling, not because no superior individuals exist.

If mass characteristics appear in a university, for example, this does not necessarily mean that the student body or the faculty is inherently incompetent. The large achievements in technical fields would be testimony to the contrary. What is at issue is cultural competence. Where the mass exists, we find the following symptoms of it: (a) the faculty is unable to reach the students as persons but merely trains them as experts; (b) conditions for the emergence and sustenance of intellectual elites on the campus are poor; (c) the faculty adapts itself to the mass character of the institution; (d) standards of conduct and of nontechnical achievement deteriorate; and (e) the meaning of the university as a culture-bearing institution is increasingly attenuated. This says nothing about the inherent competence or incompetence of the participants, but it does say something about the nature and the consequences of a type of institutional participation. The latter is consistent with the literary-philosophical critique of the mass society as the "sovereignty of the unqualified."

These remarks emphasize the difficulty of attempting to say that some given society, taken as a whole, is a mass society. But if we understand that what we are asserting is a relation between abstract characters—the nature of the mass and the quality of elites—this problem can be avoided. As in the case of any universal proposition, the statement, "In mass society the creative and culture-sustaining elites are debilitated," merely tells us what can be expected, in the absence of counter-acting forces, when social disintegration thrusts undifferentiated sectors of a population into direct contact with the areas of cultural incubation and development. Education, leisure, and politics have been most obviously affected by this process. Among its consequences is that political and educational agencies must adapt themselves to the intervention of the mass by permitting participation on the basis of low standards of knowledge and conduct.

But this adaptation is costly. Elites find it difficult to sustain their own standards, hence ultimately their special identity and function. This is most clearly evident in the institutions of higher learning: mass society threatens to transform them into institutions of specialized training. As higher education falls a prey to the mass, research as well as teaching will be affected. The student will no longer feel his relation to a community of scholarship; he is not concerned about—indeed, is impatient with—the traditional values of university life. He does not look forward to becoming a new kind of man; he expects to retain his commonness and to be distinguished from the multitude only by a certain technical competence. Like his highly specialized professor, his participation is segmental; it does not commit him as a whole man to becoming the bearer and protector of the society's aspirations. In the faculties two new types will become more prominent: the technician and the demagogue. Only these will maintain and increase enrolments; more important—the level of enrolment could indeed be steady—only these will earn the plaudits of the student body. The student will become his teacher's judge, sometimes even explicitly so. The result will be a decline in the university's ability to affect deeply the life of the student and concomitantly an increase in the vulnerability of both faculty and student to the stereotyped blandishments of the market place.[3]

Similar tendencies threaten all the highly sensitive institutions which protect existing standards and are the sources of cultural development. Even the church is not immune to this danger. Impatient of theological subtlety (not merely ignorant and deferential as in the past), uncertain and inadequate, the preacher as social worker deserts his distinctive cultural role. He becomes defensive about propagating religious values; he does not sustain the image of charitable or other activities as primarily spiritual missions. He finds new security in a feeling of oneness with the common man, but as a result he may fail as a moral and spiritual leader. Even where religion flourishes, demagogy may become the characteristic product of the times, the leader reflecting the mind and the fluctuating mood of the mass.

The strength of cultural values depends upon the ability of key agencies to transmit them without serious attenuation and distortion. But this in turn requires that these institutions be secure, that the elites which man them be able to maintain their distinctive identities. This becomes increasingly difficult as powerful solvents—science, technology, industrialization, urbanization—warp the self-confidence of the culture-bearers and, at the same time, expose them to the pressures of an emergent mass.

From a research standpoint, this analysis suggests that inquiry into institutional vulnerability should focus attention upon the conditions which affect the ability of elites to maintain those standards and self-images which invest the institution as a whole with its cultural meaning.

It should be emphasized that no commitment to established values and institutions follows from what has been said here. The problem is strictly clinical: *If* we wish to preserve the integrity of certain institutions, these are among the conditions we must investigate and control.

---

[3] It may be suggested, in the light of the foregoing analysis, that a relation to the "community of scholarship" can be core participation (see below) only through the mediation of the person-to-person relation of "disciple" to "master." It should also be noted that, while mass behavior is most obvious in the great state universities, it arises as well in many colleges sustained by and for the moneyed elites, for there, too, training is valued above education.

Whether in any specific case the institution is worth preserving must be determined on other grounds.

THE QUALITY OF PARTICIPATION

In the preceding discussion of elites in relation to the mass, we drew upon an older insight and reformulated it in clinical terms. We refer now to that idea of "mass" which associates it with such terms as "homogeneous," "amorphous," and "undifferentiated." This view in effect represents the mass man as a product of social disintegration.

Consider the transformation of the unemployed into a mass. The unemployed become a mass as their normal ties to community institutions and codes are boken down, as they break free, to reunite again in artificial ways. In other words, as family, church, and traditional political ties weaken, a psychological atomization takes place. This process is not completed overnight; nor does unemployment as such automatically create a mass. What is crucial is the change in the quality of social participation consequent upon the loss of employment in a society which values work.

Among the consequences of unemployment is, it appears, a general decline in social participation. The individual's ties to friends and to recreational and church associations weaken with prolonged unemployment. Family life suffers and cannot easily be used as a refuge. At first all this is because of the unemployed man's poverty, especially in cities, where money is so important. But ultimately the loss of self-respect and its accompanying insecurity must challenge his adherence to the codes and symbols which have sustained his earlier motivations. This loss of faith in traditional values, combined with the breakdown of older patterns of family activity, of meeting friends, of going to church, casts him loose. But he finds this new freedom less than desirable. He may take to drink, sleep more, seek out day-to-day satisfactions in gambling or sensual pleasure; he may retreat to extreme apathy; and he may search out new social and symbolic arrangements as substitutes for his lost community. He has lost his moorings to the social structure and has become part of the mass. This process of withdrawal may take a long time; it is not easy to lose established modes of behavior. But its general direction is the creation of a proletariat, in the strict sense of an alienated mass.

When the normal inhibitions enforced by tradition and social structure are loosened—and this, of course, occurs as a product of far more general and diverse conditions than unemployment—the undifferentiated mass emerges. Thus the mass has been associated with the idea of a crowd, most explicitly by Lederer. In the crowd, we find a temporary lack of differentiation, reinforced by circular response and high emotion, with concomitant loosening of inhibitions. The amorphousness of the mass is similar but is the result of a general and persistent mode of life. It does not rest upon psychological rapport but upon the atrophy of meaningful human relations, the disintegration of traditional institutional systems, and the rejection of old loyalties. Moreover, the readiness for manipulation by symbols, especially those permitting sado-masochistic releases, is characteristic of the mass as of the crowd.

The alienated mass man is in society but not of it. He does not accept responsibility for the preservation of value systems; hence he may be easily moved to new adherence. Here the insights developed by Fromm in his *Escape from Freedom* are applicable. The emergent mass is not stable. The freedom thrust upon it by the decay of social ties has significant psychological consequences. The need to belong is unfulfilled; insecurity follows and, with it, anxiety-laden efforts to find a way back to status and function and to a sense of relationship with society.

But these efforts are compulsive: enforced by urgent psychological pressures, they result in distorted, pathological responses. There arises the phenomenon of the *Ersatzgemeinschaft*, the "substitute community," in which essentially unsatisfying types of community integration—most explicitly revealed in fascism—are leaned upon for sustenance. This commitment is, however, suffused with tension and requires continuous renewal, resulting ultimately in a radical dependence of the individual upon his substitute symbols, a vain effort to escape anxiety by blotting out his own identity. This process, as Fromm describes it, is conducive to submission to totalitarian control, aggression against the weak, nihilism, and compulsive conformity. These are the symptoms of the mass when the disease is well developed.

It follows from this analysis that mass need not denote large numbers, though, of course, sheer numbers are important, especially in urban areas. Indeed, it is theoretically possible to have mass phenomena in relatively small populations and conversely to have very large and densely settled populations (e.g., on the Japanese countryside) which are not mass in nature. When we refer to a population as a mass, we are thinking of its members as undifferentiated, as forming an unstructured collectivity withdrawn from the normal, spontaneous commitments of social life. We are also thinking of the consequences which flow from this situation. Mass connotes a "glob of humanity," as against the intricately related, institutionally bound groupings which form a healthy social organism.

Prolonged unemployment, it is clear, offers only the most congenial and easily recognizable conditions for the emergence of a mass. In fact, wherever culture impinges upon the individual only superficially, the emergence of mass phenomena may be anticipated. By "culture," of course, we mean not simply the arts or manners but the basic patterns of motivation and inhibition—the aspirations and the discipline—which are transmitted from one generation to another. When the culture is transmitted only weakly, as in the cases of certain second-generation immigrant groups and of primitive peoples under the impact of white culture, inhibitions are poorly developed and withdrawal is frequent. In extreme cases we find criminality, alcoholism, and loss of initiative and self-respect. These phenomena are well known. It is necessary to recognize, however, the continuity between these consequences of cultural attenuation and earlier stages in the same process which may have different, and less obvious, roots.

It is precisely this cultural attenuation which results from the attempt to adapt the character-defining institutions of a society (e.g., the schools, the churches, the political order) to the multitude. That this should be attempted is, of course, not a matter of choice. Industrialization and urbanization tend to weaken traditional value systems by confusing the distinction between means and ends and depersonalizing the individual; at the same time they corrode the older social structure and thrust ever greater numbers into direct contact with the centers of cultural development. As the family, the neighborhood, the work place, and the local community lose their near-monopoly over the life of the individual, new burdens are placed upon those centralized institutions which have historically been far removed from the common man. As a result, the latter can only poorly perform, in their segmental way, functions which require intimate contact with the total individual; and, equally important, they become themselves incompetent to perform their essential creative tasks.

The general consequence of such conditions is the weakening of social participation, especially a superficiality in the relation of individuals to the ethos and social structure. To be sure, the breakdown of culture is never complete, and the mass may emerge even before an advanced stage of decay has been reached. It would be idle to look for some definite point at which society may be called a mass, but the symptoms are identifiable: widespread alienation, a general cultural leveling, the compulsive search for substitute sources of security, and susceptibility to propagandistic and organizational manipulation. More important, these characteristics are reflected in varying degrees in specific institutional arenas: education, religion, literature, communication, politics, and industry. Even if mass phenomena are only partially characteristic of society as a whole, they may be strikingly so of specific sectors (e.g., among the youth or in some great industry). Especially in considering relative vulnerabilities within a society, it is important to conceive of mass phenomena in terms of a set of relevant predicates which may be useful in illuminating a particular group without being necessarily characteristic of society as a whole.

It is evident, from the discussion above, that there is more in the mass character of an organization than sheer numbers. We may say that a mass organization is one in which participation is segmental, mobilization is high, and the membership is relatively unstructured save through the formal devices of managerial control and through unmediated emotional attachments to a centralized elite.

Segmental Participation

In its most obvious sense, segmental participation refers to the partial commitment which a man may give to organizations in which he has a limited interest and which do not affect him deeply. In extreme but not unusual cases, membership is of the "paper" variety, and the members themselves are easily manipulated by a small core of leaders and their supporting cliques. The mobilizability of the membership is usually low, however; and, in order to create a mass organization, the leaders must attempt to activate the ranks. Thus, to take an extreme case, it makes little sense sociologically to speak of a large "book club" as a mass organization. And those trade-unions whose members' relations to the organization are limited to the checked-off payment of dues are not mass organizations.

A more significant meaning of segmental participation invites attention not to the *extent* of participation but to its quality. Participation is segmental when individuals interact not as whole personalities but in terms of the roles they play in the situation at hand. This is characteristic of urban life and of formal organizations where only the functional relevance of participants is prized. The personalities of individuals are leveled; men deal with each other as abstractions rather than as whole persons.

The underlying distinction is sufficiently familiar: it is that between primary and secondary groups. Participation which provides needed emotional satisfactions—what Paul Kecskemeti calls "core" participation—is possible only in or through primary groups. We may have core participation in the person-to-person group, and also in the secondary group, but in the latter only by mediation through primary person-to-person groups. Without the interposition of person-to-person interaction, participation in the secondary group can only be segmental. Fully evolved mass organizations forbid such primary-group ties, because these prevent free manipulation of the members; loyalties to subleaders can only be conditional, and only loyalty to the top leader is unconditional. But the latter, while involving primary symbols, is not a person-to-person relation.

Segmental relations in a mass organization may be contrasted with the situation in large nonmass organizations, such as a church. To the extent that a church bases itself upon primary-group relations at the grass roots and builds upon the incorporation of whole families into its communion, it may become very large without being a mass organization. It is precisely this foundation, however, which the modern totalitarian party, with similar organizations, does not permit. It does not build upon, but on the contrary destroys, family and friendship ties.[4]

Mobilization

Mass behavior connotes weakened social participation, and yet mass organization is associated with a high degree of involvement. This apparent inconsistency is soon resolved, however, if we consider the meaning of mobilization. High participation in nonmass contexts is not mobili-

[4] Correlatively, Max Weber noted: "Bureaucratic organization has usually come into power on the basis of a leveling of economic and social differences. . . . Bureaucracy inevitably accompanies modern *mass democracy* in contrast to the democratic self-government of small homogeneous units. . . . This not only applies to the structure of the state. For it is not accidental that in their own organizations, the democratic mass parties have completely broken with traditional notable rule based upon personal relationships and personal esteem. . . . Democratic mass parties are bureaucratically organized under the leadership of party officials, professional party and trade union secretaries, etc. . . . Of course one must always remember that the term 'democratization' can be misleading. The *demos* itself, in the sense of an inarticulate mass, never 'governs' larger associations; rather it is governed, and its existence only changes the way in which the executive leaders are selected and the measure of influence which the *demos*, or better, which social circles from its midst are able to exert upon the content and the direction of administrative activities by supplementing what is called 'public opinion.' 'Democratization,' in the sense here intended, does not necessarily mean an increasingly active share of the governed in the authority of the social structure. This may be the result of democratization, but is not necessarily the case. . . . The most decisive thing here—and indeed it is rather exclusively so—is the *leveling of the governed* in opposition to the ruling and bureaucratically articulated groups, which in its turn may occupy a quite autocratic position, both in fact and in form" (*From Max Weber: Essays in Sociology*, ed. H. H. Gerth and C. Wright Mills [New York: Oxford University Press, 1946], pp. 224–26).

zation; it is the spontaneous product of social relationships which create an integrated life-pattern. Mobilization takes place when an unstructured population is set into motion by a controlling elite. When it is also understood, as we shall suggest below, that the very character of the mass man predisposes him to be mobilized by managerial and symbolic devices, then the bridge between the amorphousness of the mass and intense organizational activity can be readily discerned.

When the community structure and its supporting codes are viable, it may be expected that individuals will adhere only partially, with limited commitment, to those organizations which are only tangentially related to the family-friendship core of community life. Such participants may be manipulated but not mobilized; they may constitute a source of power for some organizational leadership, but this power will be only a fraction of what it might be if the individuals could be withdrawn from their institutional attachments and more fully absorbed into the organization. It is only with general alienation that the population—where and to the extent that it does not retreat into apathy and isolation—will turn for sustenance to what are usually impersonal structures. When this occurs, our analysis entails the prediction that participation remains segmental; but it is combined with a greater psychological commitment to the organization. The result is a group which may be manipulated and mobilized—hallmarks of the modern mass organization.

Symbolic and Organizational Manipulation

Mass behavior in organizations, as in society generally, is associated with a decline of the primary group and of traditional symbols. This situation leads to new types of control, both symbolic and organizational. On the one hand, alienation from older loyalties creates a need for new social symbols, new sacred objects with which the individual can identify himself and to which he can defer. But these new man-symbol relationships are unmediated; they contrast sharply with traditional symbolic controls. The latter filter through multiple agencies of social control, and especially primary groups, where the ideas symbolized can be lived and acted out. These socially mediated values and symbols express themselves in the way personalities are molded, and in the implicit understanding, the capacity to distinguish between the genuine and the fraudulent, which characterizes an effectively transmitted cultural system. The impact of traditional symbol systems is softened by long and matter-of-fact adherence; it does not necessarily interfere with rational judgment and the accommodation of interests. But when the older bonds are loosened and the shadow of values is substituted for substance, then the individual's communion with the social symbols becomes artificial and forced. He is no longer their legitimate offspring, and yet his compelling need may enforce an even more intense (but still segmental) attachment to the husks of social meaning.

The new unmediated man-symbol relationships have a manipulative directness. The individual becomes susceptible to extreme types of behavior, called for in the name of abstractions which have little to do with his daily life and which he had had no opportunity to test and reshape. Alienated from other objects of deference and devotion, the individual may focus all his deference strivings on the new symbols; but, since this is ultimately unsatisfactory, tension is not alleviated, and ever new expenditure of emotional energy is required. At the same time the individual's stake in his new attachments is very great in the absence of other sources of satisfaction. All this results in a measure of need which permits extensive manipulation.

An example of this process may be seen in alterations in the meaning of patriotism. Sentiments of this sort in a well-structured community provide a background of ideological unity which shapes the character of specific institutions. Attachments are mediated, not direct. They do not normally involve marked irrationalities (as opposed to being based upon *non*rational, custom-bound elements) or hasty aggressions against deviants. And they are consistent with a common-sense understanding of the nature of the traditional political order. But a symptom of the emergence of the mass is the direct, emotionalized adherence to patriotic stereotypes, associated with a loss of intuitive understanding and a willingness to sacrifice the traditional content of the belief in exchange for emotional release. "Americanism" as a symbol can be dangerous because it is sometimes used to arouse mass responses in ways which affront the very foundations of our constitutional order; if it were simply a name for general sentiments reflected in the core attitudes of participants in a healthy community, it would not be dangerous and, indeed, would not be a slogan at all.

Another consequence of the absence of bonds in mass groups is organizational. Symbolic identifications are reflected in and supported by the day-to-day associational behavior of individuals and groups. Again it is normal and healthy for the spontaneously evolving familial and community relations to mold such behavior. But where segmentalized relationships have destroyed the old, given pattern and are unable to create a new one, the resulting vacuum will not be filled by new symbolic attachments. This vacuum will be occupied by a secular, power-oriented machine which provides new (though inherently less satisfying) means of social participation. That is why the mass party, in which emotion-invoking symbols are combined with techniques of mobilization, is the characteristic political vehicle in a mass society.

DIAGNOSTIC SYMPTOMS OF MASS BEHAVIOR

The utility of these ideas is not that they permit us to say of some population, "This is a mass." Rather, they may help us to be forewarned concerning the emergence of mass qualities among widely disparate groups which are subject, nonetheless, to certain common pressures. These qualities may weaken without destroying, may significantly characterize yet not wholly dominate, the specific areas in which we may be interested. To put the matter another way: To analyze the mass is to identify a disease. It will be best observed when its symptoms are well developed; yet we wish to know its most general nature so that we may recognize its symptoms as early as possible.

We may now restate the major characteristics of the mass society and their implications for institutional vulnerability.

1. *Mass behavior results in the debilitation of creative and culture-sustaining elites.* At this point it need only be emphasized that a statement of this sort is to be used in investigating specific institutions and segments of society, not necessarily society as a whole.

2. *Mass behavior results in superficial adherence to stereotyped values.* Foundation for this element of the syndrome was laid in the discussion above of segmental participation and unmediated symbol attachments. A few additional remarks here will be in point.

The cultural attenuation associated with the mass manifests itself in a peculiar relation of the individual to major cultural symbols. On the one hand, he is only weakly affected by them; he does not reflect their pervasive influence in his habitual conduct. At the same time, however, he may develop a compulsive attachment to the symbols as such—not to their meaning—and to their institutional embodiments, especially if these attachments offer leverage for aggression. Thus it would be characteristic of the mass man to be only poorly influenced by the complex meaning of democracy, unable to make the necessary discriminations, with little conception of how to fulfil the value in his daily life; and yet he may be easily susceptible to manipulation by wielders of this symbol, will swear allegiance to it, and will be prepared to use any means (including those ordinarily interdicted by democratic principles) against its purported enemies. Similarly, mass elements in a church may have little understanding of basic religious principles and reflect nothing of them in their own conduct, yet they will characteristically respond with special fervor to the symbols of the church and be its most aggressive defenders. This ambiguous participation, both in symbolic and in institutional behavior, is fundamental to the mass.

Mass behavior is not a matter of a simple lack of understanding among untutored elements. Values (and their behavioral correlates) are not transmitted intellectually; they are the standards of right conduct, of proper aspiration, which are taken for granted in a healthy society. Unmediated transmission, in the sense discussed above, results in a cultural impoverishment which has significant psychological consequences.

The political import of this condition is readily apparent. When values are stereotyped, symbol and meaning become divorced. Their content can then be manipulated with impunity; acts taken in the name of the values may in fact violate their spirit. The established political order can no longer be taken for granted. It must be defended explicitly, hence held open to attack as a secular, debatable thing. In the course of the struggle the embattled system becomes overrigid, identified with specific forces in the status quo, and thus even more vulnerable. At the same time a pervasive need for new and more satisfactory relationships is created—which is in turn transformed into disposable energy by demagogic managerial elites.

3. *Mass behavior is associated with activist interpretations of democracy and with increasing reliance upon force to resolve social conflict.* Social disintegration entails the breakdown of normal social restraints, including internalized standards of right conduct, and the established channels of action.[5] This frees the mass to engage in direct, unmediated efforts to achieve its goals and to lay hands upon the most readily accessible instruments of action. Ordinarily, even in countries having democratic constitutional systems, the population is so structured as to inhibit direct decision. The electorate participates at specified times and in defined ways; it is not free to create *ad hoc* methods of pressure. The citizen, even when organized in a pressure group supporting, say,

[5] The hold of traditional techniques of political participation—balloting rather than pressure tactics—must be broken before the activist tendencies come to the fore. Bakke (*op. cit.*, pp. 54 ff.) discusses the continued hold of custom as restraining the unemployed from engaging in types of political action advocated by radicals. Increased mass behavior would be expected if unemployment were indefinitely prolonged. Bakke also suggests that radical political action "requires a greater degree of hope and confidence in the future than many unemployed can muster." However, the characteristic activist responses of mass elements do not center upon utopian visions but upon direct efforts to gain short-term release from intolerable situations: the need for immediate solutions to such problems as mass unemployment, the suffering of war, hunger, etc., and the ideological need for "some sort of answer."

a farm lobby, can vote, write letters, visit his congressman, withhold funds, and engage in similar respectable elections. Other forms of activity are strange to him. But, when this code has lost its power over him, he will become available for activist modes of intervention.[6]

It is the mass-oriented elite, Fascist and Communist alike, which is the advocate and engineer of activism. The mobilization of the mass takes place in the streets on a day-to-day basis. And it is characteristic of the Communist-led mass organization that it will engage in unorthodox pressure tactics, for example, the "invasion" of a state legislature. The meaning of such tactics—especially when they are used before any significant degree of mass character has emerged in the target population—is precisely to break down feelings of deference for the lawmaking body and to prepare for extralegal methods of intimidation. Communists attempt to *create* a mass, as well as to use it, though of course, their long-term strategy is based on the assumption that deployable mass energies will be made available as a result of more general historical forces.[7] Like other aspects of mass behavior, activism is thus a result of the withdrawal of deference to established institutions. Its extreme versions are well known, as when mass elements, impatient with the niceties of legal procedure, set up their own tribunals. These may retain the external forms of juridical administration while transforming its spirit. Such extreme measures, however, often taken in crisis, represent only the conclusion of a process which begins with the surrender to popular pressure of the values intrusted to a culture-sustaining elite.

4. *Mass behavior devalues social institutions and therewith subverts their character-defining functions.* Institutions are defended, often at great cost of life and resources, because they come to reflect society's self-image. They define its aspirations and its moral commitments; they are the source and receptacle of self-respect, of unique identity. No enemy is so dangerous as he who threatens these valued principles and structures. Like the Tenno in Japan, they are the haloed, reverenced symbols of public weal, the last bastions which dare not be surrendered, without which life itself seems worthless, cast down to a melancholy

---

[6] Cf. Neumann, *op. cit.*, p. 111: "These dispossessed taken together composed the material of the amorphous masses of modern totalitarianism. They had lost or never possessed real group life. They now were ready to merge into a great stream of political activism giving them direction and fulfillment in a life which was no longer of their own making. '"To believe, to obey, to fight' became the motto promulgated by Il Duce. It was the chief political function of the new masses."

[7] This does not mean that other groups, either Fascist or Communist, will not be forced in the direction of activism. On the contrary, it is characteristic of the emergence of the mass that pressures are generated which force reluctant leaders to engage in activist ventures.

level of hopelessness and despair. This is in no essential different from an individual's attempt to protect the extensions of his own personality. Books, a house, signs of status, manner, clothing—any components of a "way of life"—may come to be valued for themselves because they define for the individual his essential nature. These are *his*; they have symbolic meaning for him, a meaning which sustains him against the depersonalizing pressures of the outside world.

Thus as particular modes of action become infused with value, that is, institutionalized, they add to their direct functions that of defining the character of the group. The institutionalized modes of holding property, defining responsibility, transferring power, raising children, and directing traffic are developed in order to satisfy specific needs. But, like habits in the individual, they have the indirect consequence of committing the society to an integrated system of values. Taken together, these valued institutions reflect the ethos of the culture, its peculiar way of self-fulfilment.

We may take it as axiomatic that a society becomes confused and uncertain, hence vulnerable to alien doctrine, to the extent that it loses this consciousness of a unique and valued identity. This does not mean, as many too quickly conclude, that a tight doctrinal unity is a necessary condition for cultural resilience. No more than fanaticism in the individual is general subservience to dogma a sign of strength. Nevertheless, it is essential that individuals feel that they are living in a world of valued modes of life, all ultimately integrated by a sense of kinship. This does not require that men should all believe the same thing. It does require that (1) they should believe something and that (2) there should be a core of shared assumptions as to the ultimate distinction between good and evil.

In this context, however, we are concerned not with the problem of homogeneity but with that of devaluation. Splits in the community, even those leading to civil war, do not necessarily imply a general weakening of values; splits polarize values and intensify adherence, sometimes resulting in a general strengthening of over-all community.[8] The debilitation which comes from the secularization of social institutions is of another sort. The machinery of social life becomes nothing more

---

[8] A community is not necessarily defined by the locus of sovereignty or organizational boundaries, though these are often convenient indexes. A community may break into segments, because the common framework of decision-making is not adequate to deal with differences; yet these differences, though requiring organizational independence, are not necessarily such as to establish separate communions. A commonwealth of nations, a social movement, a council of churches, are examples of this ambivalent unity.

machinery, shorn of its valued, sacred quality. As culture decays, attention shifts from ends to means, from values to things.

The mass is at once a symptom of this atrophy and a contributor to it. Population sectors take on a mass quality as they are alienated from symbolic and institutional loyalties. But the movement is reciprocal. The pressure of the mass upon key social agencies—especially in education and science—results in demands for a narrow utilitarian justification. The cultural elites are insecure and do not feel that their special (but indispensable) prerogatives are justified. It is not only the general pressure of a factory system but the capitulation to the demand for commonness which leads them to accept the standards which the mass man insists must be applied to all alike. This leveling pressure, indifferent to long-run cultural meaning, combines with the demand for efficiency and service to deny to institutions any intrinsic value. The mass thus joins with other forces in industrial society to transform institutions into organizations. They become technical (and expendable) instruments for the achievement of proximate goals.

The general consequence of this process is to attenuate and confuse society's self-image; to increase the likelihood of severe shifts in behavior under the pressure of immediate exigency; and to make possible the capature of key institutions—no longer well defined in character—by organizational manipulators.

6.

THE CRISIS OF MAY–JUNE, 1960—
A CASE STUDY IN JAPANESE POLITICS (1964)

ROBERT SCALAPINO AND MASUMI JUNNOSUKE

Japan has recently experienced the greatest mass movement in her political history. Millions of Japanese participated directly in the political events of May and June, 1960.[1] They signed petitions, engaged in work

SOURCE. Robert Scalapino and Masumi Junnosuke, *Parties and Politics In Contemporary Japan*. Berkeley and Los Angeles: University of California Press, 1964, pp. 125–153. Reprinted by permission of The University of California Press and the authors.
[1] For a variety of views on the May–June incidents, in English, see "Japanese

stoppages, demonstrated in Tokyo streets, or took similar actions. Almost all of these actions, it will be noted, took place outside the framework of the party movement and the Diet or on their peripheries. In some respects, the parties never seemed weaker than in this period of troubles—*all* the parties.

The immediate issue at stake was the revised United States–Japan Security Treaty. Negotiations between the two countries over treaty revision had been long and arduous. From the standpoint of American authorities, significant concessions had been made. These related to such subjects as the disposition and use of American forces stationed in Japan. None of the concessions, however, removed the fundamental objections of the neutralists, who saw the revised treaty as a "legalization" of a condition previously imposed upon a subjugated state. The original treaty could not be defended as a product of negotiations between equals, and this fact, together with its substantive inequities, made it more vulnerable, hence potentially more temporary. To remove some or all of the inequities, and to do this in the course of negotiations when Japan was fully sovereign, was to project the American–Japanese military alliance at least a full decade into the future. Since the neutralist objection was to the alliance itself, its improvement could scarcely satisfy them.

As we noted earlier, the merits of alliance versus neutralism have been hotly debated in Japan for more than a decade. The policy of alliance with the United States has had strong support, despite the attacks leveled upon it. Its adherents have insisted that the American–Japanese alliance serves the causes of peace and prosperity. Their views, in composite form, can be set forth as follows:

a) Surrounded by formidable and hostile powers, Japan cannot risk neutralism. The Communist world does not recognize neutralism as legitimate. Hence, any agreement reached between Japan and the Communists on this basis would be violated or abrogated unilaterally by them

Intellectuals Discuss American-Japanese Relations," Introduction by Robert A. Scalapino and articles by Kanichi Fukuda, Makoto Saitō, Yoshikazu Sakamoto, and Takeshi Ishida, *Far Eastern Survey*, October, 1960, pp. 145–160; "Japan Today," Introduction by I. I. Morris and articles by Kiyoshi Nasu, Kōsaku Tamura, Kikuo Nakamura, Kazuo Kuroda, and Sadachika Nabeyama, supplement to *The New Leader*, November 28, 1960, 42 pp.; Edwin O. Reischauer, "The Broken Dialogue with Japan," *Foreign Affairs*, XXXIX, No. 1 (October, 1960), 11–26; David Wurfel, "The Violent and the Voiceless in Japanese Politics," *Contemporary Japan*, XXXVI, No. 4 (November, 1960), 663–694; "To Our Friends in America," a pamphlet containing statements by Hisaakira Kano. Takashi Komatsu, Shigeo Horie, Masatoshi Matsushita, and Seiichi Fukuoka (published by Radio Japan, n.d.).

if it suited their purposes. Experience thus far has indicated that neither the Soviet Union nor Communist China is willing to make any significant concessions to Japanese national interests. For Japan to be isolated, defenseless, or wholly dependent upon some vague international agreement would be more dangerous to its peace and security than military alliance with the United States.

b) At this juncture of world history, major war between the Communist and non-Communist forces is most likely to be avoided if a global balance of power can be maintained, it is argued. Japan has a moral responsibility to assist in the maintenance of that balance within the limits imposed upon her by constitutional provisions and internal economic-political conditions. These limitations preclude any rapid or extensive rearmament. They make impossible the use of Japanese forces overseas. They also make inadvisable the development of any nuclear weapons, or, indeed, the storing of such weapons in Japan for possible American use. But Japan can and should assist in maintaining non-Communist strength in Asia by allowing the United States to use air and naval facilities in exchange for an American guarantee to underwrite Japanese security.

c) It is also argued that what is moral happily coincides with what is politically and economically advantageous. It is proper for Japan, now en route to democracy, to align itself with a nation having similar political values and institutions. And, on balance, this alliance has fostered rather than precluded the rapid establishment of a vast network of world contacts. To have had the United States as ally and supporter has greatly facilitated the reëntrance of Japan into the world scene. She has been able to participate in international and regional organizations much earlier than would otherwise have been possible, and to assume an active, important role in world affairs. The alliance has not hindered the development of ties with the non-aligned world; on the contrary, in certain respects, especially through its economic benefits, it has aided such contacts. Despite the alliance, normal relations have been reëstablished with the Soviet Union. More than this, Japan has never been able to attain. Admittedly, the alliance has adversely affected relations with Communist China. This is unfortunate, and efforts must be made to obtain improvements. But this problem does not offset the sizable political advantages gained by Japan as a result of her alliance with the United States.

d) The most important advantage, however, has been an economic one. The American alliance, according to its proponents, must be given credit for being a major factor in the unprecedented prosperity which Japan has enjoyed during the past decade. First, by means of extensive gifts, loans, and technical aid, the United States launched Japan on the road to economic recovery and growth. All forms of assistance, including military procurement, represented billions of dollars put into the Japanese economy. There was no alternative to this support, and without it the Japanese people would have faced unending misery and crisis. But money cannot measure the worth of the most basic economic assistance, namely, the transferral of vast quantities of technical, scientific, and managerial knowledge pertaining to the whole field of economic modernization. The tremendous technological revolution now taking place in Japan can be attributed in considerable measure to the far-reaching alliance with the United States, private and public. Thousands of Japanese have had advanced training in the United States; large numbers of American technicians and counselors have taught, advised, and learned in Japan. Patent sharing and many other forms of industrial coöperation have expanded greatly in recent years. The United States and Japan are partners in a revolution that is transforming the life of every Japanese citizen.

e) Closely connected with these developments has been the great surge in trade between the two societies. In 1960, Japan exported over one billion, one hundred million dollars' worth of goods to the United States, while her imports from that country totaled more than one billion, three hundred million dollars. Approximately one third of all Japanese trade was with the United States and Canada. The United States took 28 per cent of all Japanese exports, and furnished 30 per cent of all imports. The economic future of Japan hinges upon the maintenance and, if possible, the expansion of these relations. Any shift to a neutralist foreign policy would surely jeopardize the present economic ties with the United States, and thereby affect adversely every individual in Japan.

Thus do the supporters of alliance outline and defend their case. And to meet socialist challenges of subservience, the conservative leaders have proclaimed their objective as that of "an independent foreign policy within the framework of coöperation with the West, particularly the United States." They have asserted that they are seeking partnership, not subordination. They have insisted that their firm position during the negotiations for a revised security treaty resulted in the elimination of inequities. (The conservatives did bargain in a tough fashion with American authorities on some issues.) The conservatives have also repeatedly asserted that the alliance does not preclude an independent foreign policy, including some positions differing from the policy of the United States.

Indeed, the conservatives have carried the fight over Japanese independence to the socialists. They have insisted that if Japan is to be truly independent, it must have the power to defend itself. Consequently, they have urged the repeal of the so-called antiwar clause, Article Nine of the constitution. And in answer to the objections of the Soviet Union and Communist China, Japanese leaders have argued that their military alliance with the United States is for defensive purposes only, citing the fact that their forces total only 230,000 men at present, together with some 50,000 Americans in the area, a small group in comparison to the nearly three million men in the Chinese Communist armed force.

The policy of military alliance with the United States probably has positive support from about one third of the Japanese people, with an additional third being uncertain or indifferent. However, polls on certain issues or at certain times would appreciably raise or lower that number. For example, it appears that a considerable number of Japanese now support limited rearmament for defense purposes only. It is the issue of American bases in Japan and, thus, the direct connection with American military strategy pertaining to Asia, that seems to raise the most serious doubts. While the military aspects of the American–Japanese alliance remain vulnerable, a certain counterbalance is provided by the high degree of support given the economic and cultural aspects of the alliance.

Despite the various arguments advanced for the alliance, however, public opinion polls would indicate that neutralism has had a positive appeal to at least one third of the Japanese people.[2] Many of the reasons are obvious. The disaster of World War II has not been forgotten, nor will it be forgotten soon—230,000 Japanese still suffer from radioactive diseases as a result of the Hiroshima and Nagasaki bombings, and many thousands of other victims of the fire raids or of combat injuries serve as living reminders that the last war did not pay. There is an acute awareness of the vulnerability of Japan in this age of nuclear war. Her densely packed cities are now only minutes away from Soviet or Chinese bases. Her population, approaching 93,000,000 at present, lives in an area approximately the size of California. Foreign trade is indispensable to survival. Japan must import 80 per cent of her industrial raw materials and 20 per cent of her foodstuffs. The difficulties of supply in the event of war seem enormous. There is the additional problem of trade expansion in time of peace, with the argument that neutralism would open new markets without losing old ones.

We remarked earlier that neutralism is also an expression of nationalism in foreign policy. After an era of intensive occupation, perhaps the remarkable thing is that personal relations between Japanese and Ameri-

---

[2] In each edition, the *Asahi nenkan* ("Asahi Yearbook") gives a full account of the polls and survey research undertaken by the newspapers *Asahi Shimbun*, *Mainichi Shimbun*, and *Yomiuri Shimbun*, and by other organizations.

In English, Douglas Mendel, Jr. presents and analyzes an important collection

cans have remained generally good. The United States has done well in "popularity" polls, and personal anti-Americanism has not shown any appreciable increase despite the rising nationalist sentiment and the dissatisfaction with certain American Policies.[3] Sharper reactions might

of poll data pertaining to foreign policy issues in his forthcoming book, *The Japanese People and Foreign Policy* (Berkeley and Los Angeles, 1962).

Two sets of polls on rearmament, one from the earlier period and one from a somewhat later time are as follows:

"ASAHI SHIMBUN" POLLS—1952–1954

Response	(Percentage Distribution)			
	Feb., 1952	Feb., 1953	June, 1953	May, 1954
Rearmament necessary	32	38	41	37
Rearmament unnecessary	26	29	23	30
Under certain conditions	24	14	16	15
No opinion	18	19	20	18

Source: *Asahi nenkan*, 1954, p. 306, and *Jiji nenkan* ("Current Events Yearbook"), 1955, p. 302.

POLL CONDUCTED BY THE PRIME MINISTER SECRETARIAT

Response	(Percentage Distribution)	
	Oct., 1956	Feb., 1957
For rearmament	33	28
Against rearmament	42	41
Under certain conditions	13	17
Don't know	12	14

Source: *Asahi nenkan*, 1958, p. 259.

[3] For example, in response to a Newspaper Public Opinion Survey League national poll in December, 1954, asking the question "Which country do you like?" 33.3 per cent answered, "the United States"; 26.3, "Great Britain"; 22.5, "Switzerland"; 22.3, "France"; and 11.9, "Communist China." "What country do you dislike?" got the following answers: 37.3 per cent answered, "the Soviet Union"; 30.3, "Korea"; 21.3, "Communist China"; and 10.6, "United States" (*ibid.*, 1956, p. 320).

Another national poll on the same subject, in November, 1957, produced the following results: "Which country do you like?"—26.5 per cent, "the United States," and 5.6, "India"; "Which country do you dislike?"—30.5 per cent, "the Soviet Union"; 4.0, "the United States"; and 3.7, "Communist China" (*ibid.*, 1959, p. 158).

have been expected, given the historic Japanese tradition of isolation, xenophobia, and extreme national and individual sensitivity. In spite of the relatively moderate reaction to the Occupation era, however, the demand for "full independence" has been a strong one. In politics, the socialists have kept up a drumfire attack upon conservative foreign policy as subservient to the United States. They have denounced foreign bases not merely as dangerous, but also as symbols of the fact that the Occupation has not been completely liquidated. They have insisted that only through a neutralist policy can Japan assert her independence and her proper identity as an Asian state.

For many Japanese socialists, neutralism, in addition to its other virtues, is also an article of political faith. Pacifism and Marxism have both had a deep influence on the Japanese socialist movement. Each of these now lends its weight to the neutralist cause. This may seem strange as applied to Marxism. It is true that Marxis-oriented Japanese socialists may *sound* as if they belonged to the Soviet camp. It is also true that some of them act that way. The combination of having the United States as the immediate, close-at-hand object of attack and of being trained only in Marxist terminology and methods of attack is conducive to a conscious or unconscious Communist bias.

But there is another important side of this picture. It is connected with the intricate history of Japanese socialism. The great majority of Marxists and quasi-Marxists within the Japanese socialist movement long ago broke away from the discipline of Moscow. Subsequently, the recriminations have often been bitter on both sides. Thus the postwar Japanese Socialist party, while increasingly dominated by its left wing, has not sought a broad popular front with the Communists. At home, as abroad, it has opted for neutralism. The majority of socialists continue to maintain a relatively orthodox Marxist position on many economic and political issues. This separates them decisively from the West, especially the United States. But their own experiences as well as their political instincts have caused them to seek identification with Nehru and the other Afro-Asian neutralists rather than with Krushchev. Mao, as an Asian and a Chinese, has had somewhat more personal and political appeal, it must be admitted, but it is the traditional Nehru line that has constituted the basic socialist approach to world politics.

Against the background of the above debate and a rather evenly divided public opinion, the treaty crisis emerged. Initially, the anti-treaty movement was largely confined to the "professionals." Sōhyō attempted a national campaign, but this attracted little attention. Meanwhile, the socialists fought the treaty in the House of Representatives, using such tactics of questioning and delaying as were available to them. Prime Minister Kishi had visited Washington and signed the revised treaty on January 24, 1960. On February 4, it had been introduced into the lower house, with a special committee established to examine it. Naturally, the socialist minority sought to use the maximum time in debate. Between Feburary 4 and May 19, when the treaty was forced to a vote, over a hundred days elapsed. Still, the opposition claimed that major sections of the treaty remained unclarified.

Notwithstanding the rather restricted and conventional opposition to the revised treaty prior to May 19, the foundations for a larger movement did exist, provided that some means were found to utilize these. We have noted many indications that the Japanese public has long been deeply disturbed about issues of armament and military alliance. While a majority may now accept the fact that Japan should have some type of military force for self-defense purposes, opposition to the revision of Article Nine, the antiwar clause of the new constitution, would seem to be substantial. Moreover, despite the general popularity of the United States noted earlier, the one *major* deficiency in the American image in Japan relates to issues of war and peace. More than any American "ally," the Japanese feel that the United States is making a limited contribution to peace; America is seen as being relatively military-minded.

This sentiment among the Japanese public has not been hidden from the Japanese conservatives, any more than from the socialists. It has made the former reluctant to speed up the tempo of rearmament, push for revision of Article Nine, or make any move in the direction of a regional defense pact. Too add to conservative problems, on May 2 an American U-2 airplane was shot down over the territory of the Soviet Union. This had almost instant repercussions in Japan. The socialists charged that other American U-2 airplanes were based in Japan, and that these had been used for reconnaissance missions over Communist China, North Korea, and the Soviet Union. Both the Japanese government and the United States denied that any U-2 airplanes based in Japan had been used for espionage purposes. Nevertheless, public apprehension mounted. The subsequent collapse of the summit conference and the withdrawal of Khrushchev's invitation to President Eisenhower to visit Moscow also had a drastic effect upon the Japanese political scene. The revised treaty was now being debated in the context of a more strained world situation. The cold war was being intensified, and the risk of a hot war seemed much greater than in the recent past. Moreover, the symbolic significance of Eisenhower's imminent visit to Japan had been drastically altered. Instead of coming as a representative of reduced tensions, major power accord, and coexistence—coming via Moscow—he was now scheduled to come via the Philippines, Taiwan, and Okinawa, as an inspector of American military bases in Asia. Naturally, this shift exacerbated the conservative-socialist cleavage in foreign policy, and greatly intensified the political strain upon Japanese society at large.

The Kishi government had long been in difficulties because of internal factionalism. Kishi perhaps represented the "compromise" type of leader, chosen less for his strength than for his capacity to adjust, a "neutral" in the midst of contending strong men. As we have noted, Kishi's position initially rested upon a five-faction coalition, the Kishi, Satō, Ishii, Ōno, and Kōno factions; subsequently, the Kōno faction dropped out of the coalition and the Ikeda faction was substituted. The anti–Main Current factions within the Liberal Democractic party had been mounting a formidable campaign against the Kishi cabinet in the 1959–60 period. According to the reckoning of his conservative opponents, Kishi had been in power for a sufficient period; it was time to release the office of the prime-ministership to those who had waited so long—and so impatiently. Even the Main Current faction leaders had been watching for the chance to replace Kishi. He had also accumulated a number of enemies as a result of policy actions and inactions. His socialist opponents had always emphasized Kishi's membership in the Tōjō cabinet and his active role in the militarist era. The struggle over proposed revisions in the police and security laws had evoked cries of high-pressure tactics and a resurgence of reaction.[4] Thus, in terms both of its tenure and its tactics—along with some of its policies—the Kishi administration was close to a low ebb in the spring of 1960, with opponents inside and out of the party ready to put an end to it.

Because of the above factors, it was possible to unite professional agitators with a certain portion of both the Japanese elite and the urban masses in the events of late May and early June, 1960. The catalytic force lay in the happenings of May 19. It was on this date that the Kishi government made its major drive for treaty ratification in the House of Representatives. The date was not an accident. If the revised treaty were approved by the lower house on May 19, it could come into effect one month later, at the time of the Eisenhower visit. (Under Japanese constitutional provisions, a treaty comes into effect automatically thirty days after ratification by the House of Representatives, if not approved before that time by the House of Councilors.)

---

[4] See Masumi Junnosuke, "The Problem of the Police Duties Bill and Japanese Democracy," *Shisō*, February, 1959, pp. 1–19.

It is easy to understand why an administration not overly popular at the moment, and hard pressed by its opponents on a dangerous issue, would seize upon the Eisenhower visit as an excellent political opportunity and seek to connect treaty ratification with that visit. It is equally easy to understand why all Kishi opponents, including those within the Liberal Democratic party, would seek to thwart that strategy. Thus the Kishi cabinet in developing its plans faced bitter opposition both from the anti–Main Current factions of its party and from the socialists. Because of the opposition within the Liberal Democratic party itself, the Kishi government felt compelled to cloak its strategy even from some of the members of its own party. Thus the decision to push through a motion to extend the Diet session and a second motion to approve the revised treaty on the evening of May 19 were not known to many conservatives in advance. This was, in fact, not a strategy of the Liberal Democratic party, but of the Main Current faction of that party.

Moreover, it was a strategy that had to be mounted against increasing chaos and violence within the Diet. With a portion of the Liberal Democrats looking on as passive bystanders, the socialists mounted the ramparts and, in a very literal sense, defied the government to pass. To stop passage of a Steering Committee resolution prolonging the Diet session, socialist members of the lower house sought to prevent the May 19 session from being opened by engaging in a "sit-down" movement. To keep the Speaker from reaching the rostrum, the socialists placed themselves on the floor, between the Speaker's Chamber and the front of the house. The government then ordered some five hundred police to drag the socialists off the floor. The plenary session thus opened with only conservatives taking part.

Parliamentary procedures on this day completely broke down. Along with the melee on the floor of the house, chaos reigned in a meeting of the Special Committee on the Security Treaty which was being held at approximately the same time. The socialists sought to put a vote of nonconfidence (which takes precedence over other bills), but the chairman refused to recognize the movers and later announced that the revised security treaty and related agreements had been passed by a majority of the committee. The entire meeting lasted only a few minutes and was marked by such complete confusion and shouting that no one could be certain of the actions taken.

Against this background, and with all socialists and some conservatives absent, during the midnight period of May 19–20 the Kishi elements within the Liberal Democratic party proceeded to vote an extension of the session beyond midnight and then to pass the revised treaty. These actions were accomplished with great speed, and with some anti-

Kishi conservatives later claiming that they had not been informed of the actions which were to take place.[5]

This "May 19 incident" was violently attacked by almost all of the leading Japanese newspapers. While there was some criticism of the socialist obstructionist tactics, the attack was largely concentrated upon the "anti-democratic" actions of the Kishi cabinet. The "movement to defend democracy" had its origins in this event. And suddenly many elements hitherto passive joined in the anti-Kishi movement. This gave the movement qualities of spontaneity, diversity, and enthusiasm which it had previously lacked. It is impossible to understand post–May 19 developments without realizing that numerous currents were flowing with few connecting channels. The professional agitators were still very much in the scene, occupying critical leadership positions in some areas. Now, however, they had a rank-and-file following which their own actions alone could not possibly have produced. In the all-important student arena, leaders of Zengakuren—the national student federation— exercised key leadership roles. Zengakuren has long occupied an extreme-left political position; like many organizations, its official position and that of its leaders is far more radical than the political stance of the great bulk of its rank-and-file membership.

The Japanese political situation after May 19, however, provided Zengakuren leaders with an excellent opportunity to mobilize a truly mass movement on behalf of specific objectives, those of causing the Kishi government to resign and paving the way for new elections, with the revised treaty being made the central issue before the Japanese electorate. For the first time in its history, Zengakuren had a series of issues with much broader appeal than its own set of Marxist doctrines could possibly provide. But it also faced a major handicap, namely, the ideological divisions within its top ranks. Like all other elements of the Japanese left, Zengakuren has been rent by serious ideological cleavages. In a curious reflection of postwar Japanese freedom, one portion of the student far left has seized upon such events as the Cominform criticism of Nosaka, the de-Stalinization campaign, and other traumatic events in the Communist world to declare its "independence" of international communism. New student journals of radicalism have made their debut, issuing violent criticism of Khrushchev, and sometimes of Mao Tse-tung as well. Some of these independent elements have been labeled

---

[5] For critical views of the famous midnight session see Ukai Nobushige, "Points at Issue in the Highhanded Adoption," *Shisō*, pp. 126–128, and Hashimoto Kiminobu, "It Is Legally Invalid Too," *Chūō Kōron*, July, 1960, pp. 42–46; also see the articles by Fukuda, Saitō, Sakamoto, and Ishida in *Far Eastern Survey*, October, 1960 (note 1).

Trotskyites. This Trotskyite faction came to control Zengakuren, and became its Main Current. The Zengakuren anti–Main Current group hewed to the Japanese Communist party line. Throughout the May–June period these two factions were generally in violent opposition.

Because the Communist party maintained that the central foe was American imperialism, it was natural that the students who demonstrated against Eisenhower's press secretary, James Hagerty, were from the anti-Main Current faction of Zengakuren. The Trotskyites, on the other hand, saw the main target as the Kishi government, and consequently kept their attention focused on the Diet and the anti-Kishi movement. Between these two elements, bitterness actually increased in the course of the incidents, and further fragmentation occurred.

Important though the Zengakuren leaders were, there were other student groups who participated in the post–May 19 demonstrations. Thousands of students from the five Christian universities in Tokyo paraded, and this was but one example of nonradical student demonstrators. Subsequent polls revealed that even a certain number of students favoring the Liberal Democratic party took part in one or more demonstrations. More impressive, in some respects, was the response of the mature intellectuals. For example, some 75 per cent of all faculty members of Tokyo University signed petitions demanding the dissolution of the Diet and immediate elections. Thousands of intellectuals who had not previously taken an active part in politics suddenly became involved in protest meetings, petition circulation, and demonstrations before the Diet and in the Tokyo streets. This, no doubt, acted as an enormous stimulus to students and to other citizens. Various occupational groups were organized. Such diverse groups as housewives, actresses, and Christians were mobilized for protest purposes.

Organized labor, especially Sōhyō, has represented another group frequently engaged in political agitation, and, as we have noted, Sōhyō had been a pioneer in the movement against the security treaty. But many of the past work stoppages conducted by Sōhyō had been dreary, ill-supported affairs. In the aftermath of the May 19 incident, however, on June 4 a stoppage conducted by the communications workers reportedly involved over five and one-half million workers, the largest such action in the history of Japan. Contrary to many earlier occasions, moreover, this work stoppage seemed to have considerable public sympathy.

Thus Tokyo rocked with demonstrations in the days that followed May 19. As was noted earlier, this was in many respects the most impressive mass movement ever witnessed in modern Japan. Over thirteen million citizens signed petitions urging Diet dissolution and new elections. Hundreds of thousands of people marched and demonstrated in

Tokyo and other cities. Millions engaged in work stoppages. Polls indicated that opposition to both the treaty and the Kishi government was mounting. In July, 1959, for example, a poll indicated that 31 per cent favored a new security treaty with the United States, 28 per cent were opposed, and 41 per cent either did not know or were indifferent. In February, 1960, those who supported ratification of the revised treaty were 25 per cent, those who opposed 36 per cent, and 39 per cent were the "don't know" or "indifferent" categories. A *Tōkyō Shimbun* poll taken on May 26–27, 1960, indicated that 27 per cent of the people thought the revised treaty necessary, 42 per cent believed it to be unnecessary, 11½ per cent were indifferent, and 17 per cent did not know. In this same poll, 74 per cent of those questioned favored the resignation of the Kishi cabinet, 17 per cent were opposed, and 6½ per cent did not know. Support for the dissolution of the Diet was almost equally heavy. Another poll conducted on June 3 throughout Japan indicated that 58 per cent of the people favored the resignation of the Kishi cabinet, whereas 12 per cent supported its continuance. These polls indicated that, among postwar Japanese cabinets the Kishi cabinet had reached an all-time low position in terms of public opinion.[6]

The climax to the political unrest was reached between June 10 and 19. The Hagerty incident occurred on June 10, when Press Secretary Hagerty and Ambassador MacArthur were surrounded by Zengakuren (anti–Main Current) demonstrators at the airport, had their car jostled up and down, and finally had to be taken to Tokyo by military helicopter. It is to be noted that no physical violence accompanied this or other incidents up to this point. Nor were the majority of demonstrations anti-American; they were anti-Kishi. Americans mingled freely in the crowds, and often, a holiday mood seemed to prevail. On June 15,

---

[6] At various times the *Asahi Shimbun* has asked the question, "Do you support the cabinet?" Note the results of a poll taken shortly after the May 19 incident, at the height of unpopularity of the Kishi cabinet, and compare them with the low points of other cabinets:

	Yes	No	Don't Know or Indifferent
	(Percentage distribution)		
Kishi cabinet (May, 1960)	12	58	30
Hatoyama cabinet (August, 1956)	29	41	30
Yoshida cabinet (May, 1954)	23	48	29
Ashida cabinet (July, 1948)	16	52	32

however, violence erupted in the vicinity of the Diet. It was initiated by a right-wing extremist group who apparently drove a truck into a line of demonstrators, most of whom were women. Students witnessing the spectacle stormed the Diet gates and clashed with the police. Six hundred students were injured and one woman student was trampled to death in the ensuing struggle. Violence even extended to certain side-line groups. In their excitement, police attacked some university instructors who were seeking to negotiate on behalf of the wounded students, and also attacked some newsmen covering the scene. Once again, as a result of this episode, the Kishi government was bitterly criticized by almost the entire Japanese press. But at the same time the press also began to criticize the anti-goverment movement for some of the activities taking place.[7]

On June 16, the government was forced to ask for a postponement of President Eisenhower's visit. Opposition to ratification did not cease. On June 19, over three hundred thousand demonstrators surrounded the Diet in a vain effort to demand dissolution, and there were still a hundred thousand standing in front the of the building at midnight when the treaty automatically secured Diet approval. Confronted with this *fait accompli*, the demonstrators at last retired; the crisis was over. On June 23, the ratifications were exchanged in Tokyo, and Premier Kishi announced his resignation. The Kishi government stayed in office for another month while maneuvering took place within the Liberal Democratic party to determine the new leadership. Finally, on July 18, Ikeda Hayato was formally elected premier by a special session of the Diet, after having won the presidency of the Liberal Democratic party a few days earlier. A new era had begun.

Let us now return to the questions posed at the beginning of this study. First, why did the Kishi cabinet have to resign when its party, the Liberal Democratic party, commanded an overwhelming majority in the Diet, and why did many of the conservative leaders desert Kishi at this critical period of his career? As we have seen, an answer to this question involves an understanding of the Japanese system of political factions. At no time during the crisis did the majority party act in united fashion. The anti–Main Current factions (Miki-Matsumura,

---

[7] See Arase Yutaka, "Is Speech Really Free?" *Sekai*, August, 1960, pp. 203–216, and Nakano Yoshio, "Changing Editorial Opinions," *Shisō*, August 1960, pp. 129–139.

After the June 15 clash between police and students, the press began to voice alarm about violence and unparliamentary activities. On June 17 the seven major newspapers issued a joint statement asserting that, no matter how crucial the causes for which they fought, the socialists should stop denouncing the conservatives and reënter the Diet.

Ishibashi, and Kōno) openly denounced Kishi's tactics, and helped in a variety of ways to strengthen the anti-Kishi front. Even the so-called middle factions (Ikeda, Ōno, and Ishii) although supporting the party and the treaty, directed some criticism against Kishi and Satō for their "highhanded tactics." Thus, within the Liberal Democratic party, the factions of Kishi and his brother, Satō Eisaku, tended to become isolated. This, perhaps more than any other single factor, made Kishi's resignation inevitable.

It might be argued that this situation was produced by the indignation of men who, though they were members of the conservative party, could not approve of the policies being pursued by the current leadership, or, in some cases, were antagonized by the failure of the Kishi-Satō factions to consult them concerning tactics. It might also be argued that many conservatives could not help being impressed and concerned by the trends in the press and in public opinion. There can be no doubt that a certain percentage of demonstrators against Kishi were regular supporters of the Liberal Democratic party. Subsequent polls taken among university and college students in the Tokyo area revealed this fact, and the percentage among other groups was undoubtedly higher in most cases. Despite these factors, however, it remains true that the opposition to Kishi within the Liberal Democratic party ran in accoradance with factional lines and general factional positions. The anti-Kishi factions denounced his tactics not so much because they were shocked by government actions as because they wanted to oust Kishi, supplanting him with one of their own leaders.

Once again, the supremacy of the faction as the primary unit of political loyalty in Japanese politics was revealed. Thus the loosely knit alliance of conservative factions broke under a political crisis which offered excellent chances of political realignment. Factional divisions, moreover, were equally important in the maneuvering that took place openly after the announcement of Kishi's resignation. The three "middle faction" leaders, Ikeda, Ōno, and Ishii each began to seek the party presidency and the succession to Kishi as prime minister. Ikeda hoped for the support of the Main Current Kishi-Satō factions, and the possible backing of the Miki-Matsumura faction as well, since in the days prior to the Kishi cabinet reorganization of June, 1959, his faction had been close to this group in an anti-Kishi front.

Ōno also hoped to obtain Kishi-Satō backing, since his faction had given much needed assistance during the controversy over the revised police law in the fall of 1958, as well as in the recent crisis. Ōno, however, also hoped for support from his close friend and fellow "party politician," Kōno, a prominent leader of the anti-Main Current faction.

Ishii also hoped to obtain Kishi-Satō support, and emphasized his strong position among conservatives in the House of Councilors.

The position of the Kishi-Satō factions was critical, because despite their recent adversities the two brothers controlled the votes of about one hundred and ten members of the lower house. According to informed political sources, the Kishi-Satō factions wanted the new conservative leader to preside over a five-faction alliance (Kishi, Satō, Ikeda, Ōno, and Ishii), an alliance that would exclude the three anti–Main Current factions (Miki-Matsumura, Kōno, and Ishibashi). They wanted to prevent any Ikeda-Miki or Ōno-Kōno coalition. Reportedly, Kishi spoke to each of the three "middle faction" contenders about the possibility of their becoming prime minister, but he did not initially throw his support to any one man. Kawashima Shōjirō, secretary-general of the party, served as mediator and middleman, in traditional Japanese style.

On June 24 Ikeda received important support from ex-Premier Yoshida. To meet this gain, the Ōno and Ishii forces drew together in a defensive alliance, and the factional struggle was intensified. On July 2 the Liberal Democratic party leadership agreed upon a meeting to decide its next presidency and the prime-ministership on July 13. Negotiations and bargaining were now conducted on a round-the-clock basis, Satō began to visit the three "middle faction" contenders, seeking a compromise solution. On July 6 the three met and decided to leave the decision to a "five-boss conference." But the leaders of the Main Current and middle factions were unable to reach a unanimous decision. Further mediation seemed impossible, and it was decided that the issue should be settled by a party vote. On July 8 and 9, the three contenders announced that they would each stand for the election. In addition, Matsumura (Miki-Matsumura faction) and Foreign Minister Fujiyama (Kishi faction) declared their candidacies.

The contest, however, appeared to be between Ikeda and Ōno. Ōno was now seeking to develop a "party-politician alliance" composed of the Ōno, Ishii, and Kōno factions, while Ikeda, supported by Satō, was seeking to obtain the support of the entire Main Current group and such independent elements as were backing Fujiyama. On July 13 Ōno and Matsumura suddenly withdrew in order to support Ishii as the joint candidate of the "party-politician factions." Kishi now made clear his support of Ikeda. The result of the final ballot was 302 votes for Ikeda to 194 votes for Ishii.[8]

[8] According to Liberal Democratic party rules, the president is elected by a party conference consisting of the party Diet members (at that time 286 representatives and 135 councilors), and prefectural delegates, two from each prefectural federation of party branches (at that time 92).

The new Ikeda cabinet represented an alliance of the five factions that the Kishi-Satō groups desired. Four ministers were selected from the Ikeda faction, two from Satō, two from Kishi (with an additional one from the new Fujiyama faction, formerly a branch of the Kishi faction), two from Ōno, and one from Ishii. In addition, two "neutrols" and three House of Councilor independents were selected. With respect to the new party officials, the secretary-general came from the Kishi faction, the chairman of the executive board from Satō, the chairman of the policy research committee from Kishi. The anti-Main Current factions were excluded from the cabinet. This was also a signal victory for the ex-official elements; the party-politician factions were given no major posts.[9]

It is because of these facts that the Japanese political factions deserve, in many respects, to be considered as parties in their own right. To be sure, these "parties" are closed, mutual-interest clubs, exclusive in nature. And because the constantly varying combinations of these clubs make up the larger federations which we designate as the Japanese political parties, the latter too partake of the "exclusive club" character.

But, while factional strife played a major role in bringing down the Kishi government, one cannot ignore such other factors as the adamant socialist opposition that helped to produce the May 19 incident and thereby opened the pathway to succeeding events. This again raises the question as to why the Japanese socialists have seemed so ambivalent toward the parliamentary system. Many left-wing socialists of Japan can be called believers in parliamentarism-plus. The "plus" refers to the fact that they are quite willing to go beyond parliamentarism if it does not produce the result they desire. To them, legitimate tactics represent a continuum from the Diet to the streets, from elections to sit-downs, demonstrations, and even violence. Historically, violence and suppression have interacted in Japanese politics, and this may still be a threat. But how is the position of many Japanese socialists to be explained?

The fact that a number of socialists retain a Marxist creed is a partial explanation. Marxism legalizes, indeed demands, tactics that go beyond

[9] *Asahi Shimbun,* July 19, 1960, p. 1. One year earlier, in June, 1959, the Kishi cabinet had consisted of five Kishi faction men, two Satō faction, one Ōno faction, two Kōno faction, two Ikeda faction and three councilors (one Kishi, one Ōno, and one neutral). The secretary-general had been a Kishi faction man, the chairman of the Policy Research Committee an Ōno faction man, and the chairman of the party Executive Committee had been Ishii. Such a cabinet is known in Japanese as *habatsu kinkō naikaku,* "a faction-balanced cabinet." See *Asahi nenkan,* 1960, p. 192.

parliamentarism. Especially in its Leninist forms, it is the "science" of the use and abuse of parliamentarism. In addition to this, however, there are other factors, some of them traditionally Japanese. As we noted earlier, majoritarianism is a new theory for Japan, one of dubious validity and ethical worth. Decision making, Japanese style, is based upon consensus. There is still a deep feeling in many quarters that it is immoral and "undemocratic" for a majority to govern, for decisions to be reached without compromise with the minority. Yet, as we have noted, negotiation and compromise in Japanese politics take place almost wholly among factions, not between parties. Between the major parties there is almost no communication. This is partly the result of the wide ideological separation, but it goes beyond this problem. Indeed, the difficulty of intergroup communications is a serious one in all parts of Japanese society. Once again, this seems closely connected with the closed nature of the primary social unit, the leader-follower group. *Japan represents the paradox of an open society made up of closed components.*

Beyond the Marxist and traditional obstacles that cloud socialist acceptance of Western-style parliamentarism and its rules, there also exist certain obstacles mounted by the conservatives. When the political history of modern Japan is viewed in total perspective, are not some doubts about the liberalism of Japanese conservatives in order? Has not their record on behalf of civil liberties and minority rights, thus far, been rather weak? Undoubtedly, most socialists are too quick to see "fascism" and "militarism" under every conservative proposal or action. Perhaps their fears mark them as living in a bygone era, and are partly engendered by the hope of political gain; or perhaps the old refrain is the only one with which they feel confortable. Yet, whatever the element of change and evolution in postwar Japanese conservatism, many individual Japanese conservatives do remain anti-liberal, many abhor the new constitution and regard most, if not all, of the American reforms as ill conceived. They still cherish the hope, quite probably forlorn, of making sweeping changes. They have had as little experience with genuine debate, and as little trust in Western-style parliamentarism, as their counterparts on the left.

Clearly, there were thousands of articulate non-Marxist Japanese who regarded the tactics of the Kishi government, especially the *fait accompli* of May 19, as a conservative brand of "parliamentarism-plus." This, combined with the deeply rooted intellectual suspicions of Japanese conservatism in general, produced the movement to preserve democracy against the "tyranny of the majority." One of the truly remarkable aspects of the recent crisis was the massive participation of the intellectuals. As has been noted, the journalist world was overwhelmingly anti-Kishi, and the assault of almost all leading newspapers upon the tactics of the Kishi government certainly was important in cultivating mass support for the demonstrations. In addition, hundreds of intellectuals participated in a direct political movement for the first time in their lives.

To abandon the role of scholar encased in the study-cocoon, to *act* instead of merely writing, to translate the role of social critic into that of social actionist—for many intellectuals these were novel and temporarily exhilarating experiences. In the aftermath, some inevitably had doubts, second thoughts, and uncertainties. A note of self-consciousness, even embarrassment, later made its entry into certain intellectual circles. As yet, it is uncertain whether these incidents have marked the beginnings of a deeper commitment on the part of Japanese intellectuals to active political participation. The intellectual cannot be equated with the Socialist party, nor with any organized political group. Yet in some degree, perhaps he shares the socialist ambivalence concerning Western-style parliamentarism, at least as it operates in Japan. Many of this class feel that the parties and the Diet do not reflect public opinion accurately, that the parties are closed organizations to which the people have no real access, and that elections are won or lost on the basis of funds expended, not on the basis of issues. It is for this reason that some Japanese intellectuals refuse to accept the moral right of the "majority" party. But it is also true that some talk of "qualitative democracy," a term which seeks to differentiate between an articulate elite (naturally, "progressive"), an elite which "knows the political facts of life," and the mass—particularly the rural mass—which is politically ignorant and easily bought or led. In truth, of course, this is an elitist theory or a theory of tutelage, at variance with the concepts of "quantitative" democracy upon which contemporary parliamentary institutions must rest. But it helps to account for such attempts as those by the students to go back to their home districts after the May–June incidents and "educate" the rural voters. It also provides a partial explanation for the feeling of many intellectuals that a great separation exists between the parties and the Diet on the one hand and the real interests of the Japanese people on the other. A very significant number of Japanese intellectuals believed that they were defending democracy in the only manner possible—outside the Diet, and even outside the regular political parties—in a direct appeal to the masses, which was also to serve as a method of education. But it must be recognized that these intellectuals did have as their central demand Diet dissolution and a general election focusing on the treaty revision issue. Thus, whatever their misgivings about the Japanese parliamentary system, the parties, the elections, and the common man, the basic intellectual demand was for a test of public sentiment in conventional fashion—through the ballot.

In the over-all picture of Japanese politics today, however, one fact seems to stand out clearly. Neither major party has any very deep roots among the Japanese people. Even the recent incidents illustrate this point in graphic fashion. Curiously, the Socialist party did not gain popular approval or support in proportion to the loss of strength on the part of the Kishi government. On the whole, the Socialist party displayed itself throughout the crisis as a fundamentally weak party, with shallow mass roots. It did not lead. Nor did the Communist party lead in any real sense. And in the immediate aftermath of the crisis, one poll indicated that both major parties, *including the Socialists*, had declined somewhat in popular support.[10] In short, whatever else may be faulty

[10] Note the following very interesting polls conducted by the *Asahi Shimbun:* On May 25 and 26 the question was asked: "What do you think about the activities of the conservatives (the government), the socialists, and the democratic socialists?" The results were as follows, in percentages:

	"Good"	"Bad"	"Neither Good nor Bad"
Conservative (government)	6	50	18
Socialists	11	32	31
Democratic Socialists	8	13	43

When asked which party the interviewee supported, another *Asahi Shimbun* poll gave the following percentage results in May, 1960, which can be compared with results in January, 1960, and earlier:

	May, 1960	Jan., 1960	Feb., 1959	Sept., 1958	Nov., 1957	July, 1957	Mar., 1956	Dec., 1956	Aug., 1956
Liberal Democratic	40	48	48	46	45	47	46	48	45
Socialist	30	31	36	33	33	32	33	34	39
Democratic Socialist	9	4	...	...	...	...	...	...	...
Communist	1	0	0	0	0	1	1	0	0
No party	7	5	4	4	5	5	6	4	4
No answer	13	12	12	12	16	15	14	14	12

And in August, two months after the incident, in an *Asahi* poll asking the same question the percentage showed the Socialists at a new low, with the Democratic

in the Japanese intellectuals' current analysis of democratic weaknesses in their society, their thesis of a substantial separation between the parties and Diet on the one hand and the broad public on the other has some validity. And this is why no immediate or startling changes are likely to take place in the relative standing of the parties. But this is also why political stability in contemporary Japan is a somewhat deceptive phenomenon.

In summation, there is considerable truth in the thesis that Japanese democratic institutions—the complex of parties, and parliament—have not yet been meshed very effectively with the broader patterns of rapid socioeconomic change that characterize this society. Indeed, the persistence of old political behavior and old organizational molds seems to belie the new institutions that were bequeathed Japan by American innovators. In these senses, socioeconomic changes have been moving much more rapidly than political ones. One must presume that there will be a day of reckoning. Perhaps in some measure the May–June incidents were the beginning of that day. As we suggested earlier, they represented a degree of mass participation (and one might say even more accurately, a degree of elitist participation) in some respects unparalleled in Japanese domestic politics. It is unclear, of course, whether that participation will be sustained in some fashion. Will it be nourished, and will it grow? One is aware that the "mass" element was largely confined to Tokyo and a few other large cities, and that the rural areas took relatively little part.[11] Once again, the striking political differences between metropolitan and rural areas were clearly revealed.

Liberals having gained, possibly as a result of the conciliatory statements and gestures of the new prime minister, Ikeda:

Liberal Democratic	49
Socialist	25
Democratic Socialist	6
Communist	. . .
No party	8
No answer	12

This poll was reasonably close to the November, 1960, election results, when the "undecided–don't know" vote is prorated. *Asahi Shimbun*, August 8, 1960, p. 1.

[11] For two articles on the relation between the rural areas and the incident, and also the later attempt of the students to "educate" the farmers, see Fukutake Naoshi, "The Village and Democracy," *Sekai*, September, 1960, pp. 38–45 and Fukutake Naoshi *et al.*, "The Actual Condition of the 'Voiceless Voice' in the Village," *Shisō*, October, 1960, pp. 66–78.

The basic issue, however, revolves around the question of how Japanese political processes and institutions will adjust to the new era of the mass society. The future is not easy to predict. The path ahead is strewn with boulders. As they have been structured in the past, the Japanese parties have not been suitable mass instruments. Essentially, they have been "cadre" or "Diet" parties, with very shallow grass roots. In many respects, the basic political organization has been the faction, not the party. The faction, reflective of the cultural roots of Japanese society and the nature of all Japanese organization, has occupied the vital center of the political process. For this reason, we have suggested that perhaps the most accurate description of the Japanese party system is that of two relatively stable (and unequal) federations, with each having an internal fluidity as a result of constantly shifting factional coalitions that give Japanese politics its element of suspense and change. In a broader functional sense, of course, this is a one-and-one-half-party system, with a permanent conservative majority.

The danger, however, lies in the fact that no matter how one defines the Japanese party system, up to date it has been essentially a closed system. The parliamentary process in Japan has not sufficiently encompassed the people. The parties continue in large measure to be "they" as opposed to "we" in the popular mind. Under such circumstances, mass participation is likely to operate outside party-Diet channels, as it did recently. This is conducive to variant (and, from a Western perspective, one would say questionable) theories of democracy. The left socialists are encouraged to go on holding their theory of "parliamentarism-plus"; a number of intellectuals believe in "qualitative democracy" (as do others on the right, from a different perspective); and it becomes easier to challenge majoritarianism if, in addition to a traditional practice of consensus that still commands great respect, one has reason to question the bases upon which a majority was obtained.

Yet, viewed from the democratic standpoint, there is some light on the Japanese political horizon. The emergence of multiple-interest groups, mass based and operating on behalf of self-interests, has been one of the truly important developments of postwar Japanese politics. Through these interest groups, many of them new, an ever growing number of Japanese citizens are participating in politics, and affiliating—at least, indirectly—with parties. In spite of the fact that such representation is still woefully unequal and insufficient, and in spite of the fact also that Japanese interest groups have structural and other problems derivative from their culture, the growth of interest group politics may represent the most suitable route to Japanese democracy.

The major parties, moreover, have taken increasing cognizance of the individual voter. They have shown some serious interest in having him join party ranks. They have campaigned with increasing vigor for his vote, and used more direct means, relying less upon intermediaries. The mass media have been utilized to educate the voter, and party leaders have stumped the nation in a fashion that would have astounded most politicians of the prewar era. And when the voters' position on an issue is made clear by means of accepted polls, the politicians generally pay some heed—at least, to the extent of changing the pace or modifying the stance. Polling has become a supplement to elections in the cause of Japanese democracy, the more important perhaps because elections are not necessarily an accurate gauge of public opinion.

Even with respect to voting behavior, however, a significant transition seems to be under way. The shift is from the "traditional" to the "modern" behavior: from voting as a method of ratifying authority to voting as a means of expressing one's needs and values. This transition is by no means complete. Traditional patterns are still very strong, especially in the rurual areas, but all political elements in Japan are conscious of the change that is taking place.

In some respects, curiously enough, it is the conservatives rather than the "progressives" who have thus far shown the greater flexibility in connection with the new age.[12] The Japanese socialists run some risk of being considered by history the real conservatives of this era, unable to evolve and frozen in impotence. Continuity in power has given the conservatives an important advantage in adjusting to the changing requirements of power, and continuity out of power has heightened the socialist problem of moving from the world of the past into that of the present and future. It is easy to say that the Japanese socialists should become "more responsible." But how? How does a party become responsible without power and, indeed, when it is almost without hope of power? If there is no legacy of policy to defend, irresponsibility is an omnipresent danger; the longer a party is separated from power, the greater the temptations are likely to become.

Will the Japanese conservatives, in the pattern of the conservative parties of western Europe and the United States, become truly progressive conservatives? And if so, will they retain power indefinitely? These questions raise some interesting thoughts that go far beyond Japan in their possible application. We are at a juncture in history when the "advanced" societies have accomplished, or are en route to accomplishing, many of the basic goals of democratic socialism, albeit often under

---

[12] This theme was developed in Robert A. Scalapino, "Japanese Socialism in Crisis," *Foreign Affairs*, January, 1960, pp. 318–328. We have borrowed extensively from the language used there in setting forth the concept.

different designations. Is it possible that progressive conservatives can conduct a "permanent revolution" with sufficient skill to keep the opposition out of power indefinitely? Needless to say, this would not be Trotsky's permanent revolution, but rather one in which the conservatives adjusted to the importance of the mass man, acknowledged and anticipated his most basic needs, and attuned organizational attention upon him with sufficient skill to put the opposition (however "mass oriented" in an ideological sense) indefinitely on the defensive.

Perhaps such a "permanent revolution" is not entirely possible, either in Japan or elsewhere. A depression might suddenly alter the picture—if it could not be modified by the government in power. Long continuity in power can lead to complacency, corruption, or grievous errors and thereby produce a mood for change. But there have been enough advances in the science of power and in socioeconomic trends in the "advanced" world, of which Japan is now a part, to suggest a new problem for democracy: the problem of the perennial minority. Democracy is in peril if one party knows only how to govern and the others only how to oppose.

In political terms, however, Japan does not yet belong wholly to the "advanced" world, and the above concern is in certain respects premature. Mass participation in Japanese politics is on the rise. Party policies and organization are increasingly attuned to the fact. Political behavior shows various signs of moving away from traditionalism and toward modernity. However, in comparison with the startling rapidity that has characterized socioeconomic change in postwar Japan, political change has been extremely slow and uneven. Traditional patterns of organization and process are omnipresent. Any society undergoing a very rapid transformation faces serious problems in keeping its various elements in balance. Socioeconomic change may take place at a pace much accelerated over that of political change. As the imbalance between *politics* and *society* mounts, the situation becomes increasingly explosive.

There is no question that Japan is proceeding to the status of a mass society. Mass participation in politics will steadily increase. In this sense, the May–June incidents are symptomatic of a new era. But, will this participation find channels of expression within the parliamentary process? Will the Japanese people, maturing as a result of educational expansion and economic growth, develop the type of complex, mass-based interest group structure that can reflect more fully the desires and needs of the total population and be used to pry open the exclusive nature of Japanese political organization? Will political leadership in Japan anticipate more adequately the requirements of a democratic mass society? Can the tempo of political change in modern Japan be advanced?

If not, many dangers lie ahead. Mass participation, as in the case of the May–June incidents, can circumvent parties and parliament, causing them to stand impotent and alone. Such participation can take the form of "to the streets" on the left and "via the knife" on the right. The paradox of Japan's being an open society made up of closed components must be ended. Otherwise, many perils lie ahead. And it is for these reasons that Japanese politics is both stable and unstable, depending upon how deeply one wishes to probe.

7.

PUBLIC PROTEST AND THE POLITICAL PROCESS IN INDIA (1968)

DAVID H. BAYLEY

The purpose of this paper is to explore the role played by public protest in contemporary Indian politics. Public protest of course assumes many forms. For example, there are legal and illegal forms of protest. Among the legal forms are found processions, public meetings, hartals, some strikes, and fasts. Illegal forms of protest in turn come in two varieties—violent and nonviolent. Satyagraha, or nonviolent civil disobedience, is a nonviolent but often illegal form of protest. Violent illegal protest refers primarily to riots, although it may include assassinations and coups d'état. I do not propose to examine all these forms in this paper but to focus upon those which (a) are most disruptive, that is, which pose the greatest threat to public order, and (b) have a very explicit political purpose, that is, which seek to affect governmental policy. I shall therefore be looking at the agitational activity of groups which by constituting a threat to public order seek to challenge and change the policies of government.

For convenience to the reader I have set forth the major conclusions about public protest in Indian politics in propositional form. These have been italicized in the text.

Proposition 1: Indians compel official attention and constrain decision-making by deliberately engaging in activities that threaten public order. Violence or the threat of violence has become an important instrument in Indian politics.

SOURCE. Original publication.

Group violence in India comes in many varieties; it is possible, however, to distinguish three general kinds, one of which has an explicitly political motivation and purpose. I shall call these three forms of violence the Violence of Remonstrance, the Violence of Confrontation, and the Violence of Frustration.[1] In the analysis that follows I shall differentiate among them according to the target of the violence, the precipitating or catalyzing agency, the amount of prior organization, the length of time required for the generation of violence, the visibility of the growth process, the nature of the participants, and the location of the event. The utility of this scheme depends upon the fit between these descriptive categories and the social violence of modern India.

Violence of Remonstrance refers to riots and public clashes growing out of agitational activities which have as their target governmental authority in some form. Violence is a product of interraction between protestors and representatives of that authority or of public order in general. Most commonly, this means the police. While the Violence of Remonstrance may not be organized, the activities proceeding it certainly are. The process by which the violence is generated is visible and usually prolonged, extending over several days in many cases. This kind of violence does not erupt without warning. Participants in the Violence of Remonstrance are by and large members of modern social groups—such as labor unions, universities, political parties, and professional societies. Violence of Remonstrance is more common in urban than in rural areas. Examples of this kind of violence are the anti-Hindi agitations in Madras in 1965 and 1966, the martyr's memorial agitation if Ahmedabad, 1958, student riots against higher fees, and anti–food-price campaigns in 1958 and again in 1966.

Violence of Confrontation refers to riots that grow out of the antagonism of private groups. In this kind of violence public agencies are not directly involved; they are not the immediate target of violence. The prime examples of the Violence of Confrontation are communal riots and village faction fights. In the Violence of Confrontation there is very little organization either in its conduct or in the activities leading up to it. It is generated by a process which is invisible, involving feelings and attitudes that have matured over years, sometimes over generations. The Violence of Confrontation does not generally escalate through clearly defined stages as does the Violence of Remonstrance. It is impossible to make generalizations about the time required to generate the Violence of Confrontation because the process is subterranean, almost wholly contained within the hearts and minds of people. Participants in this

---

[1] I am, of course, disregarding entirely violence perpetrated by individuals or small groups which is done exclusively for monetary gain or private revenge.

kind of violence tend to be members of traditional groups. Violence of Confrontation is primarily, though not exclusively, a rural phenomenon.

The third major type of violence I call the Violence of Frustration. The category encompasses commuter riots in large cities when trains are delayed, or attacks by mobs upon food shops that refuse to open, or when unemployed persons besiege an employment office. The Violence of Frustration does not have a definable target—unless it be society as a whole. It is not an attack upon government or upon a specific private group. It is a frenzied lashing out at a state of affairs, galling largely because of its impersonality. The pretext for this kind of violence is impersonal too. There is no organization to the Violence of Frustration; it is abrupt and spontaneous. Participants in this kind of violence may be anyone, not modern or traditional people particularly. Violence of Frustration is more common in urban areas. I might add that American society has not been free from the Violence of Frustration. Our urban riots during the past few years share most of the features of the Indian experience.

The point to underscore is that one common variety of social violence in modern India has an explicitly political motivation; it stems from a desire to shape government policy.

How prevalent is the public protest which by threatening law and order coerces governmental decision-making? Indians themselves are much more concerned about this than they used to be. For example, a recent book on the subject by Indian scholars begins with these words: "This book . . . is concerned with the growth of violence in the country which has taken a turn for the worse since the death of Lal Bahadur Shastri."[2]

Proposition 2: Political accommodation, which is real in India, is achieved at a higher level of political disorder than in any other of the world's democracies. Frankly, the United States may be catching up but for the moment the generalization holds.

Proposition 3: The amount of public protest, as well as of the Violence of Remonstrance, has increased during the past ten years. However, the subjective evaluation of its importance in politics, especially among Indians, has increased out of proportion to its objective rate of growth.

Agitational activity, even of a violent kind, is certainly not new in India. One need only recall the prolonged agitation over the States Reorganization Plan in the 1950s, several violent strikes with accom-

---

[2] S. P. Aiyar (ed.), *The Politics of Mass Violence in India* (Bombay: P. C. Manaktalas and Sons, Private Ltd., 1967, p. 15).

panying use of firearms by the police, as at Jamshedpur, 1958, and the Calcutta Secondary Teachers Strike, 1954. Some years ago, I undertook a survey of the number of riots reported in major Indian newspapers. I found that in 1955, for example, the *Times of India* reported seventy serious riots. In 1957, The *Stateman* reported sixty riots, with eighteen persons killed, over one thousand persons arrested, and sixty police firings. This evidence is not without fault, but it does demonstrate that the violence one finds today is not unprecedented.

The obstacles to determining the quantity of violence are enormous. Official statistics are of little use. The Indian Penal Code does have a category labeling "Riots" and figures are available for it. However, a riot is defined as violence involving five or more persons. Thus a toddy-shop brawl and a day of communal frenzy are equally riots. For the record, there were twenty thousand cases of riot in 1953 compared with close to thirty thousand in 1963. The rate per one hundred thousand people rose from 5.4 to 6.1 between 1953 and 1963.[3] Assuming that errors in reporting and compiling criminal statistics remained constant over this period, one can say that during the decade 1953–1963 there was a modest increase in the incidence of riotous behavior. What one cannot tell, however, is (1) whether riots springing from political protests increased as well and (2) whether the quality of the riots changed—that is, did they change in intensity, brutality, and duration?

Several years ago Rudolph J. Rummel of Northwestern University collected data about the incidence of protest and violence in India during 1955, 1956, and 1957.[4] This was part of a larger effort to study conflict behavior within and among nations. Although he was aware that his sources seriously underestimated the absolute amount of protest and violence, he thought that comparisons between different years would indicate accurately changes in the quantity of violence because systematic recording errors would be the same from year to year. Since this information is the only data from international sources that has been collected, I recently duplicated the Rummel search for the years 1964, 1965, and 1966. I *did* find that the number of riots for these later years was greater than in the earlier period—in fact almost three times

---

[3] 1953 was the first year all-India criminal statistics were issued; 1963 was the last year for which criminal statistics have been made available. The 1953 and 1963 population figures were obtained from official census data. The yearly increase was computed and the census total adjusted in order to arrive at population figures for 1953 and 1963. The increase in population per year during the decade of the 1950 was 2.1%.

[4] This study has been reported as "Dimensions of Conflict Behavior Within and Between Nations" (Northwestern University, June 1963).

greater. Moreover, during the pre-election year in each study—a year that one might assume would contain greater amounts of political activity—the later year had twice as many riots as the former. On the basis of this data, therefore, one would conclude that the amount of public protest and violence has grown considerably in the past decade.[5]

I would suggest two methods by which one might more accurately determine the changing incidence of violent protests in India. First, one could systematically search selected Indian newspapers for accounts of riots in the immediate areas. The researcher would thus be using information which was relatively complete and about which the newspaper could be presumed to know most. He would be able to avoid some of the problems of interpreting discursive reports into quantified totals that Rummel encountered using less complete, more abbreviated sources. Second, one could monitor riotous behavior in several specifically demarcated regions, such as a major city or an important district. Assuming that few research teams could achieve the coverage that the police have, police sources would have to be utilized, and this would require official sanction. The chances of obtaining permission from the government for such a venture are exceedingly slim.

On the basis of information at hand, there would appear to be an objective basis for greater concern about protest and violence today than ten years ago. I also believe, however, that the greater concern expressed by many commentators is as much a reflection of change in subjective assessments of their possible effects than of a true perception of their absolute increase. The fact is that the political environment for public protest has been transformed in the past decade. The Congress Party is no longer securely entrenched in power; it is no longer a certain winner. For members of the Opposition, the opportunity to attain power seems at last to be at hand. For Congressmen, doubts have begun to arise that loyalty to the party will be rewarded in tangible, politically significant terms. The expectations of Indian political life, which have been stable for so long, have been upset. Where once there was acceptance of Congress predominance, which bred apathy and cynicism, there is now ferment. A decade ago the government could absorb a consider-

---

[5] While this conclusion may be warranted, I must comment that the Rummel method, which uses common international news-reporting sources (such as the *New York Times*), is open to serious question. Rules for interpreting in quantitative terms ambiguous reportage of extended riots are difficult to lay down. Very slight differences in interpretation lead to very different quantitative results. Moreover, subjective factors in the choice of events to report may cause ever more differences in the amount of phenomena recorded each year. The fluctuation in totals caused by these implicit decisions is not minor but may double or halve them.

able amount of disruption. The political system seemed relatively immune from the effects of violence. Now the possibilities to be achieved through protest have been enhanced. Whether a decline in the system's capacity to ignore violence has in fact occurred would be difficult to say; it is enough that for many people a decline in capacity appears to have taken place. This being so, recourse to public protest appears much more tempting.

Proposition 4: Public protests are likely to increase in the future, at perhaps a faster rate of growth than has been evident since independence.

The prediction of an augmentation in the amount of public protest is based upon the presumption that there are now greater perceived opportunities for effective intervention in policy formation by these means. In other words, the very considerations that arouse the anxieties of observers about the effects of public protests may encourage others to resort to these methods. There are two factors that might inhibit this tendency: first, if several of the primary causes of unrest (such as a new language formula or the food problem) could be alleviated, or postponed for the moment, and second, if the tactics of opposition in a time of greater opportunity militated against a precipitate resort to unconstitutional means. It seems to me that the relative quiet in Kerala today as opposed to Bengal, and of Namboodripad's segment of the Communist Party, can be attributed to the imminence or actuality of attaining power. Indeed the debate within the Communist Party between the pro-Peking faction and almost everyone else turns on the very issue of the utility of violence in today's pregnant political situation.

One might also argue that an increase in protest and violence could be offset by a firmer policy of containment by the government. Professor Gurr . . . makes provision for this factor in his model of domestic violence. Such a move is unlikely, in my opinion, without a very substantial change in the character of government. There is even some question in my mind whether the present defense and police forces could contain widespread protest if they wanted to. One would also have to consider whether a more repressive containment policy would call forth more agitation than it would inhibit.

Proposition 5: Political protest and the deliberate use of violence are a tactic of people in the modern sector of Indian life; traditional people do not utilize these means as a matter of course but only to further particular issues about which they feel very deeply.

Modern individuals use public protests regardless of the issue. It is their stock-in-trade. Traditional persons use protests in proportion to their attachment to particular issues. For example, whenever students demonstrate there is always the danger that violence will ensue. Peasants, on the other hand, grow violent more selectively. One can argue that traditional persons are generally unsure of themselves in the world of partisan politics and authoritative governmental structures. Thus they utilize any means of access to government less readily than more modern people. If this is true, Proposition 6 may have a corollary: as traditional people become more politicized and more conscious of their rights, they will learn to use the system's agitational modes as well as its normal and institutional ones. Panchayati Raj, then, to the extent that it is a successful instrument for political socialization, may unleash forces that cannot be contained in its institutional framework.

I have no evidence that patterns of participation in protests have changed over the years. Nor do I find very different kinds of issues serving as pretexts for protest today compared with ten or fifteen years ago. Language, food prices, and student grievances are perennial issues. The possible exception is the anti–cow-slaughter campaign of 1966. Whether this is the precursor of Hindu communal issues becoming more important in the political life of the nation remains to be seen. Indian police officers, who are in closest touch with agitational activities, have not changed their assessments of the groups considered most volatile. There are students, labor unions, and leftist political parties.

A commentator might justifiably say at this point that although I have demonstrated that public protests with attendant violence exist and may have increased in number in recent years, I am making altogether too much of the matter. There has always been disorder in Indian politics and there probably always will be. Can it be argued that this disorder has affected the working of the political system in an important way? I believe the answer to this is Yes.

Proposition 6: Agitational politics is now a substitute for institutional means of exercising influence and of seeking redress of grievances.

Protests are so common that they not only supplement formal procedures but supplant them and render them irrelevant. Protests are not used only when other avenues of accommodation have been exhausted; they have become a "court of first resort." Moreover, protests are used to appeal against decisions reached openly by freely elected representative bodies. A vicious cycle may be at work. To the extent that agitational activity is perceived to be efficacious it will contribute to the decline in the perceived usefulness of formal democratic mechanisms, and this in turn will renew the temptation to utilize agitation.

Proposition 7: The din of protests has affected the relations between government and spokesmen for the people by producing deafness in ministers, legislators, and civil servants.

The Indian government is severely limited in its capacity to respond sympathetically to all demands made upon it. In a sense, this is a working definition of underdevelopment, at least with respect to material claims. Government must at times appear unresponsive to the mass of its people, even though the fault is not of its own making. People may either put up with the lack of favorable response or seek to cut through the constraints upon government by transforming their concern into a demand which is irresistible. One way to do this is to pose a threat to law and order. By means of agitational activities, in the name of a cause which has been spurned by government, people can compel official attention. If this tactic is widely adopted, as it has been in India, one result will be to make the government progressively harder of hearing. Government begins to disregard all demands not coupled with a threat to public order. Implicitly, government begins to act as if demands that do not generate public furor are unimportant. Both government and popular political leaders begin to act as if only those demands which are coupled with dramatic agitations are significant. The talisman for gaining attention becomes the size of crowds and the amount of disorder they create, replacing the merits of the demands presented. The public, for its part, despairs of commanding attention through non-agitational means. The dreadful logic of Gresham's Law begins to work: quiet demands through channels are increasingly drowned in the noise of agitations; government disregards demands not accompanied with vast public hoopla; politics becomes less a matter of accommodation in legislatures and more a matter of mass organization in the market-place. In India today, deafness is at once the defense of hard-pressed government and the cause of people raising their voices into frenzied shouts.

Proposition 8: The pervasiveness of agitational politics thrusts the issue of law and order squarely into the center of political debate. The result is that articulate dissent is continually being focused on the rules and procedures of orderly government; the "rules of the game," rather than being accepted by all, are subjects of dispute and contention.

Whenever incidents of protest and violence occur politicians are forced to choose sides between those who upset and those who preserve order. By and large few voices are raised, except in a hollow and ritualistic way, against agitational politics or even its attendant violence. Debates produce an immediate polarization between supporters and opponents of order-producing policies. Since all parties and most politicians are sometimes involved in agitational activities, politicians find it awkward to argue from principle and so take refuge in particularistic judgments involving issues and people. Politicians as a group appear very ambiguous indeed about the need, the responsibility, to defend law and order. The question is: What is the effect of these ambiguous statements

306 THE STRUCTURAL SOURCES OF PROTEST, REFORM, AND REVOLT

upon the political attitudes and practices of the public? It seems reasonable to assume that practicing politicians are among the most important tutors of democratic procedures in any society. Many commentators on unrest in the student community, for example, have noted that it is unrealistic to expect discipline from them when their political elders set so poor an example. If the practice of politics is an important formative factor in political socialization, then future generations in India are going to believe that disorder, protest, and violence are as much a part of democratic politics as the ballot box and the representative assembly.[6]

Proposition 9: The prevalence of protest and the precariousness of social order have been compelling factors behind those policies of government which since independence have infringed personal freedom most directly.

The Preventive Detention Act, 1950, and the Unlawful Activities Prevention Act, 1967, were passed and the Defense of India Rules prolonged very largely because officials in government, both state and central, believed that special powers were needed to cope with dissent conducted through agitation. Whether justified or not, these measures reflect the concern of government with protest activities. So serious have India's leaders considered the threat constituted by agitational activities that they, convinced libertarians for the most part, have been willing to abridge personal freedom and judicial review.

Proposition 10: Apart from financial stringency, the threat of violence—though not exclusively political violence—is the single most important formative element shaping the police in modern India.

The prospect of disorder affects the division of the police into armed and unarmed branches, which in turn affects recruitment, deployment, training, and relations with the public. That at least three-fifths of all police in India are armed police living in barracks and not civil con-

---

[6] A survey which I undertook in two urban areas—Bangalore and Kanpur—provided some information on this point. A majority of people in both areas thought that demonstrators who broke the law should be arrested right away. They should not be tolerated and excused. At the same time, about 30% of the respondents were for a policy of toleration. This is not a small group. The figures do show that the mass of the Indian people do not automatically and unquestioningly support law-breaking agitations. Also a great many people think that demonstrations are used too often. Forty-one per cent in Bangalore and 33% in Kanpur thought this, while 24% in Bangalore and 34% in Kanpur did not think demonstrations were overused. Half of all urban respondents thought that demonstrations were a useful way of bringing pressure to bear on authorities. Only about one-quarter didn't think so. The Indian public would seem to be a bit cynical about demonstrations, although it considers them useful in certain circumstances.

stables performing daily tasks among the public is a direct result of official fear that social stability is uncertain.

Proposition 11: The prevalence of protest places the police in a peculiarly visible and invidious position in the eyes of the public. They are seen very largely as a constraining element, not public servants working on behalf of individual citizens.

Police in India have for generations been forced to confront, constrain, and repress sections of the public. This requirement did not change appreciably in the postindependence period. While my own survey data show that public reaction to these activities by police is not as unfavorable as might be supposed, the fact remains that police appear to most Indians wholly in a martial capacity, forfeiting the opportunity to forge a link of service between themselves and the people. Policemen are continually being held up as objects of scorn for their repressive actions by politicians. Sometimes the police deserve criticism. But even when they do not, their role in the containment of protest makes them vulnerable to the charge of being brutal tools of the government in power and no friend of the citizen.[7]

Proposition 12: Protests and the deliberate use of the threat of violence have become partially institutionalized in Indian politics.

From the magnitude of protest behavior in India one might conclude that the country was quivering on the brink of anarchy and that political life was a vast free-for-all without rules or stable expectations. This conclusion would be mistaken. Protests, even illegal and violent ones, are not all normless. Indeed, they have become partly routinized. In supplementing the established means of seeking redress, protests have developed their own rules, informal regulations, and accepted uses. For example, it is not unusual for protestors to notify the police in advance about what they intend to do. This is especially true if a "Section 144" is to be violated. Ground rules for many clashes are known to both sides. In the resulting melee the participating, and observing, public

---

[7] There is in fact considerable latent support for police crowd-control activities. Indians do not have overwhelmingly critical attitudes about how the police handle demonstrations. For example, most people do not think police use firearms too often. Most important, analysis shows that having seen the police use force against a crowd—even a firing—does not dispose people to view crowd-control work unfavorably. Such people are as likely to approve crowd-control activities as those woh have not had personal experience with police and crowds. Perhaps people caught up in an unruly crowd situation experience deep anxiety and consequently welcome, rather than resent, the intervention of the police. It should be noted that the proportion of adult Indians with crowd-control experience is not small. At least a third of all respondents in Kanpur and Bangalore had seen the police use lathis or canes against a crowd; one out of six had seen a police firing.

gets an active, exciting outing; politicians have an opportunity to display their ability to mobilize a following; the police vindicate their role as custodians of public order; and disorder is kept within manageable proportions. One sees another aspect of the institutionalization of protest in the fact that among politicians no stigma is attached to being arrested as long as the individual's complicity in violence is not too blatant and self-serving. Furthermore, political parties use mass protests quite shamelessly as a means of enlisting supporters. And, like good evangelists, they recognize the value of follow-up and of maintaining momentum. Political leaders are often quite cold-blooded in their calculations about using protests; they can talk about the psychology of protests with great sophistication. There are even informal rules for calling agitations. Individual politicians are usually given discretion in the calling of local protests; major protests in the name of the party and covering wide areas must obtain the sanction of state or national party leadership.

Proposition 13: In approaching the study of political protests in foreign countries, the American student of comparative politics must be careful to avoid moralistic judgments about them. It would be a prime mistake to conclude that protests and even violence are always dysfunctional to political systems, even to democratic ones.

The role of protest, and by extension its effects, must be understood in terms of the requirements, structures, values, and habits of particular systems. To give only one illustration of the complexity of estimating effects, different systems undoubtedly have varying capacities for absorbing agitation. India, for example, presents an interesting paradox: it has a far higher level of public protest and violence than any other democratic country and yet it seems to withstand them with greater poise than other democratic countries. Could it be that these two aspects are related? Public protests may indicate, among other things, that channels of communication and response are clogged. But perhaps because they are partially clogged the system can afford a substantial amount of disruption. A system that was more responsive to political pressure might be paralyzed by frequent protests and violence. The systemic effects of disruption depend upon local circumstances. The Indian experience compared with that of other democracies certainly shows that different countries can operate stable political systems, even of similar character, at different levels of disruption.

In short, I caution those who would analyze the place of protest in the political life of a nation that they must give as much attention to the requirements of stable political interaction in any system as they do to collecting data about protests in any one system.

IV.
THE DEVELOPMENT OF
COLLECTIVE MEANINGS

Human experience seldom occurs in a pristine and objective manner. We confer meaning upon events, selecting and excluding according to what we deem significant or unimportant. Felt discontents, judgments of possibility, interpretations of official actions, and other aspects of collective action are deeply affected by the way experience is interpreted and given meaning. The language available to us and the processes of communication directly with others and through the mass media are part of the process in which discontent is signified, explained, and made into a socially agreed-upon occurrence to which specific kinds of response are credible.

Part of what a movement does for its adherents is found in the definition of the situation which is given by fellow adherents in their use of beliefs and programs. What comes to be seen as injustice must be pointed to, named, and described from among the logically possible interpretations for the potential adherents' sense of discontent. In our readings, the labor union organizer in Bernard Karsh's account of how an organizing strike developed is an excellent illustration of this process. Entering a scene of unrest, he galvanized vague and diffuse feelings into concrete explanations and evaluation. These did not arise spontaneously but emerged by agitation. The eventual consensus among many of the workers was that they were being treated unjustly and that not only was this situation unjust, it was also remediable through the strike and unionization.

The dependence of collective action on common interpretations of events makes the conditions of communication crucial for the emergence of social movements. The very fact that others share the person's meanings reinforces them and protects against contrary views and dissonant data. Rumor, especially in the absence of contradictory interpretations, plays an important role in shaping the meaning of events along lines already congruent with the interpreter's perspectives and those of his friends, neighbors, or family. In the ghetto riots of the mid-1960s both the police and the black population in the rioting areas were quick to believe what stereotyped perceptions had already indicated to them, reinforced by those around them.

Norman Jackman examines this process of communication, reinforcement, rumor, and countercommunication in an analysis of how collective protest broke out in the Japanese-American relocation camps in the United States during World War II. He shows that the absence of communications from camp officials, as well as from camp residents, gave rise to an intensive resistance to camp authority, fed on rumor as well as fact. Where opposite interpretations could also be communicated to camp residents, the residents were exposed to a balance of views. Under these circumstances they were not as likely to perceive the situation as one justifying resentment, bitterness, and protest.

The justice of collective action is implicit in the interpretation of events communicated to the adherent. Even mild reform movements justify their demands for change as legitimate and identify the established procedures as unjust, impractical, or illegitimate. The more dissident the collective action, the more it may pose a crisis of legitimacy for the adherents. This forms the focus for Gaston Rimlinger's analysis of differences in the movements among British and German coal miners. Cultural traditions made different systems of legitimation available in each country, with diverse consequences. The existence of a tradition of political and religious dissent in England made it possible for the British miners to protest their conditions of employment without attacking the basic character of British political institutions and authority. The lack of such legitimation among the German workers made their protests necessarily more revolutionary, pushing them to a more definitive break with the society.

The conditions of the Japanese relocation camps influenced the flow of communication and countercommunication among residents. Ecological properties of the environment play an important role in many of the processes of communication, control, and conflict, both indirectly influencing communications and providing opportunities for and deterrents to specific actions. Studies of riot and insurrection have often emphasized these properties of the environment. The rebuilding of Paris in the nineteenth century supposedly was influenced by the need to control the streets by military authority. Thus the radial pattern of streets, each emptying into a common center, made it possible for a few soldiers to control several arteries of traffic. In her analysis of the Los Angeles riots of 1964, Michel McCall points out how the Los Angeles pattern of urban housing and transportation differs from that of other urban communities in the United States. These differences made police techniques developed for riot control in denser areas less useful. The lack of public transportation provided fewer points of Negro-white contact, a further factor helping to isolate the ghetto and contain the rioting.

We must not imagine that meanings are fixed and unchangeable, nor that movements do not grow, change, and confront new situations. A great part of the remainder of this volume will illustrate how movements are shaped and reshaped over time. To understand the history of a movement we need to see it as it meets opposition, resistance, and contradiction, and how these encounters in turn affect the interpretation of the movement by the society and of the social order by adherents of the movement. Such encounters are crucial to the reinforcement or reformulation of belief, strategy, and loyalty.

In the public encounter between opposing sides on issues, great importance must be attached to the connotations which develop and which confer symbolic meanings upon movements. Here the role of leadership is often of great significance, since the leader's acts are more visible than those of others.

It is in this sense of collapsed events and of antagonistic opposition that the actions of leaders and the occurrence of unique and exciting events are dramatic and moving actions that define and redefine a movement. In the Civil Rights movement, for example, arrogant, oppressive, and "die-hard" Southern white supremacists often helped the movement by symbolizing the most villainous "enemies" and mobilizing sympathy and justification for the militant adherents of the movement. The lack of any such clear-cut symbols of evil in Northern events has made it less easy for black militants to gain the symbol of "goodness" in a dramatic confrontation.

We have included an excerpt from Orrin Klapp's book *Symbolic Leaders*, in which the author indicates a variety of ways in which public figures have gained or lost following and sympathy by the style of their encounters. The hero-making, villain-making, and fool-making roles of the mass media of communication are seen as having great importance in the collective meanings that emerge in judging various social movements in the public arena.

These confrontations have the quality of drama because in them the ways in which people play their roles often structure the imagery and symbolism which generate legends, heroes, enemies, and much of the emotional attachment of collective action. Because such events are often stirring and visible they compel neutrals and onlookers into attitudes and reactions. The songs, marches, demonstrations, ceremonies, and ritual of many movements provide the background for their dramatic and emotion-producing character. A movement without resistance may not be able to generate the excitement with which to continue defining the situation as urgent, critical, and demanding.

A.
The Perception and Communication of Discontent

1.

THE DEVELOPMENT OF A STRIKE

Bernard Karsh

The organization of a union in a workplace represents the formation of a new social institution. But, "institutions do not spring full-formed from the head of Zeus. Before they are institutions they are institutions in process." They represent individuals in social groups who have come to be at odds with their existing world, who have developed new or changed conceptions of themselves, their rights and dues, who have acquired new roles and new or changed values, and who strive to satisfy the conditions demanded by what they consider to be a new or altered situation.

The formation of a local union represents a degree of revolt and a new attack on collective problems. It stems from feelings of restlessness and discontent on the part of persons facing frustrating, undefined, or anxiety-producing circumstances in the factory. The disparity between

SOURCE. Bernard Karsh, *Dairy of a Strike*. Urbana: University of Illinois Press, 1958, pp. 5–6, 46–67. Reprinted by permission of the University of Illinois Press and the author.

the hopes and wishes of the individual and the realities of the work situation makes him susceptible of being organized for action along new lines. Situations of social unrest are crucibles in which new shared perspectives are forged out of old ones. Old loyalties, allegiances, and identifications are at least partially dissolved. Though the major existing values may not be directly challenged, their efficacy comes under question and the practices which stem from them come under attack. Thus, the union, as a social institution, typically emerges from conditions such as these.

Often, however, the condition of social unrest does not exist among individuals in a given objective situation. Individual unrest, frustration, or discontent represents a fluid condition which has the potentialities for differing lines of action. Indeed, the unrest is not social until it is organized; expressions of individual dissatisfaction need to be crystallized, defined, and focused. Most of all they need to be communicated and thus shared. It is in these terms that leadership plays a crucial role.

The general function of leadership is to coordinate and integrate group action. The leader defines the often highly ambiguous existing situation for his followers. He emphasizes certain aspects and ignores others; he asserts specific goals and deprecates others. He looks at the situation in an organized fashion and communicates his view to those he would lead. If his interpretation of the situation is sympathetically received by his would-be followers, a shared frame of reference or a common way of viewing the situation is developed and unified behavior is possible.

The union organizer is this kind of a leader. He seeks out situations in which workers have become disaffected from the conditions of their jobs or from the plant society. Once he finds such a situation, he designs his strategy to organize the feelings of the workers on behalf of the more or less powerful, and perhaps distant, union which he represents. He employs appropriate methods, techniques, strategy, and tactics to bind the workers together on the basis of their common membership in the union rather than on the basis of their work tasks, their employer, or other common interests. He seeks to engender a "we" consciousness among the workers which expresses their new status in the still abstract and generalized union. He knows that the union members are likely to follow his leaderhip if he is successful in winning their general acceptance of the relatively vague goals which he proclaims. He also knows that without the support of those workers whose opinions of him carry the most weight with their fellows, the workers are not likely to accept his suggestions for action or his definition of the situation. To paraphrase

Mills, the union organizer is a manager of discontent, an agent in the institutional channeling of animosity.

When a union is attempting to organize the workers in a plant, an employer is faced with a limited number of alternatives. He may quietly encourage his employees to join the union; he may adopt a policy of neutrality by not expressing his views one way or the other; or he may oppose the union and make this known to his employees. Which of the courses an employer takes depends on many factors, singly or in combination: previous experience with unions, what he conceives his prerogatives as a manager to be, the way in which he assesses the strength of the union, the possible costs involved in opposing the union, the degree of loyalty to the company which he presumes his employees will maintain, and others.

Tom Miller appeared to view the union as an alien and foreign influence at work in what he considered an otherwise harmonious situation. He felt the union sought to disrupt the relationship between himself and his workers and to wrest from him areas of control which he had always viewed as his own. Accordingly, he chose to oppose the union actively and openly.

Two days after the first open union meeting, he mailed a printed letter to each employee:

Dear Co-Worker:

It appears that a professional labor Promoter is responsible for a campaign designed to "organize" the people working at the Saylor Company. The law insures every employee the right to join a union if he so desires, and to campaign for a union. The law also insures to every employee the right to refuse to join a union and also gives every employee the right to campaign against unionization if he so desires.

THE MANAGEMENT OF THIS COMPANY DOES NOT WANT A UNION, BECAUSE WE FEEL THAT OUR EMPLOYEES WILL NOT BENEFIT BY BELONGING TO THE UNION. Just why ambitious outsiders have become so interested in "protecting" your rights we do not understand. Perhaps the sizable chunk of money which the union would get from our employees in the form of dues, assessments, etc., is the plum which the union wants to pick.

With the cooperation of our employees and without the interference of any outsiders, we have made the Saylor Company a good place in which to work. Our wages, hours and working conditions compare favorably with those of other plants in this area and with the plants of others with whom we are in competition. You have received the benefits of this high standard without having to pay initiation fees, union dues and various special union assessments. We have undoubtedly made mistakes—who hasn't. Wherever they have been made they have been, and will continue to be, corrected just as soon as they are discovered. No outsider will be required to accomplish this.

What the intervention of these strangers would mean in our relationship, no one can foretell. All of us know that unions engage in business interruptions and strikes and that frequently these cause substantial financial loss to the employees and their families. We, and you, also know that if you are a member of the union you must carry out the commands of the union officials. This frequently requires not only a financial outlay on the part of the member of the union, but picketing and similar outside union activities.

Remember these things:

1. You do not have to join any union to "protect" your jobs.

2. You can refuse to talk to union organizers.

3. You can refuse to sign a membership card. If you have already signed one, you can withdraw from membership in the union by notifying the union.

4. No solicitation is permitted under the Company rules during the working time of either the solicitor or the person being solicited.

5. While we are and will continue to do everything possible to assure you that you will not be subjected to intimidation, coercion or force, we have learned that at least one employee was told by the organizer that unless she signed the membership card and joined the union now that she would have to join at a later date at a higher cost or she would be one of the first ones laid off of work. WE AGAIN REPEAT THAT YOU DO NOT HAVE TO JOIN ANY UNION TO PROTECT YOUR JOB.

I am advised that our employees have been subjected to a lot of campaign propaganda by these union promoters. I am sure that our people will not be misled by it, and will take what they hear with the proverbial "grain of salt."

The most effective way of meeting this campaign of false promises and misrepresentations is for you, the employees, to step in to see that none of your fellow employees are misled by it. You have just as much of an interest in protecting your fellow employees from this false union propaganda as the Management has—probably more.

I am personally convinced that the intrusion of a union into our relationship here would be bad for both the Company and its employees, and for that reason the union should be opposed by the employees. I hope you will agree with that position.

If you have any questions on this subject, I wish that you would feel free to put them to me and to give me the privilege of answering them. Feel free to write to me or pay me a personal visit in my office which has always been open to you.

Sincerely,
s/T. F. MILLER
Saylor Company

The following day, on September 12, the union petitioned the National Labor Relations Board for an election. When the NLRB field examiners arrived in Saylor three days later, Phil privately pointed out to them the importance of an early election because production was at a peak and would begin to drop off in some thirty days. He felt that the company would attempt to delay an election until the slack season when many mill workers were laid off.

At the same time, Phil was concerned with the impact of Mr. Miller's letter upon the new union members. Helen reported that a few of them were frightened, but that most viewed as a joke the employer's assertions that wages paid in the mill compared favorably with those paid in the area and in the industry. "Some work needs to be done to keep up the interest," she wrote, "I had a few of the girls over to my room after the 10 P.M. shift. I bought some lunch meat and cheese crackers, bread and mustard and had lunch and drink for them. They get a kick out of that."

Two members of the "inside" organizing committee reported that at least some departmental supervisors were actively opposing the union. One supervisor said that the mill workers would be far better off without a union because if they had a union in the plant, they would have to pay dues and assessments, less work would be available, and strikes were possible. "I have the office full of people daily looking for jobs," he added.

To counter the employer's move, Phil addressed a letter to all employees, union and non-union.

> You received a letter from the company telling you that it does not want a union. Of course not. A union in the shop means better wages, decent vacations, paid holidays and paid insurance. It means job security and a voice in your everyday life in the shop. The company—just like most companies—does not want you to have it. But 16 million Americans have it and benefit greatly by it. Why shouldn't you?
>
> The letter you received tried to frighten you by referring to initiation fees, assessments and dues. Too bad the company didn't speak to the people in the shop before writing it. They would have learned—as you already know—that you pay no initiation fees, that there never are any assessments and that the dues, which will not be paid until *after* a contract is signed providing for the wages, working conditions and benefits you need and are entitled to, will be collected and controlled by the members from the shop.
>
> The letter warns you against "intimidation, coercion or force." Have you felt or heard anything like that? Why can't the company be decent and honest? Or is it so afraid of having to pay a proper wage?
>
> The letter tried to frighten you with name calling. It says the people from the union which you have met are "professional labor promoters" and "ambitious strangers." It is sad that any company will use such

tactics. Perhaps if they had taken the trouble to meet these people or to speak to you about them, the company would have known better than to use words like that.

The company is trying to frighten you with the word "strike" just as Russia is trying to frighten our country with the word "war." The workers at the mill are not frightened by the words in the letter you received any more than free Americans are frightened by Russia.

The letter is accurate in one respect. It states: *"The law insures every employee the right to join a union if he so desires and to campaign for a union."* That is true. The election by secret ballot which will soon be held will prove to the company that the workers know they are protected by the law and the union and that they want a union and a union contract.

We have said and say again that it is the desire of the workers and the officers of the union to help the company run its business successfully. But we insist on the right to a union contract with wages and working conditions comparable to those of other organized workers in the country.

It's about time that T. Miller stopped listening to his high powered supervisors who are afraid for their petty powers and started listening to the workers in the shop and to their needs.

Fraternally yours,
s/PHILIP G. DRAPER

At the same time Phil urged Helen to spend the major portion of her time seeing the "key people"—the "inside" organizing committee—to strengthen their convictions and to emphasize the need for solidarity in the face of the company's attack. Phil again wrote to Mr. Miller, claiming that 172 of the workers had now signed union membership cards and asking that the company either recognize the union or consent to an early election. The company responded by engaging a firm of Milwaukee attorneys to represent their interests. The attorneys notified Phil that the company refused to recognize the union, refused to consent to an election, and insisted that the NLRB would have to hold hearings on the union's demand for an election.

Three days later, a "captive audience"[1] meeting of all mill workers was held in the plant cafeteria. Mr. Miller stated clearly that he was opposed to the union. He told the workers that unions often made such excessive demands that companies were forced out of business. He had planned a month before to raise wages, he said, but now that the union was a factor in the situation, he could not do it because the union might bring an unfair labor practice charge before the National Labor Relations Board. He urged the union members to withdraw by writing

---

[1] This term refers to a plant meeting called by an employer during working hours which all workers are required to attend.

to the regional office of the union, and he encouraged all employees to come to him with any problems. He expressed confidence that the workers would "know how to vote" in the coming Labor Board election.

When this meeting was reported to the organizers, they were convinced that the employer was about to embark on an all-out counteroffensive. With this in mind, Phil sent another letter to all employers.

As we thought might happen, the Company held a meeting in the shop. We hope the Company will have the decency to pay you for the time you were forced to lose from your piecework jobs.

Most of the threats and insinuations made are too silly to answer. But two statements made by the Company have to be nailed down.

You were told that the National Labor Relations Board is trying to decide whether or not an election should be held. This is not true. You have the legal right to hold an election and one will be held in the very near future. The Company is trying to delay an election hoping that it can talk you out of a Union contract which will give you better wages and working conditions. But the law is on our side and the Company will not succeed.

You were also told that the Company intended to give raises in August but it cannot do it now because of the Union. What an excuse! And isn't it strange that the Company didn't think about raises until the Union was started. The Company knows now that increased wages will be put into Union contracts where they'll stick—and which cannot be taken away later.

All this fancy maneuvering on the part of the Company will soon stop—the election will be won—a Union contract signed.

In the meantime, don't let the Company fool you.

Both Phil and Helen were confident that if an election were held immediately, the union would win an overwhelming majority. They also were convinced that the company was trying to delay the election in the hope that in the interim it would destroy the union. Therefore, it was even more important for them to build and maintain as strong a union group as possible.

Helen began holding daily departmental meetings in her hotel room. Her goal was to involve all of the union members in the developing struggle and to strengthen her contact system so that the union could communicate quickly with workers inside the mill. But she was increasingly concerned at the delay in holding the representation election. She reported to Phil that "everyone is so unsettled in the shop and raising hell with me. . . . The men have been very patient and understanding, but now even they are grumbling." A few days later, the company dealt the union a severe blow. Two workers went through the plant circulating petitions notifying the union officials that the signers had withdrawn their membership. In all, about twenty-five workers signed their names.

Phil decided that the time had come to enlist some help from other unions in Saylor. He explained the situation to officials of the Trades and Labor Council, who promised that they would initiate a movement to inform their members of Mr. Miller's opposition tactics and to ask them to "spread it around town."

In the meantime Helen invited those workers who had signed the petitions to meet in her room. She told the dozen who came that the company had circulated the petitions to find out which workers were union members and that now it was all the more important for the union to win the election since only the union could protect their jobs.

At this point, Phil addressed another letter to each member.

> The Company got two of the workers to pass petitions through the shop asking you to withdraw from the Union. There are always one or two in every large group who are willing to sell themselves to the boss cheaply and in return for his favor are willing to hurt their fellow workers.
>
> The Company never knew who did or did not sign a Union card. By signing these petitions that are being circulated, those few who signed them were letting the Company know for the first time that they had signed Union cards. That was not a wise thing to do.
>
> The organizing campaign is coming to a close. Ninety per cent of the workers have joined the union and the election is not too far off. The statements made to you by Union representatives are as true today as they were when they first talked to you. Neither you nor any other workers in the shop can possibly be hurt by signing a Union card and having a Union in your shop. The Federal law protects you in this respect as it does all other workers in the country.
>
> But you do have very much to lose if the Company succeeds in frightening you away from your original intentions of having a Union. The Company will then feel justified not only in keeping wages down but in cutting them whenever it likes.
>
> This is the best chance that you ever had to bring a Union into your shop and a Union contract into effect which will give you a decent wage instead of a petty increase and the false promises that you had for these many years that the shop was in existence.
>
> Do not be deceived by traitors in your ranks. It means nothing if you were frightened by them into signing these petitions. You are still a member and you can still vote for the Union. Stick by your co-workers and insist upon a Union contract and all the good that a Union contract can do for you.

On October 10, when the union and the company received the news that the Labor Board had scheduled the representation election for October 24, both the union and company intensified their campaigns for the allegiance of the workers. The company sent a letter to all employees stating that "this vicious union drive . . . is practically turning the peaceful atmosphere of our plant and our relations with our employees, into what looks like to us guerrilla warfare," and that the "professional union organizers" were spreading lies.

> These professional union organizers . . . are constantly trying, through every means at their hand, through lies and continually badgering and bothering you in what we believe is a vain attempt to win this election.
>
> . . . It is our purpose to free you as fast as possible from this disorder which the union organizers have created here, so that you may again live in peace amongst yourselves and with us. . . .
>
> We understand also that these people are making the most extravagant promises to you as to what they are going to do for you. You have no guarantee, of course, that these promises will be fulfilled. From what we hear, they are just dreams. You can rest assured that a union is not necessary to get you anything that is possible for us to give. We will do that ourselves pleasantly and decently, without any disturbances and strife, such as you have here at the present time.
>
> As against this turmoil which now exists, we have had peace in this plant ever since we have been in business. We have had no disorders, no strikes, and no picketing. From the manner in which these union organizers are conducting this union drive, it is hard to say what may happen if the union comes in here. But, what we do know is that the history of unionism is full of cases where when the union becomes the bargaining agent, the most peaceful and pleasant relationship between employees and employers is disturbed, sometimes so seriously that those conditions never become right again. Whether this would happen here, no one can foretell. But, we ask you—Do you think the risk is worth while?

Phil scheduled a meeting at the Trades Council hall on the following Saturday. The publicity leaflet urged "everyone—those for and those against a Union . . . to exercise your rights as a citizen in a free country" by coming to the meeting. At the meeting Phil discussed the company's latest attack on the union—the contention that the company would give the employees everything possible without a union. He pointed out that the company actually was paying its employees only what the federal minimum wage law required—75 cents an hour—while other workers in the area and in the industry earned much more than that. He maintained that the company was acting like a "spoiled child who cannot have its way and now starts calling names. The company cries that the peaceful atmosphere of the plant is gone." The representation election, he stated, would give the workers the opportunity "to tell the company that you want a peaceful atmosphere, but that you also

want a union contract with better wages, job security, and union benefits." How the workers voted would determine whether the company
would continue to pay and do what it wanted or whether the workers
would have a voice in the conditions of their employment. He concluded
by saying that the company had failed its employees and it was time
for a change.

A pre-election rally was scheduled for the Saturday afternoon preceding the election. The Midwest general organizer of the union and his
chief assistant came from Chicago to be featured speakers, and the
president of the Saylor Trades and Labor Council also was on the program. The speakers outlined the union's demands: (1) union recognition,
(2) substantial raises for all job classifications, (3) company-paid insurance and retirement fund, (4) orderly grievance procedure, (5) no
cuts in piece rates after they were set.

The organizers sympathized with the Saylor Company mill workers
because their piecework rates were so low that they could earn no more
than the guaranteed minimum, and they emphasized that both minimum
rates and piecework earnings in shops organized by the union were,
on the average, 15 cents an hour higher. They added that premium
bonus rates for production over the guaranteed minimum also were
higher in organized shops. Saylor workers were told that they, in contrast, were getting a bonus for not making the minimum rate and that
this was not a bonus at all. Further, because there was no way for
the employees to determine whether or not the company-set piecework
prices were fair, workers on a given operation might be paid 10 cents
a dozen one season and only a third as much the next time for the
same operation.

The speakers took exception to the mill's "grab bag system" of distributing work: those workers who arrived first at the beginning of each
shift were allowed to pick the easiest and/or highest paying work. They
also criticized the servicing of operators: because they usually had to
leave their machines to get materials, their output and earnings were
decreased substantially. In addition, they said, many of these workers
found that they had to do a great deal of extra work on some items,
and no allowance was made for the extra work.

"Maybe you're satisfied with these conditions," Phil said. "The company
thinks so. They promise that without the union you can get along as
well as before." The speakers joined in urging the workers to take the
first step toward correcting the bad conditions in the mill by voting for
the union in the coming election. Leaflets containing the substance of
the talks were distributed as the meeting closed.

Another union leaflet was distributed at the mill gates the day before the election. Under the heading, "The Union Wants Peace in the Mill," it set forth the general demands for wage increases, an end to favoritism in the mill, vacations, health and retirement plans, and an equitable piecework system.

In the meantime, the mill superintendent was conducting "captive audience" meetings in the mill cafeteria. Workers were told of the strikes in which unions engage, of the cost of some of these strikes in terms of lost wages and permanent loss of jobs when a struck employer lost customers because he was unable to fulfill delivery commitments. Tom Miller, speaking at one of these meetings, said in effect that a nearby competitor had been driven out of business because of excessive demands made by the same union organizers at work in Saylor.

As it happened, one of the members of the "inside" organizing committee had a friend who was employed at the competing factory. She wrote to her, asking for more information about the situation there. The friend responded that the factory had been sold some three years after the union was organized and that the new owner had temporarily discontinued the operation because it interfered with clock manufacturing going on in the same building. However, the company later re-established the discontinued product. The friend reported wage levels in her unionized factory, and they turned out to be substantially higher than those in the Saylor mill. This letter was circulated by the "inside" organizing committee and appeared to spike the employer's claims effectively.

On the day of the representation election, the union distributed a leaflet to employees going into the mill to work and to vote. The leaflet, which became the basis for a seven months' delay in the final certification of election results, is quoted in full:

What is the History of the Right to Organize?

Everyone knows that, from the beginning of our industrial history, employers almost without exception have fought organization of their workers at every turn. What is organization for? It is to give each worker the strength and protection of united effort. It is to clothe the nakedness of the unorganized worker who is otherwise forced to stand single handed and alone. No bona-fide unions, free from the company domination and Russian domination, want trouble. THE RIGHT TO ORGANIZE COMES FROM ALMIGHTY GOD HIMSELF.

CATHOLIC BISHOP FRANCIS J. HAAS
GRAND RAPIDS, MICHIGAN

P.S. . . . DON'T BE FOOLED BY COMPANY PROPAGANDA.

In the election, 116 of 216 eligible mill employees voted to have the union represent them for the purposes of collective bargaining. The results made it clear that the company's counteroffensive had been more successful that the organizers had assessed. Whereas approximately 80 per cent of the workers had signed union membership cards up to the two-week period prior to the election, only 57 per cent voted for the union in the secret election.

The company's strategy now was to try to delay certification of the union as sole bargaining agency in the hope that the election could be set aside and that a new election might result in the union's defeat. Two days after the election, the company's attorneys filed objections with the NLRB regional office. The objections were based on two allegations: (1) the union leaflet quoting Bishop Haas consisted of undue and illegal pressure, and (2) the leaflet was distributed at the polling places in violation of the Board rule that no electioneering should take place within thirty feet of the polls.

Again the union representatives addressed a letter to all members stating that no matter what new "tricks" the company devised, the union would not be stopped.

> The Company told you it wanted a democratic election. It didn't mean it! The Company thought it had enough of you frightened so that you would vote the way it wanted. But when the election was held, a majority voted against the Company and for a Union.
> The Company then forgot about democracy and decided to use legal tricks to delay negotiating a Union contract with Union wages and conditions. The Company's tricks failed before and will fail again. The Union and the Federal National Labor Relations Board will take care of these stalling tactics in the near future.

Helen stepped up the meetings of the organizing committee "to keep morale up, but," she wrote, "I'm at a loss as to what to tell them. The people are awaiting the Board's decision impatiently." Union lapel pins were distributed in an effort to bolster waning morale, but members of the "inside" committee reported that very few workers were wearing them and most of the others probably would not until after the final certification of the union. Inside leaders reported to Helen that the mill superintendent was discriminating against the union members by giving them "bad work." Sue reported, "Morale is very low in the shop, and production is falling off. On top of all this, some new girls were hired in one department taking work away from some of our strong members there."

At the membership meeting on December 7, Phil told the workers that the company was using every means to "stall and delay" negotiating a contract in the hope that it could kill off the union. The organizers realized that the longer certification was delayed, the greater was the possibility of further defections from the union ranks and the greater the problem of maintaining morale among the union members. For the first time Phil suggested that strike action might be necessary.

The next day he contacted a union official in the headquarters city of the NLRB regional office and asked help in getting a quick Board ruling on the company's appeal. The Regional Director denied the company's objections on December 19. A week later the company appealed, this time by filing exceptions to the regional director's report with the NLRB in Washington. At the same time, the company confronted the union with another dilemma. It announced a general 15-cent wage increase for all employees.

Phil was faced with an important problem: could the union find a way to turn this latest company move to its own advantage? The union could file charges with the NLRB that the unilateral wage increase amounted to an unfair labor practice under the Taft-Hartley Act—refusal to bargain. But this move might give the workers the impression that the union opposed the increase, and Phil wanted to avoid this interpretation. Also, involving the Labor Board further in the case would result in more delay in certification of the union and negotiation of a contract. The whole campaign would then be more difficult for the union.

Phil decided on another tactic. He wrote a letter to all employees, arguing that the raise was given only in the hope that the union could be weakened, and asserting that without a union contract, any raises given by the company could be taken away just as easily. He pointed out that the raise was given only because of the threat of the union, and that if only the threat could produce results, the union itself could do much more for the workers. He stated that the company was spending "a fortune" on attorneys who had been hired to think up "tricks" to stop the union, and added that it would have been much wiser for the company to pay that money to the workers. He also asked everyone to come to a general membership meeting the following evening:

> I said at that meeting the Company gave them a raise simply because of the pressure brought on them by the union. I said that we could file charges with the Labor Board against them and if we won, the raise would be taken away but that's not what we're here for. They got the raise—swell, that's the first installment, and we'll go out for more.

The way in which the increase was applied convinced Phil that neither the employer nor his attorneys understood the rationale of the firm's own piecework system. In general, the system is based on the premise that workers will increase their output if a bonus is paid for extra work. But when a worker is guaranteed an amount of pay which is close to or equal to what he formerly earned including a bonus, he no longer has an incentive to do any extra work.

The minimum hourly guaranteed rates at the Saylor mill had doubled over a three-year period, but piecework bonus prices had not changed. Thus the incentives had been constantly diluted until they had all but disappeared. The latest increase in the guaranteed minimum from 75 to 90 cents actually worked to the disadvantage of both the employees and the company since it almost destroyed the incentive; when workers found it difficult to achieve the output on which the minimum guarantee was based, they were reprimanded by their supervisors for not "making out." Phil summed up the situation:

> The Company used very smart lawyers insofar, as the use of the Taft-Hartley Act was concerned. But they used very stupid lawyers insofar as the industry was concerned. They knew nothing of the industry and apparently the Company knew very little of the methods of wage payment. The increase they gave was put on the wrong end. What was logical from the factory point of view—not necessarily the union's—was to provide increases in the piece rate prices to give an incentive so that the people would turn out more than the 75 cents an hour they were already guaranteed. What they did in this situation was to actually cut down the incentive. The whole thing didn't avail the Company anything. The people were just as intent immediately after the raise as they were immediately prior to the raise to keep on going with the union.

It was not necessary for him to point out to the affected workers that the new increase actually created a new inequity.

> That particular part was brought to my attention in an awful hurry by the people who were already aware of it. Because by that time, there had been enough discussion among the people in the shop about piece rate prices and incentives in a piecework shop so that the people understood it. In fact, it seemed to me that they understood it better than Tom Miller did. And when the raise was announced, the people called it to my attention. I did point out that our need was no longer to increase the minimum but to try to bring the necessary results to both the workers and the Company. And the people pointed out to me—a lot of them said: "What the hell is the use of working if I can't possibly make that much money anyway!" There must be some differential between a minimum and the incentive—otherwise the shop goes to hell.

It now seemed to Phil that the struggle for a union contract would probably be won only through strike action. Yet both he and Helen were extremely reluctant to urge this course since they were not at all certain that the membership was ready to follow a strike recommendation. First they had to strengthen the organization. Phil wrote to the "inside" organizing committee that "the fact that the Company is so anxious to avoid a Union contract should make the people in the shop all the more interested in a contract." Anything the company wants so desperately to do without, he said, must be very precious and important to the workers.

> More than ever before, all of us will have to strive to make this understandable to the workers in the shop, to bolster up their spirits and to make them be willing not only to wait but to fight, if necessary.

Phil sent a second full-time organizer to Saylor to help prepare for a possible strike. Chuck, who was in his early thirties, had been a skilled worker in a Milwaukee plant organized by Phil and an officer of his local union before joining Phil's staff. He had had several years' experience in organizing and had been through several strikes. His assignment was to aid Helen in maintaining the morale of the group and to lay whatever groundwork was necessary in preparation for a strike.

Chuck met the "inside" committee in his hotel room and suggested that a strike might be the only way out. He told the members he wanted their reactions to this suggestion and urged that they discuss it with the people in the mill. His report to Phil on this meeting stated: "Half are eager and the remainder are those who think a little more of the consequences of a strike." Two weeks later, Chuck reported, "The story that a strike is possible if the Company keeps up its present tactics has penetrated to all corners of the shop, and it seems that it is talked about by everybody." Yet the organizers could not assess the feelings of the workers toward a strike because sentiment had not crystallized. This was a new and as yet undefined experience for the Saylor people. The organizers felt that it was necessary to build the strongest possible sentiment for a strike before it was undertaken. Further, the company's appeal to the NLRB was still pending, and the union was determined to "play the string out as far as it goes."

On February 20, almost four months after the election was held, the national Board confirmed the Regional Director's certification of the union, when it held that the leaflet distributed at the polling places fell within the realm of legitimate election propaganda and that there was no evidence of electioneering within thirty feet of the polls. The following day Phil wired the employer requesting that a date be set immediately to begin contract negotiations. A week later, the company's attorneys replied that the company was filing a motion with the NLRB, asking it to reconsider its decision.

The company now repeated a tactic which had been somewhat successful earlier. Mr. Miller addressed all the workers in the company cafeteria and urged them to write to the regional office of the union asking that their names be dropped from the list of union members. During this meeting he again hinted that other firms had either closed or moved to other towns after their work forces had been unionized. He did not state that this would happen in his case, but the impression he left seemed clear. In a community where very few or no alternative opportunities for employment existed, such inferences may carry great weight among employees. The union received sixteen letters notifying the union officials that the senders (in each instance individuals who had once before withdrawn membership by signing petitions) had withdrawn. Since the union had won the certification election with a scant 57 per cent majority, the new defections were viewed as serious.

Helen and Chuck visited each of the defectors as well as others who had signed the petition of withdrawal the previous October. The "inside" committee also contacted as many of them as possible in an effort to bring them back into the union's ranks. The union representatives were less than successful. They reported very little progress, but some hope since "the non-union people don't seem to be anti-union. They're just waiting for some sign from us of real progress before they jump on the bandwagon." Helen added that she was using a different tactic with these workers who were now referred to as "fence-sitters":

> I just call and tell them I am very surprised about their withdrawal and just wanted to talk to them, not to ask them to re-sign but to let them know what is happening. Of course I tell them I don't want them to be hurt because I've taken a personal liking to them, and when we have a strike here the fact that they are not union members, they will not be able to draw strike benefits while the union members will be taken care of. I leave without saying anything about re-signing, and I only ask them to think things over and if they want to talk to me, I will be at the hotel or I will gladly arrange to return to see them.

Chuck also emphasized that strike benefits would be paid only to union members. The "inside" committee reported to Helen that "they are talking strike throughout the shop." Phil and Helen were convinced that if the committee continued to talk about a strike, there was some chance that the defectors would rejoin. This, however, did not come about.

Helen met with leaders of the Trades and Labor Council to solicit their help in spreading the word around town that there might be a strike and that "if the girls go on the picket line at the factory, the Trades and Labor Council will be back of them and start boycotting the store because Miller is unfair to labor." The Council leaders agreed to ask their memberships for support. Phil urged Bert (now president of the mill local) to tell the people in the shop that "the Company will have to do business with us or the International Union will have to recommend to the people in the shop to go out on strike." He wanted Bert to make sure that "everyone understands fully the sort of Company that they have to deal with." At the same time, Phil wrote to Helen:

> We have not as yet reached a stage where we want to issue statements to the press or to hold any mass meetings in which to arouse the sentiments of the people both in the shop and in the community. But that step may be reached in a short time. You have been through this before and know what I mean. More than ever before, we need an aroused group in the shop.

The latest company appeal to the NLRB made it difficult for Phil to pace the strike agitation. It was the international union's policy to wait for a decision on a company's final legal resort before recommending a strike, but Phil had no way of knowing when that decison might come—how many days, weeks, or months hence. He asked the international union's general counsel in New York to do what he could to expedite the Board's decision.

The union officials, however, miscalculated the effects of the strike agitation upon the local leadership. The union policy of permitting the company to exhaust its recourse before the Labor Board was interpreted by several of the local leaders as an unnecessary delay in calling a strike. They had become convinced that only a successful strike would force the company to come to terms and that the union was responsible for delaying the showdown. One leader charged Phil with "letting grass grow under your feet. . . . The girls at the mill are all disgusted, and if you don't get going, the union will fold like a tent. . . ." Helen reported that other leaders were asking, "How much longer is Phil going to let this go on? We are beginning to believe the union is going to let the damn thing go until we lose everything. . . . Phil is stalling." The chief organizer commented:

> On the part of some people, there was a feeling of frustration and the desire to start screaming or go on strike to overcome this frustration. . . . Nothing seemed to be happening . . . we weren't much closer to a contract. They started thinking—"Well, the Company was right in the first instance—that Tom Miller and the Miller family was much too big for any union to come in and set themselves up, and that despite everything Phil had said to us, there will never be a union here. Tom Miller won again."

Phil assured the leaders by letter, by telephone, and in person that the union was doing everything in its power to avoid delays and to secure a contract. He pointed out that the union already had invested a tremendous amount of time, effort, and money to build their union. He argued that the company was responsible for the long delays and that it was necessary for the leaders to "get the people to understand the Company's delaying tactics and build up sentiments for a strike. If and when that time comes, we want to be sure that we have a large percentage of the people on the picket line and not inside the shop working." He said that the simplest course of action would be to call an immediate strike. "But it has been and continues to be the policy of our union to take every possible step before we ask our members to go on strike." Should strike action become necessary, he wrote, adequate preparation must come first.

> A responsible union does not go into a strike haphazardly any more than a country goes into a war haphazardly. . . . We will choose a time when the company's business is expanding and it will hurt the most. We will also want to be sure that we have a substantial number of people who will go on strike so that we have reason to expect a quick victory. When we do recommend strike, we will do so because we are certain that there is no possibility of getting a contract any other way.

Although Phil emphasized the strike policy of the international union in his talks and letters, his real reservation stemmed from the fact that only a very slim majority of workers stood openly for the union. He could not be sure that the majority in the shop would respect picket lines in case of a strike. He felt that the new union members still identified themselves closely with the employer—but to confess this to the local leadership would be to increase their apprehensions and to decrease their confidence in him.

Several of the local union leaders continued to blame the union for not forcing the issue, while others tended to blame the employer's attorneys. Very few felt that Mr. Miller himself held the key to the situation. The organizers continually pointed out to the local leadership that

> . . . attorneys don't do things on their own but do things under instructions from their clients. The turning point would be reached when the people understood this. It was a question of them understanding that if Miller wanted, all this would be unnecessary. It was necessary for them to understand that if Miller intended a fair compromise with the union, there would be no need for a strike or the continuance of a strike once it started.

On March 28, 1951, seven months after the election, the National Labor Relations Board denied the company's motion for reconsideration of its earlier decision. The company's recourse under the law was now exhausted. The first meeting between the employer and his representatives and the union representatives for the purpose of negotiating a contract was held April 6 in Saylor. In eight negotiating sessions during the course of the next three months, some progress was made on issues which the union considered relatively unimportant: the mechanics of the grievance procedure, the union's right to review piecework prices, improved methods for supplying workers with materials, a job classification system which would rationalize the wage structure materially, and others. However, no agreement was reached on two issues which the union leaders considered vital: union security and an across-the-board wage increase.

On June 14, Helen reported to Phil that "the workers are getting very restless—they want action. So we started a rumor that Miller was going to cut wages back to 75 cents an hour." The results far exceeded her expectations: "There is so much strike talk in the mill that the Company is working everyone at full speed—at least eight hours and some departments on Saturday. Everyone is sure that without a union they will surely face a wage-cut." She went on to report that supervisors were quietly advising non-members that they would lose their jobs if they joined the union, but that workers in the inspection department had told a forelady to "get the hell out of here before we throw you out . . ." when she suggested that the union was not really interested in the workers' welfare.

Several of the skilled craftsmen, the prestige group among the mill workers, also began making house calls to let the non-members know that they were prepared to strike for the union demands. During the negotiating session on June 29, the company's attorney insisted that some union representatives "were, in effect, badgering the employees who were not members of the union to force them to become members." Union representatives replied that such actions, if they were taking place, were without the knowledge or consent of the union. Mr. Miller stated that if the "badgering" continued, he would be forced to take disciplinary action against any union members "using this type of solicitation" or to discharge the guilty people.

The company broke off negotiations at this meeting, and both sides agreed to request assistance from the Federal Mediation and Conciliation Service. Several meetings with the conciliator spread over most of a week failed to produce a basis upon which the union representatives felt they could agree with the company. The company was willing to grant five paid holidays, some individual adjustments in piece rates, a grievance procedure, and other provisions but did not yield on the two issues which the union considered vital—the union security clause and the across-the-board wage increase. Without these concessions, the other items, when totaled by the union, did not amount to much. The company's final offer, said Phil, "would be considered a defeat by the people in the shop for all their efforts and their time." The success of the company in cutting the union's majority in the plant to what was almost a minority convinced Phil that only with a union shop could the local hope to continue in business for a year, during which time it could repair its forces and prepare for contract improvements the following year.

A complete impasse was reached late in the afternoon of the second day of almost continuous negotiations. Each side stood at fixed and deadlocked positions with the union shop and wage issues unresolved. At this point the conciliator suggested that the issues be submitted to arbitration. The union negotiators agreed to the proposal but the employer took the position that no "outsider" would be permitted to decide how the mill should be run. The union committee, now convinced that further discussion was not likely to be at all fruitful, asked for a recess and decided that there was no alternative to a strike.

Before the local could act, Phil had to call the union regional vice-president in Chicago to secure permission. Permission was granted, and the negotiating committee was sent to the mill gates at shift change to tell members of the "inside" organizing committee (by this time about twenty workers) to come immediately to a meeting in Phil's hotel room.

Phil explained the situation and recommended that the union call a strike the next day. When the committee supported the recommendation unanimously, Phil moved to call a general membership meeting for a strike vote. Since there was no time to distribute leaflets, each committee member was given a block of names and telephone numbers of union members and instructed to notify them of the special meeting that evening at the local Trades and Labor hall.

Approximately 125 mill workers were present when Phil dispassionately reported on the conduct of negotiation and the final company offer. The union's attorney spoke in detail on the company's position and how the union interpreted it. Phil again took the floor to announce that the international union was recommending a strike. He listed what he considered to be the alternatives: accept the company's final offer, which probably would result in the disappearance of the union, abandon the entire effort, or force the issue through a strike. The union had been very patient, he said; it had not taken this step until all legal procedures had been exhausted. It had given the firm every opportunity to come to a fair agreement with the union. But he insisted that any agreement had to include a union security clause, because unless the union had this protection, the company would never cease trying to destroy it. Further, any agreement had to include a "decent" wage increase. Since the company was unwilling to concede these issues through discussion, a strike was the only alternative. He promised that the strike would be fully supported by the resources of an international union with more than 400,000 members. The local union president made a short speech in support of Phil's strike motion. He was convinced, he said, that only a strike could show Tom Miller that the union members were absolutely determined to get a "decent" contract. He told the meeting that the bargaining committee stood "100 per cent" behind Phil and the strike move and that, although they had all hoped that this action might be avoided, they were unanimous in the belief that there was now no other recourse.

A short discussion period followed. Someone asked if any strike benefits would be paid. Phil replied that it was the policy of the international to pay benenfits to strikers and to make sure that no one suffered "undue hardship." He again emphasized the resources of the union, trying to assure those present that the union "would take care of them." Someone else asked if they would have to picket and Phil replied that all strikers would be asked to picket but those who felt that they could not would be given other tasks to do such as running the strike headquarters and the kitchen which would be set up. The discussion continued for about thirty minutes after which the motion to strike was put to a standing vote. About 115 of the 125 present stood for the organizer's motion. The strike was on.

2.

COLLECTIVE PROTEST IN RELOCATION CENTERS (1957)[1]

NORMAN R. JACKMAN

Following the Japanese attack on Pearl Harbor, President Roosevelt issued proclamations which subjected enemy aliens to arrest and detention on suspicion of espionage or sabotage. Certain military installations

SOURCE: Norman Jackman, "Collective Protest in Relocation Centers," *American Journal of Sociology*, 63 (November 1957), pp. 264–272. Reprinted by permission of *The American Journal of Sociology* and the author.

and defense plants and a limited area around them were designated military security zones, and enemy aliens were banned from them. They were expected to leave voluntarily. But on February 19, 1942, at the request of the War Department, which judged earlier security measures of the Department of Justice inadequate, the President authorized the army to establish military zones in the United States whose limits were to be determined at the discretion of military staff officers. The order that any group, citizen or alien, could be excluded from them was aimed primarily at Japanese aliens and Japanese-Americans from the Pacific Coast.

During the summer and fall of 1942 a mass evacuation of men, women, and children of Japanese ancestry took place. Nearly 120,000 individuals and families were moved to assembly centers and then distributed among ten relocation centers. Their release was subject to many restrictions, but most evacuees could leave and take up residence in areas outside of restricted military zones if they so wished.

The majority of evacuees stayed in the centers for the greater part of the war,[2] primarily through fear of the hostility of Caucasian soldiers and civilians. Furthermore, since the evacuees had lost nearly all their possessions, many felt that the federal government was responsible for their welfare.

Physical conditions in the centers were roughly comparable, and their formal administrative organization was identical. The frame buildings, covered with black tar paper, were in blocks designed to house from 250 to 300 persons. Each block consisted of fourteen single-story barracks, divided into four or six apartments, a mess hall, a recreation hall, latrines, and a laundry. There were also administrative, utility, and various auxiliary buildings.

Administrative responsibility was in the hands of a non-Japanese civilian staff: a project director, with assistants in operations, administrative management, and community management, a reports officer, and an attorney.

Formal authority was vested in government administrators, many of whom, at least initially, held opinions that differed from the evacuees' on such matters as the need for relocation, the oriental minority in Amer-

---

[1] The material for this article has been taken from the writer's unpublished doctoral dissertation, "Collective Protest in Relocation Centers" (Berkely: University of California, 1955).

[2] At the end of 1944 less than 40,000 people, of nearly 120,000, had left the centers. During 1945 nearly all were relocated, though much of this movement was involuntary, owing to the closing of the centers (War Relocation Authority, *The Evacuated People: A Quantitative Description* [Washington, D.C.: Government Printing Office, 1946], Table 10, p. 30).

ica, and the proper implementation of government regulations and directives. Nevertheless, the administrators were largely united in the belief
that, since the centers were a part of a government order, they must
be made to function in a reasonably orderly manner.

The long-range government policy concerning evacuation was three-
fold: to allow the residents to govern themselves, within the limitations
of War Relocation Authority regulations, to make them economically
self-sufficient, and to settle them as quickly as possible in the nation
outside of military zones.

Interaction between the evacuees and the administration centered about
the communicating of the rules and regulations to the residents and
the executing of them. Channels of communication within the centers
followed a hierarchical pattern from the top administrator, the project
director, to the individual evacuee who held no appointive or elective
post but who was linked to the camp structure through block meetings,
the camp newspaper, information bureaus, bulletin boards, occasional
mass meetings, and so on.

The functioning of the system depended mainly upon the administrative staff's interpretation of self-government. Self-government, as enacted
by the War Relocation Authority from its headquarters in Washington,
was centered in a community council composed of evacuee representatives who were American citizens. Over one-third of the evacuees were
excluded from formal community government, though the regulation was
changed to allow aliens to participate in self-government beginning in
1943. Many aliens feared that the American citizens among them would
not represent them properly. They therefore sought representation
through informal organizations which had no standing with the administration.

Self-government was impeded by the fact that the community council
was subservient, in the main, to the administration. It was thus a self-
governing body only in the narrowest sense of the term. The center
was, at best, a benevolent authoritarianism. Nevertheless, self-government bodies conducted negotiation and mediation when they had the
support of most administrators and evacuees.

The administration attempted to establish enterprises by which the
residents could become economically self-sufficient, including production
for the war effort and food for the center and recruitment as seasonal
farm labor.

The failure of community enterprises was a part of the larger failure
of self-government, the main reason for which was the prison-camp
perspective of the majority of evacuees: since the government had abrogated their civil rights, they thought it should provide completely for

their welfare. On this ground, too, they resisted resettlement, though the principal objection to resettlement was fear of adverse public opinion. Nevertheless, whereas community enterprises were a complete failure (except in the case of community consumer co-operatives), the policy of relocation was partially successful. From a quarter to a third of the evacuees were resettled throughout the nation or were serving in the armed forces by the beginning of 1945.

Resettlement was preceded early in 1943 by a leave-clearance program established to determine the "loyalty" of center residents. Concomitantly, army teams entered each center to register all male citizens over the age of seventeen for possible induction into the armed services. All registration forms, whether for draft classes or draft-exempt classes, contained the question: "Will you swear unqualified allegiance to the United States of America and faithfully defend the United States from any or all attack by foreign or domestic forces, and forswear any form of allegiance or obedience to the Japanese emperor, or any other foreign government, power or organization?"

Many evacuees refused to register. Others registered but answered the question in the negative. American citizens among them resented having their loyalty questioned, while Japanese aliens, ineligible for American citizenship, feared that an affirmative answer would denationalize them and leave them without a country. However, the response to registration varied widely from center to center. At one extreme, 36.4 per cent of the population of Tule Lake refused to register or gave negative responses to the question; at the other, only 2.6 per cent of the residents of Granada responded negatively. In an effort to segregate the "loyals" from the "disloyals," Tule Lake was designated a segregation center, and all who had not answered the question affirmatively were sent there, while those in Tule Lake who had answered affirmatively were sent to other camps. Many subsequently registered affirmatively or changed from a negative answer and were thus granted leave clearance or declared subject to the draft.

Other issues arose in every center but were interpreted differently in different centers and were therefore resolved differently Labor problems, the administration's attempt to weed out agitators, the food situation, and the shooting of evacuees by army sentries were other issues which mobilized interest.

Many evacuees did not question the legitimacy of relocation, but some were hostile to the government's efforts to make the centers function. Others felt that they had been made victims of coercive decrees which violated American democratic values. Data on how the majority of evacuees in any center came to accept the situation—whether they made some form of non-violent adjustment to it or found it unbearable and reacted violently to it—led to the formulation of the hypothesis presented below.

The data were drawn from the descriptive accounts of relocation centers collected while they were still in operation.[3] They consist of the reports of government officials, minutes of administrative and evacuee meetings, orders, proclamations and issues of center newspapers, and the like, the most important being reports by participant-observers.

The relationship of communication to conflict may be summarized as follows: the development and sharing of common symbols, which is necessary for reciprocal role-taking, depends upon situations which allow for the freest association. When free association is blocked, communication is impaired and divergent definitions are imputed to others. The development of collective protest is a function of the inability of contending parties to comprehend one another. In the absence of arbitration and negotiation, groups develop divergent definitions, and conflict ensues.

If groups are consulted on issues affecting their interests, rational discussion becomes possible. But, if they are excluded, there is little opening for controversy, for advocacy, and for defense—which introduce judgment and discrimination—and so their behavior is irrational.

Since the formal structure of relocation centers was identical, attention was focused upon the manner in which administrative policy was implemented, communicated to evacuees, and sanctioned. Hypotheses were developed for the purpose of testing the relationship between formal and informal agencies of communication, as follows:

ADMINISTRATIVE ORIENTATION. Free communication or the blocking of communication depended upon administrative policy regarding the participation of evacuees in the settlement of disputes. As long as intermediate bodies functioned between the administration and the evacuees, collective protest never reached the stage of riot.

CHANNELS OF COMMUNICATION. The greater the isolation of interest groups of the evacuees from officially sanctioned meetings, the greater

---

[3] This material, collected by the Japanese Evacuation and Resettlement Study of the University of California, plus the official publications of the United States War Relocation Authority, is held by the Documents Division of the University of California Library, Berkeley. It consists of the reports of government officials, minutes of administrative and evacuee meetings, orders, proclamations, issues of center newspapers, and reports of participant-observers employed by the University of California through funds allotted for the Evacuation and Resettlement Study. The footnotes to this article include citations to unpublished field documents, which, though inadequate, since they are in process of being recatalogued and reclassified, provide a lead to the documents held by the University of California Library.

was the divergency of meaning between them and the administration. Conversely, maximum communication reduced misunderstanding to a minimum.

DEFINITION OF THE SITUATION.   Group isolation increased the possibility of violent action stemming from divergent definitions of the situation. Conversely, the more negotiation between contending groups, the less the divergency of meanings and, therefore, the greater the probability of reasonable, non-violent behavior.

In order to test the hypotheses, the data were classified according to the degree of protest expressed in each incident. The basic unit of analysis here, the *incident*, is an issue in which the interests of the administration and those of a portion or all of the evacuees were in conflict. Any issue about which any kind of collective protest was mobilized has been considered, wherever reflected in the documents. An issue which aroused the interest of evacuees led to the formation of groups oriented toward a resolution. These groups initiated certain actions which also led to further interaction within and among the groups. Incidents were terminated by a withdrawal of interest, because either the issue had been resolved satisfactorily or another issue was interesting contending groups. In either case the resolution of the issue often had an effect on subsequent issues.

One hundred and fifteen incidents were analyzed as to degree of collective protest and classified into the following categories arranged in descending order of protest (Tables 1, 2, and 3):

SMALL-GROUP PROTEST.   These included verbal and written communications from the members of a block, a church congregation, or other special-interest group. The protests were directed against various administrative officials and concerned living conditions, minor incidents, or administrative regulations. Specific objects of protests included sanitary conditions in a mess hall or block latrine, safety and fire regulations in living quarters, and fire regulations for the entire center.

PETITIONS AND PROCLAMATIONS.   These involved a relatively large proportion of a center's population and therefore concerned issues of a more general and more important nature from the standpoint of the evacuees. They were directed against top administrative officials, usually including the project director, and concerned such issues as the shooting of evacuees by army sentries, co-operative enterprises, labor recruitment, the loyalty oath, and Selective Service.

STRIKES AND LABOR DISPUTES.   These involved bodies of various sizes in direct conflict with the administration. Specific incidents were over farm labor, motor transport, boiler-tender and carpenter strikes, disputes, and slow-downs. A limited number of persons were involved.

MASS RESIGNATIONS. These protests on the part of elected and appointed evacuees were in direct defiance of the administration and affected the functioning of the entire center. They included general strikes or the resignation of community councilmen or block leaders and of various administrative committees over such issues as the loyalty oath and Selective Service.

MASS MEETINGS. These involved the largest proportion of a center's population and were characterized by strongly expressed opposition to the administration. They occurred over incidents such as the arrest of evacuees by the Federal Bureau of Investigation for alleged subversion and over the issue of registration.

GANG BEATINGS. These were extreme forms of protest by small, well-organized under-cover groups directed against individual evacuees believed to be spying for the administration. They occurred during periods of extreme tension and served to solidify opposition to the administration.

CROWD BEHAVIOR. These protests were culminations of a series of less intensive forms of collective protest, with an intense concentration on the issue and a suspension of rational behavior.

Similar incidents involved varying degrees of collective protest as between one center and another. The type of incident has less bearing on the degree of collective protest than the already-established pattern of interaction and the actual interaction in the new situation: initially, frames of reference from old situations tended to structure the new situation, but the interaction which followed either changed or reinforced them.

Since the principal arena of communication was the meetings of self-governing bodies, most of the data was drawn from their minutes and from the reports of participant-observers. Various interest groups met to debate an event significant to them, thereby evolving definitions of formerly indefinite situations. Confused, misinformed, and varying definitions were held by the publics which mobilized immediately after a significant incident. The nature and functioning of agencies of communication (block meetings, council meetings, administrative staff meetings, mass meetings) determined the eventual definitions of the situation. Each incident was checked against the communication channels involved.

The next step was the coding of the data. Each event in the incident was entered on a summary sheet which contained space for the date and a general description in which the behavior of participating groups was classified under three categories: evacuee groups, mediation groups (if any), and administration groups. Further space was marked off for indicators of the actions from the primary sources: statements by participant-observers, minutes of meetings, formal rules and regulations passed, etc. All such statements pertaining to each incident were noted.

The entire incident was summarized on a coding sheet marked off for the listing of information pertinent to the propositions being tested. The incident was categorized according to the degree of utilization of channels of communication. Three categories comprised this rating scheme: "None"—avoidance or withdrawal; "Partial"—conflicts; and "Full"—consensus. In other words, if contending groups ceased to communicate during the process of the incident or never utilized the channels of communication, the incident was scored "None." If they communicated to some extent but tended to withdraw and return to intermittent communication, the incidents were scored "Partial." If communication was full and consistent, the incidents were scored "Full."

Another rating system was employed to categorize degree of consensus. Whenever available, statements by representatives of each group concerning various stages of the incident were compared. They were classified in order of decreasing divergency as *a, b,* and *c.*

After the incidents in all centers were classified according to degree of collective protest, they were distributed by center. Centers were then grouped in terms of three principal types of collective protest in increasing degree of intensity: "successful negotiation of differences," "passive resistance and insubordination," and "overt rebellion." Inspection of the types and frequencies of collective protest gave the classification for each center (Tables 1, 2, and 3).

Incidents were further divided by date—whether before or after segregation. (Segregation refers to the movement of individuals who refused to attest loyalty to the United States government from their respective centers to Tule Lake, and the movement of evacuees who signed the loyalty oath from Tule Lake to other centers.) This temporal distinction

TABLE 1   PROTESTS CHARACTERIZED BY OVERT REBELLION, BY CENTER

	Small-Group Protest	Petitions and Proclamations	Strikes and Labor Disputes	Mass Resignations	Mass Meetings	Gang Beatings	Crowd Behavior	Total
Tule Lake:								
Before segregation....	4	2	1	...	1	...	...	8
After segregation.....	...	...	5	1	3	...	3	12
Manzanar:								
Before segregation....	4	6	1	1	2	1	1	16
After segregation.....	...	...	...	...	...	...	...	...

TABLE 2 PROTESTS CHARACTERIZED BY PASSIVE RESISTANCE AND INSUBORDINATION, BY CENTER

	Small-Group Protest	Petitions and Proclamations	Strikes and Labor Disputes	Mass Resignations	Mass Meetings	Gang Beatings	Crowd Behavior	Total
Colorado River:								
Before segregation....	4	2	1	...	...	2	2	11
After segregation.....	2	1	4	...	1	...	...	8
Jerome:								
Before segregation....	1	...	2	...	1	2	1	7
After segregation.....	3	2	1	...	...	...	...	6
Minidoka:								
Before segregation....	2	1	...	...	...	...	...	3
After segregation.....	2	2	8	...	...	...	...	12

reveals the effect on collective protest of the changed composition of center populations as to "loyals" and "disloyals." Many observers have stated that collective protest was directly related to the percentage of "disloyals" in a given center. There is such a relationship, as an inspection of the tables indicates. However, "loyalty" is not an intrinsic personal quality: refusal to sign the loyalty oath was related to specific situations. This is shown by the percentage of the total population of each center which was segregated in Tule Lake for refusing to sign the oath. It varied from 2.6 per cent of the population of Granada to 36.4 per cent of the population of Tule Lake. Interaction between the administration

TABLE 3 PROTESTS CHARACTERIZED BY SUCCESSFUL NEGOTIATION, BY CENTER

	Small-Group Protest	Petitions and Proclamations	Strikes and Labor Disputes	Mass Resignations	Mass Meetings	Gang Beatings	Crowd Behavior	Total
Gila:								
Before segregation....	2	...	...	...	...	...	...	2
After segregation.....	1	1	2	...	3	...	...	7
Central Utah:								
Before segregation....	2	2	1	...	...	...	...	5
After segregation.....	2	3	...	...	...	...	...	5
Heart Mountain:								
Before segregation....	1	2	...	...	...	...	...	3
After segregation.....	2	1	...	...	...	...	...	3
Rohrer:								
Before segregation....	1	1	1	...	...	...	...	3
After segregation.....	1	...	...	...	...	...	...	1
Granada:								
Before segregation....	1	1	...	...	...	...	...	2
After segregation.....	...	...	...	...	...	...	...	...

and the evacuees decided the evacuees' attitudes, whether of accommodation or of hostility, and the attitudes found expression in the response to the loyalty oath. In the case of Minidoka, a much higher percentage of incidents of collective protest occurred after segregation than prior to it, which indicated that the loyalty oath was not one of the issues which mobilized protest.

Collective protest was thus seen to be related to the formal administrative structure and informal evacuee groups. Communication was channeled through block meetings, council meetings, administrative staff meetings, and mass meetings. At these meetings various interest groups met to debate an event significant to them and to evolve definitions of situations that initially were indeterminate in that there were many different interpretations of them. The severity of subsequent collective protest depended upon the definitions of situations evolved at the meetings.

The incidents now to be described are over issues which aroused interest and provoked conflict between evacuees and administration.

TOPAZ KITCHEN STRIKE

Evacuees from the Pacific Coast began arriving at Central Utah Relocation Center, Topaz, Utah, early in September, 1942. On September 14 the kitchen work crew struck. It was an advance crew from the Tanforan Assembly Center in California which had come ahead of the first large group of evacuees to arrange mess facilities. The workers refused to work for the two Caucasian chief stewards, whom they characterized as arbitrary, dictatorial, and given to issuing conflicting orders, but, at the same time, they were very conciliatory, stating that they wished to co-operate with the director but could not work harmoniously with the chief stewards.

The project director called a meeting of members of the administrative staff, house captains, and strikers. The house captains, who were elected by the evacuees, were there in the capacity of a mediation committee. They promptly presented a plan: the evacuee cooks would run the dining halls, and the chief stewards would promise to stop their abusive and dictatorial ways. The project director backed this plan strongly, rebuked the stewards, and appointed an evacuee steward as liaison between the administration and the chief cooks on matters pertaining to the kitchen.

Both sides accepted these conditions, and the strike ended. One evacuee observer wrote that, "from the point of view of the Japanese, their objectives were gained. It seems to me that the Caucasian bent over backward to win the co-operation of the Japanese cooks."

The following series of incidents illustrates the buildup of collective protest in a center where negotiating bodies were weak but never completely disappeared.

CROWD BEHAVIOR IN POSTON

On November 14, 1942, a thirty-year-old evacuee in Colorado River Relocation Center, near Poston, Arizona, was beaten by a group which he estimated to consist of eight or ten men. The next day the Internal Security Office, the evacuee police force in the center, arrested two men on charges of taking part in the beating. That night a married couple was beaten by a gang of about eight men.

On November 18 a "committee of seven," which claimed to represent all the evacuees in Poston, visited the project director and requested the release of the two prisoners. The committee was referred to the office of the Federal Bureau of Investigation, but its request was denied.

A crowd began to form before the center's jail. The project director addressed the assembled evacuees and urged them to disperse. They refused, and the crowd continued to grow throughout the day while various individuals urged a general strike. In the meantime the project director met with the community council and the Issei (Japanese immigrants) advisory board and urged them to exert their influence in disbanding the crowd. The council members replied by demanding the release of the two arrested men. When the project director refused, the council and the board resigned. Later that day the block managers resigned, and all formally recognized evacuee representation disappeared in Unit One of Poston, the section of the center where the trouble began.

In the meantime the evacuee leaders had sent two representatives from each block to meet as a governing body. This "committee of seventy-two" contained members of the three formally recognized groups which had resigned that day—the council, the Issei advisory board, and the block managers' group. This group called a general strike of Unit One, and the crowd settled down to picket the jail in shifts.

The next day, November 19, the administration met with twelve representatives from Units Two and Three (the remaining sections), who had been appointed by evacuees as a mediating body between the administration and the committee of seventy-two from Unit One. Negotiations dragged on for several more days. The administration released one of the arrested men but refused to release the other. Emboldened by this concession and by their interpretation of evacuee sentiment, the negotiating committee from Units Two and Three demanded the unconditional release of the second man.

On November 23 the project director again met with the negotiating committee, which demanded that the arrested man be unconditionally released and all charges against him dropped. The director countered by proposing to give him a trial within the center. The meeting ended in a deadlock, but the following day the committee met with the project director and accepted his terms. The arrested man was released to the custody of the evacuee police for subsequent trial in the center by legally constituted authority. This was satisfactory to most evacuees, since the main point of contention was the administration's original intention to try the arrested men outside the center, and they feared that no evacuee would receive a fair trial on the outside because of hostility toward Japanese during the war years. The strike ended the following day, the pickets withdrew from the jail, and the evacuees returned to work.[4]

These incidents illustrate the interaction which occurred when the evacuees' interest was aroused. In every incident investigated in this study, evacuee groups withdrew from communication whenever they interpreted actions of the administration as dictatorial, as taking decisions about their welfare out of their hands. This occurred when there was no established procedure for arbitration and negotiation or when the administration discouraged negotiation or negotiated in an arbitrary or dictatorial manner (hypothesis 1).

In such instances evacuee groups met mostly among themselves, and, in the absence of opposed interests, consensus developed only within the parties in opposition and not among all the interacting groups (hypothesis 2).

The definitions of the situation, initially formulated by the members of interested groups, tended to diverge greatly from the definitions of other interested groups and were reinforced. When communication broke down completely, no reinterpretation of the situation was reached by either the administration or the evacuees, and riotous conduct ensued. When there were frequent meetings of a parliamentary nature, there

---

[4] This descriptive account of several incidents at Poston was drawn principally from the following sources: "Project Director's Weekly Reports" (MS, November, 1942); Norris James, "Final Report on the Disturbances and General Strike at the Colorado River War Relocation Center" (MS, December 11, 1942); Alexander Leighton, *The Governing of Men* (Princeton, N.J.: Princeton University Press, 1946); Tsuchiyama, "Aftermath of the Strike" (MS[n.d.]).

was sufficient modification of initially divergent viewpoints, and rioting was averted (hypothesis 3).

In every case there was a relationship between the degree of collective protest and the channels of communication open at the time. In centers marked by successful negotiation of differences, channels of communication had remained open during the incident, and a high degree of consensus had been achieved among contending parties by the time the incident terminated. The degree of consensus in each center varied from incident to incident, but the pattern of communication in early incidents tended to affect subsequent incidents. In centers marked by passive resistance and insubordination, channels of communication were weak, and a growing divergence of perspectives developed. In cases marked by overt rebellion, situations became defined variously by contending groups as they refused to arbitrate and negotiate.

Collective protest in the relocation centers was related to failure in communication. Without an arena for the rational consideration of issues which were common or complementary, there was no way in which perspectives could become shared. In Cooley's terms, without a high degree of communication, there was no possibility of reciprocal role-taking, since the latter rests on the sharing of definitions, and the sharing of definitions rests on the accessibility of people to one another.

3.

SOME ECOLOGICAL ASPECTS OF NEGRO SLUM RIOTS (1968)

MICHEL McCALL

Grimshaw's stimulating paper propounding an ecological pattern in urban race riots in the United States has quickly become a classic since its publication in 1960.[1] Focusing on pre-World War II riots, Grimshaw asked: Do patterns of racial violence occur with differential "frequency and intensity" in different "types of ecological areas"? In other words, do riots take a different form in different parts of a city?

SOURCE. Original publication.

Grimshaw found that Northern urban riots before World War II typically began as "spontaneous brawls over an immediate disturbance, among bystanders,"[2] and progressed into "mass, uncoordinated battles,"[3] between groups of one race and isolated individuals of the other.[4] Within riot-torn Northern cities (excluding Harlem, which he analyzed separately), Grimshaw found the following patterns of rioting.

Most of the violence occurred in the Negro slum area, including the majority of casualties and fatalities, as well as the major looting and destruction of property. In the Northern style, conflict was most frequent (1) between groups of Negroes and occasional whites passing through the slum area (the whites being the victims in this case), (2) between white gangs invading the slum and Negro defenders, and (3) between groups of Negroes and squads of police sent into the ghetto to quell the riot. Both the Detroit riot of 1943 and the Chicago riot of 1919 saw a good deal of looting and property damage in the slum, including arson and bombing, with considerable numbers of casualties and fatalities.

The racially contested area, Grimshaw reported, was the most disordered of all areas *except* during major riots. During these riots, violence was concentrated along the borders of contested areas (as it was in white-dominated, noncontested areas) and at transportation transfer points. There were some attacks on persons and some attacks on property; the most common pattern was that of chance confrontations of isolated Negroes with white mobs.

Neither the better Negro residential areas nor the corresponding white areas experienced much actual riot-connected violence, especially if they were removed from the *centers* of the rioting.

In the central business district, violence "took the form of physical assault and usually involved large mobs of whites and individual Negroes or small groups of them."[5]

Finally, "stable" mixed neighborhoods, being defined largely in terms of their lack of overt racial conflict preceding the riots, were relatively free of riot behavior.[6]

This, then, was the ecological pattern of race riots before World War II. Grimshaw also discussed several postwar outbreaks of violence in the South, connected with the Civil Rights movement. However, he did not discuss recent changes in the Northern urban riot, for there had been no major riots until the summer of 1964.

In 1964, there were riots in Jersey City, Paterson, and Elizabeth, New Jersey, and suburban Chicago, Philadelphia, New York City, and Rochester, New York. The major riots, those at New York City, Rochester, and Philadelphia, were the most completely reported. These three will be focused upon in the following discussion. The 1965 Los Angeles riot will be discussed separately, as a somewhat special case of recent riots.

Grimshaw had viewed the 1943 Harlem riot as a deviant case from the classic pattern. He described it this way:

> The Harlem disturbances differed from other riots because of the sheer size of the local Negro population. A major invasion was inconceivable without a fairly well-equipped army, and only police forces were equipped in a manner in any way adequate to cope with the 1943 disorders. On the other hand, whites in the area were relatively few, and when outbreaks occurred, were either able to flee or to find Negroes willing to give them shelter. There were few occasions for Negro-white contacts and physical clashes were usually between the resident population and the police. Most of the violence was in the form of looting of stores and general destruction of property. While some evidence suggests that white property was singled out for attack, enough Negro establishments were attacked to leave open the question of whether the violence was racial.[7]

Thus, the Harlem pattern is characterized by (1) a lack of civilian white violence directed against Negroes, (2) a containment of the riot within the Negro slum section, (3) a preponderance of conflict between police and Negroes, (4) less physical assault, with fewer consequent injuries and less loss of life, and (5) a large amount of looting and property damage.

The outstanding fact that emerged from analysis of the recent major riots was that the "Harlem pattern" is the new pattern for Northern urban riots. Far from being a deviant case, it is now the most general pattern.

ECOLOGICAL PATTERNING AND THE NEW "SLUM RIOTS"

In all three cases in 1964, the riot was largely confined to the Negro slum area—Harlem and Bedford-Stuyvesant in New York City, the "jungle" in Philadelphia, and the Third and Seventh Wards in Rochester.

In each of these riots, the precipitating incident was an attempt by police to arrest a Negro in a Negro area. In Harlem a policeman killed a young Negro boy during an attempted arrest. In Rochester, police were called to a neighborhood dance to arrest a drunken youth. In Philadelphia, police answered a call that a car was blocking an intersection in the Negro district, and upon arrival attempted to remove the Negro occupants in order to move the car. (In the latter two cases, the riot started on the spot. In Harlem, several days passed before the outbreak of violence, but this stemmed directly from demonstrations protesting police brutality in the shooting of the Negro boy.)

Again, in all three cases, violence largely involved the police and Negro civilians. An interesting parallel is that in all three cities (and others), residents used a similar tactic in countering the police invasion—they stood on the roofs of their tenements and hurled bricks, bottles, and stones at the police below.

In these recent riots there was less personal injury and less loss of life than in the older riots. In Philadelphia, the *New York Times* reported, there were 152 injuries, including 35 injured policemen. The Governor's Commission on the Los Angeles Riot (also known as the McCone Commission) set the number of injuries in Philadelphia at 341. That body reported that there were 57 injuries in Chicago, and 46 in Jersey City, 8 in Paterson, and 6 in Elizabeth, New Jersey.[8] In Rochester, there were nearly 400 injuries, including 60 to officers. In New York City, 144 policemen and civilians were injured. There were no reported deaths in Philadelphia's disturbance, and only one in New York City and two in Rochester.

These figures may be compared with those given for the 1943 Detroit riot. Shogan and Craig report that there were 500 injuries, 38 deaths (including 23 Negroes and 15 whites), with 1000 people left homeless.[9] Lee and Humphrey's figures were 34 dead and 1000 injured.[10]

Looting and property destruction in the 1964 riots were widespread, however. The *Times* stated that about 60 stores were looted in Rochester. Rochester police listed 174 damaged businesses and set the total cost of damage at $164,000. They further reported the loss of $431,000 worth of stolen goods and an estimated $5000 in incompleted inventories. The California Governor's Commission listed 541 damaged stores in New York City, 225 in Philadelphia, 71 in Jersey City, 20 in Paterson, 17 in Elizabeth, and 2 in suburban Chicago.[11]

In addition to looting, all three cities saw a great deal of vandalism and property destruction. Windows were broken even where there was no looting of stores. Shapiro and Sullivan reported that 970 windows were shattered in Bedford-Stuyvesant alone.[12] And in many cases, items were thrown from stores into the street (including gallons of pastel paint in Rochester).

The McCone Commission's report gave comparable figures for the 1965 Los Angeles riot. They reported that during the riot, which lasted from August 11 to August 17, 34 persons were killed and 1032 were injured. In all, 3952 people were arrested. Damage to 997 stores was estimated at $40,000,000.[13]

Two additional uniformities must be mentioned, however unimportant they may seem. These riots all occurred in the summer, but more than that, they occurred when it was very hot—during the hottest July in nine years in Rochester, for example. They occurred in Negro slums where people were packed in too tightly and where there was no place to go to cool off. In the slums a rise in the temperature drives people outside and onto the streets. Once outside, they form material from which a crowd may be made, given an inflammatory incident.

Secondly, the riots were primarily weekend affairs. In Rochester and Philadelphia rioting lasted from Friday night to Monday morning. In contrast, the Detroit riots were a seven-day, round-the-clock event (there was, of course, less rioting there during the day). The combined Harlem–Bedford-Stuyvesant riots came the closest to the old pattern in this respect. However, Harlem's riot started on Saturday and ended on Monday. Rioting began in Bedford-Stuyvesant on Monday night and ended the following Thursday.

The new riots appear, then, on the basis of an analysis of extant primary materials, to follow Grimshaw's erstwhile deviant case—the Harlem riot. They do *not* follow the classical patterns laid out by Grimshaw. In fact, one can only treat one of his even ecological areas (the Negro slum) and cannot point to any evidence of residential arson, bombing, or most of his patterns of violence.

This description of the "new pattern" of Northern urban riots suggests a new name for such outbursts. I suggest that these were not "race" riots, but Negro "ghetto" riots. These riots did not involve battles between civilian members of two races, as did earlier riots. They involved, rather, Negro civilians and white (and Negro) policemen. Furthermore, as the analysis has made clear, the riots did not occur in areas characterized by integrated housing or areas of Negro "invasion." The areas involved were Negro slums. Often, from 80 to 100% of the residents in these areas were Negroes, and the areas were characterized by old and deteriorated housing, overcrowding, unemployment, lack of education, and poverty.

According to Lieberson and Silverman,

> Riots, as distinguished from lynchings and other forms of collective violence, involve an assault on persons and property simply because they are part of a given subgroup of the community.[14]

Riots may also involve aggression *by* a group of people because they are "part of a given subgroup of the community." Both may be true in the same riot. Whatever the case, in order to be considered a "race" riot, the aggressors or targets of the riot must be members of a *racial* "subgroup of the community." In recent riots, the aggressors have been members of a social and geographical (slum) "subgroup of the community." The other participants, policemen, have been both Negro and white, and thus not members of a racial subgroup.

There is mixed evidence on the question of whether the principal targets of the rioters, businesses, were singled out for attack on the basis of the race of their owners. The McCone Commission said:

> There was some evidence that businesses which were apparently Negro-owned were spared many by hastily posted signs such as "Negro-owned," and "Blood brother"—but there is also evidence of the destruction of some Negro-owned businesses.[15]

The *New York Times* and the local Rochester papers reported that Negro-owned businesses were spared in Rochester, along with CORE and Black Muslim headquarters in the riot area. As for the looting of Negro-owned stores in New York City, Shapiro and Sullivan said:

> The merchants who were boarding up, and some who weren't, both Negro and white, took another precaution. They put up signs saying, "this is a black store" or "Negro-owned." A Chinese laundryman next door to CORE posted a sign saying, "This store is owned by a black man" and emerged unscathed. How that "black man" would have fared if his establishment had stocked liquor instead of laundry is, however, open to question.[12]

There are no figures for any of the riots which show the numbers of Negro-owned stores which were attacked or spared. Because of the meager and contradictory evidence, we must agree with Grimshaw's assessment of Harlem in 1943.

> While some evidence suggests that white property was singled out for attack, enough Negro establishments were attacked to leave open the question of whether the violence was racial.[16]

One further bit of evidence supports the contention that these were not "race" riots, but ghetto or slum riots. June 12–14, 1966, residents of a Puerto Rican slum neighborhood in Chicago rioted. This riot conformed to the same pattern as have recent Negro riots. Rioting was confined to the ghetto and involved police and area residents. The precipitating incident was similar, too. The rioting began when police answered a call to stop a fight in the Puerto Rican section. The tactics of rioters were also quite similar, including throwing rocks, bricks, and bottles, setting fires, and throwing Molotov cocktails.

Thus, two different ethnic groups have been involved in very similar kinds of riots. The factor of *race* was not present in both. The factor which was present in all of the Negro riots and in the Puerto Rican riot was the residence of rioters in segregated slum areas. The recent riots have involved outbursts by a "community subgroup" which might be called the "slum-dwellers."

ECOLOGICAL PECULIARITIES OF THE LOS ANGELES RIOT

Having shown that recent Northern urban race riots conform to a new pattern, we must now discuss one such riot which was somewhat atypical. That riot is, of course, the Los Angeles riot of 1965.

Although it occurred in the same ecological area within the city as have other recent riots, there were differences. The Los Angeles riot resembled the older pattern of race rioting in its length and severity.

The Los Angeles riot lasted for seven days, as did the 1943 Detroit riot. The 1964 riots were, on the other hand, primarily weekend affairs.

Most recent riots have been less costly in lives and personal injuries than were older riots. Los Angeles was an exception. Thirty-four persons were killed and 1032 were injured. Officials said there were between 2000 and 3000 fire alarms recorded during the rioting, including 1000 during the 24-hour period from 7:00 A.M. on Friday to 7:00 A.M. on Saturday. This may be compared with the lighter injuries and single death in Philadelphia, the two deaths in Rochester, and the absence of fatalities in Harlem in 1964. In fact, the Los Angeles riot equaled America's worst, the 1943 Detroit riot, in its severity.

There were some important similarities, on the other hand. In Los Angeles the riots involved, almost exclusively, Negro civilians and police. Further, the riots occurred in a Negro slum area. The tactics which rioters used were likewise typical, with one important exception. In Los Angeles, as in other cities, rioters threw bricks and stones and cans at police, looted and damaged stores in the area, and attacked police cars and sometimes police officers. In addition, there was a great amount of arson in Los Angeles. This was not, as some observers have thought, a new development. Neither was it typical, however. Rioters started fires in the riot area buildings in other recent riots. The difference, and the final atypical feature of the Los Angeles riot, was in the number and severity of the fires.

In effect, the Los Angeles riot differed in severity, not in type. Essentially the same tactics were used by rioters in Los Angeles as in other ghetto riots; in Los Angeles the same tactics were more "successful."

The reasons for this greater success can be traced to differences in the ecology of Los Angeles as compared with Eastern riot cities. These differences in ecology influenced the success of police control tactics, which were also the same as in other riots, at the same time they influenced the success of the rioters' tactics. It is thus important to look at these ecological differences.

The principal differences between Los Angeles and most Eastern cities stem from the fact that Los Angeles is a newer city and from its location in the West.

Large urban areas in the East are, above all, crowded. They developed, in most cases, before the advent of the automobile, and their streets are narrow and few, most suitable for horses and horse-drawn vehicles. This earlier development meant that the cities did not early spread out. With poorer and slower transportation, the cities did not need to be, and indeed could not be, too spread out.

Housing units, especially in slum areas such as we are discussing, tend to be multiple-family dwellings several stories high. Individual family homes, set in yards, are rare. Finally, these cities are more likely to have some form of public transportation such as subways, elevated trains, or streetcars, which replace automobiles to some extent. These transportation systems developed before the advent of the family automobile and are necessary where streets are inadequate to handle large numbers of cars.

Los Angeles is quite different. The city developed later than Eastern cities. Los Angeles was not incorporated until 1840, and had only 10,000 citizens in 1880. In contrast, there were already 44,000 people in Philadelphia and 33,000 in New York City in 1790, at the time of the first national census.[17] This later development had a profound influence on the structure of the city.

> Author Carey Williams in the early 1920's described Los Angeles as a "collection of suburbs in search of a city." Los Angeles began taking to the suburbs too early in its urban life to have firmly rooted an urban center. Older metropolises sprouted suburbs around long-established hubs and then proceeded to choke their hubs with their automobiles. . . .
>   . . . One reason, perhaps, sprawl was considered peculiar to Los Angeles for so long may be found in the fact that the automobile appeared on the scene while the city was still in swaddling clothes. As late as 1880, Los Angeles had only 10,000 inhabitants. It grew phenomenally the following decade; even so, it had only 50,000 inhabitants by 1890. The automobile was thus able to fashion the city in fledgling form. It was able to do this at high speed because of the compatibility of the early automobile with Southern California's climate. The vehicle's

worst detractors at the time—cold weather and mud—were minimal in an area that enjoyed a long dry season and basked in warm sun. The speed of the ensuing courtship did not make it any easier to read as a portent of things to come.[18]

It has been said that there are more automobiles in Los Angeles than in any other city in the United States. There are more cars registered in Los Angeles County than in the whole of most states; only California, Illinois, New York, Pennsylvania, and Ohio have more.

There is a public transportation system of buses, but it is inadequate and expensive. The McCone Commission stated that Los Angeles is the only major city in the United States in which the operation losses of the transportation system are not subsidized by the city.[19] However, there is a highly developed system of roads and highways. One third of the entire downtown area is highways and streets, and another third is parking garages.[20] There are more streets, and these are usually wider than Eastern city streets.

In addition, housing units in residential areas are more likely to be single dwellings, with yards. The Negro ghetto is not different in these respects from other areas in the city.

Watts, now 98% Negro, is an abject slum, sociologists say, though not a slum in the Eastern sense of a rat-infested crumbling tenement, and littered streets. It is an area of small homes—90% built before the war, many surrounded by lawns. But most of the homes are rented and 20% are dilapidated.[21]

In 1965, 88.6% of the Negro population of Los Angeles lived in the riot area. The population density of the area was 4.3 persons per household on the average, as compared with a citywide average of 2.94 persons per household.

Street construction and maintenance, refuse collection, and sanitation in the riot area were described by the McCone Commission as "roughly comparable" with other areas in the city. That same body reported that "street lighting meets minimum standards, although it is not as good as in some other areas."[22] The riot area, finally, contains no movie theater, and there is no public hospital within eight miles.[23]

The ecology of Los Angeles had important implications for the greater severity of the Los Angeles riot. Police have learned how to deal with riots in Eastern urban centers. The same tactics were not so successful in Los Angeles.

The most important technique for riot control has been containment of the riot area. Police have sought to keep rioters in. In addition to the obvious reason, limiting the size of the riot, this may be partly because the areas have been Negro slums and hence property has been relatively less valuable. Furthermore, rioters who are contained within their own residential area can only damage their own homes, stores, and places of business. Finally, almost certainly police wished to avert invasion by Negro rioters into white residential areas where major battles between the races could occur.

Police have also sought to keep others out of the riot area. They have wanted to keep white civilians out, again to avert biracial clashes. They have also wanted to keep additional Negroes out; riots draw audiences and people who wish to join. Letting these people into the area could only add to the policemen's problems. Police surely feared that people coming in might bring additional weapons, too.

Containment has been accomplished by closing bus service to the riot area, discontinuing subway service to stops in the area, and stationing officers on streets that lead into the area. In addition, of course, mass media often warned city residents against entering the area.

The tactic of containment can be quite successful in a city whose major form of transportation in the subway or the bus. In New York's Harlem riot in 1964, police closed subway stops in the area, thus effectively containing the riot. No one could get in or out through the subways, and few people had any other way of getting to or from the area.

In a city like Los Angeles where there is virtually no public transportation and where "everyone" drives a car, it is much more difficult to seal off the riot area. Police would have to close hundreds of streets and stop each car which attempted to use the streets. Most people who came to the riot area drove there, leading one newspaper correspondent to label the Los Angeles riot a "drive-in" riot.

As a partial test of this analysis, I compared the residents without cars in the Rochester and Los Angeles riot areas. I expected that there would be more residents without cars in Rochester, as representative of Eastern cities. I found that whereas only 28% of the housing units in the Los Angeles riot area did not have any car available, there were no cars available for 48% of the ghetto area housing units in Rochester. This means that Negroes from the large Los Angeles ghetto could more easily drive to the center of riot activity than Rochester Negroes could travel from one Negro ghetto to the other. (Both Negro ghetto areas in Rochester contained rioting in 1964.)

Thus the tactic of containment did not work well in Los Angeles. Other typical police tactics did not work so well either. In Eastern cities, slum streets are virtually enclosed on both sides by tall buildings which sit right on the edge of the sidewalk. Police have relied on marching down the street in lines, forcing rioters inside and out of their way, thus breaking up crowds. And, if a policeman pursued a rioter, that rioter had only one place to go—down the street, unless he wanted to go inside.

Control of this sort is harder in a slum like Watts. There are yards in Watts—between houses and behind them, as well as between the houses and the street. Yards provided places for hiding when throwing objects at police and for running to when pursued. In general, rioters were not so "boxed in" in Los Angeles.

Finally, the wider streets themselves made control difficult. Wider streets allow larger crowds to congregate. They also make it difficult to force people out of the streets and into buildings by marching down the street in a column which stretches across.

Wider streets have particularly interesting implications for one new riot-control technique which has received a good deal of publicity and interest lately. Many police departments have been testing bubble-blowing machines. Soap and water are churned into a nontoxic but suffocating suds by motor-driven fans in the machines. The substance rolls over the street, breaking up crowds by forcing people out of the streets. However, it is not hard to see that such a machine would only work with narrow streets, bordered closely by unbroken rows of buildings in what are, in effect, "urban canyons."

Wide streets and front or side lawns could not easily be filled with suds. Further, the lawns would provide alternatives to going inside, and crowds of rioters are more effectively broken up when they are forced inside rather than simply moved over.

Thus, the ecology of Los Angeles made a difference to the success of typical riot-control tactics. Police were less in control than in other riot areas. On the other hand, rioters were more successful. The greater length and the increases in deaths and injuries probably reflect this.

Throughout their book, *Burn, Baby, Burn!*, Cohen and Murphy[24] give the reader a strong feeling for the loss of control by Los Angeles policemen. The rioters were aware of the loss of control, as the following quote from a young Negro male indicates.

> The first night, Wednesday, I was running with the crowds. Everytime the cops ran one bunch, another came back. The cops couldn't handle them, but they just kept hitting at them. They never took time to stand and talk. They were hitting everyone.[25]

Cohen and Murphy also document the feelings of helplessness on the part of Los Angeles policemen. One California Highway Patrolman was quoted as saying,

It is this officer's opinion that having the shotguns made all the difference in winning and losing. A Los Angeles police inspector came over and told us that we had just saved their butts, that before our arrival they were getting ready to pull out—that they could not have held the two blocks without the CHP and their shotguns.[26]

The loss of control by police was almost certainly one reason for the increase in arson in Los Angeles. Arson was the outstanding feature of that riot. There were more, bigger, and more destructive fires than in other riots of the new type. The burning of buildings—warehouses, small businesses, and even some houses—was the focus of rioters. Their slogan was "Burn, baby, burn!"

There were fires, presumably started by rioters, in other recent riots, as I have pointed out. Thus, it is not necessary to explain *why* fires occurred in Los Angeles (although we will consider that question later.) Rather, we must ask why the fires were more serious and more numerous in Los Angeles. The answer to that question lies in the lessened official control and the greater success of rioters, as these were influenced by the Los Angeles ecology.

Why were fires more numerous and serious? The reason is almost certainly the early success that rioters had. Once they found that they could set fires without being caught, and once they found that fires they set caused so much damage and such consternation to officials, they may have been encouraged to set more fires. Flames are highly visible—a visible sign of success in this case—and especially at night. Rioters felt in control, we can imagine, both because they could see their dramatic handiwork and because officials were unsuccessful in maintaining control.

The early successes, in turn, resulted from several factors. There were too few firemen available, as is often true, and dispatching may have been inefficient. The Los Angeles fire department is particularly understaffed. In 1960, there was one fireman for every 11 city blocks in Chicago, one for every 16 blocks in New York City, but only one fireman for every 34 city blocks in Los Angeles.[27] Furthermore, the organization of city government in Los Angeles probably contributed to the inefficiency in dispatching firemen. Completely decentralized, the government is considered very inefficient under the best conditions.[28]

Rioters delayed and prevented arrivals at fires by sniping at firemen, throwing objects at them, and in some cases attacking the trucks.

Firemen, about 7 P.M. during the initial moment of the riot's renewal (on Thursday, the second night), went into the neighborhood to answer alarms about torched autos. They were bombarded with rocks—and shot at. In the days and nights that followed, firemen had to retreat from many situations simply because they were unprotected. In some instances they could not even come near raging fires. In others, they fought blazes under sniper gunfire. A major task of Guardsmen and other law enforcement officers later was to protect firemen from being shot at.[29]

And, of course, rioters were successful in escaping from the scene of fires and from the scene of sniping because they could run into alleys and yards. Finally, there were many buildings available, and many were old enough and deteriorated enough that they burned easily.

One other explanation for the greater severity of the Los Angeles riot in general is almost wholly speculative, but tied to differences in ecology between that city and Eastern cities. Jane Jacobs, in her interesting book, *The Death and Life of Great American Cities*,[30] has detailed the important role played by city sidewalks in social control. She has said that where sidewalks are used by parents and children as the focus of public social life—sitting on stoops, leaning out windows, visiting on street corners, gathering in shops, and so on—children are safer and there is greater social control. She points out that this is true on an immediate level and also on a deeper level. Children are safer and more controllable because parents are right there, watching them. But more than that, she contends that neighborhood residents assume a common responsibility for maintaining social control because the social life they share on the sidewalk fosters trust.

> The sum of such casual, public contact at a local level—most of it fortuitous, most of it associated with errands, all of it metered out by the person concerned and not thrust upon him by anyone—is a feeling for the public identity of people, a web of public respect and trust, and a resource in time of personal need. The absence of this trust is a disaster to a city street. . . .[31]

She goes on to contrast the two sides of one street which she observed at the same time. On one side, the side with old buildings, there was plenty of sidewalk life, and children were under control. On the other side, there was a housing project and an absence of sidewalk life, and children were engaged in various acts of rowdyism and vandalism. She says:

> Nobody dared to stop them. These were anonymous children and the identities behind them were unknown. What if you scolded or stopped them? Who would back you up over there in the blind-eyed Turf? Would

you get, instead, revenge? Better to keep out of it. Impersonal city streets make anonymous people. . . .[32]

Later in the same discussion, she says, "Los Angeles is an extreme example of a metropolis with little public life."[33] I suggest that this results from the different nature of the streets in Los Angeles. The streets in that city, even in the slums, resemble suburban areas more than Eastern city streets. The streets themselves are wider and there are yards and single family dwellings with individual porches or stoops. Thus, the sidewalks are not the focus of social life as they are in Eastern cities. If Mrs. Jacobs is correct and violence varies inversely with the centrality of sidewalk social life, then one would expect greater violence and less internal neighborhood social control in Los Angeles than in Eastern cities.

Mrs. Jacobs contends that planned housing projects are most lacking in sidewalk social life. Such projects tend to be grouped around central courtyards and to turn their backs to the street. Nor do the areas within the projects, planned as replacements for the sidewalks, accomplish their purpose.[34] An interesting, though serendipitous, finding supported Mrs. Jacobs' analysis. I computed the percentage of buildings damaged during rioting in each of 14 riot-affected census tracts in Rochester, New York. I found that the tract with the highest percentage of damaged buildings was the one in which Rochester's only two housing projects are located.[35]

THE SUBCULTURE OF RIOTING

The startling similarity of the tactics used by rioters in all of the recent riots, including Los Angeles, suggests the existence of a "riot-making subculture." Certain tactics were probably first used because weapons—bottles, bricks, gasoline, and rooftops—were readily available. These tactics have been well reported in the mass media after each riot. Potential rioters may have learned of them through this source or by personal contact with people involved in earlier rioting. Thus, certain tactics and certain weapons, because they were available and because they worked, became the accepted modes of behavior for rioters, the accepted means of waging a riot.

We are not suggesting that Negro slum residents have planned to riot and thus mapped strategy and studied the successes and failures of previous riots. This need not be assumed in order to explain the existence of the subculture. It is more likely that individuals have learned of these successful weapons and tactics, remembered them, and then used their knowledge if they became involved in rioting.

The use of bricks, bottles, and cans, incendiary bombs, and arson, and the ways in which these have been employed, are all part of the riot-making subculture. Home-made incendiary bombs have been used in every recent major riot, first as a weapon against police and later as a means of starting fires.

One can trace the appearance of Molotov cocktails in recent riots to the 1964 Harlem riot. They may have been introduced there as "traditional weapons" in a "revolutionary uprising of downtrodden masses." Molotov cocktails were used, for example, in the Hungarian uprising of 1956, where Freedom Fighters employed them with some success even against tanks.

The continued use of these home-made bombs was quite self-conscious in Harlem, although their first use may not have been planned. Shapiro and Sullivan report that mimeographed sheets giving instructions for making them appeared on the streets on Wednesday, July 23.

> . . . Police found a teenager at 114th Street and Eighth Avenue passing out mimeographed sheets entitled "Harlem Freedom Fighters" and containing directions on "How to Make a Molotov Cocktail."[36]

INSTRUCTIONS:
   ANY EMPTY BOTTLE
      FILL WITH GASOLINE
         USE RAG AS WICK
            LIGHT RAG   TOSS AND
                                      SEE THEM RUN!

They go on to say that the instructions were reprinted the next day in the *Journal-American*. However, they do point out that instructions were probably unnecessary.

> In this day and age there were very few people in Harlem or Bedford-Stuyvesant, or anywhere else for that matter, who don't know what a Molotov cocktail is and who could not make one if they had the inclination.[37]

Necessary or not, the instructions did appear. Their appearance made the use of the bombs a very explicit part of the "riot-making subculture." Other tactics can be seen in the same way. The throwing of rocks from roofs and throwing garbage cans and bottles may have occurred "naturally." These weapons may have been chosen because they were handy and anyone could use them. It is possible, however, that certain objects would not have been chosen as weapons with such striking regularity if their previous use were not known. These other weapons were included as part of the subculture, too.

A second weapon included in the subculture was first used in the Harlem riot in 1964. The tenements in Harlem are old and many crumbling, with loose bricks on the facades. Furthermore, the roofs are flat. This combination offered a weapon and a way to use it. Rioters stood on the tops of these buildings and threw bricks down at policemen.

The tactic of throwing objects down at policemen was so successful, that is, hard to control, that it was used by rioters in very different conditions. For example, in Rochester, residents of housing projects threw objects down at police even though their buildings were rather new and did not offer the ready-made weapons. These rioters, and those in Harlem and other cities, used other "natural weapons." Many of the people in the first crowds that gathered in each riot had been sitting on their front steps, having a cool drink, when the incident which touched off rioting happened. They were thus equipped with pop bottles and beer cans, both of which made good missiles. And these objects were plentiful for later use, as for throwing down at policemen from apartment windows.

Arson is also a part of the riot-making subculture. Fires may have been an accidental outgrowth of the use of Molotov cocktails, originally. But setting fires was soon popular for its own sake. The tactic reached its peak during the Los Angeles riot. In fact, the greater number and severity of those fires in Los Angeles resulted, in additon to other factors discussed, from this element of imitation in riot behavior. Within any particular riot, techniques need not be developed, if they are available in the form of the subculture. Thus, instead of a few isolated fires which are followed by others, or a few people throwing rocks and imitated by others, the existence of the riot subculture, the knowledge that such tactics exist and are successful, shortens the process. Everyone can get down to the business of starting fires and throwing various approved objects immediately. Riots build on other riots which have gone before.

SUMMARY

Focusing upon the ecology of riot cities has allowed us to do several things. We have described an old and a new pattern of rioting based on differences in the ecological areas involved. Furthermore, within the new pattern, we have been able to explain some differences between the 1965 Los Angeles riot and several 1964 riots, on the basis of differences in ecology. Finally, we have discussed a riot-making subculture and the ways in which its development has been influenced by the availability of certain weapons, which is in turn dependent upon the ecology of the area.

REFERENCES

[1] GRIMSHAW, A., "Urban Racial Violence in the United States: Changing Ecological Considerations," *American Journal of Sociology*, 66 (September 1960), 109–119.

[2] *Ibid.*, p. 110.

[3] *Ibid.*, p. 110.

[4] "The urban program," a third pattern of violence detailed by Grimshaw, was limited almost exclusively to Southern riots, as in East St. Louis and Springfield, Illinois. In this pattern one found a full-scale assault of one group upon the members of the other—usually whites upon Negroes, with the assumption of police approval and the flight of large numbers Negroes. Grimshaw, *op. cit.*, p. 110.

[5] GRIMSHAW, *op. cit.*, p. 116.

[6] This discussion is taken from Grimshaw, *op. cit.*, pp. 110–116.

[7] *Ibid.*, p. 112.

[8] GOVERNOR'S COMMISSION ON THE LOS ANGELES RIOTS, *Violence in the City—An End or a Beginning?, December,* 1965, p. 2.

[9] SHOGAN, R., and CRAIG, T., *The Detroit Race Riot: A Study in Violence.* Philadelphia: Chilton Books, 1964.

[10] LEE, A. M., and HUMPHREY, N. D., *Race Riot.* New York: Dryden Press, 1943.

[11] GOVERNOR'S COMMISSION ON THE LOS ANGELES RIOTS, *op. cit.*, p. 2.

[12] SHAPIRO, T., and SULLIVAN, J., *Race Riots: New York, 1964.* New York: Thomas Y. Crowell Co., 1964, p. 153.

[13] GOVERNOR'S COMMISSION ON THE LOS ANGELES RIOTS, *op. cit.*, p. 1.

[14] LIEBERSON, S., and SILVERMAN, A. R., "Precipitants and Conditions of Race Riots," *American Sociological Review*, 30 (December 1965), 887–898.

[15] GOVERNOR'S COMMISSION ON THE LOS ANGELES RIOTS, *op. cit.*, p. 62.

[16] GRIMSHAW, *op. cit.*, p. 112.

[17] GORDON, M., *Sick Cities: Psychology and Pathology of American Urban Life.* Baltimore: Penguin Books, 1963, p. 16.

[18] *Ibid.*, pp. 113–114.

[19] GOVERNOR'S COMMISSION ON THE LOS ANGELES RIOTS, *op. cit.*, p. 65.

[20] GORDON, *op. cit.*, p. 32.

[21] *New York Times*, August 15, 1965, p. 1E.

[22] GOVERNOR'S COMMISSION ON THE LOS ANGELES RIOTS, *op. cit.*, pp. 23–24.

[23] MOORE, G., and RAY, B., "Watts Today", *Life*, 61 (July 15, 1966), 55.

[24] COHEN, J., anad MURPHY, W. S., *Burn, Baby Burn!* New York: E. P. Dutton and Co., Inc., 1966.

[25] *Ibid.*, p. 72.

[26] *Ibid.*, p. 104.

[27] GORDON, *op. cit.*, p. 200.

[28] A discussion of Los Angeles' city government may be found in Banfield, E. C., *Big City Politics*. New York: Random House, 1965, pp. 80–93.

[29] COHEN and MURPHY, *op. cit.*, p. 94.

[30] JACOBS, J., *The Death and Life of Great American Cities*. New York: Vintage Books, 1961.

[31] *Ibid.*, p. 56.

[32] *Ibid.*, p. 57.

[33] *Ibid.*, p. 72.

[34] *Ibid.*, Chapter 2.

[35] McCALL, M., "An Ecological Analysis of Recent Negro Slum Riots," unpublished M.A. thesis, University of Illinois, 1966.

[36] SHAPIRO and SULLIVAN, *op. cit.*, pp. 187–188.

[37] *Ibid.*, p. 188.

B.

The Legitimation of Dissent

4.

THE LEGITIMATION OF PROTEST: A COMPARATIVE STUDY IN LABOR HISTORY (1960)

GASTON V. RIMLINGER

The effectiveness of a protest movement, such as trade unionism, depends on its ability to overcome the widespread disapproval and opposition it engenders. The workers' demands and their methods of enforcing them must somehow become legitimate in the eyes of the employers, the government, the public, and the workers themselves. The present article analyzes the British and German coal miners' struggles to overcome opposition to their endeavors to rise from traditional submission to the employer to some sort of partnership in industrial government. Its main emphasis is on the development of protest ideologies over a period of time, from the late 18th century to the first World War, which spans the industrial revolution in both countries. Although many of the aspects discussed apply to the countries as a whole, it is hoped that

SOURCE. Gaston V. Rimlinger, "The Legitimation of Protest: A Comparative Study in Labor History," *Comparative Studies in Society and History* (1960), p. 329–343. Reprinted by permission of *Comparative Studies in Society and History* and the author.

by focussing on a specific and rather distinct group with a long history, some of the contrasting elements will stand out more sharply. Britain will be discussed first, and then Germany, each case starting with employer-worker relations during the pre-industrial period and tracing the broad patterns of the protest movement through the period of viable unionism.

THE BRITISH MINERS

By the end of the 17th century there was already an "almost complete divorce between capital and labor in British coal mining." But not until the early 19th century were there definite signs of a protest movement, although the miners were known for sporadic outbursts of violence, especially in bad harvest years. They had a bad reputation and were generally considered "rough and ignorant."

Their socio-economic position explains this conduct. In Britain, as elsewhere, miners were initially recruited from the peasantry living near the pits. Though there were many local variations, living and working conditions were extremely harsh. British coal mining had none of the great medieval German traditions of the noble and free miner. On the contrary, the collier's occupation had certain aspects of servility and was commonly associated with the punitive work of criminals. Wherever mines had developed beyond mere holes in the ground the protection of relatively high capital investments by continuous operation and maintenance made the securing of a steady and reliable work force a problem of the first order. The solution was to tie the worker by some means or other to his employer. The methods used to achieve this end varied from actual serfdom, made legal in Scotland in the early 17th century, to the yearly bond prevalent on the northeast coast, to long-term contracts, which were more common in the less developed fields of the Midlands and Wales. Even though the yearly bond was voluntary, for a long time it was not legally "a contract of service . . . but merely an acknowledgement by the men of a ficitious indebtedness."

The lowly position of the workers must be contrasted with that of the coal operators. On the continent, the state generally appropriated the ownership rights of coal, but in Britain, first custom and then law, reserved these rights for the landowner. It is from this politically and socially powerful group that most coal operators were recruited. Even where mines were leased to capitalist entrepreneurs, the latter were commonly drawn from the landed classes. The employer-worker relationship thus patterned itself after that between landlord and peasant, with emphasis on the social distance and power of the landlord and on absence of state interference. Or, rather, where the state did interfere it was often to strengthen the disciplinary hand of the employer, as in the case of the laws establishing collier serfdom in Scotland. In spite of the workers' frequent life-long attachment to a mine, there is little evidence of a patriarchal relationship between coal master and collier.

The colliers, of course, were not without protection. On the one hand there was the weight of custom, which was a social form of protection against arbitrary treatment by the employers, and on the other, there was the workers' well-known "riotous disposition" which was a form of self-protection. As long as the industry expanded gradually enough, local custom, which often provided for certain elementary forms of assistance in cases of accidents and in idle periods, was the guiding factor in employer-worker relations. Sudden changes in customs were likely to stir up discontent and distrust, especially if the workers suspected the motives of the change. It is clear that in spite of their subordinate social position the miners possessed enough personal independence to engage in crude forms of self-defence. This was significant for the later emergence of a protest movement. The basis for their independence lay partly in the nature of their job and partly in their social isolation, the scantiness of educational and religious institutions, the absence of employer concern with their private lives, the weakness of rural police enforcement, and the usefulness of the mines as hiding places in emergencies. It should be noted, however, that during the 18th century this relative independence did not mean that the workers were prepared to challenge the authority of their masters. Most of the outbreaks were directed not against employers but against outsiders, usually suppliers of food in bad harvest years. Struggles with employers were not entirely lacking, the point is that on the whole the miners remained loyal "servants."

These conflicts, even those with employers, differed radically from modern industrial disputes. The workers' weapon was recklessness and their strength desperation, not organization. Typically, their aim was revenge for suffering rather than redress of grievances. Yet, even these instinctive and more or less spontaneous outbursts sometimes had ideological aspects: the rioters sought to aid their cause by spreading rumors that the food suppliers tried to starve them to death while they secretly shipped grain to the Spaniards. Outbursts of anger and violence, however, were too crude a weapon to deal with the complex problems raised by the rapid expansion of the late 18th and early 19th centuries. Customs and traditions were threatened by an increasingly dynamic economy, by new mining techniques which entailed more dangerous assignments, and by the influx of new employers and workers who had little feeling for the miners' traditional rights.

The problem was to develop methods to influence the employers' decisions in a more positive manner than was feasible through mere riotous behaviour. Unlike craftsmen with a guild tradition, the colliers were ill-prepared for this task. They were not among the first to unionize; they lacked, as the Webbs observed, the "degree of personal independence and strength of character" needed to form "independent associations to resist the will of the employers." In other words, they were independent enough to have occasional outbursts, but their cultural level was too low for organized and disciplined action on their own. Moreover, they were strongly conservative; their notions of rights and duties were governed by long-standing customs. On the other hand, their conervatism furnished them with a justification for a certain type of protest: real or fancied violations of customs by the employers were felt to be strong provocation. In the old mining districts especially the miners fought most bitterly when innovations were involved, although, in all likelihood, their resistance was often motivated by discontent arising from other sources.

This backward-oriented protest justification as naturally unsuitable for the organization of a protest movement. A protest movement could develop only in so far as the workers developed a new image of themselves and of their relationship with their employers. Although the changing character of the industry, and especially the changing attitudes of the mine operators, hastened such a shift in outlook, they still had to have specific ideas to crystallize their fears and hopes and to nurture a spirit of resistance.

For the miners and other British workers, it was a fortunate historical coincidence that they could easily adopt such ideas from other widespread contemporary movements, mainly from the political reform and Methodist movements. Though none of these was designed to teach the workers how to resist the will of their masters, they nevertheless performed this educational function rather well. The spirit of reform and challenge of orthodoxy in the political and religious spheres could not be kept out of the industrial arena. The employers themselves set the example. The middle class political challenge of the entrenched aristocracy and the radical and anti-corn-law agitations became for the miners, as for many other workers, an important lesson in protest ideas and methods. There can be no doubt that the successive waves of political agitation from Peterloo to the Chartist uprisings were a strong factor in the ideological emancipation of the cooliers, in spite of the fact that their interest in politics remained slight. They sought increasingly to have a voice in the determination of their working conditions and became more and more critical of certain agelong "evils." To mention but a few illustrations: they began to organize unions, though none survived in the first half of the century; they began to object to unilateral employer interpretations of the yearly bond, especially with respect to fines; they demanded the right to measure without previous notification, the size of the corves by which their earnings were calculated; they loudly complained about their "subjection to the caprice" of the mine foremen; and by the 1840's, as one spokesman stated, "we resisted every individual act of oppression, even in cases we were sure of losing."

The role of the Methodist movement in shaping the workers' attitude was perhaps even more important than that of political agitation. In a language which both employers and workers understood and appreciated, "the Bible furnished many an economic argument, many a warning to the rich, many a threat to the oppressor. The Sermon on the Mount is an education in social equality. . . ." Nowhere did this popular religious revival spread faster than among the mine workers, and many of those who were active in spreading the Gospel became the leaders of their fellow workers. In England, but not in Wales, they even became strike and union organizers. Methodism everywhere raised the miners' cultural level and self-respect, which was a prerequisite for disciplined, voluntary association. The lay preachers enjoyed the trust and confidence of their fellow laborers, and this, it must be noted, along with the prevailing liberal emphasis of political and economic movements, was an important factor in the rise of protest leaders from the workers' ranks at an early stage of the protest movement. For, in spite of the importance of outside ideological influences, the miners' movement was not captured by outside organizations; it was independent from the beginning.

The developments considered thus far concern primarily the miners' growing will to resist their masters and their struggle for the right to resist. With the appearance of viable unions in the 1860's the problem of legitimizing protest took on a different character. Once certain basic protest rights, such as the right to organize and to strike, are recognized by society, and the workers have acquired power through unionization, the major question is one of establishing acceptable uses of the collective strength. The union leaders must take into account how much and what kind of exercises of union power a society will tolerate before taking repressive measures. This tolerance depends on how accustomed society has become to labor's new demands and on prevailing ideas about the worker's position, his rights and duties.

The third quarter of the 19th century in Britain was fairly permissive in this respect. The workers acquired political status just at the time when market conditions generally were favorable to unionization. In 1867 many miners obtained the right to vote, and in 1874 they sent two of their leaders to Parliament, the first working-class M.P.'s. The social esteem of the workingman in general had risen significantly since the early part of the century, and in the light of mid-Victorian optimism, his lot appeared more promising than in the gloom of the post-Napoleonic years. The age-old belief in the laborer's inescapable poverty, strengthened by the Malthusian vision of a continuous pressure against the margin of subsistence, had given way to hopes of economic abundance for all.

On the other hand, this period marked also the high point of free-trade, laisser-faire, and economic self-help. It was taken for granted by informed opinion that the full application of these ideas would lead to the greatest common good. Ideologically, these individualistic concepts could not easily be reconciled with unionism, especially since generations of economists had argued that unions have harmful effects on the economy and are incapable of improving the general level of welfare of the workers. In the accepted liberal creed, in economics and in politics, there was no room for private coercive organizations. The freedom and equality to which the worker was entitled in the pursuit of his own and the greatest common interest allowed him to haggle with his employer, but only as an individual. But the union leaders had already become accustomed to use this acceptance of economic self-help and of individual freedom and equality as a justification for unionism, without any concern for the potential theoretical inconsistency involved. In their thinking there could be neither self-help nor freedom and equality for the worker without unions. They won their case not be arguing against the liberal position, but by reinterpreting it to their advantage. Their success in doing so was highly significant, for it meant the transfer of important rights from the individual to the group.

Although the union leaders were neither inclined nor forced to worry about the potential theoretical consistency of their position, there were practical limits to their "opportunism." In embracing the liberal argument to justify their position they had to accept at least its major practical implications, that is, the absence of legally favored groups and of governmental interference with the laws of the market. They had to rely on self-help through the market and could not seek to advance their interest through social legislation. There was, of course, no unanimous agreement among miners' leaders on this approach, but it was clearly the dominant trend, especially on the northeast coast where the unions were strongest. Its general success, as the Webbs have pointed out, rested on the fact that the workingmen had "picked up the weapon of their opponents and left these without defense." Its chief symbol was the sliding-scale, which was widely adopted in the coal fields in the 1860's and 1870's. By tying the workers' welfare to the impersonal forces of the market the union leaders and the employers hoped to find a conciliatory solution to the troublesome wage question. For the miners' leader emphasized conciliation, some of them even denounced strikes as "a barbarous relic" of times past.

In spite of the success of this strategy, it was found increasingly unacceptable during the depression of the late 1870's and early 1880's. The reasons for a shift in protest ideologies were not merely economic. Changes developed in the pattern of union demands and methods as part of a deep transformation of social values in Britain in the late 19th and early 20th centuries which culminated in the welfare state.

The shift in the miners' orientation began to be felt in the middle 1880's. After a low point in activity, in the early years of that decade, came a powerful revival, with new ideas and methods, which radiated from the fields of central England to the other areas. The new protest ideology contained a radical reinterpretation of the worker's rights and of his position in the industrial society. His rights as an individual, in a more or less harmonious society, were no longer emphasized; on the contrary, the battle cry became class oppression and social inequality. To this change in outlook corresponded a change in methods of protest. As long as the collective rights of the workers were treated as an extension of the individual's right of contract, their welfare depended on the kind of contract possible in a given state of the market. But once these rights were treated as inherent in their class position, as social rather than civil rights, their welfare became the subject of social legislation, and their demands could legitimately transcend the laws of the unregulated market.

The first target of the new movement was the symbol of the old ideology, the sliding-scale. In its place arose a fitting new symbol, the living wage. The moving spirit of the drive, the Miners' Federation of Great Britain, formed in 1888, tested the workers' loyalty to the new principles in a gigantic lockout in 1893. It was able to maintain its position. Again in 1896, when the operators made a proposal resembling a sliding-scale, Ben Pickard, the president of the Federation, called upon the miners "to unite as one man to do battle for the living wage as this principle is the main point around which all minor points revolve." Other major new demands were the legal eight-hour day, a legal minimum wage, and finally nationalization of the mines. Not all of these demands gained immediate worker support; the idea of nationalization failed to win widespread approval until after the turn of the century. Nevertheless, there was a new militancy in union conduct and an increasing reliance on nationwide collective action as opposed to the former emphasis on conciliation and local action.

The miners' new attitude was strongly influenced by the rising socialist movement. Although they rejected the doctrinaire approach of the Social Democratic Federation and the Socialist League during the 1880's, they were receptive to the Labour Party's nondoctrinaire, ethical type of socialism. For this kind of socialism was able to capture the evangelistic and humanitarian elements which were once the strength of the Methodist movement among the miners. This rise of socialism gave the miner a view of the world that was more congenial to his interests and class position than the liberal ideology, and a field of action that was more suited to his temperament than the narrow path prescribed by the laws of the market.

In closing this section on the British miners it may be worth noting that not until the late 19th century was their protect formulated on the basis of a strictly working class ideology. Until then they adjusted to dominant ideologies rather than attacked them. The fact that workingmen could develop a protest movement in an opportunistic fashion, and largely with the ideological arsenal of their opponents, is the outstanding feature of the British case. It should be noted also that the ideological break with the employers grew not while the workers were weak and disorganized but while they were strong and united. It was a sign of strength rather than of revolutionary alienation. British society was able to allow industrial protest to develop without sowing the seeds of social revolution. The workers were able to organize a protest movement to which the employers and the state could adjust without causing irreconcilable rifts in the body politic.

THE GERMAN MINERS

The position of the German coal miners before 1850 contrasts sharply with that of the British during the corresponding stage of slow expansion. The British colliers led a "rough and ignorant" life, and outsiders looked upon them as "savages." In Germany, on the other hand, the miner's occupation had a tradition of honor and privilege. The collier's master was a wealthy landowner or capitalist lessee to whom the state left a free hand in the development of the industry, but the *Bergmann* worked either directly for the state, as was usually the case in the Saar after 1754, or for a private individual who held a mining concession from the state and who was under the detailed control and direction of the *Bergamt* (Bureau of Mines). Directly or indirectly the German miners were subjected to the disciplinary paternalism of highly status-conscious civil servants. This connection with the state was an important element in the social honor of their occupation. They also enjoyed various material privileges. They were granted exemptions from certain taxes and feudal dues and sometimes from military service. Their working conditions, including hours, wages, seniority, hiring and firing were under state protection, and they and their families received special assistance in cases of accident, sickness and death. These benefits were provided partly by law, partly by the regulations of the industry and partly by the *Knappschaften* (state controlled guild-type organizations). These organizations, with their discipline, uniforms, marching bands, parades, special holy days and feasts were another manifestation of the miners' corporative spirit and evidence of their social status.

This contrast in status between German and British miners necessarily entailed an equally sharp contrast in expected and actual conduct. The British coal-master expected little from the collier beyond his labor, but the conduct of the German miners was subject to a host of regulations and official admonitions. For instance, the Saar *Règlement* of 1797 admonished them to behave in a praiseworthy manner, to be always "modest, calm, and peaceful, without grumbling, cursing, swearing, or being insolent. . . ." It told them how late they could play cards in beer halls, when to be off the street, and when to wear their uniforms; furthermore, it ordered them to show "esteem, obedience, and respect for their superiors, and to greet them properly at all times. . . ." Similar regulations, with punishments for violation and machinery for enforcement, were passed in other areas. A Prussian ordinance of 1824 urged "to bring honor to the miners' estate and to seek the confidence of . . . superiors through good moral conduct, orderliness, industriousness, and obedience."

One of the major results of governmental tutelage was to forestall the development of independent collective action and to promote an attitude of submissiveness which lasted long after this tutelage was abolished. The *Bergmann's* honor could not be reconciled with "mutiny." Unlike their British colleagues, who were feared for their riotous disposition, the German miners rarely disturbed the peace before 1850. Even during the agitations of 1848 they stood aloof, or were hostile to reform, as in one instance where they published a statement vigorously attacking those, including many coal operators, who were trying to "subvert" the existing regime.

Significant changes in the workers' position and in their relationship with the employers began in the 1850's. Between 1850 and 1865 the state abandoned its control and supervision of the industry, except in the Saar where most mines continued to be operated by the state. Output and employment in the industry went into a headlong expansion. The miners lost their legal protection of employment conditions but received freedom of movement and contract to pursue their economic interests as they saw fit. The *Knappschaften* remained in existence but generally came under the control of the mine management.

For organizing a protest movement the workers were psychologically, socially, and legally in a very difficult position. Their own legacies of dependence and subordination and prevailing social values emphasizing obedience and deference to the master were serious tumbling blocks. Physically, little had changed; the mine managers exercised the same authority as before, except that now they were free to pursue their interests without submitting to state control. As the disciplinary system became more impersonal, some writers argue, it also became harsher. The employers remained "patriarchalisch kommandierende Feudalherren" while the government left the miner defenseless in the economic contest. Prevailing concepts of labor contract and strike rights definitely aimed at checking the "spirit of insubordination" of the worker. The Kaiser's attitude, expressed in a circular issued in 1890, was that strikes were unacceptable and that the state would intervene to correct justified grievances. Such interventions, usually by way of an investigating commission composed of *Bergamt* officials, who had close connections with the employers, were not much appreciated by the workers. The employers united in a common front to resist labor's demands, and by the eve of the first World War still considered the suggestion that unions "have a right to exist and could be trusted with a certain amount of authority" as "high treason" and regarded as proper only the "harshest attitude" toward unions.

The mine workers found it difficult to overcome the legacy of dependence on the state. They stubbornly continued to expect governmental protection, even after the mining law of 1865 had definitively established the freedom of contract in the industry. In a rather pathetic petition addressed to the King in 1869 the Essen miners bitterly complained that they were being neglected by the *Bergamt,* who "left all decisions to the capitalists." They concluded that "since we have no other possibility of being soon relieved from our distress . . . we turn to Your Majesty with the prayer that the Royal Mining Offices be advised to tolerate no longer increases in the length of the work day." They were not prepared to resist their masters. Imbusch notes that they "were so accustomed to the tutelage and wardship of the state that . . . for years it would not even occur to them to look after themselves." They appealed for the "rights of our fathers." When the Kaiser received miner delegates from the Ruhr during the big strike of 1889, they told him: "We want what we have inherited from our fathers . . . if only Your Majesty would speak a word, everything would soon change and many a tear would be dried."

In the German social and political climate the quoting of the Bible or opportunistic arguments about the rights of the individual, ideas which the British miners used so effectively, would not have been much of an ideological weapon, especially not in the service of a worker who may have been hard put to it to convince even his fellow workers. Workers with a legacy of dependence on their social superiors tend to be reluctant to shift their loyalty to a member of their own group. This shift can occur only once they have accepted the fact that they must look out for themselves. As a result, the start of the German miner's protest movement depended on the assistance of individuals of higher social status who could fashion a compelling protest ideology.

It was impossible for the miners' protest to develop along the lines dictated by their immediate economic interests. Their dependence on outside help inevitably drew them into other movements which had broader social and political aims. This had a far reaching consequence: their repudiation of the legacy of dependence and their will to defend their interests became a function of their ideological indoctrination and of the politicization of their attitude. For political parties anxious to espouse their cause were already in existence and were ready to furnish their protest with the necessary ideological justification. The miners' protest became identified mainly with two major socio-political movements. One of these was the socialist movement, represented by the Social Democratic party, and the other, the Christian Social movement, which was connected with the Roman Catholic Church and the Center party. This party became the political arm of the Christian Social unions. The many Roman Catholics among the West German miners and the political tension between the Church and the state gave the Church the position of a natural protest leader. The aim of the Christian Social movement was social reform on the basis of Christian morality. It attacked the evils of industrialization and denounced the godlessness of capitalism, liberalism and socialism. Its agitation among the miners was held responsible for the major outbreak before 1889, the so-called "Jesuit strike" of 1872 and from the ranks of those under its influence came "quite a few union leaders in later years."

The intention of the Church, however, was neither forceful action nor the formation of labor unions. The hierarchy, according to a Catholic miners' leader, was opposed to "any kind of independence for the workers . . . they were unable to divest themselves of the view that . . . workers had to be guided and led by members of the other estates."

The only labor organizations under direct clerical sponsorship were the miners' clubs, which aimed mainly at promoting good morals and good fellowship and only rarely supported strikes. Often the parish priest took the initiative in the formation of the club and played the leading role in its management. In 1886 a Catholic journalist, Johannes Fusangel, drew together some of these clubs to form the *Rechtsschutzverein,* an organization aiming at the vindication of the miner's traditional legal rights, especially with respect to the *Knappschaften. Bona fide* Christian Social miners' unions did not come into existence until the 1890's. They had workers as leaders but kept members of the clergy as advisers.

The socialists began to organize the miners in the 1860's but with little success. Like their Christian Social rivals, they waged a vigorous protest campaign on behalf of the mine workers, who, however, were slow to respond. Not until the 1890's did socialism gain a solid foothold among them. Socialistically oriented workers captured the union which grew out of the 1889 strike, but it nearly died out in the following years. Nevertheless, after 1895 it made rapid progress, expanded from the Ruhr to other areas and became by far the most powerful miners' organization in the country. On a few occasions the unions from the rival ideological camps cooperated, but usually there was strong tension between them.

There was tension also within the ideological camps regarding the role of the unions. The unions had become heirs to ideological orientations that envisaged not so much a day-to-day struggle with the employers as the remodeling of society along preconceived theoretical lines and the establishment of an industrial order which would make the daily struggle unnecessary. As the unions gained in power and prestige, they leaned more and more toward the pursuit of their immediate self-interest. Conflicts over "proper" union aims and methods were inevitable. On the one hand, there were many Church officials who felt that the Christian Social unions were becoming too independent and too materialistic, and on the other, there were influential Social Democrats who poured bitter scorn over the union's "opportunism." The workers had outgrown their dependence on a benevolent government, but to some extent they had exchanged one set of masters for another. They still could not act by themselves because they were still dependent, ideologically and politically, on outside allies.

SUMMARY AND CONCLUSION

This study has traced, at the level of employer-worker relations, the interplay of social forces determining the character of labor protest. It showed that although the British miners were nearly social outcasts in the pre-industrial period, they had enough personal independence to develop crude habits of self-defense. As their horizons widened during industrialization, they were able to learn more effective methods of self-defense and to proceed independently and opportunistically, relying, so to speak, on their opponents' ideological arsenal while the employers, the state and public opinion became accustomed to their role as a force in the industrial society. By contrast, the German miners enjoyed a state-protected status and special economic advantages during the pre-industrial period but inherited legacies of submissiveness and of dependence on the state. During industrialization they were unable to challenge their masters by themselves; their will and ability to defend their interests became a function of ideological indoctrination and politcal alliances. The result was that industrial protest, spurred by rival ideologies, and social and political reform became inseparably entangled, contributing to a deepening of the social tension not only between workers and employers, but between workers and the state and among workers themselves.

It may be permissible at this point to make somewhat speculative observations on the broader implications of this study. Where a collective labor protest movement is allowed to develop, its successful adaptation to the industrial society depends on radical changes in outlook and attitude among workers as well as among employers and government officials. Instead of being more or less resigned to obey their masters and accept their lot as God-given, the workers, if they want to control their own protest movement, must develop a will to struggle for change and an insistence on rights they did not possess in the past. The more they are bound by traditional values, especially of the kind which considers loyalty to superiors and respect for authority equivalent to self-respect and proper conduct, the more difficult the transition is likely to be. To muster the zeal and perseverance needed for the support of a protest movement, the workers must repudiate this traditionalism; a genuine protest temper demands that they be convinced of the righteousness not only of their demands but also of the novel means proposed to enforce them; they must be willing to give their loyalty to new leaders and new organizations. Employers, who see their interests and authority threatened, and government officials, who find law and order menanced, must learn to accept the challenge from below. The workers, through their spokesmen, try to make the best case they can for their cause, but to a very large extent their strategy is dictated by the kind of opposition they meet. Their strategy depends mainly on the character of existing authority relationships, on whether managerial authority can be effectively attacked within the existing system or whether the system itself must be attacked. The present study suggests that these opposite alternatives tend to yield two major types of protest legitimation: the workers' spokesmen may insist that labor and management have basically identical ideals but management fails to live up to them, or they may argue that their aims are irreconcilable but only those of labor are justifiable, either on moral or historical grounds.

The emergence of labor protest during industrialization gives the workers, in Bendix's terms, "an opportunity for self-assertion at a time when their security and self-respect are threatened." The more serious this threat, and the more difficult a society makes the legitimation of protest, the more all-encompassing and revolutionary the aims of the protest movement are likely to become. The problem is, of course, that a society has only limited control over the forces shaping the protest movement. Historical legacies do not vanish overnight, and it takes time for the ruling groups in any society to become reconciled to the challenge of the labor movement. This reconciliation is much more difficult in a rigidly stratified society where the employers are allied with a centralized ruling bureaucracy, as was the case in Germany, than in a more fluid society where the employers at times seek the support of the workers to challenge the power of an entrenched aristocracy, as was the case in Britain. Therefore, in the crucial stages of early industrialization it may not be possible to direct protest into those channels which would be most desirable in the long run.

C.

The Drama of Resistance and Confrontation

5.

DRAMATIC ENCOUNTERS (1965)

Orrin Klapp

Public men are understandably wary of dramatic encounters—televised debates, pointed questions, and personal challenges. In one city, twelve mayoralty primary candidates were invited to the same banquet to explain their positions. Of those who came, we can imagine that some had mixed feelings and poor digestions, for they knew they would not only get publicity but be put "on the spot"; they knew, also, that such a free-for-all was potentially very dangerous; but they came. A public man has to pretend to lie confrontations, or at least he must not seem reluctant to face them. Yet the question is fair: Why should a program or a reputation, perhaps the work of years, be casually jeopardized merely to satisfy some person or group? There is always more risk for a "big" man than for a small one in challenging encounters; the former has much to lose, while the latter may have everything to gain. The trouble with a dramatic confrontation is that, unlike a mere "appearance"

SOURCE. Orrin Klapp, *Symbolic Leaders*. Chicago: Aldine Publishing Co., 1965, pp. 66–67, 70–73, 75–91, 97–100. Reprinted by permission of Aldine Publishing Company and the author.

or "presentation,"[1] one puts himself and his prestige into the scales for a contest or comparison with somebody else, and in so doing may confer the gift of prestige on his opponent and meanwhile subject himself to a role crisis. . . .

The very essence of drama—the high point of its most important scenes—is usually a confrontation in which parties are thrown on their mettle, reveal and expose themselves drop their defenses, call on their personal resources to meet a crisis. *Spontaneity* is maximized. On stage, a script takes care of this, but in real life spontaneity means unexpected behavior and consequences; no one knows quite what will happen; mistakes, contretemps, or foolish roles are likely. A demagogue tries to create encounters that he can handle and his opponent cannot; witness Khrushchev, clowning, blustering, browbeating, probing into the enemy's defenses looking for a soft spot.[2] Huey Long was uncomfortable to deal with for this reason; a reporter caught this scene with Calvin Coolidge:

"What part of Louisiana are you from, Governor?" inquired Mr. Coolidge.
"I'm a hill-billy like yourself."
"The hills are a good place to come from," Mr. Coolidge responded.
"Are the Hoovers good housekeepers?" demanded Huey.
"I guess they are," answered Silent Cal cautiously.
"Well, when I was elected I found the governor's mansion in such rotten shape I had to tear it down. . . . When I'm elected President I don't want to have to rebuild the White House."

It was hard to hold a "safe" conversation with Huey in public, for he was always ad libbing for the crowd; he was, to use an expressive phrase, always "on the make."

Another potent risk-producing factor of drama is the close-up—not merely of audience with actor (made embarassingly intimate by modern

---

[1] Compare Jacqueline Kennedy's famous televised tour of the White House, which, though a smash hit, was not a confrontation but a solo performance and therefore comparatively safe. Had she undertaken a discussion or an argument with another lady about the history, art, and style of the White House, she might have glorified her partner and also subjected herself to a confrontation that could have meant "win or lose" for both.

[2] Premier Nikita Khrushchev of Russia has been called "the man of many faces." Whether making a toast at a banquet or joking with factory workers, he usually shows a nice consistency with the Soviet propaganda line of the moment. He is said to be a natural actor who can assume with zest the role suited to the occasion: the homespun, tipsy *muzhik*, the hard-headed businessman, the tough guy, the genial buffoon, the outraged puritan. He tries to force opponents into situations in which they look bad. (Eugene Lyons. "The Many Faces of Nikita Khrushchev," *Reader's Digest*, August, 1959, pp. 49–54.)

photography and high-fidelity equipment) but between the parties in personal encounter. Two giants can exist in separate fables, but bring them together and one is likely to appear smaller than the other. It is so for public men: their scale is changed by mere juxtaposition. Actors know this well and choose partners and positions on stage accordingly. If two persons stand chest-to-chest or eye-to-eye with each other, it is likely that one of them will suffer; whereas, if they perform at separate times and places, only experts can rate the differences and a "match race" to settle things is avoided. So public men should take care about whom they are matched with, billed with, or even stand next to.

Yet another hazard is the enormous importance of timing, of the right role at the right time. One can "play the hero" a moment too soon or too late and be the biggest kind of fool. The successful hero steps into a situation at exactly the moment when audience expectation and the plot call for such a part; things have gotten as bad as possible for the victim, and the crisis has been properly developed; suspense and interest are at a maximum, so no one is tired of the situation; and the balance has become so precarious that it can easily be tipped in his favor. If a man manages to do these things, it is hard to imagine how he can fail to become socially significant. On the other hand, many good deeds and worthy enterprises have failed because the time was not ripe or the ratio of forces was unfavorable. Both tragedy and comedy hinge on precarious considerations like these.

In addition, the pressure of the audience favors certain parts and outcomes. If conflict arises, people need to define a "good guy" and a "bad guy"; they will look for cues or merely cast these parts arbitrarily (as we often do at sporting contests). An audience also usually favors underdogs and victims and is very quick to find a fool, to laugh at anything funny. The man who steps into a situation, may find a part handed to him—he may unexpectedly find himself on stage, as a performer or as the subject of a joke he had not anticipated. Such pressures may seem "unfair," but it is hard to keep the proceedings sensible and objective when the atmosphere becomes dramatic.

The more general observation follows, then, that in drama outcome does not equal input. One man alone, however sincere and even if he is physically successful in what he sets out to do, cannot guarantee what his act will mean or what roles will be assigned to him and others as a result of his action. The factors that determine these consequences are outside the scope of any individual actor and do not bear a precise relationship to the physical forces mobilized or the real nature of the elements employed. A very large army, for example, could seem small and belittled in spite of its power or a noble deed could emerge as villainy. There is a capricious power in drama that might almost be called magical, for it produces astounding results from apparently insufficient means and causes changes in character like a chameleon. . . .

The point, in any case, is that the historic roles of hero, villain, and fool could not be predicted from such men's characters, intentions, or behavior, but only by knowing the particular dramatic and social situations in which they chose to act. The wide variation in dramatic results shows that, at least as far as character and motivation are concerned, outcome does not equal input in the making of heroes, villains, and fools. All we need conclude from this argument is that difference in definitions is far out of proportion to actual differences in men, that even the line of action is no key to what they will become. A little change in circumstances might allow us to see the same men and deeds in opposite parts—Custer as a villain, Ford as a hero of peace, Schweitzer as a fool, perhaps even Booth as a daring hero of self-sacrifice.

The real question of dramatic outcome involves factors having little to do with personal input, with what a man is or intends to be. The pertinent questions are these: Did he act at the right psychological moment? Did he have the spotlight? What was the mood of the audience? Did he carry his role well before the audience? Was he suitably cast for the part? Was the plot pattern favorable? Who played the parts against him, and how did they carry off their parts? If these factors are changed, all kinds of remarkable things can happen to the public character of a man.

In brief, the peculiarities of the dramatic domain are these: (1) almost anyone can steal the show, (2) a small part has an advantage over a larger one, (3) almost any kind of struggle or issue can become important, (4) spontaneity in dramatic crises and encounters favor unexpected outcomes, (5) there is great risk in close-ups, (6) timing is enormously important, (7) audience need and expectation can press hero, villain, fool, and victim roles on people and favor certain kinds of outcomes, and (8) the same kinds of character and motive (especially those called "quixotic") can elicit widely varying definitions, depending on the situation. . . .

TYPES OF DRAMATIC ENCOUNTER

For most practical purposes, there are seven important role alternatives for a public man in dramatic confrontations, ranging from a popular "hit" to downright defeat. Once he commits himself, he may come out in any of these ways. . . .

2. Hero-Making Confrontations

Hero-making confrontations are inherently risky but potentially more rewarding than honorific meetings. Three common modes can be distinguished: the benefactor, the winner in a test, and the defeat of the martyr.

The safest confrontation for a hero is with a needy party, to whom he generously makes a gift and who is in an inferior position and is showing gratitude. There is no contest between principals; indeed, the recipient may be a helpless victim. Leaders, patrons, aristocratic classes, and political bosses try to play such a role to the public. In Argentina, Eva Perón played guardian angel to working girls, unwed mothers, and the like, establishing herself as a kind of patron saint as well as reinforcing her husband's regime. Franklin Delano Roosevelt won such a role by passage of the Social Security Act and the historical accident of coming into the Presidency during the Great Depression.

Yet even such relationships between benefactor and recipient can get out of hand. One major risk is that the needy party will not show appropriate gratitude and thus make it hard for the benefactor to play his role without incurring suspicion that there is something wrong with him rather than with the recipient. (This has apparently happened in nations that view American foreign aid in terms of "ugly" Americans.) Another risk is that a competitor will steal the show with an even more exciting gift, thus making the would-be benefactor look reluctant or cheap. (To cite American foreign aid again, several times the Soviet Union has come forward with small but immediate and well-publicized token and to a needy country and stolen the show from a larger but slower program by the United States.)

The second type of hero-making confrontation—the test—is of course more risky because it requires the subject to emerge as victor in a show of strength after committing himself fully. Such an encounter is safe only with a "setup," an opponent who looks dangerous but really is unable to compete effectively. Thus, a famous news picture shows Mayor Fiorello La Guardia of New York smashing slot machines in a police raid in 1934. He cuts a fine figure, poised over the wicked machines wielding a sledge hammer, rather like Richard the Lion-Hearted with his two-handed sword. Though there is no reason to suppose that La Guardia avoided real encounters, it was much safer for him to attack machines than publicly to rebuke a live gambler.

Within the test category are at least three subpatterns: (1) the battle of rival champions, (2) the defeat of a villain (whose wickedness points up the goodness of the hero), and (3) a David-Goliath encounter in which a little man upsets a big man.

The battle of champions is illustrated by President John F. Kennedy's historic confrontation with Roger Blough, chairman of the board of United States Steel Corporation, on April 12, 1962. The chairman called on the President to inform him of an arbitrary raise in the price of steel. The President soon thereafter, in a press conference, denounced the steel industry for irresponsibility and selfishness and threatened legal and political reprisals. Within forty-eight hours, the steel industry backed down, cancelling its price increases. Said *Time:*

> The ferocity of his attack on steel alienated and angered many a businessman . . . [but] there could be no doubt that John Kennedy had won a popular victory. Beyond question, the great majority of Americans reacted angrily to U.S. Steel's price-increase announcement. That reaction was instinctive, and Kennedy exploited it skillfully. . . . He had made the steelmen look like Milquetoasts.

Though Kennedy charged villainy on the part of the steel industry, actually this was a contest between champions of rival corporate power blocs—big government versus big business. It had all the qualities of a good contest; a personal encounter between two powerful men, a conflict of wills, and a test of strength and prestige. Kennedy acted with the sturdy stance of King Arthur swinging his great sword, and Blough was obliged to back off. Blough's dramatic alternatives were to act as a villain (which he did not accept; his behavior was in no way discreditable, though some blamed him for bad timing and judgment), as the rival champion of equal strength who loses, or as the weak knight[3] who is disgraced and made a fool. While his role had aspects of all these alternatives, it was mainly the second that emerged. Kennedy also risked failure, which could have made him look like a fool (risking the power of the Presidency against a mere group of corporations and being outfoxed); the wrong tactics might have cast him as a bully, coward, swaggerer, or stuffed shirt. Blough had to be big enough to test Kennedy's mettle (there is no glory in an encounter with a stooge, a weak or humble person, or a fool) yet not big enough to overthrow him. It was very important also how Blough reacted; a more colorful man—a cantankerous Sewell Avery, a big-talking Diamond Jim Brady, a wisecracking Will Rogers—might have stolen the show. And, of course, the whole thing might have happened in some other

---

[3] Epitomized in tales of King Arthur as Sir Kay, who is overthrown by boys and fools.

way (by committees, trial balloons, or private correspondence) so that no actual confrontation would have occurred.

The second test pattern, the defeat of a villain, is safer for the "hero" because there is no sympathy to swing to the opponent if the tables should be turned. Almost any good effort against a villain receives some credit; a knockout is, of course, a "hit." The badness and strength of the villain make the hero look all the better (whereas to defeat a good man inevitably leaves the audience with some ambivalent regret). When the pattern is at its best, the hero catches a villain red-handed and at the height of a crisis, knocks him down, and carries off the prize or restores the threatened welfare. Ideally, a villain helps by confirming his own status: admitting guilt, fighting unfairly, running away, performing treachery or cruelty, and other acts well known in melodrama. President Kennedy did not have a very good villain in Roger Blough, but he had a better one in Premier Khrushchev, in the confrontation over the missile bases in Cuba in October, 1962, which followed classic lines. Here, it might almost be said, was Perseus arriving to face the dragon or Achilles girding himself to do battle for the Greeks, and the dragon backed off and withdrew his missiles, giving dramatic victory to the hero.[4] Another classic example of hero-villain confrontation was the televised hearings of a Senate crime-investigating committee headed by Estes Kefauver in 1951, which catapulted him into fame and helped make him a Presidential possibility. As chairman,

> . . . he dragged such diverse and unsavory characters as Greasy Thumb Guzik, Virginia Hill and Frank Costello into the bright lights for a classic lesson in morality. Gentle but relentless, Kefauver questioned them with painful sincerity, became to millions a pillar of log-cabin courage and small-town mores because of the contrast between his stolid ruggedness and the squirmy, shifty-eyed hoodlums he confronted. From those hearings came no important legislation, few arrests, nothing very concrete. But his investigation did center national attention on big-time crime—and on Estes Kefauver.

The third hero-making test pattern, that of David and Goliath, requires that a small hero be pitted against a large villain. It is well illustrated by Martin Luther King's organization of the strike against the bus com-

---

[4] The President personally offered a challenge to Russia by discussing on television the danger to the United States from the missile sites and the encounter of Soviet and U.S. ships. The *New York Times* described the atmosphere in the capital as a "nightmare" during these days. After an unsuccessful bid to swap Cuban for Turkish bases, Khrushchev suddenly backed down, giving dramatic victory to Kennedy, who "emerged in the West as the hero of the crisis" (October 30, 1962).

panies of Montgomery, Alabama, forcing them to modify their "Jim Crow" rules. The success of an obscure Baptist minister against the bus companies and against powerful white resistance put him in the role of David against the Goliath of segregation, which he then hit with the stone of non-violent resistance, again and again.

Ironically, another illustration is provided by an enemy of integration, Governor Ross Barnett of Mississippi, a dull political prospect who managed by a series of confrontations with the United States government to make himself a local hero and thus brighten his outlook. In an article entitled "Now He's a Hero," *Time* tells how his defiance of the federal government, for a time blocking the registration of James Meredith in the University of Mississippi, brought a "dizzying turnabout" in his political prospects.[5] We may analyze this role with profit. Prior to the event, his reputation had been that of a confirmed racist with some reputation for Christian piety (he had taught Sunday school and had vetoed a bill to raise the alcohol limit of wine), but he was a rather disappointing governor, who had a reputation as a "do-nothing." A chance to dramatize himself came with the decision of the Department of Justice to make a test case of James Meredith's entrance at the University of Mississippi. Barnett's transfiguration took place as a series of confrontations in which he defied the Goliath of the federal government as a threat to states' rights. First came a private meeting, on September 20, 1962, in which, as self-appointed registrar of the university, he rejected Meredith and the federal court order supporting his application for admission. This called some attention to him as a man who had succeeded in defying the law, but the second encounter, at the doorway of Room 1007 of the capitol building with Chief U.S. Marshall James McShane, on September 25, was more crucial. The door swung open with "theatrical timing" as Meredith appeared, backed by McShane and an aide. There stood the Governor. The officers tried "fumblingly" to hand Barnett some court orders, which he refused. Then he read off a proclamation denying Meredith admission to the university. The federal officer, James Doar, made "one last, limp try":

> "Do you refuse to permit us to come in this door?" he asked.
> BARNETT: "Yes, sir."
> DOAR: "All right. Thank you."
> BARNETT: "I do that politely."
> DOAR: "Thank you. We leave politely."

[5] Though he could not, by law, succeed himself as governor, his new popularity at home made almost any other public office in the state seem open to him. (*Time,* October 5, 1962, p. 17.)

Thus the federal government backed down. It is entirely possible that the encounter could have come out favorably for the government with more adroit handling. As it was, the federal officers were made to look inept, clumsy, and even timid; they were apparently balked by the stand of one valiant man. If they had circumvented or defeated the Governor in some way, they could have stolen his thunder.

The third encounter, next day, was also a dramatic loss to the federal forces, though Barnett, because of a missed plane, was unable to capitalize on it personally. Now the man blocking the way was Lieutenant Governor Paul B. Johnson, who stood at the doorway of the university, backed by about twenty state policemen and a dozen sheriffs.

> As before, McShane and Doar tried pleading, urging, arguing, demanding and waving court orders—all in vain. Now McShane tried using his muscles. Several times he pushed a meaty shoulder against highway patrolmen. . . . But he was outnumbered twenty to one by the troopers, some of them pretty husky too, and his scufflings with them were utterly futile, merely adding a dash of absurdity to the proceeding.

The fourth encounter, September 27, was between a motor cavalcade of marshalls and a small army of some 200 state policemen backed by sheriffs, deputies, and a mob. Again the federal forces, seeing the impossibility of making progress without serious bloodshed, withdrew. "The decision to pull back was sensible, but it looked embarrassingly like a retreat." There then followed a lull, during which President Kennedy made a speech and a federal court found Barnett guilty of contempt *in absentia*, threatening him with a 10,000-dollar-a-day fine and confinement. The Governor, seeing the handwriting on the wall, desisted, and the episode was over. He had already made himself a hero and "could quit well ahead." Why should he be a martyr to satisfy a few fanatics?

An appraisal of this episode shows that the four encounters were defeats, practically and dramatically, for the federal government, that Barnett gained corresponding credit, and that the court decision lacked the qualities of an encounter and so was not a defeat for Barnett. President Kennedy, probably fortunately, stayed out of all this personally, though if he had confronted Barnett it might have created a new pattern of drama (though one of doubtful advantage to the President). The most important thing to be noted was a buildup of forces on each side from one encounter to another that continuously operated to the disadvantage of the government. The federal forces were not strong or adroit enough to win easily. Yet, if they had built up their power and overridden the Governor and his forces, they would have offered a good opportunity of martyrdom to the rebels; while by backing off, they looked weak, hesitant, even foolish (in the comic frustration of a large by a small force). How could they have won without seeming to be Goliaths (bullies) who overcame valiant little men? Almost any kind of private or indirect dealing, it seems, would have been dramatically better for the federal government than allowing Barnett to benefit from these favorable scenes. I am not qualified to suggest alternative diplomatic tactics, but clearly the public ratio of forces was dramatically bad for the government, even though Barnett in his relation to Meredith (as a single man without federal support) was a bully oppressing the weak (at least in northern eyes). The public encounter with Barnett should have been managed with a ratio of forces that did not offer heroism or martyrdom to the defiant party. You cannot win dramatically by flouting this ratio.

Following this episode, Governor George C. Wallace of Alabama tried to carry off a similar confrontation between himself as a hero of states' rights and the federal bully. His first attempt, on June 11, 1963, was a moderate success. He stood in the doorway of the University of Alabama, "in almost pitiable solitude," opposing federal officers. (The two Negro applicants were kept out of the way in a waiting car.) Deputy Attorney General Nicholas Katzenbach asked him to "not bar entry" to the students. Wallace then read off a five-page proclamation denouncing the illegality of the central government. When he finished, Katzenbach asked him to step aside. Wallace "simply stood there" silently, "glaring with melodramatic scorn." "Very well," said Katzenbach, and then turned away to escort the students to a dormitory. The second scene followed on the same afternoon. This time General Henry Graham of the Alabama National Guard confronted the Governor to inform him that the National Guard had been federalized. Wallace read off another statement, then walked away. He had held off the federal juggernaut for four and one-half hours, then given way to superior force. Though not without certain comic features,[6] the scene, on the whole, was his. He had managed to look a bit like David by merely slowing Goliath down. Again the ratio of forces favored the underdog and worked against the big man. (But the second time Wallace tried "standing in the doorway," the results were different, as I shall point out below in discussing villain-making encounters.)

If you cannot win, you can lose heroically; and this sometimes makes a better symbol than a victory. This is especially the case for the martyr

[6] The comic touches included a lectern and chest microphone, which gave an air of pomposity to Wallace's stand; also, he was "visibly pale and trembly." (*Time*, June 21, 1963, pp. 15–16.)

role, the third and most costly hero-making route. The defeat or suffering endured by the hero is taken as a sign that, although he has lost, the cause itself will win, if only out of the loyalty of such men or the improved morale of those who remember and follow him. In contrast, a victim role, though it gets public sympathy, is not nearly so valuable; the essential difference is that it comes by accident. The martyr role must emerge from a seemingly voluntary choice for the good of the cause. One could not, for example, impose martyrdom on a fleeing victim, though if he turned and stood he might easily win the role.

The great advantage of non-violent resistance, as practiced by Hindus under Gandhi or Negroes following Martin Luther King, is that it invites martyrdom, so to speak, as a second choice to victory. It is, then, a dramatic strategy that cannot lose; the resister, being passive, is extremely hard to see as a villain, while the opponent, whether he wins or not, can hardly avoid being cast as an aggressor by an open-minded audience. The catch, of course, as practitioners well know, is in the self-control of the resister, since, if he displays the least aggressiveness, he enters the ordinary arena where he can quite as easily become a villain as a hero, and his advantage is gone.

It is not absolutely necessary to have a villain in a martyr drama; Colonel Gorgas' volunteers in the fight against malaria, for example, were martyrs, though malaria parasites could be called villains only by some stretch of the imagination. But, if the villain is present, he must play his part correctly. For example, if he overwhelms the hero without allowing him time to display fortitude and choice, he is more likely to create a mere victim, or, if he fails to be sufficiently cruel and unfair (as, for example, did Pontius Pilate), he does not make a very good persecutor and robs the martyr of his melodramatic advantage. If we begin to feel sorry for the bad guy, the affair is more likely to seem tragic than melodramatic.[7] From the standpoint of casting martyrs, then, it is partly a matter of finding a suitable villain—one who will accept his part and play it with vindictive glee, showing no remorse and not spoiling the scene by being human.

3. Villian-Making Encounters

It is sufficient to point out here two patterns of villainy: the oppression of a weaker party and the cowardly attack.

---

[7] Melodramas are, by definition, black versus white, where the villain takes all the badness on himself and gives all the goodness to the hero; whereas, in tragedy, fault is always shared by the hero.

The behavior of Eugene "Bull" Conner of Birmingham, Alabama, enormously helped Martin Luther King's civil rights cause:

> Conner became an international symbol of blind, cruel Southern racism. When King sent out his marchers, Conner had them mowed down by streams from fire hoses. Shocking news photos splashed across the pages of the world's press—of a young Negro sent sprawling by a jet of water, of a Negro woman pinioned to the sidewalk with a cop's knee at her throat, of police dogs lunging at fleeing Negroes. With that, millions of people—North and South, black and white—felt the pangs of segregation and, at least in sympathy, joined the protest movement.

The other villain-making pattern is also conveniently illustrated from the civil rights struggle in the unseen assassins who shot Medgar Evers, Negro leader, in the back, or those who bombed the Baptist church in Birmingham, Alabama, on September 15, 1963, killing four Negro children. These events, though the criminals were not caught, supplied a vivid image of the kind of person involved in such villainy; nor was there any mistaking the surge of national and world feeling for the Negro cause that followed these acts. The villains could not have done more damage to their own cause if they had used bombs and bullets on their own ranks.

In such dramas, almost any unsuspecting, helpless victim is sufficient. Of course, the height of the villainy is greatly increased if the one attacked is a popular hero; this puts the villain into a status like that of John Wilkes Booth, Judas, Mordred, or Delilah. In Governor Wallace's second attempt to make himself a hero, the federal government, presumably having profited from previous encounters with him and with Governor Barnett, refused to play the role of "Goliath"; the government did not use a superior force of soldiers embodying what Wallace would call "military dictatorship." When the Governor again proposed, on September 6, 1963, to "stand in the doorway" of the public schools of Huntsville, Alabama, the only force present was that of his own soldiers.

> Armed state troopers barred white and Negro children from four public schools . . . on orders of Governor George Wallace, stirring a rising resentment in this . . . city and other parts of Alabama.
> One brigade of determined mothers braved the line of helmeted, club-carrying troopers at one school and took their children in for registration.

Wallace himself did not appear, the state troopers (with the Governor as their absent commander) found themselves in the villain's role versus mothers and children. Local citizens were enraged. The Huntsville Board of Education and town authorities sought to defy the Governor and open the schools despite him. "You ought to be ashamed of yourselves," a mother told the troopers. By not having the superior force of the federal government to oppose and by accepting the wrong dramatic partners, he had made himself look like a tyrant depriving children of their educational rights. Again, this incident illustrates how the dramatic ratio, as much as substantive issues, determines political success. Wallace was doing almost the same thing, before the same audience, but his timing, the ratio of forces, and almost everything else about the situation were dramatically bad for him. Even the Montgomery *Advertiser,* a firm supporter of Governor Wallace, concluded that he had "gone wild."

The sequel to the incident was the second federalizing of the Alabama National Guard by President Kennedy a few days later. This action deprived Wallace of the force seriously to challenge federal force, and it was now unnecessary for the President to use federal force and thus play into the Governor's hand. Cabell Phillips said in the *New York Times:*

KENNEDY AVOIDED A SHOW OF FORCE;
  HIS STRATEGISTS THINK THEY OUTWITTED
    WALLACE AT HIS OWN GAME IN CRISES.

A strategy hastily devised at the White House between 10 o'clock last night and dawn led to the successful integration of a group of Alabama schools today without reliance upon "a Federal presence."

This was a solution toward which the Kennedy Administration had worked during the last hectic week in the face of defiance from Governor George C. Wallace. Government officials had sought means of avoiding the use of force to carry out Federal court orders to admit Negro pupils to the schools.

Their success, in view of the strategists themselves, obliterates—for the time being at least—the basis of Governor Wallace's complaint today that "I can't fight bayonets with my bare hands." For there were no bayonets in evidence today as the Negro pupils entered previously all-white schools in Birmingham, Mobile and Tuskegee.

National Guardsmen with bayonets, acting under the Governor's orders to keep the Negro children out, had taken up their posts at the beleaguered schools before dawn. But before the school bells rang, President Kennedy had federalized the Guardsmen and they had been whisked back to their armories, where they stayed, "awaiting orders."

4. *Fool-Making Encounters*

Another dramatic possibility, of course, is to be made a fool, either by one's own action or by someone else's. As noted, Governor Wallace's first, successful role had comic possibilities. For example, some mishap might have occurred as he stood before his wired-for-sound rostrum (say, a failure of power), or a soldier might have made a wisecrack good enough to report to the nation. Comic mishaps such as these can rob a performer of serious consideration unless he can turn them to his own advantage, perhaps by accepting the clown role, or by turning the tables so cleverly that the audience is more impressed by his agility than by what he intended to do in the first place. If he takes himself too seriously or lacks sufficient wit to turn it to his advantage, a public man can be in difficulty when the show turns to comedy.

While anyone can make a fool of himself merely by acting in an undignified fashion, he is likely to be made a fool by somebody else in one of two ways: a joke that he cannot turn back against the jester or a defeat by a small obstacle or a grossly inferior party. The first situation is exemplified by a "hot foot" perpetrated on a sleeping victim or a heckling wisecrack that makes a speaker lose his temper and his good judgment. The second is illustrated by the comic frustration of a large force by a small force (the mouse outwitting the elephant, a large man getting himself locked in a telephone booth). A jester can literally try to put his opponents in such situations, or he can depict them by stories, remarks, cartoons, rumors, and so on. In a later chapter some of these fool-making tactics and situations will be examined.

The main thing that keeps comedy from being used more widely in public life is that it requires more wit than does melodrama. And, in general, people protect themselves from comic predicaments rather better than they do from melodramas, where there is a tendency for sincere people to rush in. But if public men began paying gagmen as much as top comedians pay television scriptwriters, we might see a new and livelier era in politics. . . .

CONCLUSION

I have thus outlined seven outcomes of dramatic confrontation: (1) honorific ceremony, (2) hero-making (benefactor, winner, and martyr), (3) villain-making, (4) fool-making, (5) victim-making, (6) tragic, and (7) loss or draw without discredit. (More complex possibilities of role reversal will be explored in a later chapter.) Judging from these, what can be said about the principles that seem to govern? Surely there is more involved than merely the force exerted or the success of the outcome, for one can win materially yet lose dramatically.

The single most important factor in any dramatic encounter is the apparent ratio of forces. This ratio has much to do not only with how the event will actually turn out but with who will be hero, villain, fool, or victim and where audience sympathy will turn. Too great a preponderance of force on one side sets the stage for a villain who is using an unfair advantage or, if defeat looms, for a fool who could not win even when the cards were stacked in his favor. A David-and-Goliath situation is created, and the smaller party gets a role choice of hero or victim; the larger party has the possibility of victory with small credit but runs a very real chance of being villain or fool, and such an encounter is, for him, a poor bargain.[8] Apparent force, of course, is the key factor. It does not matter how many aces you have up your sleeve or tanks or henchmen hidden away; you must not display your true strength too obviously. Too large a display at the outset of a drama may make one look fearsome (as a villain), fearful (as a coward), or grandiose and pompous (as a stuffed shirt riding to his fall). For that reason, the movie hero usually underplays his strength before knocking out the bad guy,[9] and the cartoon Popeye eats his can of spinach only at the last. Buildups at the beginning are for villain and fools.

It seems plain that restraint in the early stages of an encounter has a number of consequences: (1) it avoids having the hero seem overconfident (the public welcomes the deflation of a stuffed shirt); (2) it casts the opponent as the "heavy" or the "bully"; (3) it arouses sympathy for a nice guy getting the worst of it until his wrath, valor, or potency is kindled; (4) it builds up suspense and deepens crisis; and (5) it maximizes the swing from looming defeat to victory, thus giving the audience the most exciting of emotional sleighrides. Of course, we presume a "win" or a martyr outcome; otherwise the would-be hero, instead of showing restraint, had better not appear at all.

The practical moral is that the public man, if he wishes to be popular, and regardless of how well laid his plan, how clever his tactics, or

---

[8] Perhaps this applies mainly to countries with the Anglo-American tradition of fair play and sympathy for the underdog, though I suspect that it is much more widespread, since the basic melodramatic and comic patterns can be found throughout world folklore and drama.

[9] One of the greatest of movie fights occurred in "El Cid." It followed classic lines. When El Cid fights the champion of the rival king, he is knocked off his horse, then off his feet. Getting to his feet he backs away, apparently at the mercy of the brute strength of his opponent, who swings a heavy mace. Finally, grasping a two-handed sword at the same time as his enemy, he finds himself on fair and equal terms. A furious exchange follows, in which El Cid knocks down his opponent, then with both hands plunges the sword through his prostrate form (pity is gone). El Cid lost the early rounds and then won by a knockout. Likewise, in classic Westerns, the hero shows restraint and gentility, even acting like a sissy, before he defeats the villain.

how great his resources, should always seem to act with a fair or somewhat disadvantageous ratio of force. He thus avoids being set up as
a villain by would-be martyrs or impudent challengers. If defeat comes
for him, with a safe ratio of forces he has the dramatic "outs" of the
martyr or victim or of defeat with honor. He avoids (without being
obvious about it) confrontations with small or unworthy antagonists
who can only make him look bad as villain or fool. Applying this, for
example, to the relations of the United States with Cuba in 1963–64,
we see how important it was to avoid a confrontation with Premier
Castro in which the ratio of forces would either make him look big
enough to bother or challenge the United States or, if he lost, appear
a victim or martyr in the eyes of Latin Americans, Communists, and
much of the world already disposed to see Uncle Sam as a villain.
The President of the United States should never exchange a direct public
word with such a leader whose posture is one of defiance. Military
efforts against Cuba (from a dramatic standpoint, at least) should be
indirect or by small parties. Blockades and similar tactics only create
a picture of a great villain throttling the people of Cuba. As Senator
George S. McGovern of South Dakota remarked:

> Castro not only occupies the time and energy of many of our top
> State Department, White House and CIA officials, but absorbs the atten-
> tion of Congress and threatens to be a central issue in the 1964 Presi-
> dential election.
> This animated national debate, considering the comparative weakness
> of Cuba, scarcely does justice to the dignity of the United States as
> a great world power charged with global leadership. . . .
> The President, early in his Administration, gave his sanction to the
> unfortunate Bay of Pigs invasion. This clumsy failure, the embarrassment,
> the humiliation, the sense of guilt—all these combined to produce a
> traumatic national experience for the United States. . . .
> We can best diminish Castro's prestige by ceasing to act as though
> he were the chief object of our concern.

Another principle that emerges from the cases discussed is that the
style of performance is of great importance, though not as important
as the ratio of forces. It does not matter what you do substantively
so much as how you do it. The advantage of non-violent resistance,
for example, is that its style makes it almost impossible to define the
aggressor as a villain; the worse he can be called is "troublemaker."
He is, however, naturally eligible for victim and martyr roles. Certain
qualities of style (unfairness, sneakiness, bluster, arrogance) help create
a villain in the mind of the audience, just as other qualities (modesty,
fairness, straightforwardness, pluck) set up a hero within an appropriate

ratio of forces. Again, pomposity, clumsiness, timidity, levity, or antic behavior cast one—whatever his substantive deeds—as fool, if only because the audience becomes predisposed to laugh at anything that happens to him. But style alone, without an appropriate ratio of forces, cannot govern. Governor Wallace used the same style in both his confrontations with the federal government, but President Kennedy refused to give him the needed ratio in the second.

Seeking key factors should not obscure the importance of the drama as a whole, the mutual effects of the roles of all actors as action proceeds through scenes, development, and turns. A later chapter will take up several public dramas that show how the reciprocal effects of the roles of actors, together with the style and ratio of forces, bring about interesting exchanges or reversals of role.

V.

IDEOLOGY, MYTH, AND BELIEF

As collective action becomes organized it often results in the development of systems of ideas and programs of doctrine and action. The beliefs which partisans come to hold are more or less orderly analyses of the present situation and prescriptions for its relief. They constitute justifications for dissent and provide a legitimate and intellectual basis for action. In this sense the belief system of a social movement is an incipient "social science."

The sociological analysis of ideologies involves a view which relates ideas to specific social situations. To understand beliefs we must subject them not merely to a logical analysis but to an understanding of the existence within which the believer acts. This includes bias and error but means more than the idea of bias alone. Karl Mannheim, in the reading included in this section, expresses the point well when he says, "This means that opinions, statements, propositions, and systems of ideas are not taken at their face value but are interpreted in the light of the life-situation of the one who expresses them."

The analysis of ideology, a term often given many meanings, is a basic tool of the sociologist's understanding of collective action. The word "locology" may refer to different levels of ideas. On the one hand, it may refer to a specific ideology related to a particular issue or set of issues, such as the ideology of Progressivism or of the New Deal. Here ideology refers to the beliefs of a specific social base which clash with those of others over a particular area of social controversy. At another level and in a somewhat wider sense, ideology is concerned with the set of concepts within which the very intellectual controversy may take place. Thus the conception of time used in one historical period and the system of values which legitimate intellectual controversy may vary considerably from one group to another and between historical periods. A controversy between a movement and part of a society may take place at the level of specific interests, or it may take place at the level of basic conceptual tools so that men are "talking past one another" without quite recognizing it. Karl Mannheim has called this a distinction between particular and total ideology.

No one has done more to clarify the problems of ideological analysis than the German sociologist Karl Mannheim. His work *Ideology and Utopia* deals both with the concept of ideology and with the nature of utopian ideas. In the short excerpt included here, the distinction between particular and total ideology is central for Mannheim. First, it rescues ideological analysis from the charge that it is merely debunking one set of ideas as lies or biases. Mannheim shows that our fundamental conceptions as well as our specific programs are deeply embedded in a historical and social situation. Second, by the distinction between particular and total ideology Mannheim not only clarifies a general difficulty in the way of understanding between groups and cultures, but also points to the tremendous importance of ideological analysis if one is to understand how it is that a given set of people may reject what seems to others to be self-evident. Only then, by seeing ideas in terms of the social situation of the believers, in their paradigm of experience, can we adequately understand the meanings in which they are set.

It is this phenomenon of the inability of one group to grasp the intellectual significance and legitimacy of another which makes the analysis of ideology so essential for the sociologist. It is essential because without understanding the experience from which the ideology has emerged, the student cannot see its plausibility to the actors. We clarify this idea by saying that there are *paradigms of experience* involved in the analysis of the ideas used in collective action. The partisan's experience provides for him a paradigm or model, in both moral and intellectual terms, for a system of beliefs which appear to others, with different experiences, to be foolish, insulting, or subterfuge. The industrial worker, who depends upon a job in an interdependent factory, leads a very different life from the farmer, whose existence is greatly determined by his ownership of small, private property. To the late nineteenth-century farmer his enemies—railroads and grain speculators—represented a very different kind of problem than did the employer or conditions of safety to the jobholder. In this volume we have even maintained that our very concepts—protest, reform, and revolt—have meanings derived from experiences in the modern period and are limited in utility for other contexts.

This is the value for us in selecting Martin Trow's study of McCarthyist supporters. What the small businessman brought to an understanding of Senator Joseph McCarthy's activities was the point of view and orientation of nineteenth-century American liberalism. The appeal of McCarthy to this group, and not to others, stemmed from the fact that he could be seen as a champion of beliefs which were self-evident to them but which were, in their experience, daily rejected in much of society. It is not that one group is wrong and another right in their analyses of the situation. The small businessman, from his point of view, does indeed experience that kind of existence which enables us to understand his political orientation.

Belief, however, is more than an intellectual or cognitive doctrine; it is also a prediction or prophecy about the future. There is thought which analyzes the present and defends it, and there is thought which presupposes the possibility of change and holds forth a vision of the future as an ideal capable of attainment.

To label such prophecies as "myth" is not to deny their significance or even to maintain their falsity. They are statements about the future which inspire the faith in their reality that may lead men to act so as to realize them as truth. In describing their cause as one assured of victory, myths can be self-fulfilling. In a seminal book on myth in social action (*Reflections on Violence*), Georges Sorel pointed out that myths cannot be refuted, since what is effective about myths are their consequences for action to change the very conditions which enter into the judgment of their truth or falsity. Sorel quotes the French religious historian, Ernest Renan: "The future lies in the hands of those who are not disillusioned."[1]

The future as a realization of perfection in human life has had a long history in Western societies. A number of significant movements have held out a vision of perfection capable of attainment in the immediate future. This strain of utopianism, while it has often influenced reformist action, is distinguished from the more prosaic and gradualist character of reform movements. Utopian myth and utopian thought make a sharp break between the evil, imperfect, and despised present and the world to be brought about when the movement succeeds.

Maren Lockwood Carden's account of American utopian communities of the nineteenth century effectively illustrates a perfectionism often observed in American social movements. During that period, and contin-

[1] Georges Sorel *Reflections on Violence*. Glencoe: The Free Press, 1950, p. 52.

uing even today, there were a great many communities founded by groups of people who sought to realize the perfect life, uncontaminated by the rest of the society. They were sure that it could be lived. While many of these communities disappeared soon after their origin, a number survived for several generations. The Oneida communitarians whom Professor Carden describes were a more vivid and pristine example of a utopian spirit which often deeply influenced American reformism and politics.

Utopianism has by no means been confined to withdrawal movements like those of the American utopian communities. Revolutionary and millenarian movements have been utopian in proclaiming the coming and imminent radical transformation of human life and society. The idea of the millennium has appeared in various forms not only in Western history but in contemporary times in many of the underdeveloped areas and new nations of the world. The millenarian idea, in its purely Christian or Judaic form, is a vision of the coming to earth of a messiah who will bring about the solution of all problems and the age of perfect existence. In a phrase used by theologians, it means "the end of history"—the attainment of the goals of Providence. In its general utopian form it is not specifically dependent on religious ideas. Included in our readings is a general survey of studies of millenarian movements in many areas of the world, by Yonina Talmon. In the idea of "cargo cults" the Melanesians, for example, have reproduced the millenarian idea of the West, visualizing a day in the immediate future when ships will appear bringing to the natives the goods which are now the possessions of the colonial powers.

These movements, Professor Talmon points out, have had political significance, since out of them there have often arisen the beginnings of nationalist and revolutionary action. The political significance of the millenarian myth was exemplified in "The Myth of Revolution" for Raymond Aron's *The Opium of the Intellectuals,* reprinted in Part II. Like millenarists, revolutionaries presuppose that the perfect world can be found and that the revolution will bring it about. The intensity of action, the heightened emotions, and the desperate drive to succeed become understandable when we recognize that the millenarist's and the revolutionary's dreams are for them realities close at hand. Small wonder that some observers have seen in Communism, Fascism, and other revolutionary movements a modern form of religious faith and a secular theology.

A.
The Paradigm of Experience

1.
IDEOLOGY—PARTICULAR AND
TOTAL (1929)

Karl Mannheim

In order to understand the present situation of thought, it is necessary to start with the problems of "ideology." For most people, the term "ideology" is closely bound up with Marxism, and their reactions to the term are largely determined by the association. It is therefore first necessary to state that although Marxism contributed a great deal to the original statement of the problem, both the word and its meaning go farther back in history than Marxism, and ever since its time new meanings of the word have emerged, which have taken shape independently of it.

There is no better introduction to the problem than the analysis of the meaning of the term "ideology": firstly we have to disentangle all the different shades of meaning which are blended here into a pseudo-unity, and a more precise statement of the variations in the meanings of the concept, as it is used to-day, will prepare the way for its sociological and historical analysis. Such an analysis will show that in general

SOURCE. Karl Mannheim, *Ideology and Utopia*. New York: Harcourt, Brace and Co., 1936, pp. 49–53. Reprinted by permission of Harcourt, Brace and World.

there are two distinct and separable meanings of the term "ideology"—the particular and the total.

The particular conception of ideology is implied when the term denotes that we are sceptical of the ideas and representations advanced by our opponent. They are regarded as more or less conscious disguises of the real nature of a situation, the true recognition of which would not be in accord with his interests. These distortions range all the way from conscious lies to half-conscious and unwitting disguises; from calculated attempts to dupe others to self-deception. This conception of ideology, which has only gradually become differentiated from the common-sense notion of the lie is particular in several senses. Its particularity becomes evident when it is contrasted with the more inclusive total conception of ideology. Here we refer to the ideology of an age or of a concrete historico-social group, e.g. of a class, when we are concerned with the characteristics and composition of the total structure of the mind of this epoch or of this group.

The common as well as the distinctive elements of the two concepts are readily evident. The common element in these two conceptions seems to consist in the fact that neither relies solely on what is actually said by the opponent in order to reach an understanding of his real meaning and intention.[1] Both fall back on the subject, whether individual or group, proceeding to an understanding of what is said by the indirect method of analysing the social conditions of the individual or his group. The ideas expressed by the subject are thus regarded as functions of his existence. This means that opinions, statements, propositions, and systems of ideas are not taken at their face value but are interpreted in the light of the life-situation of the one who expresses them. It signifies further that the specific character and life-situation of the subject influence his opinions, perceptions, and interpretations.

Both these conceptions of ideology, accordingly, make these so-called "ideas" a function of him who holds them, and of his position in his social milieu. Although they have something in common, there are also significant differences between them. Of the latter we mention merely the most important:—

(a) Whereas the particular conception of ideology designates only a part of the opponent's assertions as ideologies—and this only with

---

[1] If the interpretation relies solely upon that which is actually said we shall speak of an "immanent interpretation": if it transcends these data, implying thereby an analysis of the subject's life-situation, we shall speak of a "transcendental interpretation." A typology of these various forms of interpretation is to be found in the author's "Ideologische und soziolgische Interpretation der geistigen Gebilde," *Jahrbuch für Soziologie*, vol. ii (Karlsruhe, 1926), p. 424 ff.

reference to their content, the total conception calls into question the opponent's total *Weltanschauung* (including his conceptual apparatus), and attempts to understand these concepts as an outgrowth of the collective life of which he partakes.

(*b*) The particular conception of "ideology" makes its analysis of ideas on a purely psychological level. If it is claimed for instance that an adversary is lying, or that he is concealing or distorting a given factual situation, it is still nevertheless assumed that both parties share common criteria of validity—it is still assumed that it is possible to refute lies and eradicate sources of error by referring to accepted criteria of objective validity common in both parties. The suspicion that one's opponent is the victim of an ideology does not go so far as to exclude him from discussion on the basis of a common theoretical frame of reference. The case is different with the total conception of ideology. When we attribute to one historical epoch one intellectual world and to ourselves another one, or if a certain historically determined social stratum thinks in categories other than our own, we refer not to the isolated cases of thought-content, but to fundamentally divergent thought-systems and to widely differing modes of experience and interpretation. We touch upon the theoretical or noological level whenever we consider not merely the content but also the form, and even the conceptual framework of a mode of thought as a function of the life-situation of a thinker. "The economic categories are only the theoretical expressions, the abstractions, of the social relations of production. . . . The same men who establish social relations conformably with their material productivity, produce also the principles, the ideas, the categories, conformably with their social relations." (Karl Marx, *The Poverty of Philosophy*, being a translation of *Misère de la Philosophie,* with a preface by Frederick Engels, translated by H. Quelch, Chicago, 1910, p. 119.) These are the two ways of analysing statements as functions of their social background; the first operates only on the psychological, the second on the noological level.

(*c*) Corresponding to this difference, the particular conception of ideology operates primarily with a psychology of interests, while the total conception uses a more formal functional analysis, without any reference to motivations, confining itself to an objective description of the structural differences in minds operating in different social settings. The former assumes that this or that interest is the cause of a given lie or deception. The latter presupposes simply that there is a correspondence between a given social situation and a given perspective, point of view, or apperception mass. In this case, while an analysis of constellations of interests may often be necessary it is not to establish causal connectins but to characterize the total situation. Thus interest psychology tends to be displaced by an analysis of the correspondence between the situation to be known and the forms of knowledge.

Since the particular conception never actually departs from the psychological level, the point of reference in such analyses is always the individual. This is the case even when we are dealing with groups, since all psychic phenomena must finally be reduced to the minds of individuals. The term "group ideology" occurs frequently, to be sure, in popular speech. Group existence in this sense can only mean that a group of persons, either in their immediate reactions to the same situation or as a result of direct psychic interaction, react similarly. Accordingly, conditioned by the same social situation, they are subject to the same illusions. If we confine our observations to the mental processes which take place in the individual and regard him as the only possible bearer of ideologies, we shall never grasp in its totality the structure of the intellectual world belonging to a social group in a given historical situation. Although this mental world as a whole could never come into existence without the experiences and productive responses of the different individuals, its inner structure is not to be found in a mere integration of these individual experiences. The individual members of the working-class, for instance, do not experience *all* the elements of an outlook which could be called the proletarian *Weltanschauung*. Every individual participates only in certain fragments of this thought-system, the totality of which is not in the least a mere sum of these fragmentary individual experiences. As a totality the thought-system is integrated systematically, and is no mere casual jumble of fragmentary experiences of discrete members of the group. Thus it follows that the individual can only be considered as the bearer of an ideology as long as we deal with that conception of ideology which, by definition, is directed more to detached contents than to the whole structure of thought, uncovering false ways of thought and exposing lies. As soon as the total conception of ideology is used, we attempt to reconstruct the whole outlook of a social group, and neither the concrete individuals nor the abstract sum of them can legitimately be considered as bearers of this ideological thought-system as a whole. The aim of the analysis on this level is the reconstruction of the systematic theoretical basis underlying the single judgments of the individual. Analyses of ideologies in the particular sense, making the content of individual thought largely dependent on the interests of the subject, can never achieve this basic reconstruction of the whole outlook of a social group. They can at best reveal the collective psychological aspects of ideology, or lead to some development of mass psychology, dealing either with the different behaviour of the individual in the crowd, or with the results of the mass

integration of the psychic experiences of many individuals. And although
the collective-psychological aspect may very often approach the problems of the total ideological analysis, it does not answer its questions
exactly. It is one thing to know how far my attitudes and judgments
are influenced and altered by the co-existence of other human beings,
but it is another thing to know what are the theoretical implications
of my mode of thought which are identical with those of my fellow
members of the group or social stratum.

We content ourselves here merely with stating the issue without attempting a thorough-going analysis of the difficult methodological problems which it raises.

2.

SMALL BUSINESSMEN, POLITICAL TOLERANCE, AND SUPPORT FOR McCARTHY (1958)

MARTIN TROW

In the past few years social scientists have responded to the threat
symbolized by but by no means confined to Joseph McCarthy and have
made efforts to explain the variety of illiberal and repressive movements
that flourished during much of the first decade following World War
II. Such social scientists as Parsons, Reisman, Shils, Hofstadter, and
Lipset have written books or essays on the men, sentiments, and movements that came to be known as the "radical right." These writings,
and especially the essays that were collected in the volume *The New
American Right*, show an impressively high measure of agreement on
the nature of the social forces underlying such diverse popular movements as McCarthyism, the movement for the Bricker amendment, and
the many organized actions against "subversion" in schools, libraries,
the mass media, and elsewhere. In addition to the generally high measure
of agreement (or at least convergence) in these essays, they are also,
taken together, both highly persuasive and based on almost no empirical
evidence at all, at least so far as their efforts to explain the popular
support of these movements are concerned.

SOURCE. Martin J. Trow, "Small Businessmen Political Tolerance, and Support
for McCarthy," *American Journal of Sociology*, No. 64, 1958, pp. 270–281. Reprinted by permission of The University of Chicago Press and the author.

The essayists in *The New American Right* treated McCarthyism as one manifestation of the new "radical right," largely assumed its close connection with political intolerance, and discussed the nature and sources of both as part of their interpretation of the larger phenomenon. And they saw the rise of this "radical right" as largely a consequence (or manifestation) of the increasing importance during the postwar years of "status politics"—the projection of people's status anxieties and frustrations onto the political arena—and the correlative decline in the relative importance of class or "interest" politics. Moreover, say the writers, the "status politics" which underlies the rise of the "radical right" tends to flourish in prosperous times, as "interest politics" is associated with depression and economic discontent. And the essayists deal with the "radical right's" mass support chiefly by speculating on the likely locations in our society of pockets of acute status anxieties or concerns.[1] They do this job so thoroughly that they have left little room for surprise regarding the social composition of McCarthy's popular support. The essays show, and quite persuasively, how and why McCarthy got disproportionate support almost everywhere: among old Americans and among new Americans; among the upwardly mobile, the downwardly mobile, and the low status non-mobile; among Catholics, Yankee Protestants, and rural fundamentalists; among workers, small businessmen, the new middle class, and the "new rich," etc. This kind of analysis, which explains every possible or supposed appearance of the phenomenon, is, of course, in part a function of the paucity of data on the issue. But, while such an analysis precludes surprises, it also explains a good deal too much. Unless we can account for the actual distribution of support for a given issue or for a leader or spokesman of this political tendency, without finessing the crucial questions of "more or less," then our analysis loses much of its power and cogency.

A study done in Bennington, Vermont, during 1954 provided data for an intensive analysis of some of the social and social-psychological characteristics of McCarthy supporters in the general population.[2] And

---

[1] In the absence of data, these writers also attempted to *deduce* the character and composition of McCarthy's popular following from their analyses of the movement's economic and historical context and from the ideology of the movement's more prominent spokesmen. But the mass support for a movement and the grounds on which that support is granted may differ very greatly from what we would expect on the basis of an analysis of the public pronouncements of prominent men.

[2] This study of McCarthy's support was part of a larger study of political orientations and formal and informal communications carried out under the overall direction of Dr. Robert D. Leigh and supported by a grant from Columbia University. The data reported in this paper were gathered through one- to two-hour structured interviews with men living in the Bennington area. Nearly eight hundred

though the movement and its leader are no longer part of the American political scene, the Bennington study indicates that the social forces that made for support of McCarthy did not die with his power or his person but remain available to other illiberal and repressive men and movements of the radical right. If that is so, then the study of McCarthy's popular support not merely is of interest to the antiquarian but may shed light on one aspect of the continuing vulnerability of a mass democratic society to radical, right-wing movements.

The study, part of which is reported in this paper, aimed to investigate the social characteristics of McCarthy's supporters in its sample and on this basis make some inferences regarding the social sources of his popular support.[3] At the same time we were able to look into correlates of "political tolerance,"[4] explore the nature and sources of McCarthy's

---

such interviews were conducted in the area during the spring and summer of 1954, during and just after the McCarthy-Army hearings, when McCarthy was at or near the peak of his popularity and power. A national survey done in August of that year found a third of its sample giving McCarthy their support (see Charles H. Stember, "Anti-democratic Attitudes in America: A Review of Public Opinion Research" [Publication of the Bureau of Applied Social Research (New York: Columbia University, 1954) p. 52] [mimeographed]). In Bennington over half of the men we interviewed approved of McCarthy's activities, while some 40 per cent approved of his methods of investigation—that aspect of his activities which had come under sharpest criticism. Incidentally, interest in and knowledge about McCarthy were very high during the period in which these interviews were collected. In Bennington, fewer than 5 per cent of the respondents answered "Don't know" to any of the questions about McCarthy.

[3] Information on attitudes toward McCarthy was gathered through three questions in the interview: questions bearing on his activities, his methods of investigation, and the value of his investigation committee. Although these three questions could have been combined in a scale of "support for McCarthy," the decision was made to use the single question, "Just speaking of Senator McCarthy's *methods* of investigation, how do you feel about them? Do you strongly favor them, mildly favor them, mildly oppose them, or strongly oppose them?" In most of the tabulations those who favored his methods, whether strongly or mildly, were compared with those who opposed them. For the reasons this item alone was used see Trow, *op. cit.*, pp. 12–15.

[4] The measure of "political tolerance" was an index based on the three questions: "In peacetime, do you think the Socialist party should be allowed to publish newspapers in this country?" "Do you think newspapers should be allowed to criticize our form of government?" "Do you think members of the Communist party in this country should be allowed to speak on the radio?"

While these three specific attitudes were highly related to one another, there was, as we might expect, least support for the right of members of the Communist party to speak on the radio and most support for the rights of newspapers to criticize our form of government. But, on further examination, it appeared that these three questions tapped a common, more basic sentiment regarding the rights of

support and "political tolerance" separately and simultaneously, and, by contrast and comparison, throw into bold relief the similarities and differences in the forces underlying these two different sets of sentiments.[5]

McCARTHY'S SUPPORT AND POLITICAL TOLERANCE

The widespread assumption that support for McCarthy was almost always associated with political intolerance seems to gain empirical support when we observe that support for McCarthy and political intolerance were both strongly related to the amount of formal education completed. There is nothing very startling about this: we hardly need an extensive study to know that McCarthy gained much of his popular support from poorly educated, lower-class people who are, as many studies tell us, also least likely to be tolerant of unpopular political minorities and views.

But the matter becomes not quite so routine when we examine the relationship between support for McCarthy and political tolerance holding formal education constant. When we do this, the relationship between intolerance and support for McCarthy almost or wholly disappears (Table 1). On every educational level McCarthy's supporters were about as likely as his opponents to have been tolerant toward the exercise of free speech by political dissidents. In other words, while

---

people and groups hostile to our political and economic system to make their criticisms known through the media of public communication. Political tolerance involves, at a minimum, a willingness to grant to others the right to propagate their political views. The willingness to grant this right to unpopular political minorities is the sentiment common to these three items and is the sentiment we are calling "political tolerance."

The index was constructed by assigning a score of 2 to "Yes" responses, 1 to "Yes, qualified," and 0 to "No." In these tabulations the index was dichotomized, with those having a total score of 3 or more comprising the "High" group.

Identically worded questions have been included in a number of national surveys conducted by the National Opinion Research Center in recent years and provide comparisons with the Bennington sample. For further discussion of this measure see Trow, *op. cit.*, pp. 16–17.

[5] This investigation explored the relations between support for McCarthy and political tolerance and economic class, occupation, religious identification, union membership and identification, political party preference, and attitudes toward various national and foreign policy issues. The bearing of formal education on McCarthy's support and political tolerance was analyzed separately; since it was so highly related to both these sentiments, it was controlled in the analysis of all the other relationships.

TABLE 1   SUPPORT FOR McCARTHY BY POLITICAL TOLERANCE, HOLDING
FORMAL EDUCATION CONSTANT (PER CENT)

Education.......	Grade School		Some High School		High-School Graduate		Some College and More	
Political Tolerance	High	Low	High	Low	High	Low	High	Low
Favor McCarthy's methods.......	51	63	44	44	43	45	23	18
N...............	(54)	(94)	(55)	(68)	(113)	(62)	(197)	(33)

support of McCarthy and political intolerance were both related to formal education, they were very little related to each other.

The implications of this finding are many. In its simplest terms it means that, whatever the character and content of the *public* fight between McCarthy and his more prominent opponents, the sources of his support and popularity in the population at large appear to have had little relation to how strongly people support the principles of free speech.

The division over McCarthy in the population at large, at least in Bennington, was not a division between the supporters of and encroachers upon civil liberties. To see it that way is to overlook the very genuine elements of "radicalism"—of anticonservatism—in the McCarthy appeal. On the one hand, many of those who disapproved of McCarthy and his methods did so not out of any particular concern for the preservation of civil liberties or freedom of speech for unpopular minorities but rather out of a feeling that what is done to suppress "subversion" be done in conservative ways through regular legislative or judicial or administrative procedures. But these men, as their responses to our questions show, were often no more concerned with the preservation of freedom of speech than McCarthy himself and much less so than many of his followers. For many of these latter, the majority of them lower class, with little formal schooling, McCarthy's appeal was not that of a man *repressing* free speech but of a man *exercising* it, in what appeared to be bold and fearless ways. Moreover, much of his boldness, violence, and aggression was directed precisely against the conservative authorities and institutions—the "big shots," the "stuffed shirts," the "bureaucrats"— against whom many of his supporters felt anger and resentment. The men who opposed McCarthy, by and large, were solid, better educated, middle-class citizens who identified with the authorities and institutions which were McCarthy's chief targets of attack by the summer of 1954. Many an executive or engineer who watched McCarthy alternately patronize and bully Army Secretary Stevens felt, and not without reason, that he himself and men like him were also under attack.

Our finding that McCarthy's support and political intolerance were not strongly related to each other does not rest solely or even primarily on the one tabulation which shows that the apparent relationship disappears when education is held constant. That finding did indeed stimulate further inquiry in that same direction, but, as evidence accumulated, it became apparent in many other ways that the social forces underlying McCarthy's popular support were simply not the same as those making for political intolerance. And, like most empirical findings, this one posed a question: If support for McCarthy were not simply an expression of political intolerance, what were its social sources, and how did they differ from the social sources of political intolerance?

Before proceeding to report one part of our investigation into that question, it may be useful to summarize briefly some of its more general findings. In précis, we found that political tolerance is a norm or cluster of norms, very strongly related to cultural sophistication, or "cosmopolitanism," and thus to the level of formal education achieved—*and to very little else.* By contrast, popular support for McCarthy can best be understood as the channeling of certain dissatisfactions with aspects of the social, economic, and political orders. There are two elements present in that formulation: the presence of considerable discontent and dissatisfaction and the ways and directions in which those dissatisfactions are channeled. We found the highest levels of support for McCarthy in social classes and categories which, on one hand, show considerable hostility toward important elements in the social structure and, on the other hand, do not have their hostilities and discontents channeled into and through existing political and economic institutions. By contrast, neither the *level* of discontent nor the *channeling* of discontent appeared to have appreciable bearing on the levels of political tolerance characteristics of these same classes and social categories.

McCARTHY'S SUPPORT, POLITICAL TOLERANCE, AND OCCUPATION

Part of the evidence on which these general propositions are based bears on the relation of economic class and occupation to the sentiments in question. When we divide our sample into the two broad categories of "manual" and "non-manual" workers, the latter including both salaried and self-employed white-collar people, we find little or no difference between them in their support of McCarthy, holding formal education constant. Even when we divide the "non-manual" category into "lower-" and "upper-middle-class" categories, on the basis of income, we still find no appreciable differences in attitudes toward McCarthy within educational categories. But when we distinguish *within* the middle class between salaried and self-employed men, we found marked differences in their respective levels of support for McCarthy (Table 2).

In every educational category the small businessmen showed a distinctly higher proportion of McCarthy supporters than did the salaried men of similar education, and, among those who had not been to college, the small businessmen were even more pro-McCarthy than the manual workers. And the differences were substantial. For example, among the men who did not finish high school, two-thirds of the small businessmen supported McCarthy, as compared with only half the workers who did and only a little more than a third of the salaried employees who did. Among the men who had been to college the differences by occupational group are smaller but still substantial: where one in three of these better-educated small businessmen supported McCarthy, only a little over one in five of the salaried employees with this education did.

There are a number of possible interpretations of this finding, some of which were investigated and rejected in light of the Bennington data. The interpretation that gained strongest support from the data can be

TABLE 2   SUPPORT FOR McCARTHY BY OCCUPATIONAL GROUP, HOLDING FORMAL EDUCATION CONSTANT (PER CENT)

Education.......	Less than 4 Years of High School			High-School Graduate			Some College and More		
Occupation.......	Man.[a]	Sal.[a]	S.B.[a]	Man.	Sal.	S.B.	Man.	Sal.	S.B.
Favor McCarthy's methods.......	53	38	65	49	36	58	32	22	32
N..............	(188)	(53)	(52)	(59)	(78)	(38)	(35)	(124)	(44)

[a] Occupation: "Man.": manual workers; "Sal.": salaried employees, including lower and upper white collar, salaried professionals, and executives; "S.B.": small businessmen, including merchants and other small proprietors. Free professionals, farmers, unemployed, and retired people are excluded.

summarized in the hypothesis that small businessmen in our society disproportionately tend to develop a generalized hostility toward a complex of symbols and processes bound up with industrial capitalism: the steady growth and concentration of government, labor organizations, and business enterprises; the correlative trend toward greater rationalization of production and distribution; and the men, institutions, and ideas that symbolize these secular trends of modern society. These trends and their symbols were, we believe, McCarthy's most persuasive targets. Quite apart from the questions of Communists in government, and blunders or worse in foreign policy, the congruence-between McCarthy's attacks on and small businessmen's hostility to the dominant characteristics and tendencies of modern society account, we believe, for much of the disproportionate support McCarthy gained from small businessmen.[6]

This hypothesis can be explored further by looking at the connections between support for McCarthy and attitudes toward the most characteristic economic institutions of our society, that is, large corporations and trade unions. A simple but serviceable-typology emerges from responses to questions asking how the respondent feels about big companies and trade unions and permits us to distinguish empirically four important and easily recognizable patterns of orientations toward the dominant economic institutions in the population at large.[7] The group which expressed approval of labor unions but suspicion of the power of big companies, (I), is closest to the familiar "labor-liberals," who in this country gave their support to the labor-oriented, administrative liberal-

---

[6] The free professionals, chiefly doctors and lawyers, not shown in this table, were markedly low in their support of McCarthy; only one in five gave him his support. These professions, as Parsons has noted, have developed relatively well-institutionalized ways of dealing with rapid social change, so that "the dynamic process of which they are agents is not so disturbing to them" (Talcott Parsons, *Essays in Sociological Theory Pure and Applied* [Glencoe, Ill.: Free Press, 1949], p. 267). Nor do they experience the insecurities flowing from the progressive rationalization of economic life that the small businessmen do. They are, in this respect, more like the salaried employees, especially the managers, technicians, and salaried professionals.

[7] The two questions were: "Do you agree or disagree that: The way they are run now, labor unions do this country more harm than good," and "Big companies control too much of American business."

		Big Companies Control Too Much of American Business	
		Agree	Disagree
The way they are run now, labor unions	Disagree	I	III
do this country more harm than good	Agree	II	IV

ism of the New Deal and its descendants. The pro–big business, antiunion group, (IV), resemble the equally familiar "right-wing conservatives." The orientation I have called "moderate conservatism," (III), is held by people who are reconciled to the continued existence both of big companies and of trade unions; this is the dominant political orientation of both major parties today.

To the student of right-wing radicalism the most interesting of these four orientations is that which expresses hostility toward both big business and trade unions (II). At the risk of some distortion, I have called this orientation "nineteenth-century liberalism." In the middle of the twentieth century the important thing about this orientation is not its intellectual content but rather its emotional tone, its diffused anger, and its generalized suspicion toward modern tendencies of all kinds. Among our respondents, this nineteenth-century liberalism appears both as a wistful nostalgia for a golden age of small farmers and businessmen and also as an expression of a strong resentment and hatred toward a world which makes no sense in terms of older ideas and which is conducted in apparent violation of old truths and values of economic and political life.

If we look at the distribution of McCarthy support among the holders of these four political orientations (and we did this separately for better- and less-well-educated men), we find that there were scarcely any differences among holders of three of the four orientations in their proportions of McCarthy supporters (Table 3).

But among the poorly educated, as among the better educated, the nineteenth-century liberals gave McCarthy distinctly higher proportions

TABLE 3   MCCARTHY'S SUPPORT BY DOMESTIC POLITICAL ORIENTATIONS, AMONG BETTER- AND LESS-WELL-EDUCATED MEN (PER CENT)

Education.......	Less Than 4 Years of High School				4 Years of High School and More			
DPO[a]...........	I	II	III	IV	I	II	III	IV
Favor McCarthy's methods.......	44	67	51	51	32	50	29	32
N..............	(90)	(84)	(53)	(43)	(101)	(58)	(137)	(97)

[a] DPO Type I: Labor-liberal (pro-union; anti–big business)
II: Nineteenth-century liberal (anti-union; anti–big business)
III: Moderate conservative (pro-union; pro–big business)
IV: Right-wing conservative (anti-union; pro–big business)

of support than any of the other three orientations we examined. Among the men who had less than four years of high school, the difference between the nineteenth-century liberals and all the others in the proportions supporting McCarthy is the difference between two-thirds and a half. Among the better educated, the difference is between a half as compared with a third of all others who gave McCarthy their support.

There are two findings here which are perhaps of equal interest to the student of right-wing radicalism. The first—that there was little difference in the support McCarthy gained among labor-liberals, moderate conservatives, and right-wing conservatives—contradicts the widespread liberal assumption that McCarthy got much of his mass support from the traditional right-wing conservatives.[8] The other finding, with which we are chiefly concerned here, is that men holding the nineteenth-century liberal orientation toward big business and trade unions showed a markedly greater vulnerability to McCarthy's appeal. These men, as I have noted, are often angrily confused and deeply resentful of a world that continually offends their deepest values. But as important is the fact that this particular well of resentment and indignation has no effective and institutionalized channels of expression. Right-wing conservatives have substantial power in the business community and the Republican party; labor-liberals are a strong force in the trade unions, some big-city machines, and are well represented in the Democratic party; and the moderate conservatives have everything else. It is precisely the political orientation which has no institutionalized place on the political scene, little representation or leadership in the major parties, which sought that voice and place through McCarthy. And he expressed for them their fear and mistrust of bigness and of the slick and subversive ideas that come out of the cities and the big institutions to erode old ways and faiths.

It should come as no surprise to find that the small businessmen in our sample were distinctly more likely than manual workers or salaried employees to hold nineteenth-century liberal views regarding trade unions and large corporations (Table 4). Where small businessmen comprised only one-fifth of the men in these occupational categories in our sample, they contributed a third of the nineteenth-century liberals. Moreover, the small businessmen who *held* these views gave McCarthy a very high measure of support.[9] The very highest proportion of McCarthy

[8] Further investigation of holders of very conservative economic attitudes supports this finding.

[9] Even those small businessmen who held other orientations gave McCarthy more support than did workers and salaried employees with the same orientations. Looked at from another perspective, nineteenth-century liberals among workers and salaried

TABLE 4 DOMESTIC POLITICAL ORIENTATIONS BY OCCUPATIONAL GROUP, FOR BETTER- AND LESS-WELL-EDUCATED MEN (PER CENT)

Education....	Less Than 4 Years of High School			4 Years of High School and More		
Occupation...	Man.[a]	Sal.[a]	S.B.[a]	Man.	Sal.	S.B.
DPO[b]						
Group I......	42	27	19	48	20	21
Group II.....	29	25	41	12	12	18
Group III....	18	25	19	25	40	36
Group IV....	11	23	21	15	28	25
Total....	100	100	100	100	100	100
N...........	(180)	(52)	(52)	(87)	(191)	(80)

[a] See note to Table 2.
[b] DPO:
>   Group I: Labor-liberals
>   Group II: Nineteenth-century liberals
>   Group III: Moderate conservatives
>   Group IV: Right-wing conservatives

supporters among these categories was found among the poorly educated small businessmen holding these nineteenth-century liberal attitudes; almost three out of four of these men were McCarthy supporters. Here is evidence that a generalized fear of the dominant currents and institutions of modern society was an important source of McCarthy's mass appeal, not *only* among small businessmen, but perhaps especially among a group like small businessmen whose economic and status security is continually threatened by those currents and institutions.

One can hardly consider the connection between economic class and

---

men gave McCarthy more support than did men in similar occupations holding different orientations toward big business and trade unions. Occupation and these politico-economic orientations worked independently and cumulatively in their bearing on McCarthy's support.

In this study we are primarily concerned with the relationships and forces underlying McCarthy's popular support. But our findings that support for McCarthy was not highly related to political intolerance and that McCarthy gained disproportionate support from small businessmen should not obscure the fact that *most* of McCarthy's supporters were (*a*) intolerant and (*b*) manual workers. Our findings and the latter observations, of course, do not contradict one another.

right-wing radicalism in America without thinking of the analysis of the Nazi party's mass support before Hitler took power, an analysis developed by such men as Erich Fromm, Sigmund Neumann, Karl Mannheim, Emil Lederer, and Alfred Meusal. The comparison suggests itself despite, or perhaps even because of, the very great differences in the historical backgrounds and in the social, political, and economic contexts of right-wing radical movements in Europe and the United States. All the observers of naziism are agreed that lower-middle-class tradesmen, shopkeepers, and artisans gave the Nazis a disproportionately large measure of their support before the Nazis took power. And they did so, these observers agree, because of their deep-seated fear of radical proletarianism, on one hand, and of the rapid rationalization of production and distribution—that is to say, the large corporation and the department store—on the other. (These fears involved their concern with *both* material and status security.) To the small German proprietor, Hitler promised to crush radical proletarianism and control big business.

Nothing could seem further from the social scene that these writers were speaking of—societies undergoing almost continuous crisis, experiencing intense class conflicts and increasingly wide desperation and despair—than the general climate in a relatively prosperous, small New England town in 1954. The chief characteristics of Bennington's social and political climate was an absence of intense class conflict or conflict of any kind; rather there was a very considerable amount of tolerance, good humor, and the appearance of widespread optimism about the future. Similarly, nothing could seem more inappropriate to the political orientations of Benningtonians than the apocalyptic analysis applied to pre-Hitler Europe. What is perhaps surprising is that in this climate of optimism, good humor, and low-temperature politics, small businessmen in Bennington were apparently responding to the pressures of industrial capitalism in ways not wholly unlike their beleaguered cousins in the Middle Europe of twenty-five years ago, though at much lower levels of intensity.[10]

[10] This is not to identify McCarthy with Hitler, or American right-wing movements with naziism or fascism, though this is not the place to discuss the very great differences between these movements. Nor is it meant simply to equate the role of small businessmen in the mass support for those movements. Their differing historical developments and the different political situations and structures within which these movements developed heavily conditioned their actual political *consequences*. Our concern here is not with the manifold factors that affect the translation of political sentiments into action (i.e., with their consequences) but rather with the nature of those sentiments and with their location and sources in the social structure. And here, the evidence suggests, there are certain important parallels in the two situations.

McCARTHY'S SUPPORT AND SALARIED EMPLOYEES

But this comparison of the social sources of Hitler's popular support with McCarthy's shows one very striking anomaly. Students of naziism usually speak of the disproportionate support the Nazis got from the German lower middle class, in which they lump small tradesmen, artisans, and businessmen, together with lower white-collar salaried employees. The evidence would seem to justify their approach: Hans Gerth's study of the membership of the Nazi party in 1933 shows that both small proprietors and salaried employees were disproportionately represented in the membership of the Nazi party and to about the same degree, both groups supplying about twice the proportion of Nazi party members as compared with their representation in the population at large. And the students of naziism explain Hitler's support among the salaried white-collar workers in much the same way they explain the support the Nazis got from the small proprietors: largely in terms of their status anxieties—anxieties arising especially out of the discrepancy between their precarious and deteriorating economic positions and their status claims and aspirations.

By contrast, in Bennington the salaried employees not only were not as pro-McCarthy as the small businessmen but were strikingly low in the support they gave him, as indicated above. This was true not only of the better-educated managers, executives, technicians, and salaried professionals who might be expected to identify with McCarthy's high-status targets. It was also true of the less-well-educated and low-income white-collar men. Less than 30 per cent of the very large group of salaried employees gave McCarthy their approval and support, as compared with over half of all the small businessmen and merchants.

How can we account for the fact that, while the analysis of the anxieties and politics of small businessmen in pre-Hitler Germany is not irrelevant to our understanding of the political orientations of small businessmen in Bennington in 1954, the behaviors of the salaried employees in the two situations were almost diametrically opposite? The answer seems to lie in the general orientation of the two classes to modern industrial society. Salaried employees, whether in Germany or the United States, or in the new countries of the Near and Far East,[11] are in general

[11] Asoka Mehta has pointed out that in the "underdeveloped area" of Asia the Communists make their first and chief appeal not to the peasants or industrial workers but to the emerging strata of salaried employees, who respond in large numbers precisely to the promise of rapid industrialization and bureaucratization under Communist direction and to the opportunities that will be thus opened up

not alienated from the dominant trends and institutions of modern society; these trends and developments of concentration, specialization, rationalization, and bureaucratization have created the class of salaried employees and are its natural habitat. But, while accepting the general shape and direction of modern society, the salaried employees in Europe responded violently to short-run crises in capitalist society—to inflation, depression, mass unemployment, and their consequent insecurities of livelihood and social status. In this light it is not surprising that the general orientation of white-collar people in a booming and expanding economy such as the United States has had since World War II should be moderate, conservative, and generally complacent about the political economy and its direction. And this because of, not despite, the fact that the tendencies toward concentration and centralization are great and swift-moving. In pre-Hitler Germany the same classes turned to Hitler in great numbers as the large organizations which structured their lives and careers proved increasingly incapable of providing the material and status security they demanded. Their response was not against large organization but against the collapse of bureaucratic society and toward a man and a party which promised to revive and extend it.

By contrast, small businessmen react not so much to short-run crises in the economy as to its long-range tendencies and direction of development—against the society itself rather than merely to failures of its economy. The tendencies which small businessmen fear—of concentration and centralization—proceed without interruption in depression, war, and prosperity and irrespective of the party in power; thus they are *always* disaffected, though probably the acute pinch they feel in depressions makes their anxieties and angers sharper and more pointed. In this light, the small businessmen in prosperous Bennington of 1954 were not so fundamentally different in their response to the social and economic pressures of modern society from the equivalent strata in pre-Hitler Germany, or from their opposite members in the France of Poujade.

OCCUPATION AND POLITICAL TOLERANCE

It remains to be said, and with some emphasis, that the disproportionate support small businessmen gave to McCarthy is *not* evidence

---

to them (Asoka Mehta, "Can Asia Industrialize Democratically," *Dissent*, I [Spring, 1955], 152–70). See also Morris Watnick, "The Appeal of Communism to the Peoples of Underdeveloped Areas," in Bendix and Lipset (eds.), *Class, Status, and Power* (Glencoe, Ill.: Free Press, 1953), pp. 651–62.

TABLE 5   POLITICAL TOLERANCE BY OCCUPATIONAL GROUP, HOLDING
EDUCATION CONSTANT (PER CENT)

Education.....	Less than 4 years of high school			High-school graduate			Some college and more		
Occupation....	Man.[a]	Sal.[a]	S.B.[a]	Man.	Sal.	S.B.	Man.	Sal.	S.B.
High political tolerance....	36	44	50	60	68	71	81	88	86
N............	(181)	(52)	(46)	(55)	(78)	(35)	(36)	(120)	(43)

[a] See Table 2.

that they constitute a pool of repressive and illiberal sentiments of all kinds. On the contrary, we can see that, despite their vulnerability to a right-wing demagogue like McCarthy, small businessmen are no more politically intolerant than are salaried employees or manual workers of similar education (Table 5). Here again we find that occupation and economic class, and all the varied discontents that flow from membership in different class and occupational groups, seem to have little bearing on political tolerance, certainly as compared with the bearing of formal education and cultural sophistication. By contrast with support of McCarthy, tolerance of dissidence appears to be almost wholly a function of the degree to which men have learned and internalized the rules of the democratic political game: in the United States this, in turn, is closely related to general political awareness and sophistication, acquired in part through formal education and through exposure to the serious political media which support those norms, rather than through economic or occupational experience. Where political tolerance for the most part is a norm held and enforced in the sub-cultures of sophisticated men, most of whom have been to college, popular support for McCarthy, by contrast, seemed to have been largely the channeled expression of various kinds of socially engendered discontents.

THE "RADICAL RIGHT" AND POPULAR SENTIMENTS

Our findings clearly indicate that students of public opinion on political issues might well be wary of such concepts as the "radial right" and its "pseudo-conservative" members, with all the assumptions regarding a coherent if latent structure of attitudes in the general population that those terms imply. Supporters of the "radical right" have been seen not only as having supported McCarthy but also as hostile to the New Deal, organized labor, the graduated income tax, and the United Nations, as authoritarian in character, intolerant of political non-conformists, and prejudiced against racial and religious groups. Whatever may be said or learned regarding the leaders and activists of right-wing radical movements, it is not likely that these characteristics and sentiments will be found in close association in the population at large. In this respect "radical rightism" may be like "liberalism," whose articulate representatives are usually civil libertarians, internationalists, in favor of organized labor and social welfare programs, whereas in the population at large these supposed components of "liberalism" do not tend to be found together.

The relationship of public opinion to the political process is devious, indirect, and complicated. If it is misleading and dangerous to deduce the structure of political power and its behavior from the distribution of political attitudes in the population at large, as political scientists warn, it is equally erroneous to deduce the nature and distribution of public opinion from the forces and ideologies that clash on high. But the distributions of sentiments on public issues and about public leaders *can* be sensitive indicators to deep-running forces in society—social forces that have heavy political consequences, though *not* necessarily, through the public opinions that reveal them. If this is so, then there is a potentially rich source of new knowledge for political sociology in the secondary analysis of existing survey research data.

B.
Utopianism

3.
THE EXPERIMENTAL UTOPIA IN AMERICA
(1965)

MAREN LOCKWOOD CARDEN

To someone living in the nineteenth century, utopia was imminent; it was not an impractical, impossible notion. Utopia could exist: it was expounded as a legitimate hope for the average citizen and it was embodied in more than a hundred experimental communities scattered across the country.[1] Eminent men of letters toyed with the notion. A national convention of "Associationists" took place in New York in April 1844 counting among its officers Charles A. Dana, Horace Greeley, and William H. Channing.[2] One or two of such men, like Hawthorne and Alcott, actually tried the life. On the other hand, superficially it would seem today that utopia is indeed "nowhere." A few communities spot the American landscape, but we pay them scant attention. The concept utopia has dropped out of high-school text books, and, like the New Jerusalem, utopian communities seem to be part of a vague mythology, tried and found wanting. What, one wonders, has happened to the idea of the experimental community since its nineteenth-century golden age?

SOURCE. Maren Lockwood Carden, "Experimental Utopia in America," *Daedalus* (Spring, 1965), pp. 403–418. Reprinted by permission of *Daedalus* and the author. Some changes have been made by Professor Carden.

The intellectual currents of the last century, fed by the notions of the Enlightenment, looked upon the future of mankind with an optimism that is a familiar part of our national self-concept. In the nineteenth-century this optimism was not a vaguely hopeful temper of mind so much as a specific belief: man could improve himself socially and morally. For some, this came as a great surge of exultation and a sanguine faith that now men could indeed become like gods. The English poet John Addington Symonds expressed this extreme optimism in a poem that later appeared for a while in the *Methodist Hymn Book:*

> These things shall be! a loftier race
> Than e'er the world has known shall rise
> With flame of freedom in their souls
> And light of science in their eyes.
> New arts shall bloom of loftier mould,
> And mightier music thrill the skies,
> And every life shall be a song,
> When all the earth is paradise.[3]

For some, this paradise was not a distant hope, but an immediate expectation. Recent technological discoveries and theoretical reformulations seemed to have increased dramatically the pace of social change. Perhaps society was emerging into some glorious era. There were those who said this social progress lay beyond man's control, part of Spencer's organic and superorganic evolution. Others saw man a willing instrument in the process. They declared he had already made great improvements and asked could he not, with all the confidence of his new-found power, direct his destiny. Could he not begin to remodel society, men's social relationships, their work, their means of support, their very minds?

This was what the utopians asserted. When the idea of the experimental community was imported from Europe through the writings of Fourier and Owen, and through the persuasive lectures of fervent utopians like Arthur Brisbane, it found a warm response. The Yankee practicality that might well discourage such notions even worked in their favor, for the utopians too were, in this sense, practical men. Like those politicians who devised the Constitution, like the pioneers who grappled with their new land, like Franklin experimenting with electricity, they promised a demonstration of the better life. They would detach themselves from the worldly society. Freed of its imperfections, they would create an ideal social system composed of truly moral men.

This widespread expectation of improvement imbued the concept of utopia with much of its nineteenth-century vigor. But its glowing vitality was sustained simultaneously by several other prevalent social themes. These included the deep religious interest of the age, the admiration of individual enterprise and pioneering endeavor, and that prosaic enthusiasm for practical application we have mentioned. Only when such generally acknowledge and approved notions were joined with the exigencies of actual experiment did the peculiarities of utopia appear. Then the communities seemed grotesque fantasies with scarcely a feature to represent the character of their age. Thus the better life might include communalism, celibacy, free love, greatest rewards for the least attractive work, intellectual exercise combined with physical toil, religious devotion, the free expression of natural passion, industry, education, intellectual isolation—a great store of ideas drawn upon in many different combinations by the earnest utopians.

One particular utopia, the Oneida community, produced a remarkable number of exotic variations on general societal practice and combined these in a strangely harmonious and long-lived society. In these specific practices we can trace the influence of the more general social themes and show how they found a very reasonable expression in Oneida's peculiar conception.[4]

Oneida rooted its utopian idealism in religious belief. During the nineteenth century, established doctrine was threatened with radical ideas, and religion was projected into the forefront of change. While the more orthodox churches, such as the Presbyterian and Congregationalist, clung to a creed which accepted human sinfulness as their earthly lot, the radical denominations sought to introduce the vivid solace of the Enlightenment's conception of man. The Puritans had seen man as a depraved soul, who lay beneath the hand of a just but wrathful God and who was powerless to affect his own destiny. This conception gave way to the optimism of the age; the future progress of man was unbounded, and all who put themselves in God's benevolent hands could find earthly redemption. Such interpretations found many varied expressions within the orthodox churches as well as without. They were part of the great shift in the Boston churches from Congregationalism to Unitarianism. They were represented in the heretical wranglings within the divinity schools. And they found their most extreme manifestation among little groups of dissidents who, like the ascetic Shakers and the imperturbable Mormons, voiced their personal sanctity.

This enticing religious development of the theme of progress found one of its strongest statements among the groups of rebellious "Perfectionists" which appeared mostly in the northern and eastern parts of the country. In particular, it underlay the belief system of the Oneida community. Oneida Perfectionism taught that the Second Coming of Christ had occurred in 70 A.D. and that since that date all had been in readiness for the eventual perfection of this earthly life. Far more radical than Channing, who simply saw elements of divinity in man's spiritual nature,[5] it assured the individual of perfection by the simple process of accepting Christ into his soul. Such a spiritual apprehension of perfection in no way guaranteed sinless behavior. That required great personal exertion and could reach its ultimate state only in "Bible Communism," that is, in community life as practiced at Oneida.

In 1848, John Humphrey Noyes founded the Oneida community in central New York on a piece of land that not long since had belonged to the Indians. There he joined his own gifts (which were material as well as spiritual) to the farming skills of Perfectionist Jonathan Burt and engendered a community that was to survive.

In moving toward if not actually to the frontier, Noyes followed the American utopians' usual practice. With notable exceptions like Brook Farm, most earlier communities had chosen sites west of central New York and Pennsylvania and east of the Mississippi. These newly opened regions provided inexpensive, readily available land. A few communities like New Harmony bought up vast areas, but normally they were satisfied with about a thousand acres.[6] Certainly they needed land; but perhaps even more they needed freedom and seclusion. The conservative East Coast inhibited innovation and experiment. Farther west no single way of life ruled. Just as the missionary churches could alter worship forms and disregard doctrine with impunity,[7] so the utopians could expect to establish their ideal societies unmolested. To this environment Noyes introduced fifty-one charter members of the Oneida Association.[8] Once settled, they must devise some practical way to implement their lofty, idealistic principles.

Many a community floundered in its heroic efforts to earn its living. A majority, of course, turned to farming, the traditional support of utopia. In their own inimitable fashion the communities joined sides in the general conflict between industry and agriculture. Many decried industrialization. They saw it as a mistaken step in the search for improvement, and attempted to discover a better rural route for themselves. Yet this did not prevent them from incorporating elements of the expanding industrial society. The Sylvania Phalanx, for example, while rejecting the destructiveness of modern industry and city life, sought to supplement its agricultural production with the income from the manufacture of shoes. The Shakers exemplified the inventiveness of their age with ingenious gadgets to core apples or wash sheets more efficiently. They did not hesitate to sell these inventions along with their famous herbs in the markets of the commercial world.

Oneida, unlike so many experiments that have since become footnotes in history, looked to new industrial ideas to create a firm economic base. It must be admitted, too, that the early applicants came well-dowered with worldly proof of God's blessing and contributed some $108,000 in the first nine years of the community's existence.[9] With so much capital on hand the Perfectionists could afford to experiment in the best tradition of the American enterprise. Eventually, they developed a whole repertoire of sources of income. They began by canning and selling farm produce and by operating a saw mill and a flour mill; in time, they added the famous Newhouse animal trap, chain manufacture, silk thread production, and handmade traveling bags. In 1857, after years of austere living and constant work, the community finally began to show a profit.[10] From that time its energetic involvement in the American business world brought increasing prosperity and more than a touch of luxury. Accommodated in the great rambling Mansion House, which was set in spacious, tastefully landscaped grounds, the three hundred Perfectionists supplemented the regular creature-comforts with elaborate theatrical properties, musical instruments, a library of at least a thousand volumes, and even a Swedish bath.

The conflict between agriculture and industry in the nineteenth century was not simply a matter of trees as opposed to buildings, or the plough instead of the shuttles of the cotton loom. It included the vital and often unspoken issue of the relationship between the individual and those forces which directed his life. The new industry threatened to turn man into a suppressed mechanical being powerless to influence how he worked, lived, or played. Automation of the individual and alienation from his surroundings surely could not be the better life that the nineteenth century envisioned.

Many of the experimental communities did not state this issue specifically, yet it is a major inspiration behind the frequent experiments in the organization of work and underlies the whole notion of a communal enterprise. The associations frequently announced that all labor was to be paid for equally. Some, like the North American Phalanx, decreed that the more disagreeable the labor, the more reward one would receive for it. Similarly, the Clarkson Domain used Fourier's classification of jobs as "attractive," "useful," or "necessary" and awarded the most work credits to the least agreeable jobs. New Harmony established its well-known Time Store where one paid for goods in "labor notes." All of the communities, more or less, encouraged the member to participate in decisions—at times to the point of spelling their own ruin because everyone demanded the right to shirk unpleasant labor. Vainly their leaders hoped that moral education would encourage the appropriate motivation and solve the problem. But generally, of course, the community had disintegrated before these latter-day retraining programs were begun.

Members of the Oneida community did not hesitate to declare they could find perfection and happiness in work as well as all other aspects of their lives. They encouraged rotation of tasks, for example, moving people from the laundry department out on to the road for the sales department; and they worked together at "bees" to husk corn for canning or to fill a large order for traps. They also instigated formal measures to insure the individual's participation in community affairs. Each day a meeting of the whole community took place in the Big Hall or the Mansion House. Together they examined their joint endeavors. Topics ranged from the amount of butter served at dinner to a talk by Noyes on communism in the Bible; from how best to maintain good relationships with their neighbors to the merits of opening a New York City agency for the community businesses. In spite of some elements of despotism by Noyes, this system assured the survival of a sense of involvement which was being threatened everywhere by the modern industrial age.

The Perfectionists were eminently successful in their experiments in the new industrialism, but neither material progress nor individual involvement was allowed to dominate their interests as it did some of the industrialists of the age. Like the Horatio Alger heroes, who first appeared in the 1860's, they found material prosperity joined to moral earnestness. Yet the enterprising spirit of these commercial efforts and the successful application of talent that they implied were also a direct consequence of Noyes' teachings. To him, intellectual growth was an integral part of the spiritual improvement that ended with perfection. America at large viewed education as a condition for progress. Jefferson had seen it underlying true democracy. Horace Mann was busy revolutionizing the Massachusetts school system. In Boston, members of the "Charitable Mechanic Association" agreed to employ their "mechanic powers" to "assist the necessitous" and "encourage the ingenious."[11] Throughout the country, Lyceum lecturers fed men's curiosity about this new age and sustained their faith in the overwhelming power of knowledge.[12] In the communities, the numerous Owenite and Fourierist groups echoed their masters' belief in learning, although to survive they often had to forsake intellectual exercise for physical labor.

At Oneida, Noyes had declared that all forms of educational endeavor were necessary to utopia. His *Annual Report* of 1851 found "education [in the general sense] of development under the Spirit of Truth" to be "the central object and inspiration of this Community."[13] The supreme confidence afforded by constant reiteration of the belief in perfection persuaded his followers, individually and collectively, that they could master the modern world's overwhelming discoveries and solve its problems. To achieve this, they must parallel spiritual endeavor with intellectual exercise. The library was assembled and little groups of members set about reading zoology, algebra, French, or phrenology with ingenuous enthusiasm. Eventually some twenty men and women went away at community expense for medical and scientific training at Yale University and musical studies in New York City.

In the context of this sanguine exploration in the new world of science we can understand why the Perfectionists should adopt the belief that maladies of the body as well as the soul could be healed by faith. The notion, which had been a recurrent theme throughout the centuries, lay in the fertile ground between the new religious ideas and the new faith in science. Everywhere "Mesmerists" investigated the role of hypnotism in this mysterious power of the mind to control the ailments of the body. Later in the century, Mary Baker Eddy's Christian Science would link the notion with Christianity and establish a new church. Eventually, the psychologists would discard for the most part both religion and the trance and teach the mind to heal itself. But mid-nineteenth-century America was still, above all, Bible-reading and religiously-oriented. It was logical, then, that mental healing should be an integral part of Perfectionist doctrine.

While it was always part of Oneida's credo that disease represented some form of lapse from moral perfection, it is also significant that the community did not hesitate to add the resources of science to religion when faith proved inadequate. "Mutual criticism" by one's fellow Perfectionists and the "spiritual bath" of self-scrutiny and self-confession were not entirely successful in quieting the fever of diphtheria victims or in stifling children's winter sneezes. Noyes responded by sending his eldest son, Theodore, to train as a physician. Eventually, therefore, Oneida offered a faith that could conquer human ills, but backed it up with secular knowledge.

Throughout the century, the same spirit of exploration and expectation of easy success was found in the widespread interest in diet. Here, whatever his experience, a man could readily experiment with his own notions and glimpse a vision of a panacea for human sickness. Vegetarianism and Graham diets were very popular in the communities. Prairie Home and the Skaneateles Community abjured meat and stimulants. Brook Farm had its Grahamite table. Almost universally the utopias joined with the temperance organizations in their denunciation of alcohol. At Oneida, an austere diet was at first a necessity. Later such limitations remained as an adjunct to spiritual improvement and physical well-being. Though the Mansion House visitor might balk at strawberry-leaf tea, he still ate the vegetarian meals wtih a hearty appetite.

Such experiments in the organization of work, education, diet, and faith healing, and such innovations in religious belief were, as H. G. Wells said, one "part of a vast system of questioning and repudiations, political doubts, social doubts, hesitating inquiries."[14] When we, in turn, wonder why anyone inside or outside a utopian community should see these as reasonable experiments, we judge from beyond the limited perspective of the nineteenth-century man. His was a time when the sum of knowledge, though vast, could seemingly be collected and analyzed by one person if he be a Spencer or a Hegel. One expected to find scientific, social, philosophical, and literary knowledge himself, for belief in the possibility of becoming a cosmopolitan man was not yet shaken by the realization that in knowledge, too, there must be a division of labor. And it was within this context, without today's hindsight, that any potential convert would listen to the words of the founder of Oneida or any other community.

Noyes himself could produce impressive qualifications. Coming from a socially prominent family in Putney, Vermont, he had the kind of education at Dartmouth and later at Andover and Yale which lent his words authority for the intelligent but relatively untaught and uncritical farmers and artisans he selected for Oneida.[15] To these worldly qualifications was added a personal endowment that would inspire confidence in any age. He was not only intellectually superior, but also a physically impressive man, possessing charisma for men and women, adept at promoting an atmosphere at once of fellowship and challenge.

It is easy to say that Noyes' capacity to inspire confidence, combined with the peculiarities of his own psychological makeup, account for the sexual experiments that have brought Oneida lasting fame. But even sexual matters could not escape the scrutiny of the age. Whitman's "Song of Myself" celebrated the body and appealed for an enlarged sense of appreciation. Certainly, the majority preferred Longfellow's gentility to Whitman's sensuousness, but these new ideas, like those of women's rights, were not without influential sympathizers.

In the communities such issues found their usual varied expression. Most frequently they followed the example of the North American Phalanx and incorporated equal rights for women into their constitution. The Northampton Association committed itself to equal pay for both sexes, as well as all occupations. Elsewhere, more extreme views prevailed. Josiah Warren of the Modern Times community was forced to admit that "individual sovereignty" might imply free love. Because outsiders frequently associated sexual experiment with the communities, poor Fanny Wright heard her interracial experiment designed to educate freed slaves designated a "free love colony."[16] At the other extreme were the celibate Rappites and the Shaker "families" whose soulless regimen of mechanical detail drained the sisters' and brothers' lives of humor, joy, and self-expression.

The Oneida community made the most remarkable of the innovations in family life when it introduced "complex marriage" and "stirpiculture." Like the Mormons in their practice of polygamy, the Oneida Perfectionists made complex marriage an integral part of their religious and social system. For Noyes, monogamy was a form of spiritual tyranny wherein "men and women have the power to debar each other from the rights of conscience, and the enjoyment of their religious faith."[17] Exclusive attachment, or the selfish possession of another, unfitted the person aspiring to perfection from practicing a cardinal social-religious ideal, loving his neighbors without discrimination. Further, conventional monogamy in these antebellum years was denigrated by Noyes as a form of slavery. So was excessive childbearing. Women were to be freed from its burdens and the number of children born controlled by the practice of "male continence," a process also carefully detailed by Noyes.[18] Under appropriate controls the delights of "amative" intercourse were to replace the responsibilities of "propagative" intercourse.

This particular version of marriage lasted about thirty years, not so long as that of the Mormons, who lived secluded on the distant frontier, but long enough to allow Oneida to conduct a daring experiment in eugenics. At a period when Charles Darwin and Francis Galton were influencing intellectuals everywhere, Noyes (and Oneida) determined to try out their ideas. With a superior inheritance, the hope of perfection would be even brighter. Stirpiculture was a concerted effort to select those couples whose spiritual and physical qualities most fitted them to reproduce. Members of the community signed an agreement to abide by the decision of a committee as to who should conceive the stirpicults, and between 1869 and 1879 fifty-eight children were born at Oneida.[19]

From sexual matters to educational reform, Oneida explored the *avant-garde* ideas of its time. Obviously neither they nor any other communal experiment embraced every new idea. Some groups sought to improve man's mind, others to change only his environment; some sought individual expression, others immoderate conformity; some saw the ideal society in terms of an advance to modern industrialism, more wanted a retreat to earlier forms of production; and, again, some believed happiness involved activity, personal involvement, and the realization of unknown potential, whereas others grafted a notion of perfection to elements of a Puritan past and saw it as activity without involvement and regulation without the joy of self-determination. At Oneida such ideas were expressed in new interpretations of Christianity, educational reform, varied work routines, joint decision-making, dietary experiments, faith healing, complex marriage, and the stirpiculture experiment. In other communities their difference manifestations must have bewildered the fledgling utopian in search of the ideal society. Yet, behind this confusion of practices we see the basic rationality of the nineteenth-century utopia. The community was a logical place to develop several admired social themes, from spiritual improvement to stolid practicality. Some other age would deem the venture foolhardy, but nineteenth-century America justifiably believed in the reality of the utopian vision.

For one reason or another, most communities were fated to disappear by the end of the century.[20] Since then, the supply of replacements has diminished severely. A Bruderhof community flourishes in Connecticut. Koinonia, a small interracial group, lives in Christian charity and constant threat of violence in Americus, Georgia. A West Coast group may ask a social scientist's help in plannning a Pacific island utopia. We admire such valiant fortitude but see these ventures as belonging no more to the intellectual frontier than to the geographical frontier. When we survey the bizarre quasi-religious cults that still manage to find something of the frontier's seclusion in rural California, we feel even more convinced that, today, the utopian community is an anomaly, a curious revival of a dead tradition.[21]

The history of the Oneida community between 1880 and the present day illustrates the twentieth-century fate of utopia. Struggling to retain its old idealism, Oneida re-explored the social aspects of community life. Radical changes have since eliminated dreams out of keeping with the present age without removing every element of utopia.

The major reconstruction came about at the end of 1880. As John Humphrey Noyes grew older, his command faltered. In 1879 internal troubles flared. These, it seemed, could be solved only by the exchange of complex marriage for ordinary monogamous relationships and, a month or two later, by the withdrawal from common ownership of property. A joint-stock company, the Oneida Community, Limited, was formed. After each member received his portion, he could either depart to the outside world or stay on in the Mansion House and work for a salary in the community industries. Local outsiders who had long been employed in non-supervisory positions continued in their regular jobs with scarcely any change of routine. With Noyes then in retirement in Canada, his place taken by an official Board of Directors, and with disillusionment complete among the younger persons, it seemed that soon there would be nothing more utopian about Oneida than the Victorian Gothic of its great Mansion House.

The final rout of utopia was averted by one of the founder's stirpiculture children, Pierrepont Burt Noyes. In 1899 he led a successful proxy fight to rescue the company from the hands of a party of Perfectionists-turned-Spiritualists. Once in effective control, he scoured the country for able contemporaries who had left, lured them back with his design for a new utopia, and set about remodeling both the business and the idealism so that both might survive. Noyes introduced his new utopian vision to an established organization. Oneida had become a modern business with a management-owned capital investment of over half a million dollars. Without this financial backing Noyes could never have developed for Oneida Community plate a reputation to surpass that of the old community's animal trap. At the end of the nineteenth century, and certainly in the mid-twentieth century, few nascent communities could hope to produce capital on the scale required for financial independence. Noyes' contribution to the business proved more permanent than his vision of utopia. Even so, the new idealism he introduced to Oneida began to fade only in the 1940's.

Before P. B. Noyes took over in 1899, the areas in which perfection was envisioned had, one by one, been rejected; and the patent on their exploration had, in effect, been turned over to someone else. The belief that Oneida could discover ultimate religious truth was effectively quashed at the breakup. So, too, the members lost their sublime faith in complex marriage and the practicality of the stirpiculture experiment. The community never tried to repeat such ventures. Its members, like us, understood too much about the intricacies of man's psychological makeup to argue the superiority of complex marriage. Similarly, neither they nor we could pretend that a new stirpiculture scheme would improve the quality of their descendants. Eugenic change is vastly more complex than the ingenuous Perfectionists realized. In the area of education, too, there was no hope of competition with the universities and research centers of modern America.

Noyes admitted the inevitability of such changes. Under his guidance, Oneida continued to illustrate this process of the dissolution of utopia as it resigns its functions to experts, as it joins the affairs and assumes the ways of the outside society. He saw that, without the excitement and stimulation of the utopia's challenge, isolation would make Oneida a placid but enervating backwater. Consequently, everyone was perfectly free to come and go as he chose. Children attended local public schools before going to college. Those few persons who wished to do so frequented the local churches, and everyone used the stores and recreational facilities of the area roundabout. In the community itself, individual houses were built on the sites of the old orchard and vineyard so that families with growing children could enjoy more privacy. This restricted residential area, called Kenwood, seemed to borrow from the dominating Mansion House a dignity not found "on the other side of the bridge" in Sherrill.

Oneida was no longer a miniature ideal society. The grandeur of the nineteenth-century utopian spirit was irretrievable. Theologians must inquire into religious truths, the Deweys and Conants search for educational reform, and the new scientific empires direct our technological progress. Intellectual independence was no more possible than economic self-sufficiency. But, in keeping with the growing specialization of the time, Oneida could incorporate a limited number of utopian elements.

The first was a legitimate twentieth-century descendant of the nineteenth-century concept now discovered in the "garden city" idea. Introduced by English planners such as Ebenezer Howard and Patrick Geddes, it is still a central concern for such people as Percival and Paul Goodman,[22] and it has stimulated the creation of such communities as Greenbelt, near Washington, D.C. Such schemes contrast our segmented lives in supposedly dreary urban environments with the hope of an integrated life in beautiful surroundings where land use is controlled by human as well as economic criteria. These modern utopians see their plans as part of the reconstruction of our present society. For them the rainbow ends at home.

The new Oneida inherited from the old community just such advantages as many a town planner might wish. Tucked away in the rolling hills of central New York, the sales office and Kenwood formed a single unit wherein work and social relationships overlapped. Should such a rural idyl become tedious, Utica and Syracuse were within thirty miles and, for longer trips, the Midland railroad had a stop some five miles from Mansion House.

Another modern theme that lends itself to incorporation in a specialized utopia appears in the disparate threads of the cooperative movement. In the United States the ideas of the Rochdale pioneers have been transferred to a rural setting by the farmers' cooperatives of the western states. The more radical idea of producers' cooperatives is represented in the occasional effort in communal farming.[23] But economic cooperation, which has been less popular here than in Europe, has generally assumed a severely vitiated form. However, Oneida experimented with this idea also. Just as Kenwood was almost a ready-made, miniature garden city, so the company was already a cooperative endeavor. Ex-members and, later, their descendants owned most of the stock. Together with a few "outsiders" who had been brought into management posts, they were, at least until the 1930's, in complete control of the company. This meant that for the officials, for the retired members of management, and for their families the exigencies of the Oneida Community, Limited, were a vital concern. Their daily lives revolved around its operation and they depended on it for a livelihood.

P. B. Noyes used the peculiar situational circumstances that made Oneida a home, a family, and a heritage to extend its objectives beyond mere economic cooperation. He incorporated there an element missing from most of our present-day notions of utopia; a sense of personal involvement that, in its most idealistic form, allows the individual self-realization and gives him the power to influence his own destiny. Under Noyes, a new "team spirit" was devised, and the wrangling of the years following the breakup of the old community was replaced by a free exchange of ideas, interpersonal frankness, and mutual trust. He created a group of lighthearted, responsible men and women who worked together enthusiastically for the economic and the social good of the whole community.

Such a truly cooperative spirit could not survive if social distinctions were to fracture the unity of the two hundred or more members of management and their families in Kenwood. At Oneida there was, wrote Noyes in 1909, an unwritten constitution which proclaimed a "reasonable equality of wealth; a reasonable equality of opportunity; and a reasonable equality of power."[24] In Kenwood social distinctions were to be minimized. Salaries in management, unlike those in the factory, were to be held down because this would buttress the effort to make Kenwood life simple and unpretentious. Empty status-seeking pleasures, like the urgent acquisition of oriental rugs and antique furniture, were to lose out in favor of creative activities, simple social events, and individual efforts at self-development. Not that life would be Spartan; there would be waiters in the Mansion House dining room and modern conveniences in the separate homes scattered roundabout, but these were physical comforts, not psychological props. Self-respect was to come from the development of the inner man.

This theme of self-realization, so common in the nineteenth-century communities, is also echoed today throughout the larger society but without convincing expression. When a sociologist studying job satisfaction suggests that workers should realize goals of their own, he is concerned with one aspect of the issue.[25] A similar theme appears in the trade unions' gropings toward something more than increased wage rates and better working conditions. From another viewpoint, chiefly that of management, it is recognizable in the occasional, usually abortive, experiment with industrial profit-sharing. In Europe, the problem is conceptualized rather more distinctly as, for instance, by André Philip and the French Personalistic Socialists.[26] Some of their ideas are incorporated in the modern French utopias, the communities of work.[27]

The communities of work, like Oneida under P. B. Noyes, focus on a few aspects of utopia. They devote themselves to the question of self-realization and self-determination of the industrial worker. Oneida, however, was primarily concerned with cooperation and involvement in management. Yet it did make serious efforts to include the factory workers in the modern utopia. Early in the century P. B. Noyes envisioned the extension of "our society" from "the original two hundred [in Kenwood] to include the entire 2,000 who are working together toward a common end."[28] In effect he achieved this goal. Work hours were reduced, pay scales increased, pensions, profit-sharing, and "war service" wages introduced; a welfare department and recreational facilities were added; and bonuses were awarded to employees who built their own homes. The town of Sherrill became, and still is, a model community with scarcely a dilapidated house to be found. But utopia for the factory employees lacked the involvement that added such zest to the affairs of management. Everything from wages to street names in Sherrill was given to the employees by a highly paternalistic company. And in the plant, cooperation was a one-sided affair; although all were able to communicate quite freely, the power to act rested almost entirely in the hands of the company officials.

Noyes' reforms in the Oneida factory are less central to our discussion than the reforms he had instituted in Kenwood. There he saw that the old Oneida was outmoded. No community could justify changing every aspect of its members' lives. Instead it must focus on a few areas. Consequently, Noyes offered Kenwood residents an active, congenial social life in a pleasant physical setting and the chance to make a vital contribution to the affairs of both the company and the community. Moreover, echoing his father's admonitions, he urged the exercise of the intellect and cultivation of the inner man.

Although Oneida preserved these few aspects of the older utopia, the earlier vision's brilliance had faded. So also did the visions of other Americans. It is true that during the final decades of the last century the experiment and literary utopia remained a popular expression of reformers' idealism. Some twenty-eight communities were founded between 1880 and 1900,[29] and the visionary schemes of Bellamy and more than forty other writers were greeted enthusiastically.[30] Yet the principles of cooperation and socialism which they advocated never applied immediately to the larger American scene. Only in the twentieth century did would-be reformers break with the older utopian tradition and turn to the slow transformation of that creaking, infinitely complex, but apparently viable society to which they must belong. Today we find few significant experimental communities in action. A different hope stirs men's imagination. The themes of improvement, practicality, and individual endeavor can rarely be embodied in a communal enterprise. Throughout the world we discover an amazing array of alternative blue-prints for living. Which one of us can decide the best? And who, in the face of so many natural experiments, can hope to devise one better? Toward what should we direct our change when imperfections seem to riddle every society?

We are no longer sure that the future is ours. Nature's complexity is overwhelming. Those very sciences through which we look for under-standing have wrought mortal blows to the hope of perfection. The seeds of pragmatism are well rooted in our twentieth-century minds. We see no single truth, but several, no one kingdom of heaven, but several.[31] Protestantism, whose radicals once offered hope of imminent perfection, now finds the questioning theologian tentatively wondering whether utopia is to be found at home. In his book, *Honest to God*, the Bishop of Woolwich asks whether "God" and "heaven" should be conceived of as something beyond us, divorced from our secular activi-ties. Perhaps, he suggests, the Christian life might yet be seen as holy worldliness, sacred secularity.[32]

These new conceptions of man's hopes are not without some expecta-tion of human progress, for the fragmentation of utopia directs our attention to other types of improvement. We promote new educational schemes, programs for integration, trade union activity, social security programs; a presidential commision studies woman-power; and the Peace Corps is imitated at home and abroad. Our attention is fixed on the existing society, no longer diverted by the notion of the utopian community.

The shift of utopia to a national scale has one other significance. As we inevitably delegate the search for improvement to specialized groups like city planners and industrial consultants, we risk imposing utopia upon the resident of the garden city or the factory worker. Thus new visions of reform resemble those of the earliest writers on utopia. They thrust utopia on the masses and try to change man from without. Less often, they encourage man to change himself. And yet, ultimately, only he can develop that inner self which Alcott called "the living spirit within the soul."[33] . . .

REFERENCES

[1] Frederick A. BUSHEE, "Communistic Societies in the United States," *Political Science Quarterly*, Vol. XX (1905), p. 625.

[2] John Humphrey NOYES, *History of American Socialisms* (New York: Hillary House, 1961), reprint of the 1870 edition, p. 213.

[3] John Addington SYMONDS, "A Vista," in *New and Old; A Volume of Verse* (Boston: James R. Osgood and Company, 1880), pp. 226–227.

[4] The information presented here on the Oneida community is part of a larger study which analyzes the community's development from 1848 to the present. Much of the description of the modern Oneida given in the second half of the paper is based upon first-hand interviews with present residents.

[5] William E. CHANNING, "Likeness to God: Discourse at the Ordination of the Rev. F. A. Farley," *Works of William E. Channing* (Boston: America Unitarian Association, 1877), pp. 291–302.

[6] NOYES, *op. cit.*, p. 19.

[7] Whitney R. CROSS, *The Burned-over District; The Social and Intellectual History of Enthusiastic Religion in Western New York, 1800–1850* (Ithaca: Cornell University Press, 1950), pp. 104–109.

[8] Data from unpublished manuscript, "Oneida Association Family Register," presently in the library of the Mansion House, Oneida, New York.

[9] *Handbook of the Oneida Community, 1875* (Oneida, New York: Office of the *Oneida Circular* [1875?]), p. 15.

[10] *Ibid.*

[11] *Constitution of the Massachusetts Charitable Mechanic Association* (Boston: George C. Rand and Avery, 1861), p. 7.

[12] Carl BODE, *The American Lyceum: Town Meeting of the Mind* (New York: Oxford University Press, 1956).

[13] *Third Annual Report of the Oneida Association* (Oneida Reserve: Leonard and Company, 1851), p. 22.

[14] H. G. WELLS, *New Worlds for Old* (Chicago: M. A. Donahue and Company, 1907), p. 207.

[15] In 1849, the eighty-seven members of the Association included only three ex-ministers and one lawyer among those who might be presumed to have some formal education. "Oneida Association Family Register," *loc. cit.*

[16] BODE, *op. cit.* p. 127.

[17] [John Humphrey NOYES], *Slavery and Marriage* (n.p., 1850), p. 12. (Italics omitted).

[18] John Humphrey NOYES, *Male Continence*, 1st ed. (Oneida, New York: Office of the *Oneida Circular*, 1872). Between 1848 and 1869 there were probably about a dozen accidental conceptions.

[19] Hilda Herrick NOYES and George Wallingford NOYES, "The Oneida Community Experiment in Stirpiculture," *Eugenics, Genetics, and the Family*, Vol. 1. Scientific Papers of the Second International Congress of Eugenics, 1921 (Baltimore: Williams and Wilkins Company, 1923), p. 280.

[20] Why some failed, while the rare exception like Oneida survived, is beyond the scope of this paper. It has been suggested that the Shakers' celibacy resulted

in an inevitable dwindling of their numbers, that many Owenite and Fourierist groups were not selective enough in choosing their members so that incompetents and potential troublemakers proved ultimately disruptive, that some failed to insure a means of economic survival through times of panic as well as prosperity (What could have been expected of Brook Farm in this respect when Hawthorne was the head of the Finance Committee?). Some could not achieve a successful transfer of power from the original charismatic leader to the inevitable successor.

[21] Robert V. HINE, *California's Utopian Communities* (San Marino, California: Huntington Library, 1953), especially Chapter IX.

[22] Percival and Paul GOODMAN, *Communitas: Means of Livelihood and Ways of Life* (Chicago: University of Chicago Press, 1947).

[23] Henrik F. INFIELD, *Utopia and Experiment: Essays in the Sociology of Cooperation* (New York: Frederick A. Praeger, 1955), pp. 66–93.

[24] P. B. NOYES, "Basswood Philosophy, III," *Quadrangle,* Vol. II (1909), pp. 10–11.

[25] A. ZALEZNIK, C. R. CHRISTENSEN, and F. J. ROETHLISBERGER, *The Motivation, Productivity, and Satisfaction of Workers; A Prediction Study* (Boston: Harvard University Graduate School of Business Administration, 1958), pp. 421–422.

[26] André PHILIP, *La démocratie industrielle* (Paris: Presses Universitaires de France, 1955).

[27] INFIELD, *op. cit.,* p. 198. Claire Huchet Bishop, *All Things Common* (New York: Harpers, 1950). Albert Meister, *Quelques aspects méthodologiques de la recherche sociologique dans les associations volontaires et les groupes cooperatifs* (Unpublished manuscript, Harvard Graduate School of Business Administration, 1960).

[28] "Texts of Speeches given at Sixteenth Annual Banquet," *Quadrangle,* Vol. VII (1914), p. 17.

[29] BUSHEE, *op. cit.,* pp. 663–664.

[30] Allyn B. FORBES, "The Literary Quest for Utopia, 1880–1900," *Social Forces,* Vol. VI (1927), pp. 188–189.

[31] Joyce Oramel HERTZLER, *The History of Utopian Thought* (New York: Macmillan Company, 1923), pp. 312–314. Arthur E. Morgan, *Nowhere and Somewhere; How History Makes Utopias and How Utopias Makes History* (Chapel Hill: University of North Carolina Press, 1946), p. 184.

[32] John A. T. ROBINSON, *Honest to God* (Philadelphia: Westminister Press, 1963), p. 101.

[33] Edith Roelkler CURTIS, *A Season in Utopia: The Story of Brook Farm* (New York: Thomas Nelson and Sons, 1961), p. 137.

C.
The Millennial Dream

4.

PURSUIT OF THE MILLENNIUM: THE RELATION BETWEEN RELIGIOUS AND SOCIAL CHANGE (1962)

Yonina Talmon

II

Perhaps the most important thing about millenarism is its *attitude towards time*. It views time as a linear process which leads to a final future. There is a fullness of time and end of days which will bring about a decisive consummation of all history. The millennium is not necessarily limited to a thousand years; it symbolises the meta-historical future in which the world will be inhabited by a humanity liberated from all the limitations of human existence, redeemed from pain and transience, from fallibility and sin, thus becoming at once perfectly good and perfectly happy. The world will be utterly, completely and irrevocably changed. Radical millenarian movements regard the millenium as imminent and live in tense expectation and preparation for it.

Coupled with this emphasis on the apocalyptic future is the equally radical rejection of the present as totally evil and abysmally corrupt.

SOURCE. Authorized reproduction in abridged form from *The European Journal of Sociology,* II (1962), pp. 130–144.

The transition from the present into the final future is not a gradual process of progressive approximation to the final goal. It is a sudden and revolutionary leap onto a totally different level of existence. Sometimes this transformation is expected to occur suddenly and miraculously without a preparatory struggle. Yet more often than not we find that the new dispensation is born out of unprecedented cataclysms, diastrous upheavals and bloody calamities. The apocalyptic victory will be won by means of a prodigious and final struggle which will destroy the agents of corruption, purge the sinful world and prepare it for its final redemption. Millenarism is thus basically a merger between an historical and a non-historical concept of time. Historical change leads to a cessation of all change. Divine will is made manifest and realized in the historical process, yet its final consummation will come in a mythical millennium which is the end of all history.

Millenarism is a forward-looking, future-oriented religious ideology. However, while its attitude to the present is outrightly and radically negative, its attitude to the past is more ambivalent. The rejection of the present usually includes the near and often the more distant past as well. Millenarism usually has a strong anti-traditional component and preparation for the millennium has often entailed a ritualised overthrow of traditional norms. Primitive millenarian movements have engaged in a breaking of hallowed taboos and in a desecration of their most valued religious symbols, thus dissociating themselves from their traditional culture. Their main concern was often not the perpetuation or revival of their indigenous tradition but the birth of a new order. Yet this strong anti-past orientation is often mitigated when the millennium is envisaged as a return of a mythical golden age. When the millennium is regarded as a paradise regained, those elements of tradition which are viewed as embedded in it, become also components of the new order. By establishing a connection between the meta-historical past and the meta-historical future, the millenarian movement can be radically change-oriented yet incorporate traditional elements in its view of the final future.

Another important characteristic of millenarian movements is their view of salvation as a *merger of the spiritual with the terrestrial*. The millenarian view of salvation is transcendent and immanent at the same time. The heavenly city is to appear on earth. It is in this world that the saints, the elect, or the chosen people will experience the blessing, not as ethereal saints. Millenarism offers not an other-worldly hope but the fulfilment of divine purpose in a new universe and a new social order. This terrestrial emphasis is more or less evident in all the millenarian movements. In its crudest and more extreme form we encounter it in the Cargo Cults. The core of these cults is a belief that the culture hero, the devil or the spirit of the dead will return in some mechanical means of transportation such as aeroplanes, lorries or ships, loaded with a cargo of imported goods. The cargo has been made in heaven for the use of the natives, but the white men have diverted it from them. The return of the cargo to its rightful owners will bring about an era of universal plenty and happiness. The natives will be liberated from alien domination once and all and will be completely exempt from all the ills of human existence. Yet even in such a down to earth and materialistic conception of the millennium there is a more or less strong spiritual ingredient. The new order will be also a new moral order based on justice, peace and cooperation.

Closely connected with the former characteristic is the *collective orientation* of millenarism. The aim of millenarian movements is not only the salvation of individual souls but the erection of a heavenly city for a chosen people. The millenarian message is directed to an already existing group or calls for a formation of new groups of elect. It views these groups as divinely appointed bearers of the good tiding and calls on them to prepare for the imminent advent. The group is more or less collectively responsible and will enjoy the wonderful future awaiting it as a group.

What is the *role of the group in bringing about the advent?* There are many variations in this respect. Movements of this type range from the fairly passive and quietist on the one hand, to the extremely activist and aggressive on the other. There are certain elements in the millenarian ideology which work against an outrightly active definition of the role of the follower. The followers of these movements are not makers of the revolution; they expect it to be brought about miraculously from above. Ultimately, initiative and actual power to bring about change rest with divine powers. All millenarian movements share a fundamental vagueness about the actual way in which the new order will be brought about, expecting it to happen somehow by direct divine intervention. In many millenarian movements the part of the people before the change is to gather together, to watch the signs of the inevitable advent, to engage in measures of ritual preparation and purify themselves. Yet there is a strong activist militant ingredient in the millenarian ideology which more often than not outweighs the passive elements in it. Most of the radical millenarian movements define the role of the follower much more actively. In such movements, the believers have the power to hasten and retard salvation. In some cases the advent cannot come to pass without the active help of the elect. Since the vision of redemption is both transcendent and terrestrial, paving the way for it often entails the employment of both ritual and secular measures. Since the onset of the millennium is more often than not viewed as entailing a final struggle, the followers pit themselves against the powers of evil. The hope of a total and imminent salvation which will be brought about by divine powers with the active support and help of the elect throws such movements into spells of hectic and often rebellious activity. The millenarian vision instils in the movement a sense of extreme urgency and a dedication to an all-embracing purpose. Every minute and every deed count and everything must be sacrificed to the cause. The followers are driven to stake everything and spare nothing since their aim is no less than the final solution of all human problems. It would seem that the combination of the historical and the meta-historical in the millennial time conception, the vision of the unification of the transcendent and the terrestrial in a completely transformed and holy social order, the merger between individual and social destinies, coupled with a total rejection of the existing order and a view of an imminent final struggle have a powerful revolutionary potential. No wonder that in most of the movements described in these studies the millenarian ideology has precipitated and instigated active revolt against the established authorities. Comparative analysis seems to indicate that, generally speaking, the more extremely millenarian a movement is the more activist it is. As Worsley has pointed out, there seems to be a correlation between the time conception of each movement and its position in the *passivity-activity continuum*. Movements which view the millennium as imminent and have a total and vivid conception of redemption are, on the whole, much more activist than movements which expect it to happen at some remote date and consequently tend to have a more partial and rather pale conception of the millennium. It would seem that truly great expectations and a sense of immediacy enhance the orientation to active rebellion while postponement of the critical date and lesser expectation breed passivity and quietism.

This generalisation holds more or less true when examined in the material on pre-modern and primitive movements. It has to be modified to some extent with regard to such movements in modern societies. The Christadelphians have a radical millenarian ideology. They live in tense expectation of an imminent and total redemption. They rigorously oppose the social order as totally depraved and view its present difficulties with vindictiveness. Yet their attitudes are not translated into direct action against it. They defied the authorities in the matter of conscription to the army and stuck to their opposition to service in the armed forces. However, they did not oppose the authorities on other matters and did not engage in active rebellion against the established order. They have kept aloof from the world. Tense, impatient and vindictive, they await the divinely appointed time of its down fall. The same seems to be more or less true for other modern millenarian movements such as the Seventh Day Adventist and Jehovah's Witnesses.[1] Wilson hints that modern millenarian movements are less rebellious than their counterparts elsewhere mainly because there are very slender chances for successful rebellion in a modern society. He feels, however, that internal pressures towards militancy are so strong in such a movement that were a revolt at all feasible the Christadelphians would have pitted themselves against the social order and tried to overthrow it.

Most millenarian movements are *messianic*. Redemption is brought about by a messiah who mediates between the divine and the human. Most important, of course, is the figure of Jesus, but there are other figures as well. In many of the medieval movements redemption is brought about by the sleeping monarch who comes to life again and rescues his people. In primitive societies, the messiah is the culture hero or a departed leader who was persecuted and put to death by the authorities. Often it is a multiple messiah seen in the form of the spirits of the dead ancestors. Another important mediator between the divine and the movement is the *leader*. Inspired leaders who claimed to be appointed by divine powers have played an extremely important role in these movements. Sometimes these prophetic figures move from mere prophecy to become messianic incarnations of divine leadership, but more often than not the figure of the messiah and the figure of the leader remain distinct. Leaders act as precursors of the messiah and as his prophets by announcing the good tidings. They develop their special brand of millenarism by emphasising millenarian elements in their traditional culture and by seizing upon millenarian elements in the cultures which impinge on them. They interpret the millenial traditions and vulgarise them, combining disparate elements and systematising. They supply their followers with secondary exegesis when their hopes fail to materialise. They teach the new ritual and preach the new moral code. They organise their followers and lead them in preparation for the advent.

Inspired and energetic leaders have played such an important role in some of the millenarian movements that when they lost their drive or died, the movements they initiated and organized disintegrated almost immediately. Yet it should be stressed that in many cases leaders func-

---

[1] Jehovah's Witnesses have a more extreme rejection of the existing social order and have engaged in a more active struggle against the authorities. Cf. R. Pike, *Jehovah's Witnesses* (London 1954), also H. H. Stroup, *The Jehovah's Witnesses* (New York 1945).

tion as a symbolic focus of identification rather than as sources of authority and initiative. In some regions, millenarism is an endemic force
and when it reaches a flash-point it may seize upon any available figure.
The initiative in such case comes primarily from the community which
sometimes almost imposes the leadership position on its leader. Some
of the leaders are in fact insignificant and their elevation to such a
position seems to be accidental—they happened to be there and fulfilled
an urgent need for a mediator.[2] That the function of leadership is sometimes primarily symbolic is clearly seen in the cases of movements with
absent leaders. In some notable instances the influence of a leader and
his integrating power have increased enormously after he left or was
removed from his scene of operations. Death, imprisonment or mysterious
absence have increased their stature and enhanced their authority. Only
when absent did they begin to loom large as powerful prophetic figures.

Often there is also not just one charismatic leader but a multiple
leadership. First, we find in a number of instances a division of leadership between the organiser who is concerned with practical matters
and the inspired prophet. Secondly, the movements are sometimes based
on loyalty to leaders on the local level and do not have an overall
leadership. Moreover, the strong fissiparous tendencies which operate in
most of these movements work against attempts at unification of leadership. Millenarian movements suffer from frequent cessation and fission
partly because they base their recruitment of their leaders on inspiration.
A revelatory basis of recruitment facilitates the emergence of numerous
leaders and prophets since many may claim divine inspiration. That
this is only a partial explanation is suggested by the fact that millenarian
movements seem to suffer from fissiparous tendencies more than religious
movements with an equally inspirational leadership. It seems that millenarian movements are particularly prone to fissions because they
preach rebellion against authority and probably attract rebellious non-
conformist and contentious people. The denial of authority seems to
be a factor in perpetuating internecine strife. The fissiparous tendency
is particularly strong in radical but non-active movements. The attempt
to arouse and canalise rebellious feelings but to postpone active rebellion
until some future occasion resulted in the case of the Christadelphians
in the turning of rebelliousness inwards and in a proliferation of leaders.

Organisationally, millenarian movements vary from the amorphous
and ephemeral movement with a cohesive core of leaders and ardent
followers and a large ill-defined body of followers, to the fairly stable
segregated and exclusive sect-like group. The organisational form of

[2] Cf. K. Burridge, *Mambu* (London 1960), pp. 203–207, 254–259; also his "Cargo
cult activity in Tangu," *Oceania*, XXIV (1954), 241–244.

a more or less ephemeral movement is, however, more typical. This is no doubt closely related to the nature of the millenarian message. The promise of an imminent and total redemption awakes enthusiastic hopes and sweeps a large number of followers into the movement. However, its source of strength is also its source of weakness—by promising an imminent delivery and sometimes even fixing a definite date, it brings its own downfall. When the appointed day or period passes without any spectacular happenings or with not the right apocalyptic events, the movement faces a serious crisis which often disrupts and even disperses it completely.

The crisis of non-materialisation of the millennium is a severe one but it need not always lead to disruption.[3] In some notable cases the failure of prophecy did not cause disaffection and immediate disintegration. The commitment to the promise of a millennium was so intense that the shock of temporary disappointment could not shatter it. Paradoxically, non-materialization was followed in these cases by a burst of vigorous proselytizing activities and drew the believers together. These movements are sometimes able to develop a body of exegesis which accounts for the delay and keeps the hope alive. A frequent solution is the switch from a short-range radical millenarism to a long-range and more or less attenuated version of it. Another solution is refraining from fixing any definite date but still keeping the hope of a speedy delivery in full force. Wilson's study of the Christadelphians proves that such a solution is feasible and can work for a considerable length of time without serious modification of the original doctrine. Hobsbawn shows that radical millenarism has become a permanent though periodically dormant force in Andalusia for more than seventy years, suffering reversal after reversal yet flaring up again and again. The recurrent revival of the movement follows an almost cyclical pattern; the millennial outbursts follow one another after approximately a ten-year interval. Similar though not as cyclical patterns of disruption and revival can be observed in the medieval material as well as in Melanesia and Africa. Sometimes there is a hidden continuity between the different phases of the movement. When the millenarian movement suffers a reverse, it goes under cover. It remains underground until it sees a better chance for its struggle, repeatedly hiding or going out into the open but retaining its radical millenarism. It should be stressed, however, that often there is hardly any direct connection between what may seem

---

[3] See L. Festinger, H. W. Riecken and S. Schachter, *When Prophecy Fails* (Minneapolis 1956).

to be recurrent phases of the self-same movement. Continuation of similar conditions often breeds similar yet independent reactions. In many cases, there is no direct influence or any continuity of either tradition or personnel between the different movements.

Most millenarian movements are *highly emotional*. With the exception of the Christadelphians who discourage emotional release in any form and emphasise exegesis, exhortation and doctrine, almost all the other movements involve wild and very often frenzied emotional display. In many instances we encounter hysterical and paranoid phenomena—mass possession, trances, fantasies. The emotional tension manifests itself in motor phenomena such as twitching, shaking and convulsions which have swiftly spread through wide areas. Closely related to the high emotional tension is a strong antinomian tendency. Millenarian movements deliberately break accepted taboos and overthrow hallowed norms. They engage in many ritualised forms of sin and sacrilege. Sexual aberrations in the form of either extreme ascetism or sexual excess are very common as well. There is often unbridled expression of aggression. Members of such movements have swept over the country, devastating, burning and massacring on their way. Sometimes aggression is turned inwards: the members destroy their own property and even commit mass suicide.

III

What are the *conditions which give rise to* such movements and in which *social groups are they anchored?* The data clearly support the frequently posited relationship between socio-economic conditions and religious expression. Radical millenarism found support in all levels of society at one time or another but essentially it is a religion of the *deprived groups*—oppressed peasants, the poorest of the poor in cities and towns, populations of colonial countries. The millenarian hope usually flares up as a reaction to particularly severe hardships and suffering. Many of the outbursts of millenarism took place against a background of disaster—plagues, devastating fires, recurrent long droughts that were the dire lot of the peasants, slumps that caused widespread unemployment and poverty and calamitous wars.[4] Repeated historical experiences of disaster, living under constant threat of hunger, illness and untimely

---

[4] See B. Barber, Acculturation and messianic movements, *American Sociological Review*, VI (1941), 663–668 and D. F. Aberle, The Prophet Dance and reactions to white contact, *Southwestern J. of Anthropology*, XV (1959), 77–83.

and cruel death lead to rejection not only of actual history but of history as such. The fantastic hope of total redemption was often born out of abysmal despair.

Yet there is much more to it than just that. The analysis clearly shows that the development of millenarism cannot be interpreted only in terms of an extremely severe deprivation. The predisposing factor was often not so much any particular hardship but a markedly *uneven relation between expectations and the means of their satisfaction*.[5] In Cohn's and Hobsbawm's material it is predominantly the inability to satisfy traditional expectations. In medieval Europe millenarism affected mainly people who, because of the pressure of surplus population were cut off from the traditional order and were unable to satisfy wants instilled in them by it. The insidious onslaught of the developing capitalistic order on a backward and isolates peasant economy created the same basic difficulty in Spain and Italy centuries later, although there it affected not only people who were cut off from their rural base but the rural community as a whole. We encounter the same type of frustration in primitive societies as well but there it increasingly becomes not so much a problem of the lack of means to supply traditional wants but the development of a set of new expectations. The encounter with modern societies engenders enormously inflated expectations without a concomitant and adequate development of institutional means for their supply. This discrepancy creates a void which is often bridged by millenarian hope. That frustration may be much more important than actual hardship becomes evident when we consider the fact that millenarian unrest was caused in certain parts of New Guinea not by any direct contact with the white men. Though there were hardly any changes in the status quo indirect contacts brought about changed expectation and acute frustration. It should be stressed that in many cases millenarian outbursts were caused not by a deterioration of conditions but by a limited amelioration which raised new hopes and new expectations but left them largely unfulfilled.

The incongruity between ends and means is not the only source of frustration. Much of the deep dissatisfaction stems from incongruities and difficulties in the realm of *regulation of ends*. Quick change and encounter with radically different systems of values result in a more or less severe cultural disintegration. When the impinging cultural influences penetrate into the traditional setting and gain a foothold there they often undermine the effectiveness of traditional norms as guides

---

[5] On the relation between deprivation and frustration, see R. Linton, Nativistic movements, *American Anthropologist*, VL (1943), 230–240. Cf. also R. Firth, The theory of Cargo Cult: A note on Tikopia, *Man* (1955), No. 142.

of action. Even the most central traditional values cease to be self-evident and sacred. In many spheres there are contradictory claims and mutually exclusive obligations. Since conflicting claims tend to neutralise and annul each other, the impinging cultural influences often weaken and even destroy the indigenous tradition without substituting a new system of values, thus causing confusion and anomie. When the alien culture is that of a more prestigious upper class or that of a colonial ruling class, it is often willingly or unwillingly, consciously or unconsciously acknowledged as superior. This causes much self-doubt and even self-hatred.[6] Wilson stresses quite rightly that the sense of cultural deprivation and the quest for cultural reorientation are sometimes more important than economic frustration. Millenarism is often born out of the search for a tolerably coherent system of values, a new cultural identity and regained sense of dignity and self-respect.

Another important factor operative in the emergence of millenarism was found to be *social isolation* brought about by the disruption of traditional group ties. Cohn points out that millenarism did not appeal much to people who were firmly embedded in well-integrated kinship groupings and effectively organised and protected in cohesive local communities. The people most exposed to the new pressures and therefore more prone to millenarism were the mal-integrated and isolated who could find no assured and recognised place in cohesive primary groups. The importance of a breakdown of kinship and local groupings is a major theme in the analysis of pre-modern, modern and primitive societies as well.

Yet even the combination of such factors as severe deprivation, severe frustration and extreme isolation does not supply us with a full answer to our question. The most important contribution of Balandier, Worsley and Hobsbawm to this analysis lies in their insistence that millenarism is essentially a *pre-political phenomenon*. In primitive societies it appears mainly in so-called stateless segmentary societies which have rudimentary political institutions or lack any specialised political institutions altogether. When it appears in societies with fairly developed political institutions it appeals to strata which are politically passive and have no experience of political organisation and no access to political power. Instances of such non-political strata in societies with a more or less developed political structure are the peasants in feudal societies, the peasants in isolated and backward areas in modern societies, marginal and politically passive elements in the working class, recent immigrants and mal-inte-

[6] For the description and analysis of this aspect of the growth of millenarism, see K. Burridge, *op. cit.* pp. 246–254; also Z. W. Werblowsky, Messianism in primitive societies, *The Listener*, LXIV (1958), p. 684.

grated and politically inarticulate minority groups. Sometimes millenarism is post-political, appearing after the downfall of a fairly developed political system. The collapse of an entire political system by a crushing defeat and the shattering of tribal or national hopes have sometimes led to widespread millenarism. It is the lack of effective organisation, the absence of regular institutionalised ways of voicing their grievances and pressing their claims that pushes such groups to a millenarian solution. Not being able to cope with their difficulties by concerted political action, they turn to millenarism. According to this analysis, millenarism is born out of great distress coupled with political helplessness.

That the combination of all the necessary predisposing factors will actually lead to millenarism and not result in the development of other types of religious ideology is ultimately conditioned also by the type of prevalent religious beliefs. Clearly, religions in which history has no meaning whatsoever and religions which have a cyclical repetitive concept of time are not conducive to millenarism. Apocalyptic eschatology is essentially alien to religions of a philosophical and mystical cast which turn the eye of the believer towards eternity where there is no movement and no process. This is certainly the case with some nature and cosmic religions which live in the framework of ever-recurring repetitive cycles of rise and decline.[7] Another important factor operative in this sphere is a "this-worldly" emphasis. Religions with a radical, other-worldly orientation which puts all the emphasis on the here-after or on a purely spiritual and totally non-terrestrial salvation do not give rise to the vision of the kingdom of God on earth. This explains why there is apparently no apocalyptic tradition in Hinduism and why it has not occupied an important place in Buddhism.

On the whole, millenarism appeared mainly in countries which had direct or indirect contact with the Judeo-Christian messianic traditions. Christianity itself originally derived its initial élan from radical millenarism and, although the millenarian ideology was reinterpreted and relegated to a secondary position, it still played an important part in the history of Europe. The Christian missions were the most important agency for the worldwide spreading of millenarism. Several fundamentalist sects played a particularly important role in this process, but millenarism appeared also in cases where the main contact with it was mediated by less apocalyptic versions of Christianity. The millenarism is reinstated to its central position by a process of selection and reinterpretation.

When millenarism developed in primitive societies it was influenced by pre-existing religious concepts as well. Some primitive mythologies

[7] Cf. M. Eliade, *Le mythe de l'éternel retour* (Paris 1949).

contain eminently suitable beliefs such as the expectation of the future
return of the culture hero or the idea of the return of all the dead
as a prelude to a messianic era.[8] It should be stressed, however, that
these themes appeared in a rather embryonic form and did not occupy
a particularly important position in primitive mythology. They were
developed, reinterpreted and elaborated into full-fledged millenarian
conceptions only under the impact of the new situation and after the
contact with Christianity. The pre-existing primitive conceptions affected
the development of millenarism in yet another way. The prevalence
of millenarism in Melanesia and the importance of expectations of cargo
in its view of the millennium are, it would seem, due to the strong
and almost exclusive emphasis which the indigenous religion puts on
ritual activity oriented to the acquisition of material goods.

IV

What are the *functions of millenarism?* How does it answer the needs
of its followers and what does it contribute to the strata and societies
where it appears? In this sphere we find different interpretations and
different emphases. Cohn's approach to this particular problem is predominantly psychological. He regards millenarism as primarily an outlet
for extreme anxiety and as a delusion of despair. He treats it as a collective paranoid fantasy born out of irrational fears and fantastic expectations. He feels that the megalomaniac view of oneself as wholly good,
abominably persecuted yet assured of final triumph, the attribution of
demonic power to the adversary, the inability to accept the ineluctable
limitations of human existence, constitute the unmistakable syndrome
of paranoia. The irrational and hysterical emotionality, the destructive
and often suicidal activities seem to him clear symptoms of mental illness. Hobsbawm and Worsley reject this psychological interpretation
and press for a more sociological approach. Worsley strongly objects
to the description of these movements as irrational and tries to prove
that if we take into consideration the social conditions and the cultural
milieu which gave rise to them they cease to be bizarre and fantastic
and become fully understandable and not illogical reactions. The highly
emotional and aggressive behaviour is related to the revolutionary nature
of the movement which strives to overthrow the old order and establish
a new one. The severing of old ties and the rejection of old norms

[8] M. I. Pereira de Queiroz, L'influence du milieu social interne sur les mouvements
messianiques brésiliens, *Archives de sociologie des religions,* 5 (1958), pp. 3–29;
Id., Classifications des messianismes brésiliens, *ibid.* pp. 111–120.

demand an enormous effort and engender a deep sense of guilt, hence much of the hysteria and the aggression. Many of the antinomian manifestations are a deliberate overthrow of the accepted norms, not in order to throw overboard all morality but in order to create a new brotherhood and a new morality.[9] The paranoid manifestations stem from the contradictions inherent in the situation in which such movements appear and from the difficulties inherent in their revolutionary task and not so much from psychological aberrations of individual followers. Wilson treats the sociological and psychological interpretations as complementary but he too stresses the situational strains rather than the abnormality of the followers. Wilson supplies us here with a careful and balanced analysis of functions versus dysfunctions on three different levels. He distinguishes between the functions and dysfunctions of millenarism for the individual follower, for the movement and for society as a whole. By and large, he feels that millenarism has strong disruptive potentialities. While it supplies the individual follower with strong identification with a cohesive movement and gives him hope for imminent delivery, it creates serious difficulties in the sphere of canalisation of aggression. Such movements always face the crisis of non-materialisation and suffer from the turning of the aggression of its members inwards which manifests itself in numerous fissions. A millenarian movement can counteract more or less successfully the disintegrating tendencies inherent in its religious ideology for a long time but this is achieved at the cost of considerable mal-integration from the point of view of the total society. Christadelphianism institutionalises deviant tendencies without being able to bring about actual change.

A far more positive evaluation of millenarism emerges from the studies of Balandier, Worsley and Hobsbawm. The main hypothesis which underlies these studies is that millenarism is an activating and unifying force in hitherto politically passive and segregated groups and that in recent and contemporary history it has been an important *precursor of political awakening and a forerunner of political organisation.* Such functions were performed also by other types of religious movements, but radical millenarism is much more potent in this respect. The main effect of the millenarian movement is to overcome divisions and join previously isolated or even hostile groups together. Though faced by the same common problems and sometimes even sharing the same culture, these groups cannot act as a unified force except on a localised

---

[9] The most sophisticated and rigorous analysis of the development and functions of antinomian ritual in a messianic movement will be found in G. Scholem, *Main Trends in Jewish Mysticism* (New York 1946), pp. 287–324.

and ad hoc basis. When confronted by crisis and by necessity to take concerted action, they are compelled to create a new unity which transcends kinship and local loyalties. Millenarism helps to draw into activity and organise masses of people on a large scale almost simultaneously. Conversion acts as a sudden overpowering awakening. It brings about a new awareness and a change in men's attitude to life, shaking them out of their apathy. Since millenarism has a strong collective orientation and is also activity-centered, this conversion does not lead them only inwards to repentance and meditation but draws them outwards to involvement and activity in the movement. Millenarism usually evokes exceptionally intense commitment and fervour and, since exaltation eases communication, millenarism expands swiftly almost as if by contagion, cross-cutting and breaking down local barriers. It widens the horizon of identification and participation and creates wider unities.

The revolutionary nature of millenarism makes it a very potent agent of change. It demands a fundamental transformation and not just improvement and reform. The radical versions of millenarism incite the followers to active anticipation of the advent and even to active revolt. It invests their struggle with the aura of a final cosmic drama. It interprets present difficulties as signs of the beginning of the end and views every small success as proof of invincibility and as portents of future triumph. It arouses truly great hopes and therefore can make equally great demands on its followers. By promising complete salvation, it is able to liberate formerly untapped energies and generate a supreme effort without which no major break with the existing order can be achieved.

Millenarism helps to bring about a break-through to the future. Yet its special efficacy lies also in its power to bridge future and past. We have already pointed out that inasmuch as the end of days is somehow connected with the mythical beginning, the vision of the apocalyptic future includes certain traditional elements.[10] Even the most anti-traditional version of millenarism is in fact a creative synthesis between the new and old. Even when rejecting and transcending the old, it reinstates important aspects of it. It constantly reinterprets such traditional elements and places them in a new context. It invests the old with new meanings while the new elements may often have traditional connotations. Even when it negates the content of tradition it does not invalidate the principles by which truth is traditionally sought and preserved.

---

[10] Cf. A. Wallace, Revitalisation movements, *American Anthropologist*, LVIII, (1956), 264–280.

While bridging the gap between future and past, millenarism also connects religion and politics. Operating in societies or in strata completely dominated by religion, millenarism couches its political message in the familiar and powerful language and images of traditional religion employing and revitalising its age old symbols. In such milieus recruitment to new political goals is often possible only when expressed in religious terms. In many cases it is also the only means of establishing cooperation between leaders and followers. Millenarism provides an important mechanism of recruitment of new leaders. It opens up new avenues of ascent and develops a set of new statuses. Although some of the new leaders derive their authority from the their central or marginal position in the traditional order, more often than not their authority stems at least in part from their comparatively superior knowledge and greater experience in non-traditional spheres of activity and has no traditional legitimation. Millenarism helps them to establish their authority. Externalisation and sanctification of the source of authority puts the leader above sectional loyalties and helps him to avoid sectional discord. By projecting their authority to the supernatural sphere they objectify and legitimise it. Millenarism helps the leader in this respect in yet another way. It closes the gap which often develops between a more "advanced" and more politically minded leader and the more traditional mass of his followers. In many cases he cannot hope to reach his followers and really communicate with them if he does not express his protest in popular and widely understood religious terms. In some cases, the movement is started by an "advanced" and politically minded leader, but when its political ideology reaches the masses, it is spontaneously interpreted in religious terms. The best example of such a process is the development of Amicalism described by Balandier.

The resort to a religious appeal is sincere and non-manipulative in most cases. During the first stages of reorganisation most of the leaders have got little experience in the political sphere and cannot express their striving except in a religious form. During later phases of development the resort to religion may sometimes become a conscious propagandist and organisational device. The leader clothes his political ideology in religious terms because he realises that this is the only way to mobilise the masses. He often emphasises the religious components of his ideology also for the purpose of hiding his real intentions from the authorities.

Millenarism is thus essentially a *connecting link* between pre-political and political movements. It lubricates the passage from pre-modern religious revolt to a full-fledged revolutionary movement. The process of transition can be actually traced in both primitive and recent pre-modern movements. There are two main distinct avenues of transition. In some cases the movements gradually change their nature, slowly becoming less ritualised and more secular in emphasis. These movements start to pay much more attention to purely political and economic goals. They attach far more importance to strategy and tactics and organise more effectively. Yet they do not sever their ties with their millenarian tradition and continue to derive much of their revolutionary zeal from its promise of final salvation. Another major direction of development entails the complete absorption of the millenarian movement within a secular revolutionary movement.[11] When the millenarian movement fails to achieve its goals and disintegrates, its disappointed followers turn to secular revolutionism, embracing an extreme and militant version of either nationalist or socialist ideology. The millenarian movement serves in such cases as a kind of preparatory school for revolutionaries. When they "graduate" from it they are ready to go over to militant secular movements.

It should be stressed that the hypothesis which posits that millenarism functions as an integrating force and as forerunner of political action is borne out only in material on the contemporary history of Melanesia and Africa on the one hand and in the material on the recent history of Italy on the other. Most of the medieval movements were ephemeral outbursts and only a few of them had strong formative powers and lasting social consequences. Since they had little chance to change the massive structure of medieval society, most of these revolutionary revivals short-circuited and disappeared. Material on the American Indians suggests that radical millenarism has played a limited and largely disruptive role there.[12] Any movement with a revolutionary potential was quickly suppressed, leaving an aftermath of disillusion and disorganisation.[13] The task of rehabilitating and integrating the Indians was performed mainly by reformist cults oriented to peaceful accommodation to the white society.[14] Membership in millenarian movements in modern

[11] On the relations between millenarism and nationalist movements in primitive societies, see W. E. Mühlmann, Chiliasmus, Nativismus, Nationalismus, *Verhandlungen des 14. Deutchen Soziologentages* (Stuttgart 1959); G. Balandier, Messianismes et nationalismes *en Afrique noire, Cahiers internationaux de sociologie*, XIV (1953), 41–65; also J. Guiart, Naissance et avortement d'un messianisme, *Archives de sociologie des religions*, 7 (1959), 3–44; Id., Cargo Cults and modern political evolution in Melanesia, *South Pacific*, V (1951).

[12] See E. Vogt, The American Indian—Transition, reformation and accommodation, *American Anthropologist*, VLIII (1956), pp. 249–264.

[13] C. Du Bois, The 1870 ghost dance, *University of California Anthropological Records*, III (1939–1946), 1–152.

[14] Cf. G. Barnett, *Indian Shakers and Messianic Cults of the Pacific Northwest* (Carbondale 1957); see also S. Slotkin, *The Peyote Religion* (Glencoe 1958).

societies functions more as a competing alternative to membership in militant secular movements rather than as a preparation for it. All these movements reject secular movements and enjoin on their members to keep away from them. It is clear that the actual functions which any millenarian movement performs in any given situation depend on the degree of differentiation between the religious and political sphere in the society in which it operates and on the chances it has to engage in active political action and carry out a successful revolution. Much work needs still to be done before we can arrive at generally valid generalisation in this sphere.

VI.

THE ORGANIZATION OF COLLECTIVE ACTION

We have repeatedly pointed out that what characterizes a social movement as a particular kind of change agent is its quality as an articulated and organized group. It is the emergence of an organized structure that turns a sporadic demonstration, an angry crowd, or an aggregate of individual dissidents into collective action of significance for social change. Organization implies that there is some regularized method for carrying on the activities of the movement. It means that there are people who have responsibilities for specific tasks and that roles will be performed in some predictable fashion.

It is difficult to conceive of organization without some division of labor. This means that some will do one thing and some another, but that these specialized tasks are understood and anticipated. Simply to call a meeting in modern society implies that someone will obtain the items for correspondence, write them, mail them, and be assured that they will be adequately addressed. To hold a meeting one must usually obtain a hall, be sure that there are adequate facilities, and see that a program has been agreed upon. All these actions and activities which may seem minor, are parts of the regular process of organization. When we add to such detailed matters the difficult tasks of attempting to espouse a point of view in the public market, the tasks of organization require a kind of specialization and division of labor which cannot emerge spontaneously if the movement is to reach its goal in the face of opposition.

The division of labor is also a division of authority. Decisions must be made, and the movement recognized and represented in many places and arenas. The growth and development of leadership on a regular basis is again a mark of organization. Often a movement becomes synonymous with its leadership and tends to be represented by it and even, in many cases, to be named by it, as was the case with the Townsend movement, McCarthyism, and Marxism.

Precisely because it has an organization and a structure, issues of internal organization develop. The relationship between member and leader, between rank-and-file and hard-core membership, between the "fellow traveling" sympathizer and the hard core, are all matters of conflict. Crucial issues in many organizations have developed from the distinction between a powerful and authoritative day-to-day leadership and the less routine and less regular membership. Issues of internal democracy have emerged in labor unions, in temperance movements, and, as we shall see in the readings, even in revolutionary organizations.

The division between leader and member, in turn, has made for important situations of organizational style and character. On the one hand, movements are efforts to achieve change in a society. Dislodging the population from fixed beliefs and values is a crucial aspect in the development of a movement. Agitation and dramatic activity heighten excitement and intensity, bringing in converts and reinforcing partisans. On the other hand, the requirements of organization and the consequences of regularizing action often lead to a bias toward less flamboyant aspects of partisan belief, toward organizational development and long-run considerations. (We shall pay much attention to this later in this volume, where we discuss the paradox of organization.) Tension within movements has frequently arisen over just such issues. Action now to express feeling and gain public attention is contrasted with less dramatic activities designed to build future organizational strength.

The selections from V. I. Lenin are a classic discussion of some problems of organization which, while analyzed from the context of a revolutionary movement, are nevertheless found in a variety of reform movements as well. In the early twentieth century, in the period before Lenin led the Russian Revolution of 1917 and later headed the Soviet Union in its early years, he was a prolific writer on matters of organizational tactics and strategy. In arguments with his fellow revolutionaries he developed the point of view since known as Leninism. He insisted upon the importance of building an organization and the importance of a small and powerful cadre of highly committed leaders. In the selections used here, Lenin argues against committing the movement to protest action for its own sake and recommends tactics and strategy which will build organizations as strong weapons. His attack on "adventurous tactics" is the argument of the organizer against the charismatic leader.

Lenin's discussion of internal democracy and minority leadership again deals with a classic problem. He rests much of his argument against internal democracy on the characteristics of the Russian society of his time and insists that the structure of a successful movement must be related to the situation in which it is found. Being a weapon, the organizational structure must not be conceived as an end in itself. Lenin's discussion, as well as the views of revolutionist critics, has a familiar ring in the context of the American New Left of the 1960s and the debate over "participatory democracy."

This emphasis on the division of labor ignores the fact that, among other things, a social movement is an association of people with personal ties and obligations toward each other. Being a human group, it must command solidarity and loyalty. Concern for ideas and for programmatic action means that association with others in a movement is also loyalty to a set of ideas. The participants in a movement are partisans, and they bring to their membership a commitment to a belief which may deepen and be strengthened by the effective bond with other members which interaction will create. This section of the book looks at the character of this bond and its relation to partisanship. Our emphasis here is on the member and his relationship to the movement.

A variety of motivations may be involved in active participation with others in collective action. Not everyone who shares a vague restlessness about change or who is intellectually drawn to a set of ideas is a participant in a movement. Nor is participation necessarily a sign of an intially deep conviction. There are two processes which we need to consider: the conversion to a belief and the conversion to active participation. That men change beliefs and move from one perspective to another has been apparent in many of our earlier readings, such as the analysis of a strike and the development of the sense of nationalism. Because such changes in belief have been marked by vivid, emotional, and highly intense experience in religious movements, conversion as a process has been more often studied in religious psychology than in other areas of life.

The bond of fellowhip, however, is an important aspect of membership in social movements. As people interact with each other, they develop friendships and personal attachments. The relationships to the movement and to its beliefs are often highly suffused with loyalties to persons within the movement. One of the major difficulties in quitting a movement may lie in what it means for the disruption of social attachments that have emerged and around which the member has based some of his life activities.

This discussion of partisanship and membership treats movements as associational activities. We recognize, however, that some people are drawn more deeply into the pattern of activities of a movement than are others, despite what may be a common belief in its program. We can distinguish levels of membership. There is the professional, such as a full-time editor of a movement's newspaper or a full-time officer, for whom the organization has become a livelihood as well as a life. There are the hard-core activists who devote to the movement a great deal of intense dedication and time. There are the rank-and-file members, for whom the movement may have greater or less significance in their own lives. Last, there are the fellow travelers or sympathizers who share a vague consensus about programs and goals of a movement but devote very little if any time or emotional investment in its activities and aim.

This consideration suggests that there may be multiple sources of membership in collective action, involving not only diverse social bases but also a variety of personal and individual motivations. These may be highly institutional elements, such as those which explain the activity of college students in many movements as a result of their relative leisure and lack of material or familial attachments. There may be a variety of motivations, so that for some the activity and the affective bonds of fellowship are more crucially valuable in and of themselves than they are to others. Analysis of the bonds of fellowship and the sources of membership recruitment suggests a congruence of personal motivation and intellectual and sociological belief with an organized movement.

The phenomenon of partisanship is analyzed in our readings by reference to very different movements, from widely separated historical periods. Yet each has a significance beyond its specific context. In an original paper based on his participant observation in the American Civil Rights movement of the early 1960s, the historian August Meier describes the variety of motives which impelled both black and white youth to participate in the demonstrations, sit-ins, and marches in the South. It is difficult to sum up this description in any single answer to the question: Why did people participate? The partisans who made up the membership exemplify several types of persons with a variety of motives. There was, however, a linkage between the movement and the motivations which drew members toward it. This linkage forms a major source of the attraction of the recruit toward entering the movement.

Meier's descriptions of a twentieth-century movement in the United States has much in common with Michael Walzer's analysis of the Puritan revolutionaries in seventeenth-century England. In both, members found solutions to personal problems in participation and in the ideology of the movement.. Walzer emphasizes the social and general character of those problems in the disorder of seventeenth-century life. Within the network of relationships in the "band of the chosen" the Puritan member found the means to develop the orderliness which enabled him to conquer self and the King. "The band of the chosen seeks and wins certainty and self-confidence by rigidly disciplining its members and teaching them to discipline themselves" (p. 317). In analyzing the Puritan revolutionaries Walzer also presents a model of the radical and revolutionary circle of partisans. The saintliness of this circle is not peculiar to seventeenth-century England, but, as Walzer notes, has often been observed as a characteristic of the revolutionary partisan. Noting again the analogy to religious associations, one writer, Rudolf Heberle, has called such circles "political orders."[1]

[1] Rudolf Heberle, *Social Movements*. New York: Appleton-Century-Crofts, 1951, pp. 350–354.

A.
The Significance of
Organizational Structure

1.
WHAT IS TO BE DONE? (1901)
V. I. LENIN

ORGANIZATION VS. ACTION[1]

The question, "What is to be done?" has been very prominent before the Russian Social-Democrats in the past few years. It is not a matter of choosing the path we are to travel (as was the case at the end of the eighties and the beginning of the nineties) but of the practical measures and the methods we must adopt on a certain path. What we have in mind is a system and plan of practical activity. It must be confessed that the question as to the character of the struggle and the means by which it is to be carried on—which is a fundamental question for a practical party—still remains unsettled, and still gives rise to serious differences which reveal a deplorable uncertainty and

SOURCE. V. I. Lenin, *Collected Works,* Vol. IV. New York: International Publishers, Inc., 1929. Reprinted by permission of the publishers. Brackets indicate material substituted by this editor (J.G.).
[1] From *"Where to Begin?,,* Vol. IV, Book I, pp. 109–112.

ideological wavering. On the one hand, [there is a] tendency, which strives to curtail and restrict the work of political organisation and agitation is not dead yet by a long way. On the other hand, the tendency of shallow eclecticism, masquerading in the guise of a new "idea" and incapable of distinguishing between the requirements of the moment and the permanent needs of the movement as a whole, still proudly raises its head . . . today [some] quote the words of Liebknecht: "If circumstances change within twenty-four hours then tactics must be changed within twenty-four hours"; now we talk about a "strong fighting organisation" for the direct attack upon and storming of the autocracy; about "extensive revolutionary, political . . . agitation among the masses"; about "unceasing calls for organising street demonstrations of a sharply (sic!) expressed political character," etc., etc. . . .

[These people take] Liebknecht's name in vain. Tactics in relation to some special question, or in relation to some detail of party organisation may be changed within twenty-four hours; but views as to whether a militant organisation, and political agitation among the masses is necessary at all times . . . cannot be changed in twenty-four hours, or even in twenty-four months for that matter. Only those who have no fixed ideas on anything might do a thing like that. It is absurd to refer to changed circumstances and succession of periods. Work for the establishment of a fighting organisation and political agitation must be carried on under all circumstances, no matter how "drab and peaceful" the times may be, and no matter how low the "depression of revolutionary spirit" has sunk. More than that, it is precisely in such conditions and in such periods that this work is particularly required; for it would be too late to start building such an organisation in the midst of uprisings and outbreaks. The organisation must be ready when that moment arrives and immediately develop its activity. "Change tactics in twenty-four hours!" In order to change tactics it is necessary first of all to have tactics, and without a strong organisation, tested in the political struggle carried on under all circumstances and in all periods, there can be no talk of a systematic plan of activity, enlightened by firm principles and unswervingly carried out, which alone is worthy of being called tactics. . . .

The question is, Can we, at the present time, *issue* the call to storm the fortress? . . . Our military forces mainly consist of volunteers and rebels. We have only a few detachments of regular troops, and even these are not mobilised, not linked up with each other, and not trained to form into any kind of military column, let alone storming column. Under such circumstances, any one capable of taking a general view of the conditions of our struggle, without losing sight of them at every "turn" in the historical progress of events, must clearly understand that at the present time our slogan cannot be "Storm the fortress," but should be "Organise properly the siege of the enemy fortress." In other words, the immediate task of our party is not to call up our available forces for an immediate attack, but to call for the establishment of a revolutionary organisation capable of combining all the forces and of leading the moment, not only in name but in deed, i.e., an organisation that will be ready at any moment to support every protest and every outbreak, and to utilise these for the purpose of increasing and strengthening the military forces required for decisive battle.

2. COMMUNICATION AND ORGANIZATION[2] (1901)

. . . It is hardly likely that objection will be raised to the above conclusion on principle. But we are not called upon at the present moment to settle the question in principle but in practice. We must not only be clear in our minds as to the kind of organisation we must have and the kind of work we must do; we must also draw up a definite *plan* or organisation that will enable us to set to work to build it from all sides. In view of the urgency and importance of the question we have taken it upon ourselves to submit to our comrades the outlines of such a plan. We have described this plan in greater detail in a pamphlet now in preparation for the press.

In our opinion, the starting point of all our activities, the first practical step to take towards creating the organisation we desire, the factor which will enable us constantly to develop, broaden and deepen that organisation, is to establish a national [All-Russian] political newspaper. A paper is what we need above all; without it we cannot systematically carry on that extensive and theoretically sound propaganda and agitation which is the principal and constant duty of the Social-Democrats in general, and the essential task of the present moment in particular, when interest in politics and in questions of Socialism has been aroused among wide sections of the population. Never before has the need been so strongly felt for supplementing individual agitation in the form of personal influence, local leaflets, pamphlets, etc., by a general and regularly conducted agitation, such as can be carried on only with the assistance of a periodical press. It would be hardly an exaggeration to say that the frequency and regularity of the publication (and distribution) of

[2] *Ibid.*, pp. 112–116.

the frequency and regularity of the publication (and distribution) of the paper would serve as an exact measure of the extent to which that primary and most essential branch of our militant activities has been firmly established. Moreover, the paper must be an All-Russian paper. Until we are able to exercise united influence upon the population and on the government with the aid of the press, it will be Utopian to think that we shall be able unitedly to exercise influence in more complex and difficult, but more effective forms. Our movement, intellectually as well as practically (organisationally), suffers most of all from being scattered, from the fact that the vast majority of Social-Democrats are almost entirely immersed in local work, which narrows their point-of-view, limits their activities and affects their conspiratorial skill and training. It is to this fact of being scattered that we must ascribe the vacillation and the hesitation to which I referred above. The *first step* towards removing this defect, and transforming several local movements into a united national (All-Russian) movement is the establishment of a national All-Russian newspaper. Finally, it is a *political* paper we need. Without a political organ, a political movement deserving that name is impossible in modern Europe. Unless we have such a paper, we shall be absolutely unable to fulfil our task, namely, to concentrate all the elements of political unrest and discontent, and with them enrich the revolutionary movement of the proletariat. . . .

But the role of a paper is not confined solely to the spreading of ideas, to political education, and to procuring political allies. A paper is not merely a collective propagandist and collective agitator, it is also a collective organiser. In that respect, it can be compared to the scaffolding erected around a building in construction; it marks the contours of the structure, and facilitates communication between the builders, permitting them to distribute the work and to view the common results achieved by their organised labour. With the aid of, and around, a paper, there will automatically develop an organisation that will be concerned, not only with local activities, but also with regular, general work; it will teach its members carefully to watch political events, to estimate their importance and their influence on the various sections of the population, and to devise suitable methods to influence these events through the revolutionary party. The mere technical problem of procuring a regular supply of material for the newspaper and its regular distribution will make it necessary to create a network of agents of a united party, who will be in close contact with each other, will be acquainted with the general situation, will be accustomed to fulfil the detailed functions of the national (All-Russian) work, and who will test their strength in the organisation of various kinds of revolutionary activities. This network of agents[3] will form the skeleton of the organisation we need: namely, one that is sufficiently large to embrace the whole country; sufficiently wide and many-sided to effect a strict and detailed division of labour; sufficiently tried and tempered unswervingly to carry out its own work in its own way, in spite of all adversities, changes and surprises; sufficiently flexible to be able, if necessary, to renounce an open fight against overwhelming and concentrated forces, and yet capable of taking advantage of the awkwardness and immobility of the enemy and attack at a time and place where he least expects attack. To-day we are faced with the comparatively simple task of supporting students demonstrating in the streets of large towns; to-morrow, perhaps, we shall be faced with more difficult tasks, as for instance, supporting a movement of the unemployed in some locality or other. The day after to-morrow, perhaps, we may have to be ready at our posts, to take a revolutionary part in some peasants' revolt. . . . If we unite our forces for the conduct of a common paper, that work will prepare and bring forward, not only the most competent propagandists, but also the most skilled organisers and the most talented political party leaders, who will know at the right moment when to issue the call to battle, and will be capable of leading that battle.

In conclusion, we desire to say a few words in order to avoid possible misunderstandings. We have spoken all the time about systematic and methodical preparation, but we had no desire in the least to suggest that the autocracy may fall only as a result of a properly prepared siege or organised attack. Such a view would be stupid and doctrinaire. On the contrary, it is quite possible, and historically far more probable, that the autocracy will fall under the pressure of one of those spontaneous outbursts or unforeseen political complications which constantly threaten it from all sides. But no political party, if it desires to avoid adventurist tactics, can base its activities on expectations of such outbursts and complications. We must proceed along our road, and steadily carry out our systematic work, and the less we count on the unexpected, the less likely are we to be taken by surprise by any "historical turn."

SOURCE. *Iskra,* No. 4, May, 1901.

[3] It is understood, of course, that these agents can act successfully only if they work in close conjunction with the local committees (groups or circles) of our party. Indeed, the whole plan we have sketched can be carried out, only with the most active support of the committees, which have already made more than one attempt to achieve a united party, and which, I am certain, sooner or later, and in one form or another, will achieve that unity.

3. THE ISSUE OF LEADERSHIP[5]

What should be the functions of the organisation of revolutionists? We shall deal with this in detail. But first let us examine a very typical argument advanced by the terrorist. . . . *Svoboda*— a journal published especially for working men—in its first number, contains an article entitled "Organisation [sic]," the author of the which tries to defend his friends the Economist workers of Ivanovo-Voznesensk. He writes:

> It is a bad thing when the crowd is mute and unenlightened, and when the movement does not proceed from the rank and file. For instance, the students of a university town leave for their homes during the summer and other vacations and immediately the movement comes to a standstill. Can such a workers' movement which has to be pushed on from outside be a real force? Of course not! It has not yet learned to walk, it is still in leading strings. So it is everywhere. The students go off, and everything comes to a standstill. As soon as the cream is skimmed—the milk turns sour. If the "committee" is arrested, everything comes to a standstill until a new one can be formed. And, one never knows what sort of a committee will be set up next—it may be nothing like the former one. The first preached one thing, the second may preach the very opposite. The continuity between yesterday and tomorrow is broken, the experience of the past does not enlighten the future. And all this is because no deep roots have been struck, roots in the crowd; because, instead of having a hundred fools at work, we have ten wise men. Ten wise men can be caught up at a snap; but when the organisation embraces the crowd, everything will proceed from the crowd, and nobody, however zealous, can stop the cause (p. 63).

The facts are described correctly. The above quotation presents a fairly good picture of our primitive methods. But the conclusions drawn from it are worthy . . . both for their stupidity and their political tactlessness. They represent the height of stupidity, because the author confused the philosophical and social-historical question of the "depth" of the "roots" of the movement with the technical and organisational question of the best method of fighting the gendarmes. They represent the height of political tactlessness, because the author, instead of appealing from the bad leaders to the good leaders, appeals from the leaders in general to the "crowd." This is as much an attempt to drag the movement back organisationally, as the idea of substituting political agitation by excitative terrorism is an attempt to drag it back politically.

[5] From *What is to be Done?* Vol. IV, Book 2, pp. 194–201.

Indeed, I am experiencing a veritable *embarras de richesses,* and hardly know where to begin to disentangle the confusion *Svoboda* has introduced in this subject. For the sake of clarity, we shall begin by quoting an example. Take the Germans. It will not be denied, I hope, that the German organisations embrace the crowd, that in Germany everything proceeds from the crowd, that the working-class movement there has learned to walk. Yet, observe how this vast crowd of millions values its "dozen" tried political leaders, how firmly it clings to them! Members of the hostile parties in parliament often tease the Socialists by exclaiming: "Fine democrats you are indeed! Your movement is a working-class movement only in name; as a matter of fact it is the same clique of leaders that is always in evidence; Bebel and Liebknecht, year in and year out, and that goes on for decades. Your deputies are supposed to be elected from among the workers, but they are more permanent than the officials appointed by the Emperor!" But the Germans only smile with contempt at these demagogic attempts to set the "crowd" against the "leaders," to arouse turbid and vain instincts in the former, and to rob the movement of its solidity and stability by undermining the confidence of the masses in their "dozen of wise men." The political ideas of the Germans have already developed sufficiently, and they have acquired enough political experience to enable them to understand that without the "dozen" of tried and talented leaders (and talented men are not born by hundreds), professionally trained, schooled by long experience and working in perfect harmony, no class in modern society is capable of conducting a determined struggle. Numerous demagogues in Germany have flattered the "hundred fools," exalted them above the "dozen of wise men," extolled the "mighty fists" of the masses, and (like Most and Hasselmann) have spurred them on to reckless "revolutionary" action and sown distrust toward the tried and trusted leaders. It was only by stubbornly and bitterly combating every symptom of demagogy within the Socialist movement that German Socialism managed to grow and become as strong as it is. Our wiseacres, however, at the very moment when Russian Social-Democracy is passing through a crisis entirely due to our lack of a sufficient number of trained, developed and experienced leaders to guide the spontaneous ferment of the masses, cry out with the profundity of fools, "it is a bad business when the movement does not proceed from the rank and file."

"A committee of students is no good, it is not stable." Quite true. But the conclusion that should be drawn from this is that we must have a committee of professional *revolutionists* and it does not matter whether a student or a worker is capable of qualifying himself as a professional revolutionist. The conclusion you draw, however, is that the working-class movement must not be pushed on from outside! In your political innocence you fail to observe that you are playing into the hands of our Economists and furthering our primitiveness. I would like to ask, what is meant by the students "pushing on" the workers? *All* it means is that the students bring to the worker the fragments of political knowledge they possess, the crumbs of Socialist ideas they have managed to acquire (for the principal intellectual diet of the present-day student, legal Marxism, can furnish only the A.B.C., only the crumbs of knowledge). *Such* "pushing on from outside" can never be too excessive; on the contrary, so far there has been too little, all too little of it in our movement; we have been stewing in our own juice far too long; we have bowed far too slavishly before the spontaneous "economic struggle of the workers against the employers and the government." We professional revolutionists must continue, and will continue, *this kind* of "pushing," and a hundred times more forcibly than we have done hitherto. The very fact that you select so despicable a phrase as "pushing on from outside"—a phrase which cannot but rouse in the workers (at least in the workers who are as ignorant as you are yourselves) a sense of distrust towards *all* who bring them political knowledge and revolutionary experience from outside, and rouse in them an instinctive hostility to such people—proves that you are *demagogues*—and a demagogue is the worst enemy of the working class.

Oh! Don't start howling about my "uncomradely methods" of controversy. I have not the least intention of casting aspersions upon the purity of your intentions. As I have already said, one may be a demagogue out of sheer political innocence. But I have shown that you have descended to demagogy, and I shall never tire of repeating that demagogues are the worst enemies of the work class. They are the worst enemies of the working class because they arouse bad instincts in the crowd, because the ignorant worker is unable to recognise his enemies in men who represent themselves, and sometimes sincerely represent themselves, to be his friends. They are the worst enemies of the working class, because in this period of doubt and hesitation, when our movement is only just beginning to take shape, nothing is easier than to employ demagogic methods to side-track the crowd, which can realise its mistake only by bitter experience. . . .

"A dozen wise men can be more easily caught than a hundred fools" This wonderful. truth (which the hundred fools will applaud) appears obvious only because in the very midst of the argument you have skipped from one question to another. You began by talking, and continued to talk, of catching a "committee," of catching an "organisation," and now you skip to the question of getting hold of the "roots" of the movement in the "depths." The fact is, of course, that our movement cannot be caught precisely because it has hundreds and hundreds of thousands of roots deep down among the masses, but that is not the point we are discussing. As far as "roots in the depths" are concerned, we cannot be "caught" even now, in spite of all our primitiveness; but, we all complain, and cannot but complain, of the ease with which the *organisations* can be caught, with the result that it is impossible to maintain continuity in the movement. If you agree to discuss the question of catching the *organisations*, and to stick to that question, then I assert that it is far more difficult to catch ten wise men that it is to catch a hundred fools. And this premise I shall defend no matter how much you instigate the crowd against me for my "anti-democratic" views, etc. As I have already said, by "wise men," in connection with organisation, I mean *professional revolutionists*, irrespective of whether they are students or workingmen. I assert: 1. That no movement can be durable without a stable organisation of leaders to maintain continuity; 2. that the more widely the masses are drawn into the struggle and form the basis of the movement, the more necessary is it to have such an organisation and the more stable must it be (for it is much easier then for demagogues to side-track the more backward sections of the masses); 3. that the organisation must consist chiefly of persons engaged in revolution as a profession; 4. that in a country with a despotic government, the more we *restrict* the membership of this organisation to persons who are engaged in revolution as a profession and who have been professionally trained in the art of combating the political police, the more difficult will it be to catch the organisation; and 5. the *wider* will be the circle of men and women of the working class or of other classes of society able to join the movement and perform active work in it.

I invite our Economists, terrorists and "Economists-terrorists" to confute these premises. At the moment, I shall deal only with the last two points. The question as to whether it is easier to catch "a dozen wise men" or "a hundred fools," in the last analysis, amounts to the question we have considered above, namely, whether it is possible to have a mass *organisation* when the maintenance of strict secrecy is essential. We can never give a mass organisation that degree of secrecy which is essential for the persistent and continuous struggle against the government. But to concentrate all secret functions in the hands of as small a number of professional revolutionists as possible, does not mean that the latter will "do the thinking for all" and that the crowd will not take an active part in the movement. On the contrary, the crowd will advance from its ranks increasing numbers of professional revolutionists, for it will know that it is not enough for a few students and workingmen waging enconomic war to gather together and form a "committee," but that professional revolutionists must be trained for years; the crowd will "think" not of primitive ways but of training professional revolutionists. The centralisation of the secret functions of the *organisation* does not mean the concentration of all the functions of the *movement*. The active participation of the greatest masses in the dissemination of illegal literature will not diminish because a dozen professional revolutionists concentrate in their hands the secret part of the work; on the contrary, it will *increase tenfold*. Only in this way will the reading of illegal literature, the contribution to illegal literature, and to some extent even the distribution of illegal literature *almost cease to be secret work*, for the police will soon come to realise the folly and futility of setting the whole judicial and administrative machine into motion to intercept every copy of a publication that is being broadcast in thousands. This applies not only to the press, but to every function of the movement, even to demonstrations. The active and widespread participation of the masses will not suffer; on the contrary, it will benefit by the fact that a "dozen" experienced revolutionists, no less professionally trained than the police, will concentrate all the secret side of the work in their hands—prepare leaflets, work out approximate plans and appoint bodies of leaders for each town district, for each factory district, and for each educational institution (I know that exception will be taken to my "undemocratic" views, but I shall reply to this altogether unintelligent objection later on). The centralisation of the more secret functions in an organisation of revolutionists will not diminish, but rather increase the extent and the quality of the activity of a large number of other organisations intended for wide membership and which, therefore, can be as loose and as public as possible, for example, trade unions, workers' circles for self-education, and the reading of illegal literature, and Socialist, and also democratic, circles for *all other sections of the population,* etc., etc. We must have *as large a number as possible* of such organisations having the widest possible variety of functions, but it is absurd and dangerous to *confuse these with organisations of revolutionists,* to erase the line of demarcation between them, to dim still more the already incredibly hazy appreciation by the masses that to "serve" the mass movement we must have people who will devote themselves exclusively to Social-Democratic activities, and that such people must *train* themselves patiently and steadfastly to be professional revolutionists.

Aye, this consciousness has become incredibly dim. The most grievous sin we have committed in regard to organisation is that *by our primitiveness we have lowered the prestige of revolutionists in Russia.* A man who is weak and vacillating on theoretical questions, who has a narrow outlook, who makes excuses for his own slackness on the ground that the masses are awakening spontaneously, who resembles a trade-union secretary more than a people's tribune, who is unable to conceive a broad and bold plan, who is incapable of inspiring even his enemies with respect for himself, and who is inexperienced and clumsy in his own professional art—the art of combating the political police—such a man is not a revolutionist but a hopeless amateur!

Let no active worker take offence at these frank remarks, for as far as insufficient training is concerned, I apply them first and foremost to myself. I used to work in a circle that set itself a great and all-embracing task: and every member of that circle suffered to the point of torture from the realisation that we were proving ourselves to be amateurs at a moment in history when we might have been able to say—paraphrasing a well-known epigram: "Give us an organisation of revolutionists, and we shall overturn the whole of Russia!" And the more I recall the burning sense of shame I then experienced, the more bitter are my feelings towards those pseudo–Social-Democrats whose teachings bring disgrace on the calling of a revolutionist, who fail to understand that our task is not to degrade the revolutionist to the level of an amateur, but to *exalt* the amateur to the level of a revolutionist.

4. STRATEGY AND INTERNAL STRUCTURE: THE ISSUE OF DEMOCRACY[6]

The *form* a strong revolutionary organisation like that may take in an autocratic country may be described as a "conspirative" organisation, because the French word *"conspiration"* means in Russian "conspiracy," and we must have the utmost conspiracy for an organisation like that.[7] Secrecy is such a necessary condition for such an organisation that all the other conditions (number and selection of members, functions, etc.) must all be subordinated to it. It would be extremely naïve indeed,

[6] From *What is to be Done?*, Vol. IV, Book 2, pp. 208–214.
[7] The Russian word for "conspiracy" is *zagovor*, which means "conspiracy" or "plot." But the word *conspiratsiya,* "conspiracy," in Russian revolutionary literature usually means "secrecy." Hence, a conspirative organisation would be a secret organisation, but would not necessarily engage in plots. Except in the above case, when it was important to bring out the play of words, the word *"conspiratsiya"* has been rendered throughout the text as "secrecy," and the word "conspirative" was used only where the word *zagovor* has been used in the text, as in the sub-title of this section.—Ed.

therefore, to fear the accusation that we Social-Democrats desire to create a conspirative organisation. Such an accusation would be as flattering to every opponent of Economism as the accusation of being followers of Narodovolism would be.

Against us it is argued: Such a powerful and strictly secret organisation, which concentrates in its hands all the threads of secret activities, an organisation which of necessity must be a centralised organisation, may too easily throw itself into a premature attack, may thoughtlessly intensify the movement before political discontent, the ferment and anger of the working class, etc., are sufficiently ripe for it. To this we reply: Speaking abstractly, it cannot be denied, of course, that a militant organisation *may* thoughtlessly commence a battle, which *may* end in defeat, which might have been avoided under other circumstances. But we cannot confine ourselves to abstract reasoning on such a question, because every battle bears within itself the abstract possibility of defeat, and there is no other way of *reducing this possibility to a minimum* than by organised preparation for battle. If, however, we base our argument on the concrete conditions prevailing in Russia at the present time, we must come to the positive conclusion that a strong revolutionary organisation is absolutely necessary precisely for the purpose of giving firmness to the movement, and of *safeguarding* it against the possibility of its making premature attacks. It is precisely at the present time, when no such organisation exists yet, and when the revolutionary movement is rapidly and spontaneously growing, that we *already observe* two opposite extremes (which, as is to be expected, "meet") i.e., . . . the preaching of moderation, and equally unsound "excitative terro," which strives artificially to "call forth symptoms of its end in a movement that is developing and becoming strong, but which is as yet nearer to its beginning than to its end" (V. Zasulich, in *Zarya*, Nos. 2–3, p. 353). . . . *There are already* Social-Democrats who give way to both these extremes. This is not surprising because, apart from other reasons, the "economic struggle against the employers and the government" *can never* satisfy revolutionists, and because opposite extremes will always arise here and there. Only a centralised, militant organisation, that consistently carries out a Social-Democratic policy, that satisfies, so to speak, all revolutionary instincts and strivings, can safeguard the movement against making thoughtless attacks and prepare it for attacks that hold out the promise of success.

It is further argued against us that the views on organisation here expounded contradict the "principles of democracy." Now while the first mentioned accusation was of purely Russian origin, this one is of *purely foreign* origin. And only an organisation abroad (the League of Russian Social-Democrats) would be capable of giving its editorial board instructions like the following:

> *Principles of Organisation.* In order to secure the successful development and unification of Social-Democracy, broad democratic principles of party organisation must be emphasised, developed and fought for; and this is particularly necessary in view of the anti-democratic tendencies that have become revealed in the ranks of our party. (*Two Congresses*, p. 18.)

. . . Every one will probably agree that "broad principles of democracy" presupposes the two following conditions: first, full publicity and second, election to all functions. It would be absurd to speak about democracy without publicity, that is a publicity that extends beyond the circle of the membership of the organisation. We call the German Socialist Party a democratic organisation because all it does is done publicly; even its party congresses are held in public. But no one would call an organisation that is hidden from every one but its members by a veil of secrecy, a democratic organisation. What is the use of advancing "*broad* principles of democracy" when the fundamental condition for this principle *cannot be fulfilled* by a secret organisation. "Broad principles" turns out to be a resonant, but hollow phrase. More than that, this phrase proves that the urgent tasks in regard to organisation are totally misunderstood. Every one knows how great is the lack of secrecy among the "broad" masses of revolutionists. We have heard the bitter complaints of V-v on this score, and his absolutely just demand for a "strict selection of members" (*Rabocheye Dyelo*, No. 6, p. 42). And yet people who boast about their "sensitiveness to life" come forward in a situation like this and *urge* that strict secrecy and a strict (and therefore more restricted) selection of members is unnecessary, and that what is necessary are—"*broad* principles of democracy"! This is what we call being absolutely wide of the mark.

Nor is the situation with regard to the second attribute of democracy, namely, the principle of election, any better. In politically free countries, this condition is taken for granted. "Membership of the party is open to those who accept the principles of the party programme, and render all the support they can to the party"—says paragraph 1 of the rules of the German Social-Democratic Party. And as the political arena is as open to the public view as is the stage in a theatre, this acceptance or non-acceptance, support or opposition is announced to all in the press and at public meetings. Every one knows that a certain political worker commenced in a certain way, passed through a certain evolution, behaved in difficult periods in a certain way; every one knows all his qualities, and consequently, knowing all the facts of the case, *every party member can decide for himself whether or not to elect this person for a certain party office.* The general control (in the literal sense of the term) that the party exercises over every act this person commits on the political field brings into being an automatically operating mechanism which brings about what in biology is called "survival of the fittest." "Natural selection," full publicity, the principle of election and general control provide the guarantee that, in the last analysis, every political worker will be "in his proper place," will do the work for which he is best fitted, will feel the effects of his mistakes on himself, and prove before all the world his ability to recognise mistakes and to avoid them.

Try to put this picture in the frame of our autocracy! Is it possible in Russia for all those "who accept the principles of the party programme and render it all the support they can," to control every action of the revolutionist working in secret? Is it possible for all the revolutionists to elect one of their number to any particular office when, in the very interests of the work, he *must conceal his identity* from nine out of ten of these "all"? . . . You will realise that "broad democracy" in party organisation, amidst the gloom of autocracy and the domination of the gendarmes, is nothing more than a *useless and harmful toy.* It is a useless toy, because as a matter of fact, no revolutionary organisation has ever practiced *broad* democracy, nor could it, however much it desired to do so. It is a harmful toy, because any attempt to practice the "broad principles of democracy" will simply facilitate the work of the police in making big raids, it will perpetuate the prevailing primitiveness, divert the thoughts of the practical workers from the serious and imperative task of training themselves to become professional revolutionists to that of drawing up detailed "paper" rules for election systems. Only abroad, where very often people who have no opportunity of doing real livework gather together, can the "game of democracy" be played here and there, especially in small groups.

. . . The only serious organisational principle the active workers of our movement can accept is: Strict secrecy, strict selection of members, and the training of professional revolutionists. If we possessed these qualities, "democracy" and something even more would be guaranteed to us, namely: Complete, comradely, mutual confidence among revolutionists. And this something more is absolutely essential for us because, in Russia, it is useless to think that democratic control can serve as a substitute for it. It would be a great mistake to believe that because it is impossible to establish real "democratic" control, the members of the revolutionary organisation will remain altogether uncontrolled. They have not the time to think about the toy forms of democracy (democracy within a close and compact body enjoying the complete mutual confidence of the comrades), but they have a lively sense of their *responsi-*

bility, because they know from experience that an organisation of real revolutionists will stop at nothing to rid itself of an undesirable member. Moreover, there is a very well-developed public opinion in Russian (and international) revolutionary circles which has a long history behind it, and which sternly and ruthlessly punishes every departure from the duties of comradeship (and does not "democracy," real and not toy democracy, represent a part of the conception of comradeship?). Take all this into consideration and you will realise that all the talk and resolutions that come from abroad about "anti-democratic tendencies" has a nasty odour of the playing at generals that goes on there.

It must be observed also that the other source of this talk, i.e., naïvete, is also fostered by a confusion of ideas concerning the meaning of democracy. In Mr. and Mrs. Webb's book on trade unionism,[8] there is an interesting section on "Primitive Democracy." In this section, the authors relate how, in the first period of existence of their unions, the British workers thought that in the interests of democracy all the members must take part in the work of managing the unions; not only were all questions decided by the votes of all the members, but all the official duties were fulfilled by all the members in turn. A long period of historical experience was required to teach these workers how absurd such a conception of democracy was and to make them understand the necessity for representative institutions on the one hand, and of full-time professional officials on the other. Only after a number of cases of financial bankruptcy of trade unions occurred did the workers realise that rates of benefit cannot be decided merely by a democratic vote, but must be based on the advice of insurance experts. Let us take also Kautsky's book, *Der Parlamentarismus, die Volksgesetzgebung und die Sozialdemokratie.* There you will find that the conclusions drawn by the Marxian theoretician coincides with the lessons learned from many years of experience by the workers who organised "spontaneously." Kautsky strongly protests against Rittinghausen's primitive conception of democracy; he ridicules those who in the name of democracy demand even that "popular newspapers shall be directly edited by the people"; he shows the necessity for *professional* journalists, parliamentarians, etc., and for the Social-Democratic leadership of the proletarian class struggle; he attacks the "Socialism of Anarchists and *litterateurs*," who in their "striving after effect" proclaim the principle that laws should be passed directly by the whole people, completely failing to understand that in modern society this principle can have only a relative application.

[8] *The History of Trade Unionism.*

B.
The Fellowship of Partisans

2.

WHO ARE THE "TRUE BELIEVERS"?— A TENTATIVE TYPOLOGY OF THE MOTIVATIONS OF CIVIL RIGHTS ACTIVISTS (1965)

August Meier

About this time last year there were some disturbing reports emanating from Mississippi. I am not referring to the well-known facts about intimidation and oppression of Negroes in that state, but to a situation known only to those in "the movement" as Civil Rights activists refer to it. Civil Rights workers in Mississippi, especially those connected with the Student Nonviolent Coordinating Committee (SNCC), were engaged in the preliminary preparations for what later became the famous Mississippi Summer Project. At that time Northern white activists working in Mississippi found themselves, as they said, being "race-baited." These college youth, taking time out from their studies to work in dangerous Mississippi, found that the Southern Negro activists were, to put it with some detachment, ambivalent toward the presence of the whites. The

SOURCE. Original publication. From a paper given at the 43rd Annual Meeting of the American Orthopsychiatric Association, March 18, 1965.

Northern white youth discovered that their suggestions were not wanted—were in fact resented. At best the white workers were to be the tolerated followers and foot-soldiers, no matter what their qualifications.

Thus the rising tide of what has been described as Negro "nationalistic" feeling within the Civil Rights movement—a development that involved criticism of white liberals, and an assertion of the necessity of Negro leadership—appeared to exhibit itself in an aggravated form. Actually, however, I believe that there are other factors involved in what Howard Zinn has described as the "tensions and troubles, anti-white and black nationalist feelings among Negroes in SNCC, resentment expressed against white kids rushing into the movement, personal piques and gripes and explosions, and, in one setting of high nervous tension, a fistfight."[1] This paper will attempt to describe and explain at least some of these other factors.

What I intend to do is to analyze in very tentative terms the characteristics of the youth, both white and Negro, who become dedicated activists. It has been my observation that the movement has attracted different sorts of people from each racial group. By "the movement" I refer not to the total Civil Rights movement, but to its direct-action wing—including people in SNCC, SCLC, CORE, and some in NAACP. These are the people who are called activists—that is, they participate in nonviolent, direct-action demonstrations.

Some individuals have only a fleeting and superficial participation in direct action. But those I shall be chiefly concerned with are the highly dedicated ones—the "true believers" who give up jobs, postpone their education, risk physical injury and even death, and at the very least expect to be arrested and to spend some time in jail. These are the people whose life for a period of months, even years, becomes almost entirely oriented around the movement.

While I consider the movement to be a reform rather than a revolutionary movement, it does have a revolutionary mystique; and the dedicated activists would fit Eric Hoffer's definition of the "true believer," those who are completely devoted to a cause, who find meaning in life through their participation in what they esoterically refer to as "*the* movement." I recall one charming white girl with whom I spoke during the course of her month-long stay in the Annapolis, Maryland, jail, where she elected to serve out her term rather than pay a small fine. "I have thought it all over," she said, "and I have decided that I and the movement are one."

---

[1] Howard Zinn, *SNCC: The New Abolitionists* (Boston, 1964), p. 126.

The generalizations that I will set forth must of necessity be gross oversimplifications of the complexity of social reality. There are many types of people in the movement, and they enter it for diverse reasons. Obviously all of these will not be subsumed under the model types I suggest. It must be emphasized furthermore that the speaker has not done systematic research on the motivations and social backgrounds of civil rights activists. My generalizations are based in part upon four years (1960–1964) of observation as a participant in direct-action organizations in Baltimore, Maryland, and Newark, New Jersey, and in direct-action demonstrations from Cambridge, Maryland, and Atlanta, Georgia, to Syracuse, New York. In part they are based upon numerous conversations and interviews conducted during the past five years in a number of Southern and Northeastern cities, in the course of research for a book on the history of the twentieth-century Civil Rights movement. I do not claim that the people with whom I talked and worked form a representative sample. My conclusions, it must be stressed, are oversimplified and very tentative. I hope, however, to be provocative and suggestive.

When the college student sit-in movement swept the South in 1960 I was teaching at Morgan State College, a Negro institution in Baltimore. Though Morgan does have a few students from elite families, its population is mostly working-class. The majority of them come from census tracts in which average family income is $3000 or less per year. Most of them belong to the first generation in their families to go to college, and for them college is a route of upward mobility. Their parental occupational background would place the majority in the upper-lower class if they were white; but in view of the skewed nature of the Negro class structure, arising out of the lack of economic opportunity, within the Negro community these youth come chiefly from families that function as lower-middle-class.

Morgan students have been involved in sporadic direct-action demonstrations for half a dozen years prior to 1960. Practically every spring the student council would inaugurate a campaign to desegregate the movie theater and one or more of the eating facilities at the shopping center less than a mile from the campus. These efforts, some successful and others not, were ordinarily of a brief duration. Prior to 1960 not one Morgan student had been arrested on any demonstration—though in the early years police were distinctly unfriendly. In short, these student activists, had not been "true believers."

Though the revival of Morgan student demonstrations in March 1960 came after the wave of sit-ins had spread through the South, the pattern of previous years was at first followed. But something different soon happened. Three students were arrested for blocking the entrance to the restaurant being picketed. It is perhaps significant that this group did not include any of the college's political or social elite, but did involve an aggressive personality, who was seeking to overturn the student-council leadership of the demonstrations, and who eventually dropped out of school for poor grades. In two or three weeks the student-council and fraternity crowd had—with two or three exceptions—retired from active association with the demonstrations. Those students who remained active, those who sat in and walked on picket lines week after week—those, that is, who formed the small group who were the backbone of the movement—consisted for the most part of individuals obscure in campus life. They tended to be rather below average in their scholarship; and in part because their energies were monopolized by the movement, several dropped out of school and others found themselves on probation. They were not the campus leaders, not the members of sororities and fraternities, not the good students, not even the athletes. The leaders who emerged often tended, it is true, to be above-average students, though these became so involved in the movement that their grades fell disastrously. To these youth life's meaning—and their own contribution to society—came not through athletic prowess, social or political distinction in campus life, or high academic achievement, but through attacking social injustice.

This state of affairs was neatly illustrated by the response of Morgan's students to a convocation address by the college president in the fall of 1961. The president recognized the contributions made by the demonstrators, but held that just as important as the "glamorous" sit-ins and arrests that were breaking down the Negro's exclusion from American society was the work of preparing oneself academically to achieve success in the expanding opportunities of an integrating society. His remarks failed to achieve their objective. They served as an effective rationalization for the great majority of students who felt somewhat guilty because they lacked the commitment to become activists. But the president was so far from reaching the activists with his homily that they took his remarks to mean that he opposed demonstrations. Actually, he was very proud of his students' participation in the demonstrations. As he often said, while white students were engaged in panty raids, Morgan students were working for the good of society.

My observations indicate that at other colleges a similar pattern existed—though there were a few exceptions, notably in Atlanta. As the college student movements shifted from the campus to the community and drew high-school youth into their activities, they appeared to attract much the same kind of persons. In discussions of this question with a group of student leaders from all parts of the South at a workshop in Nashville in the summer of 1961, the typical observation was that the participants were youth who came from "the striving lower class." Put in more sophisticated sociological jargon, it would appear that most of the Negro college and high-school youth involved at that stage of the movement were of working-class origins, with high upward mobility aspirations. They came from the working-class, church-going "respectables," and an important part of their motivation lay in their religious faith. To them the movement was a natural, practical application of the Christian faith in which they had been reared, and which had been such a vital psychological support for them and their parents. Later, those who remained in the movement were to become increasingly secularized for a number of reasons—among them contact with Northern white students, and frustration at the slow pace of social change that the nonviolent method achieved.

But that was to lie in the future. The spirit of the Southern Negro activists in the early months of the movement was brought into sharp focus at a conference of Northern and Southern students sponsored by the National Student Association early in 1961. The Northern white students believed that the ideological basis of the movement should be rooted in such statements as the United Nations Declaration of Human Rights. The Southern Negro students, however, insisted that it be firmly rooted in Christian writ.

The ranks of these Southern Negro youth included few achievers in athletics, in Greek-letter circles, or in scholarship. It would seem, in fact, that the high achiever, especially the high academic achiever, at the Southern Negro college pictures himself as advancing both himself and the race not through protest activity but through preparing himself thoroughly for a career. Seldom does it seem possible to reconcile both roles. The upward-mobile person of lower- or lower-middle-class origins must, in view of both his financial insecurity and cultural deprivation, put all his energies into his studies if he is to succeed by the American standards of success. If he has the inclination to become deeply involved in the protest movement, he lacks the time. And he cannot afford to take a year or two off from his studies and hold his career back while engaging in a financially unremunerative pursuit. On the other hand, those Negro youth of high academic accomplishment who do become deeply involved in Civil Rights come principally from upper-middle and upper-class families, and ordinarily from the best Northern universities. Thus they are financially secure and culturally advantaged. One can, of course, think of many exceptions to these generalizations. At Morgan the ablest leader in the student movement was an extraordinarily gifted young man, who possessed erratic study habits and average grades, and who preferred to be active in the world rather than sit at home with his books.

At this point I should state that during the last couple of years there has been increasing involvement of lower-class youth and young adults, and in times of severe crisis—as at Danville, Virginia, Selma, Alabama, and Birmingham, Alabama—people from all social classes and all ages may become so deeply motivated that they participate in demonstrations and risk going to jail. In Birmingham, in Selma, in Orangeburg, South Carolina, and in certain other places, even the schoolteachers—the most vulnerable, and therefore the most conservative, group in the Negro community—have become involved, as in Selma, where two or three hundred attempted to register. Equally significant has been the growing involvement of lower-class youth and young adults during 1963 and 1964. As a factory worker who became chairman of a CORE chapter in upper New York State put it, "It's in CORE that you find the Holy Spirit."

In my emphasis upon the lower-middle-class and working-class origins of today's activists, I would be remiss if I did not point out that most of the Negroes who were active in CORE in its first years, from 1942 to 1960, were middle-class people. CORE was very tiny then, and the numbers of middle-class Negroes who participated must have been very small indeed, especially in view of the fact that down to 1961 two-thirds of CORE's members were white. The whites in direct action in these years were also middle-class people in terms of their education and occupation. They were usually professional people, highly idealistic, frequently pacifists, and often Socialists as well. Since 1961 the trend has been for CORE to become predominantly Negro and for the Negroes to come more and more from the working class, though there are still CORE chapters in which middle-class Negroes predominate and set the tone. Meanwhile those white pacifists who have not left CORE have been pushed into the background.

My first contact with large numbers of white Civil Rights demonstrators was in the winter of 1961–1962, when projects sponsored jointly by Baltimore CORE and the Baltimore student nonviolent group brought hundreds, even thousands, of people to demonstrate in Baltimore and on Maryland's conservative Eastern Shore. They came from all up and down the Northeastern Seaboard. CORE people came from Philadelphia and New York; Negro youth came from Howard University in Washington; and white students came by the hundreds from such elite institutions as Swarthmore and Brown, Queens College and New York University, Yale and Harvard. I believe that, like the first student demonstrators

I knew at Morgan, few of these white youth could have been classed as "true believers." But questionnaires answered by several hundred of these visitors and analyzed by graduate sociology students at Johns Hopkins University did reveal some interesting things about this rather unrepresentative group that could afford to spend up to thirty dollars or more for a weekend trip to Baltimore. It turned out that it consisted largely of upper-middle-class youth and professional people, liberal idealists. My own personal observations with a number of Northern college students who came to Maryland that winter and spring of 1961–1962—the winter that witnessed a Civil Rights revolution in Baltimore, and brought demonstrations to the agrarian old-fashioned Eastern Shore, thus paving the way for the later dramatic movement and tragic denouement in Cambridge in 1963—revealed a group of young people who were from the best colleges, and usually at the top of their classes. They were idealistic, liberal youth, both Jewish and Gentile, who were eager to participate in our demonstrations.

It is doubtful that most of them would have gone farther south. Maryland not only was close enough for a weekend trip, but was a place where one could demonstrate against the sort of public accommodations that were integrated at home, and thus participate in the movement, but without much serious danger of arrest. And if one were arrested—as some hoped to be—there was no danger of police brutality, and bail money was available. The Maryland demonstrations thus tended to attract a type of clean-shaven, highly intellectual, idealistic white youth, whose commitment to direct action involved considerable personal sacrifice in terms of money and time taken from pressing studies, but who were unlikely to engage in Freedom Rides in Mississippi. Some of them did of course remain in the movement and did engage in the most dangerous types of direct action, but these real true believers were a minority.

By way of contrast, earlier, in the summer of 1961, CORE's Freedom Ride to Alabama and Mississippi included a wide variety of people, both white and Negro. Among the whites were old-line CORE pacifists, college intellectuals, bearded "beatnik" types, and revolutionary Marxists. Though it is impossible to indicate precise proportions, perhaps the majority of the dedicated white activists of the period 1961–1963 were radicals and beatnik types. Both were alienated from American middle-class values, and in their rejection of these values turned either to the Marxist critique of capitalist society or, perhaps more often, took on something of the hipster personality. Many of the latter type fitted quite neatly into Norman Mailer's concept of the "white Negro." Alienated from the middle-class conventions of their parents, they glorified the most alienated and outcast group in American society, lower-class

Negroes. They accepted the stereotypes whites hold about lower-class Negroes—the stereotypes of personal sloppiness and uninhibited sexuality. Only, instead of considering these qualities bad, they regarded them as the warp and woof of a superior way of life. As one bearded Johns Hopkins graduate student gravely informed me: "Of course Negroes are more promiscuous and uninhibited sexually than whites. I envy them and wish I could be like them." Similarly, the radicals tended to romanticize lower-class Negroes as part of their romanticization of the oppressed and poor of all societies.

Such individuals find in the movement more than a peg on which to hang their alienation and criticism of American life. They find that it also provides a cause with which to identify, a meaning for life, and a sense of purpose for themselves. As one vibrant, well-proportioned lass with long, stringy yellow hair set off against a deliberately pallid complexion said to a group of Civil Rights workers in Chicago last fall: "The movement means so much to those of us who disagreed with our parents and rebelled against society. In it we have found a home."

To some, the hipster sorts are "kooks." Many of them so reject their identity as members of conventional American white middle-class society that, far from objecting to the "race baiting" of some of the Negro militants, they either revel in it masochistically or join in similar criticism themselves. A few even fancy themselves "black nationalists." At CORE's 1963 convention one such activist unsuccessfully urged a Negro to run against a white candidate for the organization's National Action Council. His reason, succinctly stated, was simple: "We don't want any more of those God-damned white people on the Council."

But over the past two years an important change has come about in the kinds of whites involved. As already suggested, from the beginning there were always a few idealistic white liberals and other intellectuals who became deeply dedicated Civil Rights activists. But the events of 1963 marked a turning point in the kind of white participation, as it did for so many other things in the movement. The key factor here was undoubtedly the formation of the Interfaith Commission on Race in January. Six months later eminent clergymen of all three major faiths were among nearly a thousand arrested in demonstrations that led to the desegregation of an amusement park outside Baltimore. At the end of the summer a quarter million people marched on Washington—an event in which the clerics played a major supporting and symbolic role. Thus by the summer of 1963 the demonstrations that culminated in Birmingham that spring, and the awakened conscience of the supposed guardians of the moral values of the community, had started a moral

awakening in America that made Civil Rights activism fully respectable,
The recent events in Selma, and President Johnson's declaration that
"We Shall Overcome" and his praise for the Negro activists, are the
most recent evidence of this growing trend.

By the spring of 1964 the fruits of this development were evident
in the large numbers of white moderates who had become so committed
to Civil Rights that they clamored for the chance to pay the money
to enable them to risk their lives in Mississippi during the summer.
In using the term "white moderates" I mean to distinguish them not
only from the radical Marxists but also from the middle-class liberals,
both of whom had been interested in Civil Rights for years. These moderates differ from all the other types of whites who had heretofore been
involved in substantial numbers, because their involvement flowed not
from any alienation and rejection of the outlook of conventional Americans, but from commitment to the traditional shibboleths and pieties.
I talked to some of these youths in Mississippi last summer, where
I was interested to find many of them along with other types. I found
them generally to be good students, from stable family backgrounds,
not terribly concerned with social issues before they become interested
in Civil Rights. Like the Southern Negro youth who first set the tone
for the Civil Rights revolution in the early 1960s, they were good Christians, sincerely motivated by their religious tradition, and some were
preparing for the ministry. The examples of the status figures in their
churches and the Civil Rights crisis of 1963 combined to make it suddenly evident to these young men and women that race discrimination
was a burning issue. And it was a burning issue to them precisely because it violated the democratic and Christian values which they had
been trained to treasure. Certainly, one must look for other personality
traits to explain the intensity and dedication that propelled these particular youths, and not others, from conventional apolitical backgrounds
to become true believers in the cause of Civil Rights. The point I
am making is that in contrast to the beatniks, the radicals, the pacifists,
and even the liberals, the commitment of these youths arises not out
of any alienation from American society, but out of a profound attachment to it.

I believe that on the basis of the foregoing analysis we can see that
the situation in COFO, described at the opening of this paper, is exceedingly complex and involves far more than Negro "nationalistic" feeling
or general Negro distrust of whites. Much of the problem stems from
the fact that the Northern white youths in the movement—liberal, radical, or moderate—have tended to be intellectuals who stand high in

their classes at the best colleges and universities. They are therefore equipped with valuable skills largely lacking among the culturally deprived Southern Negro youths in the movement, whose educational background is at best inadequate, and who are very often from the lower half of their college classes, or are not college students at all. As outsiders with superior skills, young Northern Negro intellectuals also experience similar resentments from Southern youths in the movement. Thus resentments developed and became focused on the racial identity of most of the workers coming from the North, when in fact much of the problem stems from the fact that the movement does not attract the same kinds of people from both races.

To summarize, the movement thus draws from different social types among Negroes and whites. Broadly speaking, the majority of Negro activists appear to come from upward-mobile people of working-class background. They tend to describe themselves as "striving lower-class" people, though in the context of the Negro class structure it is better to regard them as lower middle class. More recently some members of the very lowest classes have become involved. Some participants are Negro intellectuals at prestigious Northern universities, but for the most part Negro activists either have been youths without a college education or, if they have been to college, have tended to be students who have not distinguished themselves in athletics, scholarships, social life, or campus politics. The leaders, however, often tend to be people of greater versatility, especially in the skills of communication.

White youths, on the other hand, have tended to be college students or recent college graduates, often from outstanding schools, and quite frequently near the top of their class. They tend to break down into two major categories: those who are alienated from American society and those who are not. The former include beatnik sorts, who identify with Negroes as the most alienated group in America, and the radical intelligentsia, ranging from Quaker-type pacifists to Trotskyites and Maoists. This group formed a large proportion of the participations from 1960 to 1963, along with a sprinkling of upper-middle-class idealistic Jews and other liberals. Beginning with the March on Washington, when the Civil Rights movement gained greater respectability and the support of prominent white clergymen, the movement came to attract more conventional types, motivated not by their alienation from American society but by their deep attachment to its values and ideals. As the recent events in Selma indicate, it is this very important fact which, from the point of view of the historian, suggests that the Civil Rights movement may well succeed in transforming the racial relations of American society.

3.

THE BAND OF POLITICAL RADICALS

MICHAEL WALZER

II

Neither Max Weber nor any of his follwers have ever demonstrated that the Englishmen who actually became Puritans, who really believed in predestination and lived through the salvation panic, went on to become capitalist businessmen. The burden of the evidence would seem to be against such a conclusion, though this is not certain; it is possible that businessmen are simply less likely to keep records of their spiritual struggles than of their economic affairs. The weight of such diaries, letters, and memoirs as we possess, however, suggests that the most significant expression of the new faith was cultural and political rather than economic. The saints were indeed activists, and activists in a far more intense and "driven" fashion than the men who came later: English gentlemen after their conversions attended to parliamentary affairs with a new assiduousness; pious mothers trained their sons to a constant concern with political life; enthusiastic apprentices took notes at sermons and studied the latest religious and political pamphlets. The outcome of Puritan activity was godly watchfulness, magistracy, and revolution.

Had the revolution succeeded, the discipline of the holy common-wealth, as of the Jacobin Republic of Virtue, would have required an institutionalized political activism. Each utopia would have proliferated a petty officialdom, a host of minor administrators busily enforcing the new rules and regulations. The ideas of John Eliot of Massachusetts suggest an image of the holy commonwealth as an over-governed society, with every tenth man an official. These zealous and conscientious magis-trates—equipped with a realistic and intolerant sense of the sinfulness of their fellow men—would hardly constitute a modern bureaucracy, though once again their religious contentiousness may suggest the diffi-cult, half-forgotten origins of modern bureaucratic discipline. The zeal of the saints seems to have little in common with the secular competence, functional rationality, and moderate devotion required of modern officials. Yet magistracy is a far better description of the saints' true vocation

SOURCE. Michael Walzer, *The Revolution of the Saints.* Cambridge: Harvard University Press, 1965, pp. 306–320. Reprinted by permission of Harvard University Press and the author. Copyright: President and fellows of Harvard College.

than is either capitalist acquisition or bourgeois freedom. It suggests most clearly the activist role that Puritanism called upon the saints to play in the creation and maintenance of a new moral order. This activity was political in the sense that it was always concerned with government—though not only or most importantly at the level of the state. For Puritans imagined the congregation as a "little commonwealth," debated worriedly over its constitution and sought means to discipline recalcitrant members; they saw the family as a voluntary community dominated by a godly father whom they described as a governor. And finally, they saw the self as a divided being, spirit at war with flesh, and there also they sought control and government.

Once Calvinism and Puritanism have been described in the political language of repression and war it becomes easier to answer the question posed in the first chapter of this book: why did particular groups of Englishmen and Frenchmen, Scots and Dutchmen become Calvinists and Puritans? They did so, it may be suggested, because they felt some need for the self-control and godly government that sainthood offered. This is to push Weber's explanation of capitalism a step further back: he has argued that Calvinism was an anxiety-inducing ideology that drove its adherents to seek a sense of control and confidence in methodical work and worldly success. But he has not even raised the question of why men should adopt an anxiety-inducing ideology in the first place, a question to which his own concept of "elective affinity" offers a possible answer.[1] Now it is probably not true that Calvinism *induced* anxiety; more likely its effect was to confirm and explain in theological terms perceptions men already had of the dangers of the world and the self. But what made Calvinism an "appropriate" option for anxiety-ridden individuals was not only this confirmation, but also the fact that sainthood offered a way out of anxiety. Puritan "method" led to tranquillity and assurance through the "exercises" of self-control and spiritual warfare, and it then led to the political order of the holy commonwealth through the corresponding "exercises" of magistracy and revolution.

Men were likely to become saints, or rather, it is understandable that certain men should have become saints, if their social and personal experiences had been of a certain sort.[2] Three different sets of experi-

---

[1] From Max Weber: *Essays in Sociology,* trans. and ed. H. H. Gerth and C. Wright Mills (London, 1948), pp. 284–285.

[2] The notion of "appropriate" or understandable behavior is used here in the sense suggested by William Dray, *Laws and Explanation in History* (Oxford, 1957), especially Part V. But for any full scale explanation of Puritanism in these terms it would probably be neccessary to extend considerably Dray's conception of

ences have been discussed in the preceding pages: that of discontented and fearful noblemen like the French Huguenots who sought some way to adjust to a modern political order; that of clerical intellectuals, newly freed from corporate ties (and from the privileges that went along with those ties) and especially sensitive to the ambiguities of their own position and the disorder of their society; and finally that of new or newly educated gentlemen, lawyers and merchants, nervously making their way in university, parliament, and city, with a claim to stake in the political and social worlds. None of these group experiences make individual conversion predictable; each of them makes it comprehensible. Thus the modern Calvinism of a man like Philip de Mornay can be viewed as the willful effort of an educated and ambitious French gentleman to demonstrate to himself as well as to others his worthiness for political office—a demonstration that required a rigid rejection of Renaissance pleasure and extravagance. The fanatical self-righteousness of that first Puritan John Knox, a Scottish peasant's son set loose in Europe by war and revolution, can best be understood as in some sense a function of his exile. Righteousness was a consolation and a way of organizing the self for survival. When John Whitgift, the future archbishop, cruelly taunted Thomas Cartwright for "eating at other men's tables," he was perhaps suggesting an important source of Cartwright's ideas of congregational unity and ministerial status. And finally, it can be argued, country gentlemen like John Winthrop and Oliver Cromwell, educated at Cambridge, knowledgeable but uneasy in London, full of new and vague aspirations, sought in Puritanism a self-confidence equal to their hopes and became saints on their way, as it were, to becoming governors of new worlds and new societies.

It should be noted that the elective affinity of aristocrats, ministers, gentlemen, merchants, and lawyers with the Calvinist and Puritan ideologies did not lie only in the anxiety they all shared, but also in the *capacity* they all shared to participate in those "exercises" that sainthood required. They were the "sociologically competent"—as has already been argued—they were ready for magistracy and war. The Calvinist faith did not appeal to men, however anxious, below the level of such competence. Laborers and peasants were more likely, if they were free at all from traditional ways, to adopt some more pacific or chiliastic faith whose promise did not depend upon their own hard work, that is, upon the control of themselves and the cruel, unwearying repression of others.

"rational action." See Samuel H. Beer, "Causal Explanation and Imaginative Re-enactment," *History and Theory* 3:23–24 (1963).

Puritanism cannot, then, be described simply as the ideological reflex of social disorder and personal anxiety; it is one possible response to the experiences of disorder and anxiety, or rather, it is one possible way of perceiving and responding to a set of experiences that other men than the saints might have viewed in other terms. There were both merchants and gentlemen, for example, who obviously enjoyed the very freedoms that frightened the saints so much—mobility, extravagance, individuality, and wit—and who eagerly sought out the Renaissance cities and courts where such freedoms were cultivated. And from among these new urbanites undoubtedly came many capitalists and liberals. It would not be easy to explain in particular cases why the court of James I held such attractions for some members of the English gentry while it was vicious and iniquitous in the eyes of others. No more is it readily comprehensible why some of the newcomers to the burgeoning city of London merged into the mob or explored the exciting underworld, while others hated the "wickedness" of the city and sought out virtuous brethren and a sense of security and confidence in the Puritan congregations. All that can be said is that some of the men living in this age of social transformation found what was for them a suitable response in Calvinist ideology. In England, Puritanism was their effort to capture control of the changing world and their own lives—hence the insistent concern of the saints with order, method, and discipline.

III

The Puritan concern with discipline and order, however, is not unique in history. Over and over again since the days of the saints, bands of political radicals have sought anxiously, energetically, systematically, to transform themselves and their world. The choice of sainthood, then, need not be described simply as a reasonable choice for sixteenth and seventeenth-century Englishmen to have made; it can be related systematically to other choices of other men in similar historical circumstances.

The very appearance of the Puritan saints in English history suggests the breakdown of an older order in which neither Protestant autodidacts, political exiles, nor voluntary associations of lay brethren were conceivable. At the same time that breakdown provides the context within which the choice of sainthood seems reasonable and appropriate, though not in any individual case predictable. It is possible to go further than this however, and argue that given the breakdown of the old order, it *is* predictable that some Englishmen would make that reasonable choice. And further than this: given similar historical circumstances, Frenchmen and Russians would predictably make similar choices. Englishmen became Puritans and then godly magistrates, elders and fathers in much the same way and for many of the same reasons as eighteenth-century Frenchmen became Jacobins and active citizens, and, and twentieth-century Russians Bolsheviks and professional revolutionaries—and then in Lenin's words "leaders," "managers," and "controllers."[3] The Calvinist saints were the first of these bands of revolutionary magistrates who sought above all control and self-control. In different cultural contexts, at different moments in time, sainthood will take on different forms and the saints will act out different revolutions. But the radical's way of seeing and responding to the world will almost certainly be widely shared whenever the experiences which first generated that perception and response are widely shared, whenever groups of men are suddenly set loose from old certainties.

That older order in which Puritanism was unimaginable has been described in the preceding pages as a traditional society, that is, a society in which hierarchy is the fundamental ordering principle; patriarchy, personal loyalty, patronage and corporatism are the key forms of human relations; and passivity is the normal political posture of common men. At some point in the later Middle Ages, the complex institutional structure of European traditionalism began to weaken and erode; its philosophical rationalizations were called into question by bold speculators free, more or less, from traditional controls. Then there began a long period of transition, in which moments of rapid and explosive change alternated with moments of stalemate and frustration. Individual men experienced at once a new and exhilarating sense of freedom and mobility and an acute anxiety and fearfulness, both of which may be summed up in the Puritan notion of "unsettledness." Only gradually, at different times in different countries, did there emerge a new society, whose members were at least formally equal, their political relations impersonal, based either upon negotiation and contract or upon a uniform coercion. In this society the activity of the organized "people" was as necessary to social discipline as was popular passivity in the traditional world.[4] The

[3] Lenin, *The Immediate Tasks of the Soviet Government* (1918) in *Selected Works* (New York, 1935–37), VII, 332–333. It was necessary, Lenin wrote, "to discover real organizers, people with sober minds and a practical outlook, people who combine loyalty to socialism, with ability without fuss (and in spite of fuss and noise) . . ." Compare this with Cromwell's plea for men "conscientious in employment."
[4] The importance of "participation" in modern politics is urged by Daniel Lerner, *The Passing of Traditional Society* (Glencoe, Ill., 1958), esp. pp. 57 ff.

old order was imagined to be natural and eternal, but it is in the nature of the new that it be regularly renewed. It is the produce of art and will, of human doing. If traditionalism was stable, modernity is founded upon change. Even so, however, it represents a routinization of the frenetic mobility that marked the period of transition and of the zeal and anxiety that drove men forward during that exciting and painful time.

The significance of Puritanism lies in the part it played between 1530 and 1660. Those were crucial years of struggle and change in England and those were the years when Calvinism was a forceful, dynamic faith. After the Restoration, its energy was drawn inward, its political aspirations forgotten; the saint gave way to the nonconformist. Or, Lockeian liberalism provided an alternative political outlook. But Puritanism cannot be explained by reference either to its survivals or its transformations; it is necessary to confront the historical reality of those years when it was still an integral creed. In those years, Puritanism provided what may best be called an *ideology of transition*. It was functional to the process of modernization not because it served the purposes of some universal progress, but because it met the human needs that arise whenever traditional controls give way and hierarchical status and corporate privilege are called into question.[5] These needs can be met in other ways: by ideologists of nostalgia, for example, who glorify the old security and the old bondage. But they are met most effectively by doctrines like Puritanism that encourages a vigorous self-control and a narrowing of energies, a bold effort to shape a new personality against the background of social "unsettledness." Once such a personality has been achieved, the saints proceed to shape society in the image of their own salvation; they become what the ideologists of nostalgia can never become: active enemies of the old order. Thus when country gentlemen have experienced a conversion like Cromwell's, they are transformed not only into saints but also into parliamentary intransigents, attacking the traditional hierarchy root and branch and experimenting with new forms of political association.

But though they appear in history as revolutionaries, who destroy the old order and kill the king, the primary source of the saints' radical character lies in their response to the *dis*order of the transition period. The old order is only a part, and not the most important part of their experience. They live much of their lives amidst the breakdown of that order or (as with the clerical intellectuals) in hiding or exile from it.

---

[5] This view of radical ideology was first suggested by Adam Ulam in his study of Marxist thought, *The Unfinished Revolution* (New York, 1960).

Much as they hated bishops and courtiers, then, the Puritan saints hated and feared vagabonds more and dreaded the consequences of the vagabonds in themselves, their own "unsettledness." "Masterless men" are always the first products of the breakdown of tradition and the saints hardly thought such men less dangerous than did their former masters. Without the experience of masterlessness, the Puritans are unimaginable. Sainthood is one of the likely results of that experience, or rather one of the ways in which men seek to cope with that experience. Hobbist authoritarianism is another way—and the contrast between Hobbes' appeal to sovereign power and the Puritan's struggle for self-control suggests the difficulty of describing sainthood, in Erich Fromm's terms, as an "escape from freedom."[6]

Fromm is certainly right, however, in viewing the saint in the context of "freedom." The Puritans were in no sense the products of a new order slowly growing up within traditional feudal society, as Marxist theory would have it. They were the products—though that word hardly suggests their extraordinary activism—of disorder. They inherited the critical and destructive work of writers like Machiavelli and Luther and they continued that work only after they had organized themselves to survive in the midst of criticism and destruction. They were second-generation men: they arrived in a world where courageous heretics and philosophers had already challenged the traditional masters; they encountered the difficulties of this world by being born again, by rejecting masterlessness and finding a new master in themselves and a new system of control in their godly brethren.

Coping with disorder meant being reborn as a new man, self-confident and free of worry, capable of vigorous, willful activity. The saints sometimes took new names, or gave new names to their children, to signify this rebirth. If the experience of "unsettledness" had made them anxious, depressed, unable to work, given to fantasies of demons, morbid introspection, or fearful daydreams such as Calvin had suggested were common among fallenmen, then sainthood was indeed a triumph of character formation. Here the analogy with the Bolsheviks is worth pursuing. Lenin's diatribes against "slovenliness . . . carelessness, untidiness, unpunctuality, nervous haste, the inclination to substitute discussion for action, talk for work, the inclination to undertake everything under the sun without finishing anything" were intended first of all as attacks upon his fellow radicals and exiles—whatever their value as descriptions of the "primitive" Russia he hated so much.[7] The first triumph of Bolshe-

[6] Erich Fromm, *Escape from Freedom* (New York, 1941), pp. 84–98.
[7] *How to Organize Competition* (1917, repr. Moscow, 1951), p. 63; also *Letters*, trans. and ed. Elizabeth Hill and Doris Mudie (New York, 1937), p. 113.

vism, as of Puritanism, was over the impulse toward "disorganization" in its own midst: here, so to speak, was Satan at work where he is ever most active—in the ranks of the godly. It should not be forgotten, however, that this was a triumph also over the impulse toward free thought and spontaneous expression that manifests itself with especial vigor in the period of masterlessness and with which modernity has, up to a point, made its peace. This was the sacrifice which the saints found necessary in their terrible struggle for self-control. The Puritans vigorously attacked Renaissance experimentation in dress and in all the arts of self-decoration and hated the free-wheeling vagabonds who roamed the countryside and crowded into cities, never organizing themselves into families and congregations. They dreaded the dance and the drama, tore down maypoles and closed playhouses; they waged a long, bitter and unending war against fornication. In a similar fashion, the Jacobin leader Robespierre attacked the hedonism and censured the morals of the new bourgeoisie and spitefully connected the radical free thought of the Enlightenment with anti-revolutionary conspiracy. Atheism, he declared, is aristocratic.[8] And again Lenin, preaching with all the energy of a secular Calvinist against free love: "Dissoluteness in sexual life is bourgeois, [it] is a phenomenon of decay. The proletariat is a rising class. . . . It needs clarity, clarity and again clarity. And so, I repeat, no weakening, no waste, no destruction of forces."[9]

In fact, Lenin's morality had little to do with the proletariat and the "dissoluteness" he attacked had little to do with the bourgeoisie. He might as well have talked of saints and worldings as the Puritans did. The contrast he was getting at was between those men who had succumbed to (or taken advantage of!) the disorder of their time—speculators in philosophy, vagabonds in their sexual lives, economic Don Juans—and those who had somehow pulled themselves out of "unsettledness," organized their lives and regained control. The first group were the damned and the second the saved. The primary difference between them was not social, but ideological.

All forms of radical politics make their appearance at moments of rapid and decisive change, moments when customary status is in doubt and character (or "identity") is itself a problem. Before Puritans, Jacobins, or Bolsheviks attempt the creation of a new order, they must create new men. Repression and collective discipline are the typical

[8] Quoted in A. Aulard, *Christianity and the French Revolution* (Boston, 1927), p. 113.

[9] Quoted in Klara Zetkin, "Reminiscences of Lenin," in *The Family in the U.S.S.R.*, ed. Rudolf Schlesinger (London, 1949), p. 18.

methods of this creativity: the disordered world is interpreted as a world at war; enemies are discovered and attacked. The saint is a soldier whose battles are fought out in the self before they are fought out in society. Revolution follows from Puritan sainthood—that is, from the triumph over Satanic lusts—and also from Jacobin virtue and from the Bolshevik "steeling" of character; it is the acting out of a new identity, painfully won. This connection between sainthood and revolution is nicely illustrated in John Milton's eulogy of Cromwell: "A commander first over himself; the conqueror of himself, it was over himself he had learnt most to triumph. Hence he went to encounter with an external enemy as a veteran accomplished in all military duties. . . ."[10] In traditional societies, this self-conquest is not necessary—except for relatively small numbers of men who for personal reasons choose monasticism as a way of life. In modern societies, it is routine. But there is a point in the modernization process when large numbers of men, suddenly masterless, seek a rigid self-control; when they discover new purposes, dream of a new order, organize their lives for disciplined and methodical activity. These men are prospective saints and citizens; for them Puritanism, Jacobinism, and Bolshevism are appropriate options. At this point in time, they are likely options.

This is not to reduce political radicalism to the psychological therapy of "unsettled" men. The "unsettledness" which Knox, Cartwright, and Cromwell experienced, with all its attendant fearfulness and enthusiasm, sometimes disfiguring and sometimes ennobling, was only a heightened form of the feelings of many of their fellow Englishmen—for ultimately the sociological range of the Puritan response was very wide. Of course, "unsettledness" was not a permanent condition and so sainthood was only a temporary role. The Puritans failed in their effort to transform England into a holy commonwealth and, in one way or another, their more recent counterparts have also failed. Sainthood mediated the dangerous shift from one social routine to another; then it survived only as a remembered enthusiasm and a habitual self-control devoid, as Weber's capitalism is, of theological reason. What this suggests, however, is not that holiness was an impractical dream, the program of neurotic, muddled, or unrealistic men. In fact, Puritan ministers and elders (and fathers) had considerable political experience and the holy commonwealth was in part achieved—among those men who most needed holiness. Nor is it correct to argue from the inability of the saints to retain political power that Puritanism represented only a temporary triumph

[10] Milton, *Works*, ed. F. A. Patterson et al. (New York, 1932), VIII, 213.

of "ideas" over "interests," of the holiness doctrine over the ultimately more significant secular purposes of gentlemen, merchants, and lawyers.[11] For what needs to be explained is precisely why the saints over a long period of time acquired such an intense interest in ideas like predestination and holiness. Puritan ideology was a response to real experience, therefore a practical effort to cope with personal and social problems. The disappearance of the militant saints from English politics in the years after the Restoration suggests only that these problems were limited in time to the period of breakdown and psychic and political reconstruction. When men stopped being afraid or became less afraid, then Puritanism waas suddenly irrelevant. Particular elements of the Puritan system were transformed to fit the new routine—and other elements were forgotten. And only then did the saint become a man of "good behavior," cautious, respectable, moved only by a routine anxiety and ready to participate in a Lockeian society.

IV

It is now possible to suggest a model of radical politics based on the history of the English Puritans and developed, at least in part, in their own terms. Such a model may serve to reveal the crucial features of radicalism as a general historical phenomenon and to make possible a more systematic comparison of Puritans, Jacobins, and Bolsheviks (and perhaps other groups as well) than has been attempted here.

(1) At a certain point in the transition from one or another form of traditional society (feudal, hierarchical, patriarchal, corporate) to one or another form of modern society, there appears a band of "strangers" who view themselves as chosen men, saints, and who seek a new order and an impersonal, ideological discipline.

(2) These men are marked off from their fellows by an extraordinary self-assurance and daring. The saints not only repudiate the routine procedures and customary beliefs of the old order, but they also cut themselves off from the various kinds of "freedom" (individual mobility, personal extravagance, self-realization, despair, nervousness, vacillation) experienced amidst the decay of tradition. The band of the chosen seeks and wins certainty and self-confidence by rigidly disciplining its members and teaching them to discipline themselves. The saints interpret their ability to endure this discipline as a sign of their virtue and their

[11] This is the view of revolutionary enthusiasm suggested in Crane Brinton's book on the French Revolution, *Decade of Revolution* (New York, 1934), and again in his *Anatomy of Revolution* (New York, 1938).

virtue as a sign of God's grace. Amidst the confusion of the transitional period, they discover in themselves a predestination, a firm and unelevating sense of purpose, an assurance of eventual triumph.

(3) The band of the chosen confronts the existing world as if in war. Its members interpret the strains and tensions of social change in terms of conflict and contention. The saints sense enmity all about them and they train and prepare themselves accordingly. They keep watch and continually calculate their chances.

(4) The organization of the chosen suggests the nature of the new order they seek, but also reflects the necessities of the present struggle.

(a) Men join the band by subscribing to a covenant which testifies to their faith. Their new commitment is formal, impersonal, and ideological; it requires that they abandon older loyalties not founded upon opinion and will—loyalties to family, guild, locality, and also to lord and king.

(b) This commitment is voluntary, based upon an act of the will for which men can be trained, but not born. It is not possible to take one's place in the chosen band through any sort of patronage. To be chosen, one must choose.

(c) The commitment and zeal of prospective saints must be tested and proven. Hence it is not easy to choose sainthood and the band of the chosen remains exclusive and small, each of its members highly "talented" in virtue and self-discipline. Even after men have been accepted as saints, they must still demonstrate their godliness on every possible occasion. They are subject to examination and as they could once have been rejected so they can always be purged. The godly tension which the saints maintain is thus in vivid contrast to the apathy of worldings, secure and at their ease with their customs and traditions.

(d) Within the band of the chosen, all men are equal. Status counts for little. Members are measured by their godliness and by the contributions they can make to the work at hand.

(5) The acting out of sainthood produces a new kind of politics.

(a) The activity of the chosen band is purposive, programmatic, and progressive in the sense that it continually approaches or seeks to approach its goals. This activity may be defined as an organized effort to universalize sainthood, to reconstruct or reform the political or religious worlds according to objective criteria (revealed, predetermined, written), without any regard for the established forms.

(b) The activity of the saints is methodical and systematic. Politics is made into a kind of work, to which the chosen are required to commit themselves for long periods of time. At work they must suppress all purely personal feelings and behave in a disciplined fashion.

They must learn to be patient and to concern themselves with detail. Above all, they must work regularly and hard.

(c) The violent attack upon customary procedures sets the saints free to experiment politically. Such experimentation is controlled by its overriding purposes and the right to engage in it is limited to the chosen few who have previously accepted the discipline of the band. It is not a grant of political free-play, but it does open the way to new kinds of activity, both public and secret. The saints are entrepreneurs in politics.

(6) The historical role of the chosen band is twofold. Externally, as it were, the band of the saints is a political movement aiming at social reconstruction. It is the saints who lead the final attack upon the old order and their destructiveness is all the more total because they have a total view of the new world. Internally, godliness and predestination are creative responses to the pains of social change. Discipline is the cure for freedom and "unsettledness." As romantic love strengthens the bonds of the conjugal family, so ideological zeal establishes the unity of the nonfamilial brethren and makes it possible for men to feel secure outside the traditional system of connections.

One day, however, that security becomes a habit and zeal is no longer a worldly necessity. Then the time of God's people is over. In this world, the last word always belongs to the worldlings and not to the saints. It is a complement word and it comes when salvation, in all its meanings, is no longer a problem. But the saints have what is more interesting: the first word. They set the stage of history for the new order.

Once that order is established, ordinary men are eager enough to desert the warfare of the Lord for some more moderate pursuit of virtue. Once they feel sufficiently secure as gentlemen and merchants, as country justices and members of Parliament, they happily forego the further privilege of being "instruments." Hardly a moment after their triumph, the saints find themselves alone; they can no longer exploit the common forms of ambition, egotism, and nervousness; they can no longer convince their fellow men that ascetic work and intense repression are necessary. The experience of other revolutionaries has been similar: the history of their success is brief. An enthusiastic poet of the Bolshevik Revolution, for example, wrote as early as 1924 that his verse was no longer needed.[12] The vanguard, he suggested (not quite accurately) had settled down to a new routine:

[12] Sergei Esenin, "Soviet Russia," trans. George Reavey, *Partisan Review* 28:379–382 (1961).

> I see before me
> Villagers in Sunday best
> Transact a meeting as if attending church.

The good old cause had quickly become only a memory:

> Wrinkling his reminiscent forehead,
> A lame Red Army man with drowsy face
> Grandly expatiates upon Budyonny
> And the Reds who captured Perekop by storm.

And the "rebel soul" felt like an alien again:

> What a misfit I've become
> . . . I feel a foreigner in my land.

So too the Puritan saint was a stranger before his revolution, and after. There was a difference, of course, for the new routine embodied many aspects of his radical faith. But the enthusiasm, the battle-readiness, the confident enmity, the polemical eagerness, the sense of unity among the brethren, the first pride of self-control—all these were gone. Something of the tension, vigilance, and excitement they suggest might have been maintained in the holy commonwealth, but not in the world of the Restoration or the Whigs. They had helped carry men through a time of change; they had no place in a time of stability. They had been elements of strength in an age of moral confusion and of cruel vigor in an age of vacillation. Now it was suggested that saintly vigor had its own pathology and conventionalism its own health; peace had its virtues as well as godly warfare.

VII.

SOME CONTINGENCIES OF COLLECTIVE ACTION

Social movements exist over periods of time. Because they have histories, they are deeply affected by new events and new conditions of action. Whether or not they will achieve their initial goals is always a matter of doubt. In the process of developing organization they undergo change. Over periods of time the structure of the society itself changes, and the social base of the movement, as well as its existence, may no longer be what it was in the initial stages of collective development. New circumstances arise, and the history of the movement is often influenced by the contingencies it must face.

To some extent there may be patterns of development involved in the histories of many social movements. Some sociologists have utilized a *natural history* approach to the study of social movements and have attempted to describe characteristic stages of a movement from its initial enthusiastic burst to the acceptance of its goals and their enshrinement as institutions. One can think of the process of institutionalization in two senses. In the first sense the movement itself becomes regularized and routinized in organized ways. In the second sense the movement achieves some of its goals and now the organization and/or its program becomes part of the social order. The tendency of sects to become churches and thus lose their disident character is an apt illustration of this phenomenon. The advent to power of a dissenting political movement is another good illustration of the process of institutionalization.

The contrast between a movement as it regularizes or as it succeeds and its earlier enthusiastic and somewhat utopian spirit has been a prevalent subject among students of social movements and collective action.

The idea that movements have careers, and that they can succeed or fail, leads us to recognize that in the process of response to changed conditions and to its own internal changes a movement may transform its goals. A movement that has reached success, like the Infantile Paralysis Foundation, may deliberately seek to change its goals. A movement that meets with stronger opposition or with a shift in its base to another group or to slightly different interests may find pressures arising to shift and displace itself from one set of goals to another. It is worth noting that the present cornflake industry, now quite correctly characterized as a business, developed from a health movement which sought to displace meat by healthy cereal foods. Goals may change, and transformation is an important aspect in understanding both the outcome of movements and the ways in which a given structure, a movement's organization, is utilized for a variety of purposes and functions.

Considerations such as these have made many analysts of social movements look to the general theory of formal organization for some understanding of what happens to many social movements. The consequences of bureaucratization have occupied a number of social scientists since Max Weber developed his famous theory of bureaucracy. Such analysis has stressed the ways in which the development of structure for specific purposes often leads to the structure itself, its enhancement and continuance, becoming a major goal of the movement. Thus the interest in organizational survival and aggrandizement may become paramount over the earlier mission of the movement.

This problem has been discussed with great vigor both by students and by activists in social movements who have been dismayed by the paradox that the structure necessary to achieve purposes may itself become a barrier to the success of its mission. In Lenin we have already seen a defense of the importance of organizational structure. Nevertheless, many activists have taken strong measures to secure a high degree of flexibility and fluidity which would avoid tendencies for leadership to become permanent, for experts to replace enthusiasts, and for the movement's values to be overtaken by those of organization for its own sake.

The first two of our readings deal with these issues both as problems of analysis and as policy matters that movements must confront. H. Richard Niebuhr's analysis of the Methodist movement in England and the United States is a classic presentation on the theme of the churches of the disinherited. Niebuhr is concerned with the tendency of religious enthusiasm and spiritual values to become accommodated to those of the society around which they exist and to lose their dissenting status of sectarian criticism of society.

This paradox of organization is examined in a number of areas by Mayer Zald and Roberta Ash in their paper on growth and change in social movements. Zald and Ash refer here to a large body of literature, including studies of a number of different kinds of movements, and especially the point of view of Robert Michels in his work *Political Parties*. Michels formulated a famous "iron law of oligarchy" which states that as organizations get bigger they tend to become ruled by a small minority and tend to displace their original goals by those of organizational needs. As Zald and Ash indicate, this is by no means a necessary conclusion from the fact of organization, and they suggest a number of instances in which the "law" is not applicable.

As collective action continues it becomes susceptible to the pressures of change in the society around it and within its own organization. Change produces new problems and dilemmas for adaptation and decision. Thus movements go through crises in which they must make decisions that influence their own futures to a very great degree. They are confronted with new situations for which their periods of generation and development may not have prepared them. The Indian independence movement, for example, after many years of battle against Great Britain, was confronted with a crisis of decision in relation to independence in 1947, when the goal of national independence became possible but at the cost of partition between India and present-day Pakistan.

Certain events in history may thus be crucial turning points for a movement, deeply affecting its direction from that point forward. The description of such turning points is crucial to any understanding of a movement's history. Sometimes these emerge as policy decisions within the movement. When the Soviet Union concluded its pact with Hitler in 1939 it represented a great change in the policy which had existed for several years before Individual national Communist parties were confronted with an event of considerable importance for their future. Many went along, but at a certain cost to the character of the movement. Sometimes the turning points may be products of events over which the individual movement has little choice. The Prohibition movement in the United States was affected by the depression of 1929–1933. More than any other event, the depression was crucial to the success of the Repeal movement, which succeeded in repeal of the Eighteenth Amendment.

It is not only the conditions within or without the movement that change. The adherents who make up the constituency of a movement may themselves undergo changes. Thus the policies that the government follows or the increased or decreased resistance to it in the society may have important repercussions in the willingness or the ability of the members to remain committed to the movement. The fact of defection, or loss of commitment, is a typical crisis which movements confront.

Defection and commitment, however, can be seen not only as responses to events but also as functions of change itself. People die, get older, marry, have children—these changes have important repercussions for a movement because they mean that what was taken for granted in one stage of the movement may no longer be taken for granted. The death of a leader and the problems of succession are among the many problems which movements face over time.

Excerpts from *The Appeals of Communism* by Gabriel Almond indicate some sources of defection. In this case they emerged through the tension between dedication to the Communist movement and to other roles and loyalties which the individual retained. Loyalties to values, to families, or to other job demands all played a role in minimizing the commitment of the member to the movement, especially in the face of policy decisions which seemed to him inconsistent.

There is an ambiguity about the realization of goals which the student of social movements must face. This ambiguity sometimes has made people question the worthwhileness of collective action and to suggest that deep-lying social trends are more crucial and important than the noise and fervor of ideological discussion. An opposing view, however, suggests that without explicit development of demands for change social institutions would remain static and inertia-ridden. Movements act to topple the social order when underlying trends are ready for it, and also to give direction to change. Neither answer is wholly acceptable. Instead the specific conditions under which movements develop and act must be understood before their effective accomplishments can be assessed. The tendency of some movements to dissolve in the very process of realizing their goal has been a matter of considerable note in this volume. Both failure and success may destroy the solidarity and organizational base of a movement. The effort to find new goals may reveal considerable schism within the organization or may provoke factional controversies over how the changes should be managed.

Yet collective action may have an impact on the society even though only through the development and maintenance of public sentiment and opinion. It is fallacious to judge the consequences of a movement solely by how its programmatic aims are realized. Some movements have achieved legislation, as in the case of the Progressive movement's achievement in antitrust, but have seen the legislation become an ambiguous instrument. Others, such as many third party movements in the United States, have seldom succeeded in achieving the election of officials or adoption of the specific policies that they enunciated. Though such movements have themselves dissolved, their impact and imprint on public opinion has often been quite considerable and a strong source of changes in institutional policy.

The institutionalization of movements is a complicated and complex problem. Passage of legislation may not be followed by its enforcement, as was true in part of the Prohibition movement in the 1920s. In the achievement of power, a political movement may find itself compromising the very programs and goals with which it began, so much that the utility of its victories is in doubt. Yet the consequences of the movement may not be clearly related to its success or failure as an organizational and programmatic effort. The consequences of the movement cannot necessarily be spelled out by the analysis of what happened to the organization or what happens to specific campaigns to achieve its program.

Our final reading provides an excellent illustration of the fact that even failures can be successful. In his analysis of what has happened to the American antitrust movement, the American historian Richard Hofstadter agrees that neither ineffective enforcement nor in the maintenance and growth of public sentiment were the antitrust aspects of the Progressivist era very lasting. Nevertheless, Hofstadter points out that antitrust legislation became most effective in the late 1930s, when it was utilized by experts and technicians in powerful positions in the government. While the legislation and enforcement may have been limited, the effect of possible development and resurgence of antitrust sentiment and antitrust action has acted as a powerful force in business circles. While the antitrust movement, as a vehicle of public sentiment and as an organized effort to achieve specific legal action, had disappeared, its aura enabled institutionally effective persons to utilize it for a much wider enforcement. Hofstadter's analysis is a very good illustration of what he himself says: "Institutions are commonly less fragile than creeds."

A.

The Transformation of Mission

1.

THE CHURCHES OF THE DISINHERITED

H. RICHARD NIEBUHR

I

That astute historian of the social ethics of the churches, Ernst Troeltsch, once wrote: "The really creative, church-forming, religious movements are the work of the lower strata. Here only can one find that union of unimpaired imagination, simplicity in emotional life, unreflective character of thought, spontaneity of energy and vehement force of need, out of which an unconditioned faith in a divine revelation, the naïveté of complete surrender and the intransigence of certitude can rise. Need upon the one hand and the absence of an all-relativizing culture of reflection on the other hand are at home only in these strata. All great community-building revelations have come forth again and again out of such circles and the significance and power for further development in such religious movements have always been dependent upon the force of the original impetus given in such naïve revelations as well as on the energy of the conviction which made this impetus absolute and divine." This passage not only describes the character of

SOURCE. H. Richard Niebuhr, *Social Sources of Denominationalism*. New York: Living Age Books, 1957, pp. 29–33, 54–75. Reprinted by permission of Mrs. H. R. Niebuhr.

the religious movements which originate in the culturally lower strata of society but also indicates wherein the religious expatriation of these classes consists and shows the dialectic of the process which gives rise to ever new movements.

The religion of the untutored and economically disfranchised classes has distinct ethical and psychological characteristics, corresponding to the needs of these groups. Emotional fervor is one common mark. Where the power of abstract thought has not been highly developed and where inhibitions on emotional expression have not been set up by a system of polite conventions, religion must and will express itself in emotional terms. Under these circumstances spontaneity and energy of religious feeling rather than conformity to an abstract creed are regarded as the tests of religious genuineness. Hence also the formality of ritual is displaced in such groups by an informality which gives opportunity for the expression of emotional faith and for a simple, often crude, symbolism. An intellectually trained and liturgically minded clergy is rejected in favor of lay leaders who serve the emotional needs of this religion more adequately and who, on the other hand, are not allied by culture and interest with those ruling classes whose superior manner of life is too obviously purchased at the expense of the poor.

Ethically, as well as psychologically, such religion bears a distinct character. The salvation which it seeks and sets forth is the salvation of the socially disinherited. Intellectual naïveté and practical need combine to create a marked propensity toward millenarianism, with its promise of tangible goods and of the reversal of all present social systems of rank. From the first century onward, apocalypticism has always been most at home among the disinherited. The same combination of need and social experience brings forth in these classes a deeper appreciation of the radical character of the ethics of the gospel and greater resistance to the tendency to compromise with the morality of power than is found among their more fortunate brethren. Again, the religion of the poor is characterized by the exaltation of the typical virtues of the class and by the apprehension under the influence of the gospel of the moral values resident in its necessities. Hence one finds here, more than elsewhere, appreciation of the religious worth of solidarity and equality, of sympathy and mutual aid, of rigorous honesty in matters of debt, and the religious evaluation of simplicity in dress and manner, of the wisdom hidden to the wise and prudent but revealed to babes, of poverty of spirit, of humility and meekness. Simple and direct in its apprehension of the faith, the religion of the poor shuns the relativizations of ethical and intellectual sophistication and by its fruits in conduct often demonstrates its moral and religious superiority.

Whenever Christianity has become the religion of the fortunate and cultured and has grown philosophical, abstract, formal, and ethically harmless in the process, the lower strata of society find themselves religiously expatriated by a faith which neither meets their psychological needs nor sets forth an appealing ethical ideal. In such a situation the right leader finds little difficulty in launching a new movement which will, as a rule, give rise to a new denomination. When, however, the religious leader does not appear and religion remains bound in the forms of middle-class culture, the secularization of the masses and the transfer of their religious fervor to secular movements, which hold some promise of salvation from the evils that afflict them, is the probable result.

The development of the religion of the disinherited is illustrated not only by the history of various sects in Christianity but by the rise of that faith itself. It began as a religion of the poor, of those who had been denied a stake in contemporary civilization. It was not a socialist movement, as some have sought to show, but a religious revolution, centering in no mundane Paradise but in the cult of Christ. Yet it was addressed to the poor in the land, to fishermen and peasants, to publicans and outcasts. In Corinth as in Galilee, in Rome as in Antioch, not many "wise after the flesh, not many mighty, not many noble were called"; and this condition continued far down into the third century. Origen and Tertullian as well as the opponents of Christianity, notably Celsus, bear ample testimony to the fact that "the uneducated are always in a majority with us." But the new faith became the religion of the cultured, of the rulers, of the sophisticated; it lost its spontaneous energy amid the quibblings of abstract theologies; it sacrificed its ethical rigorousness in compromise with the policies of governments and nobilities; it abandoned its apocalyptic hopes as irrelevant to the well-being of a successful church. Now began the successive waves of religious revolution, the constant recrudescences of religions of the poor who sought an emotionally and ethically more satisfying faith than was the metaphysical and formal cult Christianity had come to be. Montanism, the Franciscan movement, Lollardy, Waldensianism, and many similar tendencies are intelligible only as the efforts of the religiously disinherited to discover again the sources of effective faith. Yet on the whole it is true that the Roman Church, with its ritual, its pageantry, and its authoritative doctrine, supplied to the unsophisticated groups a type of religion which largely satisfied their longings; for under the necessity of adapting itself to the inundation of the northern tribes it had evolved a system of leadership and worship congenial to the naïve mind and had learned to set forth salvation in terms not abstract but tangible and real though remote. The Roman Church, despite the evident failings of scholasticism and papal policy and sacerdotal luxury, was unable to maintain its integrity not so much because it did not meet the needs of the lower strata as because it did not sufficiently accommodate itself to the new middle classes represented by humanism, the new capitalism and nationalism, as well as for reasons not primarily connected with the economic and cultural stratification of society. . . .

The Quakers, no less than their predecessors among the churches of the poor, soon settled down to an "equable respectability." They accommodated themselves to the social situation and confined their efforts toward social reformation to the work of gaining converts to their faith, to the works of charity and to occasional efforts to influence public opinion on social questions. A number of factors were responsible for this decline in revolutionary fervor. The effect of persecution has been pointed out. Another important factor in the development of such denominations from revolutionary groups to settled social bodies, content with their place in the scheme of things, is the substitution of a second generation, which holds its convictions as a heritage, for a first generation which had won these convictions painfully and held them at a bitter cost. But most important among the causes of the decline of revolutionary churches into denominations is the influence of economic success. The churches of the poor all became middle-class churches sooner or later and, with their need, lose much of the idealism which grew out of their necessities. There is no doubt of the truth of Max Weber's contention that godliness is conducive to economic success. From the days of Paul at Thessalonica onward, Christianity has not failed to exhort its adherents "that with quietness they work and eat their own bread," while at the same time it has commanded them to abstain from luxury, but, having "food and covering," "therewith to be content." Monastic asceticism, supported by a dualistic view of life, carried the second of these ideas to its extreme, and was rejected by Protestantism, but the Reformers introduced in place of the "extra-worldly" asceticism of the monks an "intra-worldly" asceticism, which regarded work in trade and vocation as the primary duty of life and a service to God; yet they continued to condemn any indulgence in the comforts and luxuries of life as sinful. Restrictions on consumption accompanied by emphasis upon production have their inevitable result in an economic salvation which is far removed from the eternal blessedness sought by the enthusiastic founders of the Protestant sects, but which is not less highly valued by the successful followers of later generations. This process, which is repeated again and again in the history of Christian sects, also took place in the case of the Quakers. In the second and third generations, with the aid of the prosperity prevailing in the days of good Queen Anne, this church of the disinherited became a more or less respectable middle-class church that left the popular movement from which it originated far behind. It continued to hold the tenets of its social program but now as the doctrines of a denomination rather than as the principles of inclusive social reconstruction. In America, especially, the economic rise of the Quakers was speedy and permanent.

Once more, therefore, the poor were without a gospel. The Millenarian hopes which had fired the popular movement of the seventeenth century with enthusiasm were definitely left behind. The ethics of Jesus was dissolved completely into a mild morality of respectability. Eighteenth-century England, ecclesiastical and academic as well as political, feared nothing so much as enthusiasm. Its reaction against the tense emotionalism of Civil War and Revolutionary days, its disillusionments, its lack of vital energies, exhausted as it was by the turbulent passions of religious and political revolt, left it sterile and cold in religion, enamored only with the bleak beauty of mathematically-minded philosophy or, more frequently, indifferent to the claims of any ethical or religious idealism. Lecky, describing the religion of the period, writes, "The sermons of the time were almost always written, and the prevailing taste was cold, polished and fastidious." "As is always the case, the habits prevailing in other spheres at once acted on and were influenced by religion. The selfishness, the corruption, the worship of expediency, the scepticism as to all higher motives that characterized the politicians of the school of Walpole; the heartless cynicism reigning in fashionable life which is so clearly reflected in the letters of Horace Walpole and Chesterfield; the spirit of a brilliant and varied contemporary literature, eminently distinguished for its sobriety of judgment and for its fastidious purity and elegance of expression, but for the most part deficient in depth, in passion, and in imagination, may all be traced in the popular theology. Sobriety and good sense were the qualities most valued in the pulpit, and enthusiasm and extravagance were those which were most dreaded."

Whatever were the contributions which the Enlightenment made to the progress of religion—and that they were important none need doubt—it is evident that the period had nothing to offer the untutored and the poor by way of escape into emotional salvation nor by way of promise of social redemption. "The interval between the accession of Anne, in 1714, and the death to George II, in 1760, is a period in the religious history of England to which neither Churchmen nor Dissenters can look back without shame and regret," writes Fisher. "Puritanism had not only lost a great part of its influence, but also a great part of its vigor. A prevalent indifference and scepticism, the spread of vice, partly a heritage from the last Stuart kings, and the ignorance of the clergy, did not lessen a whit the acrimony of ecclesiastical disputes." Lecky has drawn a vivid picture of the low estate of the clergy. They were largely recruited from the lower economic classes, it is true, and so they might have been in a position to interpret Christianity to the people; but, on the one hand, they were too closely attached to the gentry, from whom they derived their livings, to feel any real concern for the needs of their fellows, while, on the other hand, too many were grossly ignorant of the content of Christianity and without appreciation of its meaning. Bishop Burnet wrote in 1713 of those who came to be ordained that "they can give no account, or at least a very imperfect one, of the contents even of the Gospels, or of the Catechism itself." The "moral and intellectual decrepitude" of the universities, which were "the seed-plots of English divinity," in part reflected, in part brought about the low estate of the clergy.

Such was the religious situation. Social and economic conditions presented a different aspect. England was more prosperous in the first half of the eighteenth century than it had been for many years. But that prosperity, as is usually the case, only tended to accentuate class differences by flaunting in the faces of the poor the luxury which they helped to create but could not share, and by calling forth in the fortunate that sense of superiority which flourishes where possession has no relation to merit. Class distinctions were apparently more real in the days preceding and during the Methodist revival than they had been at any time since the rise of Puritanism. This stratification of society played its part in excluding from the churches of the nobility and the middle class the unwanted and uninterested poor—uninterested in the comfortable, æsthetically pleasant, and morally soft religion of the well-to-do.

During the second half of the eighteenth century, moreover, this tendency toward stratification in English society was greatly accelerated by the industrial revolution. The old ties which had bound laborer and employer together in the feudal relationships of agriculture or in the patriarchal connection of master and apprentice were broken by the coming of the factory. The wage system and uncertainty of employment, rising capitalism and the competitive order, the growth of the cities and the increase of poverty widened the cleft between the classes. Lecky summarizes the situation by writing that "wealth was immensely increased, but the inequalities of its distribution were aggravated. The contrast between extravagant luxury and abject misery became much more frequent and much more glaring than before. The wealthy employer ceased to live among his people; the quarters of the rich and of the poor became more distant, and every great city soon presented those sharp divisions of classes and districts in which the political observer discovers one of the most dangerous symptoms of revolution."

II

Revolution occurred, as it had always occurred under similar conditions in the past, and again it was a religious revolution, for these disinherited classes furnished the material for the Methodist revival. As a religious movement, it is true, Methodism was not as spontaneous in character as had been the insurgencies which preceded the rise of the Quakers or of the Mennonites; it was much more dependent upon leadership than these had been. But the need was present and the highly trained Oxford Methodists offered the poor a type of faith and religious life which met their needs. While the primary leadership was supplied by the upper classes the secondary leaders, the lay preachers and the membership, with little exception, were derived from the lower economic and cultural orders of society. The people who gathered in the Foundery in London were of the lower economic class with some small sprinkling of the well-to-do. The weavers of Bristol, the miners of Kingswood, the colliers and keelmen of Cornwall and Staffordshire and Wales—these were the groups whence Methodism drew most of its converts. In his "Advice to the People Called Methodists" John Wesley himself points out to his followers that they "have been hitherto, and do still subsist, without power (for you are a low insignificant people), without riches (for you are poor almost to a man, having no more than the plain necessaries of life), and without either any extraordinary gifts of nature, or the advantages of education; most even of your teachers being quite unlearned and (in other things) ignorant men." The opponents of the movement frequently seemed to think it a major argument against its value that it was composed of a "rag-tag mob," of "a set of creatures of the lowest rank, most of them illiterate and of desperate fortunes," while its leaders were called "the heads and spiritual directors of hot-brained cobblers." It is true of course that converts were also gained from other ranks of society. A description of a Methodist congregation mentions not only numbers of poor people, "thieves, prostitutes, fools, people of every class" but also "several men of distinction, a few of the learned" and merchants. Cowper belonged to the movement himself and testified to the presence of some members of the upper classes of society in the couplet "We boast some rich ones whom the Gospel sways, and one who wears a coronet and prays," referring to Lord Dartmouth. The Countess of Huntingdon's adhesion to the movement was responsible for making it rather fashionable in some circles. But the attitude of the upper classes on the whole was probably truly, if somewhat extravagantly, represented by the Duchess of Buckingham in her letter to Lady Huntingdon: "I thank your ladyship," she wrote, "for the information concerning the Methodist preachers. Their doctrines are most repulsive and tinctured with impertinence and disrespect towards their superiors, in perpetually endeavouring to level all ranks and do away with all distinctions. It is monstrous to be told that you have a heart as sinful as the common wretches that crawl the earth. This is highly offensive and insulting, and I cannot but wonder that your ladyship should relish any sentiments so much at variance with high rank and good breeding." If such honesty was rather singular the attitude was not. It is evident from all sources that persons of wealth and influence were comparatively rare in eighteenth-century Methodism and that when the division between the conventicle and the established church was finally completed it was the group of the disinherited which found its home in the chapel while those whose social position allied them with Anglicanism found it quite possible to maintain their Evangelicalism within the pale of the establishment.

The characteristic features of the new denomination also marked it off as a church of the poor. Its emotionalism made it at the same time an abomination to the enthusiasm-hating upper classes and the salvation of those for whom religion needed to mean much more than prudential counsel and rationalized belief, if it was to mean anything at all. The emotionalism of Methodism, evident in the extravagances of the Bristol revival and the whole tenor of its preaching and experience, had the same significance as had the demand for direct experience among Anabaptists and Quakers. It was the only way religion could become real to the class which composed the movement; it furnished that group with a psychologically effective escape from the drudgeries of an unromantic, unaesthetic life. "To an ordinarily cultivated mind," as Lecky well states the situation, "there was something extremely repulsive in [the Methodist teacher's] tears and groans and amorous ejaculations, in the coarse anthropomorphic familarity and the unwavering dogmatism with which he dealt with the most sacred subjects, in the narrowness of his theory of life and his utter insensibility to many of the influences that expand and embellish it, in the mingled credulity and self-confidence with which he imagined that the whole course of nature was altered for his convenience. But the very qualities that impaired his influence in one sphere enhanced it in another. His impassioned prayers and exhortations stirred the hearts of multitudes whom a more decorous teaching had left absolutely callous. The supernatural atmosphere of miracles, judgments and inspirations in which he moved invested the most prosaic life with a halo of romance. The doctrines he taught, the theory of life he enforced, proved themselves capable of arousing in great masses of men an enthusiasm of piety which was hardly surpassed in the first days of Christianity, of eradicating inveterate vice, of fixing and directing impulsive and tempestuous natures that were rapidly hastening towards the abyss." The moral effectiveness of this emotional religion was, of course, its most significant feature. Religious enthusiasm declined in later days because Methodist Christianity became more literate and rational and because, with increasing wealth and culture, other escapes from the monotony and exhaustion of hard labor became available. The substitution of education for conversion, finally, played its part in making revivalism less important for successive generations.

The lay character of the movement, no less than its emotionalism, was also typical of the poor man's Christianity. The use of lay preachers in Methodism, as among Anabaptists and Quakers and in related medieval movements, was due to many factors connected with the economic and social status of the membership: to the unwillingness of a settled and salaried clergy to participate in the popular religious revolt, to the people's antagonism to a professional class which they regarded—sometimes wrongly, sometimes correctly—as being without real understanding of and sympathy with the needs of the disinherited, to the ability of the lay preacher to meet the new group on its own terms, to the simple fervor and naïvely genuine piety of the unsophisticated missionary. A conversation between Robinson, Archbishop of Armagh, and Charles Wesley illustrates several of these points. "I knew your brother well," said the bishop; "I could never credit all I heard respecting him and you; but one thing in your conduct I could never account for, your employing laymen." "My Lord," replied Wesley, "the fault is yours and your brethren's." "How so?" asked Robinson. "Because you hold your peace and the stones cry out." "But I am told," objected the bishop, "that they are unlearned men." "Some are," answered the Methodist, "and so the dumb ass rebukes the prophet." His lordship, as Tyerman adds, said no more.

The ethics of Methodism distinguished it no less from the churches of the middle class and the gentry, although at this point the movement represented a marked departure from the religious revolts of the poor in preceding centuries. It has been maintained with some right that the Methodist movement had the same significance for England that the Revolution had for France. Its democratic character—religious as it was in inspiration and effect—had a marked influence upon the social order. It was responsible for creating a considerable sentiment for greater democracy among many of the wealthier citizens of the nation, whether or not these became adherents of the movement and despite the fact that the majority may have shared the sentiments of the Duchess of Buckingham. It inspired among these an extensive philanthropic activity which resulted in the founding of scores of eleemosynary institutions and in the humanitarian legislation of the early nineteenth century, which was sponsored, in large part, by the Evangelical disciples of Wesley in the Church of England. Among the poor members of the societies it fostered, as all such movements have done, a high degree of mutual aid and co-operation and laid the foundations for popular education. After all Methodism largely represented the religious aspect of that great revolutionary movement of the eighteenth century which placed the individual at the center of things and so profoundly modified all existing institutions.

Despite these influences upon social ethics, however, Methodism was far removed in its moral temper from the churches of the disinherited in the sixteenth and seventeenth century. Briefly, the difference lay in the substitution of individual ethics and philanthropism for social ethics and millenarianism. It has been pointed out that the distinctive ethical note of the churches of the poor in the earlier periods was due to the interest of the constituency in salvation from social evils, from class inferiorities, injustices, and oppressions and that these movements derived much of their driving force and enthusiasm from the millennial hope. A second characteristic of their ethics, the emphasis upon humility, frugality, and democracy, was partly religious in origin, partly due to a natural tendency to exalt the typical virtues of the poor, supported as these virtues are by the teaching of Jesus. With respect to the first point, the ethical approach of Methodism was apparently quite different from that of Anabaptism or seventeenth-century millenarianism. It had some interest in the economic fortunes of its constituency and in the social inequalities from which they suffered, but it was much more interested in the correction of their vices, from the point of view of their religious fortunes. The ethics which it had in mind was not the social ethics of the Sermon on the Mount but the sober, individual ethics of "The Serious Call" and of Moravian piety. It was in one sense of the word much more of a religious and less of an ethical movement than were its predecessors. The religious interest preceded the social and social idealism remained more or less incidental, while the hope of a thoroughgoing social reconstruction was almost entirely absent. Indeed, it may be maintained that the socially beneficial results of Methodism were never designed, but that they accrued as mere by-products of the movement.

This difference in temper between the earlier churches of the poor and Methodism doubtless had much to do with the latter's success in a class-governed world, which feared nothing so much as social revolution and easily defeated the enthusiastic millenarianism of previous movements. Despite the mob-violences from which Wesley and other Methodist preachers suffered in the early years of the revival, persecution in their case was not comparable with that meted out to Baptists and seventeenth-century democrats. Methodism was never subject to the same official oppressions and grew respectable in a much briefer time than these required.

The difference in ethics was due to a number of causes but primarily, it seems, to the fact that the Methodist movement remained throughout its history in the control of men who had been born and bred in the middle class and who were impressed not so much by the social evils from which the poor suffered as by the vices to which they had succumbed. The character of a religious movement is probably more decisively determined by its definition of the sin from which salvation is to be sought than by its view of that saving process itself. The primary question to be asked for the understanding of a Fox, a Paul, a Luther, a Wesley as well as of Old Testament prophets and of the founders of non-Christian religions, such as Buddha, Zoroaster, Mohammed, is this: what did they mean by sin or evil? from what did they want to save men? Now it is evident in Wesley's case that he envisaged sin as individual vice and laxity, not as greed, oppression, or social maladjustment. Sin meant sensuality rather than selfishness to him and from Wesley the entire Methodist movement took its ethical character. Wesley was more offended by blasphemous use of the name of God than by a blasphemous use of His creatures. He was much more concerned about swearing in soldiers' camps than about the ethical problem of war and the useless sacrifice of soldiers' lives or the righteousness of their cause. "My soul has been pained day by day," he wrote to the mayor of Newcastle, "even in walking the streets of Newcastle, at the senseless, shameless wickedness, the ignorant profaneness, of the poor men to whom our lives are entrusted. The continual cursing and swearing, the wanton blasphemy of the soldiers in general, must needs be a torture to the sober ear, whether of a Christian or of an honest infidel. Can any that either fear God or love their neighbor hear this without concern? especially if they consider the interest of our country, as well as of these unhappy men themselves. For can it be expected that God should be on their side who are daily affronting Him to His face? And if God be not on their side, how little will either their number, or courage, or strength avail?" Apparently Wesley believed that the justice of a cause was quite secondary in the eyes of God to the personal purity of its defenders. In the rules for the band societies the same conception of sin meets us: their members are to abstain from evil, especially from buying or selling on the Sabbath, tasting spiritous liquors, pawning, backbiting, wearing needless ornaments such as rings, ear-rings, necklaces, lace, and ruffles, and taking snuff or tobacco. It is not to be denied that Wesley achieved an eminent success in delivering the poor from many of their worst vices by the one-sided emphasis upon sin in its individual aspects, and it may be that the vices of eighteenth-century English colliers and soldiers stood in such high relief that social evils appeared insignificant beside them; yet one must remember that the usual picture drawn of the brutalization of the working classes of the time was largely inspired by the Evangelical view of the situation. In the much greater moral problems involved in the new social relationships brought about by the industrial revolution or present in the age-old relations of the classes Wesley and Methodism had no real interest.

Even in so far as social interests and influences were present Methodism betrayed the bias of its middle-class leadership. The reform movements were supported largely by the Evangelical party in the church of England and did not represent the efforts of the poor to help themselves. Wilberforce and Hannah More, Kingsley and the Christian socialists set forth the social spirit of the movement; there were no leaders of the people of the type of Winstanley or Harrison. The social ethics of Methodism was an ethics of philanthropy and humanitarianism, which regarded movements toward equality as concessions made out of love rather than as demands of justice, and this philanthropy suffered the constant danger of degenerating into sentimental charity. But the typical social ethics of the poor is an ethics of reconstruction whose excrescences appear in violence rather than in sentimentality. Thus Methodism was adapted from its beginnings to become a church of the respectable middle class, even though the emotionalism of its religion continued to make a strong appeal to the untutored.

Other factors, beside this original middle-class point of view in Methodism, were responsible for its early rise into a higher economic and cultural stratum. Wesley himself faultlessly described the process whereby other churches of the disinherited, and his own with them, sloughed off their original character. "Wherever riches have increased," he wrote, "the essence of religion has decreased in the same proportion. Therefore I do not see how it is possible in the nature of things for any revival of religion to continue long. For religion must necessarily produce both industry and frugality, and these cannot but produce riches. But as riches increase so will pride, anger, and love of the world in all its branches. How then is it possible that Methodism, that is, a religion of the heart, though it flourishes now as a green bay tree, should continue in this state? For the Methodists in every place grow diligent and frugal;

consequently they increase in goods. Hence they proportionately increase in pride, in anger, in the desire of the flesh, the desire of the eyes and the pride of life. So, although the form of religion remains, the spirit is swiftly vanishing away. Is there no way to prevent this—this continual decay of pure religion? We ought not to prevent people from being diligent and frugal; we must exhort all Christians to gain all they can, and to save all they can; that is in effect to grow rich. What way then can we take, that our money may not sink us into the nethermost hell? There is one way and there is no other under heaven. If those who gain all they can, and save all they can, will likewise give all they can, then the more they gain, the more they will grow in grace, and the more treasures they will lay up in heaven." It is quite significant that Wesley omits all reference to the manner in which Christians are to gain all they can. But the passage well describes the rise of Methodism in the Old World and later in the New from a church of the poor to a middle-class church, which, with its new outlook, abandoned the approach to religion which made it an effective agency of salvation to the lower classes in the century of its founding. In England this development was not dissimilar to that of the Quakers, and Methodism remained somewhat sectarian in character, but in America the result, for reasons which will become apparent, was the growth of a church in the true sense of the word which attracted to itself the most substantial classes of the citizenry. In both cases, however, the economic and cultural character of the movement underwent profound modification and, sooner than was the case with the other movements, this religion of the disinherited became a respectable church of respected classes. Originally urban in character it retained the loyalty of the tradesmen and workers who, rising in the social scale through their thrift and diligence, became the small and later often the great capitalists of the growing cities of the nineteenth century. More than Presbyterianism or Congregationalism Methodism came to be the religion of business classes. Methodism left behind the emotionalism of its earlier years and adapted its ethics, never typically lower-class in character, to the needs of its rising clientele. It abandoned lay preaching in favor of a regular and theologically trained ministry; it modified and softened in many ways the original stringency of its methods; it gave up its old program of mutual aid, so typical a feature of the religion of the poor; it left aside the semi-ascetic character of its early communities and arranged its rules to accommodate those whose interests made the world-fleeing ethics even less practicable than it was for the poor. Once more a religious revolt, issuing in the formation of a sect, led finally to the establishment of a middle-class church, a yielding servant of the social order.

III

The Methodist revival was the last great religious revolution of the disinherited in Christendom. And it was not wholly a popular movement. Perhaps that is one reason why it was the last. It is a striking fact that the revolutionary tendencies of the poor in the nineteenth century were almost completely secular in character, while in preceding eras they were always largely religious in nature. The socialism of 1848 and later years was closely akin in many ways to Anabaptism and Quakerism as well as to Lollardy and the Waldensian revolt. It cherished as these did the hope of an inevitable social renewal which would cast down the mighty from their seats and exalt them of low degree. Like these it provided the oppressed with an emotional escape from the weariness and grime of uneventful and profitless labor. Like these it brought to consciousness the latent sense of social solidarity and endowed the impoverished individual life with the significance of participation in a cosmic event. But for the angels who fought on the side of Baptists and Quakers it substituted economic laws, and in place of the early coming of the Son of Man it anticipated the class struggle and the dictatorship of the proletariat. What were the reasons for this change?

The conditions which preceded the rise of socialism were not dissimilar to those which formed the background of the religious revolutions of previous centuries. There was present the actual exclusion of the poor from churches grown emotionally too cold, ethically too neutral, intellectually too sober, socially too aristocratic to attract the men who suffered under the oppression of monotonous toil, of insufficient livelihood and the sense of social inferiority. There was present also the awakening of the disinherited to the consciousness of their human dignity and worth. But the result was not a religious revolt. On the contrary socialism often assumed the character of an anti-religious movement. Its secularism was doubtless due to many causes—to the growth of the scientific temper and of nineteenth-century materialism, to the prevalence of the mechanistic conception of life which industrialism fosters, to the determinism of the Hegelian philosophy in which Marx had been trained, to the bare fact that the leaders of the movement were not religious men. But among the causes of this secularism the absence of an effective social idealism within any of the Christian churches was of especial importance. The last previous religious movements among the disinherited, Methodism and Pietism, had failed to follow in the steps of the Baptists and Quakers. They had allowed the millenarian hopes to lapse; they had substituted for the concept of the kingdom

the symbol of heaven; they had been concerned with the redemption
of men from the hell beyond the grave alone and had held out little
promise of salvation from the various mundane hells in which the poor
suffer for other sins besides their own. So they had failed to keep alive
within the church those realistic hopes which had always been the source
of new religious uprisings in the centuries before; and they had joined
with the older churches in proclaiming a purely other-worldly hope.
In any other century of Christian history this failure to keep alive the
promise of social amelioration through Christian ethics and by divine
miracle might have had less far-reaching results. In the century of inventions and of industrial production, in a time so largely occupied with
the present world and its values, the absence of this social element
from the preaching of the gospel was fatal to the religion of the disinherited. It is significant that much of the leadership of the social movement
now came from a group which had been nurtured in the ideals of Old
Testament prophecy, and which even when it lost its religious faith
did not fail to give expression to ideals which had been derived from
that religion. The leadership of the Jews in the social revolutions of
the nineteenth and twentieth centuries had these religious sources; it
was the only effective substitute for the Christian leadership which had
once been unfailingly available in every crusade for justice but which
had died out, perhaps as a result of attrition in the theological and
other-worldly church.

2.

SOCIAL MOVEMENT ORGANIZATIONS: GROWTH, DECAY, AND CHANGE (1966)

MAYER N. ZALD AND ROBERTA ASH

Social movements manifest themselves, in part, through a wide range
of organizations. These organizations are subject to a range of internal

SOURCE. Mayer N. Zald and Roberta Ash, "Social Movement Organizations:
Growth, Decay and Change," *Social Forces*, 44 (March 1966), p. 327–340.
Reprinted by permission of the University of North Carolina Press and the authors.

and external pressures which affect their viability, their internal structure and processes, and their ultimate success in attaining goals.

The dominant line of approach to the sociological study of the transformation of social movement organizations (hereafter referred to as MO's) has been the institutionalization and goal displacement model of organizational transformation. This model, which stems from Weber and Michels, takes the following line of analysis: As an MO attains an economic and social base in the society, as the original charismatic leadership is replaced, a bureaucratic structure emerges and a general accommodation to the society occurs. The participants in this structure have a stake in preserving the organization, regardless of its ability to attain goals. Analytically there are three types of changes involved in this process; empirically they are often fused. The three types of change are goal transformation, shift to organizational maintenance, and oligarchization.

Goal transformation may take several forms, including the diffusion of goals, in which a pragmatic leadership replaces unattainable goals with diffuse goals, so that the organization can pursue a broader range of targets. However, according to the Weber-Michels model, whatever the form of goal transformation, it is always in the direction of greater conservatism (the accommodation of organization goals to the dominant societal consensus).

Organizational maintenance is a special form of goal transformation, in which the primary activity of the organization becomes the maintenance of membership, funds, and other requirements of organizational existence. It too is accompanied by conservatism, for the original goals must be accommodated to societal norms in order to avoid conflicts that could threaten the organization's viability.

Oligarchization may be defined as the concentration of power, in the Weberian sense, in the hands of a minority of the organization's members. (For our purposes, bureaucratization is that form of oligarchization which stresses a hierarchy of offices and prescribed rules for conducting affairs.) Of course, some MO's begin with a relatively oligarchical structure and de-oligarchization may occur. But the Michels part of the model treats mainly of the movement from democratic decision structures—a situation of dispersed power, to centralization and oligarchy. (This process is typically evaluated as morally wrong and as a prelude to member apathy and organizational conservatism.)

This line of sociological analysis has a distinguished place in the literature—if only for its imaginative concepts—goal displacement, iron law of oligarchy, routinization of charisma, and the like. Nevertheless, as a statement on the transformation of (social) movement organizations it is incomplete. There are a variety of other transformation processes that take place including coalitions with other organizations, organizational disappearances, factional splits, increased rather than decreased radicalism, and the like. And in fact, the Weber-Michels model[1] can be subsumed under a more general approach to movement organizations which specifies the condition under which alternative transformation processes take place.

An essay in theoretical synthesis, here we attempt to specify some of the major factors influencing the direction of change of MO's and to provide illustrative propositions. Each section contains several of these, but only a few propositions and predictions that summarize and sharpen the argument will be listed and set off.

We follow the general sociological approach to organizations most explicitly stated by Selznick and often called organizational or institutional analysis. The approach can be applied to any kind of association or organization, not just those with bureaucratic structures. Briefly, large scale organizations are seen as a collection of groups harnessed together by incentives of various kinds to pursue relatively explicit goals. Both the ends and means of subgroups may conflict with those established by the authoritative elements in the organization; there may be conflict over the distribution of power and rewards within the organization. Organizations exist in a changing environment to which they must adapt. Adaptation to the environment may itself require changes in goals and in the internal arrangement of the organization. This view of organizations treats goals as problematic, and as changing in response to both internal and external pressures. It is especially useful for the study of MO's precisely because it focuses on conflict, environmental forces, and the ebb and flow of organizational viability.

Our first task is to define the analytic characteristics of movement organizations—how does an MO differ from other complex or formal organizations? A social movement is a purposive and collective attempt of a number of people to change individuals or societal institutions and structures. Although the organizations through which social movements can manifest themselves may have bureaucratic features, analytically they differ from "full-blown" bureaucratic organizations in two

---

[1] Although Michels' iron law of oligarchy was originally applied to political parties of the left, while Weber's routinization of charisma referred to a more general process, both deal with the adaptation and subsequent accommodation of social movements to the society. We treat them as one general line of analysis. Weber stresses the process of rationalization of organizational structure to a greater extent than does Michels. For any single organization, Weber is more concerned with internal processes than is Michels, who focuses more on goals.

ways. First, they have goals aimed at changing the society and its members; they wish to restructure society or individuals, not to provide it or them with a regular service (as is typical of bureaucracies). For example, proselytizing and usually messianic religious groups, melioristic political organizations, and conspiratorial parties are movement organizations by our definition. Goals aimed at change subject movement organizations to vicissitudes which many other types of organization avoid. For instance, if the society changes in the direction of the MO's goals, the organization's reason for being no longer exists. On the other hand, its goals of change may incur great hostility and repressive action in the society.

Second (and related to the goals of change), MO's are characterized by an incentive structure in which purposive incentives predominate. While some short-run material incentives may be used, the dominant incentives offered are purposive, with solidary incentives playing a secondary role. Organizations which rely on purposive incentives often have the problem of maintaining membership commitment and participation, for the values represented by the MO's goals must be deeply held in order for the organization to command time and loyalty in the face of the competition of work and the demands of family and friends.[2]

As we have noted the Weber-Michels model predicts changes in goals (conservatism and organizational maintenance) and in structure (oligarchization). Although we will comment on the latter aspect of organizational change, we focus more on the transformation of and the interplay of goals and structure. On this point we challenge the Weber-Michels model by limiting its predictions to certain types of MO's, and by suggesting conditions under which alternatives are possible.

In this paper we first discuss the relation of movement organizations to the environment in which they exist—both the society at large and more narrowly the social movement of which they are a manifestation. The ebb and flow of sentiments, the results of success and failure in attaining goals, and the problems of coordination and cooperation among movement organizations are treated. The purpose of the first section

[2] Of course, if members devalue material incentives or have independent access to them and if organizational goals represent central life interests of members, gaining and maintaining membership commitment represents less of an organizational problem.

In a very different context V. I. Lenin recognized that the central problem of movement organization is gaining and maintaining commitment. Where most people think of organizational structure as pyramidal, Lenin described structure in terms of concentric circles of lessening commitment and participation. See V. I. Lenin, *What Is To Be Done?* (New York: International Publishers, 1929). Arthur Stinchcombe first drew our attention to this point.

is to show how the transformation of MO's is conditioned or determined by factors outside of itself. The second, briefer, section focuses to a greater extent on internal processes related to goals and commitment. There we discuss two topics, the cause of factionalism and schismogenesis and the relation of leadership to organizational transformation.

ENVIRONMENT AND ORGANIZATION

The environment of MO's consists of two major segments. One segment is the broader social movement, which consists of potential supporters—members and financial backers and other movement organizations. The people who identify with the movement represent the potential support base for the organization. The other major segment of the environment is the society in which the social movement exists. The larger society may contain the target structures or norms which the movement organization wishes to change; but even in cases where the MO's goal is to change individuals, members or not, the larger society affects the MO because the attitudes and norms of the larger society affect the readiness of movement sympathizers to become members, and the readiness of members to participate fully.

There are at least three interrelated aspects of the environment of MO's which critically affect both their growth and transformation. Changing conditions in the society increase or decrease the potential support base of an MO; there is an ebb and flow of supporting sentiments. Second, the society may change in the direction of organizational goals, or events may clearly indicate that goals will not be attained; the possibilities of success or failure sharply influence member and potential member sentiments and attachments. Third, MO's exist in an environment with other organizations aimed at rather similar goals. Similarity of goals causes an uneasy alliance but also creates the conditions for inter-organizational competition.

The Ebb and Flow of Sentiments

Any MO is dependent on the readiness for mobilization of potential supporters. This readiness is dependent on the ebb and flow of sentiments toward an organization, which in turn is a function of at least two major variables: (1) the extent to which there are large numbers of people who feel the MO's goals and means are in harmony with their own; and (2) the extent to which groups and organizations in the larger society feel neutral toward, reject, or accept the legitimacy and value of the social movement and its organizational manifestations. The attitudes in the larger society toward the movement and the MO condition the readiness of potential supporters to become actual supporters.

The difference between the ebb and flow of sentiment for a *social movement* and for a given MO has important consequences for organizational growth. Under some conditions there may be a strong sentiment base—at the same time that there is strong hostility to a particular organization in the society. "Front" organizations are attempts to capitalize on such a situation. The dimensions are partially independent. The ideal condition for organizational growth is obviously a strong sentiment base with low societal hostility towards the movement or its MO's. Periods of great religious revival are characterized by this condition. On the other hand, the more interesting case may be when there is a weak sentiment base and no or low societal interest. A petulant stance and organizational decline as in the Women's Christian Temperance Union may be the consequence.

The processes of change predicted by the Weber-Michels model are thus affected by the organization's relations to its environment. Organizational maintenance and other forms of goal transformation are the outcomes of a struggle to maintain membership in the face of changes in the larger society. The changes in the society that threaten the MO's viability may be either favorable (the goal is achieved and the MO seems to lose its *raison d'être*) or unfavorable (widespread hostility arises).

However, the ebb and flow of sentiments does not effect organizational transformation at equal rates in all MO's. Two dimensions of movement organization mediate the extent to which MO's are effected by the ebb and flow of sentiments: (1) the extent of membership requirements, both initial and continuing, and (2) the extent to which operative goals are oriented to change of member or individual behavior rather than oriented to societal change. These two dimensions are related to the defining characteristics and recurring problematic foci of MO's stated earlier. Variability in them means that MO's can take a broad variety of organizational forms.

1. MEMBERSHIP REQUIREMENTS. The "inclusive" organization requires minimum levels of initial commitment—a pledge of general support without specific duties, a short indoctrination period or none at all. On the other hand, the "exclusive" organization is likely to hold the new recruit in a long "novitiate" period, to require the recruit to subject himself to organization discipline and orders, and to draw from those having the heaviest initial commitments. When such an organization

also has societal goals of changing society it may be called a vanguard party.

Inclusive and exclusive MO's differ not only in recruitment procedures and requirements, but they also differ in the amount of participation required. The inclusive MO typically requires little activity from its members—they can belong to other organizations and groups unselfconsciously, and their behavior is not as permeated by organization goals, policies, and tactics. On the other hand, the exclusive organization not only requires that a greater amount of energy and time be spent in movement affairs, but it more extensively permeates all sections of the member's life, including activities with nonmembers. Any single MO may have attributes of both the inclusive and the exclusive organization; even the inclusive movement must have some central cadre.

The ebb and flow of sentiments in the society more markedly effect the inclusive than the exclusive organization. For example, membership figures compiled by Mike Muench indicate that the Socialist party had a more rapid decline in membership than the Socialist Worker's party during the McCarthy era, and a more rapid rise following the Irish peril. This, despite the fact that the SWP's ideology was more left-wing and more subject to charges of un-Americanism. (The Communist party had an exclusive orientation and declined greatly, but it was under heavier and more direct attack than the other two.)

The inclusive MO's membership declines and rises faster than that of the exclusive's because competing values and attitudes are more readily mobilized in the inclusive organization. While members of both organizations may have similar goals, the members of inclusive organizations are more likely to be subjected to conflicts in the face of threats or in the face of competing social movements that appeal to other values. Their allegiances to other groups and values lead them to rather switch than fight.

2. Changing Individual and Member Behavior versus Changing Society. In many ways, as has often been noted, the religious sect and the vanguard party have much in common and, in our terms, are both exclusive organizations. The separation from other roles or positions, the total allegiance and discipline, the messianic vision are parallel phenomena. But a key distinction is their strategy for attaining fundamental goals: What are they trying to accomplish in the here and now? Some MO's, especially those with religious affiliations, have as operative goals the changing of individuals. As such, they *may be* less threatening to dominant values and other institutions. At least to the extent that operative goals are restricted to membership proselytization and are

not relevant to control of institutional centers, to political action or to central societal norms counter pressures are less likely to be brought to bear on them. Furthermore, the commitment of members in this type of movement organization is less dependent on the external success of the organization. Commitment is based to a greater extent on solidary and/or expressive incentives than on purposive incentives.

Of course, the growth of religious sects is related to the ebb and flow of sentiment in the society. But it is possible that once recruits are gained the organization can maintain its members. First, focusing on member change, the sect may threaten the society less, calling forth fewer punishments for belonging. (In a theocratic state, however, the religious sect would be a direct challenge to the larger society.) Second, if the sect is not milleniastic, it is not subject to the problems of success and failure in the environment. Therefore, the rate of attrition is likely to be a function of the life careers of members rather than of wide swings in societal attitudes affecting members. Third, the organization that attempts to change individuals, especially its own members, is less constrained by the definitions of reality of the broader society.

Proposition 1: The size of the organizational potential support base, the amount of societal interest in the social movement and its MO's and the direction of that interest (favorable, neutral, or hostile) directly affect the ability of the organization to survive and/or grow.

Proposition 2: The more insulated an organization is by exclusive membership requirements and goals aimed at changing individuals, the less susceptible it is to pressures for organizational maintenance or general goal transformation.

INTER-ORGANIZATIONAL COMPETITION: THE PRESS TO LEFT AND RIGHT. Thus far our discussion of the ebb and flow of sentiment has been presented as if within a social movement there was consensus on goals and tactics. However, there may be many definitions of proper goals and tactics and these may shift over time. Competition among MO's for support requires them to be responsive to these differences and to shifts in sentiment towards goals and tactics. It is our thesis that these shifts are a major determinant of the transformation of organizational goals.

The major thrust of the iron law of oligarchy deals with the internal bureaucratization of MO's; officials gain a vested interest in maintaining their positions and in having a stable and nonconflictful relation to the society. In the process of accommodating to the society, the goals of the MO become watered down. Over time, the prediction runs, MO's shift to moderate goals or even to goals of maintaining the status quo. But the competition for support among movement organizations leads to shifts in goals which may be towards the center, but *which may also be towards the extremes.*

In *An Economic Theory of Democracy,* Anthony Downs argues that in a two-party, issue oriented political system, there are strong pressures to make the difference between parties minimal. If the parties are relatively well-balanced, movement away from the center of the distribution of attitudes by one party means loss of votes to the other party and, therefore, loss of the election. The competition is for election, not directly for long range goals. Only if there are large pools of abstaining and alienated voters at the extremes, does a movement away from the center promise greater support than a movement towards the center. The notion of the distribution of sentiments in social movements permits an analysis similar to that of Downs.

This analysis uses as its example the case of the Civil Rights movement. Consider the situation before the Supreme Court's school desegregation ruling in 1954. The goals and tactics of the Urban League and the NAACP were in agreement with most active supporters of the movement. However, the number of actives was relatively small, and there were large segments of the potential supporters who were not active at all—college and high school students, working class Negroes, in both the north and south, and the clergy. After 1954 and especially after the Montgomery bus strike in 1958, the sentiment base of the movement changed—there was an increased readiness for mobilization of potential adherents, adherents expected more rapid change in a wider range of areas, and tactics acceptable to adherents became more militant. Furthermore, new or previously marginal organizations, such as CORE and SNCC, began to compete for the support of the enlarged potential support base. As a response both to the new opportunities for change presented by the society *and* the competition from other organizations, the stance of such organizations as the NAACP and the Urban League became more radical. *Failure* to respond to these pressures would have led to either a smaller relative support base and/or a less prominent role in the leadership of the Civil Rights movement.

This analysis is, of course, too simple. It ignores cleavages within movements; for instance, in the case of the Civil Rights movement differences in sentiment can be found between financial backers and between members of the same organizations, between class groups and generations. Furthermore, it ignores the polarization processes whereby the growth of intense attitudes on the left generates a larger number of people with intense attitudes on the right. Lastly, it ignores the very complex problem of the competition and interaction of organizations with different primary goals that draw from the same pool of supporters—for instance, SANE, NAACP, and ACLU. Nevertheless, the essential point is clear.

Proposition 3: Goal and tactic transformation of a MO is directly tied to the ebb and flow of sentiments within a social movement. The inter-organizational competition for support leads to a transformation of goals and tactics.

FAILURE AND SUCCESS IN ACHIEVING GOALS.[3] The first problem of MO's is to gain support. But, a MO, like any organization, must have a payoff to its supporters. Aside from the joys of participation, its major payoff is in the nature of a promise; its goals or at least some of them must appear to have a reasonable chance of attainment. In a sense, the perfectly stable MO which avoided problems of organizational transformation, goal displacement, and the like, would be one which over time always seemed to be getting closer to its goal without quite attaining it.

A MO succeeds when its objective is attained; a MO is becalmed when, after achieving some growth and stability, its goals are still relevant to the society but its chances of success have become dim; a MO fails when the society has decisively rejected the goals of the organization and the MO as an instrument is discredited. Although the sources of the change in MO status differ in the three cases, in all three cases incentives to participate decline and the survival of the organization is threatened. Survival depends, partially, on the ability of the MO to muster solidary, material, or secondary goal incentives.

SUCCESS. There are various kinds of movement success. At the very least, one must distinguish between the actual attainment of goals and the assumption of power assumed to be a prerequisite to attaining goals. The analysis of the transformation of the MO ends when it or the movement it represents accedes to power; at that point, analytic concepts applicable to party structure and governmental bureaucracy become

[3] Success or failure in goal attainment effects the ebb and flow of sentiment toward the social movement and its organizations. We treat the topic separately because (1) it represents a determinant of the ebb and flow of sentiment, not just a dependent consequence; (2) success or failure may be the result of organizational activity, whereas we have been treating the ebb and flow of sentiment as to a great extent being a resultant of the conditions in the larger society; (3) success or failure may question the validity of a given organization regardless of the sentiment for the social movement, and (4) because we have a lot to say about it.

more relevant. The operating dilemmas of MO's that have assumed power have been well described by S. M. Lipset and others.[4]

But what happens when the goals of the MO are actually reached; what happens when a law is enacted, a disease is eradicated (for instance, women get suffrage, the threat of infantile paralysis is drastically reduced), or social conditions change, thus eliminating the ostensible purpose of the organization? Two major outcomes are possible: New goals can be established maintaining the organization or the MO can go out of existence.

The establishment of new goals to perpetuate the organization is more likely to occur if: (1) The MO has its own member and fund raising support base. (2) There are solidary or short-run material incentives that bind members to each other or to the organization. In order to continue obtaining such rewards, the members support a new goal. It must be noted that lacking such support, the organization leaders cannot maintain the organization. It is not the existence of a bureaucratic structure and office holders per se that guarantees continuance, if the rank and file or the contributors do not share the desire to continue the organization.

In some cases, however, the solidary and material incentives alone become sufficient to hold the allegiance of some of the members. This is the extreme case of a shift to organizational maintenance. Such an organization can hardly be classified as a part of a social movement, since it has abandoned both defining characteristics—purposive incentives and change goals. The remains of the Townsend movement represent such an ex-MO. The New Deal and old-age pensions cut away much of its programs and goals. But its solidary incentives, minimal membership requirements, and material resources from the sale of geriatric products allowed it to maintain itself, albeit at a minimum level of functioning.

Several propositions about the relation of organizational change to success follow:

Proposition 4: MO's created by other organizations are more likely to go out of existence following success than MO's with their own linkages to individual supporters.

[4] S. M. Lipset *et al.*, *Agrarian Socialism* (Berkeley: University of California Press, 1950). The organization in power is limited by its coalition dependencies—its links to other organizations; it is limited by the range of variables outside of its control, such as the general state of world economy; it is limited by lack of experience and competence, by its dependency on the holdover office holders; and whereas incentives were earlier of a purposive and idealistic sort, now material incentives become the rules of the day—the organization loses its romantic idealism.

Proposition 5: MO's with relatively specific goals are more likely to vanish following success than organizations with broad general goals.

Proposition 6: MO's which aim to change individuals and employ solidary incentives are less likely to vanish than are MO's, with goals aimed at changing society and employing mainly purposive incentives.

Proposition 7: Inclusive organizations are likely to fade away faster than exclusive organizations; the latter are more likely to take on new goals. (These predictions apply to the failing as well as to the successful MO.)

THE MOVEMENT BECALMED.   Many MO's do not represent either successes or failures. They have been able to build and maintain a support base; they have waged campaigns which have influenced the course of events; and they have gained some positions of power. In short, they have created or found a niche for themselves in the organizational world but their growth has slowed down or ceased. Members do not expect attainment of goals in the near future, and the emotional fervor of the movement is subdued. As in the case of the successful organization, it is the existence of extra-purposive incentives which is a fundamental condition for maintaining the organization.

However, the goals of the MO are still somewhat relevant to society. Thus, the organization is able to maintain purposive commitment and avoids losing all of its purposively oriented members to competing causes.

It is such a becalmed movement that is most susceptible to processes predicted by the Weber-Michels model. (1) The lack of any major successes produces periodic bouts of apathy among the members. Membership is maintained, but attrition takes place over time and no new blood is attracted. (2) Leadership becomes complacent, resting on its control of material incentives. The leader's control over access to such material rewards increases their power, perhaps to the point of oligarchization. (3) The leaders become more conservative, because the pursuit of the MO's initially more radical goals might endanger the organizations' occupation of secure niches by provoking societal and, perhaps, members' hostility, consequently endangering the power of the leaders and their access to material rewards.

Proposition 8: A becalmed movement is most likely to follow the Weber-Michels model because its dependence on and control of material incentives allows oligarchization and conservatism to take place.

FAILURE.   Where the successful organization loses members because it has nothing more to do, the failing MO loses members because they no longer believe their goals can be achieved with that of instrument. The leadership cadre may attempt to redefine goals and to define external reality as favorable to the organization; nevertheless members are usually not fully shielded from societal reality and have independent checks on the possibility of attaining goals.

A MO may also fail because its legitimacy as an instrument may be discredited. Discreditation may happen rapidly or may take several years. Central to the discreditation process is the MO's inability to maintain *legitimacy* even in the eyes of its supporters. Discreditation comes because of organizational tactics employed in the pursuit of goals. For instance, many moderate organizations have lost support when they appeared to accept support from extremist groups. The consequences of failure are not discussed by scholars using the Weber-Michels model.

One consequence of the failure of a MO is the search for new instruments. Where the member leaving a successful movement may either search for new goals and social movements or lapse into quiescence, different alternatives seem to be open to members leaving the failing organization: Either they search for a more radical means to achieve their goals within the movement, decrease the importance of their goals, or change the focus of discontent. A Mertonian analysis of anomie might be relevant to this point.

Interaction among Movement Organizations

Under some conditions the tactics of a MO in attempting to succeed or avoid failure involve it in direct interaction and coordination with other organizations from the same social movement. Above we discussed competition among MO's, but our analysis did not focus on direct interaction and exchange. Here, in our last topic under the heading of the relation of MO's to their environment, we treat of mergers and other aspects of inter-MO relations. Such relations could be treated as an organizational outcome. But we are chiefly concerned with how interaction affects member commitment and ultimately the goals of the involved organizations.

We distinguish three types of interaction: cooperation, coalition and merger. Typically, cooperation between MO's is limited. Except during full scale revolutions or total movement activities, MO's do not engage in a complex division of labor. It occurs primarily in situations where special competencies are required for legislative lobbying or legal work, and a simple symbiotic relationship may develop that does not lead to transformation in either organization.

More interesting are the creation of coalitions and mergers,[5] for here the interaction may lead to new organizational identities, changes in the membership base, and changes in goals. The coalition pools resources and coordinates plans, while keeping distinct organizational identities. It will take place if it promises greater facilities, financial aid, or attainment of goals. Thus coalitions are more likely when MO's appear to be close to the goal than at other times, for then the costs of investing in the coalition seem small in comparison with the potential benefits.

Some coalitions resemble mergers in that only one organization retains an identity. However, within the MO the old MO's retain identities and allegiances. Such coalition-mergers are most likely to take place when there is one indivisible poistion or reward at stake, e.g., one governor or president can be elected, one law is required.

Each organization then may have a distinct role in the overall plan of attack. The coalesced organization is ruled through a committee or umbrella organization. Such an organization may be riven by factional positional jockeying if the leadership is not fully committed to the coalition. Furthermore, not all MO's are equally capable of mergers or coalitions. The level of outgroup distrust and the unlikelihood of shared perspectives makes it difficult for an exclusive MO to participate in mergers or coalitions.

A merger or coalition leads to a search for a common denominator to which both parties can agree. The more conservative party to the merger finds itself with more radical goals and vice versa. The goals of the more conservative party can remain nearly the same only if both organizations are trying to persuade a broader and even more conservative public.

A true merger leads to the suppression of previous organizational identities. Because of the likelihood that the basic stance of the MO's involved will change, a true merger does not necessarily broaden the support base for its program. The more conservative members of the conservative partner and the more radical members of the radical partner

---

[5] By and large, mergers and coalitions require ideological compatibility. Although extremist parties from both sides may work for the overthrow of the government (as in the Weimar Republic, for instance), they do not engage in planned coordinated attack. They do not support the center against the other extreme, and they independently work against the established government. For the role of ideological compatibility in coalitions see William Gamson, "Coalition Formation at Presidential Nominating Conventions," *American Journal of Sociology,* 68 (September 1962), pp. 157–172.

may find that the goals (or tactics) of the newly formed organization are no longer congenial. Both extremes drop away. Furthermore, now only one organization speaks for the movement, whereas before several voices clamored for change. The merging of movement organizations may make the movement appear smaller from the outside.

Since true mergers may have such potentially drastic effects on the support base, it is possible that they only occur when the leadership of one or both MO's feel their cause is lost, there is growing apathy, or the like. Then the merger appears as a way of preserving some vestige of vitality.[6]

Proposition 9: Inclusive MO's are more likely than exclusive MO's to participate in coalitions and mergers.

Proposition 10: Coalitions are most likely to occur if the coalition is more likely to achieve goals or lead to a larger resource base—when success is close or when one indivisible goal or position is at stake.

INTERNAL PROCESSES AND ORGANIZATIONAL TRANSFORMATION

All of the topics discussed in the previous section have dealt with the effects of external events or problems on the growth and change of movement organizations. However, external events are not the only causes of change. Emerging bureaucratic structures, internal ideological factions, leadership styles, and other, essentially, internal factors also cause organizational transformation. Here we focus on MO factions and on leadership changes.

When discussing external factors the task of separating dependent from independent variables was relatively simple. The effects of the environment are mediated through membership recruitment, requirements, and incentives, or through the organizational structure, and ultimately affect goals. But here we deal with the influence of internal variables on each other; the cause and effect sequences cease to be analytically (much less empirically) distinct; vicious circles as well as causal chains are possible. Consequently we can no longer so clearly

---

[6] These problems have arisen in the recent attempt to merge two MO's oriented to military disarmament, SANE and United World Federalists. These two organizations have differed in that the UWF has had historic attachments to the upper class, to Quakers, and to proper institutional types. It has been more educative and persuasive in technique. SANE has had a nervous, more alienated, liberal base, and has used heavier handed propaganda techniques. The proposed merger has been sharply questioned by members.

distinguish goals as our dependent variable. However, we still offer alternatives to the Weber-Michels model and point to a broader range of organizational outcomes.

Factions and Splits

Schismogenesis and factionalization has received but little attention from sociologists. A faction is an identifiable subgroup opposed to other subgroups, a split occurs when a faction leaves a MO. There are two major internal preconditions for splits and the development of factions, heterogencity of social base and the doctrinal basis of authority.

The role of heterogenity in creating conditions for organizational splitting needs little discussion. Richard Niebuhr's discussion of the role of class and ethnic factors in denominationalism remains the classic statement of the need for internal homogeneity in a MO with no ultimate and accepted internal authority. Consciousness of kind and the solidary incentives gained from homogeneity lead to the development of schisms.

What is true for religious sects and denominations is also true for political MO's. The early history of the American Communist party as described by Theodore Draper, was marked by fights based on disputes between the left and the right and connected to the European (particularly, Dutch, Lettish, and German) versus American base of the party. In this case, factions within the party were only finally suppressed by the use of the great external authority and legitimacy of the true revolutionaries, the Bolsheviks.

Factions and schisms occur not only because of the heterogeneity of a MO's support base, but also because of concern with doctrinal purity. MO's concerned with questions of ultimate ideological truth and with theoretical matters are more likely to split than MO's linked to bread and butter issues. It is not concern with ideology per se that is central to this proposition, but rather that ideological concerns lead to questioning the bases of organizational authority and the behavior of the leadership. Miller has argued that the difference between Catholic sects which remained in the church and those which left depended on the acceptance of the ultimate authority of the Word as revealed in the Bible, and interpreted by the Fathers of the Church, versus the word of contemporary church authorities: The Montanists of second century Phrygia and the Feeneyites of twentieth century Boston both rested their authority on the former and left the church, whereas St. Francis bowed to the latter.

Unless the nonreligious movement organization possesses the prestige of success and material incentives, as did the Bolsheviks in relation to the American Communist party, the bases for authority are difficult to establish. In this respect, the inclusive organization with its looser criteria of affiliation and of doctrinal orthodoxy is more split-resistant than the exclusive organization. The inclusive organization retains its factions while the exclusive organization spews them forth. Given internal dissension, it may be that the inclusive organization retains its support base, but is crippled in its capacity for concerted action. Splitting, of course, leads to a decrease in membership in the original movement organization. For a short period of time, at least, it leads to higher internal consistency and consensus. As such, it may also transform organizational goals away from a conservative or organizational maintenance position, for the remaining remnant is not encumbered by the need to compromise.

Proposition 11: The less the short-run chances of attaining goals, the more solidary incentives act to separate the organization into homogeneous subgroups—ethnic, class, and generational.[7] As a corollary, to the extent that a becalmed or failing MO is heterogeneous and must rely heavily on solidary incentives, the more likely it is to be beset by factionalism.

Propostion 12: The more the ideology of the MO leads to a questioning of the bases of authority the greater the likelihood of factions and splitting.

Proposition 13: Exclusive organizations are more likely than inclusive organizations to be beset by schisms.

Leadership and Movement Transformation

Initially we suggested that the Weber-Michels model is a sub-case of a more general set of concepts explaining MO transformation. Using such concepts as the ebb and flow of sentiments, potential and actual support base, membership requirements, incentives, and goals, we have attempted to explain a number of organizational processes. In simplified terms, the Weber-Michels model predicts changes in organizations stemming from changes in leadership positions and leadership behavior; it also predicts what organizational changes lead to changes in organizational behavior. If our more general approach is to be of value, it must be able to deal with the same problems.

Analysis of leadership phenomena [is] an even more crucial aspect

[7] It may be that the relation of splitting and developing factions to chances of attaining goals is curvilinear rather than linear. As movement organizations approach gaining power, latent conflicts over means, ends, and the future distribution of power, which have been suppressed in the general battle, rise to the fore.

of the study of MO than of other large scale organizations. Because the situation of the MO is unstable, because the organization has few material incentives under its control, and because of the nonroutinized nature of its tasks the success or failure of the MO can be highly dependent on the qualities and commitment of the leadership cadre and the tactics they use. Three aspects of leader-organization relations are discussed—the organizational transformation following the demise of a founding father, the factors affecting the commitment of leaders to goals, and the consequences for the organization of differences in leadership style.

THE REPLACEMENT OF CHARISMA. Following the death of a charismatic leader, several changes in MO's can be expected. But the more bureaucratized the MO the less the replacement of a leader causes organizational transformation. Three kinds of change are likely in the less bureaucratized MO's.

First, there is likely to be a decline in membership and in audience as those drop away whose commitment was more to the man than to the organizational goal and sentiment base. Furthermore, we would expect the outer circle of those who were weakly committed to drop away first.

Secondly, the death of a charismatic leader can lead to factionalization. The divergent tendencies of subgroups and the power struggles of lieutenants may have only been suppressed by the authority of the leader. His "word" now becomes one ideological base for intra-organization debate as the factions seek their place in the distribution of reward and the definition of goals and tactics.

Finally, there occurs the professionalization of the executive core and the increased attempts to rationalize the administrative structure of the organization that is heir to the charismatic leader's own organization. The routinization of charisma is not only an institutionalization and rationalization of the goals and guiding myths of the organization but also a change in the incentive base of the organization—from gratifications related to the mythic stature of the leader and the opportunity to participate with him to the gratifications afforded by the performance of ritual and participation in a moral cause. Rationalization also produces a routinization of material incentives.

Proposition 14: Routinization of charisma is likely to conservatize the dominant core of the movement organization while simultaneously producing increasingly radical splinter groups.

GOAL COMMITMENT OF LEADERS. More relevant to the Michels argument than the problems discussed above are the organizational changes

attendant on officers' increased attachment to their offices and perqui-
sites. While attachment to office may lead leaders to be more interested
in organizational maintenance than pursuit of goals, organizational maintenance seems to displace radical goals following the creation of a
bureaucratic structure only under three prerequisite conditions: (1) A
base support independent of membership sentiment; in labor unions the
payroll checkoff insures a constant flow of funds and permits the leadership to remain in office and to replace the original goals of the MO
(the union) by the goal of clinging to their own relatively lucrative
offices. (2) The commitment of leaders (and followers) to other goals—
to social position to a stable life, to a family (as Jesus Christ recognized); leadership concern with the maximization of non-MO goals is
a major cause of decline in intensity in any organization. (3) The co-
optation of leaders by other groups with subsequent transformation of
goals; co-optation is the most extreme result of what Gusfield terms
"articulating leadership." The growth of "statesmanship" in labor unions
is one example of articulating leadership producing changes in goals
and tactics of a MO.

However, none of these three conditions is in itself sufficient to produce a long range change in goals or tactics. A necessary precondition
for leaders to become concerned with organizational maintenance is
a change in member sentiment—a growing lack of interest.

Under some conditions, however, a decline in member interest may
actually allow a movement to grow more radical. As members permit
other concerns to tempt them away from the MO, they insist less on
their right to participate in decision making. The decision-making apparatus of the organization thus falls into the hands of the persons with
the greatest commitment to the movement goals. In some cases, these
persons may actually form a cadre of professional organizers. As the
MO becomes oligarchical, contrary to Michels, it may become *more*
rather than less radical in its goals.

*Proposition 15: If a leadership cadre are committed to radical goals
to a greater extent than the membership-at-large, member apathy and
oligarchical tendencies lead to greater rather than less radicalism.*

LEADERSHIP STYLE. Gusfield distinguishes between the articulation
function of leaders and the mobilizing function. In brief, mobilization
refers to reaffirming the goals and values of the organization and building member commitment to the goals, while articulation means linking
the organization and its tactics to those of other organizations and to
the larger society. There is an almost inherent dualism and conflict between these roles, for mobilization requires a heightening of the ideologi-

cal uniqueness of the MO and the absolute quality of its goals, while articulation often requires the uniqueness of the organization to be toned down and an adoption of the tactics of compromise. In the simple interpretation of the Weber-Michels model mobilization is followed by articulating leadership. But, as Gusfield has shown in the case of the WCTU, no such simple progression holds—indeed, demands from the membership required Francis Willard, an articulating leader, to use a more mobilizing leadership style. And at a much later date, when organizational needs changed, more articulation followed the retirement of a mobilizing leader.

Not only is the notion of a simple and inevitable progression from mobilizing to articulating a false notion of leadership transformation, but different kinds of MO's make different demands on leaders. For instance, the exclusive organization is restricted in its possibilities of articulation.

Proposition 16: An exclusive organization is almost certain to have a leadership which focuses on mobilizing membership for tasks, while the inclusive organization is readier to accept an articulating leadership style.

Proposition 17: The MO oriented to individual change is likely to have a leadership focused on mobilizing sentiments, not articulating with the larger society. Organizations oriented to changing the larger society are more likely to require both styles of leadership, depending on the stage of their struggle.

CONCLUSIONS: THE RELATION OF GOALS AND STRUCTURE

While there is often an association between growing institutionalization and bureaucratization *and* conservatism, there is no evidence that this is a *necessary* association. Instead it is a function of the cases examined and the frame of reference with which scholars have approached the study of social movement organization. In particular, many of the studies of movement organization have been conducted out of a "metaphysical pathos" of the social democratic left. Left-leaning scholars have noted that the radical organizations of their youth have changed their goals and structure. The concepts they employed or which "caught on" both summarized the movements' trend *and* implied the emotional evaluation of the trend. In this paper we have attempted to work out of a relatively neutral frame of reference to account for organizational transformation. Furthermore, we have used a fairly general approach and set of concepts which, we think, allows us to examine the transformation of any MO, whatsoever.

To briefly recapitulate, we have examined the impact of a number of internal and external processes on the transformation of MO's. By examining the ebb and flow of sentiments and incentives available to organizations and interrelating these with the structural requirements for membership and the nature of organizational goals, two crucial analytic factors, we have made predictions about how different movement organizations will grow and decline and in what direction their goals will change. We have paid less attention to the internal authority structure, although it would be relatively easy to incorporate such analysis into our framework. We see one of the main advantages of our approach as raising to the center of sociological analysis a number of phenomena that have only rarely been at the center. For instance, the problems of mergers, of factions and schisms, of alternating leadership styles, and of inter-organizational competition all deserve greater attention than they have been given.

Our focus has been on organizational change, and we have examined the sequence from the environment and sentiment base to goals *and* structure rather than from goals *to* structure. But, the organizational leadership's commitment to a set of goals may also influence the structure. In some cases, goal commitment can act as a deterrent to the process of bureaucratization. To implement the more radical goals, an appropriate structure can be imposed on the organization: Members must invest more time and effort, sometimes to the point of professionalization; members are recruited from groups that have low commitment to a family or a career; workers are paid little and are frequently transferred to prevent attachment to the material rewards of office, and to prevent the creation of local support or empire building; the MO has a localized branch or even a cell structure with frequent meetings. In short, the militant MO is given a quasi-exclusive structure not only to implement goals, but also to maintain them in the face of pressures to become more conservative. The organization of CORE and SNCC illustrate some of these structural devices against goal displacement.

In focusing on change of organization we may have introduced our own metaphysical pathos; we have not looked at the other side of the coin, organizational stability, although the conditions are often the obverse of those discussed for change. However, some differences would enter in. For instance, Gusfield has discussed the problem of generations in the WCTU. There, the circulation of elites in an organization is related to the rate of growth and the organization's relation to the larger social movement as well as to internal structural and constitutional conditions.

As a general problem, the problem of stability can be encompassed within our framework.

We have proposed some general hypotheses specifying conditions of membership, goal type, success and failure, environmental conditions, and leadership that determine the extent and nature of the change of organizational goals. We have illustrated our propositions, but illustration is not proof. What is now needed is a systematic testing of the propositions, using large numbers of historical and contemporary case studies—in short, a comparative analysis of social movement organizations.

B.
Crises and Turning Points

3.

DEFECTION IN THE COMMUNIST PARTY
(1954)

Gabriel Almond

For most of our defectors, multiple dissatisfactions were involved. Similarly, for most of them, becoming dissatisfied with the party was cumulative. Thus an individual may join the party in some doubt as to the wisdom of his decision. He may resent the impact of party activities on his non-party interests and relationships. He may be offended by the process of indoctrination by slogans. But even though dissatisfactions may accumulate at each one of these stages, his original momentum and party pressure keeps him in line until some sharp impingement on his interests, feelings, or values takes place. Even at this point inertia may keep him in the party, even though he has already defected in spirit. He may wait until a general party crisis makes it possible for him to withdraw with a minimum of conflict and publicity.

What is interesting in our findings as to these processes of assimilation into and defection from the Communist movement is that so few of the respondents fully perceived the esoteric party at the point of defection

SOURCE. Gabriel Almond, *The Appeals of Communism.* Princeton: Princeton University Press, 1954, pp. 299–313, 324–327. Reprinted by permission of Princeton University Press and the author.

or in their subsequent thinking about their experience. In other words, most of them did not perceive the esoteric party when they joined and were not fully aware of it when they left. To the extent that perception of, and repulsion from, the esoteric party was involved in defection, it typically took the form of a realization that the "real" party to which they had finally become exposed was different from what it had been represented as being, and that this "real" party either involved risks and costs which the respondents were unwilling to incur, or was felt to be intrinsically evil in some general way. But it was the rare case who could generalize about the party or explicate this feeling beyond offering such vague characterizations as "The leaders are all corrupt"; "They're out to line their pockets"; "What these boys want is power"; "They're just Russian puppets"; and the like.

This finding should not occasion surprise, since clarity in the perception of one's political associations and affiliations is generally rare. What is of importance in this connection is that this is probably as true of most Communists as it is of other groups. This may suggest that the widespread view that all party members are, or that all former party members were, in the same sense participants in the "conspiracy" is quite inaccurate.

The variety of meanings which Communist affiliation may have has already been discussed. Our problem now is to describe the varieties of needs, interests, and values which may come into conflict with assimilation into the party, and contribute to defection. We have classified dissatisfactions with the party into five categories: (1) career-related dissatisfactions; (2) pressures on personality and personal relations; (3) pressures on other group loyalties; (4) pressures on values; and (5) pressures on moral standards. The task of the present chapter is to describe and illustrate these types of dissatisfaction, and then to indicate how they are distributed among the various party groupings.

CAREER-RELATED DISSATISFACTIONS

Considerably more than half of our respondents had made their careers as party functionaries or as paid officials of party-controlled organizations such as trade unions. A good many others held low-ranking unpaid positions in the party apparatus. A common cause of defection among these functionaries and unpaid officeholders was some interruption or disturbance of their party careers. Twenty-two per cent of the respondents attributed their defection in whole or in part to career reasons. Sometimes these career-related dissatisfactions simply involved a party decision to replace a man in his post. Thus an English respondent reported that after his war service, ". . . I returned to the Midlands and found that new people had taken over control of the party there. I naturally resented that these people had usurped my place and I was now only part of the machine." An American trade unionist remarked, "In the shop unit I was frequently asked to step aside when due to become a full-time paid union organizer in favor of someone brought in from the outside. They asked me as a 'true member of the proletariat' to step aside, and told me that I was best in the rank and file. I swallowed this to the very end." A similar situation arose with a British trade unionist, but the conflict had a different outcome: "I was informed by a party member just before the annual union election that they had decided to put up another nominee as union delegate. I told them I would go forward and stand or fall by the judgment of the men. At the time of the nomination meeting I was away convalescing after illness and the party tried to have me ruled ineligible. But the meeting went against the opinion of the Communist chairman, and at the pit-head ballot I was re-elected by a substantial majority. I left the CP and applied to join the Labor Party. I was accepted with cheers." There were several cases involving intra-party struggles for power, as in the instance of the British high party official who was accused by a colleague of having misappropriated party funds. ". . . I tore into him and knocked him unconscious. After that, the party decided I was run down and needed a long rest."

In Italy the high rate of defection from the party for career reasons was due to the fact that the party bureaucracy was hastily recruited after 1943 and had not been fully trained and indoctrinated. Thus many officials withdrew when party discipline began to be imposed. Such was the case of the Italian woman who was assigned the job of organizing a unit of the Communist-controlled Union of Italian Women. She was quite successful and recruited women of all political persuasions, and instituted an effective and popular educational program. After getting the unit under way, she was ordered to turn over the job to a woman who had just completed a course at the party training school in Bologna. She herself was sent on to another village to organize a new unit. She soon learned that the work she had undertaken in the first village was being undone by the new party leader, who followed a policy of declaring war on all the non-Communists in the village—the priest, the mayor, the doctor, and the pharmacist. All of the Catholic women were ordered to withdraw from the organization by the priest. She went to the federation headquarters to protest, and explained that all her work had been undone and that the party had lost an excellent opportunity to carry its propaganda among all classes in the village. She was bitterly critical of the party training school, stating, "If in the party schools they implant confusion in the minds of the comrades, I am proud of never having gone there." She was interrupted by the federation secretary, who asked her, "What use are the non-Communists? You come from a family of property owners and of exploiters of the poor and can never be a real Communist; that is the reason you kept reactionary elements in our ranks." The following day her expulsion was announced in *L'Unità* and party members were instructed to avoid her because of her reactionary affiliations.

An Italian party intellectual who was used in propaganda work was summoned to cell headquarters, where he was told that he deviated from the directives in his speeches. "From that day," he said, "I was conscious that there was an extra listener to my speeches who would report any deviation." He refused to mend his ways and was suspended from his duties for fifteen days. He thereupon resigned.

Activity in the party often conflicts with one's career outside the party. Some 13 per cent of the respondents reported that their defection was influenced by conflicts between party activities and career interests. This is particularly the case with individuals who are moving ahead in their work and find the party a handicap. One British party intellectual got a university post and ". . . didn't like pushing rather crumby pamphlets around the senior common room." Another Britisher who had a bright future as a member of a local council reported, "I felt I could be of more use if I were free of ties with the CP. I realized I ran the risk of being accused of being a Communist and getting kicked out." There was a French Communist who was given a government post because of his outstanding services in the resistance movement. While doing this work, he was summoned to Paris by the party to take part in the formation of the French Communist youth organization. He replied that since he had been sent by the government he could not return until his mission was completed. When he finally did come back, the party broke him to the ranks for punishment. He gave up all party activity and at length resigned.

Sometimes this disruption of careers by the party involved efforts to force individuals to engage in work which conflicted with their professional interests and values. There were many cases of writers who felt that party activities were destroying their talents. Thus, an American writer remarked, "In the movement you always ran across the 'leather jacket' party people who looked with scorn on the writer and admired the proletariat. I felt that I was doing something good, ethical, but the price I was paying was the abortion of my talent. I had no time to write, to brood, etc. As time went on, I began to ask for leaves of absence to do writing. To get these leaves I had to get into more and more arguments. Finally, the thing that made me break was the realization that I would kill something very precious in me if I stayed in the party."

A British writer who had the same problem said, ". . . my writing seemed to be getting worse. There were two things conflicting for my energy. I only spent a quarter of my time on party work, but the effect was bad. I had to choose between being a writer and a politician. I just went to live in the country, very largely to break contact with the party. They never bothered to keep track of me."

A young French historian was forced to make a choice between the study of history and the party. "The party asked me to show them the first draft of my thesis. I was summoned to party headquarters and told that I had to choose between going on with my thesis and remaining a Communist."

PARTY DEMANDS AND PERSONALITY

The party often makes demands on people which force them to act out of character, to violate personal standards of conduct. It may require that they act without mercy, that they manipulate other people, tell them one thing while meaning another. It also may require that they sacrifice their own individuality, give themselves up fully to the party's purposes. Nine per cent of the respondents reported that their defection was influenced by being required to do "cruel" things, or by witnessing them; 17 per cent were revolted by being compelled to manipulate other human beings or by observing the manipulative patterns in the party; and 24 per cent were repelled by the destruction of individuality in the party, the depersonalization which they were forced to undergo or which they observed taking place about them.

Some of the French and Italian Communists were revolted by acts of cruelty during the liberation purges, and carried these memories on their consciences. An Italian partisan had been set to guard a Fascist prisoner whose face had been beaten to a bloody pulp. Two of his comrades asked to be permitted to finish the prisoner off. He refused to permit this. ". . . they returned with a political commissar, who commanded me to let them pass. When I opposed this, they called me a reactionary and I was obliged to threaten to open fire to force them to leave. . . . Another time I assisted at the destruction of all the furnishings, goods, and chattels in a house owned by a Fascist. The Fascist had escaped, but his wife and little girl were there and were insulted and maltreated." He commented that the cruelest among the liberators were those who had suffered least. Those who had returned from the concentration camps had really suffered and were more inclined to understand and forgive.

Some of the respondents reported incidents from the Spanish Civil War which had horrified them. A French party leader visited the French battalion of the International Brigade and made a speech. "After the speech some men came to see me and gave me letters for their relatives in Paris. Later on I had dinner with André Marty in his sumptuous villa, where he was guarded very heavily (he was always afraid). He told me, 'Give me those letters! I know that you have several, and they must be censored.' I refused. He said, 'This is an order. It is necessary for security reasons.' I gave him the letters and later learned that one of the men had been shot."

One of the British International Brigade leaders had a subordinate who was having difficulties with the party leadership. He instructed his subordinate not to expose himself in action. "A little later I heard that G. had been killed in a Fascist ambush. There were conflicting stories about his death. One of the American Communist leaders who had been wounded in the same action told me that G. had been shot in the back. I sent my men to find G.'s body. After some trouble they located it and found it had a small hole in the back of the head and a large one in the forehead. He had been shot in the back of the head at close quarters."

The cruelties involved were not always acts of physical violence. These were, on the whole, rare events and usually occurred in war situations. More frequent were comments about the humiliations imposed on party members for minor acts of deviation and disobedience. Individuals committing such offenses were often required to confess their errors publicly. Some of the British respondents first began to doubt the party when British soldiers and officers who had been stationed in Russia during the war and had married Russian girls were refused permission by the Soviet Union to take their Russian brides home with them.

The problem which troubled the consciences of quite a few of our respondents was the party's practice of using people, manipulating them, misrepresenting the party's purposes. Seventeen per cent of the respondents referred to these manipulative practices as factors contributing to their defection. A British trade unionist remarked, "Before I joined the CP, I could go to a meeting, sum up what was being said, and make up my own mind. But when I joined the party I found it was all worked out beforehand, who was to say what, who was to get up and second. . . . They tried to work up the feeling that anyone who disagreed was disloyal to the rest of the men. Then the vote would be taken by a show of hands. The last thing they wanted was a ballot. So about half a dozen could carry a meeting of two thousand."

An Italian intellectual developed this theme of manipulativeness more explicitly: "I sincerely loved the masses whom I addressed, but little by little I became aware that the party machine—that is, the whole hierarchy—did not love them at all, but was merely maneuvering them as a shapeless mass, absolutely lacking personal or, rather, individual intelligence. In fact, the party needed only a collective brain, and wanted of me, as an intellectual, aid in this depersonalization."

More common among the respondents were reactions against threats to their own individuality. A simple Italian fireman, who had joined the party during partisan days, remarked after serving for a few years in the party, "I felt that my personal character was becoming, day by day, more styled and repressed. . . ." Another Italian said, ". . . to express my own personality had become almost a physical necessity. And it was my personality which was opposing this absorption of personality which the Communist Party was trying to obtain from the masses." An Italian intellectual spoke of the party as tending to "crystallize my brains." Still another remarked, "Leaving the party gave me the feeling of having reacquired the right to my own personality." A French intellectual who had served eighteen years in the party talked about the changes he observed among his intellectual comrades. "They spoke like characters out of Kafka; they were dried up; they read only *L'humanité*. I felt hideously alone among these French comrades, and I could not stay with them. For them, if you have a single doubt you ought to be killed. Their humanity is deformed, atomized, disintegrated. They are monstrous people. They have lost their souls." An American commented in similar terms: "These people interfered most viciously in my personal life. They were the ones who destroyed my spontaneity, who made me express myself in the most stereotyped forms."

The most common class of dissatisfactions with the party were simple repulsions from the atmosphere of the party and from party associates. Almost half of the respondents described their problems of adjustment in the party in these terms. Middle-class party members often felt uncomfortable while working in the same cells with unemployed or foreign workmen. Working-class party members were repelled by the pedantry and intellectual gymnastics of the intellectuals, or the bohemianism of some of the middle-class members ". . . who found it exotic to be Communist." Some of the British and American respondents were offended by the bohemianism and sexual immorality of groups with whom they came in contact. Others felt that many of the party members were "queers," neurotics, misfits. Still others were repelled and frightened by the dogmatism and fanaticism of the party militants. A young Negro remarked, "The regular party people were so intense, like maniacs, they scared young people." A Britisher was offended by the dogmatism and humorlessness of the party atmosphere: "I found the word 'comrade' repellent, with its heaviness and artificiality. The first time someone said, 'Comrades, we are in a revolutionary situation,' I expected something to happen. But not the tenth time. . . . I was prepared to work quite hard for the party, but found it quite a strain that no one could ever think the CP funny."

There were those who were troubled by the conspiratorial atmosphere. An American remarked, "They said Communism was twentieth-century Americanism, but couldn't make a phone call without making it sound conspiratorial." Others referred to the scruffiness and dirtiness of the comrades. Still others were appalled by the inefficiency of the party. This was particularly true of the British and American respondents who came into contact with the upper echelons. An American who worked for a while in the party headquarters in New York reported, "I was almost immediately appalled by the bureaucracy. The party functionaries were wasteful, inefficient, solvenly. They had no files, did no research. The top men came in at 11 a.m. and went out for two-hour lunches. They didn't look like professional revolutionaries to me."

PRESSURE ON PERSONAL RELATIONSHIPS

If the ideal of the party is to have the individual give up his personal moral standards and individuality, it also tears at his personal relationships—with parents, siblings, spouse, and friends. Twenty-nine per cent of the respondents cited pressure on personal relationships as factors leading to defection. There was an Italian engineer whose father was the manager of a plant, apparently a man of simple dignity who had not opposed his son's decision when he joined the party. When the Cominform was established, the plant was struck and the son took his turn on the picket line. When his father came out for lunch at noon, forty Communist pickets sent from a neighboring town surrounded him and his car. "My father leaned out of the car window, asking what they wanted of him. No one spoke, but as he got out of the car one of the pickets spat in his face. Offended and furious, careless of the fact that he was one against forty, he invited the coward who had spat to come forward and settle it man to man, saying that he was talking not as the factory manager but as a man offended in his personal dignity." The pickets withdrew. After this incident, the son found his membership in the party intolerable and resigned.

Many of those who defied their parents when they joined the party had uneasy consciences which troubled them until they finally left the party and rejoined their families. Certainly, many of the children of Catholic families in France and Italy must have experienced tragic scenes similar to that described by an Italian respondent: "My mother appealed to my Catholic sentiments, asking me how I could deny the religious principles in which I had been raised. She saw in the party a movement which would destroy the family and society, and was heartbroken when my young brother followed my example and joined the party." A number of the respondents reported as causes of defection actions taken by the party against wives or husbands or friends.

CONFLICTS OF GROUP LOYALTIES

Most individuals when joining the party are not fully aware of the integral loyalty demanded by the movement. They consider that there is an identity of national or trade union interests with that of the party, or at least that the two interests do not conflict. It is quite evident that this exclusive claim upon loyalty is not fully perceived by a large proportion of party members at the time of joining, since so many defections occur at the point at which the party insists that national loyalty, trade union loyalty, or minority group loyalty be subordinated to party loyalty. Thus the Nazi-Soviet Pact reduced the parties in the West to mere fragments of themselves, since the subordination of the various national movements to Russian policy was made so dramatically clear. One French respondent who was a top party leader in the 1930's reports that even Maurice Thorez was sympathetic to the idea of a party independent of Moscow after the announcement of the pact. He went to see Thorez, who was then in the army serving as chauffeur to an officer. They had a long talk about their common ideas and Thorez seemed to agree with the proposal that the French party ought to become autonomous and support France in its war against Hitler. Party loyalty won out in Thorez' case. Shortly after this meeting, he deserted from the French army and went underground.

Since the end of World War II the establishment of the Cominform has posed a similar problem for party leaders and members. Both Thorez and Togliatti were required by the Cominform to make public statements that in the event of a war with the Soviet Union, Communists would not fight against Russia. This policy had an especial impact in Italy, where a number of provincial party leaders, led by Magnani and Cucchi, resigned and formed a rival "national Communist" organization. Magnani had previously presented a resolution at a provincial congress of the party in Reggio Emilia in 1951. The resolution supported the opposition of the party to the Atlantic Pact, but also declared that Communists would defend their national territory from aggression from any quarter.

The subordination of trade union interests to the interests of the party also is a common cause of defection. In recent years, the political strikes in France and Italy that were called to protest the participation of these countries in the Marshall Plan resulted in the defection of large numbers of party members and a general loss of membership in the Communist-controlled trade unions. An Italian trade union leader commented, ". . . the moment always comes in which one recognizes that the Communist Party is not trying to help the masses to better their condition, but to endure in their present poverty. . . . As a union official, there came a point at which I felt shame at the use of such weapons as 'chain strikes,' 'quickie strikes,' and the like." He felt that the entire purpose of the unions was being subverted, that the discipline essential to production was being destroyed without any material advantage to the working class.

Similar efforts to use the unions for political purposes provoked crises in the British and American trade unions. A Scottish trade union leader reported that in the postwar period the Scottish Communists had captured the Glasgow Trades Council. "Having gained control, they recklessly steam-rollered resolutions that had nothing to do with trade union work, for instance, about peace and the Americans' handling of Scottish students going through Austria to the Berlin Congress. This was going against the declared policy of the Scottish Trades Union Congress and they must have known they were risking a head-on collision. Now the Scottish T.U.C. has withdrawn its support from them and is forming a new Trades Council." Similarly, the efforts of the American party to use the Communist-dominated trade unions in the Wallace campaign precipitated a crisis. One union leader recalled, ". . . a few of us decided that the third-party idea was bad and that the gains under FDR would be lost. We wanted the union not to take a stand but the leaders jumped on us to plug for Wallace regardless of how the union felt. About half a dozen of us dropped out all at once, and they went after us hammer and tongs. It really busted the union up."

Another American trade union leader said, ". . . the CP got the union to take many rash steps after Korea. . . . I got disgusted, went out for a double rye, and decided that I wanted nothing more to do with the CP. I went on working as a business agent."

Similar resistances are created when the party subordinates group interests to its purposes. Some of the Negro and Jewish respondents reported that they left the party when it became clear to them that the party had no real interest in Negro or Jewish problems as such, but was simply using them as a basis for propaganda and recruitment. One young Negro was sent to Moscow to participate in the making of a film on the Negro problem. For some reason, the Russian changed their minds about producing the film. He protested the decision and was invited to spend a weekend with a top Russian party leader. In the course of a long discussion, the Russian asked him, "Are you a Communist or a Negro?" He told the Negro he had to forget his birthright, that the problem is the same for black or white, Christian or Jew. "That was too much. I couldn't agree and said so." Other Negroes working with non-Communist Negro organizations complained that the party could never be relied on. Sometimes it took a stand on race questions and sometimes it didn't. Gradually they became aware of the fact that the party used the Negro problem when it suited the party's purposes, and not when it suited the needs of Negroes.

In a country such as Italy many party members are believing Catholics. In the years after the liberation of Italy neither church nor party forced the issue. The party statutes did not require that a member leave the church, and the church did not formally prohibit party membership. Since 1947, the pressure of the church has increased, and threats of excommunication have been directed at Catholics voting the Communist and Left Socialist tickets. This threat, however, has not been effectively enforced and there continue to be many Italian party members who are believers, churchgoers, and even continue to receive the sacraments. Sometimes this conflict between religious faith and Communist faith becomes clear only *in extremis,* as was the case of an Italian who fell ill: "I grew worse and was at the point of death, and then my old religious faith, the constant support of my family, came back stronger than ever. . . . I commended my soul to God . . . and took a vow to quit Communism if my life would be spared. . . . God granted me my life. I had been a long time in the hospital, which gave me the opportunity to think over my purposes much more clearly than I had thought at the time of my joining the CP."

That religious feelings of many party members in Italy are still alive is reflected in the reported successes of a Catholic lay organization specifically active among Communist workers and peasants. The organization was founded by former Communist Party members who had left the party for the church. Members of the organization are on a constant lookout for Communists who still show signs of the persistence of their religious faith. Such individuals are approached on admittedly false pretenses. They are invited to spend three or four days on a free vacation where they can play cards, bowl, listen to accordion concerts, and the like. An Italian whose defection was precipitated by such a "vacation" described his experience as follows: "The house was large and very beautiful, profoundly silent, and surrounded by a garden with tall pine trees. We entered a long corridor and each one of us was assigned a small bedroom with a window opening on the garden. The exercises lasted three days. A Jesuit gave about four lectures daily in a chapel, sermons in which from time to time he touched on all those subjects which were most stinging to us who had denied the faith. . . . The rest of the time was spent in our rooms in meditation, alone and in absolute silence.

"In this complete solitude, the priest's words kept running in my brain and repeating themselves, until all resolved themselves into one phrase: I had denied God, that same God who had sustained me in the most unhappy of my days of imprisonment, and in whose name my mother reproached me for my friendship and work with Communists. Nevertheless, something in me resisted that constant call to redemption, something which was probably due to the unfeeling iron discipline to which I had been subjected in the past years; so that while almost all who had taken part with me in the spiritual exercises ended by confessing and taking Holy Communion on the second day, I resisted in a state of anguish until the third day: only then was I able to break down all reserve and void my soul of all that had weighed it down. Not one of those who were with me refused or abandoned the 'Villa del Sacro Cuore' before the termination of the three days and all of us left restored, after having undergone the same process of conversion. Up to three days before, if we wanted to insult someone, we called them 'priest.' Today we saw in the priest the benefactor, the liberator."

VALUE CONFLICTS

Loyalty to the party and its decisions often puts pressure on ideals and principles other than those already implied in the material discussed above. The value conflicts reported by the respondents could be classified under the headings of intellectual, aesthetic, political, and economic. Intellectual and aesthetic conflicts were primarily reported by party journalists, scientists, and artists. Conflicts over economic values were mainly reported by trade unionists, factory officials, or administrators of such party enterprises as cooperatives. Political value conflicts were generally reported among all groups of party members.

The Nazi-Soviet Pact created a crisis of conscience among many party journalists. In their capacity as journalists, they had to elaborate and defend a policy which flew in the face of everything the party had stood for in the period of the Popular Front and "collective security." Even party journalists who had the reputation of being "tough Bolsheviks" found it difficult to stomach this role. Thus one of them remarked that when he first heard of it, he viewed it as "hard-boiled realpolitik." ". . . the Western powers deserved what they got. They would have turned the Germans on the Russians if it had been possible, but the Russians turned the tables." But, as time went on, his troubles began. While he could accept the pact as tough politics, he could not go so far as to view the Western powers as responsible for the war. He was too much of a journalist. "I couldn't take this intellectually." He protested among his colleagues and was told to "trust Stalin," take matters on faith. This he could not do, and when the fall of France showed him dramatically what the consequences of the pact had been, he resigned from the party. . . .

PATTERNS OF DISSATISFACTION

Thus we have seen that defection may be influenced by the pressure of the party on any one or a combination of the interests, values, and relationships which the individual brings with him into the party. But these types of dissatisfaction are not distributed in a random manner among the various types of party members. It was of interest that the Italian respondents complained with particular frequency of threats to their individuality. Forty-five per cent of the Italian respondents were repelled by this aspect of their experience. This especially high proportion may be due to the fact that the Italian respondents came into the party in 1943 largely as a reaction against Fascist suppression. To them the party meant liberation. The impact of party discipline would be felt with especial poignancy by persons coming to the party with these libertarian expectations.

The American and British respondents were repelled far more frequently by the atmosphere and associations of party life than the French and Italians. This may be accounted for by the fact that the conspiratorial, dogmatic, and authoritarian pattern of the party clashes most sharply with the political and associational patterns of British and American society. The especially high proportion of American respondents who were repelled by the associations and atmosphere of the party may be attributed to the ethnic and social heterogeneity of the American movement. The French, Italian, and British respondents were largely of native stock and of the dominant religions. The Americans, on the other hand, were very frequently foreign-born or first-generation native-born (and of many different national origins), the religious mixture was not like that of the society at large, and the proportion of bohemian intellectuals was substantial. Hence almost every group found something in the party which was repelling. Those from the older ethnic stocks were sometimes repelled by the foreign aspect of the party. Working-class members were repelled by the bohemian intellectuals and artists. Some of the whites were uncomfortable among the Negroes and the Negroes were ill at ease among the whites.

SOCIAL CLASS AND PATTERNS OF DISSATISFACTION

A number of interesting differences emerged from a comparison of the dissatisfactions of the middle-class and working-class respondents. Table 1 groups together the types of dissatisfaction most characteristic of these two groups. More of the working-class respondents complained about conflicts in connection with their party careers. This probably results from the fact that a greater proportion of the working-class respondents were employed by the party or by party-controlled trade unions. Complaints about pressure on individuality occurred twice as often among the middle-class respondents. This is not a difficult finding

TABLE 1   TYPES OF DISSATISFACTION WITH PARTY BY SOCIAL CLASS[a]
(IN PER CENT)

	Working Class	Middle Class	All Respondents
Disruption of party careers	27	17	22
Loss of individuality	16	32	24
Party associates and atmosphere	40	53	47
Trade union–party conflict	46	14	29
Russian domination of party	19	28	24
Party vs. intellectual values	11	47	29
Party vs. aesthetic values	1	12	6
Party vs. political values	25	34	29
Party vs. economic values	10	7	9

[a] Multiple responses.

to interpret, since middle-class people tend generally to be more individuated, to have more elaborate interests than working-class people.[1] Hence they are more likely to feel the threat to their individuality resulting from party discipline and to resent the pressures for conformity.

As might be expected, the working-class respondents were caught in trade union–party conflict far more frequently than the middle-class respondents. On the other hand, the middle-class respondents were more troubled by the Russian domination of the party. This may be due to the fact that the middle-class party member tends to see the party in its general and international manifestations, while the working-class party member tends to be more locally oriented. Conflicts with intellectual and aesthetic values were more characteristic of the middle-class members, while the working-class members complained somewhat more frequently of the effects of party policies on the efficiency and productivity of enterprises with which they were identified. In general, the repulsions from the party of these two groups resulted from the party's impingement on their vocational interests. In the case of the middle-class respondents, many of whom were intellectuals, the impingement was on such values as honest reporting and interpretation of news for journalists, or aesthetic freedom for artists. In the case of the working-class members, the impingement was on career interests (as trade union functionaries, in most cases), or on trade union interests in general.

4.

WHAT HAPPENED TO THE ANTITRUST MOVEMENT? (1965)

RICHARD HOFSTADTER

I

The antitrust movement is one of the faded passions of American reform. Historians have always been interested in the old romance, but with

SOURCE. Richard Hofstadter, *The Paranoid Style in American Politics.* New York: Alfred A. Knoff, 1965. pp. 188–195, 212–215, 222–224, 228–236. Reprinted by permission of John Wiley & Sons, Inc., and the author. Copyright: John Wiley and Sons.

[1] See Richard Centers, *The Psychology of Social Classes* (Princeton: Princeton University Press, 1949), pp. 141 ff.

remarkable unanimity and an uncharacteristic lack of realism, they have neglected to tell us what happened when it was over. The writers of our general history books deal with the antitrust issue when they tell of the rise of the great corporations and the passing of the Sherman Act and then, again, in discussing antitrust sentiment in the Progressive era and the enactment of further regulatory laws. Most of them touch on it briefly once more when they take up the New Deal antitrust revival, Thurman Arnold, and the T.N.E.C. Then, for the most part, they drop the subject; the student or the general reader must study law, economics, or business administration to become aware that the antitrust enterprise has more significance in contemporary society than it had in the days of T.R. or Wilson, or even in the heyday of Thurman Arnold.

Presumably the historians drop the subject of antitrust at or around 1938 not because they imagine that it has lost its role in our society but because after that point it is no longer the subject of much public agitation—in short, because there is no longer an antitrust *movement*. The intensity of public concern is, of course, a poor guide for historians, but here their neglect embodies a certain self-protective wisdom. They ignore antitrust for the same reason the public ignores it: it has become complex, difficult, and boring. In any case, the intricacies, both legal and economic, of regulating monopoly and competition are intricacies of a sort the historian is ill equipped to handle. It is simpler for him to sweep the whole thing under the carpet, and retire, along with the general public, from the baffling maze of technical refinements which the lawyers and economists have created.

Perhaps, at the risk of oversimplifying a little, the source of the problem can be put in this paradox: once the United States had an antitrust movement without antitrust prosecutions; in our time there have been antitrust prosecutions without an antitrust movement. In its day the antitrust movement had such consequences for our political and intellectual life that no historian who writes about the period 1890–1940 can safely ignore it. But the antitrust enterprise, as an institutional reality, now runs its quiet course without much public attention, and we lose sight of it. In failing to take more cognizance of its work, the historians are missing one of the most delicious minor ironies of our reform history and one of the most revealing facets of our institutional life. In the very years when it lost compelling public interest the antitrust enterprise became a force of real consequence in influencing the behavior of business.

For a long time liberal historians held to a kind of mythological history of the antitrust experience which, though it was not entirely false at any point, ended somehow in being entirely misleading. Antitrust, as

an ideology and a movement of reform, always contrasted so sharply
with its actual achievements in controlling business that it tempted
our powers of satire. The conventional history went something like this:
In 1890, as a largely meaningless and cynical gesture to appease public
sentiment, an ultra-conservative Congress passed the Sherman Antitrust
Act. The act was couched in such vague terms as to confirm our doubts
that those who passed it expected that it could ever be enforced. Its
early history fully warranted such doubts. From the beginning it was
rendered a dead letter by administrative neglect and judicial hostility.
Though it had little effect on the big business firms that were supposed
to be its main object, it was used with greater success against labor
unions. By the time Theodore Roosevelt took office, when the Sherman
Act was little more than ten years old, it had become all too clearly
a charade behind which the consolidation of big business, notably accelerated between 1898 and 1904, went on apace. It was easy and amusing
to debunk the reputation of T.R. as a trustbuster when one considered
the infrequency and superficiality of his prosecutions, as well as his
own doubts about the value of the whole enterprise, and to compare
his robust rhetoric with the comic and pathetic image of the Antitrust
Division of the Justice Department sallying out against the combined
might of the giant corporations with a staff of five lawyers and four
stenographers.

Subsequent statutory efforts under Wilson to strengthen regulation
of monopolistic conduct, whatever one is to say of their value and the
intent behind them, had to be recounted by the historians with a full
sense of the denouement in mind. And the denouement required us
to say that the antitrust effort went down the drain with the attempt
to organize industry for the First World War; that the ensuing saturnalia
of reaction during the 1920's, another period of business consolidation,
undid the Wilsonian reforms—indeed, that the Federal Trade Commission was converted from an agency to control business into an agency
controlled by business. Finally the revival of antitrust under F.D.R.,
the creation of the Temporary National Economic Commission, and the
installation of Thurman Arnold's reforms seemed to be largely a movement of desperation, a return to the old antitrust charade, on the part
of an administration which had exhausted its capacity to reform and
was having indifferent results in its efforts to bring about recovery. The
very appointment of Thurman Arnold as head of the Antitrust
Division—a man whose books had effectively ridiculed the antitrust
laws as a facade behind which the concentration of American industry
could go on unimpeded—seemed to underline perfectly the whole comedy of the antitrust enterprise. And here, for the most part, as I have

observed, the standard history of antitrust breaks off, perhaps with a few words about the difficulties Arnold confronted, and how his honest efforts were circumvented during the Second World War. . . .

II

The history of antitrust may be divided into three phases. In the first, from about 1890 to 1914—the era of the founding fathers of anti-trust—the opening steps were taken, in statutes and in the courts, to define what form the antitrust efforts of the federal government might take and to see how they would work. The great outburst of business consolidation quickened antitrust sentiment, which was strong through-out the Progressive era. Often a common hostility to big business was the one link that bound together a variety of interest groups that di-verged on other issues. The Progressive era, which culminated in 1914 with the passing of the Clayton Act and the creation of the Federal Trade Commission, probably marks the high point of anti-big-business sentiment in our history. As a movement, through hardly as an adminis-trative reality, antitrust was in high gear.

The second phase, lasting from the First World War to about 1937, might be called the era of neglect. Efforts at prosecution during the 1920's were almost minimal, and even the New Deal in its opening years suspended the antitrust laws to accommodate the N.R.A. codes. The present phase, which may be dated from 1937, is the phase of revival, opened by the New Deal's reactivation of the Antitrust Division and the T.N.E.C. investigation. The sharp legal and administrative activ-ity of this period has taken place without any corresponding revival of public sentiment against big business, indeed in the face of a growing public acceptance of the large corporation. Antitrust has become almost exclusively the concern of small groups of legal and economic specialists, who carry on their work without widespread public interest or support.

Whereas the first of these three phases was marked by tentative efforts at enforcement with nearly negligible results, and the second by minimal or token enforcement, the comparative vigor of the third may be mea-sured roughly by the number of prosecutions. During all the years from 1891 to 1938, the government instituted an average of 9 cases a year. The peak years of this barren half-century were 1912 and 1913, with 29 and 27 prosecutions repectively. For about thirty years after 1913 the typical load was about 12 cases, often considerably fewer, and the objects chosen for prosecution were not often vital points in American industry. In 1940, with the Roosevelt-Arnold revitalization well on its way, the number of cases jumped to 85—only two less than the number instituted during the entire first *two decades* of the Sherman Act. Thereafter the number of cases, though still fluctuating, stayed at a level considerably higher than that maintained before 1938. In 1962 the Antitrust Division, employing 300 lawyers and working with a budget of $6,600,000, instituted 92 cases. Figures, of course, are crude, but a qualitative analysis of the legal victories of the antitrust revival would show that the decisions it has won from the courts, particularly since 1940, have greatly amplified the possibility of enforcement. Despite the collapse of antitrust feeling both in the public at large and among liberal intellectuals, antitrust as a legal-administrative enterprise has been solidly institutionalized in the past quarter-century. . . .

IV

There are two salient differences between the problem of bigness as it was perceived about sixty years ago and the problem as it is perceived now; the first is that it is no longer a new problem, and the second is that the economy has performed in a way hardly dreamed of before the Second World War. In 1965 we are as remote in time from the passage of the Sherman Act as the men of 1865 were from the first term of George Washington. The public has had almost three-quarters of a century of experience in living with big business, and analysts of the big-business problem no longer make the same frightening projections as to its future dangers that could be made with entire plausibility sixty or seventy years ago. At the same time, the public is hardly unaware that the steepest rise in mass standards of living has occurred during the period in which the economy has been dominated by the big corporation. Whatever else may be said against bigness, the conception of monopolistic industry as a kind of gigantic, swelling leech on the body of an increasingly deprived and impoverished society has largely disappeared.

About the change in public attitudes from those prevailing sixty years ago we can make only an educated guess. Today we can check our impressions of the public mind against opinion polls; for the earlier era we have impressions alone. But it is very difficult for anyone who reads widely in the political literature of the period 1890–1914 to believe that public concern today over big business has anything like the sense of urgency that it had then. In 1951 the Institute of Social Research of the University of Michigan published the results of an illuminating survey, *Big Business as the People See It*. Its findings show some residues of the old popular suspicion of bigness, but the noteworthy thing is public acceptance. Americans have always had to balance their love of bigness and efficiency against their fear of power and their regard for individualism and competition. The survey indicates that this ambivalence has been largely resolved in favor of the big business organization.

A quarter of the population, as represented in the Institute's national sample, showed some concern over big business and an awareness that it had an important effect on their lives. But a substantial majority reacted favorably to big business. Asked to give a general characterization of its social effects, the respondents answered as follows:

The good things outweigh the bad things	76%
They seem about equal	2
The bad things outweigh the good things	10
Don't know	5
Confused; evaluation not ascertainable	7
	100%

Plainly, big business was no longer a scare word to the public at large. Eighty-four per cent of those polled reacted without apparent emotion to the question, and only a small minority reacted unfavorably. Questioned on particulars, respondents spoke with especial favor of the productive powers of big business and its ability to give jobs and keep prices down. The most critical responses about big business dealt mainly with its effect on "the little man" and the destruction of competition. Very little concern was expressed about the power of big business over its workers (it is commonly regarded as a good employer) and surprisingly little about its influence on government.

Whereas fifty years before, fear of an indefinitely continued increase in the political power of big business was commonplace, the typical expectation expressed in the poll of 1951 was that the power of big business would decline, and properly so. As in the Progressive era, there was a strong preference for a balance of power and a conviction that wherever there must be a clear preponderance of power it should rest in governmental and not private hands. But the existing state of business power was not widely considered to be dangerous. In fact, big-business power was ranked third among five forces—behind national government and labor unions and ahead of state governments and smaller business. Stronger feeling was shown against labor unions than against big business. There was a fraction of the public that saw big business as more powerful than labor unions and would have liked to see the situation reversed; but there was a fraction almost twice as large that saw the unions as more powerful and would have preferred to see the situation reversed. . . .

V

It is easier to account for the decline of the antitrust movement as a matter of public sentiment than it is to explain the persistence and growth of the antitrust enterprise as a legal and administrative fact. But the fate of antitrust is an excellent illustration of how a public ideal, vaguely formulated and often hopelessly at odds with stubborn realities, can become embodied in institutions with elaborate, self-preserving rules and procedures, a defensible function, and an equally stubborn capacity for survival. Institutions are commonly less fragile than creeds.

The antitrust revival originated in the closing phases of the New Deal. It was a response to the recession of 1937–8, which itself brought about a crisis in the thinking and the political strategy of the New Dealers. The recession gave to the Brandeis liberals, who had always been present in New Deal councils, a chance to reassert their ideas about competition and their suspicion of big business. In 1934, long before the cartelization of the N.R.A. was abandoned, the economist Gardiner C. Means, then economic adviser to the Secretary of Agriculture, had prepared a memorandum on administered prices that provided the economic rationale for a new approach to the depression. Early in 1935 this memorandum was published by the Senate. Means contrasted market prices, which were made and remade in the market as the result of interactions between buyers and sellers in the fashion of traditional economic theory, with administered prices, which were set by administrative action and held constant for a considerable period of time. Market prices are flexible and respond readily to a fall in demand; administered prices are rigid. Means considered the disparity between flexible and rigid prices to be an important aggravating force in the depression. Although he did not identify administered prices with monopoly, he focused attention once again on those industries in which market power was sufficiently concentrated to make administered prices possible. Some of his contemporaries seized upon the conception as a rationale for stepping up antitrust activity, and Franklin D. Roosevelt invoked it in his message of 1938, calling for the creation of the T.N.E.C. At the same time, other New Deal theorists, notably Assistant Attorney General Robert Jackson, who was then head of the Antitrust Division of the Department of Justice, and

Secretary of the Interior Harold L. Ickes, became convinced that the organized power of big business was attempting to sabotage reform through a "strike of capital" and that a new assault on business power must be undertaken as a basis for further attempts at recovery. The old argument that business power was a threat to democratic government itself thus entered into Roosevelt's T.N.E.C. message.

The new attack on business power took two forms; the first was the elaborate, if inconclusive, T.N.E.C. investigation, which yielded a mass of factual information, much of it new, but no programmatic proposals in which the investigators themselves had any confidence. The second was the stepping up of antitrust activity under the leadership of Thurman Arnold, the new chief of the Antitrust Division. Congress doubled appropriations for Arnold's division in 1939 and then doubled them again in 1940. Between 1938 and 1943 its staff grew almost fivefold.

In retrospect it is instructive to see what results came from uncertain and, at times, ill-considered beginnings. Today the Jackson-Ickes view of the recession seems quite partisan and fanciful; the T.N.E.C. investigation, for all the information it gathered, was from a pragmatic point of view a fiasco; the value of Means's emphasis on administered prices is highly controversial among economists; and Thurman Arnold's experiment with antitrust enforcement can be judged, at least from one angle of vision, a substantial failure. And yet, as in the case of so many of the gropings of the New Deal, there was a valuable outcome, which in this case can best be got at by looking at the core of success wrapped up in Thurman Arnold's frustration.

Arnold's story is replete with ironies. He had written of the antitrust enterprise with a devastating note of mockery, and the appointment of a man with such views, especially by an administration that had only recently resorted to the wholesale cartelization of the N.R.A., was looked at askance by antitrust-minded senators as a possible effort to sabotage the Antitrust Division. But Arnold proceeded to recruit and inspire a splendid staff and to rehabilitate the entire antitrust function. His goal was not to attack bigness or efficient mass production or efficient marketing, but rather to discipline the pricing policies of business at the vital points where abuses seemed most important. Antitrust was thus to become an instrument of social and economic policy, aimed to stop firms from setting prices above reasonable levels, to prevent businesses from holding new processes off the market, and to reduce unemployment. All this was to be achieved not so much by isolated cases or by responding to this or that complaint, but rather by systematic action against whole industries—motion pictures, petroleum, radio broadcasting, drugs, housing.

From a short-run point of view, Arnold's regime could be judged a failure. His program for housing was spiked when the Supreme Court made it impossible to act effectively against the labor unions, which constituted a linchpin of restraint of trade in that industry; his plan for the food industry lost its point during the war; his program for transportation was put off by the War Production Board. He could not wholly reform a single industry, much less bring about important general structural changes in the economy. And yet he succeeded in demonstrating the usefulness of the antitrust laws. In actually *using* the Sherman Act, thanks to the enlarged staff that Congress had given him, he showed for the first time what it could and could not do. Although it could not alter the fundamental character of the economy or make it less liable to cyclical instability (as Arnold had promised it would in his book *The Bottlenecks of Business*), it could significantly affect the conduct of business within the framework of the existing structure. Arnold's division soon won a number of decisions from the courts—particularly in the Alcoa case of 1945 and the American Tobacco case of the following year—which opened new possibilities for enforcement. It won from Congress a permanent reversal of the former policy of niggardly support. And finally, it put the antitrust enterprise on such a footing that it could flourish under both Democratic and Republican regimes.

The return of the Republicans under Eisenhower did not bring a remission of efforts to use the Sherman Act or a retrenchment of the Antitrust Division. Instead, the Eisenhower administration set up the Attorney General's National Committee to Study the Antitrust Laws, which in 1955 returned a unanimous judgment in favor of antitrust policy and of the current state of case law, under which enforcement had been tightened. Although the Committee did not make any dramatic recommendations for more rigorous enforcement, the effect of its work was to reaffirm the bipartisan character of the antitrust commitment by ratifying the achievements of Democratic administrations in the preceding fifteen years. Nor should we forget that the most spectacular and revealing case involving a criminal price conspiracy—the General Electric case—took place during the Eisenhower administration.

What makes it possible to institutionalize antitrust activities at the higher plateau that has been maintained since 1938 is not a consensus among economists as to its utility in enhancing economic efficiency, but a rough consensus in society at large as to its value in curbing the dangers of excessive market power. As in the beginning, it is based on a political and moral judgment rather than economic measurement or even distinctively economic criteria. "It must be recognized," says Edward S. Mason, "that there is an element of faith in the proposition that maintaining competition substantially improves the efficiency of resource use." The option for a minimal level of competition to be underwritten by public policy, although it can be backed by substantial economic arguments. "rests basically on a political judgment," write Carl Kaysen and Donald F. Turner in their inquiry into trust policy: "In our democratic, egalitarian society, large areas of uncontrolled private power are not tolerated." "We found," write J. B. Dirlam and A. E. Kahn in their book *Fair Competition,* "that the decisions [of courts and commissions] could not be fully understood or fairly appraised by economic standards alone. Hence we concluded that the appropriate question for economists to ask about antitrust policy is not whether this is the most efficient way of structuring or reorganizing the economy, but the inverted one: Does antitrust seriously interfere with the requirements of efficiency?" "The rationale of antitrust," writes A. D. Neale, a British student of the American experience, "is essentially a desire to provide legal checks to restrain economic power and is not a pursuit of efficiency as such." "For most Americans," concludes John Kenneth Galbraith, "free competition, so called, has for long been a political rather than an economic concept."

In any case, the state of antitrust enforcement seems to correspond with a public consensus. Economists and lawyers differ profoundly on how effective the antitrust laws have been and on how effective they could be if they were more amply enforced, but there is hardly a major industry that has not seen a significant lawsuit or two, and in most industries in which intervention might be thought desirable, government action has had more than negligible effects. It is also one of the strengths of antitrust that neither its effectiveness nor its ineffectiveness can be precisely documented; its consequences rest on events of unknown number and significance that have *not* happened—on proposed mergers that may have died in the offices of corporation counsel, on collusive agreements that have never been consummated, on unfair practices contemplated but never carried out. Liberals can support it because they retain their old suspicion of business behavior, and conservatives support it because they still believe in competition and they may hope to gain an additional point of leverage in the battle against inflation. No one seems prepared to suggest that the antitrust enterprise be cut back drastically, much less abandoned, and Congress has consistently supported its enlarged staff. The existing state of enforcement conforms to the state of the public mind, which accepts bigness but continues to distrust business morals. Even business itself accords to the principle of antitrust a certain grudging and irritated acceptance, and largely confines its resistance to the courts. Visitations by the Department of Justice are a nuisance, lawsuits are expensive, and prosecution carries an odious stigma, but the antitrust procedures can be considered an alternative to more obtrusive regulation such as outright controls on prices. At any rate, big business has never found it necessary or expedient to launch a public campaign against antitrust enforcement; the pieties at stake are too deep to risk touching.

A final element in antitrust enforcement rests on the fact that the government itself is now a major consumer, and the points of exposure of industrial prices to official concern and reaction have been multiplied. One of the reasons for the antitrust revival in 1938 was the irritation of government officials over the prevalence of what seemed to be collusively priced bids. Thurman Arnold's hope that consumers could be mobilized behind the new antitrust enforcement was out of keeping with the historical passivity and disorganization of American consumers. But the presence of the government as a consumer may supply some of the leverage he was looking for.

Antitrust reform is not the first reform in American history whose effectiveness depended less upon a broad movement of militant mass sentiment than upon the activities of a small group of influential and deeply concerned specialists. In ceasing to be largely an ideology and becoming largely a technique, antitrust has taken its place among a great many other elements of our society that have become differentiated, specialized and bureaucratized. Since no layman can any longer concern himself with the enormous body of relevant case law or with the truly formidable literature of economic analysis and argument that has come to surround the issue, the potentialities of antitrust action have become almost exclusively the concern of a technical elite of lawyers and economists. Indeed, the business of studying, attacking, defending, and evaluating oligopolistic behavior and its regulation has become one of our lively small industries, which gives employment to many gifted professional men. No doubt this is another, if lesser, reason why antitrust has become self-sustaining: it is not our way to liquidate an industry in which so many have a stake.

Author Index

Aberle, D. F., 443
Ahluwalia, Sagar, 244
Aiyar, S. P., 300n
Alcott, B., 419, 433
Ali, Syed Amir, 28
Almond, Gabriel, 500, 538
Altbach, Philip, 193, 225, 244
Appleton, 17
Aragon, L., 142
Arendt, Hannah, 193
Arnold, Thurman, 553–555, 559, 560, 562
Aron, Raymond, 87, 134, 398
Ash, Roberta, 499, 516
Ashida, H., 286n
Atarashiki, Mura, 95–100, 102
Ataturk, Kemal, 138
Aulard, A., 490n

Baguénier-Désormeaux, H., 49n
Bakke, E. Wight, 271n
Balandier, G., 445, 448, 450, 451n
Baldwin, Roger, 128
Balzac, H., 141
Banerjea, S., 24
Banfield, Edward C., 362n
Barber, Bernard, 443n
Barnett, G., 451n
Barnet, Rose, 384–385, 388
Barnes, Gilbert H., 16, 17
Bassett, T. D. Seymour, 95, 105
Bateson, Gregory, 65
Bayley, David, 194, 298
de Beauchamp, Alphonse, 49n
Beegle, J. Allen, 44
Beer, Samuel H., 485n
Bellah, Robert N., 104, 106
Bendix, Reinhard, 119, 192, 195, 376, 416n
Bennett, John W., 104, 106
Bernanos, G., 146
Bestor, Arthur, 93, 95, 106
Birney, James Gillespie, 16n, 20
Bisgambilia, Antoine, 115

Bishop, Claire Huchet, 435n
Blake, William, 117
Bloch, Jean-Richard, 142
Bloch, Marc, 58
Blough, Roger, 382, 383
Blum, Leon, 142
Blumer, Herbert, 5, 149, 150n, 189
Bode, Carl, 434n
Boguslaw, Robert, 106
Bois, Paul, 49, 57–59, 62
Bontemps, Arna, 158n, 165n, 189
de Bourniseaux, P. V. J. Berthe, 49n
Bracher, Karl D., 39n, 40n, 41n, 43n
Bremme, Gabriele, 41n
Breton, Andre, 142
Brinton, Crane, 50, 492n
Brisbane, Arthur, 420
Brothers, Richard, 117
Brown, H. Rap, 218
Bryan, William Jennings, 127
Bryce, James, 36n, 37n, 131
Burke, Edmund, 70, 79–80, 122, 126, 210
Burnet, G., 507
Burridge, K., 441n, 445n
Burt, Jonathan, 422
Bushee, Frederick A., 433n, 435n

Cabet, 94, 100
Campbell, Angus, 256
Carden, Maren Lockwood, 397–398, 419
Carlyle, Thomas, 210
Carmichael, Stokely, 183, 219
Cartwright, Thomas, 485, 491
Castro, Fidel, 392
Cavanaugh, J., 216
Celsus, 504
Centers, Richard, 552n
Chalier, 19
Channing, William Ellery, 19
Channing, William H., 419, 434n
Chassin, Ch.-L., 49n
Chessman, Caryl, 6

563

Subject Index